CORRECTIONAL ADMINISTRATION

INTEGRATING THEORY AND PRACTICE

SECOND EDITION

Richard P. Seiter

Prentice Hall

Boston   Columbus   Indianapolis   New York   San Francisco   Upper Saddle River
Amsterdam   Cape Town   Dubai   London   Madrid   Milan   Munich   Paris   Montreal   Toronto
Delhi   Mexico City   Sao Paulo   Sydney   Hong Kong   Seoul   Singapore   Taipei   Tokyo

Vice President and Executive Publisher: Vernon Anthony
Senior Acquisitions Editor: Eric Krassow
Editorial Assistant: Lynda Cramer
Media Project Manager: Karen Bretz
Director of Marketing: David Gesell
Senior Marketing Manager: Adam Kloza
Senior Marketing Coordinator: Alicia Wozniak
Production Manager: Holly Shufeldt
Creative Director: Jayne Conte
Cover Designer: Karen Salzbach
Cover Illustration/Photo: Fotolia
Image Permission Coordinator: Karen Sanatar
Full-Service Project Management/Composition: Integra Software Services Pvt. Ltd.
Printer/Binder: Courier

Library of Congress Cataloging-in-Publication Data
Seiter, Richard P.
    Correctional administration : integrating theory and practice / Richard P. Seiter.—2nd ed.
        p. cm.
    Includes bibliographical references and index.
    ISBN-13: 978-0-13-511362-2
    ISBN-10: 0-13-511362-8
    1. Corrections—Administration. 2.   Correctional institutions—Administration.
3. Prison administration.   I. Title.
HV8665.S29 2012
365.068—dc22

                                                                    2010033679

V036 10 9 8 7 6 5 4

Prentice Hall
is an imprint of

www.pearsonhighered.com

ISBN 10:   0-13-511362-8
ISBN 13: 978-0-13-511362-2

To my son, Matt, who every day, brings me pride and joy.

Love, Dad

Creating a Safe & Secure Enviroment
& Managing Disrupting Inmates

Contents

13

14

part five
Issues for Now and the Future 425

15

Preface

This textbook has been written to help students learn and enjoy the past, present, and future of corrections; the functions of correctional administrators; and the issues that drive administrators as they create new operational approaches to respond to new challenges. As the title indicates, it is an integration of theory and practice, providing the background and relevant theory that guides practice and the administration of correctional agencies. The book is organized into five sections, each providing readers with essential history and background, an understanding of critical issues, the important functions of correctional operations, and projections for future needs and adjustments to correctional administration. The goal of the textbook is to provide a framework for understanding and action. As correctional practitioners confront some of the issues and critical functions presented in this text, they should be able to put them in both historical and managerial perspectives, and avoid mistakes that might occur without such an orientation.

Part 1 of the text (Correctional Management and Administration) provides a discussion of the environment and influences impacting corrections from past to present. It includes a description of management development in the private sector and how that management expertise was transferred and reorganized to meet public sector bureaucracies. There is also a description of the development of correctional administration and how evolving theories and criminal justice philosophies resulted in certain management practices.

Part 1 also delves into the important area of leadership. Corrections is a "people business," and leadership style and quality are essential to accomplishing the mission of a correctional agency. Readers of the first edition suggested a leadership theory chapter; accordingly Chapter 2 provides this so that students can link style and correctional challenges and recognize how various leadership approaches could be useful in the administration of correctional agencies. Chapter 3 then describes the practical application of these theories and illustrates how management differs from leadership and how the complex issues of the future will require leaders to modify traditional styles of leadership. Finally, this section includes a discussion of how administrators can guide their organizations through planning exercises that create a vision and mission while identifying future challenges and appropriate responses. By the end of Part I, you have a solid background of management and leadership, the issues that drive correctional administration, and the approaches to "reach ahead" and proactively confront the future of a correctional agency.

In Part 2, we move into the management and administration of the most important resource for a correctional agency—the staff. We begin with the role of staff in Chapter 5, as students learn of the variety of positions and staff functions in a correctional agency. Chapter 6 addresses the specific human resource management activities that must occur to maximize the productivity of the critical staff resource. We address hiring, training and development, succession planning, performance appraisal and staff discipline, and collective bargaining in a correctional agency. We then move to organization, as Chapter 8 describes the principles of organizing staff and functions to meet mandates and produce expected outcomes. We address the roles of headquarters and field organizations, and specifically examine how prisons and community corrections agencies are organized.

The final chapter in Part 2 focuses on how we supervise this resource. As we have come to understand, you can't just hire and train staff and then send them on their way. They must be continually mentored and coached, they must be guided and encouraged, and they must be directed and work delegated to them. But the traditional ways of supervising staff are no longer effective with the current workforce. They desire involvement and to understand not only what they need to do but also why they are doing it. So a major section includes how to "empower" the workforce and move them toward accomplishing the vision of the organization.

Part 3 is "managing the environment." Correctional administration must operate in a very complex and dynamic environment and must have expertise in many areas that were less important in their world thirty years ago. First, we now face an unprecedented budget crisis in our country, and correctional agencies are thus required to deal with significant budget challenges. Chapter 9 describes some of the approaches being taken to address these budget issues. In Chapter 10, we discuss how correctional administrators manage risk and use the many actuarial methods to predict and respond to the risk of additional crime or misbehavior by offenders. Chapter 11 describes the tremendous challenge of managing the external environment. Today everyone cares about corrections. Administrators must know how to manage issues of the public, the elected officials, and the media to successfully lead their organizations through challenging times.

In Part 4, we focus on the management of prisons, and specifically the three main areas of prison operations: security, programs, and services. Chapter 12 provides critical security issues of design and physical security, inmate accountability and control of contraband, responding to inmate violation of rules, controlling prison gang activities, and preparing for emergencies and riots. We then focus on the provision of prison programs, as the most important responsibility of a prison is to release offenders better able to be successful law-abiding citizens. The varieties of programs (education, substance abuse, mental health, work, religious, and recreation) are all described. We conclude Part 4 with a description of how prison administrators manage and provide quality services that are basic to successful prison operations. These include health care, food service, visiting, mail, and inmate commissary operations.

Finally, our study of correctional administration is concluded with a look to the future. Many issues that will confront correctional administrators over the next decade are presented and discussed. You will realize that correctional administration is not a static event; it evolves in anticipation and response to issues that must be confronted. Many such issues deal with the types of special management of groups of offenders (aging, juveniles, women, and sex offenders). A significant issue over the past decade that has changed the expectations for the next decade is prisoner reentry. We conclude our study of correctional administration with questions for the future. Where are we going? How will community supervision of offenders change? How will technology impact correctional administration? Will there be a rebirth of rehabilitation?

This text was written with several goals in mind, but the most important goal was to give those who are considering corrections as a career or who are preparing for the role as a correctional administrator a realistic appraisal of what their intended vocation looks like. I also suggest that students read, if they have not already done so, my book *Corrections: An Introduction* (Third Edition), which is also published by Pearson Education (2011). This text lays a more basic groundwork of the real-life activities of someone who works in corrections and the clients served by correctional agencies. There are also outstanding videos we shot of correctional administrators and line staff, elected officials, judges, and inmates and offenders under community supervision. These videos really illustrate the practical world of corrections.

For this book *Correctional Administration: Integrating Theory and Practice*, we attempted to convey the difficulty of the work in this arena, as well as the potential enjoyment and fulfillment that can accompany doing a challenging job well, while contributing to the public good. With the combination of background, philosophy, policy, and current practice, you get an authentic and pragmatic understanding of the world of correctional administration.

This text includes a variety of learning tools and aids. Practical Perspectives present real case studies of correctional administrators, the challenges they faced, and the decisions they made to handle a situation in a certain manner. The Key Terms reinforce your understanding of the terminology of corrections and correctional administration. Like any discipline, correctional administration has a language unto itself, and familiarity with the terms and their uses helps you learn and become comfortable in your study. In the feature You're the Correctional Administrator, you are put into the role of an administrator that must act and make a decision. The decision is not always simple and there may be no obvious "right" choice. But struggling with the situation you find must use knowledge and resources to respond to a problem and develop a solution. Web Link Exercises provide you with Web site addresses that relate to the topics being studied. Not only are you instructed to visit the Web sites but you are also assigned learning activities to complete. You also have Group Exercises for each chapter that give you a group assignment that is both a learning opportunity and a great way for a classroom group to work together and learn from each other.

Overall, this text is geared toward building knowledge of correctional administration that can be used throughout your careers. The examples and case studies convey not only the types of substantive issues that must be addressed but also the thought processes that are often used in considering optional solutions to problems. Corrections is not a career for those who do not want to be challenged, who do not want to be in a "people business," and who do not want to contribute to the protection and safety of society. It is for those who are willing to expose themselves to public scrutiny, second-guessing, and even life-and-death decision making. This text is designed to prepare you for these career challenges.

Richard P. Seiter, Ph.D.

Acknowledgments

I wish to acknowledge the many people who helped to make this book possible. First, thanks to my colleagues in academia and in practical corrections. I have learned from and served with so many fine professionals that model outstanding correctional administration and provided much fruit from which to pick and enrich chapters with. Second, I thank the many people who provided information, pictures, and feedback to make the book more interesting and useful to students. Many correctional agencies provided information and photographs. Special thanks go to the Federal Bureau of Prisons, the Ohio Department of Rehabilitation and Correction, and Correctional Corporation of America that provided several pictures that will help bring this book to life for students. Anne Diestel, archivist at the Federal Bureau of Prisons and Julie Walburn, Communications Chief for the Ohio Department of Rehabilitation and Correction spent much time finding and providing pictures. And Corrections Corporation of America allowed me access to take pictures and access to their photo bank so that challenges and opportunities for correctional administrators are illustrated as well as described. And special thanks go to Professor Mike Montgomery of Tennessee State University. Mike assisted in updating much of the information, wrote all of the Web and Group Exercises, and wrote a first draft of Chapter 2.

Second, I thank the staff at Pearson Prentice Hall, who assisted in many ways. Eric Krassow is the acquisitions editor for criminal justice and I thank him for his guidance and support. I especially appreciate the work of Jessica Sykes, Production Project Manager at Pearson. Jessy not only gave me considerable advice and information and guided the development of the second edition. I also wish to thank Todd Hobson, Redlands Community Center; Darrell L. Legg, Marshall University; and James S. Opolot, Texas Southern University. They reviewed the first edition of this textbook and provided several suggestions for organization, topics, and student learning opportunities. I found their suggestions extremely valuable to improving the text, and making it more readable and useful for students of correctional administration.

Finally, I thank my many friends and family members who encouraged and supported me during the writing of this book. My son Matt, to whom both editions of this book are dedicated, not only provides me common sense on my work and industry, but also is a model for a strong work ethic, and provides humor and encouragement. Thank you Matt; I am so proud of you. And thanks to my wonderful wife Riffi O'Brien, who not only took some of the pictures used, but also heard all of the complaints of how hard I was working, and was a constant source of motivation.

I owe you all a debt of gratitude. Thank you.

Richard P. Seiter, Ph.D.

1

Correctional Administration: Past to Present

What Is Correctional Administration?

Is management the same as administration? Is leadership the same as management? Does the administration of a correctional agency differ from the administration of some other public agency? These are the kinds of questions this textbook is designed to answer, while providing the student or practitioner of correctional administration a framework for understanding the essential functions of a correctional agency and the role of managers and leaders in that agency.

First, it is important to have a common understanding of terms. For purposes of this textbook, *administration* is a broad term which encompasses both leadership and management and includes all the activities and functions that leaders and managers must do to guide and direct an agency toward today's mission and tomorrow's challenges. **Correctional administration** is guiding and directing an agency responsible for the safekeeping of criminal offenders and includes the traditional management functions of planning, organizing, staffing, directing, and controlling. It requires a thorough substantive knowledge of corrections and correctional issues. And, it includes showing leadership by empowering staff and guiding them toward the future. While there are currently many private, for-profit companies that contract with governments to conduct this function, this textbook will primarily address the role of public correctional administration.

As we begin our study of correctional administration, keep in mind the definition of correctional administration—*guiding and directing an agency responsible for the safekeeping of criminal offenders. Safekeeping* of criminal offenders is herein used as a broad term to include protecting the public from further crimes committed by offenders, through both supervising and preparing them to be successful and law-abiding citizens after completion of their period of supervision from a correctional agency. In that sense, safekeeping of criminal offenders can take place in the community as well as in a prison or other residential setting. Safekeeping also represents a balance between supervision and programming for offenders and cannot be achieved to its fullest with an emphasis on one function over another.

Guiding and directing an agency are used herein to convey a unique aspect of administration. When most people think of administration, they think of "running something" and being the boss who tells people what to do. Administration is far more complex than that. Organizations must have a vision, mission, and goals; they must have a focus, and staff must work together to move the organization toward accomplishing the goals. Administrators have the very challenging task of bringing together the resources of an agency (staff, budgets, and facilities) in a coordinated fashion to put the organization in the best position to accomplish their mission. In that sense, an administrator is like a football coach, who puts certain players on the field, gives them scouting reports of what to expect from their opponent, and modifies the game plan as the game progresses and the situation changes. The coach's job is to put the team in the best possible position to win the game and let them accomplish as much as they can with their God-given abilities.

Guiding and directing has a future as well as a present context. Not only must administrators maximize the use of resources and coordinate functions so their agencies can accomplish their missions in the current state, but they must also envision the future and guide their agencies in a direction to increase performance and success in coming years. This requires understanding the forces and pressures that currently face an agency, anticipating change and developing trends, and preparing the agency to meet future expected and unexpected challenges.

For the purpose of definition, the textbook will use four levels of delineation for correctional staff. **Line staff** are employees or personnel responsible for carrying out the prescribed procedures and activities of the agency. Examples of line staff are correctional officers in a prison who conduct security functions and supervise inmates, parole or probation officers who monitor whether offenders meet the conditions of their parole or probation, and drug treatment counselors who conduct group and individual counseling for offenders required to participate in such programs as a part of their criminal sanctions. **Supervisors** are the next level of staff that oversee and direct the work of line staff. Their specific duty is to ensure that the work of staff is within required procedures while promoting efficiency and compliance with agency policies.

The third level of staff are **managers**, responsible for setting their department or division goals and objectives and ensuring their successful completion. Managers are responsible for controlling resources, such as budget dollars and staff allocations, and disbursing those resources in a manner that best accomplishes their goals and objectives. The final level are **leaders**, who provide direction, empower staff, and deal with external agencies and political leadership. Their external interactions are critical to gain support for allocation of resources and establishment of the authorities under which the agency functions.

This delineation of four staff levels (as illustrated in Figure 1-1) is an oversimplification of a general table of organization for a public agency. There can be, and usually is, overlap in these roles and functions. Many supervisors are also managers under these definitions. Many managers are also leaders. Although perhaps an oversimplification, these broad definitions will assist the reader in understanding material presented later in this text.

Why Is It important to study correctional Administration?

Correctional administration is one of the most challenging, unpredictable, and varied professions of any public or private management operation. Correctional administration students soon understand the diverse challenges that face a modern-day correctional administrator. Over the past twenty years, corrections is the most rapidly growing public

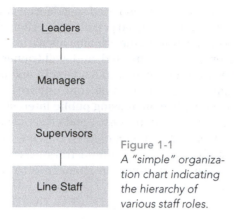

Figure 1-1
A "simple" organiza-
tion chart indicating
the hierarchy of
various staff roles.

sector function and perhaps, other than information technology, the most rapidly grow-ing "business" in the American economy. Corrections is growing in the number of offend-ers it handles, it is growing in the staff required to carry out the functions, it is growing in the quantity of tax dollars directed to its operation, and it is growing in public interest. Consequently, the administration of correctional agencies is also becoming more com-plex, and this complexity may require a need to rethink the traditional ways correctional agencies operate and also our long-held beliefs on how we manage and punish criminal offenders. The future challenges for correctional administrators mandate that future correctional leaders will have to be innovative, aggressive, and bold as they approach their roles and responsibilities.

The growth of corrections is expected to continue. Despite the fact (see Figure 1-2) that both violent and property crimes have been on a continual decline since 1993, the pubic fear of crime continues. However, a 2008 Gallup poll indicated a concern, as 44 percent of citizens polled still believed that there was more crime now than the year before.[1] With fear of crime continuing, even with the actual reduction in the likelihood of

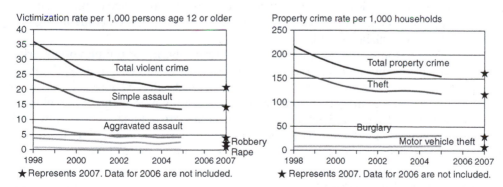

Figure 1-2
Violent and property crime rates: 1998–2007. Source: Michael R. Rand, "Criminal Victimization, 2007," National Crime Victimization Survey (Washington, D.C.: U.S. Department of Justice, December 2008), pp. 2–3.

victimization, elected officials respond by increased spending on law enforcement, expanded definitions of criminal activities, and enhanced penalties for criminal offenses. The end result is more and more resources going toward the criminal justice and correctional system.

This creates a need for talented, educated, and well-trained individuals to enter the field of corrections and moving their way into leadership and administrative positions. The issues that correctional administrators must confront are some of the most complex in the public sector. And even with an increasing public interest, there is a lack of understanding of corrections, and its operations, costs, and effectiveness. Correctional administrators must therefore educate the public, elected officials, and even their staff. It is important for students to study correctional administration as proficient and professional correctional administrators are needed today and tomorrow to guide corrections through this rapid growth and uncertain future.

The Background of Correctional Administration

As we begin the study of correctional administration, it is valuable to understand its history from two perspectives. The first is how the discipline of both private and public sector management has developed throughout the history of the United States. The second is how the more specific discipline of correctional administration has developed, mirroring the prevalent theories of corrections, and how those theories have influenced the practice of correctional administration.

In this regard, correctional administration should be studied as an interactive entity, influenced by general management theory and by public expectations regarding the role of correctional agencies. When referring to the private sector, the term "management" is used rather than "administration." "Administration" is almost exclusively a "public sector" term, without a parallel in the private sector. Yet, "administration" as defined above for the public sector is similar to the more general term of "management" in the private sector.

It is easily argued that corrections is influenced both by the broader approaches to private and public management and by public opinion and political reaction regarding the issue of crime. What makes correctional administration and management so complex today is that corrections is a highly visible activity, a large percentage of public funds go toward its operations, and criminal justice is one of the top issues confronting every elected official and legislative body.

The first section of this chapter presents a brief history of public versus private management approaches and continues with the development of correctional theory and the impact that theory has had on management practices. As already noted, it is important to understand general management practices and how they incrementally developed to where we are today. Theory and practice in any discipline are not just created; they evolve in an incremental fashion from past theory and practice. By understanding from where a discipline has come, it is possible to better understand where it will go.

Private Sector Management

Throughout history, public sector governments have copied the private sector in terms of styles of management and organization. For private sector companies, no matter how they started or how technologically sophisticated their product or processes have become, most can trace their work styles and organizational roots back to the prototypical pin factory that Adam Smith described in *The Wealth of Nations*, published in 1796.[2] Smith recognized that the technology of the industrial revolution had created unprecedented opportunities for manufacturers to increase worker productivity and thus reduce the cost of goods, not by small percentages, which one might achieve by persuading an artisan to work a little faster, but by orders of magnitude. From his studies of industry, Smith developed what he called the principle of division of labor.

Smith's principle embodied his observations that some number of specialized workers, each performing a single step in the manufacture of a pin, could make far more pins in a day than the same number of generalists, each engaged in making whole pins. Today's airlines, steel mills, accounting firms, and government agencies all have been built around Smith's central idea—the division or specialization of labor. Usually, the larger the organization, the more specialized is the worker and the more separate steps into which the work is divided.

Another development in the way in which organizations operate resulted because of innovative changes in the ways in which goods could be shipped. In the 1920s, Americans began to build railroads. To prevent collisions on single-track lines that carried trains in both directions, railroad companies invented formalized operating procedures and organizational structure and mechanisms to carry them out. Management created a rule for every contingency they could imagine, and lines of authority and reporting were clearly drawn. The railroad companies literally programmed their workers to act only in accordance with the rules, which was the only way management knew to make their one-track systems predictable, workable, and safe. Requiring workers to conform to established procedures remains the essence of bureaucracy even today. The command and control systems in place in most companies and government today embody the same principles introduced in the railroad industry almost a century ago.

Soon thereafter, Henry Ford improved on Smith's concept of dividing work into smaller, repeatable tasks with the invention of the assembly line, thereby bringing the work to the worker. Alfred Sloan, head of General Motors, created the prototype of the management system that Ford's efficient factory system demanded. Sloan created smaller, decentralized divisions that managers could oversee from a small corporate headquarters simply by monitoring production and financial numbers. He was applying Smith's principle of division of labor to management just as Ford had applied it to production, as corporate executives did not need general expertise in all areas such as manufacturing or marketing. They could oversee these operations simply by creating and monitoring quantitative goals. Companies created divisions dealing with production, quality, shipping, and finance. And similarly, government agencies created departments such as finance, human resources, delivery of program services, and operations.

The final evolutionary step in the development of corporations came about in the United States between the end of World War II and the 1960s, a period of enormous economic expansion. Through elaborate planning exercises, senior managers determined the various types of businesses in which they wanted the corporation to be involved, how much capital they should allocate to each, and what returns they would expect the operating manager of these businesses to deliver. Large staff of corporate controllers, planners, and auditors acted as the executives' eyes and ears, ferreting out data about performance and intervening to adjust the plans and activities of operating managers. During this period, the consumer had money to spend, and after being deprived of material goods (first by the Depression and then by the war), customers were more than happy to buy whatever companies had to offer, regardless of quality or service. The chief operational concern of managers, and how they responded to the needs placed upon them, was to expand capacity or increase the ability of the company to produce and deliver their products to their customers. Most corporations were organized as a pyramid, well suited to expansion by simply adding workers to the bottom of the organizational chart, and then filling in the management layers above them. This type of organization is also well suited to control and planning and therefore proliferated through much of the twentieth century.

The Public Sector

Following the private sector models, government similarly developed its organization and structure. Government has always been based on a bureaucratic model. When developed over 100 years ago, the term *bureaucracy* had a much more positive perception than it does today. At that time, bureaucracy connoted a rational, efficient method of organization. Mirroring the division of labor created by Adam Smith and the need for procedures and control developed by the early railroads, bureaucracy was designed to replace the arbitrary exercise of power by authoritarian regimes. Following periods when strong political bosses operated government agencies as they desired, policies and procedures, command and control, and civil service systems were put in place as reform measures for government agencies. Bureaucracy was seen as precision, speed, and reduction of ambiguity.

Today, things have changed. The bureaucratic model of government developed when society was slower paced and change was incremental. Bureaucracy began with the use of a top-down hierarchy, when only those at the top of the organization had enough information to make informed decisions. It developed in a society of people who worked with their hands, not their minds. It developed in a time of mass markets, when most Americans had similar wants and needs.

We now live in an era of rapid change. We live in a global marketplace and an information society in which people get access to information almost as fast as their leaders. The economy is knowledge based, in which educated workers bridle at command and control and demand involvement and the authority to act. In the public sector, employees are important customers, and managers and administrators must recognize the culture and expectations of their employees/customers.

In this fast paced and continually changing environment, bureaucratic institutions created during the industrial era are often ineffective. Today's environment demands organizations that are extremely flexible and adaptable, that deliver high-quality goods and services, that are responsive to customers, and that empower workers and citizens. Correctional organizations were modeled after traditional, bureaucratic organizations. They have historically been inflexible, highly structured, and with strong central authority. But even in a correctional setting, organizations have had to change to respond to the world in which we live, use educated employees to their benefit, and use information technology to improve operations.

Practical Perspectives

Life as a Correctional Administrator

Correctional administration is a very difficult career. It is probably one of the most complex of public sector management and requires the skills of a surgeon, the leadership of Churchill, the charisma of JFK, the wisdom of Job, the diplomacy of Kissinger, the patience of a loving parent, the skin of an elephant (tough), and the stomach of a goat. By this, I mean able to eat and digest almost anything. There has probably never been a more difficult time to be a correctional administrator. Inmates are serving longer sentences with little hope for early release; there are more violent and gang-affiliated offenders. We are not sure how we want to supervise offenders in the community. Budgets are so tight we are cutting to the bone, and the public and elected officials have no tolerance for error. So, why does anyone want to be a correctional administrator?

Good question. Obviously, some people still do, or there would be no course in correctional administration and no need for this book. There are those who have entered the field of corrections knowing it is not an easy job, but with a commitment to serve and try to make a better life for our citizens, to help their staff reach their career goals, and to help inmates improve their skills and motivation to be successful and avoid future criminality. And thank goodness, they make the decision to serve and do what they can to improve the corrections profession and all those who it serves.

Life as a correctional administrator is much different now than it was a few decades ago. My entire career has been in corrections and I have been in some administrative role for over thirty years. What is different? Almost everything. The offenders are different. There are many more; they are more violent; they serve longer sentences; the communities in which they live or to which they will return are unstable and unable to provide them much support. They have more program needs such as substance abuse, need for education and training, and preparation to take a job in a more complex job market. The staff are different in that Generation X and Y are not believed to be as committed to their employer, want to be involved in forming policy and decision making, and seek more immediate gratification in terms of pay, benefits, and time off work. They are a very skilled workforce, however, and if administrators are able to meet their needs, they can deliver and adapt to change very quickly.

Correctional organizations are different, as they have more demands to manage the external environment and respond to the high visibility of corrections in the public domain. Comparing a correctional system headquarters now and one three decades ago is like a comparison of The Spirit of St. Louis and the Space Shuttle. And the issues faced by correctional administrators are much more complex than they were in the past. Later in this chapter is a description of how correctional philosophy has influenced correctional administration. The philosophy under which administrators must work and lead today has evolved to a level more complex than in any public sector agency. Administrators are expected to punish and deter offenders through Spartan prisons with few amenities and through monitoring those in the community to a point that reduces the chance they commit further crimes. They are also expected to rehabilitate offenders by understanding and meeting their needs for self-improvement. Somehow, it seems that no one sees how these two diverse goals can make it more difficult to accomplish one or the other.

And leadership today is much more multifaceted than in the past. The description of transactional leadership in Chapters 2 and 3 illustrate how out-of-date it is. However, it certainly was easier to accomplish. More contemporary transformational leadership provides the opportunity to grow and cultivate an organization into one that can meet the challenges of tomorrow. However, being a transformational leader is much more difficult to accomplish and takes a more sophisticated person than in the past. Thanks to those who are and desire to become correctional administrators. Your country, the profession, and the clients and staff need you and need you to be successful. I hope through your study and personal development you reach your personal goals and lead your agencies to reach theirs as well.

The Evolution of Correctional Philosophy and Its Effect on Administration

Since public agencies are to carry out the will of their citizens, management practices usually develop to reflect the mission and philosophical approach of the era. Throughout the history of corrections in the United States, there has been an evolution of focus resulting in changing missions of corrections. During early periods in the nation's history, correctional agencies focused almost exclusively on the punishment of offenders. At other times, the focus included the need for rehabilitation. More recently, there has been a blend of punishment and rehabilitation, resulting in an emphasis on public safety. The following sections provide a brief overview of how the evolution of correctional philosophy has influenced the managerial approach to correctional administration.

Stages of Correctional Development

Throughout the history of corrections, the overriding philosophies and expectations of correctional sanctions influenced what correctional administrators did and the practices they put in place. As our nation was in its infancy, methods and approaches for dealing with criminals were related to prior experiences in England, yet often reflected a desire to do things differently than in the "mother country." The creation of prisons as a criminal sanction occurred in the United States when the Walnut Street Jail in Philadelphia converted a wing to hold sentenced prisoners in 1790. For the next eighty years, U.S. prisons continued the focus on strict discipline, hard work, and inmates doing penance for their discretions. But during the latter part of the 1800s, things began to change.[3]

From 1870 until 1910, corrections was in the **reformatory era**, driven by a need to respond to the overcrowding of prisons and the building and operation of prisons to alleviate it. U.S. prison administrators followed the early work of Captain Alexander Maconochie, who in 1840 had taken over the British penal colony on Norfolk Island, and Sir Walter Crofton, who built on the ideas of Maconochie when he became head of the Irish penal system. These two men used the concept of indeterminate sentencing, emphasizing preparing offenders for release, an opportunity for inmates to gradually reduce control and work their way to a less restricted environment, and release on a conditional basis when administrators determined the offender was prepared to return to the community. The concept of conditional release led to the development of parole in the United States. Correctional managers in the reformatory era had to change their focus from punishing the offender while they reflected on their past behavior. The reformatory era emphasized looking forward, and prisons provided education and other programs so that offenders could concentrate on avoiding crime in the future.

Soon after the turn of the century, American corrections turned to the **industrial prison era**, which lasted from 1910 to 1935. During this period, the number of inmates in U.S. prisons grew over 170 percent,[4] resulting in the construction of several new prisons designed to hold large numbers of inmates in harsh, work-oriented environments. The emphasis was on having inmates work and produce products that could help to make the prisons self-sustaining. Using their free labor, prisons became very

Staff at the McNeil Island (WA) Federal Penitentiary (c. 1895). Correctional administration was much simpler in the 1980s, when there were few staff or inmate issues.
(Courtesy of the Federal Bureau of Prisons)

successful at this, prison management emphasized production as much as security and rehabilitation, and the volume of prison-made products sold on the open market increased considerably.

However, the success of prison industries brought challenges from organized labor. As a result, the U.S. Congress passed two laws, the Hawes–Cooper Act in 1929 and the Ashurst–Sumners Act in 1935, which was amended in 1940, that severely limited the sale of prison-made products on the open market. These statutes tolled the death knell for the industrial prison, and thousands of inmates who had previously been working were forced into idleness. With nothing for inmates to do, prison administrators had to find another approach. From 1935 to 1960 was the **period of transition**, as enforced idleness, a lack of professional programs, and the excessive size and overcrowding of prisons resulted in an increase in prisoner discontent and prison riots. Prison managers were constrained in what they could do with the large facilities they had inherited, and struggled to find alternative approaches to maintain control of very difficult to operate prisons. As a result of all the problems prisons were experiencing, the U.S. Supreme Court ended its **"hands-off" doctrine**, which had restricted judicial intervention in the operation of prisons and the judgment of correctional administrators. By accepting cases filed by inmates under the Fourteenth Amendment to the U.S. Constitution, the Court opened a "Pandora's box," and the floodgates opened to decisions by federal courts demanding certain procedures or operations be instituted in prisons.

With the federal courts mandating it, correctional officials themselves also looked for ways to reform their operations. They realized that they could not provide a safe and secure environment for inmates or staff with a large number of idle inmates. Reforms included the professionalizing of staff through recruitment and training and implementation of many self-improvement programs to take the place of the industrial work programs.

Inmates working in the prison factory at the Lewisburg (PA) Federal Penitentiary (c. 1935). Prisons during the industrial era had large factories to keep inmates busy. When these factories and the inmate workers were idled, new methods to maintain security were needed.
(Courtesy of the Federal Bureau of Prisons)

As such, prisons entered the **rehabilitative era**, which lasted from 1960 to 1980. During this time, prison programs provided by professional staff took the place of the industrial prison with a focus on work.

During the rehabilitative era, corrections adopted the **medical model** of managing inmates. With the medical model, offenders were believed to be sick, or "inflicted" with problems that caused their criminality. A medical approach was therefore appropriate for management, and offenders were diagnosed and treated in a "hospital"-like setting. It was believed that offenders' problems could be resolved through programming and they could be returned to the community "well" and able to successfully lead a crime-free life.

Correctional officials realized that while the medical model made sense, it left out the importance of the transition to the community after release, and "reintegration" joined the focus on rehabilitation. **Reintegration** represented the inclusion of the community into the medical model, as it was understood that the transition from prison to free citizen in society was a difficult step for most offenders to make. Community correctional programs were in their heyday, and dollars and ideas on how to bridge the gap between the prison and the community were readily available.

The Death of the Medical Model

In the early 1970s, Robert Martinson completed a review of all correctional research to determine what worked in the treatment of offenders. Martinson and his colleagues analyzed over 200 separate studies of the effectiveness of correctional treatment programs in reducing recidivism. While there were a few isolated correlations between a treatment program and a reduction in recidivism, there were no consistent findings of the effect of any single treatment program significantly reducing recidivism.[5] Therefore, the Martinson review concluded that "**nothing works**." This revelation spelled the death knell for the medical model, and public officials looking for a way to reduce costs and make corrections more punitive had their statistical support. Soon, rehabilitative programs were not being funded in many jurisdictions, and parole was eliminated in several states. The theory was that if these programs did not help keep the public safe or change offender behavior, why spend money on them.

The Last Twenty-Five Years

Developments over the past twenty-five years of correctional history represent the most dramatic changes in philosophy, policy, and practice of correctional administrators. As a result of the criticism over the medical model, correctional administration sought safe cover and their retreat led to a philosophy and practice of improving management and focusing on corrections as a part of the criminal justice process. The primary mission became protection of society. Correctional administrators emphasized managing the criminal justice process in an efficient manner, accepting that corrections could not change offenders, and therefore they would do their jobs with competence and professionalism. Corrections would continue to offer programs; however, it was the offenders' responsibility to take advantage of opportunities and change if they wanted to. This period emphasizing "efficient management" unfortunately resulted in almost a generation of correctional administrators forgetting why most people sought a career in corrections—to help make a difference in offenders.

The practical advantage of this period was that the corrections profession became better managed. Interestingly, the most career-enhancing postgraduate degree for correctional workers changed from masters in social work to masters in public administration. Objective risk assessment resulted in corrections doing a better job of classifying and supervising offenders according to danger and risk; information technology helped in the management of information for both efficiency and better decision making; training and staff development became more professionalized; and budget development and management systems were improved. This era also resulted in corrections strengthening its links with other criminal justice components, as the mission was perceived to be very similar to that of law enforcement and the court system.

The "Get Tough on Crime" Mentality

As crime increased during the 1980s, the public fear of crime and criminals increased, and corrections (which had almost been totally ignored in the public mind) became very important to the society and elected officials. Throughout the 1990s, constant media coverage of tragic and senseless violence created a fear of and anger about the crime issue. Political rhetoric emphasized the need to be tough on criminals, keep them away from law-abiding citizens, and make them serve "hard" time. Correctional administrators, therefore, were forced to rethink and reposition their priorities. Corrections had to react to the need to be tough, offer few amenities to prisoners, and emphasize public safety

Inmates wearing stripes. The "tough on crime" era has even resulted in going back to forcing inmates to wear striped clothing, chain gangs, and other ways to be punitive.
(Courtesy of Maricopa County (AZ) Sheriff's Office)

over all else. This "get tough" approach resulted in administrators avoiding even minimal risks that could allow offenders to commit new crimes and create a media and political frenzy. With this retrenchment and avoidance of risk, there was little advancement in knowledge and professional development.

During this period, judicial discretion was limited and the legislative branch of government began to dominate sentencing practices in many states and the federal government. Legislative reforms of sentencing included implementation of mandatory minimum sentences and three-strikes law to require lengthy prison terms for some criminals, emphasizing a "just desserts" approach to crime and punishment. During the 1980s, there was concern that some offenders were getting probation when the severity of their crime should have resulted in a sentence to prison. In response, mandatory minimum sentences were adopted by forty-eight states and the federal government to require that for certain crimes (violence, use of a gun, and drug distribution) and types of offenders (habitual criminals and sexual predators) there must be a sentence to prison for a set minimum term.

Several states also passed the three-strikes law requiring judges to sentence third-time felons to extremely long prison sentences (often twenty years, thirty years, or life). These laws were intended to incapacitate habitual and dangerous law violators who commit three felonies so that they could not continue to prey on law-abiding citizens. The initial passage of such a law by the state of Washington in 1993 was intended to target repeat violent offenders. In 1994, California expanded the definition of those who come under the law and allowed some second-felony offenders to be included. At this time, twenty-six states have passed three-strikes law. As with other mandatory minimum sentences, the three-strikes laws is often an overreaction to crime-control efforts.[6]

Recent Developments in Correctional Philosophy

Even as a punitive attitude about crime, sentencing, and offenders developed, there has never been a complete withdrawal of support for rehabilitation. In fact, a recent survey found that 87 percent of the U.S. voting public is in favor of rehabilitative services for prisoners as opposed to a punishment-only system.[7] And more than 90 percent of those surveyed support providing a variety of programs by rating providing job training, drug treatment, mental health services, family support, and housing guidance to inmates as "important."[8]

Another positive development is that recent studies have indicated considerable evidence of positive results from treatment programs. Since the Martinson "nothing works" findings, the use of more sophisticated techniques for reviews of research has provided evidence of the success of correctional treatment. One technique is the use of meta-analysis, which allows researchers to examine many different outcome studies of programs, identify their individual indicators of success, and link those to each other to determine overall success of any particular treatment modality.[9]

Researchers have also begun to measure the quality of correctional programs in assessing their effectiveness. Reviews have defined high-quality treatment programs as those that are based on identified offender needs, targeted at high-risk offenders, delivered outside the correctional environment, fully implemented, and include follow-up after completion of treatment.[10] Using these updated methods, many reviews of treatment programs now conclude that certain categories of treatment programs are effective when implemented in a quality fashion.[11]

The new information regarding the effectiveness of correctional treatment has led to increased support by elected officials and policymakers and to a rebirth in rehabilitation. While the public wants criminals punished, there is support for providing offenders rehabilitative programs. And rehabilitative programs often prove that they are cost-effective and save the government at least as much money as they cost. It is much easier for a correctional official to argue for expending funds for correctional programs by citing data that illustrate how investing in the program reduces recidivism and protects society.

Correctional populations

The number of adults under correctional supervision has grown dramatically over the past three decades. As indicated in Table 1-1, in the United States, only 1.8 million adults were on probation and parole and in jail and prison in 1980. By 1988, this number had doubled, and by 2008, there were more than 7.3 million adults under the supervision of correctional agencies.

A significant percentage of the growth in the correctional population comes from increases in the prison population. As a result of the "get tough on crime" era, incarceration as a criminal sanction has skyrocketed over the past thirty years. In 1980, the rate of sentenced inmates incarcerated per 100,000 population was only 139. By 2008, the rate of sentenced adults incarcerated per 100,000 population had reached 762.[12] Although the incarceration rate increased every year during the period and more than doubled between 1980 and 1990, the rate of increase has continued to grow from 2000 to 2008. However, a major change that will be addressed later in this textbook is that

Table 1.1
NUMBER OF PERSONS UNDER CORRECTIONAL SUPERVISION 1980–2008

	Probation	Jail	Prison	Parole	Total[a]
1980	1,118,097	183,988	319,598	220,438	1,842,100
1981	1,225,934	196,785	360,029	225,539	2,008,300
1982	1,357,264	209,582	402,914	224,604	2,194,400
1983	1,582,947	223,551	423,898	246,440	2,476,800
1984	1,740,948	234,500	448,264	266,992	2,690,700
1985	1,968,712	256,615	487,593	300,203	3,013,100
1986	2,114,621	274,444	526,436	325,638	3,241,100
1987	2,247,158	295,873	562,814	355,505	3,461,400
1988	2,356,483	343,569	607,766	407,977	3,715,800
1989	2,522,125	395,553	683,367	456,803	4,057,800
1990	2,670,234	405,320	743,382	531,407	4,350,300
1991	2,728,472	426,479	792,535	590,442	4,537,900
1992	2,811,611	444,584	850,566	658,601	4,765,400
1993	2,903,061	459,804	909,381	676,100	4,948,300
1994	2,981,022	486,474	990,147	690,371	5,148,000
1995	3,077,861	507,044	1,078,542	679,421	5,342,900
1996	3,164,996	518,492	1,127,528	679,733	5,490,700
1997	3,296,513	567,079	1,176,564	694,787	5,734,900
1998	3,670,441	592,462	1,224,469	696,385	6,134,200
1999	3,779,922	605,943	1,287,172	714,457	6,340,800
2000	3,826,209	621,149	1,316,333	723,898	6,445,100
2001	3,931,731	631,240	1,330,007	732,333	6,581,700
2002	4,024,067	665,475	1,367,547	750,934	6,758,800
2003[b]	4,120,012	691,301	1,390,279	769,925	6,924,500
2004	4,143,792	713,990	1,421,345	771,852	6,995,000
2005	4,166,757	747,529	1,448,344	780,616	7,051,900
2006	4,215,361	765,819	1,492,973	799,875	7,182,100
2007[c]	4,234,471	780,174	1,517,867	821,177	7,274,300
2008	4,270,917	785,556	1,518,559	828,169	7,308,200

(continued)

Table 1.1   Continued

Note: The jail and prison counts represent the custody populations, which refer to the number of inmates held in local jails or state and federal prisons, respectively. The custody population is not comparable to the jurisdiction population, which refers to the entity having legal authority regardless of where the inmate is held. For more details, see "Definitions" in *Prisoners in 2008* (PDF file 1.5M).

[a]Because some offenders have multiple statuses (i.e., held in a prison or jail but remain under the jurisdiction of a probation or parole authority) totals for 2007–08 exclude probationers and parolees held in jail or prison and parolees who were also on probation. Totals for 2005–06 exclude probationers and parolees held in jail or prison. Totals for 2000–04 only exclude probationers held in jail or prison. For these reasons, details do not sum to totals.

[b]The 2003 probation and parole counts were estimated any may differ from previously published counts.

[c]Some states were unable to provide data for 2007. See *Methodology* in

Probation and Parole in the United States, 2007 - Statistical Tables (PDF file 355K) and Prisoners in 2007 (PDF file 195K).

Source: Bureau of Justice Statistics, Correctional Populations, *Key Facts at a Glance,* http://www.bjs.ojp.usdoj.gov/contents/glance/tables/corr2tab.htm (accessed April 20, 2010).

early estimates suggest that in 2009, the state prison population actually decreased for the first time in nearly forty years. The Pew Center for the States collected data that indicate that as of January 1, 2010, there were 1,403,091 inmates in state prisons. That is a decrease of 5,739 from the number of inmates on December 31, 2008.[13] The projections for change in the future and what it might mean for correctional administrators is addressed in Chapter 16.

The Goals of Corrections

The goals of corrections include punishment, deterrence, incapacitation, rehabilitation, and restitution. The most dominant correctional goal has historically been **punishment**, the infliction of pain or suffering. Through punishment, society can maintain order and show fairness to those who do not violate the law. People need to see that those who demonstrate inappropriate behavior receive their "just desserts," or what is coming to them.

The idea of *lex talionis* (Latin for "law of retribution") is similar to the biblical adage of "an eye for an eye" and indicates that offenders should get the punishment they deserve. Punishment is primarily focused on the past, in that it is in exchange for the commission of a criminal violation. However, it is closely linked to more future-oriented correctional goals, such as deterrence or rehabilitation. Punishment is necessary for deterrence, and the presence of punishment encourages rehabilitation. Punishment is also reactive in that it focuses on the act or crime, rather than on the offender's particular circumstances or needs. Society believes that it is only fair and just that criminal offenders receive punishment for their crimes.

Our criminal codes must specify how much punishment is appropriate for the commission of a crime. The U.S. Supreme Court addressed this and created the "test of proportionality" in the 1983 case of *Solem v. Helm*, by declaring that "a criminal sentence must be proportionate to the crime for which the defendant has been convicted . . . and be guided by objective criteria, including (i) the gravity of the offense and the harshness of the penalty; (ii) the sentences imposed on other criminals in the same jurisdiction; and (iii) the sentences imposed for commission of the same crime in other jurisdictions . . . ."[14]

Deterrence is a goal focused on future actions (or the avoidance of certain actions) by both individuals and society. The expectation is that, as a result of offenders receiving punishment, society will be deterred from committing crimes in the future. Jeremy Bentham, in his 1789 concept of hedonistic calculus, argued that if the sanction for committing a crime inflicted a greater amount of pain than the pleasure resulting from the offense, crime would be prevented. When an individual commits a crime and receives a punishment, the punishment is designed to result in **specific deterrence** of that offender from committing further crimes. The idea is that the punishment the offender received created such an unpleasant situation that he or she will not want to experience it again. This certainly seems logical, but requires that offenders receive punishment that is swift, certain, and specifically linked to the criminal act. Unfortunately, justice today often does not end with these results.

Deterrence philosophies are also expected to have an effect on the general society. **General deterrence** presumes that others in society will not commit crimes, because they see that there is a punishment for such acts and that individuals do receive the prescribed punishments. This requires logic and rationality. The theory often breaks down, as criminals do not believe they will get caught, think they can get out of trouble with a good lawyer, or do not fear the available punishment enough for it to deter them from the criminal act.

Incapacitation is a goal that reduces offenders' ability or capacity to commit further crimes. Correctional sanctions restrict offenders' opportunity to continue their criminality and, through this restriction, society is protected from potential criminals. Incapacitation can be seen as both reactive in that it is a punishment for past crimes and proactive as it anticipates offenders' future actions. Carlson and colleagues argue that "Like retribution, incapacitation is reactive, and yet, like deterrence, it attempts to predict and influence future behavior."[15]

Blumstein suggests that there are two ways to define and view the correctional goal of incapacitation: "The most narrow is that incapacitation (through a sentence of imprisonment or death) makes it literally impossible for offenders to commit future crimes. In this view, incapacitation serves to [avert crimes] in the general society by isolation of the identified offenders during periods of incarceration."[16] Thus, incapacitation is believed to reduce crime by focusing on the offender who is being incapacitated or imprisoned, while the person is under the control of the authorities carrying out the punishment. Incapacitation is based on the belief that most criminals commit several crimes over their lifetimes and therefore, during the time of their criminal sanction, crime is being prevented by their reduced opportunity. Blumstein notes that incapacitation operates on the assumption that "punishment can take a slice out of an individual criminal career."[17] However, even a person who is in prison or on death row is capable of committing crimes against victims. In prison, inmates commit crimes of assault against other inmates or prison staff. Offenders in prison still use or deal in drugs. However, society is protected, even while those who work or live in prison are still potential victims of crime.

The second way to consider incapacitation is under a broader definition whereby offenders' opportunities to commit further crimes are lessened by the imposition of the criminal sentence. For instance, house arrest using electronic monitoring to ensure that an offender remains at home at prescribed times reduces the opportunity for criminal activity. Whenever an offender serving a sanction while in the community is under the supervision or monitoring of correctional staff, his or her opportunity to commit crime is reduced. As already noted, incapacitation is based on a belief that most criminals repeat their criminality. Studies have shown that most offenders commit more than one crime, and a small group of offenders commit a large percentage of crimes.[18]

These findings led to efforts to identify offenders with the greatest potential of committing a high number of crimes and sentence them to long prison terms, an approach referred to as **selective incapacitation**. Greenwood argues that to maximize the incapacitating result of imprisonment, scarce prison and jail space should be reserved for the most dangerous, violent, and repeat offenders.[19] It had earlier been concluded that if selected offenders who commit repetitive crimes were imprisoned and incapacitated for three or even five years, significantly fewer crimes would have been committed.[20]

The next goal of corrections is to rehabilitate offenders, that is, return them to society better able to avoid criminality and less likely to commit further crimes. In the case of criminal offenders, **rehabilitation** means to prepare them for a crime-free and successful life. The emphasis of rehabilitation is on preventing future crimes. Corrections attempts to rehabilitate offenders in many ways. First, correctional programs are aimed at trying to reduce offenders' motivation to commit further crimes. Although there are many reasons why people commit crimes, correctional agencies offer psychological counseling to help offenders understand the factors that trigger certain behaviors, anger management and other programs to help offenders recognize dangerous situations in which they may act wrongfully, and sensitivity training to get offenders to understand the impact of their criminal actions on victims and their families.

Second, correctional programs try to build competencies in offenders that may help them avoid problems that heighten their likelihood of committing crime. Such programs are designed to help offenders to increase their educational level, develop a vocational skill, or reduce the use of drugs or alcohol. Finally, correctional programs may simply have a goal of improving offenders' decision making. Why do offenders choose selling drugs over getting a legitimate job? Why do offenders choose to act out violently rather than avoid confrontation or seek nonviolent resolutions to problems? Or why do offenders steal others' property to make an easy buck? Some correctional programs help offenders improve their decision-making skills while considering the values and potential outcomes of their criminal actions.

The first four goals of corrections are widely acknowledged. Less mentioned is the goal of **restitution**, or making right by repaying society or victims for the wrongs done by offenders. Criminal sentences have historically included fines and victim restitution, but the principle of *restoration* of the damage resulting from crime has increased in importance, and many more criminal sentences include the opportunity for restitution as the sanctions are carried out.

Over the past two decades, **restorative justice** emerged as an alternative to traditional criminal sentencing. Restorative justice sentencing emphasizes involving the victim while holding offenders accountable for the harm they caused and finding opportunities for them to repair the damage. Freeman describes restorative justice as "a process that focuses on the injury resulting from the crime and works to repair the injury by shifting the role of the offender from passive recipient of punishment to active participant in reparation."[21] Because of the current recognized value of holding offenders responsible for "making right" the harm they have done with their crimes and the importance of involving the victim in the criminal justice process, restitution is now recognized as a goal of corrections, with importance comparable to that of the other four goals. In fact, and because of these reasons, this goal will probably continue to be seen as important in sentencing criminal offenders.

Correctional organizations today

The above information regarding correctional philosophy and goals provides students a background on which to understand the dynamics and trends that influence corrections and correctional administration. Correctional administrators face a much different environment today than they did 100 or even twenty-five years ago. There are several ways in which today's situation is different from the past. First, public opinion and political involvement in correctional policy and practice is very active, while in past years it was very passive. Crime is one of the nation's most visible issues and one that almost all citizens perceive affects them. Most citizens have an interest in the public policy regarding defense, environment, or economic development. However, they usually trust the details of the policy and practice is carried out by the professionals in these topic areas. However, with crime policy, there is not only high public interest but most people also have a strong opinion and take positions regarding how policies should be developed and implemented.

Second, correctional budgets make up a large percentage of the total budget of the federal, state, and local governments. With so much money allocated to any one area, a high amount of scrutiny is likely to follow. Big budgets get the attention of everyone: general citizens, interest groups for other social service programs, and elected officials. Supporters of increased budgets for education, child development programs, economic development, and other public programs see the increasing correctional budget as a threat to their interests. As such, these special interest groups generate support for their budget concerns, which are frequently in conflict with the growth of correctional budgets. Elected officials would like to avoid pouring more money into correctional operations. However, they never want to be seen as "soft on crime," and therefore do not want to change sentencing statutes in a way that would reduce the number of offenders under correctional supervision. These budget tensions created by no reduction in demand but often a reduction in funding forces correctional administrators to constantly reassess what they do and how they do it.

Finally, because of the extensive media coverage of high-profile crimes and sentencing practices, citizens develop a strong interest and opinion of how criminals should be dealt with. Most people are fed up with crime and support criminals receiving a sentence they perceive as punitive to hold offenders accountable for their behavior. As elected officials try to react to this concern and continue to enhance sentences, they end up with the same policy issues to confront—how tough to be and how much it costs.

Debates regarding these issues create even more visibility and interest in how correctional agencies operate and spend their public dollars.

Correctional administrators face many challenges in this highly charged environment. There is great interest in what they do. They require more resources to carry out their mission, yet there is little philosophical support for allocating the resources it takes to operate continually growing agencies. Even the most supportive and responsible elected officials would rather spend less on corrections and more on "politically popular" public programs. As a result, while corrections received little interest twenty-five years ago, correctional administrators in today's environment face a variety of issues.

SUMMARY

This chapter outlines the history of correctional administration, the evolution of correctional theory and how it impacts correctional administration, and the issues confronting corrections now and into the future. The remaining chapters of this text will expand on these topics. You will now have an understanding of how correctional administration is one of the most difficult roles in the public sector. As well, you should have an understanding of the importance of studying correctional administration, and think of it as a distinct profession, requiring a combination of education, experience, and personal preparation to perform effectively.

Correctional administration has developed into a unique discipline, and has been influenced by administrative theory and practice in both the public and private sectors. It has also been influenced by public opinion and the correctional philosophy prevalent over various periods and eras. Especially over the past twenty-five years, the public and political interest in correctional policy has not only caused administrators to focus on the internal operations of their agencies but also on the external environment and the forces and trends that impact public opinion. Successful correctional administrators must be adept at managing the external environment as well as successfully performing traditional management roles. At this early point in your study, you have the framework and understand the background of issues linked to administration in a correctional agency. The remainder of this text will build on this framework, and continue to challenge you to merge the theoretical and practical applications of correctional administration.

KEY TERMS

Correctional administration	Period of transition	Specific deterrence
Line staff	"Hands-off" doctrine	General deterrence
Supervisors	Restorative justice	Incapacitation
Managers	Reintegration	Selective incapacitation
Leaders	"Nothing works"	Rehabilitation
Reformatory era	Punishment	Restitution
Industrial Prison Era	Deterrence	Medical model

YOU'RE THE CORRECTIONAL ADMINISTRATOR

1. You are a probation administrator in a large metropolitan county. You have been increasingly concerned over the past decade about the trend toward surveillance and monitoring of probationers and the lack of support for rehabilitative programs like substance abuse and vocational training. There are more and more rules being passed down about the need to do urine tests for drug use, and a "zero tolerance" once someone tests dirty. Probation revocation rates are going up dramatically. While you agree that probationers who fail to meet their responsibilities should be revoked and sent to prison, you think the current reactive approach doesn't put enough emphasis on helping offenders, and many who are trying but have relatively small failures end up being sent to prison. You believe we need a more balanced approach to supervising probationers. How would you do this? What type of public message would you create about rehabilitative programs? How would you try to sell the need for these programs to your politically sensitive leadership?

2. You are in charge of planning for a correctional agency. You believe that challenges for correctional administration are usually influenced by the development of new correctional philosophies. You have been asked to speculate on the "next era" of correctional philosophy that will develop from the current "get tough" approach. This is important because the agency can begin to consider how the philosophy might impact the operations. How do you go about thinking about the future? What type of information is important to consider? How do you go about the task of predicting the future? Once you decide how you will make the prediction, what do you think is the "next era" of correctional philosophy?

WEB LINK EXERCISES

Go to http://www.libraryindex.com/pages/313/History-Corrections-Punishment-Prevention-or-Rehabilitation.html

After opening the webpage you will notice a section called, Additional Topics. Each topic examines a different era in correctional history and addresses the issue of whether it was a punishment or rehabilitative era. Open these short historical accounts and see if you can determine at what times in our history we were more punishment oriented in our dealings with criminal offenders.

Go to http://justice.uaa.alaska.edu/directory/c/correctional_history.html

Upon opening this website click on *Correctional Photo Archives* and examine what is available. Click on *Access the Collections* to see the many different photos depicting correction history from around the United States. After examining these photos, go back to the main page and scroll down to *Louisiana State Penitentiary Museum* to view the resources of the history of Angola Prison. There are some great photos of this infamous prison which should provide an excellent understanding of southern prisons.

GROUP EXERCISES

Each group will be assigned a goal of corrections: protection of society, retribution, incapacitation, deterrence, and rehabilitation. Students will present their topic, addressing the tenets of each goal, how it actually operates in corrections, how it relates to sentencing, an historical perspective, how it works in consort with the other goals, how it is ranked in importance in today's correctional environment, and the probable future importance of the goal.

ENDNOTES

1. Sourcebook of Criminal Justice Statistics Online, Table 2.36.2008, *Attitudes toward Level of Crime in Own Area,* http://www.albany.edu/sourcebook/pdf/t2362008.pdf (accessed August 23, 2009).

2. Adam Smith, *An Inquiry into the Nature and Causes of the Wealth of Nations* (Philadelphia, PA: Thomas Dobson, 1796).

3. A good history of the evolution of correctional philosophy can be found in Richard P. Seiter, *Corrections: An Introduction,* 3rd ed. (Upper Saddle River, NJ: Pearson Prentice Hall, 2011), Chapter 1.

4. Margaret Calahan, *Historical Corrections Statistics in the United States: 1850–1984* (Washington, DC: U.S. Department of Justice, 1986), p. 36.

5. Douglas Lipton, Robert Martinson, and Judith Wilks, *The Effectiveness of Correctional Treatment and What Works: A Survey of Treatment Evaluation Studies* (New York: Praeger, 1975).

6. For an overview of three-strikes laws across the country, see Walter J. Dickey and Pam Hollenhorst, "Three-Strikes Laws: Five Years Later," *Corrections Management Quarterly* 3 no. 3 (1999): 1–18.

7. Barry Krisberg and Susan Marchionna, "Attitudes of U.S. Voters toward Prisoners Rehabilitation and Reentry Policies," *Focus: Views from the National Council on Crime and Delinquency,* http://www.famm.org/Repository/Files/Attitudes_of_US_Voters_toward_Prisoner_Rehabilitation_and_Reentry_Policies%5B1%5D.pdf (accessed August 17, 2009).

8. Ibid.

9. Paul Gendreau, Claire Goggin, and Paula Smith, "Generating Rational Correctional Policies: An Introduction to Advances in Cumulating Knowledge," *Corrections Management Quarterly* 4 no. 2 (2000): 56–57.

10. For discussions of qualitative assessments of treatment programs and matching of offenders to program services, see Sharon Levrant, Francis T. Cullen, Betsy Fulton, and John Wozniak, "Reconsidering Restorative Justice: The Corruption of Benevolence Revisited?," *Crime and Delinquency* 45 (1999): 3–27; Edward J. Latessa and Alexander Holsinger, "The Importance of Evaluating Correctional Programs: Assessing Outcome and Quality," *Corrections Management Quarterly* 2 no. 4 (1998): 22–29; Paul

Gendreau and Donald Andrews, *The Correctional Program Assessment Inventory*, 5th ed. (Saint John, Canada: University of New Brunswick, 1994); Gendreau, et al. "Generating Rational Correctional Policies," pp. 52–60.

11. For examples of studies that indicate a positive treatment effect, see Francis T. Cullen and Brandon K. Applegate, eds., *Offender Rehabilitation: Effective Treatment Intervention* (Aldershot, England: Ashgate, 1997); Gerald G. Gaes, "Correctional Treatment," in *The Handbook of Crime and Punishment*, edited by Michael Tonry (New York: Oxford University Press, 1998), pp. 712–738; Vernon L. Quinsey, "Treatment of Sex Offenders," in *The Handbook of Crime and Punishment*, edited by Michael Tonry (New York: Oxford University Press, 1998), pp. 403–425; Douglas S. Lipton, "Prison-Based Therapeutic Communities: Their Success with Drug-Abusing Offenders," *National Institute of Justice Journal* 230 (February 1996): 12–20; William G. Saylor and Gerald G. Gaes, "Training Inmates through Industrial Work Participation and Vocational and Apprenticeship Instruction," *Corrections Management Quarterly* 1 no. 2 (1997): 40; Federal Bureau of Prisons, *TRIAD Drug Treatment Evaluation Six-Month Report: Executive Summary* (Washington, DC: U.S. Department of Justice, 1998).

12. Heather C. West and William J. Sabol, *Prison Inmates at Midyear 2008–Statistical Tables* (Washington, DC: U.S. Department of Justice, Bureau of Justice Statistics, March 2009), p. 2.

13. 2010 figures were compiled by the Pew Center for the States in partnership with the Association of State Correctional Administrators. Data reported in Pew Center for the States, *Prison Count 2010: State Population Declines for the First Time in 38 Years* (Washington, DC: Pew Charitable Trusts, March 2009). The 2008 figures come from William J. Sabol, Heather C. West, and Matthew Cooper, "Prisoners in 2008," *Bureau of Justice Statistics* (Washington, DC: U.S. Department of Justice, December 2009).

14. *Solem v. Helm*, 463 U.S. 277 (1983).

15. Norman A. Carlson, Karen M. Hess, and Christine M. H. Orthmann, *Corrections in the 21st Century* (Belmont, CA: West/Wadsworth, 1999), p. 16.

16. Alfred Blumstein, "Selective Incapacitation as a Means of Crime Control," *American Behavioral Scientist* 27 no. 1 (1983): 93.

17. Ibid., p. 94.

18. Marianne W. Zawitz, ed., *Report to the Nation on Crime and Justice* (Washington, DC: U.S. Department of Justice, Bureau of Justice Statistics, 1983), p. 35.

19. Peter Greenwood, *Selective Incapacitation* (Santa Monica, CA: RAND Corporation, 1983).

20. Stuart Miller, Simon Dinitz, and John Conrad, *Careers of the Violent* (Lexington, MA: Lexington Books, 1982).

21. Robert M. Freeman, *Correctional Organization and Management: Public Policy Challenges, Behavior, and Structure* (Boston: Butterworth-Heinemann, 1999), p. 397.

2

Theories of Leadership and Management

Introduction

Correctional administrators manage and lead. Chapter 3 describes in more detail the types of activities they undertake in this regard. It addresses the difference in management, leadership, and administration and also examines the evolution of predominant styles of leadership used throughout the history of corrections. To precede Chapter 3, this chapter presents the historical and relevant theories of leadership and management in correctional service. Chapter 2 will enable you to better understand how these theories affect the thinking and practice of correctional administration.

Corrections is not only a discipline similar to many others but also a discipline in which leadership may be more important than almost any other discipline. Leadership is often considered extremely important in the military, in which followers risk their lives to accomplish a mission executed through the orders of their leaders. In many ways, corrections is similar. The mission of supervising criminals and getting them to rethink their lifestyles and improve their chance of success after release is daunting in itself. In addition, the fact that many of these "clients" are violent and affiliated with gangs makes the mission even more challenging. Correctional staff do put their safety in peril each and every day. And they dedicate their work to accomplish a mission that is difficult but important to society. They must trust their leaders and their leaders must believe in them.

Corrections is also a complex discipline with staff supervising white collar offenders in the community as well as death row inmates in maximum security prisons and includes staff responding to prison riots with force to conducting substance abuse or religious counseling. It seems reasonable to wonder if there is any one leadership theory that fits this wide scope of situations. Another reasonable question is whether leadership theories can be tested to determine if they really work in a correctional environment. And do varying styles of leadership work with the wide range of staff functions (physicians and psychologists, teachers and chaplains, correctional and parole officers, maintenance and food workers, and accountants and human resource managers) that are common in corrections? These are the issues and questions that are addressed in this chapter.

Babbie defines theory as "a systematic explanation of the observations that relate to a particular aspect of life.[1] Theory explains what is and not what should be, while social theory informs us of what is and why. And scientific social theory is developed through inductive reasoning and tested through deductive reasoning. As we examine leadership theory and how it relates to correctional administration, it is important for students to understand the interactions of management and line staff. As already noted, Chapter 3 presents distinctions between leadership and management in practice. Some of these differences are also described here to help put leadership and management theories into perspective. A simple way to differentiate management and leadership is that managers have subordinates and leaders have followers. Another difference is that leaders do the right things and managers do things the right way.

There are many ways to describe leadership and management. DePree points out that, "The first responsibility of a leader is to define reality. The last is to say thank you. In between the two, the leader must become a servant and a debtor."[2] Hersey and Blanchard state that management is "the process of working with and through individuals and groups and other resources to accomplish organizational goals," while leadership "occurs anytime one attempts to influence the behavior of an individual or group."[3] And Cohn distinguishes the two as follows:

> While the manager attends to daily functions to ensure that the organization fulfills its mission and according to declared processes, it is the leader who looks to the future, anticipates and attempts to control the future, and otherwise has a vision that is not only acceptable to subordinates, they do their best to ensure it becomes reality.[4]

We now move to a description of the major leadership theories.

Leadership Theories

There is a large body of literature on the theories of leadership that are helpful to gain an understanding of perspectives of leadership in public organizations. And most of the discussions focus on examples and styles for use within private sector businesses. Less attention has been paid to public agency leadership. Montgomery Van Wart states that "Although the literature on leadership with a public-sector focus is a fraction of that in the private sector, it has been substantial albeit unfocused."[5] Research in leadership has been conducted for the better part of the twentieth century and has provided an enlightening array of theories on how we direct and energize people to achieve goals. Early theories focused directly on the characteristics of the leader, but later theories have distinctively moved away from focus on the leader to concentration on leader relationships with employees. These contemporary theories emphasize that without followers there can be no leaders.[6]

There are countless leadership approaches and models, but one way to organize these varied theories is through clustering them into eight major groups.[7] These eight categories will be used to organize theories and will be described in more detail here.

1. Great man theories—Leadership qualities are inherent and that leaders are born, not made.
2. Trait theories—Presume that some people inherit particular traits that make them suited for leadership. These traits are generally personality or behavioral characteristics.
3. Contingency theories—The leadership style is related to environmental characteristics as determined by the situation and quality of followers.

4. Situational theories—Different styles of leadership are appropriate for certain types of decision making.
5. Behavioral theories—Based on the premise that leaders are made, not born. People can learn to be leaders through teaching and observation.
6. Participative theories—The ideal leadership style allows input of others, and encourages participation from groups. Decision making is more group related.
7. Management theories—Also known as "transactional theories," which base leadership on a system of rewards and penalties for employees. These theories focus on the role of supervision, organization, and group performance.
8. Relationship theories—Also known as "transformational theories," which base leadership on motivation and inspiration of employees. There is a focus on the performance of groups and individual potential. Ethical and moral standards are important.

Following is a discussion of predominant leadership theories that have existed in American culture.

Great Man Theories of Leadership

Great man theories were proposed years ago, when gender issues were not considered and almost all leaders were men. It was believed that there were traits that great leaders were born with, and it was only a matter of time before they were in a situation in which their leadership qualities came into play and they showed their abilities. Research into the **great man theory** showed that these men were already great leaders and focused more on what their qualities were than how they acquired them. With examples such as Jesus or Mohammed, Churchill or Roosevelt, and Gandhi and Martin Luther King, it was believed that in times of need, a great man would arise and provide the leadership necessary to overcome whatever challenge was before him.

Trait Theories of Leadership

If Great Men as leaders had certain qualities, it was an easy transition to trait theories of leadership, from which researchers believed that there were certain traits that made leaders effective. The research focused on identifying the human traits that were characteristic of effective leaders. Some of the traits included physical traits such as height and "presence," personality traits such as enthusiasm and persistence, and intellectual traits such as intelligence and foresight. **Trait theory** like the great man theory suggested that leaders were born with inherent traits. However, from its beginning, there was much debate over both great man and trait theories. In 1927, Mary Parker Follett questioned the trait theory of leadership:

> Only a short time ago people were telling us that leadership was an 'intangible capacity', you could never acquire it. We are coming to think now that executive leadership can in part be learned. This is the point about leadership I like most to emphasize, for unless this is true, there is not much hope for men in subordinate positions being able to rise, and also, if it were not possible for men to learn to be leaders, our large, complex businesses would not have much chance of success, for they require leadership in many places, not merely in the president's chair.[8]

Over the years, there has been mixed support for trait theory. However, there has consistently been recognition that effective leaders as a group do possess certain common traits. These traits include vision, creativity, tenacity, courage, empathy, and enthusiasm. Other research indicated that persons with varied personality and environmental and hereditary backgrounds can make effective leaders, leading to a belief that traits in themselves are an inadequate way to describe why someone makes a good leader.[9] And other research demonstrated that even with these traits, leadership effectiveness cannot be guaranteed as the situation often determines which traits are most useful or important.[10] Consequently, trait theory was subsequently replaced with more balanced approaches to predict leadership effectiveness.

Even with the evolution of theories away from trait theory, there is still a belief that certain traits are inherent in most leaders. From his research into leaders during the 1980s, DePree established a list of leadership traits and attributes to include the following:

1. Integrity—Behavior is the only score that is kept
2. Vulnerability—Trust in the ability of others and allow them to exercise that ability
3. Discernment—A quality that lies between wisdom and judgment
4. Awareness of the human spirit—Personal skills always precede professional skills
5. Courage in relationships—Facing tough decisions with ruthless honesty
6. Intellectual energy and curiosity—Frantically learn what your followers can teach
7. Respect for the future, regard for the present, and understanding of the past
8. Predictability—Leaders are not free to follow a whim, tend to your vision
9. Breadth—A leader's vision has room for contributions from all staff
10. Comfort with ambiguity—Healthy organizations exhibit a degree of chaos; a leader will have some sense of it
11. Presence—Leaders stop to ask and answer questions

Other logical support for theories of trait leadership often cites or constructs leadership traits or practices of prominent people who are accepted as good leaders. For example, Rudolph Giuliani was the mayor of New York City during the terrorist attacks on September 11, 2001, on the World Trade Center buildings. In his book *Leadership* (2002), he discusses traits he believes are the primary attributes of a good leader:

1. Put first things first
2. Prepare relentlessly
3. Everyone is accountable, all of the time
4. Surround yourself with great people
5. Reflect, then decide
6. Underpromise and overdeliver
7. Develop and communicate strong beliefs
8. Be your own man (don't let critics set your agenda)
9. Loyalty, the vital virtue
10. Weddings discretionary, funerals mandatory

11. Stand up to bullies
12. Study, read, and learn independently
13. Organize around a purpose
14. When you make a deal, keep it (pp. 29–324)

Contingency Theories of Leadership

Contingency theory begins to blend theories of personal traits with the situation around the leader. Developed by Fred Edward Fiedler in the 1960s, **contingency theory** contends that while each leader may have a permanent leadership style, the style will not work the same in every situation. The theory takes into account a broad view that there are contingent factors to include the leader capabilities and variables in the situation that affect how effective the leader's style is. The leader's ability to lead successfully is believed to depend on factors such as the types of challenges faced and the skills and behaviors of their followers. Accordingly, contingency theory focuses more on the environment than on the person. It is not believed that there is one right way to lead, and one style may be successful in some situations and not in others. Success depends more on how that style fits with the characteristics of followers and the aspects of the situation. Fiedler's premise was that leaders should understand their style and attempt to work in situations that would best benefit from their personal style, and organizations should place leaders in situations to match their styles.[11]

To separate and better understand this theory of leadership, Fiedler used the least preferred coworker (LPC) scale.[12] The LPC scale was developed by asking the leader to complete a questionnaire on the employee the leader would least like to work with and then score that person on a number of personal characteristics. The ratings were on a range of scales with both positive factors (friendly, helpful, and cheery) and negative factors (moody, gloomy, unfriendly, and unhelpful). Results from several studies indicated that two types of leaders emerged: the high LPC leaders who gave more favorable ratings to the LPC, and low LPC leaders who rated coworkers much more unfavorably. The low LPC leaders were task oriented and the high LPC leaders were more relationship oriented. However, both styles of leadership can be effective contingent upon a good match between the skills and traits of the leader and the situation or needs encountered. The studies also found three contingencies prioritized by their impact on effectiveness: (1) leader–member relations; (2) task structure; and (3) position of power of the leader. The most effective setting for the leader is when the three contingencies are rated high. A mix of ratings of the contingencies determines moderate settings, and the least favored settings are when all are rated low. The focus of this theory is to identify leaders' beliefs about people, and specifically if they saw others as more positive or negative. Fiedler believed it was the responsibility of the organization to alter the setting to fit the leader.[13]

Another type of contingency theory was developed by House in 1971 and is known as path–goal theory.[14] In simple terms, path–goal theory emphasizes followers more than leaders, and describes the way that leaders encourage and support their followers to achieve goals. They do this by creating a path that followers can follow to make the chance of successful accomplishment of goals as high as possible. The leaders' role includes not only identifying and clarifying the path but also removing any impediments that slow down or stop followers from going down the path and creating rewards along the route as progress is made. Leaders can take different approaches to how they do these things.

They may be directive or just suggestive in telling followers about the path. They may be proactive and try to remove all roadblocks or they may let followers try it themselves and then step in to help if necessary. And they may only give minimal encouragement or they may make the rewards very enumerative.

House and Mitchell then identified four styles of leadership in terms of how active or passive the leader was in addressing these three needs.[15] Supportive leaders consider and are very much concerned about the welfare of followers and try to create a friendly work environment. They focus on making jobs interesting and building self-esteem. Directive leaders just tell followers what the path is, what needs to be done, and give guidance and feedback along the way. They reduce role ambiguity by giving staff a plan, schedule, and expectations for performance. This style works well with complex work and inexperienced followers. Participative leaders consult followers and get their ideas before creating the path. When followers are skilled and have as much information and expertise as the leader, this is the best approach. And achievement-oriented leaders set challenging goals and the path may be difficult, but the leader helps achieve the goal while showing faith in followers. If done well, this approach usually results in performance beyond what followers think they can do.

Leaders must match their directive, supportive, participative, or achievement-oriented styles to both the characteristics of the group and the demands of the task. But path–goal theory believes that the leader best knows the one right way to move down the path, as they are more knowledgeable or experienced. This theory is also based on understanding that leaders can elevate motivation among subordinates when they help them along a path toward goal completion. To do this effectively, the leader must convey a high value of the goal outcome to the subordinates and must assist in removing barriers to the outcomes.

One additional contingency theory is the Normative Decision Model developed by Vroom and Yetton in 1973.[16] This theory suggests that many complex decision situations that result in unpredictability can be simplified and reduced to a limited set of options. The theory is "normative" in that it is defined more by logic than by observation. Using this model, leaders create a complex decision tree to assist with improving the quality of decision making and the degree by which the decision will affect subordinates. The decision tree guides the leader through eight questions to determine the importance of the decision, to include if enough information is available to make a good decision, if the decision will generate conflict among the subordinates, and if acceptance of the decision is important to the subordinates. As a result of the decision quality, the selection of the best alternative is likely to be accomplished, and acceptance of the decision is more likely by followers.

Situational Theories of Leadership

Situational theories of leadership move one more step away from trait theories and are beyond contingency theories in that they consider the environment in which the leader operates as more important than specific traits and style of the leader. **Situation theory** is based on the premise that different situations require different styles of leadership, and the most effective leaders do not have one single approach, rather they are able to use different styles based on the situation they face and that will be most effective in the situation. The capability of staff, for example, is a situational factor that influences how a leader operates. The more willing and capable the staff, the less the supervision required. The opposite is also true as the less willing and capable the staff, the more the guidance and direction required.

One of the first to recognize the impact of the environment on a situation were Tannenbaum and Schmitt, who in 1958 identified three forces that combined result in the actions taken by a leader: (1) forces from the situation; (2) forces from followers; and (3) forces in the leader's own style and comfort zones.[17] They developed a continuum of leadership behavior that combined the approach leaders take with how much authority they grant to followers. The model identifies on one extreme a highly authoritarian model used in a situation in which leaders do not trust followers and results in most decisions being made by the leader whose focus is much more task oriented. The other end of the continuum has democratic leaders who recognize that they have a capable workforce and can trust more decision making to them. These leaders encourage participation in decision making by employees and give them more freedom to determine how to reach organizational objectives. Between the two extremes is a full continuum of behaviors balancing trust and freedom to employees with the experience and skill of the workforce. Leaders recognize their followers' abilities and lead according to their needs. Maier soon thereafter added that leaders consider not only the skill of followers in deciding on their style but also how critical, time sensitive, and important the task is. Leaders become more directive when the risk of failure is greater.[18]

Hersey and Blanchard developed a similar situation leadership model. First introduced as life cycle leadership, in the 1970s, the model became a situational leadership theory.[19] Like other situational theories, they agreed that there is no best style, and they suggested that successful leaders must adapt their style to the "maturity" of their followers. Maturity includes the followers' capacity to set high goals that can be attained, willingness and ability to take responsibility for reaching goals, and the education and experience of the group. This model establishes four primary leadership styles for a leader and matches them to the developmental level of the group. If the group is low in experience and motivation on a task, then the leader must use a high task and low relationship style. Conversely, if the group is experienced and motivated on a particular task, the leader can use a low relationship and low task style as the group requires little leadership.

The model describes four styles of leadership (S1–S4) that are matched to four levels of development (D1–D4) of the followers. The leadership styles are on a continuum of how much the leader focuses on task accomplishment versus employee relationship building. The followers' maturity is on a continuum of low to high competence and commitment. S1 is a Directing or Telling style with a high focus on task and is used when followers are not prepared or motivated to doing their jobs. To further analyze the needed style, leaders also examine why followers are not capable (experience, skill, and effort) or motivated (lack of confidence and lack of support for mission) of achieving. S2 is a Selling or Coaching style for which followers are more motivated and capable than in S1. Leaders listen more and attempt to coach staff about the importance of the mission and help them improve their capabilities.

S3 is Participating and Supporting style in which followers are competent but not fully committed. In this style, leaders do not need to coach or sell, but try to understand why followers may be resistant or not fully committed to the goals and use their skills to increase commitment. And S4 is Delegating and Observing for which followers are both highly competent and highly committed. In this situation, leaders can step back and trust employees will perform. They can be more "hands off" and just guide rather than direct, and can spend their time looking into the future for potential challenges and opportunities.

Situational theories of leadership have been strongly supported over the many years since they were first presented, in part because they seem logical and in part because practicing leaders all recognize they do not lead in the same way in every situation. Anyone who has supervised employees knows that you treat people differently, and the highly capable employee who always performs at a level beyond expectations is not supervised or led the same as one who is constantly underperforming and whose commitment is questionable. No matter what theory that seems most reasonable and effective in contemporary society, it seldom seems the case that leaders will use the same style across all situations.

Behavioral Theories of Leadership

We now move one more step forward as behavioral theories of leadership are almost 180 degrees counter to trait theories, in that they assume leadership capabilities are learned and not inherent. Instead of researchers conducting psychometric tests to see what traits leaders have, behavioral theories focus on the types of training, development, and activities to build leadership skills. The nice thing is that it opens the door to anyone to become a leader with proper developmental activities. **Behavioral theory** also focuses not on what traits or capabilities leaders have, but what they actually do. With this approach, researchers identify and then correlate specific behaviors with leadership success.

Zenger describes behaviors of leaders with the following list of qualities and actions:

1. Leaders create values through communication
2. Leaders develop committed followers
3. Leaders inspire lofty accomplishments
4. Leaders model appropriate behavior
5. Leaders focus attention on important issues
6. Leaders connect their group to the outside world.[20]

Role Theory

Role theory is one of the types of behavioral theories. **Role theory** proposes that people define roles for themselves and others based on what they expect should be done and the influences others have on them. People subtly encourage others to act and meet the expectations they have. For example, leaders are influenced by their followers. Leaders and followers participate in leadership and management training and they all know the types of behaviors experts define as important for success. So leaders know that people are watching and evaluating them against these behaviors, and many followers actually remind leaders of these behaviors. Leaders are believed to be sensitive to the feelings of their followers and do respond positively to such influence.

In addition to concern for employees, leaders must also be concerned about organizational outcomes and success (accomplishing tasks). Therefore, they must pay attention to both, and there has been much research in terms of how they prioritize these two components. In 1964, Blake and Mouton developed a managerial grid to describe five basic styles of leadership based on how much emphasis (low, medium, or high) they put on concern for people and concern for production/tasks.[21] The five styles were as follows: (1) Authority-Compliance, in which the leader focuses on maximizing production with a minimum concern for people; (2) Country Club Management, with a minimum concern for production and maximum concern for people; (3) Impoverished Management, with low emphasis on both and the leader does the minimum and avoids as much work as possible; (4) Middle-of-the-Road Management, with a medium balance on both people and work, and little push toward either one and just accept the status quo; and (5) Team Management, in which people are committed to the task and the leader is committed to them.

In the 1940s and 1950s, considerable role theory research was conducted at the Ohio State University and the University of Michigan. The Ohio State researchers examined 1,800 examples of leadership behavior reported on a 150-item questionnaire given to workers to report on the behavior of their supervisors.[22] Ten dimensions were initially identified and then they were reduced to two factors. The first (consideration) referred to the leader's relationships with subordinates in terms of support, trust, respect, and friendliness. The second (initiating structure) clarified the relationship between the leader and the followers and emphasized set standards and procedures for assigning roles and accomplishing organizational objectives. Workers preferred supervisors high on consideration, while mid-managers preferred leaders high on initiating structure. Consequently, research revealed that leaders high on structure were rated higher by superiors and had higher producing work groups. Yet, leaders rated high on initiating structure had high grievance and turnover rates among employees.

The University of Michigan study focused on organizations of high producing units and compared them with organizations of low producing units. From their research, they developed two categories of leaders: production-centered leaders and employee-centered leaders.[23] Findings revealed that most productive work groups tend to have leaders who were employee centered and effective leaders emphasized group decision making as opposed to individual decision making. According to these two important studies, effective leaders should emphasize high productivity and develop good interpersonal relationships.[24] These two studies have been the basis of much of the later research of behavioral theories of leadership.

Participative Theories of Leadership

Participative theories of leadership involve the degree to which leaders include followers in the decision making of the team or organization. Participative leaders involve others in the decision making process rather than making decisions themselves and with little input from peers, supervisors, other stakeholders, or followers. Continuums in the **participative theory** include autocratic leaders who make all decisions themselves to full delegation for decision making to the team. It seems reasonable to believe that either ends of the continuum are poor models and that there may be circumstances in the middle that influence and dictate a changing style depending on the situation.

The level of participation can also vary with the type of decisions being made. There are several decisions that require the leader taking a stand and going against the popular will of employees, particularly in corrections. No employee likes to be at risk, but corrections has inherent risks and leaders must often decide whether the risk is worth the outcome. This does not force employee involvement. For example, a probation official may decide that officers will not carry firearms when making home visits. However, the official may then ask a group of probation officers to come up with other policies and practices to increase safety other than carrying a firearm.

There are believed to be several benefits of participative leadership:

- The quality of decisions is improved by the involvement of others, particularly those responsible for carrying out the decision.
- People are more committed to decisions in which they have been involved.
- Interactions of the team to come to a decision are important learning and team-building opportunities.
- People become more focused on the team and are more collaborative when they work on jointly developed goals.
- People feel more committed to an organization and their morale increases proportionately to the level of involvement they have in decision making.

There are also obvious limits to the types of situations in which participative leadership can be useful. Leaders cannot abdicate their responsibility by adopting a participative style, and there are many times when too much involvement by followers only causes confusion and is demoralizing. Similar to participative styles are often referred to as consultative or empowered leadership. These are often more useful, as leaders consult with employees and receive their input before making a decision. Empowered often means employees are thoroughly involved or make decisions that are important to them but not to the organization. A good example is when I was warden of a prison. We did training in firearms for all employees every year, and the training could occur during January through March, when few people wanted to take vacation but it was often cold on the firing range, or during warmer months, when employees would like to take vacation. Both could not be done at the same time as too many people off their correctional posts would drive up overtime. If I made the decision, people would complain about it, and all we cared about was that both got done with little increase in overtime. This was an excellent example of empowering staff to decide as it was important to them and either worked for the organization.

Participative theories of leadership have been around for several decades. In 1930, Lewin, Lippitt, and White conducted research and identified three styles of leadership around the way decisions were made.[25] Styles included autocratic, democratic, and laissez-faire. Autocratic leaders made decision without consulting others, causing a high level of discontent among employees. Democratic styles involved people in decision making, but the decision may ultimately be made by leaders after consultation. This style was appreciated by employees, but could be problematic if there were strong and a wide range of opinions among staff. And laissez-faire styles allowed people to make their own decisions with little guidance or involvement by leaders. Even though people got to make the decisions, it often causes more problems among the workforce and often results in more rather than less discontent.

In the 1960s, Rensis Likert identified four styles of leadership in terms of how much involvement employees had in decision making.[26] In "exploitative authoritative," leaders have low concern for staff and are authoritative and threaten staff to get conformance to the decision. There is little communication up, and staff feel ignored and uninvolved. With "benevolent authoritative," leaders still make decisions but are concerned about how they will be received. Therefore, they use rewards to encourage performance and commitment to the goals of the organization. With "consultative" styles, leaders seek upward flow of information, and listen and consider the feelings of employees. However, major decisions are still made centrally by the leader. And the fourth style is "participative," in which leaders engage people throughout the organization in decisions. In all four of these, the primary flow of information is top-down, but that was not unusual in leadership of that era.

Management Theories of Leadership

We next move to the **management theory** of leadership, which focuses on how the transactions between the leader and the follower are managed in an organization. Also referred to as transactional leadership, this theory begins with the assumption that people are motivated by rewards and punishments, and that the role of their leaders is to direct them on what to do. **Transactional leadership** revolves around the leader–follower relationship in which the leader motivates the followers by recognizing their needs and providing rewards to fulfill those needs in exchange for support and performance. The leader must be in a position to reinforce the subordinates for completing their part of the bargain. So, a transaction is negotiated in which the subordinate receives rewards for performance and loyalty, all worked out within the constraints of the organization. Leaders tell followers what needs to be done and rewards them for doing it, or punishes them for not doing it. It is often suggested that as limited as it seems, it is still used by many supervisors today, but often more on the "management" than the "leadership" role in which tasks are simple yet must be done with preciseness (such as a job on an assembly line or some would say an assignment as a correctional officer).

Transactional leaders are usually found in well-defined chains of command and in which the functions required by subordinates are also clear. Rewards come from following orders and punishment comes from not performing the job as prescribed. The transactional part of the roles is that employees are given a salary by the company and thereby accept the authority of the leader. Work is allocated to employees who are then responsible for it and are personally at fault when they do not succeed. Once the transaction of hire and commit to the reward (salary), the leadership role is a style of "telling" rather than coaching or encouraging. The old style warden was believed to use transactional leadership, as "guards" were expected to carry out their duties to move inmates, unlock and lock doors, and maintain security. When something went wrong, it was believed to be because they did not perform as they were told, not that the system broke down.

The Leader–Member Exchange Model (LMX) developed by George Graen and colleagues in the 1970s describes how leaders assert their positions through tacit exchanges with their followers.[27] The LMX model also describes the importance of loyalty to the leader and explains why one group in a unit may form a cohesive team while another will be excluded. Simply stated, LMX argues that leaders develop close working relationships with one group (the in-group) and exclude relationships with another group (the out-group). The in-group is believed to work harder and is more committed to the organization. They are trusted and seen as thoroughly loyal to the leader, and in exchange, they receive higher levels of responsibility, more involvement in decisions, and more access to resources. Traits that make the in-group seemingly supportive of the leader include empathy, reasonableness, sensitivity, and good at seeing the viewpoint of the leader.

The out-group is treated more formally and is less likely to achieve good teamwork. They are not treated as well and have to pave their way through harder work, more commitment, and showing more loyalty to the leader if they ever hope to move into in-group status. The out-groups often have traits of aggression, sarcasm, and views that may be counter to the leader that keep them from being seen as loyal and committed. As often happens, the out-group members can recognize that they are not receiving the promotions or benefits of the in-group. They can then decide to either emulate the in-group traits or try to move into it, or they may accept their role in the out-group and even escalate behaviors that lead them to be seen as nonloyal. In a transactional leadership environment, this usually ends up with them leaving the group, either through getting fired or they find another job with less of an LMX requirement for success.

Leaders have to nurture and play on these relationships to maintain the belief by all that you have to work your way into the in-group to succeed.[28] And oftentimes, the relationship between leaders and workers is based on factors unrelated to performance, such as same gender, race, religious affiliations, or even things such as whether followers share hobbies or interests (playing golf) with leaders. Howell and Shamir describe how effective transactional leaders work to develop a "mature partnership" with the in-group to continue to nurture performance and build commitment no matter what the costs.[29]

There are several steps that occur throughout the LMX process, and begin soon after a person joins the group.

- Role taking: Soon after joining the team, the leader assesses the talents and abilities of a new member. This may come about as new members are given opportunities to demonstrate their capabilities.
- Role making: In this phase, the leader and member informally negotiate a role for the new member with the understanding that opportunities and benefits will come in return for acceptance of the leader's power and loyalty to the leader's position. Relationship as well as work factors go into the negotiation and understanding of role.
- Routinization: In this phase, the ongoing pattern of exchanges takes place between the leader and member and a firmer hold on status (in-group or out-group) takes place.

Relationship Theories of Leadership

Relationship theories of leadership are also known as "transformation" leadership styles. **Relationship theory** is much broader than management theories in that the complexity of leaders, followers, and organizational vision and values are all integrated to guide what needs to be done and how it is to be accomplished. James MacGregor Burns distinguished transformational theory from transactional theory in 1978.[30] **Transformational leadership** differs from transactional styles in that rather than rewarding followers for following orders, they encourage employees to help to "transform" the organization into one in which all (in-group and out-group) are welcome and staff are given more latitude to create better ways to accomplish goals rather than follow set routines. The weaknesses of transactional styles are that few workplaces are simple with tasks that are always the same. Judgments must be made along the way, and transactional leaders do not accept too much decision making from line staff without their specific review and approval.

Transformational leaders believe that working collaboratively is better than working as groups of individuals, and this is more effective than the appeal to selfish concerns in transactional styles. Transformational leadership was considered by Burns as an ongoing process rather than discrete exchanges as in the transactional approach. As transformational leaders work to change the organization, they attempt to motivate workers for goals that are beyond self-interests and are seen to be good for the group or organization. Some research has shown that transactional leaders can progress to transformational styles and remain effective.[31]

Transformational leaders focus on the big picture, they do not micromanage as this tends to show a lack of trust in followers. But details of an organization must be tended to and it is important that there be forces within the organization (a policy department or a strong second in command) that can ensure there is guidance or work out conflicts that will arise. There are multiple steps that transformational leaders take to move the organization and the followers to the desired higher level of both performance and employee satisfaction. These include the following:

1. Development of a vision: Transformational leaders recognize and begin with establishing a vision for the organization. The vision is the guidepost for action; employees understand it and can take actions to move the organization further toward the vision.

2. Selling the vision: The leader must sell the vision to employees, telling them how important it is to the organization and to them to reach it. This cannot happen if the leader does not truly believe in and model the vision at all times. Employees will gladly accept and follow a vision they believe important, but will quickly turn away if they believe it is merely a motto or the organization is not fully committed to it.

3. Plotting the course: While the vision provides the direction, it does not provide the details on how to get there. Transformational organizations often use strategic planning to involve many employees to chart the course to reach the vision. As progress is made, it is communicated to employees who can enjoy the success and strive even harder to continue to make progress.

4. Continuing to lead the change: Transformational leaders must always remain central to the transformation and move the organization toward the vision. There are always many distractions along the way, but the leader must continue to guide the ship and make in-course corrections when the organization veers off course. When transformational leaders fail, it is often because they accept another path or let forces push them in another direction and lose sight of the vision. This does not mean a vision can never change, but only major changes in the environment should result in a redirection. The leader's role is to accept challenges and lead the organization beyond them without losing track of the vision.

When Burns first wrote about transformational leadership, he emphasized its importance and the actions of leaders to transform an organization. Soon after, Bernard M. Bass focused on the effect of transformational leaders on their followers, who can be themselves "transformed" in three ways: (1) heightening their understanding of the importance of value rather than just task; (2) getting them to focus first on organizational goals rather than their own interests; and (3) activating their higher order needs (as described in Maslow's hierarchy of needs below).[32] Followers tend to trust, admire, and respect a transformational leader, and leaders tend to be charismatic in that they are personally identified with the vision and greater good of the organization. Bass further

Transformational leaders communicate constantly with staff, coaching them, and helping them to learn the values of the organization, while seeking their input on policies and procedures.
(Photo by Richard P. Seiter)

noted how transformational leaders are grounded in moral aspects of their own character, their ethical values linked to the vision, and the reasonableness of the social ethical choice and action that they should collectively pursue to reach the vision.[33]

Dubrin, in writing about the competencies of effective leaders, suggested they possess four qualities useful in contributing to transformations: (1) charisma, vision, and sense of mission; (2) inspirational leadership with the ability to inspire group members to exceed their expectations; (3) intellectual stimulation that creates an environment that encourages creativity and forethought; and (4) individualized consideration or investing time in one-on-one communications with group members.[34] The charismatic leadership suggested as important by both Bass and Dubrin is not the same as "heroic leadership" or the great man theories in which the leader single-handedly determined the success or demise of organizations.

Charismatic leadership as a component of transformational leadership results in leaders almost pushing the emphasis away from themselves and onto the organization and followers. Transformational charismatic leaders spend time being supportive of subordinates, model behavior to which the subordinate would want to be like the leader, focusing attention on value and ideological convictions, and encouraging the collective identity of the group.[35] As a result, followers identify with the leader, match the leader's beliefs and values, and are motivated to achieve the missions and goals of the leader.[36] Howell and Shamir also described how personal identification with the leader and a desire to become like the leader results in a group social identification that drives the group to see organizational successes and failure as personal successes and failure.[37]

A step even beyond transformational leadership is presented in Greenleaf's book entitled *Servant Leadership*. In the book, Greenleaf added a new insight suggesting the study of leadership even more away from leaders and toward followers. Servant leaders establish relationships with subordinates to serve their needs and collaborate with them to achieve organizational goals. Beyond that, servant leaders empower their workers to achieve their potential. Trust becomes the cornerstone of the servant leader theory as cooperative relationships are based on mutual respect.[38]

Transformational leadership has been well received as it blends the importance of personal leadership with a focus on followers and how the organizational vision becomes the guiding principles for both tasks and values. It is "behavioral" in that it illustrates the effect of both leaders and followers in reaching a higher level of organizational need. As such, it moves workers further along in Maslow's hierarchy of needs.

Maslow's Hierarchy of Needs

One of the most prominent leadership and management theories developed by Abraham Maslow in 1943 is still useful today. Maslow created a Hierarchy of Needs and was one of the first humanist approaches to management (see below). Everyone begins with a desire to meet his or her physiological needs for good health, food, sleep, and shelter. If those are met, they focus on safety needs of stability, law, protection, and order. They then move into group needs of belonging and love, desiring affection and a relationship to a group. From that comes a need for esteem, in which they desire recognition of status and reputation from the group. And finally, they reach a level of self-actualization, with a desire for personal growth and fulfillment.

In many ways, transformation leadership works to move the individual up the hierarchy beyond group belonging, beyond recognition, and to self-actualization. Transformational leadership can result in the entire group gaining fulfillment from the organization moving toward its vision. Good leaders often suggest that a vision is "a journey and not a destination." It may not be possible to reach a vision, as being the best

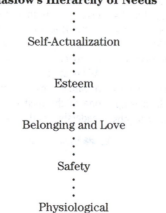

Maslow's Hierarchy of Needs

Self-Actualization

Esteem

Belonging and Love

Safety

Physiological

Practical Perspectives

From Transactional to Transformational Leadership

A prison warden who was very experienced and competent faced a new challenge that he was not only unfamiliar with but was also somewhat perplexed as to the solution. A riot occurred in the facility (described in Practical Perspectives in Chapters 4 and 12), and staff confidence was shaken. The facility was in its first year of operation and two-thirds of the staff were new and had never worked in corrections before. Several staff were injured in the riot, and the facility was heavily damaged. Staff were becoming very critical of everything: the leadership of the warden and executive team, the policies and procedures, the communications (or lack of), and the training and equipment they had to deal with the riot.

While the entire leadership team was experienced and competent, they had all been brought up in corrections in a different era, in which you did as you were told and were loyal to your organization and leaders. They had trouble understanding a workforce that so quickly turned on them and became so negative. They knew the riot had been traumatic, but were disappointed that the staff did not respond and return to normal operations more quickly, as they believed things were headed the right way and the facility was back into control of the inmates and the reasons for the riot were behind them.

The executive team was doing a lot. They were listening to staff and trying to fix the issues they heard. They increased the number of briefings and other avenues to improve the frequency of communications and availability of information to staff. They changed policy and procedures to respond to some of the problems staff pointed out. They hardened the facility by adding bars over windows and replacing wood with steel doors. They expanded training, especially for emergency preparedness. But for everything they did, the morale did not improve; staff were still dissatisfied, and the employee union was feeding their discontent. While they seemed to be doing the right things, the problem was that "they" were doing it for the employees.

As noted, the leadership team was concerned, committed, and competent; they all practiced transactional leadership. They hired and trained staff, and expected them to do their jobs to the best of their abilities. They had all been successful with their leadership style. It worked fine in the past in a fairly rigid chain of command, a fairly stable environment, and one with older and more experienced staff. However, they found themselves in a situation in which their style not only did not work but also made things worse. Staff were just not responding to all that they were doing. They keep hearing from staff things like, "you guys need to. . . ."

Finally, the warden realized what was wrong. He was reading some leadership literature and recognized that they needed to move to a more transformational style while empowering staff and bringing them into the process of finding and implementing solutions. There were many steps they took in the process. First, they committed and told staff they were going to be empowered; meaning that they would be given responsibility and be involved in the decision-making process. Second, they worked with staff to create a vision statement (see Chapter 4). Third, they told department heads what was expected and encouraged them to work with their teams to find the best way to accomplish it. Fourth, they formed a line staff advisory committee and charged them to get ideas from other staff but to come forward with a solution and not just a problem. Finally, they supported an active employee club with activities for staff and their families to have fun and play as well as work together. Then, they stepped back and watched it work.

Things went great from then on. Staff no longer complained and said "you guys need to," but instead said "we need to." They took responsibility and worked with their department heads to improve procedures. Through their involvement in decisions that affected them, they were committed to the solutions and made them work. Every component of the prison became high performing, and morale improved. The warden said it was the easiest job he ever had. All he had to do was organize, encourage, and recognize and reward success. The staff pulled together and made the prison one of the best in the entire system. It was truly a staff, leadership, and organizational transformation.

or achieving excellence are terms that have no reachable point and the end result is ever changing. It is similar to how hard it is to repeat as NFL Super Bowl champions; it is said to be easier to win than to repeat. If an organization gets to be the best, it will not stay the best unless it continues to progress and improve, as other organizations will get better and pass them by. This concludes our discussion of transformational leadership and the description of the many theories of leadership. The following section describes some of the practical applications of leadership and their relevance to corrections.

Practical Applications of Leadership

There are many different approaches to what leaders do to move an organization and achieve the levels of quality and accomplishment desired. While theories of leadership are instructive, it is sometimes more difficult to use them to suggest what leaders should do to show leadership. The following represent many current ideas of what leaders should do to lead.

A good example of practical leadership comes from the five practices of what Kouzes and Posner call "exemplary leadership:"

- Model the way
- Inspire a shared vision
- Challenge the process
- Enable others to act
- Encourage the heart.[39]

These five practices illustrate that leaders must be role models for their followers, and not only inspire but also "live" the vision of the organization. As described in Chapter 4, the vision is a roadmap for an organization in terms of how to act rather than what to do. By modeling the vision, employees can act in accordance with the principles included in the vision. And as explained in Chapter 8, employees then need to believe that they are "empowered" to act and get things done. But what exactly does a leader do to model behavior?

Daniel Goleman contends that the fundamental duty of leaders is to create good feeling in their subordinates, and therefore, the primary activity of leadership is emotional rather than practical. By conducting research on how a random sample of 3,871 executives thought of and practiced emotional intelligence, Goleman developed six leadership styles that may all be used on a regular basis depending on the situation. The six styles are as follows: (1) Coercive leaders who demand immediate compliance; (2) Authoritative leaders who mobilize people toward a vision; (3) Affiliative leaders who create emotional bonds and harmony; (4) Democratic leaders who build consensus through participation; (5) Pacesetting leaders who expect excellence and self-direction; and (6) Coaching leaders who develop people for the future.[40]

And Stephen Covey in his best-selling book, *The 7 Habits of Highly Effective People*, compiles a list of principles with which to live and behave.[41] These leadership principles have been cited and used by private corporations and public organization leaders for a number of years:

1. Be Proactive—The principle of personal vision
2. Begin with the End in Mind—The principle of personal leadership
3. Put First Things First—The principle of personal management

4. Think Win-Win—The principle of interpersonal leadership
5. Seek First to Understand, then to be Understood—Principle of empathic communication
6. Synergize—The principle of creative cooperation
7. Sharpen the Saw—The principle of self-renewal

In an article suggesting the value of collaborative leadership for criminal justice agencies, Carter compares a collaborative leader to a symphony conductor whose job is to get the orchestra to act together—powerfully.[42] The conductor or leader points out where the group is headed. Just as the conductor stands on the podium and sees the big picture of the composition, leaders have the view of what is obvious, and must communicate to the followers a sense of how things should be and how they can achieve the vision. In a criminal justice organization, the skills needed to be effective include the following:

- Political knowledge and skills—These are the types of skills to form a team, negotiate relationships, and secure external support for the teams' work.

- Interpersonal knowledge and skills—These are consensus building, conflict management, and building trust. They must be able to communicate their beliefs and commitment, model the expectations for behavior, and develop leadership qualities in others.

- Process knowledge and skills—These include the ability to organize the team, establish work processes, and lead the team to accomplish its goals. Leaders must focus the group's attention on the important work, ensure participation from all team members, and make sure the team develops and accomplishes a work plan.

In another practical and fun book on leadership entitled *Lead or Get Off the Pot*, Pat Croce (formerly owner of the Philadelphia 76ers NBA basketball team) provides several insights into leadership. He suggests leadership is about compassion, hard work, dedication, and tireless enthusiasm for what you do and the people you do it with. Some of his most meaningful quotes are, "Vision without action is a daydream. Action without vision is a nightmare" (p. 3) and "You can delegate authority and decision making, but you can never delegate responsibility" (p. 21).[43]

I advocate a practical leadership approach termed "**leadership by attention**," which is based on the theory of "what gets attention gets done," and an extension of it that "what gets measured gets done." By this is meant that what leaders do in their organization is give attention to the things that they want to reinforce and the things that need to be accomplished. Through those actions alone, the organization is likely to make the type of progress desired. There are two steps in leadership by attention: (1) setting quantifiable measures of success and (2) paying attention to things considered important. Following are the steps for setting measures of success:

1. Set annual goals that if accomplished, move the organization closer to the vision. For example, if the vision of a correctional agency is to be the "best correctional system in the United States," annual goals may be to operate safe and secure prisons for staff and inmates and to provide all services in line with American Correctional Association (ACA) standards and in a high-quality fashion.

2. Create a scorecard for measuring progress toward the goals. Following the earlier example, the scorecard may include reducing acts of violence (fights, assaults, use of force, and so on) by 5 percent from the previous year and improving audit scores measuring quality by 5 percent from the previous year.

3. Create metrics to measure the progress. This seems easy, but there must be clear and consistent definitions for violent acts and a good record keeping so that all acts are reported and documented. Each month can then be compared to the same month of the previous year as can the year to date numbers of violent acts. For the audit scores, there can be the percent of all audit findings (many agencies have 500 or more specific standards as do the ACA standards) that are determined satisfactory or not deficient.

4. Every component of the organization must develop plans of action to accomplish the goals and reach the desired metrics.

5. Review all metrics on a monthly basis. The leaders review the metrics with all other organizational executives and managers to determine how they are doing. As a part of the review, the components that reach the goals describe the best practices they used to accomplish this so that others can learn from their success. Those that do not reach the goals must also demonstrate what actions they will take to get back on course with the target metrics.

6. Celebrate success by recognizing the organizational components that accomplish the goals.

The second part of leadership by attention is for the leader to model and encourage certain types of performance and actions by paying attention to those things. The following are suggested actions that leaders can take to pay attention to things to reinforce.

- Purpose—Leaders should constantly reinforce the vision and purpose of the organization. By talking about it all the time, by referring to it in organizational publications, and by setting goals and creating strategies to move the organization toward its vision, the leader is likely to get followers to keep purpose at the forefront of their thoughts and themselves attempt to move the organization in that direction.

- People—A leader should both recognize good performance by staff and take actions that demonstrate that they care about staff as individuals. Examples are writing personal notes thanking someone for a job well done or calling individuals to wish them a happy birthday. Leaders should share in the joy and sorrow of people's lives. When staff know their leaders care about them, they will care about what is important to the leader and the organization.

- Performance—By setting up the metrics already noted and monitoring their progress, leaders let followers know these goals are important. Many leaders and organizations set goals, but few do a good job of measuring and conducting regular reviews of their progress.

■ Professionalism—This refers to the style and how people do their jobs. Goals can be accomplished and policies followed through many approaches. The hard-charging, demanding, and intimidating approach will get things done, but usually only in the short term as this style wears on people and their performance is likely to wane over time. Yet, if they constantly stress professionalism, trusting staff, and encourage organizational learning, the progress is likely to continue to improve.

SUMMARY

This chapter is a good way to move into our study of correctional administration. Corrections, like almost every other discipline, must have effective leadership to meet its very challenging mission of protecting society while supervising criminal offenders. In the first part of this book, we focus on the elements of leadership. We begin with a description of correctional administration, how it has evolved over the years, the link of philosophy and administration, and the goals and current environment of corrections that administrators must tend to. We then move to leadership in two ways. First, we describe the current belief as to the best methods to lead in corrections as well as how and what correctional administrators manage. We finish the first part of this book with a key component of leadership, how leaders set the tone, create the vision, and move an organization forward toward its goals.

Before we move too far into leadership and these components, it is important for students to understand the many theories and how they have evolved. All theories have been used and can be seen in the history of corrections. Warden Joseph Ragen is a great example of great man, trait, and transactional leadership. We describe the theories that move from a focus on leaders to how they involve and shape their followers. And we move to how they build an entire organization, focusing on the team and the greater principles and values of the organization. Students can see many benefits of almost every theory listed, and they will see several challenges for correctional leaders who attempt to use a specific style.

Most of you will nod affirmatively as you read about situational leadership, believing that no one can ever lead the same way in every situation. Yet, you will also find it reasonable in that there are some traits that can make a leader more effective, no matter what the situation. And you will warm to the suggestion that transformational leaders move their organization far beyond what others could, especially in an era of complexity and rapid change. You will overall find this chapter more interesting than you would think a "theory" chapter might be. That is because you will use your own knowledge and experience to put the theories into perspective, thinking how you would lead if you tried to use the approaches described by each theory. And moving forward in the book, you will have opportunity (through Practical Perspectives and You're the Correctional Administrator) to think of how you could use any of the styles of leadership to meet the many challenges facing correctional administrators of today.

KEY TERMS

Great man theory

Trait theory

Contingency theory

Situation theory

Behavioral theory

Role theory

Participative theory

Management theory

Transactional leadership

Relationship theory

Transformational leadership

Leadership by attention

YOU'RE THE CORRECTIONAL ADMINISTRATOR

1. You are a new chief probation officer (CPO) in a large urban department. The agency urged the last CPO to retire as there was much dissatisfaction and discontent among employees. They seemed committed to their jobs and were continuing to supervise probationers as required. However, they were going in different directions and no one seemed to know what was expected of them and did not perceive the agency was doing enough to meet their concerns or add resources to meet a growing probation population. What do you want to do in terms of how you lead them? First, decide what theory of leadership seems best for this situation and list the key activities you need to undertake to get the agency back on the right track. Then outline the first major speech you will deliver to the employees. What are the kinds of things you will tell them?

2. You are the chief of staff for the state director of corrections. He has been in the position for almost twenty years, and has always been effective and has a very good reputation. However, the department is going through many changes to include a tremendous increase in the number of inmates, a new wave of gang violence in the prisons, and serious budget cuts. People are whispering that "the old man" may not still have it and perhaps they need a change of leadership. He has picked up on this and asked you what you think. You do think his transactional style is past its time; but you believe he is still an able leader and the right person to lead the department through these difficult times. You talk in general about changing leadership styles, and he asks you to write him a two-page memo outlining what you suggest. Create the outline for the memo with the reasons for the change and what key things he should do to modify his style of leadership.

WEB LINK EXERCISES

Go to http://nicic.gov/Downloads/PDF/library/020475.pdf

An excellent report on correctional leadership to assist supervisors and managers (1st report) and executives and senior leaders (2nd report) is *Correctional Leadership Competencies for the 21st Century* by Nancy M. Campbell (2006). You should examine this report, especially the executive summary to see what the report includes, as it is very comprehensive. If you choose a career in corrections, this manual will become valuable as it covers many topics of professional leadership. Also, the last chapter provides an excellent overview of the criminal justice system. Pick one area (supervisors, managers, executives, or senior leaders) and list the three competencies you believe are most important for leading in a "transformational" way.

Go to http://www.corrections.com/podcasts

This is the Corrections.Com Web site. Listen to an interesting podcast on *Budget and Corrections —A National Challenge—UMUC-DC Public Safety*. Click on DC Public Radio, aired January 8, 2010. To be successful, correctional leaders need a good understanding of budgets and the budgeting process. After listening to it, think of situational leadership and list how contemporary leaders can respond and lead their organizations through these challenging times.

GROUP EXERCISES

Divide into five groups with each one assigned one leadership theory: transactional (management), relationship (transformational), participative, behavioral, or situational leadership. Groups will present a basic description of how their leadership theory works, the primary factors of the theory, what kind of correctional environment it may work best (prison, community corrections, etc.), and the strengths and weaknesses of the theory within corrections.

ENDNOTES

1. E. Babbie, *The Basics of Social Research*, 4th ed. (Belmont, CA: Thompson Wadsworth, 2008), p. 13.

2. M. DePree, *Leadership is an Art* (New York, NY: Doubleday, 1989), p. 9.

3. Paul Hersey and K. H. Blanchard, *Management of Organizational Behavior: Utilizing Human Resources* (Englewood Cliffs, NJ: Simon & Schuster, 1993), p. 5.

4. A. W. Cohn, "The Failure of Correctional Management: Rhetoric versus the Reality of Leadership," *Federal Probation* 62 no. 1 (1998): p. 30.

5. M. Von Wart, "Public-Sector Leadership Theory: An Assessment," *Public Administration Review* 63 no. 2 (2003): 214–229.

6. E. P. Hollander, "How and Why Active Followers Matter in Leadership," in *The Balance of Leadership and Followership*, edited by E.P. Hollander and L.R. Offermann(College Park, MD: Academy of Leadership Press, 1997).

7. K. V. Wagner, *Leadership Theories: Eight Major Leadership Theories* (2009), About. Com. http://pyschology.about.com/od/leadership/p/leadtheories.htm?p=1 (accessed January 1, 2009).

8. H. C. Metcalf and L. Urwick, *Dynamic Administration: The Collected Papers of Mary Parker Follett* (New York, NY: Harper & Brothers Publishers, 1942).

9. W. Wayne Scott and Lloyd F. Spaulding, *What Do We Know About Leadership?* (Washington, DC: Education Resources Information Center, 1972).

10. A. J. Dubrin, *Leadership Research Findings, Practice, and Skills* (New York, NY: Houghton Mifflin Company, 2001).

11. A. J. Dubrin, *Leadership: Research Findings, Practice, and Skills* (New York, NY: Houghton Mifflin Company, 2001).

12. Fred E. Fiedler, *A Theory of Leadership Effectiveness* (New York, NY: McGraw-Hill Publishers, 1967).

13. H. G. Rainey, *Understanding and Managing Public Organizations*, 3rd ed. (San Francisco, CA: John Wiley & Sons, Inc, 2003).

14. R. J. House, "A Path–Goal Theory of Leader Effectiveness," *Administrative Sciences Quarterly* 16 (1971): 321–339.

15. R. J. House and T. R. Mitchell, "Path–Goal Theory of Leadership," *Contemporary Business* 3 (Fall 1974): 81–98.

16. V. H. Vroom and P. W. Yetton, *Leadership and Decision-Making* (Pittsburg, PA: University of Pittsburg Press, 1973).

17. A. S. Tannenbaum and W. H. Schmitt, "How to Choose a Leadership Pattern," *Harvard Business Review* 36 (March/April 1958): 95–101.

18. N. R. F. Maier, *Problem-Solving Discussions and Conferences: Leadership Methods and Skills* (New York, NY: McGraw Hill Publishers, 1963).

19. Paul Hersey and Kenneth Blanchard, *Management of Organizational Behavior: Utilizing Human Resources* (Upper Saddle River, NJ: Prentice Hall Publishers, 1969).

20. J. H. Zenger, "Leadership: Management's Better Half," *Training* (December 1985): 44–52.

21. R. R. Blake and J. S. Mouton, *The Managerial Grid* (Houston, TX: Gulf Publishing Company, 1964).

22. Roger M. Stogdill and Alvin E. Coons, "Leadership Behavior: Its Description and Measurement," *Research Monograph No. 88* (Columbus, OH: Ohio State University Bureau of Business Research, 1957).

23. D. Katz and R. L. Kahn, "Some Recent Findings in Human Relations Research," in *Readings in Social Psychology*, edited by E. Swanson, T. Newcombe, and E. Hartley, (New York: Holt, Reinhart and Winston, 1952).

24. See A. J. Dubrin, *Leadership: Research Findings, Practice, and Skills* (New York, NY: Houghton Mifflin Company, 2001) and H. G. Rainey, *Understanding and Managing Public Organizations*, 3rd ed. (San Francisco, CA: John Wiley & Sons, Inc., 2003).

25. K. Lewin, R. Lippit, and R. K. White, "Patterns of Aggressive Behavior in Experimentally Created Social Climates," *Journal of Social Psychology* 10 (1939): 271–301.

26. Rensis Likert, *The Human Organization: Its Management and Value* (New York, NY: McGraw-Hill Publishers, 1967).

27. F. Dansereau, Jr., G. Graen, and W. J. Haga, "A Vertical Dyad Linkage Approach to Leadership Within Formal Organizations: A Longitudinal Investigation of the Role Making Process," *Organizational Behavior and Human Performance* 13 (1975): 46–78.

28. For a good history of LMX leadership, see G. B. Graen and M. Uhl-Bien, "The Relationship-Based Approach to Leadership: Development of LMX Theory of Leadership over 25 Years: Applying a Multi-Level, Multi-Domain Perspective," *Leadership Quarterly* 6 no. 2 (1995): 219–247.

29. J. M. Howell and B. Shamir, "The Role of Followers in the Charismatic Leadership Process: Relationships and Their Consequences," *Academy of Management Review* 30 no. 1 (2005): 96–112.

30. James M. Burns, *Leadership* (New York, Harper and Row Publishers, 1978).

31. See B. M. Bass, "Does the Transactional–Transformational Leadership Paradigm Transcend Organizational and National Boundaries?," *American Psychologist* 52 no. 2 (1997): 130–139 and M. Van Wart, "Public-Sector Leadership Theory: An Assessment," *Public Administration Review* 63 no. 2 (2003): 214–229.

32. Bernard M. Bass, *Leadership and Performance Beyond Expectation* (New York, NY: Free Press, 1985).

33. Bernard M. Bass and Paul Steidlmeier, *Ethics, Character and Authentic Transformational Leadership* (Binghamton, NY: Center for Leadership Studies at Binghamton University, 1998).

34. Dubrin, 2001.

35. Ibid.

36. H. G. Rainey, *Understanding and Managing Public Organizations*, 3rd ed. (San Francisco, CA: John Wiley & Sons, 2003).

37. Howell and Shamir, "The Role of Followers in the Charismatic Leadership Process".

38. Robert Greenleaf, *Servant Leadership: A Journey into the Nature of Legitimate Power and Greatness*, 3rd ed. (Mahwah, NJ: Paulist Press, 2002).

39. James M. Kouzes and Barry Z. Posner, *The Leadership Challenge*, 4th ed. (San Francisco, CA: Jossey-Bass, 2007).

40. Daniel Goleman, "Leadership that Gets Results," *Harvard Business Review* (March/April 2000), pp. 78–90.

41. Stephen R. Covey. *The 7 Habits of Highly Effective People* (New York, NY: Simon & Schuster, 1989).

42. Madeline M. Carter, *The Importance of Collaborative Leadership in Achieving Effective Criminal Justice Outcomes* (Silver Springs, MD: Center for Effective Public Policy, 2006).

43. Pat Croce, *Lead or Get off the Pot* (New York, NY: Simon and Schuster, 2005).

3

Leadership and Management of Corrections

Leadership and Management in Corrections

In this chapter, we examine correctional leadership and management and clarify how the two terms are similar and distinct. *Leadership* is perhaps the most overused word in the English language. Everyone talks about the importance of leadership and the impact strong leaders can have. But trying to explain what that means in terms of everyday behavior is not so simple. *Webster's* defines *leadership* as directing the operations, activity, or performance of an organization, and *management* as the judicious use of means to accomplish an end. These definitions imply a subtle difference between "guiding" and "doing," or "showing the way" and "making something happen." While leaders do the right things, managers do things the right way. Most authors propose that leadership and management are different, while others suggest they are similar. Carlson seems to combine the two, noting how "strong, involved management does not preclude the chief executive officer from exuding many intrinsic leadership qualities."[1]

In this book, three terms are used to describe and distinguish the roles of those responsible for correctional agencies or operations. The first term is **leadership**. Correctional leaders are responsible for setting the direction and guiding the agency through both internally and externally created challenges. Leadership is associated with the higher-level functions of mission and vision. Managers conduct traditional supervision of activities to ensure that the day-to-day functions of an organization are accomplished efficiently. In this regard, the second term, **management**, is more likely linked to policy and procedure than mission and vision. And throughout the book, the third term, **administration**, is used when including both the functions of leadership and management and those staff who fill these roles. *Correctional administrators* include both leaders and managers of correctional agencies and the roles they play in the organization.

Traditional Correctional Administration

Throughout the history of corrections, the terms *leadership* and *management* had a very different meaning than they do today. Historically, correctional administrators focused their activities on managing the internal organization, did not have to be concerned with stakeholders external to corrections, and there was little interest in what they did to those outside the correctional system. Through most of the history of corrections, prison wardens and agency heads wielded almost autonomous authority, established policy and procedures, and hired and fired staff as they desired. Management was autocratic, and the vision of leadership was "barking orders" in the General George S. Patton mode than in the empowered staff mode of modern approaches. Today, we think of leadership as guiding an organization through difficult times, setting agendas and priorities, empowering staff, and urging continuous improvement through total quality management.

The focus of "management" as a discipline separate from "leadership" came about with the advent of bureaucracy, when managers were seen as the people who made sure operations were efficiently completed according to the dictates of those in charge. Managers were almost considered a career in itself, and management was thought to include the functions of planning, organizing, directing, and controlling. Midlevel management positions were created to supervise organizational entities (departments, divisions, or sections). Managers were charged with these four functions of management within their area of responsibility, were held accountable to ensure the entity completed the tasks for which they were responsible, and were to do everything necessary to contribute to the overall mission of the organization.

These roles and functions of leadership and management continued with little change until the 1980s, when elected officials and politicians became more interested in corrections. Until that time, corrections was a small part of state or federal budgets and, therefore, did not attract the attention of elected officials. Little attention was paid to correctional operations, assuming that correctional administrators were doing a good job if there were no problems that surfaced and had to be dealt with at a level above the correctional department. Policy and practice were totally within the discretion of the correctional administrator, with little political intervention. Today, public correctional administration has changed radically. Politicians are interested in what is done, how it is accomplished, how much it costs, and how successful the results are. Therefore, the role of both leaders and managers of correctional agencies has changed dramatically. The section that follows gives an illustration of this, and the management of the external environment is the topic of Chapter 11.

A Change in Correctional Leadership

Correctional agencies are paramilitary organizations, taking many of their key operational functions from the military model of command. Line correctional officers wear uniforms; ranks such as sergeants, lieutenants, and captains are often used; and the need to follow the chain of command is understood by both staff and offenders. Wardens were historically perceived as generals in that successful wardens had to be assertive, strong, and let it be known that they were in charge. Wardens were usually autocratic leaders, wielding power over all things in their domains, totally controlling the prison, staff, and inmates. The warden not only thought of as the authoritative boss but also as the highest ranking person in the organization; he or she was believed to be the smartest and most powerful, the person who always knew what to do and how to do it.

An example of this type of leadership is described by Jacobs in *Stateville: The Penitentiary in Mass Society*, where Warden Joseph Ragen ran that prison for more than thirty years until the 1960s.[2] Stateville was a maximum-security prison that held almost 4,000 violent inmates in a space designed for 1,600. Ragen ruled the prison with an iron fist and demanded strict adherence to rules by both staff and inmates and meted out

Practical Perspectives

How Things Have Changed

Recently, a state correctional director from a decade ago was musing about the political oversight of current state directors. She told the story of using new technology to change policy and practice to improve the prison environment and benefit taxpayers. The state had many prisons built in the 1930s through 1950s. These prisons used traditional methods for perimeter security to keep prisoners from escaping. The prisons usually had a set of two fences around them, and armed guard towers every one hundred yards or so to watch the fence and shoot inmates who tried to escape.

The problem with guard towers is that they are only as effective as the staff member's ability to see the fence, and accurately shoot an escaping inmate. The staff member also has few options to using deadly force. They cannot leave the tower and respond to the area of attempted escape. However, new developments in physical fence security offer new approaches. Many medium security prisons have moved to upgrading the fence security using layers of razor ribbon, which makes it extremely difficult for inmates to move through and get to the fences without being seriously cut and injured. Also, electronic detection devices can be set up on the fences, and alert staff to an attempted breach of the fence, even if the staff are not present or cannot see because of fog or other bad weather conditions. Finally, instead of having eight to ten guard towers around the prison fence line, two or three armed "roving" patrols are often used. Roving patrols are correctional officers in vehicles specially equipped with electronic pictures of the fence line that visually show the point of attempted breach. The vehicles continuously drive around the perimeter, and two or three patrols provide more improved coverage than eight or ten towers.

The director told of how she had staff research the possible replacement of the towers at the medium security prisons in the state. The findings were that for approximately $150,000 per prison, the physical security of the fences could be improved with razor ribbon, electronic detection devices could be installed, and roving vehicles could be purchased and equipped. Two roving patrols operated twenty-four hours per day, seven days per week, could replace ten towers, which also had to be operated continuously, saving eight staff posts. These eight posts required forty staff to cover. A post that must be covered twenty-four hours per day, seven days per week, is calculated at approximately five to one. In other words, calculating the need for around the clock coverage, sick and annual leave by staff, it takes five people to fill one post. At an average of $35,000 dollars in salary and benefits, these forty staff not needed could save $1,400,000 per year.

The director decided to invest the money in upgrading the fences and eliminate all the towers in the medium security prisons. The staff saved from the tower posts would be used to implement unit management. When the plan for the first prison was announced, the local union objected. They suggested that the change would not be as effective as the current guard towers. However, in reality, some of the correctional officers liked working alone in the towers, with no contact with inmates and little contact with their supervisors. The union even put an advertisement in the local newspaper saying how eliminating the towers would increase the chance of inmate escape and endanger the local community.

The prison warden and director developed a plan to reduce the union opposition and inform staff of the benefits of the change and of implementing unit management. First, they sent several staff to another state prison, about seventy miles away, to observe the nontower fence system and talk to staff at that prison about its effectiveness and the benefits of unit management. Second, the warden let union leadership try to get through the razor ribbon and climb the fence without setting off the alarm and having the roving patrol quickly respond. They could not do it. Finally, the warden and director briefed local politicians about the effectiveness, benefits, and potential cost savings of the new system. These efforts were successful, and six medium security prisons eliminated towers, and several new prisons were built without towers.

The director enjoyed telling how the change was beneficial to her state. She then bemoaned how she had just read a January 2000 Associated Press article about New Jersey Governor Donald T. DiFrancesco ordering state prisons to continue manning guard towers, reversing a cost-cutting measure imposed by his predecessor, Governor Christie Whitman. The Whitman administration had previously ordered prisons to begin vacating the towers as new electronic perimeter fencing was installed. The article noted how complaints from correctional officers and community residents persuaded DiFrancesco to change course.

severe punishment to anyone who violated his rules.[3] Jacobs describes Ragen as one of the last of the warden "village chieftains" who vanished as their society modernized.

Traditional correctional leaders like Warden Ragen had much greater control over their environment and their operations than contemporary leaders. These leaders without question or interference managed the *internal* operations of the correctional agency. With few policy directives from their political supervisors, these leaders focused on the internal operations of the agency and were not accountable to anyone about why they made a particular decision or took a particular action. These correctional leaders were autocratic, most likely not because they wanted to be, but because there were no standardized and accepted best practices and no written policy or procedure with step-by-step guidance for implementation. Therefore, they were left to their own devices about what should be accomplished and how it should be done.

Today, the world in which correctional administers operate is totally different. There are rules and regulations for every activity, judicial and political interest and oversight, and policies for everything from hiring staff to spending a budget to supervising an offender. Today's complex environment for corrections, along with the close oversight by elected officials, the courts, and the media, require them to also be good *external managers*.[4] Corrections is now of interest to everyone. With crime a major public concern and domestic priority, what correctional agencies do, how they do it, and how much it costs is of great interest to the public and elected officials. Only a few decades ago, the courts would not get involved in correctional management issues. Today, they are regularly and intensively involved in corrections and at times take over a correctional operation and direct how some correctional agencies must be managed. Media sources seldom reported on activities or occurrences in prisons. However, print and television media now regularly present stories about criminal justice and correctional programs and operations. These stories are of high interest, sell newspapers, and attract viewers.

Modern Leadership for Corrections

For the reasons cited above, correctional leadership in the twenty-first century is very different than correctional leadership in the past. In Chapter 2, transactional and transformational leadership were defined. This evolution was particularly relevant to corrections. Historical correctional leadership was based on the position rather than the person. Leaders were those in the top position who exercised power by giving orders and making decisions. Leaders offered rewards and resources to followers in exchange for assistance in reaching the organization's goals. These leaders practiced "transactional" approaches that involved exchange relationships between leaders and followers.[5] **Transactional leadership** involves essentially immediate, short-run exchanges. It is bounded in that it affects the immediate situation of a group of individuals but has little consideration for the public or society as a whole.

Transactional correctional leaders gained their position and power from their experience and extensive knowledge of the substantive area in which they worked. With their experience, they were able to provide answers and direction for any issue the agency confronted. This knowledge resulted in staff respecting them and looking to them for more guidance and direction. Whenever anything occurred that challenged the organization, everyone stopped and waited for the boss to tell them what to do.

This type of transactional leadership worked fairly well in the relatively stable correctional environment of the past, when most situations were within the realm of experience of the leader.

It is easy to think of the traditional role of the warden as transactional leadership. Wardens rose to their positions after a long tenure in the prison, and they were the substantive experts with the experience and background to know how to deal with any situation. If they did not have the answer, they knew where to find it for any circumstance. In this model of leadership, the person in the highest position of authority is frequently expected to know more than they actually do. This puts pressure on the leaders and often forces them to "play the expert" even when they know they are not, because it is what staff expects of them.

Modern leadership demands more sophistication and intellect in dealing with issues and followers. The challenges of today and tomorrow often result from the fact that rapid change occurs in almost every workplace and, therefore, there is less likelihood that experience only gives a leader the tools to solve problems. As issues and the environment change, there will be many problems that are new or have a new twist to them. Therefore, the type of leadership that best suits this situation is "transformational." As noted, **Transformational leadership** is much broader than transactional leadership and is based on principles rather than practice and on motivating people to jointly address challenges and find solutions to new problems. Modern correctional leaders know they cannot be there to make or influence every decision a line correctional officer makes during a day. In a study of decision making by police officers, Murphy and Drodge identified the way leaders can share values and beliefs and emphasize how officers can apply them to their own knowledge for better field decision making.[6]

Transformation correctional leaders begin with a vision that has a set of values and principles as guidelines to use in responding to issues. They inspire staff to focus on the broader vision and higher-level goals, and help staff and the organization to learn and work through problems in an adaptive manner. They know they cannot jump to conclusions or rush to find quick and easy answers to many questions. They must involve staff in creative and innovative solutions. Modern correctional administration requires the ability for leaders, managers, and line staff to work together, involving and empowering staff to adapt to change and deal with difficult and frustrating issues.[7]

One important role of transformational leaders is to help set, define, and reinforce the desired culture of the prison. **Organizational culture** includes the values, beliefs, and behaviors that form the way of life within the organization. From the first day of recruiting a prospective staff member and throughout the basic training employees receive before they begin work in a prison, correctional agencies instill the desired organizational culture. For effective correctional agencies, the culture includes being professional, striving to meet high standards, being ethical, positively interacting with inmates, rewarding staff for good performance, and using state of the art correctional practices. Correctional leaders set the tone and play critical roles in creating and reinforcing organizational culture. Staff take their cues on meeting standards, communicating with offenders, and rewarding excellence from the agency leader. DiIulio, in *Governing Prisons*, writes, "the individual who heads a prison, or a prison system, can shape the organization in ways that help to determine the quality of prison life."[8]

What Correctional Administrators Manage

As noted, managers are charged with carrying out the essential functions that help ensure the entity completes required tasks that are often required by statute and contribute to organization's mission. Management is very different from "doing," in that managers have to learn how to delegate and get things done through people. Keenhold suggests, "If you are doing it all yourself, you are not managing."[9] It could be said that the managers tend to the functions required to accomplish the day-to-day activities of their organization. Phillips and McConnell suggest that management is the effective use of resources to accomplish the goals of the organization.[10] Koontz and O'Donnell point out that managers are responsible for planning, organizing, staffing, directing, and controlling.[11] These traditional management functions are the mainstay of correctional managers, as they are with other public sector or private sector managers.

Planning

For the first three-quarters of the twentieth century, correctional administrators were not required to conduct any extensive level of planning. Simply put, **planning** is looking into the future and deciding what an agency and its workers must do to respond to the issues and challenges they face. Historically, planning has been deficient for correctional administrators, because most correctional planning that was accomplished was neither complex nor long term. Leaders just dealt with what was in front of them at the time. There are two types of planning: strategic and tactical. Chapter 4 describes strategic planning, or charting the long-range direction and activities for an agency. Most planning in corrections is more tactical and focused on short-term (perhaps six months) issues such as creating next year's budget, dealing with staff shortages, expanding to meet an increasing institutional or community program population, or implementing a new program or initiative.

The history of correctional management is not replete with discussions of planning activities or how administrators planned to respond to changes in policy or philosophy. And most correctional planning has been incremental, in that staff begin with the status quo and decide if they need to change what they are doing in moderate ways. Planning is seldom a perfect process; a major planning activity does not often result in a listing of goals and objectives for the future. Forces thrust on corrections more often spur planning, as administrators decide how to respond to these forces, which frequently results in knee-jerk reactions and "Band-Aid" solutions.

For instance, in the 1930s, when the Ashurst–Sumners and the Taft–Hartley Acts forced idleness in prisons by almost eliminating prison industry work opportunities for inmates, prison wardens had to modify operations to ensure the secure and safe operation of their facilities. They did this by increasing security and limiting programs. These changes were not the result of a regular planning activity to anticipate the future but reactions to a change forced on wardens at that time. It was more reactionary; we have too much violence, let's stop it.

Today's correctional managers have to be more sophisticated about even their short-term planning processes. For instance, most government operations require detailed budget information regarding the changes expected by an agency, what these changes will mean for management, and how the agency's budget submission responds to these changes. Second, the environment in which correctional managers operate today is fluid, and because of rapid changes in conditions, corrections managers must be flexible, plan, and replan throughout the year. Most correctional agencies have created an organizational unit responsible for planning. Staff assigned to the planning unit do conduct planning, but most of their effort is to collect information that is important to consider in monitoring compliance and progress on administrative or statutorily required activities.

Organizing

The development of bureaucracy and the division of work forms the basis of **organizing**. By organizing work, an agency links staff functions to the accomplishment of the organization's mission. The first step in organizing work in a public agency is understanding the product or outcome expected by the government entity. Administrators then identify the specific tasks that must be accomplished to produce the product or outcome, and assign each task to an organizational component, resulting in a table of organization. A typical table of organization for a prison is presented in Figure 3-1. Tables of organization are narrower at the top than at the bottom. They often include department or unit titles, and they communicate expected lines of authority and reporting. Each person noted in the table of organization has a specific responsibility that is to be accomplished to contribute to the agency mission.

An example of organizing tasks in a probation office begins with the dual mission of supervising probationers to ensure they are following conditions of their supervision and not committing crimes, while providing them programs that help improve their likelihood of success in the community. To do this, probation officers conduct office visits at which probationers report, provide documentation of work or other required activities, and have urine tests to detect if they have used illegal drugs. As well, officers work with community mental health and substance abuse agencies which enroll probationers and provide treatment for their problems. These activities are assumed to "roll up" to an outcome that the probationers avoid further criminality and deal with their mental health or substance abuse problems that cause them to fail as productive citizens. Probation officers have

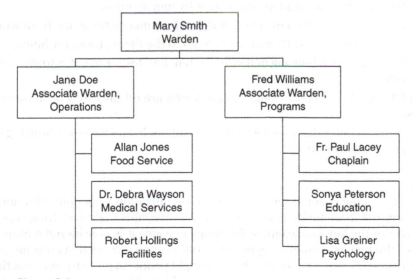

Figure 3-1
Typical organizational chart for a prison.

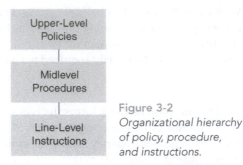

Figure 3-2
*Organizational hierarchy
of policy, procedure,
and instructions.*

procedure manuals describing how to write presentence investigations, conduct offender home visits, or arrest violators.

The method for completing tasks at each level is detailed through written policy and procedure. Organizations generally have a similar hierarchy of policy and procedures that somewhat mirrors the table or organization. As an example of how this might look organizationally, see Figure 3-2. Upper-level administration is responsible for setting policy for activities to be accomplished. Midlevel managers create procedure—how policies are to be carried out. And the lowest levels (individual employees within an organization) have specific instructions about how to perform their functions.

In a jail, the instructions are called **post orders**, which are detailed descriptions of the activities that are required to be performed throughout the day. Post orders are specific to the assignment and detail what to do rather than how to do it. As an example, the post orders for a housing unit officer on the day watch may include a schedule similar to the following list:

- 7:00 A.M.—Report for duty and read the logbook of the prior shift's activities.
- 7:30 A.M.—Open the housing unit doors for ten minutes to let inmates go to work.
- 8:00 A.M.—Start sanitation assignment by inmate crew.
- 10:30 A.M.—Open the housing unit doors for inmates returning from work.
- 11:00 A.M. to noon—Allow inmates to go to the dining room for lunch.
- 12:30 P.M.—Open housing unit door for ten minutes for inmates to go to afternoon work call.
- 1:00 P.M.—Do a census count. Inmates who are off duty may be allowed to go to recreation yard.
- 3:00 P.M.—Enter day's activities into the logbook, and sign over housing unit keys to evening shift officer.

Staffing

Staffing is assigning specific tasks within the organization to people with appropriate skills to carry out those tasks. In contemporary management texts, staffing is not always listed as one of the key management functions because it is considered a more specific function of the human resource department, rather than a general management activity. However, managers must ensure they have the right people in place to carry out the duties. An experienced human resource executive has told me his job is "to get the right people in the right place doing the right thing." The human resource departments complete the technical requirements of staffing, such as identifying competencies for each job, recruiting staff with backgrounds to provide a foundation for skills required, following legal hiring practices endemic to public agencies, and assigning employees to a work unit.

Staffing is particularly challenging in a twenty-four-hour operation like a prison, jail, or some community supervision operations like electronic monitoring. After deciding that you need a person to fill a specific role, deciding how many people it takes to fill that role twenty-four hours a day and seven days a week (24/7) requires developing a **relief factor**, or the number of full-time staff that must be included in the staffing and budget resource to provide coverage for an assignment. The relief factor takes into account that people are off the job for training and leave and that scheduling is difficult to fill seven days when people normally work five days. As an example, it takes approximately 5.5 staff to fill a 24/7 assignment.[12]

Managers, however, are the key people that monitor employee performance, mentor staff to improve their understanding of the organizational culture and standards, suggest training, take disciplinary actions for nonperformance, and make assignments to proper staff. These staffing functions are the responsibility of managers. While human resource managers put a person with the right education and experience into a job, the department manager makes sure that the person gets the right level of work and continuously attempts to efficiently match an employee's skills and work assigned.

Directing

An area in which correctional managers excel is directing operations. **Directing** involves the supervision of functions to be accomplished, through clear policies, procedures, and chain of command. Perhaps because corrections is a "paramilitary" organization, correctional supervisors are very good at giving direction to line staff regarding how to understand policy, follow procedures, and accomplish work. The success of a correctional agency is often the result of clear direction to staff, with little or no variance in carrying out established policy. The role of supervisors is, therefore, to ensure that written policies are followed, both by staff and by inmates.

In correctional agencies, directing staff comes from two elements: written policy and a clearly understood chain of command. Prisons and community correctional agencies usually have a lengthy policy and procedure manual, guiding staff on how to carry out all types of tasks in detailed fashion. As noted previously, prisons use post orders to direct correctional officers on particular shifts regarding the activities they are to perform at specific times during their shifts. There are regular checks by supervisors to ensure that these activities are accomplished.

The second element of directing staff involves a clear chain of command. As illustrated in Figure 3-1, correctional agencies have tables of organization that indicate who works for whom. As in the military, lower-ranking staff take orders and direction from their higher-ranking officials, and according to the culture of these agencies, orders are communicated and passed through the ranks. These traditional lines of authority have historically been very rigid, and it was considered a "cardinal sin" to not follow the chain of command. With more modern methods of leadership and empowerment, these traditions are changing, and communications are more flexible and free flowing.

Correctional leaders now interact with all levels of staff and seek their input on a variety of issues. However, effective outcomes require that all staff complete their responsibilities in a consistent manner, and all levels of supervision know what others are doing. Therefore, leaders will not "jump" the chain of command to give orders directly to a line staff member several levels below them without advising or passing the instruction through the supervisory chain. However, in these complex and changing times, administrators realize that policies and orders cannot cover every act and decision that must be made by a correctional employee. Therefore, correctional administrators attempt to instill in all employees the important principles and values that should be considered when staff act independently. Through this empowerment, staff not only receive orders continuously through the chain of command but also carry out their duties in line with the principles and philosophy expected.

Controlling

Controlling is a management function most often viewed as taking action to ensure that activities and procedures are completed as directed, and result in accomplishing the organizational objectives. A weakness in correctional management has been that there is often not enough resources put into evaluating the effectiveness of programs and operations, and therefore adjustments in policy or procedure to improve work outcomes often do not occur. It is relatively easy to create a policy and give a directive to carry it out. However, it is much more difficult to follow it up, measure results, and revise the policy in a way that improves the intended outcome.

Supervisors monitor activities and control the behavior of line staff in a variety of ways. In some situations, they may actually watch activities being performed and make adjustments on the spot. Once they know staff have performed a specific procedure, supervisors may follow up procedures by discussing with the staff any problems the staff encountered or any questions they had about the task. Or, supervisors may be able to determine the successful completion of the procedure by reviewing the end results. Probation or parole supervisors receive regular records of violation rates and know what percent of offenders fail during supervision. And prison managers regularly get feedback from staff and inmates as to the effectiveness of a procedure or program. In this sense, correctional managers effectively monitor and control operations by continuous and regular feedback and make adjustments in procedure, even though they do very few if any formal evaluation of policy effectiveness.

A great example of controlling is the continuous review of data to improve accountability and drive progress toward goals. The motto of the New York City Department of Corrections (DOC) under the leadership of Marty Horn was that "if you don't measure it, you can't manage it."[13] One focus of the DOC was to reduce the numbers of stabbings of inmates (there were more than 1,000 in 1995) through monitoring and tracking, and by 2008 they reduced the number to 19. They credit the reduction to data-driven management and holding each jail leadership team accountable for bringing violence down. Monthly data are collected, stabbings are mapped as to where they occur in the jail, and senior officials of the DOC do regular reviews with facility leadership as to their initiatives to reduce violence. These reviews of actual data have been shown to drive performance and be an outstanding method for controlling staff behavior.

Issues Facing Correctional Administrators

As already noted, corrections has changed significantly, and to meet the demands of these changes, a new model of correctional leadership and management has developed. This section identifies some of the issues that have evolved and require correctional administrators to move their agencies to address these challenges or respond to new initiatives. As with any public administration function, correctional administrators have a dual role. They must manage the substantive areas of corrections, such as security, offender programs, and operational procedures, while adapting to changes in policy and philosophy. And, they must manage the administrative areas standard in public administration, such as budgeting, human resources, and facility maintenance.

These are not times for "weak-spirited" correctional managers and leaders. There are few public departments and organizations that face a more difficult challenge and a more rapidly changing environment. Correctional administrators are required to be some of the best leaders and managers in government service. Throughout this text, there are many detailed descriptions of practical issues that confront correctional administrators. To put these specific issues into perspective, the following discussion presents these issues in four general categories: (1) substantive issues of correctional operations; (2) administrative issues of organization within a correctional department; (3) policy and philosophical issues of what correctional agencies should do and how they should be accomplished; and (4) issues in the management of the "external" environment.

Substantive Correctional Issues

Correctional administrators face a variety of challenging issues that require futuristic planning, innovation, and the effective management of change. **Substantive issues** within corrections are those that are a part of the knowledge specific to the practice and profession of corrections, and include such factors as how to deal with increasingly overcrowded prisons, and how to manage prisoners who are serving extremely long (possibly life without parole) terms. Managers of community-based correctional operations must consider what is often referred to as a new narrative for community supervision, one that deals more with supervision and public safety than with assistance and counseling for offenders.[14]

Both community and correctional institution administrators must deal with classification and risk issues as to which inmates should be supervised in the community rather than incarcerated. Other challenges for both prison and community correctional staff are how to deal with offenders who are younger, more violent and more likely to be associated with gangs, and how to respond to the needs of a much more diverse offender population in terms of gender, age, and program needs.

From 1980 to 1996, the number of prisoners in state and federal prisons went from 330,000 to 1,054,000, an increase over threefold.[15] During this period, the prison population grew more rapidly than at any other period of time since prisons were first established in the late 1800s.[16] In 1985, there were 256,615 inmates held in local jails, a number that more than doubled to 567,079 by 1997.[17] This growth continued, and by mid-2002, the population of the nation's prisons and jails for the first time reached 2 million. On June 30, 2008, there were 2,396,120 offenders incarcerated in the fifty states, the District of Columbia, and federal government prisons and local jails. One-third of these were in jails (785,556), and two-thirds were in prison (1,610,584).[18]

After tremendous growth in the number of incarcerated offenders for the last two decades of the 1900s, there has been a slowdown of the growth in the past few years. For the decade preceding the year 2000, the inmate population average annual growth was 8.7 percent.[19] However, from 2000 to 2006, the average increase was only 2.6 percent per year, with state prison populations increasing by 1.7 percent, federal prisons by 5.3 percent, and local jails by 3.6 percent. And, during the first six months of 2008, sixteen states actually had a decline in their prison population.[20]

There are several reasons for the slowdown in the growth of incarcerated offenders. First, after such growth during the late 1990s, there had to be a slowdown some time. If, as proponents of the use of incarceration argue, incapacitating offenders in prison reduces crime, then at some point a large number of potential criminals will be in jail and prison, and the increase in new admissions will have to slow down. Second, many states are getting results from increasing their use of alternatives to incarceration. Many of these alternatives have proved effective and less costly when the risk of offenders is properly identified and matched to correctional sanctions.[21] Moreover, jail pretrial release programs have been added in many local jurisdictions and have also effectively slowed the increase in the number of jail inmates.

Finally, the continually increasing costs to government for building and operating correctional facilities challenge a jurisdiction's budget, and if the recession of 2008 continues for some period, there is likely to be an even greater slowing of the incarcerated population. In a report regarding methods to alleviate jail overcrowding (that is also relevant to prisons), the authors noted, "Construction and operation of local jails are extremely expensive propositions. Over the years, the view that a jurisdiction can solve its jail crowding problem through building has proved to be wrong."[22] Governments facing serious budget challenges are looking for less expensive ways to manage their criminal populations. The changes and politics around the use of incarceration are discussed in detail below.

One of the driving forces of growth in the inmate population has been the lengthening of prison sentences. As state legislatures and the U.S. Congress lengthen sentences, adopt three-strikes law for repeat offenders, and expand the number of crimes for which offenders must serve a "natural life" sentence, new issues are created for correctional administrators. Flanagan notes, "Prisoners incarcerated for long periods present correctional policymakers and administrators with several formidable problems. These problems stem from two principal characteristics of this prisoner population: (1) its diversity and (2) the serious offenses that eventuated in the inmates' long prison sentences."[23] Correctional administrators must consider changes in the design and construction of prisons to house long-term inmates, determine how these longer sentences affect traditional motivations for inmate discipline and incentives for good behavior, and redesign prisoner reentry strategies that respond to someone releasing to the community after long terms of separation.

Proponents of longer sentences argue that they maximize the correctional goals of incapacitation and deterrence, result in maturation of offenders (offenders usually reach their peak criminal activity during their late teens to early twenties[24]), and reduce crime, which justifies the significant cost resulting from the increase in the number of inmates.[25] Opponents, however, argue that this increase in prisoners creates other collateral issues that must be factored into the consideration of the benefit of this policy. Clear notes ten unintended consequences of the growth of imprisonment, including social consequences such as the recruitment of younger offenders to replace those criminals arrested and incarcerated and the depreciation of the family that results from removing the parent-age male from the home. He also notes fiscal consequences such as the reduction of funding for schools and other public services and the growth of future generation debt to fund prison construction and operation, even at a time when crime is decreasing.[26]

For most of the decade of the 1990s, community supervision (probation and parole) has undergone a transition from helping and counseling offenders to one of risk management and surveillance.[27] The focus on risk management is accompanied by new allocations of resources toward incarceration rather than probation and parole, and management of internal system processes. This perspective is referred to as the "new penology."[28] Rhine describes this perspective as one in which

> crime is viewed as a systemic phenomenon. Offenders are addressed not as individuals but as aggregate populations. The traditional corrections objectives of rehabilitation and the reduction of offender recidivism give way to the rational and efficient deployment of control strategies for managing (and confining) high-risk criminal populations. Though the new penology refers to any agency within the criminal justice system that has the power to punish, the framework it provides has significant analytic value to probation and parole administrators.[29]

While community corrections and prison administrators struggle with how to deal with longer sentences and new strategies of supervision, they also must confront a basic and critical issue, managing an offender population that has changed dramatically over the last twenty-five years. Seiter describes these changes as follows:

> A variety of characteristics separate the contemporary offender from his or her historical counterpart. As a group, today's offenders are more prone to gang involvement and violence, are younger and more impulsive, are serving longer sentences, and have little hope or belief that they will successfully return to the community as law-abiding citizens. The number and percentage of females involved in crime have increased too. Many more offenders are dealing with medical and mental health issues. Last, juvenile offenders increasingly act like adults in their sophistication and types of crimes.[30]

A changing offender population requires correctional administrators to deal with several new problems, including how to handle violent, impulsive inmates while ensuring staff safely, how to provide medical and mental health programs to respond to increased offender needs and demands, and how to plan facility construction or renovation to house an increased number of female and juvenile offenders. And correctional administrators must confront a wide variety of problems in substantive areas such as prison security, offender programming, and facility and bed space management.

Administrative Correctional Issues

Many of the substantive issues described above drive or lead to **administrative issues**, or those topics dealt with by administrators that include areas such as budgeting, human resource management, construction, maintenance, and planning for the future. Budgeting for correctional agencies used to be a relatively simple process, with few controversial issues, and with little interest or concern by elected policy makers. However, correctional budgets have grown and now demand a larger share of the governmental resources. With this growth has come increased political and public scrutiny. In 1981, it was reported that correctional expenditures totaled over $7.9 billion.[31] This amount has increased almost 400 percent in less than twenty years, as the budget for state correctional agencies was reported to be over $29 billion in 1999.[32] By fiscal year 2006, these budgets more than doubled again and totaled $68.7 billion.[33] And in 2007, state correctional agencies consumed 6.8 percent of state general funds.[34] This growth is expected to continue, and another $25 billion will be needed to fund state and federal correctional budgets by 2011.[35] Correctional administrators are being forced to find ways to cut funds without undermining public safety, as corrections has become governments' primary focus of how to reduce costs to meet budget challenges.

Another very complex administrative issue is the multitude of human resource management issues and challenges that result from rapid expansion, particularly when the work environment is difficult and sometimes dangerous. These challenges include recruitment, training and staff development, retention, professionalizing staff, and labor relations. Over the past several decades, correctional agencies have more fully recognized the critical value of their "people resources" to accomplish their mission. Freeman even named an era in correctional management history after this recognition. He calls the period from the 1970s to the 1980s "The Human Capital School," and notes how this approach "emphasized that employees are much more than just factors of production or individuals who only respond on the basis of feelings or needs. Employees are valuable investments that provide long-term returns to the organization if they are effectively developed and utilized."[36]

As the number of inmates increased so dramatically, the number of correctional staff also grew, resulting in the burden on correctional agencies to expand the numbers and train new staff to take over challenging duties. However, new staff is only the bottom level of the organizational pyramid—with supervisors, managers, and administrators at each step above this level. With each new prison or community-based unit, there must be new supervisors, managers and administrators, as well as new line employees. Rapid growth requires rapid development of management staff, which must quickly move up in the organization and be prepared to assume more responsibilities. In the past, the "maturation" and development of staff to assume upper-level positions came from years of experience. Unfortunately, during this period of rapid expansion, time for development is not available, and therefore correctional agencies must create specialized training and developmental activities to meet this need for an accelerated development of staff.

Another human resource issue is dealing with labor organizations. Although a few states (Connecticut in the 1940s and New York and Washington in the 1960s) have had unions for some time, collective bargaining is relatively new to most state correctional agencies. By the 1970s, more than twenty states had formally authorized collective bargaining by public employees, and by the end of the twentieth century, more than half of the states had collective bargaining for at least some correctional employees. Due to the mission of safety and security and the role of supervising felony offenders, collective bargaining is more complex for correctional agencies than for many other public and private organizations.

There are several reasons for the large number of unions representing correctional employees. First, with the decline of the number of industrial jobs in the United States, unions have concentrated on organizing and representing employees in the public sector.

Second, in an environment in which employees face risks to their personal safety (like police and corrections), there is likely to be strong employee involvement in unions. It is natural for employees to seek all of the support they can for the safest and most comfortable working condition they can have. Finally, with tightening budgets, salary increases often do not occur, causing discontent that can also lead to more interest in joining unions by correctional employees.

A third organizational issue is how to plan for the future. Correctional agencies have had almost two centuries of very slow change, and most strive for routine and consistency rather than being organizationally prepared for change. From the founding of the first prison in the United States in 1790 until approximately 1980, there were only a little more than 300,000 inmates in state and federal prisons. In less than thirty years, this number has grown six times, and the correctional world we knew has changed dramatically. Freeman notes, "Correctional managers must constantly respond to changing circumstances in the internal and external environment."[37] Continued change should be anticipated, and the dilemma administrators face is how to position their organizations to adapt to these changes. Leaders must reposition their correctional agencies to be learning organizations, and more fluid and able to respond to a changing environment. Implementing change requires an organizational ability to recognize factors that could bring about a need to change, establishing efficient decision-making processes, and the capability to modify policy and procedures as required. Many inexperienced managers think that making change is easy. However, effectively managing change is one of the most difficult things a manager must do.

Issues of Correctional Policy and Philosophy

Driven by shifts in policy and philosophy, changes in the use of incarceration, supervision of community offenders, and correctional policy have come about "fast and furious" over the last three decades. For example, increase in the number of incarcerated offenders has been influenced by many factors, but more by sentencing and incarceration policies than anything else. Blumstein and Beck examined the growth of imprisonment between 1980 and 1996 and concluded that 88 percent was due to changes in policy, including sentencing to prison rather than probation (51 percent) and lengthening time served by offenders (37 percent). Only 12 percent of the growth was the result of changes in the crime rate or the makeup of criminal offenders.[38]

And, as correctional administrators have to confront issues of policy and philosophy, they find that these issues also drive the substantive and administrative issues discussed earlier. Never in the history of corrections has there been so much attention and action by elected officials to dictate correctional policy. Seiter writes, "However, in an attempt to seem tough on crime, many correctional professionals believe that they (elected officials) may go too far in trying to influence what professional administrators should be doing."[39] Courtless continues this theme:

As we have seen, corrections must deal with legislative actions and judicial decisions. Legislatures have been moving toward statutes based on philosophies such as "truth in sentencing," "just deserts," with determinate sentences, and variations on life without parole terms of imprisonment such as "three strikes and you're out," and harsher forms of probation and parole. The correctional administrator has little choice but to follow these laws when offenders enter the correctional domain.[40]

Why have elected officials become so involved in correctional policy and why have they specifically moved to a "tough on crime" position? The watershed political event regarding politics and correctional policy occurred during the 1988 presidential campaign, when Vice President George Bush successfully used the public's fear of crime as a campaign tool against his opponent, Governor Michael Dukakis of Massachusetts. Bush used campaign ads presenting Dukakis as soft on crime for allowing a Massachusetts furlough program and suggesting that it led to the commission of a tragic murder by Willie Horton, a furloughed inmate, while he lived in a halfway house. Other candidates for public office saw the effectiveness of "tough on crime" policies and the dangers of being labeled "soft on crime." Campaign promises to keep dangerous offenders in prison longer became the rallying cry for elections across the country.

Another major change in policy was President Ronald Reagan's War on Drugs, which resulted in legislation to toughen drug laws and require mandatory prison terms for federal drug offenders. The dramatic increase in the federal prison population resulted primarily from these policies, to the point that almost two-thirds of the federal prison population is currently drug offenders. These laws were a good example of the mood to move away from treatment and understanding of the causes of crime to punishment and deterrence.

However, it is interesting that the politics around the "tough on crime" policies are not that clearly supported by the general public. Some of the major changes in sentencing included the implementation of sentencing guidelines, determinate sentencing to replace parole boards, and **mandatory sentencing**. All these reduce discretion by judges and correctional professionals, who can consider the individual risks of each offender and their chance for successful rehabilitation. As Petersilia writes, "One of the most distinguishing characteristics of U.S. crime policy since the 1980s has been the gradual chipping away on individualized decision making and its replacement with one-size-fits-all laws and policies."[41]

Public attitudes today are less punitive than they were in the past. In 1994, only 48 percent of Americans favored addressing the causes of crime and 42 percent preferred the punitive approach. However, in 2002, a public opinion poll found support for addressing the root causes of crime over strict sentencing, by 65 percent to 32 percent, and poll respondents favored more rational sentencing for offenders. Only 28 percent of those surveyed believed that the most effective way to reduce crime is to keep offenders off the street as long as possible. Nearly two-thirds of those surveyed believed that the most effective way to reduce crime is to rehabilitate prisoners by requiring education and job training.[42]

In 2006, a National Council on Crime and Delinquency poll found that 87 percent of the U.S. voting public favored rehabilitative services for inmates as opposed to a punitive approach to sentencing.[43] Respondents also expressed concern with the overreach of **three-strikes laws**, as 56 percent favored elimination of mandatory sentencing laws and giving judges more discretion to choose the appropriate sentence. In general, only 35 percent supported the direction of the nation's crime approach and 54 percent believed we are on the wrong track.[44] Greenwood and colleagues suggest that legislators who found voting for the legislation politically attractive later reversed themselves and found that voting against funding the act's implementation was just as politically attractive.[45]

The challenge for correctional administrators is how to respond to the expectations that criminal offenders must be punished for their crimes. They cannot overreact and totally accept punishment as their "marching orders," but must take the responsibility to advise and counsel elected officials on the importance of rehabilitation, deterrence, and incapacitation as well as punishment to ensure a safe environment for staff and improved opportunity for the future success of offenders. And correctional administrators have to deal with pressure to create approaches to move offenders deeper into more restrictive correctional sanctions and reduce the use of diversion and community-based programs. The public does have little tolerance for offenders who commit additional crimes while under community supervision, and it is difficult to resist the urge to violate every probationer or parolee that commits a technical violation of their supervision. Correctional officials have responded by increasing the use of classification and risk management (attempting to predict the chance of success) to help guide decisions and make community supervision explainable when it results in failure.

Issues in Managing the External Environment

Linked closely to the challenges of dealing with issues regarding policy and philosophy is the issue of "managing the external environment." The **external environment**, as related to corrections and correctional administration, includes interest groups outside the correctional organization, such as the media, political supervisors, the legislature, other criminal justice and social service agencies, and a variety of interest groups from victims to offender families. The external environment is the arena in which philosophy around correctional issues is turned into public policy.

For correctional administrators to effectively influence public policy, they must be adept at operating in the external environment. Historically, this has not been the case. With little public interest in correctional policy or practice, correctional administrators could do almost whatever they wished, with little oversight or concern, and therefore developed few skills in working with outside groups. Today, correctional administrators must be much more sophisticated and have a much wider breadth of leadership skills. In acknowledging the scope of talents required of someone in a high-level executive position in correctional agencies, Riveland writes:

> I would suggest that the ideal candidate for corrections director positions in the future would have the following qualities: well-grounded experientially and academically in correctional operations and theory; in management skills and techniques; and in major public policy development and political skills. Many have the first two, few have all three.[46]

Many correctional administrators bemoan the fact that they sometimes spend more time on issues external to the organization than any internal issue. They must regularly deal with interest groups, both those who support and those who disagree with the agencies' policies. They often must give media interviews, to explain a policy or describe a situation or incident. They regularly inform or respond to questions from executive branch leaders or members of the legislature. If they want their policies to be supported by these elected officials, they must educate and convince them that they are in the public and the officials' constituent interests.

There are two types of external issues: those to which the administrator must react, and those that require a proactive approach of education and coalition building. The reactive type of issues often come from a serious incident, such as an escape from prison, a serious crime committed by a parolee, a disturbance or riot, or a union picket or walkout. The proactive issues usually result from a challenge to an established policy, or the administrator's interest in changing a policy. Both reactive and proactive issues take considerable time, and both require considerable patience, excellent communication skills, and a foundation of trust and confidence in the administrator by others. Managing issues in the external environment is the topic of Chapter 11.

SUMMARY

The issues facing corrections have changed dramatically over the past few decades, requiring correctional leadership and management to change accordingly. Historically, leaders were autocratic and ruled correctional organizations with an iron fist. Few states had central departments of corrections, none had standardized policies and procedures, and prison authorities decided on their own how the prisons would operate. Managers performed the traditional functions of planning, organizing, staffing, directing, and controlling. Even those functions, however, were unsophisticated and performed without guidelines or bureaucratic standards.

Today's environment for corrections is sophisticated and complex and requires standard, bureaucratic processes for almost everything. Change is rapid, and new problems must be confronted almost daily. Corrections has become a very visible discipline, with high public interest and intense involvement by political officials. No longer are correctional administrators left alone to manage their organizations without interference. The public demands that they be protected and that offenders be held accountable for their actions. Over the past three decades, elected officials have enhanced sentences and toughened sanctions, leading to dramatic increases in the number of incarcerated offenders and correctional budgets.

All of these changes have demanded a different style of leadership by correctional administrators. Leaders must now be as concerned with understanding and managing the external environment as they are with the internal organization. Therefore, they must spend their time looking forward, identifying new trends and challenges, being proactive, creating a vision, and empowering staff with that vision. They must become transformational leaders by focusing on the principles, values, and vision of their organization rather than on efficiency and procedures. Because procedures must still be performed efficiently and consistently, leaders must encourage midlevel managers to oversee day-to-day operations, meet agency goals, improve policy and procedures, and mentor and develop staff.

As the many issues that confront correctional administrators continue to change, the sophistication of those who lead correctional agencies must also increase. Today, the challenges of more offenders to supervise, conflicting philosophies by elected officials on how they should be managed, tightening budgets requiring difficult choices on resource allocations, and employees who demand involvement and inclusion make correctional administration one of the most difficult and complex leadership challenges in society. Throughout the remainder of this textbook, the issues that must be confronted and the best practices in dealing with them will be further presented.

KEY TERMS

Leadership	Planning	Controlling
Management	Organizing	Substantive issues
Administration	Post orders	Administrative issues
Transactional leadership	Staffing	Mandatory sentencing
Transformational leadership	Relief factor	Three-strikes law
Organizational culture	Directing	External environment

YOU'RE THE CORRECTIONAL ADMINISTRATOR

1. You have been appointed as an associate warden of a prison that has operated in a very traditional fashion for the past forty years of its existence. The warden has been there for a long time, operates in a very autocratic fashion, but is becoming increasingly ineffective. Line staff have been joining the union at increasing numbers, their morale is very low, and they complain that they are never told what is going on or when a threat of conflict is developing between inmate groups. The midlevel managers or departments believe they do not have the authority to make any decisions without getting them approved by the warden. Do you simply blend in and accept the situation as it is, or do you try to make changes? If you want to change things, what risks do you run, and how do you gain the approval of the warden? What types of changes should be made, and what are some actions you would take to make the changes? What end results do you hope for from the changes?

2. You are the director of corrections for a midwestern state. The agency has operated well, and there have not been any serious incidents for a while. However, the state legislature has become increasingly interested in the department and has passed some bills to lengthen sentences, reduced the ability of corrections staff to award good time to inmates, and reduce what they consider "amenities" in the prisons. There seems to be a continuous increase in the political rhetoric around how the prisons should be managed, in order to make offenders feel punished for their crimes. You believe that the legislature's involvement in the operation of the department will continue but do not know what to do to change it. They do not consult you when considering new legislation. Where do you begin, what can you do, and how do you go about it? Develop a plan that will ensure thoughtful discussion of correctional legislation and, hopefully, result in the department not being required to implement policy that you believe will have a negative impact on your ability to run safe and controlled prisons.

WEB LINK EXERCISES

Go to California Department of Corrections (CA DOC) http://www.cdcr.ca.gov.

Go to the section regarding news for the California Department of Corrections. Go to Press Releases and pick one news release from 2010 Press Releases (or the most recent year) and read it. In this chapter, there was a discussion of the importance of managing the external environment to include constituencies, the media, and the political arena. From the news release, what do you think was the intent of the CA DOC? What message were they trying to send? What group(s) were they trying to influence and how?

Go to http://www.collaborativejustice.org/docs/The%20Importance%20of%20Collaborative%20Leadership.doc

The Web site is for an article produced by the Center of Effective Public Policy in conjunction with the National Institute of Corrections. This is a short article that you should read to learn about the author's eight Lessons of Effective Leadership entitled, *The Importance of Collaborative Leadership in Achieving Effective Criminal Justice Outcomes.* You should remember these lessons as you will want to incorporate them in your career to assist your promotional progress. After reading the article, how important do you think the eight lessons are and why?

GROUP EXERCISES

Each group will be assigned one of the functions of correctional administrators: Planning, Organizing, Staffing, Directing, and Controlling. Groups will make a presentation on the how each function operates in a correctional environment and its importance to organizational management. To instill competition among the groups, each group will attempt to depict their function as the most important for a successful correctional operation.

ENDNOTES

1. Peter M. Carlson, "Organization and Management," in *Prison and Jail Administration: Practice and Theory*, edited by Peter M. Carlson and Judith Simon Garrett (Boston, MA: Jones and Bartlett Publishers, 2008), p. 204.

2. James B. Jacobs, *Stateville: The Penitentiary in Mass Society* (Chicago: University of Chicago Press, 1977).

3. Nathan Kantrowitz, *Close Control: Managing a Maximum Security Prison; the Story of Ragen's Stateville Penitentiary* (Albany, NY: Harrow and Heston, 1996).

4. For an excellent discussion of the "new" role of correctional leaders in this era, see Chase Riveland, "The Correctional Leader and Public Policy Skills," *Corrections Management Quarterly* 1 no. 3 (1997): 22–25.

5. See James MacGregor Burns, *Leadership* (New York: Harper & Row, 1978).

6. Steven A. Murphy and Edward N. Drodge, "The Four I's of Police Leadership: A Case Study Heuristic," *International Journal of Police Science and Management* 6 no. 1 (2004) 1–15.

7. See M. Kay Harris, "A Call for Transformational Leadership for Corrections," *Corrections Management Quarterly* 3 no. 1 (1999): 24–29.

8. John J. DiIulio, Jr., *Governing Prisons: A Comparative Study of Correctional Management* (New York: Free Press, 1987), pp. 188–189.

9. David G. Keenhold, "What Do Managers Get Paid to Do?," *American Jails* 22 no. 3 (2008): 65–72.

10. Richard L. Phillips and Charles R. McConnell, *The Effective Corrections Manager: Corrections Supervision for the Future* (Boston, MA: Jones and Bartlett Publishers, 2005), p. 39.

11. H. Koontz and C. O'Donnell, *Principles of Management* (New York: McGraw-Hill, 1968).

12. A good description of this is found in John Wetzel and Rod Miller, "Staffing Analysis: Comparing "Relief Factor and Net Annual Work Hour' Calculations," *American Jails* 21 no. 4 (2007): 58–62.

13. Martin F. Horn, "Data-Driven Management Systems Improve Safety and Accountability in New York City Jails," *Corrections Today* 70 no. 5 (October 2008): 40–43.

14. Edward E. Rhine, "Probation and Parole Supervision: In Need of a New Narrative," *Corrections Management Quarterly* 1 no. 2 (1997): 71–75.

15. Jill Furniss, "The Population Boom," *Corrections Today* 58 no. 1 (1996): 38–43.

16. Albert Blumstein, "Prison Populations: A System Out of Control," in *Crime and Justice: A Review of Research*, edited by Michael Tonry and Normal Morris (Chicago, IL: University of Chicago Press, 1988).

17. Bureau of Justice Statistics, *Prison and Jail Inmates, 1997* (Washington, DC: U.S. Department of Justice, 1997).

18. Bureau of Justice Statistics, Press Release, "Growth in Prison and Jail Populations Slowing: 16 States Report Declines in the Number of Prisoners" (Washington, DC: U.S. Department of Justice, released March 31, 2009), http://www.ojp.usdoj.gov/bjs/pub/press/pimjim08stpr.htm (accessed August 16, 2009).

19. See Allen J. Beck and Paige M. Harrison, *Prisoners in 2000, Bureau of Justice Statistics Bulletin* (Washington, DC: U.S. Department of Justice, 2001).

20. Bureau of Justice Statistics, Press Release.

21. For a description of intermediate sanctions that have proved effective, see Richard P. Seiter, *Corrections: An Introduction* (Upper Saddle River, NJ: Pearson Education, 2011), pp. 131–133.

22. Pretrial Services Resource Center, *A Second Look at Alleviating Jail Overcrowding: A Systems Perspective* (Washington, DC: U.S. Department of Justice, Bureau of Justice Assistance, October 2000), p. 66.

23. Timothy J. Flanagan, "Correctional Policy and the Long-Term Prisoners," in *Long-Term Imprisonment: Policy, Science, and Correctional Practice*, edited by Timothy J. Flanagan (Newbury Park: CA: Sage Publications, 1995), p. 249.

24. A. Blumstein, J. Cohen, J. A. Roth, and C. A. Visher, *Criminal Careers and "Career Criminals"*, Vol. 1 (Washington, DC: National Academy Press, 1986), Chapter 3.

25. Edwin W. Zedlewski, "Why Prisons Matter: A Utilitarian Review," *Corrections Management Quarterly* 1 no. 2 (1997): 15–24.

26. Todd R. Clear, "Ten Unintended Consequences of the Growth of Imprisonment," *Corrections Management Quarterly* 1 no. 2 (1997): 25–31.

27. J. Simon and M. M. Freely, "True Crime: The New Penology and Public Discourse on Crime," in *Punishment and Social Control*, edited by T. G. Bloomberg and S. Cohen (New York, NY: Aldine De Gruyter, 1995).

28. M. M. Greeley and J. Simon, "The New Penology: Notes on the Emerging Strategy of Corrections and Its Implications," *Criminology* 30 no. 4 (1992), pp. 449–474.

29. Rhine, p. 73.

30. Richard P. Seiter, "Offenders and Issues Force Managerial Change," *Corrections Management Quarterly* 1 no. 2 (1997): iv.

31. Edmund R. McGarrell and Timothy J. Flanagan, *Sourcebook on Criminal Justice Statistics—1984* (Washington, DC: U.S. Department of Justice, 1985), p. 2.

32. Camille Graham Camp and George M. Camp, *The Corrections Yearbook, 1999: Adult Corrections* (Middletown, CN: Criminal Justice Institute, 1999), p. 85.

33. Camille Graham Camp and George M. Camp, *The 2002 Corrections Yearbook: Adult Corrections* (Middletown, CT: Criminal Justice Institute, 2003), p. 92.

34. National Association of State Budget Officers, "State Expenditure Report FY 2006," December 2007, http://www.nasbo.org/Publications/PDFs/fy2006er.pdf (accessed August 16, 2009).

35. *Public Safety, Public Spending: Forecasting America's Prison Population, 2007–2011*, Public Safety Performance Project (Washington, DC: The Pew Charitable Trust, February 2007), p. ii.

36. Robert M. Freeman, *Correctional Organization and Management: Public Policy Challenges, Behavior, and Structure* (Boston, MA: Butterworth Neinemann, 1999), p. 24.

37. Freeman, p. 363.

38. Alfred Blumstein and Allen J. Beck, "Population Growth in U.S. Prisons: 1980–1996," in *Prisons: A Review of Research*, edited by Michael Tonry and Joan Petersilia (Chicago: University of Chicago Press, 1999), pp. 17–62.

39. Richard P. Seiter, "Setting Correctional Policies," *Corrections Management Quarterly* 1 no. 2 (1997): 81.

40. Thomas F. Courtless, *Corrections and the Criminal Justice System: Laws, Policies, and Practices* (Belmont, CA: Wadsworth Publishing, 1998), pp. 387–388.

41. Joan Petersilia, *When Prisoners Come Home: Parole and Prisoner Reentry* (New York: Oxford University Press, 2003), p. 221.

42. As cited in Peter D. Hart Research Associates, *Changing Public Attitudes toward the Criminal Justice System* (New York: Open Society, February 2002).

43. Barry Krisberg and Susan Marchionna, "Attitudes of U.S. Voters toward Prisoners Rehabilitation and Reentry Policies," *Focus: Views from the National Council on Crime and Delinquency* (San Francisco, CA: NCCD, April 2006).

44. Ibid.

45. Peter Greenwood, et al., "Estimated Benefits and Costs of California's New Mandatory Sentencing Law," in *Three Strikes and You're Out*, edited by David Shichor and Dale K. Sechrest (Thousand Oaks, CA: Sage, 1996).

46. Chase Riveland, "The Correctional Leader and Public Policy Skills," *Corrections Management Quarterly* 1 no. 3 (1997): 24.

4

Setting the Tone: Vision, Mission, and Strategic Planning

Introduction

The concepts of strategic planning, vision, and mission statements are "old hat" to the private sector but have only more recently become a regular element of management in public agencies. In particular, it has only been in the last two decades that correctional administrators began to think about and implement planning into the management routine. Corrections has historically been very reactionary in its management, and thoughtful, strategic planning, including an examination of external factors and forces, agency strengths and weaknesses, and expected future challenges, has historically not been used extensively. Gibbons and Pisciotta note,

> As the corrections industry begins to look more and more like a multibillion dollar business, so must the leadership of each individual agency and facility, given the dynamic and complex operating environment of corrections and the limited funding, stringent federal regulations and exploding offender populations. Correctional agencies need a vision and a plan for how to manage burgeoning inmate populations while retaining a motivated workforce.[1]

Correctional agencies now face intense public scrutiny, rapid technological and environmental changes, continually increasing demands for services (more offenders), and a proportionately reduced supply of resources (budgets and staff). To address these challenges, correctional agencies must constantly look into the future and plan for how to respond to both known and unknown challenges. Traditionally, planning for public agencies was around the budget cycle, as needs and resources for the coming few months were anticipated. This was satisfactory when there was little or only moderate growth in clients to be served, minimal changes in operations and conditions, and few outside pressures on an agency. However, this type of planning is no longer satisfactory to meet the current fluid environment that confronts corrections.

This chapter outlines approaches used by private corporations, public organizations, and correctional agencies in order to understand the future, create a vision, and develop a plan that meets their needs well into the twenty-first century. Planning for the future is complex, and requires commitment and effort from leadership, management, and line staff. All play a critical role in the planning process, and all must be involved and contribute at every step along the planning route. Only with a concerted effort by all staff within an organization, as well as with input from political leaders and other constituent groups and stakeholders, can planning be successful in meeting future challenges that confront the field of corrections.

This chapter also provides an understanding of strategic planning. This section includes much more than a step-by-step account of how to conduct a planning initiative. It also describes the more subjective issues of the role of leaders in the planning activities, the creation of a vision and its impact on organizational culture, and the critical importance of leaders and managers tending to the communications and change process that line staff will go through when implementing the strategic plan. This chapter also includes a discussion of vision, mission, objectives, and goals; a description of the planning process; and the need for emphasis on the implementation of the plan.

Distinguishing Vision and Mission

Organization mission statements have been around almost as long as organizations, and the military has always made "accomplishing the mission" a key part of its training and communications. Almost every report, article, or book on management includes a discussion of the purpose, or mission, of the organization. However, the concept of **vision** for an organization is relatively new in organizational literature, and is even more recent in the practice with public correctional agencies. But what is meant by vision in an organization or agency?

Vision is often confused with mission, goals, statement of purpose, and many other terms used by organizations. In the context used in this textbook, and in the context used by most agencies that really understand vision, it is not the same as the other terms. Kouzes and Posner define *vision* as "an ideal and unique image of the future."[2] In *The Empowered Manager*, Peter Block notes, "A vision is the preferred future, a desirable state, and ideal state. It is an expression of optimism despite the bureaucratic surrounding or the evidence to the contrary."[3] Bennis and Nanus state, "A vision articulates a view of a realistic, credible, attractive future for the organization, a condition that is better in some important ways than what now exists."[4] As is apparent, vision is a general statement encompassing the direction an agency wants to take and the desired end result once it arrives there. As employees of an organization think of their vision, it is simply what they want the organization to be.

A **mission**, however, is more focused on the specifics of what an organization does or is to accomplish. It differs from a vision in that it focuses on function, is accomplishable and measurable, and is often statutorily or bureaucratically established. Eadie states that the mission of an organization "is a statement of its basic purposes, often in terms of broad outcomes that it is committed to achieving or the major function it carries out."[5]

A mission can also be the reason an agency exists. When staff meet to write a mission statement, they often begin by asking themselves, "Why do we exist? What is it we are supposed to accomplish?" For public sector agencies, the mission is often legislatively established. When a legislature creates an agency, it almost always states its purpose, function, or mission. For a state correctional agency, a common mission often is "to supervise criminal offenders during the period of their sentence, protect the public, and offer programs that assist in the rehabilitation of criminals."

As well as stating the purpose or function of an organization, a mission can also be value laden, going beyond what is to be accomplished, and communicating some of the principles and values that accompany the function. Freeman states, "A well-developed mission statement also states the strategies, values and commitments that provide guidance and direction to both managers and employees as they pursue accomplishment of the objectives."[6] The incorporation of values into the mission statement is not the usual approach, because most correctional mission statements are very focused on function. Mission statements that emphasize values and principles blur the usual distinctions between mission and vision.

An Example of Mission and Vision

The Federal Bureau of Prisons (BOP) has been a leader as a correctional agency in strategic planning, communicating, and reemphasizing the mission of the organization to employees. The mission statement of the Federal BOP, as stated on its Web site, is

> The Federal Bureau of Prisons protects society by confining offenders in the controlled environments of prisons and community-based facilities that are safe, humane, cost-efficient, and appropriately secure, and that provide work and other self-improvement opportunities to assist offenders in becoming law-abiding citizens.[7]

Many federal prisons restate that mission statement as their own purpose or function within the overall Bureau of Prisons operation. For instance, the Federal Correctional Institution (FCI) at Greenville, Illinois, which was constructed and opened in 1994, states the mission as

> FCI Greenville protects society by confining offenders in a controlled environment that is safe, humane, and appropriately secure for both staff and inmates. FCI Greenville provides work and other self-improvement opportunities to assist offenders in becoming law-abiding citizens. As stewards of the public trust, cost efficiency will be a guiding principle at this facility.[8]

However, to be more future oriented, FCI Greenville also created a vision statement. The vision statement was value laden, future oriented, and an ideal of what the staff wanted the organization to be. The vision of FCI Greenville is, "We [the staff] envision FCI Greenville as a safe, pleasant and empowered workplace."[9]

One of the positive characteristics of this vision statement is its simplicity. Although the vision clearly presents certain key values in describing and defining the institution, it is not so complex that it is difficult to communicate. One of the problems often associated with vision statements is that they are extensive, hoping to cover all aspects of the company's or agency's values and principles. They, therefore, end up being difficult to communicate to employees, clients, customers, and external stakeholders. And, as discussed later in this chapter, the communication of the vision is the most important reason to have one. If all associated with the agency do not know the vision, it is a waste of time to develop one. As an example, the vision for the Federal BOP is as follows:

> The Federal Bureau of Prisons, judged by any standard, is widely and consistently regarded as a model of outstanding public administration, and as the best value provider of efficient, safe and humane correctional services and programs in America. This vision will be realized when ...
>
> The Bureau provides for public safety by assuring that no escapes and no disturbances occur in its facilities. The Bureau ensures the physical safety of all inmates through a controlled environment, which meets each inmate's need for security through the elimination of violence, predatory behavior, gang activity, drug use, and inmate weapons. Through the provision of health care, mental, spiritual, educational, vocational and work programs, inmates are well prepared for a productive and crime free return to society. The Bureau is a model of cost efficient correctional operations and programs.
>
> Our talented, professional, well trained, and diverse staff reflects the Bureau's culture and treat each other fairly. Staff works in an environment free from discrimination. A positive working relationship exists where employees maintain respect for one another. The workplace is safe and staff performs their duties without fear of injury or assault. Staff maintains high ethical standards in their day-to-day activities. Staff is satisfied with their jobs, career opportunities, recognition, and quality of leadership.[10]

Although this vision statement is excellent at communicating values and principles when it is read, it is very complex to communicate. The FCI vision of a "safe, pleasant and empowered workplace" is probably remembered and easily repeated by most staff who work there. However, it is unlikely that many staff could recite more than one or two elements of the Bureau of Prisons' vision. Vision statements should be brief and clear. Brevity allows communication of the message through mottos, posters, symbols, or any other approach used to communicate and remind employees and stakeholders of the vision. Acceptance of a vision statement by stakeholders cannot occur unless they fully understand it.

Leadership and the Vision

When establishing a vision for an agency, leaders must first determine their role in the process. Most current literature on organizational leadership notes that providing a vision for an organization is the responsibility of a leader, and even goes so far as to conclude that all good leaders have a vision for their organization. As quoted in Kouzes and Posner's *The Leadership Challenge*, Robert L. Swiggett, chairperson of Kollmorgen Corporation, stated, "The leader's job is to create a vision."[11] Bennis and Nanus note that an essential element of leadership is the articulation of direction or vision.[12]

There are others who dispute the almost sole responsibility of the leader to create a vision for the organization. Ensuring and guiding the development of a vision for an organization is one of the key activities of leadership:

> Agencies and organizations must have a vision and understanding of where they want to go and what they want to be. Leaders must provide this for their agencies. This does not mean that the leaders do this for the organization, as leaders involve employees in setting the vision. . . . it is critical to involve employees in creating a vision and setting the direction for the future of a public agency.[13]

Leaders have the opportunity to hear firsthand the opinion of elected, political officials regarding their expectations of correctional agencies. They spend more time talking to external stakeholders than other agency managers and line employees. They also deal with other agencies in developing budgets and acquiring resources. As a result of these opportunities, leaders should be aware of trends, expected changes, and future challenges to the agency. Leaders should have a strong cognitive ability to process this information, understanding what is important, and what issues are most likely to impact the future of the agency. The end result of this gathering and processing of information is that the leader becomes the repository of information that is essential when creating a vision for an agency.

Practically, organization leaders should use this knowledge to help in the creation of a vision. From the preceding statements regarding the leader's responsibility to create the organization's vision, one gets the impression that after processing the information, the leader may already have a vision of what the future of the agency should be. However, this individual formulation of a vision neglects to take advantage of the collaborative experience and information that lies within other employees of an organization. It is better for leaders to share and communicate their acquired information with staff. The leader then participates in, and may even direct, the process of staff discussing historical situations, current operations, and future trends and challenges, as they jointly create a vision for the agency.

Developing and Promoting the Vision

Although it can be argued that it is not the sole responsibility of the leader to create a vision, it can also be argued that it is the sole responsibility of the leader to guide staff through the vision development process and to promote the vision in every way possible. After a vision is created, the leader should do everything possible to make it a part of the agency culture. The following case study provides a good examination of a vision being established.

The case study is a good demonstration of a process that can be used to create a vision for an organization. Based on the activities presented, several key steps can be enumerated:

1. Educate staff about what a vision is and why it is important. In this case, the warden began talking about a vision for the future, not what it should be, but what it could mean for the facility. It would be more difficult to jump into a planning session to create a vision before the staff understood and had the chance to discuss and accept why

Practical Perspectives

Creating a Vision Statement for an Organization

In a western prison, the warden had read the recent leadership and management literature and wanted to establish a vision for the institution. However, she was convinced the vision would mean more to all staff if they participated in developing it rather than it being her idea only. Although the staff respected the warden's intellect and believed she was forward thinking, they had been through a rough few years. The institution had a serious riot, with several staff injured. After the riot, the employee labor union went on the offensive, demanding certain changes to ensure staff safety. This created a divisive situation, whereby staff were not sure if they were to support the union or the administration. Because the prison had been in operation less than three years, there was no entrenched culture to reemphasize as a guiding principle to staff.

As a result of these problems, the warden and her executive staff had been emphasizing the need to involve staff in decision making, push decisions down to the lowest possible level, empower midlevel managers to take charge of their areas, and be very visible in communicating with line staff about issues, problems, operations of the prison, and why certain decisions were made. These activities seemed to be working, but the warden wanted a single focus for building a positive culture for the institution. Creating a vision, an impression in every employee's mind, of what the prison should be and could be, was important, and it would make an excellent activity to give these individuals an overarching goal or approach.

The warden began talking about a vision statement, what it was, and what it could mean to the future of the institution. She emphasized it was the staff's responsibility to take the best of what the institution was, and build that into a model for the future. The institution had several small groups of staff, in addition to the various departments that made up the formal organizational structure. These included the department heads, the labor union, the lieutenants (the ranking security officers who supervised correctional officers), the employees club (a voluntary group of employees that sponsored social functions for staff), a line staff advisory committee (created by the warden to hear directly from line staff about issues important to them), and the executive staff. The warden used these groups as discussion groups about the vision. She asked each group to discuss what the vision should be for the institution, seeking their input on the most important elements of what they do. Flyers were put up notifying all staff that their input was important and giving them ways to communicate their ideas and suggestions even if they were not a part of any of the groups.

The warden then organized a retreat to discuss the vision. Representatives of all the groups were invited to attend. It was to be a roundtable discussion, with no hierarchy. All employees were equal in their roles, regardless of their job or rank in the institution. The warden played the role of facilitator, organizing the discussion, providing information, and getting everyone involved. She sought out opinions from each group and the kinds of things that were important to them in the operation of the prison. As ideas were presented, the warden began to blend them into similar areas and shape them into a vision statement. At the end of the discussion, the group agreed on a brief, clear statement that espoused the values that were important to them. This became the accepted vision for the future.

a vision was important. It also would not have been as effective if the warden created and then announced a vision for the prison. Staff hear all types of pronouncements from upper-level management, and announcing a vision would have been little different than announcing a minor change in procedures.

2. Develop a process to involve all staff in creating the vision. The positive steps taken by the warden to begin to seek input from staff, giving every staff person the opportunity to be involved, not only ensures a better product but it also ensures increased acceptance. As staff acceptance increases, the likelihood that the vision will be integrated into the organizational culture also increases.

3. Ask for specific input from the various groups within the organization. In this case, the warden also asked each group to provide input so that it could be considered at the planning retreat. Not only is there the opportunity to provide input but it also requires each group to discuss and consider the topics important to them. This can be particularly important when there are groups of staff who do not contribute but will criticize decisions or processes after the fact. Although no one likes to admit it, all organizations have "naysayers" who do this. Through this process, those who would not contribute and provide recommendations feel peer pressure by the other groups to encourage them to do so. If they do not contribute to the discussion, it is less likely that staff will give their after-the-fact criticism much credibility.

4. Hold a planning session or retreat to gather input and shape the vision statement. In the case study, the warden held a retreat, inviting all groups to send a representative, and treating each person as an equal in terms of the value of their input. The retreat allows excellent discussion, each group hears what is important to the others, and they most likely find out that they all share common ground and desire the same outcome.

5. The leader should share information, lead the process, and shape the vision statement. It is important for the leader to "be the leader" in this group process. Some argue it is better to use a trained facilitator and let the leader only be a participant in the process. But the leader cannot totally abdicate leadership, even if he or she is trying to get everyone involved. A facilitator would naturally seek the leader's opinion throughout the discussion, and the other participants would simply wait to see what the leader says and wants. This stymies discussion. If the leader facilitates the discussion, he or she can encourage input yet still provide personal opinions and desires during the process.

6. Draft the vision statement. At the end of the retreat, the vision statement should be drafted, at least for distribution and further comment. The retreat should not end without a product. Some leaders are hesitant to end a process and do not want to create a vision without more opportunity for comment. This delay can have negative consequences. If a process with the opportunity for staff involvement, as in the case study, has been completed, it is time to draft the vision. There is nothing wrong, however, with calling it a draft and encouraging comments. However, it is unlikely there will be any significant suggestions after such a thorough process and opportunity for discussion.

7. Communicate and reinforce the vision to staff. Once the vision is established, it is critical to communicate it to all levels of staff throughout the organization. The vision does little in guiding staff and giving direction if all levels of staff are not aware of it and use it as guidance. It is critical for leaders and other staff to constantly reinforce the vision. Typically, an organization develops signs and posters to communicate the vision to staff, discusses the vision at staff meetings, and takes advantage of opportunities addressing large groups of staff to reinforce the vision. These are important steps, but the most effective way to reinforce the vision is to use it to begin the planning process, to build it into supervisor–employee discussions of performance, and to create awards and recognition programs based on activities and accomplishments that are consistent with the agency vision.

This process describes the specific steps that can be taken to develop a vision statement for an agency, as well as the key role of leaders in making the process a success. The vision is a desired state, sets a direction for the future, and guides employees in the day-to-day functions within their job responsibilities. After establishing and communicating the vision statement throughout the organization, it is important to align it to the agency mission, along with the goals and objectives. The next section explains the meaning of these terms, and later sections explain a strategic planning process used to develop activities to accomplish the mission.

Mission, Objectives, and Goals

As noted, vision statements provide a direction of where an agency wants to go. The mission, objectives, and goals should be aligned to move the agency toward the vision, and are developed through a planning process to create and promote shorter-term activities that should occur. These activities should focus on overcoming obstacles and moving the agency toward reaching the vision. King and Cleland note that "The objective of the planning process is the establishment of a mission, goals, strategies, programs, and allocations of resources that will enable the organization to best cope with and influence an uncertain future."[14]

Figure 4-1 illustrates a simple hierarchy of organizational plans, and the elements that can align organizational purpose with activities to accomplish that purpose.[15] It should be noted that the use and definitions of specific terms is not universal, and many agencies use "goals" as the broader activities between mission at the top and specific steps to be taken at the bottom of the hierarchy. Even though the terms and definitions can vary, in general there is a broad mission statement that is to be accomplished and more detailed and

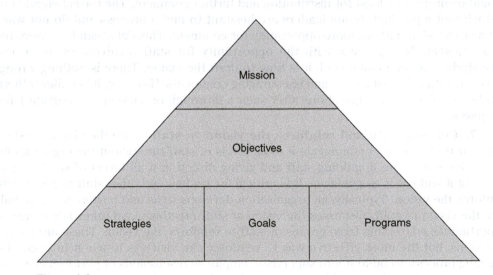

Figure 4-1
Relationship of strategic choice elements.

specific activities at the bottom of the hierarchy that support the accomplishment of the mission.

At the top of the hierarchy is the organization's mission. As previously stated, the mission is the key function that the organization is to accomplish. As an example, a mission statement for a prison could be "to confine offenders in a controlled environment that is safe, humane, and appropriately secure for both staff and inmates." At the next level are **objectives**, which specify the accomplishments that need to be completed to fulfill the mission statement. As an example, three objectives that could be listed for the prison include the following:

1. Have no inmate escapes.
2. Have no serious staff or inmate injuries from assaults by inmates.
3. Have a positive pattern of staff and inmate interaction and communications.

King and Cleland suggest that, based on these objectives, the organization chooses its next level of the hierarchy, "its strategy (general direction), goals (specific targets), and programs (objective- or goal-focused collection of activities). . . . A strategy may be oriented toward the accomplishment of a single objective, or an array of objectives. Goals are more detailed and specific states to be achieved within the framework of objectives and strategy. Programs may relate to goals or objectives or both."[16] Figure 4-2 illustrates an example of an entire hierarchy that could be created for the prison to accomplish its mission.

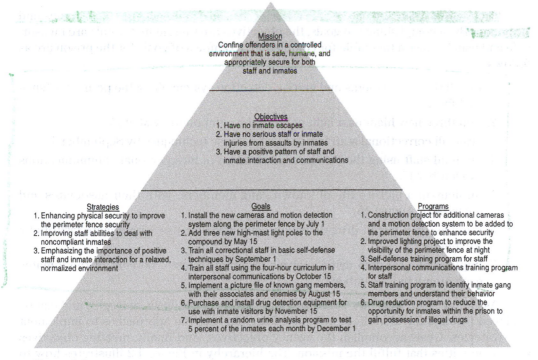

Figure 4-2
Mission, objectives, strategies, goals, and programs for FCI Greenville.

Strategies are the general approaches that are taken to accomplish objectives. Strategies listed in Figure 4-2 include enhancing physical security to improve the perimeter fence security; improving staff abilities to deal with noncompliant inmates; and emphasizing the importance of positive staff and inmate interaction for a relaxed, normalized environment. Strategies help communicate the approaches that are believed will accomplish the objectives and the institution mission.

Programs are made up of projects and activities that are linked to strategy to accomplish a specific goal. In this sense, all three of the elements at the bottom of the pyramid link together to accomplish the goals. Examples of possible programs to accomplish the goals for the prison are as follows:

1. Construction project for additional cameras and a motion detection system to be added to the perimeter fence to enhance security.
2. Improved lighting project to improve the visibility of the perimeter fence at night.
3. Self-defense training program for staff.
4. Interpersonal communications training program for staff.
5. Staff training program to identify inmate gang members and understand their behavior.
6. Drug reduction program to reduce the opportunity for inmates within the prison to gain possession of illegal drugs.

The **goals** are specific activities to be accomplished as a part of the strategies and programs. By accomplishing the goals, the objectives are therein met. Goals are measurable and usually have a timetable for completion. Examples of goals for the prison are as follows:

1. Install the new cameras and motion detection system along the perimeter fence by July 1.
2. Add three new high-mast light poles to the compound by May 15.
3. Train all correctional staff in basic self-defense techniques by September 1.
4. Train all staff using the four-hour curriculum in interpersonal communications by October 15.
5. Implement a picture file of known gang members, with their associates and enemies by August 15.
6. Purchase and install drug detection equipment for use with inmate visitors by November 15.
7. Implement a random urine analysis program to test 5 percent of the inmates each month by December 1.

As can be seen, goals are the actual activities resulting from strategies and can be achieved through the identified programs. Programs are the approaches to implement the strategies. Goals accomplish the agency objectives. And finally, meeting objectives are the activities that fulfill the mission. The hierarchy in Figure 4-2 illustrates how to visualize the linkages of all these activities to successfully reach the mission of a safe, humane, and secure prison.

Strategic Planning: Identifying Mission, Objectives, and Goals

How does an organization create a mission statement, and identify objectives and goals (as well as strategies and programs)? The answer is through a process called strategic planning. Strategic planning originated in the private sector during the 1960s. One early definition is as follows:

> Strategic planning is the process of deciding on the objectives of the organization, on changes in those objectives, on the resources used to attain these objectives, and on the policies that are to govern the acquisition, use and disposition of these resources.[17]

Strategic planning is a process involving many staff, resulting in alignment of the mission statement to objectives and goals, and identifying actions to be taken by the agency to accomplish these objectives and goals. In essence, it results in a "road map" for how an agency gets to where it wants to go. Strategic planning is future oriented rather than about where the agency has been. In a strategic plan, agencies clarify future directions, obstacles to getting there, and steps that must be taken to overcome the obstacles.

Why (or When) to Plan?

Most purists would suggest that strategic planning be continuous and that there is no particular time or issue generation that spurs planning. Most would also agree that an agency should always be reaching into the future, scanning the environment, and modifying plans. In most organizations, however, the planning process is not continuous, and is usually bounded and defined. Once completed, it often takes some event or major change in the organization to spur another strategic planning cycle. Some of the following represent events or opportunities that often encourage the beginning of a planning activity.

A change in leadership.
A change in leadership is a very good opportunity for developing a new plan. New leaders want their own "thumbprint" on the organization, and strategic planning provides this and communicates changes to the organization. The planning process not only creates a road map for the future, but it is also a great chance to communicate with employees, hear their concerns as well as their optimism about the future, let them hear the leaders' vision, and identify employees who have specific skills the leaders may be need to move the organization forward.

Changes in the external environment that necessitate a response by the organization.
External pressures that develop and challenge correctional agencies include new sentencing laws, a major change in budget allocation, an identified change in the types of offenders supervised, or expected growth or even reductions in the number of offenders. These influences almost always require an agency initiating strategic planning to be sure they understand the change, identify potential impacts, and develop action plans to respond to the change.

Changes in the internal environment of the organization.
At times, agencies reorganize and modify the responsibilities of various units. When this occurs, it can be helpful to conduct a planning process, because various staff interactions and

roles can shift. The planning process is a good opportunity to discuss these in relationship to the desired outcome and to clarify who will be responsible for certain activities.

When staff morale is low or when staff need direction.
It is naive to think that staff are always dedicated and excited about their jobs and their roles in an organization. At times, even the best of staff can become disenchanted with the agency, certain policies or procedures, or their leadership. Strategic planning process can provide a constructive forum to address these concerns without being a "gripe session," but by emphasizing how to as a team address the future successfully. As staff are involved in setting the direction for the future, they can be reinvigorated and recommitted to the agency and its goals.

When there is a major change in policy or procedure.
Many things can prompt a need to change an agency's policies and procedures. If the changes are significant enough to affect a large number of staff, it is valuable to have a planning session to be sure staff understand how the new policy will be implemented and to determine whether there are any unexpected outcomes that may be identified by staff that also need to be addressed.

In addition, there are many situations that undermine an organizations ability to meet its potential. One that often occurs is when an organization becomes too bureaucratic and immersed in process rather than outcome, and reactionary rather than proactive. King and Cleland identify several symptoms that require a planning process to change the focus of the organization from reactionary to future oriented. These include the following:

1. A tendency for managers to view a current domain from the standpoint of the discipline in which credentials were first acquired, regardless of its broader scope and the requirements for more diverse considerations.
2. A "tunnel vision" phenomenon, in which managers fail to recognize the multiple objectives of the organization even though they have moved to a general management position and can no longer afford the luxury of the simplistic efficiency-oriented objectives that are the forte of managers at lower levels.
3. A bureaucratic organizational structure designed more for maintaining efficiency and control in current operations than in fostering long-range innovation.
4. The lack of an "organization" or process designed specifically for fostering the managerial participation and innovativeness for developing new products and services.
5. An assumption that the chief executive or, alternatively, a professional planning staff should *do* the planning.
6. An incentive system wherein performance oriented toward the production of short-range results is rewarded more highly than a system oriented toward long-range opportunities.
7. The introduction of radically new planning systems into organizations without proper concern for their effect on the motivations and behavior of those managers who must use them.[18]

These symptoms should be a trigger for agencies to reconsider their leadership and management approaches and ensure they have a culture that involves staff in planning and focus on the future.

Organizational Culture and Strategic Planning

Every organization has a **culture** in terms of the way employees interact; the manner in which the organization interacts with other entities; the emphasis that is placed on certain traits, processes, and goals; and the style of leadership and management that is utilized. Wilson defines organizational culture as "a persistent, patterned way of thinking about the central tasks of and human relationships within an organization."[19] The culture of an organization can also be viewed as "the integrated system of acquired behavioral patterns in the organization that are characteristic of the members of the organization and that influence the attitudes and the modus operandi of the organization."[20]

The culture of an organization is an important consideration when doing strategic planning. Stojkovic and Farkas suggest that "Changing and shaping the work culture must be a part of any strategic management plan."[21] There are three ways in which organizational culture links to strategic planning. First, when an organization has a culture endorsed and appreciated by employees, they have a sense of mission about the agency's work. In contrast, when the agency mission is vague, employees are less committed to the organization's role, and there is little sense of dedication to the organization and what it is trying to accomplish. Strategic planning can clarify mission, goals, and everyone's role in accomplishing the mission, resulting in a culture focused on this accomplishment. Second, if an agency has a culture that accepts strategic planning as a basic part of their operations, they are likely to be more focused on the future. Those organizations that do not share such a culture are unlikely to be successful at planning. Therefore, effective planning can assist in the development of a culture being mission driven, and a future-oriented culture can lead to effective planning. Both culture and planning contribute to one another.

And finally, the culture of an organization impacts how employees are involved in the strategic planning process. Seiter suggests that one of two types of culture that develops in a prison setting (also true in other correctional organizations) is the **management culture** that puts into practice how leadership deals and communicates with subordinate staff and falls into a continuum between *autocratic* and *empowered* (illustrated in Figure 4-3).[22] In an autocratic culture, staff strictly follow rules and do not make decisions without approval if they fall outside of established policy. With an empowered culture, employees are fully understanding of, and are expected to make decisions consistent with, the principles, values, and desired outcome of the organization. The more empowered the environment, the more likely employees at all levels are invited to contribute and be included in the strategic planning process.

Autocratic	Moderate	Empowered
Staff must follow policy or check with supervisors before making decisions		Staff make decisions with full knowledge and consistent with prison principles and values

Figure 4-3   *A continuum of management cultures in a prison.*

To have a strategic plan that is effectively communicated and implemented, an organization must have developed a culture that looks toward the future, accepts change, is mission driven, and constantly strives to improve its operations. All organizations do not have this culture, and culture cannot be developed or changed overnight. For correctional agencies, it may be particularly difficult to establish a culture of focusing on the future. Correctional agencies are by nature reactionary, and routine and consistent repetition of procedures is a desirable trait. For a correctional leader to suddenly declare that the agency must look for different ways of doing things and not be wedded to the past is almost counterintuitive to the way a generation of correctional workers has learned to do their jobs.

Therefore, the planning process is not the time for leadership to suggest an organization look to the future. For effective strategic planning, the leaders must be committed to a culture of planning and constantly lead and manage to reinforce this emphasis. Perhaps the most effective activities by leaders and managers is to constantly discuss the future and ask employees what the organization must do to get ready for it. Even if leaders and managers do function in this manner, a culture that emphasizes planning will not quickly develop. But with persistence, empowerment, and encouragement, the end result will be an organizational culture emulating these traits.

The Planning Process

For purposes of simulating a planning activity, two assumptions will be made. First, an agency has an event that creates an opportunity for planning, or the agency has recognized symptoms that reflect the need for developing a plan. Second, the agency has a culture that values planning, and seeks to identify future challenges and create responses to them. The organization is now ready to conduct a strategic planning exercise.

There are several steps that are key elements in strategic planning. The following activities are identified by Sorkin, Ferris, and Hudak as basic to the process:

1. Scan the environment.
2. Select key issues.
3. Set mission statements or broad goals.
4. Undertake external and internal analysis.
5. Develop goals, objectives, and strategies with respect to each issue.
6. Develop an implementation plan to carry out strategic actions.
7. Monitor, update, and scan.[23]

These steps should result in the end product of the planning process. It is important to remember, "Plans are not the objectives to be achieved through planning. The objective of the planning process is the establishment of a mission, goals, strategies, programs, and allocations of resources that will enable the organization to best cope with and influence an uncertain future."[24]

Before describing each of these seven steps, it is important to understand two issues of logistics: how long strategic planning should take and who should participate. Planning cannot be accomplished in only a few hours, and it also should not take several days. The first part of strategic planning (steps 1 through 5) can be accomplished, if a strategic planning process is well organized, in two to three days. The required follow-up of developing an implementation plan and monitoring progress and making necessary modifications is a long-term and continuous process. The first two- to three-day session should be organized to take each of steps 1 through 5 sequentially, because each builds on the information developed and the discussion points made in the earlier steps.

The second logistical determination is who should attend the planning exercise. As noted earlier, a benefit in strategic planning is that it is an opportunity for many people to be involved in creating a road map for the future of an agency, so that they bring their knowledge to the discussion, and take a commitment to implementation away from it. In the early days of strategic planning, planning usually included only small groups of upper-level management. However, participation from all levels of staff results in more thoughtful and realistic planning.

A good example of broad and fruitful participation is the example of the development of a strategic plan for Federal Prison Industries (FPI). FPI is a government corporation that manages the prison industry program within the Federal BOP. FPI executives included approximately thirty FPI staff and other interested parties in the planning process. The staff included were all of the corporate officers (approximately five), all of the division managers (approximately eight), three or four factory managers, one or two quality assurance supervisors, representatives from the sales staff, representatives from the financial department, and a three-person planning group. Interested parties included six to eight wardens who oversee the factories within the prisons they supervise and three or four other executives from the Bureau of Prisons.

To ensure that the group had input from outside parties, yet to prevent the group from getting too large, a facilitator conducted interviews with additional relevant individuals prior to the planning session. Those interviewed were all seven members of the FPI board of directors, a few representative customers (federal government officials who purchase FPI products), a few private sector company officials who sell products in competition with FPI, and selected members of the U.S. Congress. At the beginning of the planning process, the facilitator presented the results of these interviews to set the stage and create an understanding of the environment in which FPI was operating. Through the interview process, FPI not only benefited from the diversity of the planning group but also were able to broaden the input considered without expanding the number of planning participants.

Although not every stakeholder is included in the group, strategic planning processes usually can accommodate fairly large numbers, perhaps as many as 75 or even 100, so they allow and encourage all participants to present their points of view and allow for active discussions. The large group usually is together for overall presentations and directions; however, they break into smaller groups for discussion. These small groups then present a summary of their discussion back to the larger group.

Scan the Environment

Environmental scanning is usually the first step in a planning process, and allows the organization to look both internally and externally to determine what current or future trends will influence the organization's ability to accomplish its mission. Denhardt, in describing environmental scanning, states that "the organization is not assumed to exist in a vacuum, but rather both the organization's objectives and the steps to achieve those objectives are seen in the context of the resources and constraints presented by the organization's environment."[25]

The strategic planning group engages in a variety of activities to seek input on significant issues that will impact their organization. In correctional planning, this is especially important. Over the past twenty-five years, the environment has changed on almost all fronts—legal, political, supply and demand, financial, types of clients, and even levels of competition. The following represents some of the sources to review to identify potential changes in the correctional organization's environment:

- Trends in the number of offenders the agency supervises.
- Budgets approved by the legislature, and the proportional increases (or decreases) related to the number of clients.
- New legislation or political proposals regarding the agency policy or operations.
- The makeup of clients (age, offense, and history of violence).
- Changes in staff retentions rates.
- Changes in incidents of violence by clients/inmates.
- Changes in rates of program completions.
- Recidivism rates.

Select Key Issues

The next step in strategic planning is to select the issues believed to have the most impact on the organization and need to be addressed. For correctional agencies, these usually include the growth in the number of offenders to be supervised, fewer per capita financial and staff resources, offenders who are becoming violent and dangerous, the effectiveness of treatment modalities, advancements in technologies of equipment available to supervise offenders, and increased scrutiny from the public and political leaders.

Develop an Implementation Plan

Surprisingly and regretfully, even the best developed plans are often poorly executed. You would expect that an agency that completed every step of planning would also do a good job of implementation. However, as noted by Bossidy and Charan,

> When companies fail to deliver on their promises, the most frequent explanation is that the CEO's strategy was wrong. But the strategy by itself is not often the cause. Strategies most often fail because they aren't executed well.[26]

Because of the chance of poor execution, correctional administrators must tend to the implementation even more than to the development of the plan. The plan is not the objective. The end objective in a planning process is the effective implementation of goals, objectives, strategies, and programs in a way that improves the agency's ability to meet its mission in the face of any challenges.

A rather common phenomenon occurs some months after a plan is developed when top managers realize that they have not been effective in meeting the challenges they identified during the planning process. They are often quick to doubt the plan and question whether they accurately identified environmental challenges, goals, strategies, and programs that would effectively meet their objectives. They may even begin another planning process to identify where they went wrong. However, if they objectively examine the process, they are likely to discover that the plan in itself was fine, but their implementation of the plan was ineffective.

There are four steps essential to effective execution of a strategic plan: (1) successfully communicating the plan; (2) fully empowering middle management with responsibility for the implementation; (3) developing action steps, measures of outcome, and target dates for completion of the steps; and (4) regular monitoring and holding staff accountable for progress. All four steps are essential, but the most critical is effectively communicating the plan.

Communication of the plan begins even before the planning process. The reasons for planning, how the process will occur, and interest in staff input should be made known to staff. These activities are important for effectively communicating the plan once it is complete. Selection of a diverse group of staff to attend the planning function allows them to become informal communicators of the plan and its importance to the organization. The completed plan should be documented in writing and communicated to as many staff as possible. The key is to then widely distribute the plan in whatever form is available to the agency (intranet, employee bulletin boards, or at staff meetings).

Organization leaders should then discuss the plan with as many staff groups as possible. This could be through staff meetings, union meetings, or even videotape or written communications if staff is dispersed over a large geographic region. Effective communication of the plan lets staff know the plan is important, that it should be taken seriously, and it allows leaders to explain some of the reasons for the plan and its strategies and programs. Staff are able to ask questions and provide input on implementation strategies. Through these communication efforts, staff feel involved in and committed to the planning process.

After the plan has been communicated, and agency leadership has demonstrated their commitment to it, the plan should then be passed to middle management for implementation. There are several reasons for this, but the most important is that a plan's success or failure usually rests in the hands of middle management, who can easily stall a plan simply by not aligning work and resources to focus on the elements of the plan. Middle managers should meet with the line staff they supervise; develop action steps and target completion dates for implementing goals, strategies, and programs; and identify measures of outcome. Because they are charged with its implementation, middle managers and their staff should develop the activities necessary to accomplish the plan.

The final step in the plan is to monitor its implementation, hold middle management accountable for the target dates they set, and recognize and reward staff for making positive progress. An old, but still true, strategy for implementing change is to identify success stories and reward staff responsible for the success. This creates enthusiasm and momentum toward completion of the overall plan. Completion of activities by the identified target dates should be publicized, and staff should be visibly recognized and rewarded. This recognition is an incentive for those who have not yet reached their target dates and shows all staff that progress is being made in the plan.

Monitor, Update, and Continue to Scan

Even when a plan is effectively executed, it should never be considered "set in stone." Situations and conditions change, especially in today's fluid and rapidly changing correctional environment, and leaders and managers must constantly monitor the plan, continue to scan the environment for unanticipated outcomes, and update the plan as necessary. Leaders should resist the urge to make dramatic changes in a plan before it has been fully implemented or the results measured. However, there should be no hesitancy to make modifications when factors do change, and it is obvious that a revision of the plan is necessary.

Monitoring and constantly seeking improvement is consistent with the advice that organizational consultants often give managers—to seek a culture of continuous improvement. The old adage, "if it ain't broke, don't fix it," is usually not true in today's environment. A technique widely used in government agencies seeking continuous improvement is **total quality management (TQM)**. TQM is a strategy to constantly review operations, with the goals of continuous improvement in all an organization does. TQM requires that clients be recognized as consumers and that correctional organizations become more consumer oriented. But to make the best use of TQM, correctional agencies need to accomplish two things. Agencies must first be committed to doing things differently and casting aside the philosophy of doing them the way they have always been done. Also, they need to better assess who the consumers are; that is, are the consumers the legislators, governor, general public, offenders, or some other entity? "Until this question can be answered with some degree of certainty, TQM can only be a possibility, not a reality, in corrections management"[27]

An excellent example of implementing TQM in a correctional agency is the Ohio Department of Rehabilitation and Correction (ODRC), the state agency that oversees the operation of the state's prisons and parole functions.[28] The ODRC began to focus on the concept of total quality management in 1992 when the then governor George Voinovich required implementation of TQM in all state agencies. ODRC Director Reginald A. Wilkinson was committed to the concept, appointed a coordinator for its implementation in the agency, and began to train staff in the focus and activities required of TQM. The goal of this inclusion of TQM in the management of the ODRC was to empower staff to continuously look for ways to improve the agency's efficiency. This effort has succeeded, and the Ohio correctional system is recognized throughout the United States as a model for TQM and staff involvement.

Another approach to monitoring an agency's performance is through the implementation of **performance-based measures**. Performance-based measures provide an agency with a mechanism for assessing what they do and how well they are doing it. All agencies, government and private alike, get overly encumbered with processes, the repetitive functions that staff repeat on a regular basis, and therefore forget what was to be accomplished. A serious problem results when an organization focuses more on processes than outcome. The use of performance-based measures focuses attention on outcome and measuring results, rather than on merely counting activities.

A successful correctional example is the American Probation and Parole Association, which in the late 1990s began to develop performance-based measures for community corrections. Their work resulted in a monograph entitled *Results-Driven Management: Implementing Performance-Based Measures in Community Corrections.*[29] In the monograph, the authors developed six goals for a hypothetical agency and demonstrated how performance-based measures could be developed for each. The six goals examined are to assist decision makers, enforce court/parole board ordered sanctions, protect the community, assist offenders to change, support crime victims, and coordinate and promote the use of community services. Similar to TQM, incorporating performance-based measures is an excellent method to ensure that an agency accomplishes its mission in a quality manner.

Strategic Management in Corrections

An important part of organizational culture is how well an organization aligns its work and resources toward accomplishing the goals resulting from strategic planning. The management of an organization in line with its expectations of outcomes is referred to as **strategic management**. Strategic management is a process carried out at the top of the organization, which provides guidance, direction, and boundaries for all aspects of operational management. Strategic management differs from strategic planning, because strategic management exists when organizations move beyond planning to develop mechanisms for implementation of strategies. Another way to differentiate the two is that strategic planning creates the plan and strategic management pulls the organization together to execute the plan. The emphasis of strategic management is on organizational adaptation to environmental demands and opportunities. It requires the alignment of organizational capacities, managerial capability, culture, leadership, and organization structure.

Strategic management emphasizes the linkage of scanning and understanding the ever-changing environment, creating opportunities to move an organization forward, and implementing change in response to needs. It can be useful to analyze how leaders guide their agencies through challenges and opportunities, create support for their strategies and goals, and effectively motivate staff to implement change.

The Strategic Management Triangle

Professor Mark H. Moore of the Kennedy School of Government at Harvard University has presented a conceptual framework developed by faculty at the Kennedy School to help public sector managers assess their potential and actively pursue initiatives.[30] In the framework, called the strategic management triangle, the three points of the triangle define particular calculations that managers must make in deciding whether an enterprise is worth pursuing and the particular activities that they must undertake to ensure the success of their venture.

The first aspect is to determine whether there is *public value* in the results desired or imagined by the manager. Correctional administrators often take for granted that what they do has public value or that it is important to the taxpayers and citizens that corrections serve. Obviously, protecting citizens from crime has public value. It is more difficult to determine which programs and operations have value, or are worth the resources in time and money that are required to carry them out. Should an intensive probation supervision program be implemented? Should a literacy program be established in a county jail? Should serious juvenile offenders be bound over to adult courts and correctional agencies? Should amenities in prisons, such as weights, college programs, and recreational activities, be reduced? At this first point of the strategic triangle, the question to ask is whether making the change or implementing the program has value. In other words, is the correctional agency better able to accomplish its mission by implementing the change, to the point that it is worth the organizational resources required?

The second point of the strategic management triangle is to determine whether a goal or initiative will be *politically and legally supported*. Moore suggests "managing upward," toward political leaders, to invest the agency purpose with legitimacy and support. This is particularly true in corrections, where many elected officials respond to the public and political rhetoric. This rhetoric too often results in emotion rather than fact becoming the determining factor as to whether political leaders will support a correctional initiative. It is the responsibility of correctional leadership to educate both the public and elected officials regarding the merits and value of a correctional program or initiative.

The final point of the strategic management triangle is to determine whether implementation of an initiative is *administratively and operationally feasible*. This point of the triangle is to "manage downward," toward improving the organization's capabilities for achieving the desired purposes. Strategic management assumes a changing political and task environment, and, therefore, implementation strategies must take into account an ever-changing landscape. Too often, public administrators take this step for granted, believing that by issuing policy changes, modifications in line staff behavior will follow. It takes all three of the points of the triangle for public leaders to effectively identify, implement, and accomplish an initiative. The description by Moore is an excellent lesson in the complexities involved in implementing new initiatives in a government setting.

Setting the Tone: The Importance of Leadership

In this chapter, we have examined the importance of creating a vision, mission, and strategic plan to accomplish both. Throughout the discussion, the role of leadership has been alluded to. However, the importance of management and leadership in accomplishing the mission of a correctional agency cannot be assumed. No matter how talented, experienced, and educated the staff are, without proper leadership to set a tone and set expectations, a correctional organization's performance will deteriorate. According to Wright,

> When one enters a facility (prison) for the first time, it does not take long to determine the quality of management. An unused mop leaning against the wall in the entry way lets you know that the institution lacks administrative attention to detail . . . hallways may be dank and dark, with walls in need of painting and floors not recently shined. In poorly run prisons, inmates mill around with no particular destination or work to do. You hear shouts, insults, and incessant testing of one another. Violence occurs routinely and inmates easily acquire drugs and alcohol. Low-quality management produces depressed staff morale and low job-satisfaction. Professional pride among the staff and hope among the inmates rarely develops in poorly run prisons.[31]

What can correctional administrators do to set a tone or "show" leadership in a correctional agency? Is leadership evident when an individual manages authoritatively, making all decisions and barking orders constantly? Is leadership the ability to take charge when a riot occurs? Is leadership making staff get approval for any initiative they believe would better the prison operation? Most correctional administrators would say no, none of these examples explain fully what leadership really is in a prison or other correctional agency. In fact, most of these are poor examples of good leadership. What are the types of activities or measures of impact that leaders have on their agencies?

In *Governing Prisons*, DiIulio suggests three consequences that are affected by the quality of prison management: order, amenity, and service. Order is the absence of individual or group misconduct that threatens the safety of others. Amenity is anything that enhances the comfort of inmates, such as clean cells or good food. Service is that intended to improve the life prospects of inmates, such as treatment programs.[32] Effective correctional leaders attend to details within their environment and set high standards for order, control, good communication between staff and inmates, and excellence in professionalism.

How a leader sets the tone and how a leader carries this out is another story. There is no standard routine for successful management. In a study of how correctional leaders manage staff to get the most from their performance, the authors examined four correctional agencies, and interviewed many correctional administrators. They concluded that "Each administrator subscribes (either formally or informally) to a particular philosophy or style of management. Accordingly, approaches to the actual task of managing the workforce differed among the administrators interviewed."[33]

There are perhaps two keys to setting the tone to accomplish an agency mission. One of the keys to achieving quality is to "pay attention" to the fundamental values that a leader determines are important to the agency.[34] A leader attends to fundamental values (security, sanitation, staff pride, order, etc.) in many ways. The most important is visibility or **managing by walking around (MBWA)**. Good correctional administrators do not sit in their offices; they move around a prison or visit various community components of their agency, talk to staff where they work, and comment on the factors that they want to encourage. Many administrators believe that the things that get staff's attention and get done are those things that the staff hear administration mention or ask about.

A second key is to develop performance metrics for the goals desired to accomplish. As already noted, progress must be measured and the outcomes must be clear. If there is a goal to reduce violent incidents by 5 percent in a prison, those must be measured and routinely presented to staff. If the probation office has a goal of reducing missed appointments by clients by 10 percent, the number and percentage of missed meetings must be calculated. The saying is that "what gets measured and gets attention, gets done" is so true. Leaders set the tone and accomplish their goals by creating metrics, measuring progress, MBWA, and asking about staff's progress in achieving their goals. The character of leadership is important, but the actions of leaders are even more important.

SUMMARY

In this chapter, we examined how a public agency creates a forward-looking approach to its management and the accomplishment of its mission. Through a vision of how the agency sees its own future, staff can understand the subjective values and direction that the organization holds as important. Organizational culture is extremely important to success, and leaders must promote a positive organizational culture that supports the vision of the agency. Equally important is how an agency develops its plans for the future, using strategic planning to involve staff, identify future challenges, and create and implement programs and strategies to move beyond these challenges.

This chapter goes beyond strategic planning and introduces the concept of strategic management. With strategic management, an agency can determine activities that are valuable in accomplishing its mission, focus on gaining support of external political leadership, and work to successfully initiate the change throughout the internal organization. Whereas strategic planning guides staff in the creation of the agency practices and procedures in response to future challenges, strategic management goes even further by helping staff envision the bigger picture of how public policy is made outside the agency boundaries and aligns resources to accomplish goals and objectives.

The first section of this textbook has presented the challenges facing correctional administration in the new millennium, examined the roles of leaders and managers within their organizations, and demonstrated the process of strategic planning for developing an agency's agenda. In the next sections, there is an examination of the role of correctional staff, the importance of human resources management, and how staff are organized and supervised. In this examination, we come to realize the essential elements of the people business of corrections, and how staff are recruited, organized, and developed to result in an effective correctional agency.

KEY TERMS

Vision	Goals	Performance based measures
Mission	Strategic planning	Strategic management
Objectives	Culture	Managing by walking around
Strategies	Management culture	(MBWA)
Programs	Total Quality Management (TQM)	

YOU'RE THE CORRECTIONAL ADMINISTRATOR

1. You are the director of a community halfway house. You know the challenges facing community correctional agencies, and you believe you and the staff of the halfway house should begin to do some planning for the future. You decide to begin by discussing with the staff a "vision" for the halfway house. Anticipate some of the discussion that would result, and develop with a vision for the halfway house. Write the vision, and highlight some of the key discussion points that influenced the selection of the vision by the staff. List five statements made by staff that had general agreement and were important to the vision statement.

2. You, as director of the halfway house, now want to begin a strategic planning process. You plan to follow the outline of the process illustrated in this chapter. The first decisions, however, you must make are who to invite to the planning session and what type of information should be collected before the session begins. First, list the groups you would invite to the session and the reasons why they should be invited. Second, list the types of information you want to have in hand before you begin the strategic planning process. Also, describe where this information is found and how it can be collected.

WEB LINK EXERCISES

Go to American Probation and Parole Association (APPA) www.appa-net.org

This is the Web site for the APPA. Read some background information on the organization, and find their mission statement. After you read the mission statement, describe how you would develop a strategic plan to implement the mission. Include the steps you would take to involve members and the activities you would use to accomplish the mission.

Go to http://www.12manage.com/methods_swot_analysis.html

When performing a strategic plan for your organization, or one for in which you hope to work, it is helpful to have some format to follow to accomplish this task. One method is called a SWOT Analysis. After examining the Web site explaining a SWOT analysis, choose an organization for which you have some familiarity and do a simple SWOT analysis on the organization. You will quickly see how this can help you with constructing your strategic plan.

Go to http://www.quintcareers.com/SWOT_Analysis.html

After gaining an understanding of how to conduct a SWOT analysis, look at the next Web site to see how you apply SWOT to your career in criminal justice.

GROUP EXERCISES

Each group will be assigned to develop a vision statement, mission statement, and strategic plan for a 10 percent expansion for one of the following correctional operations: Maximum Security Prison, Halfway House, Pretrial Electronic Monitoring Program, 500 Bed Jail, and a Probation and Parole Office.

ENDNOTES

1. Rodney Gibbons and Frank Pisciotta, "Corrections in the Twenty-First Century," *Corrections Today* (July 1999), p. 62.

2. James M. Kouzes and Barry Z. Posner, *The Leadership Challenge* (San Francisco: Jossey-Bass, 1987), p. 85.

3. Peter Block, *The Empowered Manager: Positive Political Skills at Work* (San Francisco: Jossey-Bass, 1987), p. 103.

4. Warren Bennis and Burt Nanus, *Leaders: The Strategies for Taking Charge* (New York: Harper & Row, 1986), p. 89.

5. Douglas C. Eadie, "Strategic Management by Design," in *Strategic Planning for Local Government: A Handbook for Officials and Citizens*, edited by Roger L. Kemp (Jefferson, NC: McFarland & Company, 1993), p. 85.

6. Robert M. Freeman, *Correctional Organization and Management: Public Policy Challenges, Behavior, and Structure* (Boston, MA: Butterworth-Heinemann, 1999), p. 32.

7. Federal Bureau of Prisons, www.bop.gov (accessed August 28, 2009).

8. Federal Correctional Institution, *1998 Strategic Plans: FCI Greenville,* unpublished document (Greenville, IL: Federal Bureau of Prisons, 1998), p. 1.

9. Ibid.

10. Federal Bureau of Prisons, *State of the Bureau 2007, Bureau of Prisons Staff: Everyday Heroes* (Washington, DC: U.S. Department of Justice, 2008), p. 5.

11. Kouzes and Posner, p. 81.

12. Bennis and Nanus, p. 89.

13. Richard P. Seiter, "The Leadership and Empowerment Triangle," *Corrections Management Quarterly* 3 no. 1 (1999): 4.

14. William R. King and David I. Cleland, *Strategic Planning and Policy* (New York: Von Nostrand Reinhold, 1978), p. 45.

15. Ibid., p. 133.

16. Ibid., p. 134.

17. R. N. Antony, J. Dearden, and R. F. Vancil, *Management Control Systems* (Homewood, IL: Irwin, 1965), p. 4.

18. King and Cleland, p. 7.

19. James Q. Wilson, *Bureaucracy: What Government Agencies Do and Why They Do It* (New York: Basic Books, 1989), p. 91.

20. King and Cleland, p. 274.

21. Stan Stojkovic and Mary Ann Farkas, *Correctional Leadership: A Cultural Perspective* (Belmont, CA: Wadsworth/Thompson Learning, 2003), p. 128.

22. Richard P. Seiter, *Corrections: An Introduction,* 3rd ed. (Upper Saddle River, NJ: Pearson Education, 2011), pp. 403–404.

23. Donna L. Sorkin, Nancy B. Ferris, and James Hudak, *Strategies for Cities and Counties: A Strategic Planning Guide* (Washington, DC: Public Technology, Inc. 1984).

24. King and Cleland, p. 45.

25. Robert B. Denhardt, "Strategic Planning in State and Local Government," *State and Local Government Review* 17 no. 1 (1985): 175.

26. Larry Bossidy and Ram Charan, *Execution: The Discipline of Getting Things Done* (New York, NY: Crown Business, 2002), p. 15.

27. G. Larry Mays and L. Thomas Winfree, Jr., *Essentials of Corrections,* 4th ed. (Belmont, CA: Wadsworth, 2009), p. 291.

28. For a detailed description of the application and process Ohio used regarding TQM, see State of Ohio, Department of Rehabilitation and Correction, "Commitment to Quality" (Columbus: State of Ohio, 1993), an unpublished document available through the National Institute of Correction Information Center, Longmont, Colorado.

29. Harry N. Boone, Jr. and Betsy Fulton, *Results-Driven Management: Implementing Performance-Based Measures in Community Corrections* (Lexington, KY: American Probation and Parole Association, The Council of State Governments, 1995).

30. Mark H. Moore, *Creating Public Value: Strategic Management in Government* (Cambridge, MA: Harvard University Press, 1995).

31. Kevin N. Wright, *Effective Prison Leadership* (Binghamton, NY: William Neil Publishing, 1994), p. 6.

32. John J. DiIulio, Jr., *Governing Prisons: A Comparative Study of Correctional Management* (New York: The Free Press, 1987), pp. 11–12.

33. George M. Camp, Camille G. Camp, and Michael V. Fair, *Managing Staff: Corrections' Most Valuable Resource* (Washington, DC: National Institute of Corrections, 1996), p. 31.

34. Wright, p. 25.

5

The Role of Staff in Corrections

Introduction

Part 2 of this text examines the management of correctional staff and the critical role that staff play in the operations and mission of a correctional agency. Many people think of "corrections" as bars and fences, prison cells, and violent offenders. However, staff are the most valuable resource of a correctional agency, and are far more important than secure prison construction, policies and procedures, or technology. Corrections is a people business, in that the work is not accomplished by bars and fences, prison cells, or the use of electronic monitoring. The work of corrections is accomplished by people, staff supervising offenders to carry out the sentencing orders of the courts, and monitoring and guiding behavior in what will hopefully be a crime free and productive completion of a criminal sentence. The four chapters in Part 2 will provide students with an understanding of some of the key activities that must occur in agencies to create the most valuable correctional resource—the staff.

In Chapter 5, there is an explanation of the roles and functions of staff. Chapter 6 provides how correctional agencies are organized and the activities they carry out to manage their human resources. Chapter 7 describes how staff and correctional operations are organized. And Chapter 8 presents key elements of staff supervision and the importance of empowering staff to carry out organizations' vision and mission.

As a student of corrections, you are likely to consider a career in corrections or may already be working in corrections but seek to improve your knowledge and opportunities for advancement. Therefore, Chapter 5 describes some of the entry-level jobs of correctional staff, including the roles of correctional officers, counselors or caseworkers, probation or parole officers, or social service workers. It is important for you to thoroughly understand what these staff do in their jobs, either to consider whether to seek such employment or to be able to effectively administer a correctional agency. As staff advance in their organizations, they are much more effective if they fully understand the role of each staff person. A football quarterback can have exceptional individual skills, such as running or throwing a football. However, even the most athletically gifted quarterbacks will be ineffective at moving the team toward a touchdown if they do not know and consider the role of every player on every play and can adjust and modify the play as situations change and the unexpected occurs.

Therefore, this chapter thoroughly describes the actual functions of correctional staff, as well as the considerations, challenges, and stresses that are a part of the job. By the end of this chapter, you should clearly understand what it is to be a correctional officer or a halfway house counselor. You will know some of the critical issues concerning correctional staff. You will recognize the importance of agency culture and leadership in setting the tone for the daily performances of staff. And you will be able to envision some of the future needs and challenges to meet the increasing difficulty of maintaining the effectiveness and efficiency of corrections' most valuable resource—correctional staff.

The Importance of Correctional Staff

It almost goes without saying that correctional staff are important to accomplishing a correctional mission. As noted previously, corrections is a business of people interacting with people. Approximately 65 percent of a correctional agency budget is spent on staff salaries. And, especially over the past two decades, there has been a tremendous increase in the number of correctional staff. For all these reasons, when correctional administrators think in a broad way about their profession, they think of their staff performing the day-to-day activities necessary to accomplish their mission.

The public's focus on crime control, a push for stiffer sentencing practices, the increase in length of prison terms, and the more restrictive supervision in the community by probation and parole officers necessitated a significant increase in the number of staff required to supervise offenders. On January 1, 1998, state and federal correctional agencies employed almost 415,000 prison staff,[1] there were more than 57,000 probation and parole staff,[2] and jails that held 200 or more inmates employed another almost 70,000 staff,[3] with approximately 550,000 people working in corrections throughout the United States. That was almost as large as the number of autoworkers in September 2000, when the United Auto Workers reported approximately 750,000 members in both the United States and its international affiliates.[4]

However, the number of correctional staff has grown significantly since then. The *Bureau of Justice Statistics, Expenditure and Employment Extracts 2005* reports a 37 percent increase since that time, as there were 755,239 correctional staff working at the federal, state, and local levels in the United States in 2005.[5] Most people do not know the wide range of jobs available to correctional staff. They have an understanding of what correctional officers and wardens do, and to a lesser extent the functions of a probation or parole officer. However, those are only a few of the types of jobs available to those seeking a career in corrections. Spertzel lists the following as examples of correctional jobs.[6] It is obvious from this list that the variety of correctional jobs is extensive and offers opportunities for employment for students in many fields of study.

- Budget administrator
- Chaplain
- Computer specialist
- Correctional officer
- Employee development specialist
- Facility manager
- Financial manager
- Food service manager
- Health system administrator
- Industrial specialist
- Institution administrator

- Juvenile caseworker
- Medical officer
- Ombudsman
- Personnel manager
- Probation/parole officer
- Psychologist
- Recreation specialist
- Safety manager
- Teacher
- Training instructor

Historically, the role of correctional staff, especially those who worked in prisons, was very narrowly defined and did not attract the most educated or professional staff. In prisons, the custodial staff have always made up the largest group of employees. In fact, in early U.S. prisons, uniformed custodial officers made up almost the entire staff, except for a few clerks and administrators. As an illustration, the picture of the staff of the U.S. Penitentiary in Leavenworth, Kansas, in the late 1800s shows only uniformed guards. And not only have the scope of roles of those working in corrections broadened but also the functions and expectations have gotten much more complex.

Staff at the U.S. Penitentiary in Leavenworth, Kansas (c. 1915). During the early years of prisons, almost all of the staff were "guards" or custodial personnel.
(Courtesy of the Federal Bureau of Prisons)

Probation and parole officers must now focus on a wide variety of issues related to supervising offenders in the community. As was historically the case, once offenders are granted probation or paroled from prison, it is the responsibility of the officers to supervise and enforce compliance with conditions of their probation or parole. Modern officers have a complex, dual, and sometimes conflicting, responsibility. The primary purpose of supervision is to maintain surveillance, enforce conditions of their community release, and guide offenders into treatment to protect the public from further crimes. To fulfill this purpose, officers first monitor offenders' activities through a combination of office visits (offenders report to the officer at the field office), verification of offenders' activities by visiting their homes and contacting their employers or program providers, and monitoring activities such as drug testing of probationers. But in addition, officers help offenders succeed by determining program or treatment needs and placing them in social service programs that address their needs for education, mental health counseling, vocational training, or substance abuse programming. There is nothing simple about the responsibilities of these officers. They must constantly meet the goals of both public safety and offender rehabilitation.

The complexity of the role of correctional staff is also illustrated by the change in the role and terminology for correctional officers. Until approximately the 1970s, correctional officers in a prison were referred to as **guards**, because that term implied most of what they were hired to do. The role of guards, also referred to as "turnkeys," was to simply guard inmates, unlock and lock their cells (hence the term turnkeys) when necessary, march inmates from the cell houses to other locations for work or eating, and brutally enforce rules and discipline. Duffee writes, "In the early penitentiary, there was not a great deal of concern about goal conflict among the prison staff. Staffing patterns were rather simple, and guards played a prominent role in both guarding and supervising work."[7] Goffman, in his classic study of the harsh treatment and deleterious effect of imprisonment on inmates, described the great social distance of inmates and staff, which was formally dictated and reinforced.[8]

And, there was little discretion or decision making required by guards during early prison operations. Cressey even suggests about this simple role, "Most guards have nothing to do but stand guard; they do not use inmates productively any more than they themselves are used productively by prison managers."[9] In a description of the role of prison guards prior to 1970, Jacobs and Crotty write about their work in Statesville (Illinois) prison:

> In the course of a day's work, the guard stationed at the cell house gate is required to open and close the steel-barred cell house. Another guard may distribute medicine, mail, and laundry; answer telephones; and supervise maintenance activities. A third guard is positioned in an enclosed observation post in the middle of the cell house where he can see into every cell. The most important responsibility of the cell house guard is conducting the "count"—determining several times a day if all inmates are accounted for.[10]

The role of custodial staff in modern prisons has changed considerably, even to the point that it is now a misnomer to refer to them as merely "custodial" staff. As noted, the

WHEREAS, the duties of correctional personnel whose primary responsibility are custody and control require extensive interpersonal skills, special training and education; and WHEREAS, correctional personnel are skilled professionals; and WHEREAS, the term "guard" produces a false and negative image; THEREFORE BE IT RESOLVED that the American Correctional Association adopt the term "correctional officer" as the official language in all Association publications, meetings, events and communications to describe custodial/security personnel; and THEREFORE BE IT FURTHER RESOLVED that the Association actively promote the use of the term "correctional officer" and discourage the use of the word "guard" by the media, general public, educational institutions and publishers.

Figure 5-1
ACA's resolution on the term correctional officer.
Source: American Correctional Association, "Resolution on the Term 'Correctional Officer'," *Corrections Today* 60 (April 1993): 146.

contemporary term of **correctional officer** is more descriptive and accurate to describe the complex role of staff that carry out security functions within a prison. The changing role of custodial staff prompted the American Correctional Association (ACA) in 1993 to pass a resolution to encourage the use of the term *correctional officer* rather than *guard*, because it much better describes their responsibilities of custody and control, which "require extensive interpersonal skills, special training and education, and . . . correctional personnel are skilled professionals."[11]

The complex roles played by correctional staff are the focus of this chapter. You will come to understand not only the functions but also the challenges and the discretion required for effective correctional workers. This chapter examines the role of various correctional staff, issues affecting staffing, the change in the environment and the expectations for them, and the importance of management and leadership in making a difference in the future of corrections.

The Role of Professional Staff

As might be expected, the manner in which staff do their jobs will have a significant impact on the success of a correctional agency. Perhaps the most important skill required of correctional workers is communication. Compliance is gained through communications, not through the threat of a revocation of probation or parole or a disciplinary infraction within a prison. And, correctional workers must treat offenders with dignity and respect if they are to expect like treatment and a commitment to change behavior. If staff communicate with offenders in a courteous manner, it has a positive impact on reducing tension in a prison and opens the door to discussion about successful community supervision. Positive interaction between staff and offenders opens lines of communication that can lead to inmates providing staff advance warning about plans to escape or a planned assault of another inmate. It can lead a probationer to openly admit challenges they are facing and their considering a return to crime. While correctional workers can never become friends with offenders, there must be mutual trust and respect to accomplish correctional objectives. An example of this is a report by George and Camille Camp that discusses the importance of staff and inmate communications in crowded prisons:

> Lack of effective communication can lead to frustration. Impatience within the system can cause discontentment, disenchantment and even disturbances. Keeping staff and inmates informed of the administration's concerns and plans for dealing with crowding becomes extremely important. Communication is a valuable means of ensuring stability and providing opportunity for feedback before implementation of specific programs.[12]

Below are descriptions of the roles of many correctional workers in both a community and an institutional setting. As will be illustrated, their roles have changed and are more complex than ever before, yet the success of correctional agencies depends on their effectiveness. In addition to the roles of a variety of correctional workers that is described, the increasingly important opportunities to use volunteers and contract workers is also presented.

The Correctional Officer

The first job function to be examined is that of the correctional officer. The segment of the criminal justice system with the most rapid growth has been institutional corrections, and the largest job category in an institution is that of correctional officer. On January 1, 1998, there were almost 240,000 correctional officers employed in state and federal prisons,[13] but by 2005, the number of state and federal prison correctional officers had grown to 295,261.[14] In addition, the *Sourcebook of Criminal Justice Statistics, 2008*, reported an estimated 250,944 staff employed by jails in 2005,[15] and it is estimated that approximately 72 percent (or 180,500) of these are correctional officers.[16] In total, there are by now 500,000 correctional officers in the United States.

Unfortunately, many individuals who receive a two- or four-year college degree do not seriously consider correctional officer positions. They often think of correctional officers as unskilled, poorly paid, and not using their education. However, as previously noted, the role of correctional officers has changed, education and good decision-making skills are important, and the pay has become more competitive in order to keep positions filled and maintain quality staff. Also, many correctional agencies have officer positions as the entry level for all employees, recognizing the value of this experience in learning security and developing skills in managing inmates. Promotion or selection of staff for other professional positions, such as caseworkers, counselors, or teachers, is often based on the current pool of correctional officers.

What Correctional Officers Do

Correctional officers face ambiguous and sometimes in-conflict goals, and must be intelligent and well trained. The role of correctional officers has evolved for many reasons. Crouch suggests three factors that have changed the work of correctional officers: (1) an increased emphasis on the goal of rehabilitation, (2) growth in the size and changes in the composition of the inmate population, and (3) judicial intervention.[17] Perhaps even more important than these three is the fact that these factors all occurred over approximately the same period of time and interacted with each other in such a way as to almost mandate a new role for correctional officers.

Correctional officers' roles have considerably changed over the history of corrections. As noted in Chapter 1, during the 1950s and 1960s, corrections began to emphasize the importance of rehabilitation as a correctional goal. As such, many new professionals, including psychologists, educators, and administrators, were brought into the prison environment. As the emphasis on rehabilitation developed, the importance of the overall prison experience on inmates was recognized. This included the interaction of correctional officers with inmates, and officers were therefore trained in interpersonal communications so that they could take on a broadened responsibility beyond security functions. In addition, the immigration of professionals sympathetic to the plight of inmates into the prison changed the culture and communications among staff. Previously, the dominant personality style of staff was machismo and authoritarianism. Even though this style continued with many correctional officers, those who wanted to adopt a more helping style found support for their approach.

Guard on duty at the U.S. Penitentiary in McNeil Island (WA), c. 1909. The role of correctional officers has considerably changed since the time they simply watched inmates, guarded doors, and "keyed" locks. Today, correctional officers' roles are complex, requiring education, training, and good interpersonal skills.
(Courtesy of the Federal Bureau of Prisons)

The 1980s brought the beginning of the prison construction boom, with dramatic increases in the number of prisoners and the number of prisons and staff to operate them. As many prisons became overcrowded, officers often felt overworked and frustrated and were in fear of losing control. Totally outnumbered, the authoritarian style was less effective and correctional officers who were good communicators gained better compliance of inmates and maintained order. Both the move to rehabilitate and the increase in the use of prisons as criminal sanctions created frustration and some uncertainty in the role of correctional officers, and many officers became more punitive "to the extent that they assault or misuse disciplinary action against inmates."[18] Prison administrators, therefore, focused their hiring practices on officers with good communication skills who were comfortable working with the multiple goals of custody and rehabilitation.

As federal courts began to examine many aspects of the prison environment and the overall conditions of confinement, there were many judicial decisions that dictated certain requirements or practices within the operation of prisons. Many correctional officers and prison administrators believed that this intervention undermined their control of prisons and overall prison security. However, the courts were not to be deterred, and judicial intervention in prison operations continued extensively into the early 1990s. The effect was that those correctional officers who could not work in an environment of judicial intervention retired or found other jobs. Newly hired officers accepted the involvement of federal courts in prison operations and found that they could work comfortably in a prison setting that emphasized staff–inmate interaction and communication.

To describe the changing role of contemporary correctional officers, Johnson suggests, "In the prison, the skills that matter are human relations and human service skills. These are the skills that can be used to develop relationships and hence to reduce tension, defuse crises, and conduct daily business in a civilized (and potentially civilizing) manner."[19] Not only has the role of correctional workers changed but also college educated individuals, minorities, and women have been recruited into correctional positions in much greater numbers. All of these developments have changed the current and future outlook for corrections.

The importance of staff on the correctional environment dovetails closely with the recognition of the importance of management and leadership. As noted in Chapter 3, early prisons were simple to manage through strict discipline and enforcement of rules on both staff and inmates. Today, prison order is more involved with fairness and equity, leadership and empowerment, and organization and management. As suggested by Dilulio,

> The answer to be offered . . . is that the quality of prison life varies according to the quality of prison management. The evidence will lead us to the conclusion that prison management is the strategic variable, one that may be subject to change with predictable and desirable consequences.[20]

Although the role of correctional officers has changed considerably over the past thirty years, there are still some basics that remain true about the position. Correctional officers are responsible for overseeing individuals who are detained in jail while awaiting trial or who have been convicted of a crime and are serving a sentence in prison. Their basic responsibility is to maintain order and contribute to the secure operation of the institution. As such, officers are assigned and oversee various sections of an institution, such as a housing unit, yard or compound, perimeter fence, or inmate work or program area. Prisons and jails usually have written policies and procedures (post orders) for the operations of these areas, and correctional officers' first responsibility is to carry out the prescribed duties of their post orders. Lombardo identifies seven basic roles or areas of responsibility for correctional officers:

- Living unit officers supervise inmate housing areas.
- Work detail officers oversee inmate work assignments.
- Industrial shop and school officers control and provide security to these areas.
- Yard officers supervise inmate movement and maintain accountability.
- Administration building assignments perform office functions.
- Perimeter security is maintained through armed surveillance.
- Relief officers fill in when others have days off.[21]

There are many tedious and detailed functions that must occur in the maintenance of security and order. For instance, officers must control doors and grills and lock and unlock them to allow only approved inmate movement. Officers must search inmates and areas, because constant efforts to find contraband such as drugs and weapons are a key element of security. Officers must conduct "inmate counts" in order to maintain inmate accountability and prevent escapes. Officers ensure inmates obey rules and initiate disciplinary action when they do not. And officers must oversee inmate work crews, such as those assigned sanitation responsibilities, and ensure that the inmate crew performs the work at the accepted standard. Although some prospective officers may find these details of the job unexciting and uninteresting, they are basics that must be accomplished.

There are many other challenging roles for correctional officers. According to Seiter, "Officers have to be a variety of things to a variety of people. Their bosses expect them to be exact in performing their security duties, while being professional in their interaction with inmates. . . . And inmates expect them to be fair and not hassle them for minor things."[22] This provides an excellent example of how an officer may feel role conflict or ambiguity. It is difficult to never show favoritism in handing out discipline or enforcing prison rules or policy. Yet, many of these roles require understanding, communications, and recognizing the individualism of every inmate. Less successful correctional officers are those who show favoritism under the guise of treating each inmate as an individual.

And there is considerable stress on correctional officers. Sources of stress include the threat of violence, inmate demands and manipulations, and problems with coworkers. Although there are no data available for the past decade, inmate assaults against correctional staff in state and federal prisons increased between 1990 and 1995 by nearly one-third (10,731 to 14,165), while the number of correctional officers increased by only 14 percent.[23] And the number of deaths in the line of duty has also increased. Data from the Correctional Peace Officers Foundation (an organization created to support surviving families of correctional officers slain in the line of duty at the hands of incarcerated felons) show that there were fourteen deaths between 1965 and 1979, twenty-seven between 1980 and 1989, ninety-eight between 1990 and 1999, and seventy-six between 2000 and 2007.[24]

The responsibilities of modern-day correctional officers are broad and challenging. The challenges stem from the fact that correctional officers must maintain order and gain compliance from offenders who are incarcerated against their will and who have a natural inclination to resent those who try to control them. Jacobs and Kraft describe the

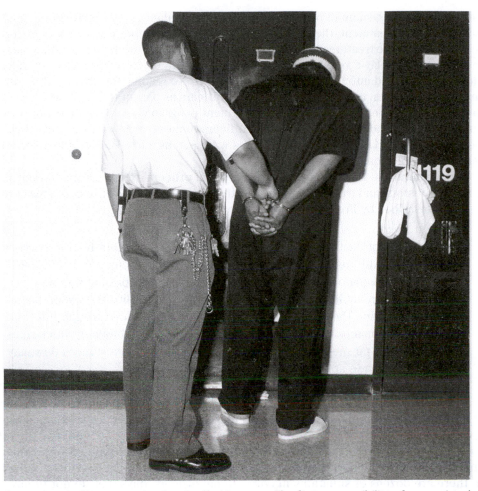

Correctional officer escorting handcuffed inmates. The first responsibility of correctional officers is to maintain safety and security in prisons and jails.
(*Courtesy of the Federal Bureau of Prisons*)

situation as "structured conflict."[25] Some uninformed about the operations of prisons have difficulty understanding why gaining compliance is not an easy task, because "inmates are in prison and have to follow the rules." However, if staff have to make inmates comply with rules, by resorting to disciplinary action or using force on a regular basis, prisons become the tense, violent, and dangerous world that these people envision. Effective correctional officers and other prison staff gain compliance by communicating expectations, fairly enforcing rules, and treating inmates with respect and dignity. Officers who constantly "write up inmates" for insubordination or failure to follow an order usually do not last long on the job and are not respected by either staff or inmates.

One of the responsibilities that make the job of correctional officers difficult is contributing to the rehabilitation of offenders. As corrections moved away from the strict authoritarian management of prisons toward a setting balancing the correctional goals of punishment and treatment, there were concerns over the proper contribution of correctional officers to the treatment aspects for prisoners. Most administrators agree that correctional officers play a role in treatment, but it is difficult to determine how this role should be integrated into the daily duties of officers. To resolve this issue, a few correctional agencies began to consider correctional officers as part of the treatment team and expected them to be aware of inmates' treatment programs, even, at times, to provide counseling for offenders. However, asking officers to move very far away from their traditional custody and security responsibilities was seen as a loss of control by some and as an unworkable conflict by others.

Throughout the 1960s and 1970s, correctional officers' requirements to contribute to both the custody and treatment aspects within prisons caused confusion. This conflict in roles is described by Freeman:

> The dual roles of custody and treatment create a role conflict for the correctional officer. Although the central goal of an officer's custody role is well defined (maintaining order and security), the central goal of the treatment role (assisting in the rehabilitation of the inmate) entails flexibility, the use of discretionary justice, and the ability to secure inmate compliance through informal exchange relationships that deviate from the written rules. Knowing which rules can be bent, how far they may be bent, and under which circumstances they may be bent is not always apparent or understood by the officer.[26]

This description of officers' struggles with how far to "bend the rules" to recognize and treat inmates as individuals is not acceptable to most correctional administrators. According to correctional administrators, correctional officers should not bend the rules, because once they begin to do so, they lose their ability to maintain required rules or standards for other inmates. The conflict of custody and treatment is evident in the fact that there are dozens of situations in correctional officers' days that do not fit any rule or policy, and officers must use their own discretion in deciding how to handle them. An inmate may tell an officer he or she is depressed about something that happened at home. An officer may see two inmates in a mildly heated argument. An officer may find an inmate has nuisance contraband (property not allowed, yet not a security risk, such as extra clothing or magazines). How to handle these issues is not always spelled out in prison policies, nor are they always addressed in a rule. In these types of situations, correctional officers must recognize their custodial roles, yet they can use their knowledge of individual inmates in deciding how to handle each situation.

Today, most correctional agencies have clarified the conflicting roles of custody and treatment by establishing a realistic and practical role for officers in the rehabilitation of inmates. This role includes three aspects: (1) contributing to an environment of control without threats and tension, (2) communicating with inmates on a professional basis, and (3) focusing on providing human services. None of these three aspects require the officer to be a counselor or treatment specialist. Officers contribute to the rehabilitative aspect by the manner in which they conduct themselves and do their jobs, not by trying to befriend or advise inmates about personal problems.

Correctional officer discussing an issue with an inmate. Correctional officers must constantly communicate with inmates. Although they are not counselors, listening to inmate concerns helps ease tension and blurs the line between custody and treatment personnel.
(Courtesy of the Federal Bureau of Prisons)

Perhaps more than any other staff, correctional officers impact the tone and environment of a prison. Officers contribute to the overall prison setting by carrying out their security activities, such as searches for contraband and maintaining inmate accountability, in a thorough and constant manner. By doing so, inmates realize that staff control the prison, and they do not have to be overly concerned with their personal safety or join a gang for protection. They can relax and become involved in rehabilitative programs without fear of looking weak to other inmates or appearing to be **snitches** (inmates believed by other inmates to cooperate with staff by giving them information regarding misbehavior by other inmates) because they spend time talking to staff.

Correctional officers' roles in offender rehabilitation involve providing "human services." A variety of authors conclude that a human services role is beyond what is usually expected of correctional officers,[27] and there is still a lack of clarity as to what is expected of officers in this regard. Johnson and Toch note that providing inmates with human services "should not be confused with providing treatment."[28] Whereas treatment is proactive, the officers' human service role is usually reactive. For instance, an inmate who may not be able to talk to a counselor or prison psychologist tells a correctional officer about problems the inmate's family is experiencing. An inmate may not have been able to get to the laundry to pick up clean sheets and needs some help or intervention by the officer to resolve the issue over the weekend when the laundry is not open. A correctional officer, acting in a human services role, may contact a counselor or psychologist about the inmate experiencing family problems or may ask a supervisor if clean sheets can be provided for the inmate. These basic, yet sympathetic, responses to real issues in the lives of inmates are considered the appropriate human services role of correctional officers.

Although correctional officers spend their days maintaining order and providing security, the manner in which they perform their tasks and communicate with inmates has a major impact on the overall prison environment. A brusk and harsh manner, an unwillingness to recognize genuine inmate issues, or a lack of respect for inmates creates an environment with constant tension between inmates and staff. However, a fair and impartial upholding of prison rules, a pleasant personality, a respect for individual dignity, and an understanding of correctional officers' role in prisoner rehabilitation contribute to a relaxed environment with positive interaction between staff and inmates. The role of correctional officer has moved well beyond that of guarding inmates; it now requires knowledge, training, good interpersonal communications, and sound decision making.

Correctional Officer Pay and Requirements

Although the salary for correctional officers is still relatively low, it has increased steadily throughout the 1990s. As reported in the *Corrections Yearbook, 1998*, the average starting salary for correctional officers on January 1, 1990, was $17,521, which increased to $21,088 on January 1, 1998.[29] In 2008, annual salaries for correctional officers ranged from $27,540 in Texas to $45,288 in California.[30] In addition, correctional officers also regularly work overtime, and it is not unusual for officers to make an additional 20 percent of their base salary. Most prison systems do not require a college education for officers, but many require either experience or a two- or four-year degree. Many states and the federal prison system use correctional officer jobs as the entry level into the prison system; staff who are successful as officers gain communications and security skills that serve them well throughout their careers and often help them get promotions and additional career opportunities.

Today, many agencies require correctional officers to have college degrees, although most jurisdictions still only require correctional officer candidates to have completed high school, have some experience in law enforcement or the military, and have no criminal convictions.[31] Even though most correctional agencies still have relatively low requirements for the position of correctional officer, these positions have become very competitive, and candidates selected usually have qualifications well beyond the minimum requirements. Advanced qualifications are also important for promotion within correctional agencies. The *Occupational Outlook Handbook*, 2010–11 edition, reports that "Some state and local corrections agencies require some college credits, but law enforcement or military experience may be substituted to fulfill this requirement."[32]

During the screening of correctional officer candidates and the selection process, some agencies do psychological testing, and others do extensive interviews to determine whether there are ethical issues in the candidate's background (recent drug use, financial problems, or unfavorable termination from a job) that may indicate the possibility of a candidate being compromised by inmates. Most agencies also conduct an interview to determine the candidates' interpersonal skills and decision-making abilities. And almost all agencies performed drug tests on correctional officer applicants.

As corrections has become more complex, and as more correctional agencies look toward promotion and filling of other professional jobs from the ranks of correctional officers, education at the entry level for officers has become more important. The *Occupational Outlook Handbook*, 2010–11 edition, notes that

> The Federal Bureau of Prisons requires entry-level correctional officers to have at least a bachelor's degree; 3 years of full-time experience in a field providing counseling, assistance, or supervision to individuals; or a combination of the two.[33]

Raising the educational requirement for hiring correctional officers is being reconsidered because the job complexity requires it and because it will result in an increase in professionalism. There is usually no requirement for a specific college major, because correctional agencies believe that the exposure to higher education with any topic of study improves individuals' maturity, decision making, ability to prioritize, and understanding of diversity. Employment as a correctional officer is challenging and rewarding. It is an excellent opportunity for entry to a correctional career, and correctional officer work builds a foundation of knowledge and skills that will improve an individual's performance in other prison jobs.

The Counselor or Caseworker

Another position in prisons that is often considered as an entry-level job (especially for recent college graduates) is that of a counselor or **caseworker** (also called social worker in some agencies). These are professional positions in correctional agencies that are responsible for working directly with inmates to create a plan for program and work participation throughout the period of confinement, and in preparation for release. Duties of a caseworker include (1) obtaining case histories and descriptions, (2) solving immediate problems involving family and personal relationships, (3) exploring long-range problems of social adjustment, (4) providing supportive guidance for inmates about to be released, and (5) providing supportive guidance and professional assistance to probationers and parolees.[34]

Caseworkers often work as part of a team with prison educators, mental health professionals, and substance abuse counselors to create treatment plans and monitor inmates' progress toward their goals. Some casework staff actually perform counseling, but in most state and federal prisons their principle role is to guide inmates through all aspects of their prison sentence, including the legal sanction and expectation for release, an understanding of their individual treatment needs, and the availability of prison programs to meet these needs. Caseworkers can also act as liaisons with services outside the prison (job assistance, family counseling, or halfway house agencies) to assist inmates in their prison-to-community transition.

Casework duties usually require good interpersonal, decision making, and writing skills. Although some states do not require a college degree for casework positions, most states find that completion of college is highly beneficial. When a college degree is required, the college major varies with the specifics of casework duties. According to the *Occupational Outlook Handbook*, "Some employers require a master's degree in criminal justice, social work, psychology, or a related field for candidates who do not have previous related experience. Different employers have different requirements for what counts as related."[35] If caseworkers do a considerable amount of therapeutic treatment themselves, they may be required to possess a clinical degree in mental health or social work. When their work is primarily as liaisons to other resources, there may be no single major specified, although a four-year degree with a certain amount of hours in sociology or social work is usually recommended. Although the salary for most state or federal casework jobs is usually 15–20 percent higher than the starting pay for a correctional officer, caseworkers usually have less opportunity to earn additional overtime pay.

The Probation and Parole Officer

Probation and parole officers supervise inmates at the two ends of the sentencing continuum (incarceration being in the middle). However, the work is very similar for the two jobs. **Probation officers** supervise offenders with a suspended prison sentence, monitoring their behavior in the community, and their compliance with the conditions of their probation and suspended prison sentence. **Parole officers** supervise inmates who have been conditionally released from prison and returned to the community. Similarly, parole officers monitor released inmates' behavior and compliance with the conditions of their release. Both probation and parole officers' primary responsibility is to supervise these offenders with "conditional" placement in the community, enforce the rules governing their supervision, and report any violation to the body that authorized their community placement and placed conditions on their behavior (the court for probation and the parole board for parole).

Even though prisons and issues focusing on incarceration receive much of the attention and most of the resources, probation and parole still play a critical role for correctional systems across the United States. In 2008, the Bureau of Justice Statistics reported a total of 7,308,200 adults under correctional supervision. Of these, 4,270,917 were on probation and 828,169 were on parole.[36]

Average caseload sizes vary considerably from jurisdiction to jurisdiction. The *2002 Corrections Yearbook* reports that the average size of officer caseloads is very large, as the regular supervision average caseload size was 127, ranging from 314 cases per officer in Rhode Island to 15 cases per officer in Pennsylvania.[37] Large caseload sizes make it very difficult for probation and parole to be effective sanctions in providing services to offenders, monitoring their behavior, and reducing recidivism. And high caseloads were reported as one of the primary causes of stress among probation and parole officers.[38]

In a report of the American Probation and Parole Association in 2007, a recommended caseload approach was described, as presented in Table 5-1.

Table 5.1
SUPERVISION CASELOAD APPROACH

Case Priority	Hours Per Month	Total Caseload
High	4 hours	30 cases
Medium	2 hours	60 cases
Low	1 hour	120 cases[a]

Source: Matthew T. DeMichele, *Probation and Parole's Growing Caseloads and Workload Allocations: Strategies for Managerial Decision Making*, APPA Perspectives (Lexington, KY: Council of State Governments, May 2007), p. 16.
[a]Based on a 120 work hour per officer per month.

The expectations and approach to probation and parole supervision have been changing. Even while the public recognizes that not every criminal offender can be sent to prison and that almost all are released, there is little tolerance for offenders not following all requirements of their supervision and many are revoked and sent to prison. This has impacted the manner in which a parolee or probationer is supervised. Until the late 1960s, probation and parole supervision focused on the casework style of supervision, or restoring offenders to the community.[39] However, over the past twenty years, there has been an increasing reliance on surveillance, or closely monitoring offenders to catch them when they fail to meet all required conditions. Rhine, in describing this change in supervision style, suggests that it brings about a new paradigm in the supervision of offenders in the community:

> Despite their importance to public safety, the past 20 years have witnessed a marked devaluation of traditional probation and parole supervision. Acknowledging this trend, many administrators in the field have adopted a set of practices and a discourse that represent a discernible shift toward risk management and surveillance. This shift in the mission and conduct of supervision reflects a new narrative, the plausibility of which has yet to be established.[40]

The transition from casework to the surveillance style of supervision could be less of a philosophical than a pragmatic change, as caseload sizes have been increasing, and with less time to provide individual attention to probationers, officers must resort to surveillance tactics. For example, caseloads in California over the last few decades of the twentieth century increased dramatically; in the early 1990s they reached 500 per officer, and "some 60 percent of Los Angeles probationers were tracked solely by computer and had no face-to-face contact with a probation officer."[41]

Probation and parole officers usually require college degrees, and important skills include those similar to a prison caseworker, such as good interpersonal communication, decision-making skills, and writing skills. Carlson, Hess, and Orthmann note, "A significant part of a probation or parole officer's job involves understanding human nature, something that cannot be learned in a classroom."[42] Probation and parole officers serve as agents of the court or the parole board, and their decisions and recommendations can lead to the loss of offenders' freedom and placement in or return to prison. It is important for probation and parole officers to recognize the legal due process rights for offenders, and the legal nature of their jobs, and their written reports support the fact that most agencies require at least an undergraduate college degree.

Probation and parole officers operate much more independently, or with less supervision, than most prison staff. Probation and parole officers are trained in the techniques for supervising offenders and then assigned a caseload. Their daily activities are much less regimented than the routine of prison work and they must manage their time and create their own work plans. They schedule their day to include meeting with offenders in the probation or parole office, contacting employers and law enforcement agencies, making home or workplace visits, and conducting urine tests for drug use. A Missouri probation officer states, "No one tells me how to spend my day. They expect me to manage my case load within the policies and guidelines of the state. I, as closely as possible, monitor the activities of my case load, and must report any violations of the conditions to the court or to the parole board."[43]

Pay for probation and parole officers also varies considerably, but the starting pay is not bad for entry into a career. For example, certified probation officers in Florida can earn from $33,500 to $51,500 per year.[44] In California, county probation officers begin around $26,500 per year but can make up to $57,500 per year and state parole officers begin at almost $40,000 and can reach up to $55,000 per year.[45] In many jurisdictions, supervision of both parolees and probationers is done jointly by the same agency and many times by the same officers. In a survey of states in 2001, the average starting salary for parole officers was $31,652 per year.[46] And a college career Web site reported that in 2004 the median salary for all parole officers was $39,600 per year, with the highest 10 percent earning $66,660 per year.[47]

A controversial issue regarding probation and parole officers is the carrying of firearms. Some agencies require, others permit, and still others do not allow officers to carry firearms. Officers must make home and employment visits in the neighborhoods in which offenders live. These areas are not always safe for anyone, and probation and parole officers are often considered law enforcement officers and seen with mistrust. In some situations, officers plan to revoke offenders and may even need to make an arrest and take them to jail. It is easy to imagine how uncomfortable an officer would be in an offender's home, informing him or her of a recommendation for sending the offender to prison, or actually taking him or her into custody pending the revocation decision. A 1993 study by the Federal Probation and Pretrial Officers Association (see Table 5-2) revealed more than 2,600 violent acts against officers from 1980 to 1993 and illustrated the danger to officers in the line of duty.

Although these data make it seem obvious that officers should carry a weapon, many agencies do not allow their officers to take offenders into custody, and if an arrest is necessary, officers are to file an arrest warrant that will be executed by the police. Many probation and parole agencies believe that if officers carry weapons, they are perceived differently and are unable to perform as counselors and encourage offenders to take up treatment and self-help programs. There is no standard policy for probation and parole agencies regarding carrying weapons and even officers themselves are not in agreement

Table 5.2
VIOLENCE AGAINST PROBATION AND PAROLE OFFICERS, 1980–1993

Murder or attempted murder	16
Rape or attempted rape	7
Other sexual assaults	100
Shot or wounded or attempts	32
Use or attempted use of blunt instrument or projectile	60
Slashed or stabbed or attempt	28
Car used as weapon or attempt	12
Punched, kicked, choked	1,396
Use or attempted use of caustic substances	3
Use or attempted use of incendiary device	9
Abduction or attempt	3
Attempted or actual unspecified assaults	944
Total	**2,610**

Source: Phillip J. Bigger, "Officers in Danger: Results of the Federal Probation and Pretrial Services Association's National Study on Serious Assaults," *APPA Perspectives* 17 (1993): 14–20.

as to whether they should be armed. Champion reports that 59 percent of officers believe they should have the option to carry a firearm on the job, yet 80 percent of female and 69 percent of male officers disagree that they should be required to carry a firearm.[48] Some states classify probation and parole officers as peace officers and grant them the authority to carry a firearm both on and off duty. It seems perhaps the best policy regarding officers' carrying of weapons is that established by the American Probation and Parole Association (APPA), which in 1994 adopted a weapons "position statement." Essentially, APPA does not support or oppose officers' carrying weapons but suggests that the decision should be based on the need, officer safety demands, and local laws and policies.[49]

The Community Residential Staff

Community residential centers (CRCs) or **halfway houses** are used either as an intermediate sanction between probation and prison or to assist released inmates make the transition between prison and the community. CRCs provide a combination of supervision, structure, accountability, and programming to aid in the community supervision of probationers or parolees. They are seen as cost effective, and are less expensive than a prison. In 2008, the average cost per day for a prison term was $78.95[50], considerably more than the 2001 average cost for a halfway house operated by the department of corrections ($46.15 per day) and for contracted halfway houses ($43.41).[51] And in most halfway houses, residents must pay a portion of the cost of their stay through wages they earn while in the community.

These facilities are usually an old boarding house, a YMCA, or some other large residential structure in an urban area. They range in size from 30 to 200 residents. While they have limited physical security to keep residents from leaving (usually standard residential locks, with cameras throughout the center to assist in supervision), residents are not free to come and go as they please. Residents must stay at the center unless they are approved to go to work or attend an authorized program. If they are complying with center rules, they may receive a weekend pass to visit family or friends.

Community residential programs offer good opportunities for employment for individuals who want to work with offenders in the real-life setting of the community rather than in a prison.

Most individuals enter one of two positions when beginning work at a halfway house. The first is a paraprofessional position often called a desk monitor. Desk monitors control access into and out of the facility. The monitor ensures that residents sign in, and are in the house when required. In many ways, it is equivalent to the role of a correctional officer in a prison. When not watching the desk, monitors do room checks to make sure there is no contraband (items not allowed in the possession of residents) or activities such as drinking or drug use. They also search for contraband in rooms or other locations throughout the house. These positions are often paid between $10 and $15 per hour and have limited

Halfway houses are usually large, older homes located in central cities so that public transportation and other services are available to residents. (Courtesy of the Corrections Corporation of America.)

benefits. However, they are very good part-time positions for students preparing for a corrections career and good entry-level jobs to get experience working in a criminal justice agency and with offenders. This experience is very good preparation for work as a police officer, probation or parole officer, or correctional officer.

The second category of halfway house jobs is professional positions, such as counselor, case manager, or substance abuse specialist. Counselors and case managers are assigned a caseload of residents and are responsible for guiding them through their stay by suggesting (or requiring) participation in certain programs, initiating disciplinary action for violation of probation or parole when required, and overseeing the collection of fines or costs for staying at the house. A college degree in criminal justice, social work, psychology, or one of the other social sciences is usually required. These jobs are very interesting and very challenging. These staff must be directive with residents and hold them accountable for following the rules. They must be knowledgeable of programs and job-finding resources to assist residents. And they must deal with the difficult situation of offenders being restricted in their activities and movements—all in a non-secure facility in the community where they go on almost a daily basis.

There were many jobs in halfway houses; as of 2005, there were 221 community-based correctional facilities in the United States.[52] The requirements for halfway house counselor positions are similar to those of a probation or parole officer or a prison caseworker, usually requiring a college degree with several curriculum hours in social work or sociology. Most halfway houses are operated by the private sector, most are nonprofit, and most had their originations with a church or religious organization. Perhaps because of their history of service, salaries are usually low, and there is considerable turnover of staff in both the paraprofessional monitors and the counselor positions. Even with the low pay and challenging work, these positions provide excellent experience, opportunities for staff to develop a variety of skills, and excellent opportunities to network with other criminal justice, and social service agencies.

Volunteers and Contractor Services

Volunteers and contract staff play a critical role in delivery of services and operations of correctional institutions. Volunteers are defined as nonpaid and intermittent providers of a service to a correctional agency. In contrast, contract staff are paid, regularly scheduled providers of service to a correctional agency. Even though contract staff are paid, their contracts are usually much less expensive than full-time staff, as they receive no paid benefits, such as sick and annual leave, health insurance, or retirement. Also, contract staff usually work considerably fewer hours than the full-time staff. There are three reasons why agencies use volunteers and contract staff. First, to expand the volume of services that can be provided to offenders. Second, to provide specialized services that full-time staff are not qualified to provide. And finally, the use of volunteers and contractors brings community citizens into the operations of correctional agencies and helps spread the word and gain support for their mission.

These staff are critical for agencies, especially in times when correctional budgets are stretched with increasing numbers of offenders and reducing financial resources. To provide services that are deemed important, yet cannot be afforded with the available budget, correctional agencies use volunteers and sometimes contract staff. The use of volunteers in community corrections has been around for fifty years in both halfway houses and probation. The formation of Volunteers in Probation occurred in the early 1970s, and a 1979 national review found that there were approximately 300,000 volunteers serving 2,000 probation jurisdictions and contributing over 20 million hours of service per year.[53] In prisons, religious service departments have historically used volunteers to assist with religious services and provide faith-based counseling. Most prisons have one or two full-time chaplains, and contract a few hours per week with ministers to provide for the specific needs of faith groups with small numbers of inmates (such as Muslims, Jews, or Buddhists). A review of the use of religious volunteers in Kentucky prisons found that most had long tenures (had volunteered an average of over seven years) and provided services such as preaching and teaching inmates on issues of their faith.[54]

Volunteers and contract staff both in prisons and for probationers and parolees provide substance abuse counseling and facilitating programs such as Alcoholics Anonymous or Narcotics Anonymous. These are valuable not only for provision of services but also because they allow a smooth transition into such programs in the community. Prisons' recreation and hobby craft programs often make use of volunteers and contract staff to teach painting or music classes, instruct inmates on diet and healthy lifestyles, and even provide competition for inmates' sports teams.

Over the past decade, there has been a significant increase in the use of faith-based volunteers in jails and prisons. A 2003 survey found that forty-four of the state correctional systems provided faith-based programming.[55] Volunteers are critical for the provision of these programs. Most are not funded or receive little public funds to operate. However, there seems no shortage of committed volunteers who provide their time to work in training and counseling offenders interested in learning more about and live according to the tenets of their faith. An interesting case (*Americans United for Separation of Church and State v. Prison Fellowship Ministries*) was recently decided regarding the use of public funds to offer faith-based programs to inmates. An Iowa state prison provided inmates a chance to live together and participate in the InnerChange program conducted by Prison Fellowship Ministries, which was dominated by Bible study, religious revivals, and church services. In 2006, the Southern District Court of Iowa ruled that the program was "pervasively sectarian" and therefore unconstitutional as it violated the separation of church and state.[56] Inmates in the program received privileges other inmates did not (more privacy, family visits, and computer time), and there were no equivalent nonreligious programs. The 8th U.S. Circuit Court of Appeals affirmed the District Court decision, noting that inmates had "no genuine and independent private choice" to receive rehabilitation services from an organization other than the one run by Prison Fellowship.[57]

Contract staff are used regularly in jails and prisons to supplement full-time staff and provide specialty services that are not available or not needed on a full-time basis. For example, prisons and jails have medical departments that are similar to community family practice medical offices and provide treatment for general illnesses and injuries. Medical conditions requiring a specialist are referred to contract practitioners such as surgeons, dermatologists, or physical therapists. Another high use of contractors is in prison and jail educational department, where specialized programs or courses such as English as a second language or reading for inmates with learning disabilities require part-time contract staff.

In addition to the value that volunteers and contract staff add to fulfilling the mission of a correctional agency, their use is also an excellent way to involve the community in the agency and mobilize support and understanding for correctional issues and operations. With correctional issues so much a political interest and financial drain of public budgets, it is important for members of the general public to be educated about the difficult role these agencies play. Not only do volunteers and contract employees play a role in this, but community service clubs are also sometimes invited to form chapters within prisons and jails to provide leisure time activities for inmates and to link the community to the prison. Toastmasters International and the Jaycees are service clubs that often have chapters in prisons and jails. And church congregations often assist both institutional and community correctional agencies by providing inmate visitors with transportation or accommodations or by providing support to inmates transitioning from the prison to the community.

While volunteers and contract staff can be very valuable and helpful in many ways, engaging them can also be problematic, and they must be well organized and monitored to ensure effectiveness. Ogburn suggests the following steps in establishing and maintaining an effective volunteer program:

1. Evaluate needs.
2. Develop goals and job descriptions.
3. Involve staff in planning and implementation of the volunteer program.
4. Actively recruit volunteers.
5. Educate volunteers about inmates and the potential for manipulation.
6. Explain security needs to volunteers.
7. Give volunteers the big picture about the prison mission and the volunteers' roles in accomplishing it.
8. Evaluate volunteer program effectiveness.
9. Recognize volunteers' contributions.[58]

Most of these guidelines hold true for contract staff as well as volunteers. By following these guidelines, the volunteer and contract services are likely to be effective and successful.

The Importance of Diversity in Corrections

Important to the operation of correctional agencies is staff diversity. Having a staff that is diverse in terms of gender, race, and ethnicity is important for many reasons. First, with such a large percentage of offenders under correctional supervision being minorities, race and ethnic diversity aid in the management of prisons and community correctional agencies. Second, diversity of staff enriches and develops all staff as they continuously learn from each other. Diversity in terms of gender, race, and ethnicity provides experiences for staff that enable them to more effectively supervise a diverse group of offenders. And, having women within a correctional workforce brings a calming and normalized influence to men's prisons and doubles the available pool for recruiting talented individuals.

The racial make up of offenders has changed over the years, and there is now an overrepresentation of minorities under correctional supervision. In 1986, whites were 65 percent of all offenders in prisons and jails and under community supervision. By the end of 2007, the imprisonment rate of men per 100,000 population was 955 for whites, 3,138 for blacks, and 1,259 for Hispanics.[59] The black imprisonment rate has actually decreased since 2000, when it was 3,188.[60] The proportion of minorities increases when considering the seriousness of the criminal punishment. Of the 2,311,200 inmates in prison and jail on June 30, 2008, 807,000 (34.9 percent) were white, 913,800 (39.5 percent) were black, and 460,400 (19.9 percent) were Hispanic.[61]

This disproportionate representation of minority offenders makes it even more important that correctional agencies aggressively recruit minority staff in order to have the staff be somewhat representative of the offender makeup. The problems resulting from an almost all-white workforce supervising an inmate population that was primarily minority became expressly clear after the riot in the New York State Penitentiary in Attica in 1971. A significant problem at Attica was the guarding of urban black and Hispanic inmates by rural white staff who were very different in culture, which resulted in mistrust and a lack of communication. Whites from rural New York State had little understanding of the culture of the urban black and Hispanic inmates. There was little communication between staff and inmates and these differences grew into hostility as inmates perceived race and discrimination to be the basis for many of the prison policies.

Even though there is no conclusive evidence that the criminal justice system is inherently racist in practice or policy, the high numbers of minorities in correctional systems create a phenomenon that causes management problems for correctional officials. Therefore, correctional agencies use **affirmative action programs** to recruit and develop a workforce that mirrors to the greatest extent the client base. Race and ethnicity are not always a barrier to effective communication between inmates and staff. However, a diverse workforce reduces the perception by offenders that the system is racist and that they therefore have an excuse to commit crimes, misbehave, or not follow prison or community supervision rules.

Since the Attica riot, there has been significant progress in diversifying the correctional workforce. By January 1, 2002, of the total of 435,688 staff employed by prisons and jails, 69.0 percent were white, 20.1 percent were black, and 7.6 percent were Hispanic.[62] While there is still a large percentage of the workforce that is white, the percentage of nonwhite employees has increased from 28.8 percent in 1994 to 30.8 percent in 2002.[63] Probation and parole agencies have done somewhat better, as a 2002 survey of sixty probation and parole agencies reported that of 50,640 people employed, 66.7 percent were white, 23.5 percent were black, and 7.2 percent were Hispanic.[64]

These advances have not been easy. Irwin points out that when minority staff were first recruited to rural prisons with predominantly white staff, some white staff felt that the nonwhite, urban officers would be more pro-inmate and less trustworthy and might undermine security and did not easily accept them.[65] Studies have found that nonwhite correctional officers experience more stress than their white counterparts, and black officers are more likely to quit their jobs than white officers, primarily because of conflicts with supervisors.[66] When there is not a diverse workforce, minority staff do not feel accepted into the workplace and can become bitter and perceive their supervisors' actions as racially motivated.

There are many reasons for affirmative action programs in corrections. First, as public agencies, there are affirmative action laws that mandate efforts for aggressive recruitment of minorities. Second, the culture and expectations of many correctional agencies encourage affirmative action and encourage their human resource offices to set and attain diversity goals. However, in addition to the *legal* and *personnel* reasons for affirmative action, correctional agencies pursue cultural diversity as a *management necessity*. Offender management is most successful when there is interaction and communication between staff and offenders. Although this does not mean that white staff cannot communicate with African American offenders, tension is reduced when the workforce and client group are similarly represented. In discussing the prison workplace, Carlson suggests, "The staff must 'look like' the inmates; the ideal is to have the same proportions of Caucasians, African Americans, and Hispanics in staff and inmate ranks."[67]

Similarly, opening opportunities for women to work as correctional officers in male prisons began as a legal and civil rights requirement, yet it quickly became valuable for management purposes. While the integration of women into the correctional workforce can have a very positive impact on prison and jail environments, until recently there were several reasons why women were barred from working as correctional officers in male prisons. First, there was concern that women could not physically respond to violence or protect themselves against inmate assault. There was even the concern that the presence of women working in solitary situations may spur a sexual attack by predatory inmates. Second, it was believed that having opposite sex correctional officers working in housing units or other remote areas of prisons would result in an increase in romantic involvements of staff with inmates. And finally, there was a question about how to deal with the privacy concerns of inmates, because correctional officers must supervise all areas of a prison, including bathrooms, showers, and sleeping rooms.[68]

Gender Issues in Correctional Staffing

This section examines the significant issues of gender regarding staffing of correctional agencies. It is not surprising to most people that only within the past two decades women have been accepted as equally able to perform as male correctional officers in male prisons. On hearing that women work in male prisons, many people express surprise, expecting it to be too dangerous, male inmates would prey on women officers, that women would be unable to effectively control male inmates, and that it would cause privacy problems of supervising men when they were showering and sleeping. As a result, the only female employees in men's prisons held jobs with no inmate contact, such as clerks, secretaries, or mail workers.

However, with the passage of the 1964 (and then amended in 1972) Civil Rights Act, employment discrimination on the basis of race, religion, sex, and national origin was prohibited, and women had the legal right to seek employment as correctional officers in men's prisons. However, a provision of Title VII of the Act states that some discriminatory practices might be allowed if there is "a **bona fide occupational qualification (BFOQ)** reasonably necessary to the normal operation of that particular business or enterprise."[69] Most correctional agencies used this exception, arguing that the risk to security and loss of privacy for inmates would be considered an acceptable BFOQ exception.

Practical Perspectives

Increasing Minority Staff

When I became the director of the Ohio department of corrections, the department had a very low proportion of minority staff. While I did not believe that the department had a racist attitude or discriminated against minorities, there just had not been a focus on the importance of this issue. Most of the prisons were in rural locations, and there was no easily available pool of minority applicants from which to hire. And since so much recruiting comes by word of mouth and from current employees, the predominantly white workforce continued to fill vacancies with other nonminority staff. And there was not a base of minority leadership from which to gain momentum, as the department had no minorities as senior administrators in the headquarters and no minority wardens.

The governor who appointed me, Richard Celeste, came into office with a commitment to increase minority employment in the state and was well aware of the poor record in my department. A large percentage of his cabinet was African Americans, and he quickly put in place an affirmative action hiring program. In one of my first major personnel moves (within a few weeks after becoming director), I promoted a current warden as my chief deputy and replaced him with an outstanding black staff member. His appointment was welcomed by the black community and by our staff, who knew him to be extremely capable and deserving.

Nowhere was the lack of minority employees worse than at the maximum-security prison in Lucasville, at the most southern tip of Ohio, at which there was only one black person in a staff of more than five hundred employees. Lucasville was the sole maximum-security prison for adults; more than 50 percent of inmates were black, and more than half were from Cleveland and other northern Ohio cities, more than 200 miles from Lucasville. On my first visit to the prison, I heard a story about the warden having to discipline a correctional officer for making a racist comment over the loudspeaker as he called for all inmates to leave the yard and return to their cells.

To guide our affirmative action program, I hired a black human resources professional from Dayton who had experience and good ties with community action programs providing job and training assistance for urban minorities. Fred was full of energy and immediately set out to build ties between the prisons and the closest communities with a substantial minority population. He began to hold job fairs in communities, using local community action groups to host them and encourage attendance by minorities. I attended many of these job fairs myself, as a show of the department's commitment to hiring minority staff.

When we held the job fair in Portsmouth, a town about ten miles from Lucasville, we got an earful. Fred had organized the event, and the chief of personnel for the Lucasville prison and I attended. There was a really good turnout, with approximately fifty people (mostly African American) attending. Fred started with an overview of the types of jobs available and the reasons we were reaching out to the minority community in our recruitment efforts. But he was quickly interrupted with questions and complaints about our past hiring practices. There were allegations of racism in hiring and of driving off black staff members; allegedly in one case by putting sand into the gas tank of his car. I was really taken aback and could only reaffirm our commitment to do things differently at this point. The people there were not convinced, but simply said they would encourage applicants and see how we responded.

I am pleased to say that we were successful. We made good on our recruitment and hiring emphasis, and by the time I left Ohio, Lucasville had more than fifty black employees and was well on its way to ending the history of a predominantly white staff supervising a predominantly black inmate population. This did not only occur at Lucasville but also across the state in other prisons, as our leadership team began to recognize the importance and value of having a diverse workforce. We received considerable praise and support from minority elected officials from across the state, and the department was much stronger and did a much better job of supervising offenders in both the community and in prisons. We had come a long way since that contentious job fair in Lucasville.

Women quickly filed several cases with the Equal Employment Opportunity Commission (EEOC), claiming discrimination and the inappropriate use of the BFOQ. In 1977, the U.S. Supreme Court first addressed the BFOQ exception in the case of **Dothard v. Rawlinson.**[70] Rawlinson had been denied a position as a correctional officer in an Alabama men's prison because the state prohibited women in any position that would require contact with male inmates. The Court ruled that a BFOQ prohibiting female correctional officers was allowable because of the deplorable conditions of the Alabama prisons and the presence of predatory male sex offenders as inmates. In 1979, in **Gunther v. Iowa**, the U.S. District Court of Iowa did not find the same predatory environment in an Iowa prison and therefore determined that inmate privacy was not a valid reason to refuse to hire women as correctional officers, and that the state could create staffing and assignment patterns to avoid infringing on inmate privacy.[71] After the *Gunther* decision, most states abandoned their BFOQ and moved quickly to hire women.

By January 1, 1993, women represented 17.3 percent of the approximately 169,000 correctional officers in state and federal prisons; by January 1, 2002, 22.7 percent of the 218,000 total U.S. correctional officers were women,[72] and by 2005, 26 percent of all correctional officers in state prisons were women.[73] Progress did not come easily, however, as the historical bias and assumption that female officers would have different attitudes and carry out their duties differently from their male counterparts persisted. A 1986 survey reported that

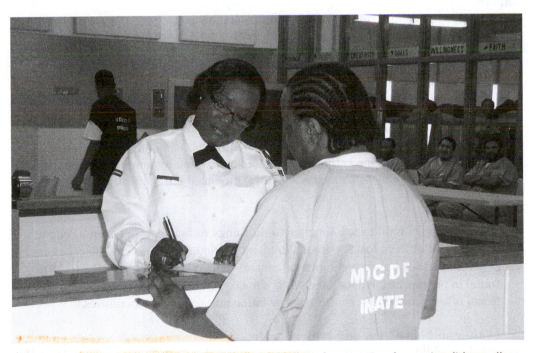

Female correctional officer performing her duties. Although correctional agencies did not allow women as correctional officers in male prisons until the past three decades, they are now fully integrated into the correctional workforce and have significantly aided in the management of prisons.
(Photo by Deborah L. O'Brien)

Out of a hundred men interviewed, only a handful were at all supportive of [women working as correctional officers]. . . . The most frequently voiced reasons for opposing the presence of women were that they impair the security of the institutions as a whole and jeopardize male guards' own safety.[74]

A study of gender relationship in San Quentin (California) Prison found gender conflicts, competition, divisions among workers, and an uneasy social order in the prison.[75] Another California prison study found that male officers and male inmates perceived that women were less effective in responding to violent situations requiring physical strength. However, the study (when analyzing actual performance instead of perceptions) found that women actually performed their jobs as well as male officers.[76]

Other studies have found either no or only minor differences in relation to the attitudes and job performance of women compared to men.[77] A study of female correctional officers in California in 1983 found that women performed as well as men as correctional officers. However, men continued to perceive women as less effective when the situation required physical strength or a violent emergency existed.[78] A study within the Federal Bureau of Prisons also found no lapse in performance, but did find that female correctional officers experienced hostility and sometimes sexual harassment from male staff and inmates.[79]

Interesting findings resulted from a survey of male inmates who were asked to rate female correctional officer performance compared to male correctional officers. Cheeseman and colleagues found that higher-security inmates were more likely to favorably rate the performance of female officers than lower-security inmates. The authors write, "Specifically, prisoners classified as close custody were significantly more likely than minimum or medium custody inmates to agree that female staff performed as well as male staff when responding to stabbings, responding to physical fights, settling verbal disputes among inmates, and preventing riots or disturbances."[80]

Today, correctional agencies find that there are many benefits to women working as correctional officers. One is that the style of supervision by female correctional officers of male inmates may bring a calming and normalized influence to a prison. Pollock writes

> Women officers tend to ask inmates to do things rather than tell them. Female correctional officers foster personal interest in the inmate and use the relationships they develop as a technique of control. This relieves some of the tension found in prisons for men and encourages male prisoners to interact with correctional officers rather than cultivating isolation and separate subcultures.[81]

Other authors agree, and even note that "Women in corrections have demonstrated their ability to meet or exceed the required levels of performance."[82] At this point, women are fully integrated into the workforce. Correctional administrators recognize that women are well able to perform the role of correctional officers in male prisons.

Basic training for correctional workers. Diversity of the correctional workforce is critical to accomplishing the mission. This basic training class reflects the diversity of their workforce.
(Courtesy of Corrections Corporation of America)

SUMMARY

One thing is without question: There is nothing more important to the quality operation of a correctional agency than staff and leadership. The manner in which staff understand and work toward accomplishing the agency mission, the skill and pride with which they carry out their duties, and the concern and attention of leadership all contribute to the success of a correctional agency. Correctional jobs are challenging, and they are unlikely to be successfully accomplished without highly trained staff working together for high quality and high standards. Although staff are the most important resource of a correctional agency, that resource can never be taken for granted. It must be carefully assembled, prepared, and properly led in order to meet the complex responsibilities and far-reaching goals of correctional agencies.

This chapter reviewed the types of jobs that are available in the correctional profession, including descriptions of the workplace, types of functions to be fulfilled, and challenges. Issues of pay, career opportunities, and entry-level requirements have been presented. The importance of a diverse workforce was addressed, and the movement away from a predominantly white, male correctional staff was described. As noted in earlier chapters, leadership in a correctional agency also plays a significant role, and leadership's impact on staff cannot be overstated.

In following chapters, we address the way we manage, organize, and supervise correctional staff. Human resource management elements include the recruitment, training, and continued development of correctional staff. The importance of good supervision and the vital elements of supervision, whether they occur in a correctional, or other public or private sector, environment, will also be examined. On the completion of this chapter, you should clearly understand the value of correctional staff and how staff must be nurtured and developed to maximize their potential.

KEY TERMS

Guards
Correctional officers
Snitches
Caseworker
Probation officers

Parole officers
Halfway houses
Staff diversity
Affirmative action programs

Bona fide occupational
  qualification
Dothard v. Rawlinson
Gunther v. Iowa

YOU'RE THE CORRECTIONAL ADMINISTRATOR

1. You are the human resource manager of a state correctional agency. Your department just finished a very good strategic planning exercise, and you identified the need to "reinvent" the role and competencies of your correctional officers. You found that many had not kept pace with the changes in the types of skills and attitudes needed for success, and there have been increasing conflict and tension among the current group of CO's and inmates. You have decided to attempt to both recruit differently to get a very skilled person who wants to begin a career and promote within the agency. And you have decided to put in place a training program for current COs to get them thinking about the current role needed. Prepare an outline of the type of person you would try to recruit and where and how would you try to communicate with them? Also prepare an outline of a training program to get current CO's more in tune with the skills and competencies needed in contemporary prisons.

2. You have just been appointed the volunteer coordinator for a county probation department. Your bosses have decided with budget cuts, they will try to supplement a shortage of staff with volunteers. They do not know exactly how they want to do this; that's why they appointed you. You are to create a plan on how volunteers can be used in the department and then create a training program for them. First, outline the plan to include the types of activities volunteers will do and how they will work with current probation staff. Second, outline the training program they will need to make them truly effective.

WEB LINK EXERCISES

Go to Federal Bureau of Prisons (BOP): www.bop.gov

This is the Web site for the Federal Bureau of Prisons (BOP). Find the employment information. Research the description of duties, requirements, and process for applying for a job as a correctional officer. From the other information available on the Web site, list the key requirements for obtaining a job as a correctional officer in the BOP. Stay at the Web site for the BOP.

Also, examine the pay schedule for the position of correctional officer. Is this a salary you can live with while preparing for promotion? Look at the benefits, as these generally amount to about 35 percent of the amount of the salary. Benefits are important to all workers today and the federal government provides excellent benefits.

Stay at the Web site for the BOP. Find the employment information.

GROUP EXERCISES

Each group will present a description of how the following positions operate in a prison environment: Correctional Officer, Counselor, Accreditation Compliance Officer, Unit Manager, and Chaplain.

ENDNOTES

1. Camille Graham Camp and George M. Camp, *The Corrections Yearbook, 1998* (Middletown, CT: Criminal Justice Institute, 1998), p. 130.

2. Ibid., pp. 196–197.

3. Ibid., pp. 262–265.

4. Web page of the United Auto Workers, http://www.uaw.com (April 8, 2001).

5. U.S. Department of Justice, Federal Bureau of Investigation, Crime in the United States 2007 Table 1, http://www.fbi.gov/ucr/cius2007/data/table_01.html (accessed October 13, 2008).

6. Jody K. Spertzel, "A Correctional Career Guide," *Corrections Today* 55 no. 1 (1993): 37.

7. David E. Duffee, *Corrections: Practice and Policy* (New York: Random House, 1989), p. 388.

8. E. Goffman, *Asylums: Essays on the Social Situation of Mental Patients and Other Inmates* (Garden City, NY: Doubleday & Company, 1961).

9. Donald Cressey, "Prison Organization," in *Handbook of Organizations*, edited by J. March (New York: Rand McNally, 1965), p. 1024.

10. James B. Jacobs and Norma Meacham Crotty, *Guard Unions and the Future of the Prisons* (Ithaca, NY: Institute of Public Employment, 1978), p. 3.

11. American Correctional Association, "Resolution on the Term 'Correctional Officer'," *Corrections Today* (April 1993): 60.

12. George M. Camp and Camile G. Camp, *Management of Crowded Prisons* (Washington, DC: U.S. Department of Justice, 1989), p. 51.

13. Camp and Camp, *The Corrections Yearbook*, 1998, p. 132.

14. James J. Stephan, "Census of State and Federal Correctional Facilities, 2005," *National Prisoner Statistics Program* (Washington, DC: U.S. Department of Justice, October 2008), p. 4.

15. Bureau of Justice Statistics, Data Online, *Expenditure and Employment*, http://wwwbjsdata.ojp.usdoj.gov/dataonline/Search/EandE/state_emp_next.cfm (accessed December 29, 2008).

16. James J. Stephan, *Census of Jails, 1999*, NCJ 186633 (Washington, DC: U.S. Department of Justice, Bureau of Justice Statistics, August 2000), p. 25.

17. Ben Crouch, "Guard Work in Transition," in *The Dilemmas of Corrections; Contemporary Readings*, 2nd ed., edited by K. C. Haas and G. P. Alpert (Prospect Heights, IL: Waveland Press, 1991).

18. Michael Welch, *Corrections: A Critical Approach* (New York: McGraw-Hill, 1996), p. 138.

19. Robert Johnson, *Hard Time: Understanding and Reforming the Prison* (Belmont, CA: Wadsworth, 1996), p. 224.

20. John J. Dilulio, Jr., *Governing Prisons: A Comparative Study of Correctional Management* (New York: The Free Press, 1987), p. 95.

21. Lucien X. Lombardo, *Guards Imprisoned*, 2nd ed. (Cincinnati, OH: Anderson Publishing Company, 1989), pp. 51–57.

22. Richard P. Seiter, *Corrections: An Introduction*, 3rd ed. (Upper Saddle River, NJ: Pearson Education, 2011), p. 390.

23. Cited in Peter Finn, *Addressing Correctional Officer Stress: Programs and Strategies* (Washington, DC: U.S. Department of Justice, 2000), p. 11.

24. From the Correctional Peace Officer Foundation, http://www.cpof.org/page/3361250.htm (accessed April 7, 2009).

25. James B. Jacobs and Lawrence Kraft, "Integrating the Keepers: A Comparison of Black and White Prison Guards in Illinois," *Social Problems* 25 (1978): 308.

26. Robert Freeman, "Correctional Officers: Understudied and Misunderstood," in *Prisons: Today and Tomorrow*, edited by Jocelyn M. Pollock (Gaithersburg, MD: Aspen Publishers, 1997), pp. 319–320.

27. See, Robert Johnson, "Informal Helping Networks in Prison: The Shape of Grass-Roots Correctional Intervention," *Journal of Criminal Justice* 7 no. 1 (1979) 53–70, and Lucien X. Lombardo, *Guards Imprisoned: Correctional Officers at Work* (New York: Elsevier, 1981).

28. Robert Johnson and Hans Toch, *The Pains of Imprisonment* (Newbury Park, CA: Sage, 1982), p. 287.

29. Camp and Camp, *The Corrections Yearbook*, 1998, p. 149.

30. Texas Department of Criminal Justice (Corrections), http://www.tdcj.state.tx.us/vacancy/coinfo/cosalary.htm and California Department of Corrections and Rehabilitation, http://www.cdcr.ca.gov/Career_Opportunities/POR/docs/payandbenefits.pdf (accessed April 17, 2010).

31. For a good overview of the need for a college degree for correctional officers, see Ray Bynum, "Does a Correctional Officer Need a College Education?," *American Jails* 22 no. 6 (February 2009): 19–25.

32. *Occupational Outlook Handbook*, 2010–11 Edition, U.S. Department of Labor, Bureau of Labor Statistics, *Correctional Officers*, http://www.bls.gov/oco/ocosl156.htm (accessed April 20, 2010).

33. *Occupational Outlook Handbook*, 2010–11 Edition.

34. Vernon Fox, *Correctional Institutions* (Englewood Cliffs, NJ: Prentice Hall, 1983), p. 71.

35. *Occupational Outlook Handbook*, 2010–11 Edition.

36. Bureau of Justice Statistics, *Key Facts at a Glance: Correctional Populations*, http://bjs.ojp.usdoj.gov/content/glance/tables/corr2tab.cfm (accessed April 23, 2010).

37. George M. Camp and Camile G. Camp, *The 2002 Corrections Yearbook* (Middletown, CT: Criminal Justice Institute), p. 191.

38. Peter Finn and Sarah Kuck, "Stress Among Probation and Parole Officers and What Can Be Done About It," *NIJ Research for Practice* (Washington, DC: U.S. Department of Justice, June 2005).

39. David I. Rothman, *Conscience and Convenience: The Asylum and Its Alternatives in Progressive America* (Boston, MA: Little, Brown, 1980).

40. Edward E. Rhine, "Probation and Parole Supervision: In Need of a New Narrative," *Corrections Management Quarterly* 1 no. 2 (1999): 72.

41. Dan Richard Beto, Ronald P. Corbett, Jr., and John J. Dilulio, Jr., "Getting Serious about Probation and the Crime Problem," *Corrections Management Quarterly* 4 no. 2 (2000): 3.

42. Norman A. Carlson, Karen M. Hess, and Christine M. H. Orthmann, *Corrections in the Twenty-First Century: A Practical Approach* (Belmont, CA: West/Wadsworth, 1999), p. 448.

43. An interview by the author with a State of Missouri probation officer. (October 20, 2000).

44. Florida Department of Corrections Web site, Probation Officer Careers, http://fldocjobs. com/paths/cpo/salary.html (accessed November 10, 2009).

45. California Employment Development Department, "Probation Officers and Parole Agents," http://www.calmis.ca.gov/file/occguide/PROBOFF.HTM (accessed November 10, 2009).

46. Ibid., p. 225.

47. "Parole Officer Job Description, Career as a Parole Officer, Salary, Employment—Definition and Nature of the Work, Education and Training Requirements, Getting the Job," http://careers.stateuniversity.com/pages/728/Parole-Officer.html (accessed April 14, 2009).

48. Dean Champion, *Probation, Parole, and Community Corrections*, 2nd ed. (Englewood Cliffs, NJ: Prentice-Hall, 1996), pp. 429–430.

49. American Probation and Parole Association, *APPA Position Statement: Weapons*, Approved 1994, http://www.appa-net.org/eweb/Dynamicpage.aspx?site=APPA_2& webcode=IB_PositionStatement&wps_key=e2e80331-3bed-4d64-a044-ea98ee53bd17 (accessed November 11, 2009).

50. The Pew Center (March 2009), p. 2.

51. Ibid., p. 145.

52. Stephan, p. 2.

53. Chris W. Eskridge and Eric W. Carlson, "The Use of Volunteers in Probation: A National Synthesis," *Journal of Offender Counseling, Services, and Rehabilitation* 4 no. 2 (Winter 1979): 175–189.

54. Richard Tewksbury and Sue Carter Collins, "Prison Chapel Volunteers," *Federal Probation* 69 no. 1 (2005): 26–30.

55. Cece Hill, "Faith-Based Programming," *Corrections Compendium* 28 no. 8 (2003): 8–20.

56. Americans United for Separation of Church and State v. Prison Fellowship Ministries, 432 F. Supp. 2d 862.

57. Americans United for Separation of Church and State v. Prison Fellowship Ministries, 509 F.3d 406 (2007).

58. Kevin R. Ogburn, "Volunteer Program Guide," *Corrections Today* 55 no. 5 (1993): 66.

59. Heather C. West and William J. Sabol, "Prisoners in 2007," *Bureau of Justice Statistics Bulletin* (Washington, DC: U.S. Department of Justice, December 2008), p. 19.

60. Ibid., p. 4.

61. Bureau of Justice Statistics, "Prison Inmates at Mid-Year 2008—Statistical Tables," (Washington, DC: U.S. Department of Justice, March 2009), http://www.ojp.usdoj.gov/bjs/abstract/pim08st.htm (accesed April 23, 2010).

62. Camp and Camp, *2002 Corrections Yearbook*, p. 154.

63. Ibid., p. 155.

64. Ibid., p. 219.

65. John Irwin, "The Changing Social Structure of the Men's Correctional Prison," in *Corrections and Punishment*, edited by D. Greenberg (Beverly Hills, CA: Sage, 1977), pp. 21–40.

66. Susan Philliber, "Thy Brother's Keeper: A Review of Literature on Correctional Officers," *Justice Quarterly* 4 no. 1 (1987): 9–33.

67. Peter M. Carlson, "Diversity of Correctional Officers," in *Prison and Jail Administration: Practice and Theory*, 2nd ed., edited by Peter M. Carlson and Judith Simon Garrett (Boston, MA: Jones and Bartlett Publishers, 2008), p. 245.

68. For a review of the constitutional bases for inmate privacy and equal employment opportunity for women, see Susan L. Reisner, "Balancing Inmates' Right to Privacy with Equal Employment for Prison Guards," *Women's Rights Law Reporter* 4 no. 4 (Summer 1978): 243–251.

69. 42 U.S.C. 2000e-2 (1976), p. 703(e).

70. *Dothard v. Rawlinson*, 433 U.S. 321 (1977).

71. *Gunther v. Iowa*, 462 F., Suppl. 952 (N.D. *Iowa* 1979).

72. Camp and Camp, *2002 Corrections Yearbook*, pp. 159, 164, 165.

73. Stephan, p. 4.

74. Lynn E. Zimmer, *Women Guarding Men* (Chicago: University of Chicago Press, 1986), pp. 53–54.

75. Barbara A. Owen, "Race and Gender Relations Among Prison Workers," *Crime and Delinquency* 31 no. 1 (January 1985): 147–159.

76. H. Holeman and B. Krepps-Hess, *Women Correctional Officers in the California Department of Corrections* (Sacramento: California Department of Corrections, 1983).

77. See Nancy C. Jurik and Gregory J. Halembia, "Gender, Working Conditions and the Job Satisfaction of Women in a Non-Traditional Occupation: Female Correctional Officers in Men's Prisons," *Sociological Quarterly* 25 (1984): 551–566. Also see Lincoln J. Fry and Daniel Glaser, "Gender Differences in Work Adjustment of Prison Employees," *Journal of Offender Counseling, Services and Rehabilitation* 12 (1987): 39–52.

78. Herbert Holeman and Barbara Krepps-Hess, *Women Correctional Officers in the California Department of Corrections* (Sacramento: California Department of Corrections, Research Unit, 1983).

79. See Kevin Wright and William Saylor, "Male and Female Employees' Perceptions of Prison Work: Is There a Difference?," *Justice Quarterly* 8 (1991): 505–524.

80. Kelly A. Cheeseman, Janet L. Mullings, and James W. Marquart, "Inmate Perceptions of Security Staff across Various Custody Levels," *Corrections Management Quarterly* 5 no. 2 (2001): 44.

81. Joycelyn M. Pollock, "Women in Corrections: Custody and the 'Caring Ethic'," in *Women, Law, and Social Control*, edited by Alida V. Merlo and Joycelyn M. Pollock (Boston, MA: Allyn and Bacon, 1995), p. 111.

82. Carlson et al., *Corrections in the Twenty-First* Century, p. 441.

6

Human Resource Management for Corrections

Introduction

The key resources of a correctional agency include prisons and office space, budgets, equipment, and staff. There is almost no one working in a correctional agency that would disagree that corrections is a "people business," and that staff are the most important resource, and salaries make up the largest portion of any correctional agency budgets. Apart from the initial outlay of capital cost to build a prison, nearly 85 percent of annual operating funds is committed to the salaries and benefits for prison employees. In probation and parole organizations, the percentages are sometimes even higher. With staff as such an important and costly commitment, this "human resource" must be created, cultivated, and continually supported. The challenge for these activities rests with the staff working in human resource departments of correctional agencies.

Human resource (HR) departments face significant challenges. First and foremost is the challenge resulting from the tremendous growth of correctional agencies in clients served and numbers of staff (as illustrated in Table 6-1). While the increase in the number of prison inmates receives the most attention, there has also been significant growth in the number of offenders under probation and postprison supervision. This growth in clients naturally requires an increase in the staff to oversee or supervise them. In most prisons, there is approximately one staff member for every three inmates. Therefore, as the inmate population grows, the number of staff also grows by about one-third of that number. Probation and parole caseloads often average 75–100 offenders for each officer, and staff numbers grow for community corrections as well. Human resource departments must recruit and hire this large number of staff to keep up with the growth in the number of offenders and successfully assimilate them into the correctional culture in which they will work.

After they are hired, new staff must be trained and prepared for taking over very difficult and potentially dangerous assignments. Corrections has a higher turnover rate than most jobs, and stability can be improved through sound training so that staff are confident and well prepared for the challenging jobs they will take on. And the rapid growth also requires that correctional staff be developed in a faster-than-normal pace, in order to be prepared to quickly assume supervisory and management functions. Correctional agencies must have effective performance evaluation systems to identify and improve staff weaknesses. There must be employee recognition programs to reward

Table 6-1
INCREASE IN THE ADULT CORRECTIONAL POPULATION, 1980–2008

	Number of persons under correctional supervision				
	Probation	Jail	Prison	Parole	Total[a]
1980	1,118,097	183,988	319,598	220,438	1,842,100
1981	1,225,934	196,785	360,029	225,539	2,008,300
1982	1,357,264	209,582	402,914	224,604	2,194,400
1983	1,582,947	223,551	423,898	246,440	2,476,800
1984	1,740,948	234,500	448,264	266,992	2,690,700
1985	1,968,712	256,615	487,593	300,203	3,013,100
1986	2,114,621	274,444	526,436	325,638	3,241,100
1987	2,247,158	295,873	562,814	355,505	3,461,400
1988	2,356,483	343,569	607,766	407,977	3,715,800
1989	2,522,125	395,553	683,367	456,803	4,057,800
1990	2,670,234	405,320	743,382	531,407	4,350,300
1991	2,728,472	426,479	792,535	590,442	4,537,900
1992	2,811,611	444,584	850,566	658,601	4,765,400
1993	2,903,061	459,804	909,381	676,100	4,948,300
1994	2,981,022	486,474	990,147	609,371	5,148,000
1995	3,077,861	507,044	1,078,542	679,421	5,342,900
1996	3,164,996	518,492	1,127,528	679,733	5,490,700
1997	3,296,513	567,079	1,176,564	694,787	5,734,900
1998	3,670,441	592,462	1,224,469	696,385	6,134,200
1999	3,779,922	605,943	1,287,172	714,457	6,340,800
2000	3,826,209	621,149	1,316,333	723,898	6,445,100
2001	3,931,731	631,240	1,330,007	732,333	6,581,700
2002	4,024,067	665,475	1,367,547	750,934	6,758,800
2003[b]	4,120,012	691,301	1,390,279	769,925	6,924,500
2004	4,143,792	713,990	1,421,345	771,852	6,995,000
2005	4,166,757	747,529	1,448,344	780,616	7,051,900
2006	4,215,361	765,819	1,492,973	799,875	7,182,100

(continued)

Table 6-1   Continued

	Number of persons under correctional supervision				
	Probation	Jail	Prison	Parole	Total
2007[c]	4,234,471	780,174	1,517,867	821,177	7,274,300
2008	4,270,917	785,556	1,518,559	828,169	7,308,200

Note: The jail and prison counts represent the custody populations, which refer to the number of inmates held in local jails or state and federal prisons, respectively. The custody population is not comparable to the jurisdiction population, which refers to the entity having legal authority regardless of where the inmate is held. For more details, see "Definitions" in *Prisoners in 2008* (PDF file 1.5M).

[a]Because some offenders have multiple statuses (i.e., held in a prison or jail but remain under the jurisdiction of a probation or parole authority) totals for 2007–08 exclude probationers and parolees held in jail or prison and parolees who were also on probation. Totals for 2005–06 exclude probationers and parolees held in jail or prison. Totals for 2000–04 only exclude probationers held in jail or prison. For these reasons, details do not sum to totals.

[b]The 2003 probation and parole counts were estimated and may differ from previously published counts.

[c]Some states were unable to provide data for 2007. See *Methodology* in Probation and Parole in the United States, 2007 - Statistical Tables (PDF file 355K) and Prisoners in 2007 (PDF file 195K). *Source*: Bureau of Justice Statistics, *Key Facts at a Glance*, available at www.bjs.ojp.usdoj.gov/content/glance/tables/corr2tab.cfm (accessed April 21, 2010).

outstanding performance and motivate employees to excellence. And there must be systems to fairly discipline staff for unethical behavior or inability to perform duties at an acceptable level.

Human resource departments also administer collective bargaining programs within correctional agencies. Although the percentage of manufacturing workers who are members of labor unions has been steadily declining, the percentage of public employees who are union members has been on the increase. Much of this increase is the result of the growth of criminal justice employees whose work environment is both stressful and dangerous. Other areas of responsibility for human resource departments involve maintaining diversity in the workforce and overseeing affirmative action and equal employment opportunity programs. The scope of activities in human resource departments is very broad, and the complexity of this work is increasing. This chapter presents the many facets and challenges facing correctional agencies as they recruit, hire, train, and develop their staff.

An Overview of the Growth in Correctional Staff

The number of offenders supervised by correctional agencies continues to grow. By the end of 2007, there were more than seven million offenders either in prison, in jail, or under supervision in the community. Table 6-1 illustrates the growth from 1980 until 2008, during which there was a 400 percent increase in the number of offenders under correctional supervision. While the largest percentage increases have come in the adult prison population, there has been significant growth in all segments of correctional populations. The number of prisons and jails has also increased. On December 30, 2005, there were 1,821 state and federal prisons and 3,300 jails in the United States.[1]

The number of staff employed by correctional agencies has also increased steadily over the past decade. On January 1, 1998, there were 413,318 employees in adult correctional agencies and another 57,317 employees in probation and parole agencies.[2] But by 2005, the *Bureau of Justice Statistics, Expenditure and Employment Extracts 2005* reported that there were 755,239 correctional staff working at the federal, state, and local levels in the United States.[3] And these figures do not include the privately operated correctional prisons, halfway houses, and social service agencies that provide assistance to offenders under correctional supervision.

The role of staff in correctional agencies is even more critical than the role of staff in most other government agencies or private companies. This is because of the mission of corrections. First, correctional agencies are responsible for protecting the public, and they do so by taking away or severely limiting offenders' freedoms. These two items are a serious responsibility. If correctional staff fail to effectively perform their duties, innocent citizens may suffer the consequences of becoming victims of crime. When correctional staff supervise inmates and take away their individual freedoms, they do so under the authority of law. Staff must be aware of their legal obligations in this regard and the high ethical standards expected of this responsibility.

In some jurisdictions, correctional staff are also sworn peace officers. In thirty-one of the fifty-one state or federal correctional agencies, probation or parole officers are given **peace officer status**. This status affords correctional staff the authority to carry weapons when off duty and to make arrests. With this status comes the additional requirement to carry out these duties in a fair and impartial manner, and to do so in a manner that maintains safety for the community. Carrying a weapon is a tremendous responsibility, and it requires good judgment and respect for authority. When sworn peace officers are granted the authority of law to use deadly weapons, it is incumbent on the persons who commission this authority to ensure the individuals have both the training and the mental preparation to carry out this duty responsibly.

Another point that makes the role of correctional workers difficult is that, although there are many policies and procedures, there is also considerable personal discretion that accompanies the performance of duties. Policy statements explain the agency mission, goals, and standards expected of agency operations. Procedures are standardized methods for carrying out the agency policy. However, policy and procedure cannot address every situation that correctional staff encounter. Staff use policy and procedure as guidelines and principles to follow when they are confronted with new situations that require the use of individual, professional judgment. It is much easier to train employees on the techniques and steps required to carry out job duties than to create an understanding of principles and the effective use of them to guide actions under a variety of unanticipated situations. And finally, correctional staff must be flexible and able to deal with change. Many forces within corrections (new types of offenders, new laws, external pressures to change policy, and new technology) bring about change in operations and procedures. Correctional staff must be able to incorporate these changes into their own roles and responsibilities.

Human resource management is complicated by the growth of corrections and the issues they face that may not totally be within their control. The functions of human resource staff are not simply performing bureaucratic duties to recruit, hire, and fire staff. They are also charged with finding high-quality individuals, encouraging them to consider corrections as a career, training them in the competencies required, and developing employees to conform to the agency mission and goals. As such, they must recruit individuals with the proper background and maturity for correctional work. They must train staff to capably perform standardized procedures and to consider agency ethics and principles as they use their own judgments to perform day-to-day activities. They must also help staff develop by increasing their skills and preparing them to take on greater responsibilities.

Correctional Systems and Subsystems

In terms of human resource management, corrections has many systems and subsystems. The two major categories of correctional agencies are institutions and community corrections. There are two types of correctional institutions: jails and prisons. The majority of jail inmates are pretrial offenders who are being held without bond until their trial. Jails also hold misdemeanor offenders and minor felons who are serving short jail terms as the punishment for their crimes. Prisons almost exclusively house more serious felons who are serving a year or more as a criminal sanction. Even with these differences, jails and prisons have similar staffing patterns and similar human resource management processes.

Community corrections includes probation and parole agencies, as well as halfway houses and other agencies that administer community sanctions, such as house arrest (often using electronic monitoring), intensive probation, community service programs, or other intermediate sanctions. Some probation and parole agencies are historically public, halfway houses and other community providers are usually private or not-for-profit agencies. The categories of staff needed for these diverse agencies often vary considerably.

Prisons and jails both have a large portion of their workforce categorized as correctional officers. In 2005, there were 295,261 correctional officers working in state and federal prisons in the United States,[4] and correctional officers and supervisors are approximately two-thirds of all staff in state and federal prisons. A large majority of correctional officers in state prisons (74 percent) are male.[5] And the growth of the inmate population creates a challenge for correctional officers, for example, between 2000 and 2005, the number of inmates grew at a faster rate than the number of correctional officers, and the ratio of inmates to correctional officers increased from 4.8 to 1 in 2000 to 5.1 to 1 in 2005.[6]

The job of a correctional officer is a challenging one and human resource staff must keep the role in mind as they recruit and train individuals into these roles. Correctional officers basically assist in the accomplishment of the mission of a jail or prison by maintaining control and order. They are responsible for constant supervision of inmates and implementation of security procedures. Their world is both highly technical in that they must be very routine and precise in following prescribed security procedures and highly interactive in that they must continuously communicate with inmates.

Officers have to accept change and have a variety of expectations placed on them. Their bosses expect them to be exact in performing their security duties, while being professional in their interaction with inmates. Their peers expect them to support them and not show weakness in performing their job and supervising inmates. And inmates expect them to be fair and consistent and not hassle them for minor things they don't think are important. Prout and Ross write, "The most successful [correctional officers] have a genuine interest in their work and a real desire to serve the needs of the correctional system, on the one hand, and the requirements of the inmates on the other. . . . They recognize the social and political position of the prison in the larger society beyond the prison walls."[7]

Being professional as a correctional officer is extremely important, and much has changed in the perception of the role over the past few decades. Previously, most correctional agencies and the general public used the term *guard* for the prison or jail staff who did security work. However, with the movement toward professionalism in correctional agencies and the realization that correctional security staff do much more than "guard" inmates, the term **correctional officer** became more commonly used. The term *correctional officer* more accurately conveys the many activities (security, interacting with inmates, monitoring standards, and recommending improvements in procedures) required of correctional staff who perform security duties in a prison or jail. Today, the term *guard* is considered as derogatory; however, it is still regularly used by the media and the public when describing prison or jail security staff.

Other prison and jail staff positions include support (maintenance, business office, or medical) and treatment (mental health, education, or counseling professionals) staff. These groups vary in terms of the types of experience and education required. Some of these professions require graduate degrees, yet others are entry-level positions. Teachers and counselors must be certified in their specialty area. Business office staff usually need accounting degrees and background, while medical personnel require the same types of preparation as a physician's office or hospital. And maintenance workers often must have a background and sometimes a license in areas such as plumbing, electrical, or building maintenance.

Since 1975 the number of offenders under community supervision has risen from less than 1 million to nearly 5.1 million by 2008, of which 4,270,917 were on probation, 828,169 were on parole, and only 2,304,115 in jail or prison.[8] Therefore, the greatest number of correctional staff work for community correctional agencies. Today, probation in the United States is a federal, state, and local activity administered by more than 2,000 separate agencies. Although probation began as a service to the courts, today, in all but eleven of the states, adult probation is located in the executive branch of government, and in more than half of the states, probation operations are a part of the state department of corrections. In approximately eight states and the federal government, probation and parole services are provided by the same state agency that supervises both probationers and parolees.

Parole and probation officers play a variety of roles for their agencies. First and foremost, they supervise offenders in the community, ensuring that offenders meet the requirements of their supervision. Second, they conduct investigations. Probation officers do presentence investigations for the sentencing courts, and parole officers investigate prospective release plans for inmates. Finally, officers assist in the operation of other community correctional programs. They may supervise intensive probation or parole caseloads, or they may be assigned special caseloads, consisting only of offenders with drug abuse problems, mental problems, or those with a history of sex offenses. Parole and probation officers are also often responsible for collecting financial sanctions, such as offender restitution and victim compensation. They may also be required to monitor offenders under house arrest, sometimes using electronic monitoring.

Professionalism and Corrections

Over the past several decades, corrections has taken many steps to be recognized as a profession by incorporating several facets ascribed to a "profession." Organizational components associated with a profession include (1) a systematic body of theoretical knowledge acquired through lengthy academic study and not possessed by those outside the profession, (2) community interests rather than self-interest as a motivator of professional behavior, (3) self-regulation, and (4) a system of rewards.[9] In each of these components, corrections has made progressive strides to be recognized as a profession.

First, although not all correctional jobs require "lengthy academic study," corrections certainly does have its own body of theoretical knowledge that is acquired through either experience or academic study, and is not possessed by those outside the profession. As already noted , there are many positions in correctional agencies that do require an undergraduate degree, professional education beyond the baccalaureate, or a specific license or certification. And a few correctional agencies such as the Federal Bureau of Prisons require candidates for correctional officer positions to have either a four-year college degree or two years' experience working in a correctional or law enforcement setting. In addition, while not required, the **American Correctional Association (ACA)** has certification processes available for correctional officers, managers, and executives. This certification requires study and successfully passing an examination.

There continues to be a developing body of knowledge for the field of corrections. Over the past thirty years, there have been a number of professional journals, research reports, and monographs published regarding the practice of corrections. In describing the development of a body of knowledge for corrections, Williamson writes, "The support provided by the Law Enforcement Assistance Administration (LEAA), which began in 1968, was a primary contributor to a significant increase in research and expansion of the theoretical knowledge base."[10]

There is no question that correctional staff operate for "community" rather than "self" interest. Salaries for correctional workers are often less than for positions requiring like-experience or education. Correctional work is stressful and can be dangerous. Therefore, correctional staff must be motivated by public service, or by work in a helping profession, rather than by personal financial gain. Researchers have found that correctional staff are similar to other law enforcement personnel, who want to help their fellow citizens, and do work that is difficult, yet they recognize that it contributes to the public good.[11] With the continued growth and visibility in corrections, more staff not ordinarily interested in correctional work (psychologists, teachers, medical personnel, attorneys, and the clergy) have opted for correctional employment.

In the early 1970s, corrections also made a strong push to improve its ability to self-regulate and be considered a profession. In the 1970s, the American Correctional Association created the Commission of Accreditation for Corrections (CAC) and a process whereby facilities and agencies can be accredited against a set of professional standards that are updated regularly through review by a select group of practicing professionals. Agencies may apply for consideration and, after extensive auditing and on-site visits, may be accredited by the CAC. The first accreditation audits were completed in 1978. Through the development of standards and self-review of compliance, correctional agencies meet the component of being "self-regulating." According to the ACA, the purpose of this process is

> to promote improvement in the management of correctional agencies through the administration of a voluntary accreditation program and the ongoing development and revision of relevant, useful standards. . . . The recognized benefits from such a process include improved management, a defense against lawsuits through documentation and the demonstration of a "good faith" effort to improve conditions of confinement, increased accountability and enhanced public credibility for administrative and line staff, a safer and more human environment for personnel and offenders, and the establishment of measurable criteria for upgrading programs, personnel, and physical plant on a continuing basis.[12]

Part of being self-regulating involves having a professional code of ethics. The ACA adopted a code of ethics at the 105th Congress of Corrections in 1975 and updated it in 1994. The ACA Code of Ethics (see Figure 6-1) is a guideline for correctional professionals in terms of accepted behavior. However, unlike other associations (the American Medical Association or the American Bar Association), which certify individuals and can impose sanctions against them for violating the professional standards, the ACA neither certifies nor imposes sanctions. Discipline for unprofessional conduct (discussed later in this chapter) is the prerogative of the agency that employs the staff member.

Finally, professions provide a system of rewards. Without an organization that "certifies" individual correctional professionals, there is no recognition for reaching certain levels of competence as there is in the legal and medical professions. However, there is recognition of correctional agencies and organizations through the accreditation process. Agencies that meet the accreditation standards often use this recognition as a defense to inmate lawsuits, and find accreditation helpful in explaining to their political oversight groups and legislative funding committees why certain functions and operations are important. In 2009, ACA listed eighty-nine affiliated professional organizations (see Figure 6-2).[13]

ACA Code Of Ethics

Preamble

The American correctional Association expects of its members unfailing honesty, respect for the dignity and individuality of human beings and a commitment to professional and compassionate service. To this end, we subscribe to the following principles.

1. Members shall respect and protect the civil and legal rights of all individuals.
2. Members shall treat every professional situation with concern for the welfare of the individuals involved and with no intent to personal gain.
3. Members shall maintain relationships with colleagues to promote mutual respect within the profession and improve the quality of service.
4. Members shall make public criticism of their colleagues or their agencies only when warranted, verifiable, and constructive.
5. Members shall respect the importance of all disciplines within the criminal justice system and work to improve cooperation with each segment.
6. Members shall honor the public's right to information and share information with the public to the extent permitted by law subject to individuals' right to privacy.
7. Members shall respect and protect the right of the public to be safeguarded from criminal activity.
8. Members shall refrain from using their positions to secure personal privileges or advantages.
9. Members shall refrain from allowing personal interest to impair objectivity in the performance of duty while acting in an official capacity.
10. Members shall refrain from entering into any formal or informal activity or agreement which presents a conflict or interest or is inconsistent with the conscientious performance of duties.
11. Members shall refrain from accepting any gifts, services, or favors that is or appears to be improper or implies an obligation inconsistent with the free and objective exercise of professional duties.
12. Members shall clearly differentiate between personal views/statements and views/statements/positions made on behalf of the agency or Association.
13. Members shall report to appropriate authorities any corrupt or unethical behaviors in which there is sufficient evidence to justify review.
14. Members shall refrain from discriminating against any individual because of race, gender, creed, national origin, religious affiliation, age, disability, or any other type of prohibited discrimination.
15. Members shall preserve the integrity of private information; they shall refrain from seeking information on individuals beyond that which is necessary to implement responsibilities and perform their duties; members shall refrain from revealing nonpublic information unless expressly authorized to do so.
16. Members shall make all appointments, promotions, and dismissals in accordance with established civil servicerules, applicable contract agreements, and individual merit, rather than furtherance of personal interests.
17. Members shall respect, promote, and contribute to a work place that is safe, healthy, and free of harassment in any form.

Adopted by the Board of Governors and Delegate Assembly in August 1994.

Figure 6-1
Code of ethics of the American correctional association.
Source: American Correctional Association, *Code of Ethics* (Alexandria, VA: American Correctional Association), http://www.aca.org/pastpresentfuture/ethics.asp (accessed April 8, 2010).

DUAL MEMBERSHIP CHAPTERS

Dual-Membership Chapters of American Correctional Association.

- Arizona Probation, Parole and Corrections Association
- Colorado Criminal Justice Association
- Connecticut Criminal Justice Association
- Correctional Association of Massachusetts
- Department of Corrections and Rehabilitation of Puerto Rico Chapter of the American Correctional Association
- District of Columbia Criminal Justice Association
- Hawaii Criminal Justice Association
- Illinois Correctional Association
- Indiana Correctional Association
- Iowa Correctional Association
- Jamaica Federation of Correctional Officers
- Kansas Correctional Association
- Louisiana Correctional Association
- Maryland Criminal Justice Association
- Michigan Corrections Association
- Missouri Corrections Association
- Nebraska Correctional Association
- Nevada Correctional Association
- New Jersey Chapter Association
- New Mexico Criminal Justice Association
- New York Corrections and Youth Services Association
- North Carolina Correctional Association
- Ohio Correctional and Court Services Association
- Oklahoma Correctional Association
- South Carolina Correctional Association
- Virginia Correctional Association
- Washington Correctional Association
- Wisconsin Correctional Association

PROFESSIONAL AFFILIATES

Professional Affiliates are national or international organizations that represent a major professional discipline engaged in corrections or a related field.

- Alston Wilkes Society
- American Association for Correctional Psychology
- American Correctional Chaplains Association
- Association of Correctional Food Service Affiliates
- American Correctional Health Services Association
- American Institute of Architects
- American Jail Association
- American Probation and Parole Association
- Association for Correctional Research and Information Management
- Association of Paroling Authorities International
- Association of State Correctional Administrators

Figure 6-2

ACA dual membership and affiliated professional associations.

Source: American Correctional Association, *Membership Chapters,* available at www.aca. org/membership/chapters.asp (accessed April 25, 2010).

- Association of Women Executives in Corrections
- Association on Programs for Female Offenders
- Correctional Accreditation Managers Association
- Correctional Education Association
- Council of Juvenile Correctional Administrators
- Family and Corrections Network
- Historical Association for Corrections
- International Association of Correctional Officers
- International Association of Correctional Training Personnel
- International Community Corrections Association
- International Correctional Arts Network
- International Correctional & Prisons Association
- Juvenile Justice Trainers Association
- National Association of Adult and Juvenile State Corrections Mental Health Directors
- National Association of Blacks in Criminal Justice
- National Association of Juvenile Correctional Agencies
- National Association of Probation Executives
- National Correctional Industries Association
- National Council on Crime and Delinquency
- National Organization of Hispanics in Criminal Justice
- National Juvenile Detention Association
- National Major Gang Task Force
- North American Association of Wardens and Superintendents
- Parole and Probation Compact Administrators Association
- Prison Fellowship
- The Salvation Army
- Volunteers of America

GEOGRAPHICAL AFFILIATES

Geographical Affiliates are organizations that represent all disciplines engaged in corrections, or a closely related field, within a local geographical location.

- Caribbean Correctional Association
- Integrated Correctional Association of the Philippines (ICAP) Inc.
- Middle Atlantic States Correctional Association
- Southern States Correctional Association
- Western Correctional Association

STATE AFFILIATES

State Affiliates are organizations that represent the entire continuum of corrections within a state of the United States, a province of Canada, or a similar formal territorial jurisdiction in another country.

- Alabama Council on Crime and Delinquency
- California Probation, Parole, and Correctional Association
- Florida Council on Crime and Delinquency
- Kentucky Council on Crime and Delinquency
- Minnesota Corrections Association
- Oregon Criminal Justice Association
- Pennsylvania Association on Probation, Parole and Corrections
- Tennessee Correctional Association
- Texas Corrections Association
- Utah Correctional Association

Figure 6-2 Continued

STUDENT CHAPTERS AND AFFILIATES

- Appalachian Student Chapter of the American Correctional Association
- Central Missouri State University Student Chapter of ACA
- Eastern Kentucky University Corrections and Juvenile Justice Student
- Moraine Park Technical College Corrections Club
- Northern Illinois University Academic Justice Association
- Pierce College Criminal Justice Club
- Richmond Community College Student Chapters of ACA
- St. Augustine College Student Chapter of the ACA

Figure 6-2 Continued

These organizations also recognize and give awards to agencies and individuals for noteworthy performance.

The movement to professionalize corrections is important to the focus and goals of human resource management. Employees should "join" the profession and commit to it as their life's work. Through the entire process of human resource management (recruitment, staff development, retention, rewards, and recognition), there is an emphasis on hiring staff committed to a career in corrections and developing them to contribute fully to the enhancement of their chosen profession. Critical to success is the fact that staff must believe they have ownership in their careers. Ownership can be developed through the following four important steps:

1. Allow people to work on important issues.
2. Trust their judgment and provide them with the freedom to do their jobs.
3. Give praise and recognition.
4. Build relationships for people, connecting them to sources of power and resources and to opportunities to learn and develop.[14]

The following sections of this chapter illustrate how human resource management attempts to guide staff through their careers, while building ownership, commitment, and competence.

Recruitment, Hiring, and Retention of Correctional Staff

Recruiting is simply the process used to attract candidates with skills and background that match competencies needed for the job you are trying to fill, and is the "lifeblood" of corrections. There are never enough candidates for correctional jobs that just walk in off the street and apply. Therefore, it is critical that correctional agencies identify the types of employees they want and target locations and methods to communicate with potential candidates that have the skills and backgrounds that are desired. It is impossible to reach the level of professionalism and excellence in managing correctional agencies if the available pool of applicants to hire does not have the requisite experience, education, attitude, motivation, and commitment to work in the difficult environment of institutional or community corrections.

Recruitment of correctional staff has improved considerably over the past thirty years. Previously, correctional agency recruitment was all too often like the following situation:

> Massachusetts in the 1970s had a depressed economy with high unemployment. At the same time, the Massachusetts prison system had a high turnover rate among officers and a chronic need for new officers. Yet the Massachusetts Department of Correction was hard pressed to fill each new training class with recruits. The waiting list of applicants to police and fire departments were years long, while corrections with its similar salary and benefits was in reality a "walk-in" job. Screening and selection were largely limited to investigation of possible criminal records of applicants. So haphazard was the system that the correction officer exam was not even given for six years. The prison officer recruit was largely self-selected.[15]

In the Massachusetts description, there was little actual recruitment occurring. The most common way a new employee was recruited was through encouragement by relatives or friends who were already employed, and "recruitment in these cases was often casual in nature."[16] There was no plan by which characteristics of successful employees were identified, organizational needs considered, and an aggressive recruitment effort implemented. As a result, most correctional agencies ended up hiring new employees with little experience, academic training, or diversity. As the review of Massachusetts correctional hiring reported, "Most of the Massachusetts recruits who were a part of this study were young, white men who had no formal education beyond high school and who had a history of blue-collar employment."[17]

Recruitment by correctional agencies has become much more sophisticated. Prompted by problems of high turnover and the challenge of a growing workforce, correctional agencies began to invest in quality recruitment material, make targeted recruitment trips and participate in job fairs, and screen candidates against the qualities identified as desirable for employees. Corrections, first and foremost, needs individuals with excellent interpersonal skills and an ability and interest in working with others. Even entry-level staff must make numerous decisions during a daily shift, and therefore, good judgment and decision-making skills are critical. Finally, although staff should not be overly empathetic to the problems of offenders, they should not have a bias against offenders, minorities, or people with different backgrounds from their own.

To recruit a professional workforce into corrections requires what is referred to as "relationship-based recruiting." This means identifying places to find potential recruits, going to those locations, and talking one-on-one or to small groups. As noted by Baker and Carrera, "Recruiting for correctional facilities is unique because of the stigma and false information associated with such employment."[18] Correctional recruiting requires breaking stereotypes and educating people about the realities of working in a prison, jail, or community corrections environment. And there are many positive factors that can be reinforced about correctional work. In a recent survey of jail employees, primary reasons people accepted their job included job security (67 percent) and salary and benefit packages (62 percent), and these are often strong points for working in corrections.[19]

There are several rich targets for recruiting future correctional workers. First, the military is a significant recruitment opportunity, as individuals leaving the military make outstanding correctional workers. Their history of working in large organizations with a clear chain of command and being on a team with a diverse group of individuals, and having a focus on accomplishing the organization mission makes the career transition to corrections fairly easy. Second, correctional agencies recruit from both public and private social service agencies. Many staff with this type of work background have knowledge of community resources and have worked with disadvantaged clients with a variety of needs.

Correctional agencies also successfully recruit from community and four-year colleges. One of the fastest growing college majors is criminal justice, and with this course of study, graduates understand the way correctional systems are organized to meet their mission and roles. Probation and parole agencies regularly recruit candidates for parole and probation officer positions from college campuses. Prisons now recruit college graduates for entry-level correctional officer jobs. Some college graduates have the perception that correctional officer jobs are "below" their educational accomplishments. However, as they learn more during the recruitment process, they often understand how working as a correctional officer is excellent experience for developing skills in security and managing inmates. These proficiencies are an important foundation for success in other corrections jobs that the individual may later acquire.

Even with the more sophisticated approach to recruitment, the most effective recruitment is still by referral of current employees. Correctional administrators hope and expect that their employees would be good ambassadors and encourage friends and associates to apply at the agency. But even this "informal" recruitment must be done properly. Employees need to be educated as to the type of people the agency desires, they need to know the minimum qualifications, and they need to be able to explain and "sell" the prospect of working in corrections. Etter suggests that while most correctional employees do not see themselves as salespeople, when recruiting, that is exactly what they are doing. He writes that "You are selling your customers (potential applicants) on your job and on your jail as a good place to work."[20] Yet, you also cannot oversell. Osborne describes the need to be consistent in the message, and "Inform them on what your agency's requirements are and what it can offer. Don't sell them a bill of goods that you cannot deliver."[21]

The Hiring Process

The goal of recruiting is to generate a large pool of qualified applicants. From this pool, human resource staff then screen applicants to find those best qualified and

A job fair for a new prison. Although recruiting the right people is sometimes a challenge, in today's economic climate, there are often plenty of applicants. Here is a picture of the crowd filling out applications for the opening of a new prison.

(Courtesy of the Ohio Department of Rehabilitation and Corrections)

suited for correctional employment. Agencies identify the characteristics important to success and then create a screening process to rate applicants' abilities on these areas. For instance, following are examples of skills needed to be a successful correctional officer:

- Good interpersonal skills (both oral and written)
- Ability to make sound decisions
- Lack of prejudice toward criminal offenders
- Understanding of the need to treat each client and inmate in a fair and consistent manner
- Ability to "think on one's feet"
- Ability to supervise others
- Good presentation of self

To identify applicants' abilities in these areas, several screening and rating mechanisms have been instituted. First, a candidate for employment must complete a fairly extensive application, which includes past educational, military, and job experience. In some agencies, the previously listed skills are included on the application, and candidates are requested to provide examples of past experiences that are indicative of these abilities and traits. Government correctional agencies are required to use a competitive hiring process. To ensure all candidates receive equal consideration, their applications are scored anonymously, and the candidates with the highest scores are considered first for employment.

Many public agencies require hiring through a process called the rule of three. The hiring organization (a state prison, for instance) will receive the names of the three highest rated candidates. They then complete the interview and screening process on these three, and hire the one they determine best meets their needs. They will not even be allowed to consider other than these three applicants unless one is later determined to be "unqualified," rather than simply "not liked." The rule of three assists in providing fairness and objectivity in hiring. If an organization was allowed to consider anyone who met minimum standards, preferential treatment would more likely result, and agencies might end up hiring less qualified candidates. The rule of three ensures that the most qualified candidates receive the best opportunities for employment.

After identifying the best group of candidates from their applications, screening usually includes a personal interview, review of a writing sample, and an interview to determine integrity concerns. In the personal interview, interviewers ask candidates questions that allow them to be rated on each of the important skills. Interviewers often try to put candidates in stressful situations to see how they approach and handle a correctional situation. As an example, interviewers may ask candidates if they would tell their supervisor if another staff member was showing preferential treatment toward one inmate. Candidates are often required to provide a writing sample, which is scored both on the ability to communicate in writing and on the judgment shown in the situation they have to describe.

Staff who work in corrections are continually confronted with the opportunity to benefit personally from giving offenders favored treatment, either by allowing them something they should not have, granting them additional privileges, or smuggle contraband into a prison or jail. For that reason, agencies do criminal and sometimes financial background checks. The **integrity interview** is a relatively new process in correctional agency screening of candidates. Integrity interviews seek information such as financial difficulty, current drug or alcohol abuse, or other conditions that could put a correctional worker into a compromising situation. Agencies follow guidelines for the types of integrity issues (recent drug use, arrests for a felony, recent termination from another job, and financial problems) that disqualify a candidate for employment.

After these screening processes, the candidate rated the highest is usually offered employment, although it is usually a "conditional offer," contingent on their passing a physical examination, passing a test for drug use, or completing mandatory training. Over the past decade, more agencies are requiring candidates for employment to take a test to determine recent drug use. Almost all correctional agencies now require correctional staff to pass a drug test before hiring. If candidates pass the physical exam and the drug screening, they are officially hired and a date is set to begin their employment.

Problems of Retention

Turnover of staff is a problem for all correctional agencies. A 2003 survey by the ACA found that the average national turnover of correctional officers was 16.1 percent, and noncompetitive compensation was the most frequently cited reason for recruitment difficulty and the second most cited reason for retention. Demanding work hours, stress and burnout, and employees not understanding and finding they were not suited for the job were other factors in turnover.[22] Another reason for high turnover rate is the stressful and dangerous nature of correctional jobs. Both institution and community correctional workers must work with difficult clients and (even though the incidents are infrequent) risk assault and potential serious injury.

To reduce turnover, many correctional agencies are identifying and addressing the most serious issues to retention and the recession and rising unemployment rates are making more people consider working as a correctional, probation, or parole officer. Salary is consistently cited as a reason for turnover. In recent years, Delaware, Louisiana, North Dakota, Vermont, Virginia, and West Virginia have raised pay for correctional officers to make them more comparable to law enforcement officers. Delaware reported that after raising pay by 18 percent in 2006, their vacancy rate was the lowest in five years.[23] The state of Alaska is attempting to improve hiring practices by shortening the time it takes to hire, as they have discovered that they lost many qualified candidates because of the long lag time between application and hiring. Correctional Commissioner Marc Antrim noted that "The goal is to keep the hiring process to no more than 60 days . . . a successful applicant generally should be able to walk in for their first day of work within 60 days of applying for the job."[24] In 2008, the Texas prison system increased correctional officer starting pay by 10 percent to just over $25,000 and within six months officers are paid approximately $28,500. In addition, in 2009, Texas also provided a $1,500 recruiting bonus if an applicant agrees to work at one of four designated understaffed correctional institutions.

The way correctional agencies are improving recruitment and retention is positively changing the culture of their organizations. In a case study of Florida and Pennsylvania departments of corrections, it was noted that assessing and enhancing the workplace could reduce staff turnover.[25] And Corrections Corporation of America, the largest private prison company with over 17,000 staff, conducted interviews with staff to determine workplace satisfaction, and identified that the way correctional officers were treated by their first-line supervisors had a major impact on turnover. As a result, the company implemented a values-based training program for supervisors and has seen their retention rates improve as a result.[26]

Retention can also be improved by enhancing the confidence of staff in their ability to do the job. One suggested approach to reduce turnover is to improve the on-the-job training (OJT) that usually occurs as a part of the training for new employees. In addition to several days or weeks of classroom training, most correctional agencies provide some OJT to give new employees the chance to do the job with another experienced employee. However, OJT programs are often unsuccessful and do not contribute (and even may hurt) to improved employee performance and turnover. This was addressed as Ohio developed a structure OJT program for specific job classifications. The six-step process they put together models a National Institute of Corrections program to better equip correctional officers to perform their duties. The Ohio OJT program includes a formal process by which the trainee watches an element of a job, and then performs it under the supervision of a mentor/coach who offers feedback and suggestions. At the time the program was implemented in 2005, the agency turnover rate was 37 percent, but decreased over the next 3 years by 16 percent.[27]

In an article in *Corrections Today* discussing strategies to recruit and retain correctional employees, McVey and McVey suggest two other practices that can positively affect retention.[28] The first is to streamline hiring practices. Government bureaucracies often take unneeded time to meet requirements of the civil service system, military preferences, EEO, union agreements, and other hiring inefficiencies. Many very qualified candidates will not wait for these and take other jobs before the process is complete. And the second is to increase the flexibility of work schedules, shifts, job sharing, part-time employment, and accommodating special family needs. While these are not always possible, and many correctional agencies are unwilling to even consider them, they present a great opportunity to increase the potential pool of employees and respond to the needs of current employees.

Although recruitment and retention are improving among many correctional agencies as a result of thoughtful improvements in pay, culture, and working conditions, perhaps the biggest impact on reduced turnover is the recession. With severe economic times comes layoffs and high unemployment. During these times, individuals look for what they consider to be more stable employers, and correctional agencies are perceived to be "recession proof." And many workers are putting off retirement due to the economy and staying in the correctional workforce.[29] What remains to be seen is whether the improvements made by these agencies will help in retaining employees as the economy improves and jobs in noncorrectional agencies are again available.

Training and Developing Correctional Staff

As new employees are hired by correctional agencies, the first and perhaps most critical activity is to provide them with "basic" training and to prepare them to perform their assigned duties. Basic training is designed to accomplish two major goals: to develop skills needed to effectively do the job for which they were hired, and to instill the organization culture and expectations into them. Neither of these goals is a simple task. Correctional workers perform such a diverse range of functions, that basic training must be very broad to cover all the types of required activities. Correctional workers also come from various backgrounds, and melding them into a unit with an understanding of purpose and culture is a difficult challenge.

Staff training continues throughout the careers of employees. Even if employees never change jobs, there are changing techniques, legal requirements, changing offender population, and external pressures that require staff skills and knowledge be continuously upgraded. Very few, however, correctional workers stay in the same job throughout their careers. Most receive promotions, and move up in their organization by accepting more responsibility or becoming supervisors. Others change job roles and move from one function to another (e.g., prison security to casework or probation officer to administrator). These career progressions also require retraining and the development of new skills.

Correctional training takes many forms. Basic training takes place within the first few weeks of hiring (during the employees probationary period) and is designed to provide the basic skills necessary for correctional work. In-service training takes place on the job and is designed to improve skills in the particular work area assigned to the employee. Developmental training can occur at any time in an employee's career in corrections and prepares the employee to progress into another function or area of responsibility. Specialty training can add to an employee's skills, either in general correctional practices or in very specific duties performed in addition to the employee's regular duties. The following sections describe all four of these areas of correctional training.

Basic Correctional Training

As noted, **basic training** both develops skills for job performance and instills the organizational culture in new employees. Whether hired into probation or correctional officer role, certain technical skills are required. Table 6-2 lists the curriculum for the Federal Bureau of Prisons basic training provided at the Federal Law Enforcement Training Center in Glynco, Georgia. After a one- to two-week institution familiarization training period, new employees attend the Introduction to Correctional Techniques training for three weeks at Glynco. These two training courses cover *technical* skills as diverse as firearms use, emergency communication devices, controlling inmate use of tools, and supervising inmate visits. There are also several topics of study that help develop the *human* skills necessary in a prison environment. These include stress management, communication skills for correctional workers, and avoiding problems with routine orders and requests. Finally, there are courses that help instill the agency *culture* into new recruits, which cover the mission of the Bureau of Prisons, the history of the Bureau of Prisons, and managing diversity.

Table 6-2
TOPICS AND HOURS IN THE FEDERAL BUREAU OF PRISONS BASIC TRAINING COURSE

Topics	Hours
Administrative processing	6 1/2
Affirmative action	1/2
Introduction to the Bureau of Prisons (BOP)	1
Mission of the BOP	1
Legal and ethical issues	1
Employee conduct and responsibility	1
Role of the employees' club	1/2
Tour of prison	2
Glynco preparation	1
Organization of institutions	1
Inmate programs	2
On-the-job training (OJT)	8 1/2
Individual personal protection	1
Logs, memos, and incident reports	1
Daily safety and security checks	1
Emergency communication devices	1
Review of disturbance plan	1
Disturbance control program	2
Use of fire extinguisher and hoses	1
Use of restraints	3 1/2
Key control and use	1 1/2
Staff library	1
Use of force	1 1/2
Monitoring inmate mail	1
OJT—living unit	1
Supervisor's responsibility	1
Escorting inmates	1/2
Controlling inmate use of tools	1/2
Correctional officers and the control center	1/2
Control center observation	1/2

(continued)

Table 6-2   Continued

Topics	Hours
Orientation to religious services	1
Self-study test	1 1/2
Identifying and accounting for contraband	2
Drug and alcohol testing and phone monitoring	1 1/2
Metal detection devices	1
Administering the pass system	1 1/2
BOP hostage policy	1
Incident reports performance tests	1
Self-study	1
Managing diversity	1
Employee assistance program and suicide prevention	1
Orientation to prison industries	1
Orientation to the labor union	1
Communicable diseases	1
Basic first aid	1 1/2
CPR training	1 1/2
Conducting pat searches	1
Conducting visual searches	1
Conducting area searches	2
Inmate counts and accountability	3
OJT—observing count	1
Computer training	3

The Bureau of Prisons and many states take a general view of basic training focused on developing "correctional workers," and all employees (not just correctional officers) attend the same basic training program. The **correctional worker concept** recognizes all employees as the same, regardless of their job specialty as correctional officer, secretary, nurse, plumber, or any other role. All prison and jail staff perform similar functions of security, inmate supervision, self-defense, and disturbance control and are trained in how to search an area or inmate, how to control contraband, how to enforce the inmate disciplinary system, and how to manage a hostile and aggressive inmate. With the correctional worker concept, there is no separation of staff into treatment, operations, or custody, and this contributes to a feeling of one team working to complete the same mission. Some jurisdictions provide a short training session for all employees except correctional officers, as they believe that correctional officers have the most inmate contact and are primarily responsible for the security of the prison and enforcement of institution rules.

Introductory or basic training ranges from 40 hours to 400 or more hours, with an average of 232 hours of introductory training among the 42 state and federal correctional agencies included in a recent survey.[30] The introductory training includes both classroom and on-the-job training. The difference between those states with the lowest hours of introductory and those with the highest hours is usually based on the philosophy of when the employee is believed to be ready to perform correctional duties. The lower number of hours accepts the employees' familiarization with duties and then assigns them to a correctional post to do the job as they continue to learn and become proficient with their duties. These employees often receive closer supervision during the first few weeks on the job. The agencies with the highest number of hours do not assign employees to a post until they become proficient with duties to be performed.

Training for probation and parole officers is similar in that it may be a combination of classroom and on-the-job training. In some cases, the training for probation and parole officers is very similar to basic training for prison staff, because the human relations requirements and skills are very similar, and the need for self-defense and dealing with hostile clients is necessary in the community as well as in prison. Table 6-3 presents an outline of a basic curriculum for the Missouri Board of Probation and Parole. The first

---

Table 6-3
TRAINING TOPICS FOR PROBATION AND PAROLE OFFICERS, MISSOURI DEPARTMENT OF CORRECTIONS

Phase I: Taught to all Missouri Department of Corrections employees

	Course	Hours
Week 1	Overview of the criminal justice system	4
	The profession of corrections	8
	Restorative justice	4
	MoDOC response to substance abuse	4
	Stress management	3
	Conflict resolution through communication	4
	Gender and sexual harassment issues	6
Week 2	Managing diversity	6
	Verbal judo	16
	Infectious diseases	2
	Constitutional law in corrections	10

(continued)

Table 6-3   Continued

Phase II: Taught only to probation and parole staff (a separate training program is available for all other MoDOC employees)

	Course	Hours
Week 3	Vision, values, and principles	1
	Offender rights and restrictions	3
	Confidentiality	1
	Cognitive restructuring	4
	Reality therapy	12
	Sex offender	12
Week 4	Interview and assessment process	6
	Presentence investigation	8
	Supervision strategies and community corrections tracking	4
	Substance abuse	12
	Education, vocation, and employment	4
Week 5	Domestic violence	6
	Case summary	4
	Mental health	4
	Violation process	8
	Interstate compact	2
	Parole policy	6
	Institutional reports	3
	Time management	1

Phase III: Safety Training (for probation and parole officers who choose to carry a weapon)

	Course	Hours
Week 6	Use of force	8
	Safety awareness	4
	Pepper spray	2
	Physical safety skills	16
	*Introduction to firearms	30 minutes

Source: Eastern Regional Human Resource Center, Missouri Department of Corrections (Park Hill, Missouri, August 2000).
*Developed for correctional service trainees (CST), the entry-level position for probation and parole officers, this class provides information regarding carrying a weapon.

two weeks (Phase I) are provided jointly to prison and community corrections employees and covers topics such as an overview of the criminal justice system, the profession of corrections, stress management, conflict resolution, managing diversity, verbal judo, and constitutional law. Phase II is specifically for new probation and parole officers, providing them skills in interview and assessment, presentence investigations, supervision and community tracking, managing substance abusers, violating offenders, writing reports, and time management. In Missouri and several other states, probation and parole officers may elect to carry a weapon, but they are not required to do so. Every new officer receives a 30-minute overview about carrying firearms, and those who will carry weapons receive an additional one week of training (Phase III) on both firearms safety and physical safety skills.

Missouri currently provides their new probation and parole officers with 200 hours of training (240 hours for those officers who elect to carry a weapon), which is just below the average for other states combining probation and parole (243 hours required) but above the average for those who have separate probation and parole agencies and training programs (101 hours for probation-only agencies and 146 for parole-only agencies).[31] Even though the combined agencies have almost twice the number of average hours of training for their officers, there is really no reason that this combined training should require more time.

Firearms training as a part of basic training. Although correctional staff seldom have to use a weapon, they must be very familiar and proficient with a variety of firearms. Here, new recruits are practicing firing the pistol.
(Courtesy of the Federal Bureau of Prisons)

Self-defense training as a part of basic training. All staff should have training in self-defense, whether they will work as a probation officer, correctional officer, counselor, or secretary. *(Courtesy of the Federal Bureau of Prisons)*

In-Service Training

As noted, corrections is a rapidly changing enterprise, and staff need to be continually updated on developments and new procedures or programs. Each year brings new legal cases, new information regarding inmate and street gangs, new technologies, and new legislation impacting correctional practices. To keep staff aware of changes, correctional agencies offer **in-service training** to provide employees annual updates and refreshers of many of the key aspects of their jobs.

In-service training is important for correctional agencies for many reasons. First, there are many technical skills that require practice and "refresher" training. Some of these activities are essential to correctional work (self-defense and disturbance control tactics) but may not be used often, which can result in an erosion of skills. In-service training provides an opportunity to practice these skills and be reeducated regarding the philosophy and approach to be considered when confronted with a need to use these skills. Second, in-service training is used to update employees in changes in laws, rules, policies, and procedures impacting the agency.

In addition, in-service training can reemphasize an existing practice or concern that may be a problem and requires a reminder to staff of the problems that can result if they are not sensitive to the concern. For instance, if an agency has had a "rash" of incidents in which staff developed sexual relationships with inmates or offenders supervised in the community, in-service training can be a reminder of how these relationships can develop (for instance, if an employee is vulnerable as a result of personal problems), and the severe criminal and administrative penalties that result from such conduct. If agencies discover that inmates are trying to mail drugs into the prison using a newly discovered technique, in-service training can be used to remind staff of the importance of thorough searching using mandated procedures.

Developmental Training

As staff progress in their careers, they often consider changing career specialties, seek a promotion, or even move to another prison or community region to broaden their experience. To aid staff in making decisions about career choices and to prepare them for taking on jobs with additional responsibilities, agencies often provide **developmental training** for staff. Developmental training can often be accomplished in two ways: by providing staff cross-training in another correctional job specialty or by appointing staff to an "acting" promotional assignment.

Cross-training involves assigning a staff member to work in an area other than his or her job specialty in order to experience a different type of work and to identify the staff member's skills and aptitude for a new type of work. For instance, correctional officers who are interested in being counselors or case managers may be designated to work in that job specialty area for a short time to fill a vacancy or cover for another staff member who is on sick or vacation leave. By doing this, the correctional officer receives some experience and can decide if he or she wants to pursue that type of work in the future. Case managers or counselor supervisors also get the opportunity to see how well the correctional officer performs and the potential they have for success in that role.

Vacancies also exist (in between appointments or for leave purposes) in supervisory and management positions. Line staff may be temporarily appointed as "acting" in a supervisory or management position, with all the authority and responsibility they would have under a permanent appointment. As an example, a case manager may be appointed to "act" as the unit manager, or a senior correctional officer may be appointed to "act" as a lieutenant or other correctional supervisor. The acting position is usually in the same job category in which the employee already works, but in a higher-level or supervisory position. Acting assignments provide excellent training for staff to experience the more challenging role and to develop their own skills in supervision or performing different tasks.

In addition to the two primary ways that staff develop and move from their own discipline, correctional staff must also be kept up-to-date in developments in their own specialty area. Chaplains, medical personnel, psychologists, and educators are only a few of the staff who must stay apprised of new knowledge or findings in their professions. Most correctional agencies fund travel and training costs for these purposes. The ACA also promotes these activities through their accreditation standards, one of which states

The institution encourages and provides administrative leave and/or reimbursement for employees attending approved professional meetings, seminars, and similar work-related activities. The institution should encourage participation in outside training and educational programs, including membership in local, state, and national professional organizations. Adequate funds for this purpose should be included in the budget.[32]

Specialty Training

The final area of training provided for correctional staff is **specialty training**. Specialty training is some skill that will add to an employee's contribution to the agency, either in general correctional practices or in very specific duties. Three common types of specialty training are supervision training, training for newly appointed management positions, and training to develop a special technical skill required by the agency. An example of training in supervision is the correctional officer who has just been promoted to a supervisory correctional position or a food service employee who becomes the assistant food service manager. These staff now need general supervisory training to understand the responsibilities and practices of a supervisor. They must learn how to change their job behaviors from "doing" to "supervising." Keenhold suggests that managers "get paid for what subordinates do, and not what they do,"[33] meaning that supervisory training must focus on how to delegate and get work completed effectively through others. This type of training usually includes completion of supervision surveys so individuals understand their own styles and supervisory preferences, procedures to complete employee performance appraisals and counsel employees regarding their performance, and management of a budget.

One particular skill essential for managers is to learn how to be coaches. In general terms, workplace coaching helps people achieve their potential. More specifically, the role of mentor or coach is to help people learn the important aspects of a job through their own experience, and instead of detailed technical training, it is more advisory to focus on how something worked or what the employee learned from an experience. Gomez notes that correctional coaching helps "build and maintain an atmosphere that attracts dedicated people, optimizes performance and retains those who are committed to the goals of the organization."[34] In that sense, it not only helps individual employees reach their potential, it helps organizations reach their potential as well.

All four types of training (basic, in-service, developmental, and specialty) contribute to the creation of a professional and competent correctional staff. In such a challenging, rapidly changing, and dangerous work environment, it is essential that agencies invest in their staff by providing extensive and well-rounded training opportunities. By doing so, the agencies provide staff with the abilities needed to perform their duties both now and in the future. As would be expected, the state and local correctional agencies that have the best reputations for management excellence are usually those that take training seriously and commit financial and time resources.

Succession Planning

Although not a type of training, the end result of effective staff training and development is that there are staff prepared to fill upper-level organizational roles when they become available. The end result is that an organization has the "bench strength" needed to continue high-quality performance regardless of the person that fills any job. **Succession planning** is a process for identifying high potential individuals and developing their skills, knowledge, and abilities to have the competencies required to fill a key position in the organization. It ensures that capable and experienced employees are ready to step into these roles. Succession planning is another integral element of human resource management, as it requires a specific set of activities to ensure the process is in place that when key positions are available, there are people who are not only in "line" for the promotion but are also "prepared" for it. A recent article by Perroncello describes this process for correctional agencies to include identifying the elements of every key position, the competencies required of it, and communicating to staff what they must do to prepare themselves for any job.[35]

There are four stages to developing an effective succession plan:

- Identifying roles for succession
- Developing a clear understanding of the capabilities required to undertake those roles
- Identifying employees who could potentially fill and perform highly in such roles
- Preparing employees to be ready for advancement into each identified role.[36]

The first step is to create a process whereby you identify the key roles that must have a prepared person always ready to fill it if it becomes vacant. HR managers often begin with, "what would you do if tomorrow Ms. Blank got hit by a bus?" The second step is to fully understand the capabilities and requirements of any job. In most cases, this is beyond technical skills that can be developed through standard training. In public correctional agencies, ability to represent the agency in the public political process, building coalitions and collaborating, and problem solving are some important skills. The next step is to identify high potential employees who could fill the job and finally to begin to prepare them (training, experience, and special assignments) so that they could easily and without much letdown in performance fill the role.

Succession planning is another area of increased sophistication for which corrections has not spent much time in the past but is critical for meeting the challenges of the future. With the current growth in corrections, promotions come faster and the development that used to come from years of experience must now be developed through a deliberate focus on succession plans and leadership development. Ruddell and Cecil suggest that "A key part of correctional managers and executives' succession plans should be to create learning opportunities for the new generation of leaders."[37] They cite as an example the Foundations training conducted by Corrections Corporation of America, a one-week program to develop knowledge and skills of the company's leaders in three areas: finance and business acumen; correctional operations; and human resource management. The goal of this training is to accelerate the development of leaders who can continue to move the company toward its vision to be the best correctional system in the United States.

Performance Appraisal and Recognition Systems

Performance appraisal and recognition systems are important in the management of human resources for many reasons. First, these systems provide the formal opportunity for staff and their supervisors to discuss their performance. Discussions about an employee's performance are not easy, unless the employee is one of the very few who have no faults and no need to improve their performance. No one likes to hear that they are not doing as well as they could, even when the criticism is offered constructively, with the primary intention of helping them perform better for their own success. A formal performance appraisal system provides a process and creates the expectation that certain elements important to job performance will be discussed and suggestions made for improvement. This process makes evaluations less "personal," and more businesslike.

Second, performance appraisal systems are targeted toward improving employees, not criticizing them. If they are done well, staff evaluations spend little time discussing the past and most of the time discussing how performance can be improved in the future. Evaluations allow both the supervisor and the employee to jointly discuss and agree on a plan for improvement. This plan may include additional training, more regular review and feedback on employee performance, or informal mentoring and coaching to discuss job issues and problems. When they include these aspects, performance appraisals provide both employees and supervisors a road map that can lead to improvement and the chance for successful careers.

Third, an evaluation system is a motivator for staff. If staff believe that the evaluation process is fair and consistent, they are motivated to perform well and receive a high rating on their evaluation. Most people want to perform well and please their supervisors. Everyone wants to be successful, and the evaluation process allows positive feedback and a reaffirmation of successful work. Also, every agency considers evaluations for promotions or other assignments. Employees who cannot perform their current jobs well are usually not promoted or given expanded responsibility. Likewise, employees who do perform well prove they are ready for a greater level of responsibility. In the formal, competitive process used to determine who gets promoted in most public agencies, evaluations may often count for up to one-third of the consideration of employees' readiness for advancement.

Finally, a recognition system is a way to differentiate and reward staff who consistently perform at a high level. Every agency has a disciplinary process (discussed later) to respond to unprofessional conduct or poor performance. Truly exceptional agencies have just as sophisticated and meaningful a recognition program to identify and reward those staff who are professional and demonstrate job excellence. Agencies have a variety of recognition programs. Public agencies do not give "bonuses" as does the private sector. However, the formal evaluation system in public agencies will often result in a higher pay increase or even a cash award. Agencies often have a pool or "merit pay increases," which are awarded at a greater amount or percentage to employees with the highest performance ratings. In addition, correctional agencies usually have awards such as "employee of the month," or more specialized forms of recognition such as "correctional or probation officer of the month." Although the recognition of a job well done is enough for many outstanding employees, there is usually a small monetary award that accompanies this recognition.

The overall value of appraisal and recognition systems is that they differentiate high-performing from low-performing staff, giving attention to those who need encouragement and improvement, and recognizing those who deserve to be rewarded. As important a resource as staff are to accomplish the correctional mission, a meaningful and well-administered performance appraisal and reward system is critical.

Disciplining Staff

Most correctional staff perform at expected levels and act professionally. Unfortunately, not all do; therefore, agencies must have a disciplinary system to respond to poor performance or inappropriate behavior. A comprehensive, fair, and well-communicated disciplinary process is important for any organization, and perhaps even more important for a correctional agency. Correctional agencies supervise law breakers who are used to manipulating and blaming others for their problems. Correctional clients try to compromise staff by tricking or bribing them to provide them favorable treatment. Since inappropriate behavior can result in termination, the disciplinary process needs to conform to legal requirements of fair and consistent treatment.

An employee disciplinary system encompasses many facets and is not the same thing as "punishment." **Employee disciplinary systems** are designed to educate employees about unacceptable behavior and provide a fair process to address such alleged behavior. Just by having a disciplinary system that specifies and trains staff on expected behavior, much unethical behavior can be avoided or reduced. It could be argued that the disciplinary system has failed when it actually results in punishment. This proactive approach is captured in the following:

Discipline can be defined as orderly conduct based on definite standards catalyzed by effective leadership, and encompasses three interrelated factors.[38]

1. The framework of policies, rules, and procedures established by the organization.
2. The employee's and supervisor's attitude toward, and degree of compliance with, this framework.
3. The leadership process—example, instruction, training, and so on—exercised by the supervisor that largely determines the employee's attitude and compliance.

Although there is nothing wrong with punishment as a motivator for compliance with agency policy, supervisors seek to instill *positive* rather than *negative* discipline. Positive discipline is the self-control that most people have that drives them to succeed, to do their jobs well, and to please their supervisors and themselves. Both human resources staff and supervisors have a role to play in positive discipline. Human resources staff must ensure that there are punishments for poor performance and rewards for good performance. Supervisors must show employees how the employees and the organization benefit from their compliance with expected performance.

Negative discipline is used as a last resort, when a positive, informal approach for gaining compliance has not worked, and the agency and supervisor must resort to punishment to change the employee's behavior. This approach, if administered with certainty and uniformity, can achieve compliance. However, it can also achieve only the minimum compliance necessary to avoid discipline and penalties without encouraging employees to perform at their fullest. Although no supervisor enjoys using negative discipline to gain compliance, it must be practiced when necessary in order to differentiate between positively and negatively performing staff.

There are several keys to an effective disciplinary system:

■ Clarifying expectations for acceptable behavior and punishments for non-compliance.
■ Training staff in the disciplinary process.
■ Training supervisors in the disciplinary process.
■ Separating the review of performance from decision making regarding punishment.
■ Administering the disciplinary process in an impartial, timely, and consistent manner.
■ Allowing for appeals from the disciplinary process.

Agencies clarify expectations by publishing a list of prohibited behavior and the range of punishments that coincide with each type of behavior. No circumstance is exactly the same, and agencies usually provide a wide range of punishments for each type of misbehavior. This allows the decision maker broad discretion in considering mitigating and aggravating circumstances. All staff must be trained and must understand the disciplinary process. They must know there will be consequences when agency rules are violated. Staff should never be surprised that poor conduct results in discipline. They should have been given a list of prohibited acts and punishments, and the topic should be covered each year during in-service training. Supervisors play a key role in identifying inappropriate conduct, especially when it has to do with failure to perform duties, and they must be sure to follow the process as prescribed. Dowling and Syles suggest the following for supervisors administering discipline:

> Timing . . . the supervisor shouldn't procrastinate in administering discipline. The longer he postpones reproof or punishment after he has observed the violation, the more likely he is to get a 'who—me?' Follow-through . . . Once he (the supervisor) has disciplined a subordinate, it's crucial that he treat him as he did before his reproof. Consistency . . . Obviously, it's unfair when one supervisor, all other things being equal, imposes a penalty harsher than that imposed by another supervisor.[39]

The best way to reduce inconsistency is to separate the decision making regarding punishment from first-line supervisors. This also encourages supervisors to instill positive discipline. In fact, most legal reviews of staff disciplinary processes require this separation. The process usually requires that a first-line supervisor or department manager states the violation and proposes discipline, an objective third party investigates the incident, and an upper-level manager decides on guilt and imposes discipline. One advantage of this approach is that it limits the number of individuals who actually impose punishment and, therefore, there is likely to be more consistency of punishments.

The disciplinary process should be administered in an impartial, timely, and consistent manner. The most difficult dilemma for an administrator is to have to impose discipline on an employee who has a history of dedication and following the rules. However, if the administrator gives the good employee "too much of a break," it becomes almost mandatory to give the same break to a poorer employee who commits the same violation. The imposition of discipline must be impartial. A like act deserves a like penalty, and although prior discipline can be considered, prior performance and commitment usually cannot. Staff must believe that the system is fair and equitable. If they believe that the decision maker "plays favorites" and shows partiality, the credibility of the system is undermined.

Finally, the system must provide for appeals for disciplinary actions. A fair process for appeal adds credibility to a system. Also, disciplinary actions almost always are seen as personal, because employees feel like victims, and their supervisors and managers feel betrayed. Knowing there is an appeal process reduces personalizing the process to a certain extent, and it forces decision makers to step back and consider how the punishment will be viewed in other's eyes.

Negative discipline is never preferable to positive discipline. However, there will always be a failure by some staff to fully comply with standards of conduct for correctional agencies. When this occurs, it is imperative that the agency has a fair and equitable process to investigate and administer discipline. Corrections is a profession that must have public trust, allow for redress of wrongs against inmates and offenders, and prove itself to be above reproach. The type of disciplinary system described is very important to accomplishing these requirements.

Collective Bargaining in Correctional Agencies

Collective bargaining is relatively new to corrections, although a few states (Connecticut in the 1940s, and New York and Washington in the 1960s) have had public employee unions for some time. For other states, collective bargaining among public employees started in the East and moved to the South and to the West. In the 1970s, more than twenty states formally authorized collective bargaining by public employees, and by the end of the twentieth century, most states had some recognition of labor organizations to represent public employees. The first time that collective bargaining was a part of the ACA program agenda was in 1977, when at least one-third of the states had collective bargaining agreements covering correctional agencies.[40] The movement to collective bargaining has, perhaps, had even more of an impact on corrections than on most public agencies, because of the mission of security and public protection, and the interaction among line staff and their unions, management, and inmates.

There were several historical developments in corrections that spurred the emergence of unions. First, corrections, and especially prisons, had unpleasant working conditions, low pay, and low job prestige. Second, the advent of prisoner rehabilitation during the late 1950s and 1960s clouded the security mission of prisons and threatened correctional officers with a loss of discipline and control over inmates. The move to professionalize corrections, pushing for increased educational requirements for staff and bringing treatment and program staff into prisons, also threatened the traditional strong role of correctional officers. Finally, during the 1960s and early 1970s, prisons experienced a number of riots, and violence against staff increased. Staff had less confidence in the administration to provide for their personal safety, and they sought help from unions to argue for policies to protect them and reclaim their lost authority.

In general, **collective bargaining** is the formal recognition of employees, along with their right to negotiate with management regarding issues in the workplace. The purposes of collective bargaining lead one to question why anyone would oppose it. Collective bargaining includes the right

- To establish and protect employees' rights.
- To improve working conditions and benefits.
- To establish and maintain more harmonious employer–employee relationships.
- To establish a participative role for employees in management decisions that affect employees.[41]

However, in the early days after authorization of collective bargaining, many correctional administrators feared it would diminish management authority and undermine staff discipline and prison security. It was also believed that unionization would bring more emphasis on **seniority** of staff in post assignment and promotion. Seniority allows the employees who have been employed the longest their choices of work assignments, days off, or shift schedules. At times, it is even considered for promotions. The administrative concern is that correctional managers need the utmost discretion in placing staff with unique abilities in the positions that require these strengths. At the same time, managers do not want to place inexperienced staff, or those with certain weaknesses, in critical positions. There is no question that correctional administrators prefer the maximum flexibility to make decisions with no guidelines and without challenge. However, over the years that collective bargaining has been in place with correctional agencies, the early fears have not materialized, and the benefits of "shared governance" by line staff and management has led to better decisions and higher morale.

The Collective Bargaining Process in Corrections

When a state or local government authorizes public employees to organize and engage in collective bargaining, the first step is for the employees to select a labor organization to represent them. A major decision that must be made early in the collective bargaining process is how to align employee groups for representation. Seldom are all correctional employees a part of the same bargaining unit that negotiates for their working conditions. For instance, all correctional employees may be represented by one labor organization, or employees may be clustered into logical groups (all correctional officers, all trade employees, and all treatment staff) to be represented by a union. After the employees are grouped for representation, the group votes to elect the labor organization that will represent them in negotiations and contract management.

There are many national labor organizations that represent public sector and correctional employees. These include the American Federation of Labor and Congress of Industrial Organizations (AFL-CIO), the American Federation of State, Federal and Municipal Employees (AFSFME), and even the International Brotherhood of Teamsters. Several organizations can vie for representation of correctional employees. The election process can be extremely difficult for both management and employees. The elections are often very highly contested, and the competing unions seek to find issues and convince staff they can best represent their interests.

After a labor organization is elected to represent employees, the parties prepare for negotiations. Most of the issues involve pay and benefits for the public employees, and they are usually negotiated statewide or countywide, including noncorrections as well as corrections employees. However, there will also be separate issues in negotiations regarding correctional employees about the role of seniority. Unions always want seniority to be the determining factor in many decisions. For instance, the labor position for promotions is that the most senior person is selected from all candidates found to be "qualified." Management wants to be able to select the "most qualified" person, and be able to consider affirmative action and other management needs. Unions also want seniority for "job bidding," or allowing correctional officers by seniority to pick the post they want to work.[42] Negotiations will also include many issues specific to correctional employees, such as how staff are selected for overtime, the type of clothing provided to staff by the agency, and possibly the coverage by correctional officers in areas such as educational programs and the medical clinic.

After the contract is negotiated, each prison or community corrections office must implement and administer it. Unfortunately, there are always questions that come into dispute about the true meaning of the contract. In these instances, management can make a decision, and the union can file a grievance to argue it. A **grievance** is a formal complaint that the decision is not within the language or intent of the labor contract as negotiated, and the grievance must go through a formal process for resolution. The grievance is usually reviewed by the next level of agency and union officials to see if they can resolve it. If not, it may go to a labor mediator to assist in its resolution, or the parties may have agreed to "binding arbitration." With binding arbitration, the parties have previously agreed that any grievance will go to arbitration, and the decision is final; it may not be further appealed by either party. One thing is clear in a collective bargaining environment: If either or both parties want to be confrontational and argue almost every minor contract issue, they will spend a tremendous amount of time and money to resolve their disputes.

The following case study describes the stages of collective bargaining in one state correctional agency during the early 1980s.

Collective Bargaining Implications for Corrections

Collective bargaining is now well entrenched in prisons and other correctional agency operations, and it will continue to have an impact on policy and practice. There is, however, much dispute about the implications of collective bargaining. Those who oppose it argue that collective bargaining interferes with management's rights and need for flexibility, and undermines the historical solidarity that is important for prison staff working in a stressful and dangerous environment. Those who favor collective bargaining suggest that the sharing of power in a correctional setting between management and staff benefits all parties, and labor unions can even be a strong voice to the legislature for additional staff and financial resources.

One significant issue involves the impact of collective bargaining on staff solidarity. Historically, prison wardens were autocratic rulers who could hire, promote, discipline, and fire at will, and who demanded allegiance to those in command. As unfair as this may seem, this allegiance resulted in solidarity of staff, because they pulled together to maintain prison security. Collective bargaining has changed that, resulting in a clear distinction

Practical Perspectives

Implementing Collective Bargaining in a Correctional Agency

A state in the central United States had an "ugly" history of collective bargaining. There had been some unofficial and nonstatutory negotiations in the department of corrections in the 1960s, which resulted in agreements with several labor groups that represented small numbers of correctional employees. The result was constant friction among the unions and between labor and management. A walkout of correctional officers occurred at several prisons, and inmates rioted and several escaped from a high-security prison during one of the strikes. As a result, the conservative governor stopped all negotiations and had the unions disband. Since that time, the state legislature several times passed a statewide collective bargaining bill, but the governor vetoed the bill. After a new governor was elected with the support of labor, he signed a collective bargaining bill passed by the legislature. The department of corrections, with the history they had, was very hesitant to move forward and implement the new law. The director describes the events and stages of the next several months as follows.

The first stage was the organizing and election process for correctional staff to select the labor union that would represent them. It was horrible. We are a large state, and our employees would end up being several thousand union members. I thought management had a really good relationship with staff, and I personally spent a lot of time with line staff whenever I visited the prisons. I know they appreciated it and respected me for my concern and leadership. All of a sudden, the three national unions vying to represent them were campaigning and trying to find issues to get employee attention. Since there really were no major issues regarding safety or prison management, they had to make things up. It was a personal affront to me with some of the things they came up with. I couldn't believe some of the nefarious schemes they came up with to suggest why we made certain decisions. Fortunately, the least professional and most untruthful of the labor groups quickly lost credibility. I was glad to see our employees elected the union I felt was the most sophisticated and professional during this campaign period.

The next step was the statewide negotiations. We, even though a large agency in state government, did not have a lot of say at the table, since it was a negotiation with all state employee organizations. The key issue our employee union wanted was "pick a post." This means that correctional officers could "bid" on the job or post assignment in the prison they wanted by seniority. We drew the line in the sand, and would not negotiate it at all. So, we had to go to arbitration before a third party. I remember to this day the testimony I gave, and the experts that the union brought in from other states to say why pick a post would work. I worked hard with our attorneys to research and prepare my testimony, and made the point that pick a post could result in the more junior correctional officers with the most difficult assignments or security jobs in the SHU or high security housing areas. We won the arbitration, but the union continued to fight for seniority to be recognized in other ways.

In some of the prisons, they took a really hard stance in their interpretation of what the contract actually said, and it seems we almost had to do individual prison renegotiations on several of the issues we thought had been addressed. I remember a few prisons where we had really difficult union leadership and really stubborn management staff. It seems all we did was respond to grievances, and use staff resources to answer complaints by union stewards. I admit, we were as much at fault as the union, but we just couldn't get an understanding of what the contract meant with all parties. It probably took three to four years before everyone found a comfortable communications point, and things began to level off. Today, the union and management really work well together, and collective bargaining does serve everyone well. But, for a long while, I questioned the whole process, and whether it would ever work in our department. I guess the history of the 1960s left too many scars that had to be forgotten before we could start over again, and approach collective bargaining for the positive, shared interest and communications it could provide.

between line staff and management. Managers are no longer seen as looking out for line staff, because union leadership promotes their own version of staff advocacy and downplays management efforts as self-serving. Jacobs and Crotty suggest, "It [collective bargaining] has redefined the prison organization in adversary terms so that wardens are bosses and complaints are grievances."[43]

A second major issue involves the "right to strike." Most public safety organizations are not allowed to strike, taking away a major tactic to getting the government to accept labor's demands during negotiations. One can only imagine, however, the crises that would occur if police and correctional officers were allowed to strike. However, unions representing these groups sometimes sanction informal job actions (known as "blue flu," for the blue uniforms traditionally worn by the police) to get the attention of management and force them to consider the union positions. There have also been illegal strikes by correctional officers. In New York state, the Taylor Law sets penalties whereby strikers lose 2 days' salary for each day they are on strike.[44] However, this did not deter a 1979 strike by New York state correctional officers. A study of this strike found that officers believed they had lost status and authority, and racial tensions had mounted within the officer workforce as well as between officers and inmates. An analysis of the strike found that collective bargaining was not well suited to resolve these types of problems and may have even aggravated them.[45]

Another concern regarding collective bargaining is its impact on correctional policy and efforts toward rehabilitation. As previously noted, the rehabilitative movement spurred concern by officers and unionization within prisons. In the late 1980s and 1990s, rehabilitation was replaced by a renewed emphasis on inmate accountability and prison security and control. There was fear that prison unions would, using a concern for staff safety issues, subtlety lobby against any reemphasis of rehabilitation. Others suggest that interests of prisoners and officers are intertwined, and as one group benefits, so does the other. Improved working conditions for staff must also include improved living conditions for inmates. Also, rehabilitative programs that improve inmate morale, reduce idleness, and enhance security result in benefits to the staff who work in a prison.

Overall, it is not the allowance or the process of collective bargaining that seems to have negative or positive implications for corrections; it is the attitude of agency administrators and union leaders and the relationships that they develop that signals the type of impact that collective bargaining has on correctional operations. If both parties communicate with and listen to each other, show mutual respect, and are reasonable in their positions, collective bargaining can have a very positive effect on a correctional organization. However, if the parties let the issues get personal, and become overly adversarial in the relationship, collective bargaining results in few positive and many negative outcomes.

SUMMARY

Effective human resource management is a key to the successful operation of a correctional agency. The quality of a community or institutional correctional organization directly depends on the quality of the staff. In this chapter, we examined the human resource activities and challenges that go into recruiting, hiring, and training staff and the importance of evaluating staff performance and the potential impact of collective bargaining on accomplishing correctional missions. The message is that the staff are the most important resource available to a correctional agency, and therefore these roles played by human resource managers cannot be over-emphasized.

The management of human resources is an ever-evolving and never-ending undertaking. Outstanding correctional agencies (every organization, for that matter) are those that invest in these activities and pay particular attention to maintaining the best staff possible. In good economic times, well-qualified recruits do not apply for correctional jobs that do not require education and relationship building. Even the best-qualified, new staff need to be provided adequate technical skills, and they need to understand the culture and guiding principles of their organization. Correctional staff need training to prepare for supervision and management, and other positions of increasing responsibility. Performance appraisal and recognition systems are critical to continuing to motivate staff to perform at their highest level. And when staff fail, or behave in less than a professional manner, they must be fairly and impartially disciplined in order to maintain high ethical standards.

Human resource management is in the middle of the section entitled "Managing Correctional Staff." This is appropriate because the people who manage the human resource of correctional agencies bind the roles, organization, and functions of staffing with the more interpersonal and leadership approaches to getting the most out of your staff. In the following two chapters, we continue to examine some of the "people" issues of corrections. Chapter 7 reviews the way people and functions are organized to accomplish a correctional mission, and Chapter 8 presents the vital function of supervising people in correctional organizations, activities that effective supervisors must undertake, and the importance of empowering staff to fully enhance their contribution to the organization.

KEY TERMS

Peace officer status
Correctional officer
American Correctional
  Association
Recruiting
Competitive hiring process
Rule of three

Integrity interview
Basic training
Correctional worker concept
In-service training
Developmental training
Specialty training
Succession planning

Performance appraisal and
  recognition systems
Employee disciplinary system
Collective bargaining
Seniority
Grievance

YOU'RE THE CORRECTIONAL ADMINISTRATOR

1. You are the newly appointed manager of human resources for a rural prison. The prison has a history of hiring relatives of current employees who reside in the local area. This has resulted in a lack of diversity in prison staff, some problems of potential nepotism, and the need to avoid assigning relatives to work for other relatives. The staff believe this

system is fine, however, and that their relatives deserve an opportunity to be hired before "outsiders." This trend is now causing problems in quality of staff, a lack of staff diversity reflective of the inmate diversity, and administrative problems because "everyone is related to each other." How do you go about changing this situation? First, address the types of recruitment and hiring processes you want to implement. Then, address the process you would go through to convince staff that changing the current practice of hiring relatives is a good idea.

2. You are the chief of labor relations for the state correctional agency. You have been asked by the local prison to mediate a dispute they are having that is not addressed in the local or state labor contract. The local union members want to have "pick a post" by seniority: They want the most senior correctional officers to have first choice to work their preferred correctional assignment. There are many posts, including security/fence towers, outside the prison security, educational building, food service, control center, front desk processing of visitors, inmate housing units, and inside compound security. The prison administration wants to avoid "pick a post," arguing that the best and most senior correctional officers will select jobs with little or no inmate contact and the most junior and inexperienced staff will have to work in the housing units, in which an error of judgment can cause serious problems. Also, the administration argues that there are some more technical and highly sensitive jobs that involve a risk of undermining the overall security of the prison if the wrong staff member is assigned there. Your first step is to objectively list some of the issues that the two sides will agree on and some that they will dispute on this topic. Then suggest a process that they can use to reduce their disagreements before you attempt to mediate the dispute. Finally, list the arguments you assume the two sides will present to you as mediator. Although a mediator does not make decisions, list the decisions you would make to resolve this dispute if you had the authority to do so.

WEB LINK EXERCISES

Go to AFSCME Chapter for Correctional Workers: http://www.afscme.org/201.cfm

Go to the Web site for the American Federal, State, County, and Municipal Employees union. Look at the left side of the webpage and click on Publications. Then click on AFSCME Corrections United and open the latest newsletter. This presents the latest news of AFSCME union members in correctional departments around the United States. The newsletter will give you an idea of the issues of the union leadership. Read the publication and express some written comments about your personal feelings of the necessity and effectiveness of this union. Are the members making prisons, jails, and community corrections a better place to work and are they concerned with the public's concerns with and safety financial issues?

Go to The Bureau of Justice Statistics: http://bjs.ojp.usdoj.gov/

Look on the left side of the page and click on *Employment and Expenditure*. Scroll down to *Corrections*. How much money is being spent on the corrections sector of the criminal justice system? What percent of correctional employees are serving at the state, local, and federal levels? Continue scrolling to see the valuable publications, reports, and charts regarding employment and expenditure levels of the national criminal justice system.

GROUP EXERCISES

Each group will present a plan for a 1,000-bed prison for the following staffing issues: recruitment, hiring process, training, retention, and promotion.

ENDNOTES

1. James J. Stephan, *Census of State and Federal Correctional Facilities, 2005* (Washington, DC: U.S. Department of Justice, Bureau of Justice Statistics, October 2008), pp. 1–2.

2. Camille Graham Camp and George M. Camp, *The Corrections Yearbook: 1998* (Middletown, CT: Criminal Justice Institute, 1998), pp. 131, 196, and 197.

3. Bureau of Justice Statistics, *Sourcebook of Criminal Justice Statistics, 1994* (Washington, DC: U.S. Department of Justice, 1995), p. 26.

4. Stephan, *Census of State and Federal Correctional Facilities, 2005*, p. 4.

5. Ibid.

6. Ibid., p. 5.

7. Curtis Prout and Robert N. Ross, *Care and Punishment: The Dilemmas of Prison Medicine* (Pittsburgh, PA.: University of Pittsburgh Press, 1988), p. 152.

8. Bureau of Justice Statistics, *Key Facts at a Glance: Correctional Populations*, http://bjs.ojp.usdoj.gov/content/glance/tables/corr2tab.cfm (accessed April 21, 2010).

9. E. C. Hughes, "Professions," in *The Professions in America*, edited by Kenneth S. Lynn (Boston, MA: Houghton-Mifflin, 1965), p. 4.

10. Harold E. Williamson, *The Corrections Profession* (Newbury Park, CA: Sage, 1990), p. 77.

11. C. Cherniss and J. S. Kane, "Public Sector Professionals: Job Characteristics, Satisfaction, and Aspirations for Intrinsic Fulfillment Through Work," *Human Relations* 40 (March 1987): 125–136.

12. American Correctional Association, *Standards for Adult Correctional Institutions*, 4th ed. (Lanham, MD: American Correctional Association, 2003), p. vii.

13. American Correctional Association Web site: http://www.aca.org/ membership/chapters. asp (accessed April 6, 2010).

14. Rosabeth M. Kanter, *The Change Masters: Innovation for Productivity in the American Corporation* (New York: Simon and Schuster, 1983).

15. Kelsey Kauffman, *Prison Officers and Their World* (Cambridge, MA: Harvard University Press, 1988), p. 167.

16. Ibid., p. 168.

17. Ibid., p. 167.

18. Nicole Baker and Max Carrera, "Unlocking the Door to Relationship-Based Corrections Recruiting," *Corrections Today* 69 no. 1 (February 2007): 36.

19. Jeanne B. Stinchcomb and Susan W. McCambell, "The 21st Century Jail Workforce," *American Jails* 23 no. 2 (May/June 2009): 15–20.

20. Gregg W. Etter, "Recruiting the Best!" *American Jails* 22 no. 2 (May/June 2008): 22.

21. Roderick S. Osborne, "Recruiting for Corrections in Today's World," *American Jails* 22 no. 3 (July/August 2008): 22.

22. Jane Lommel, "Turning Around Turnover," *Corrections Today* 66 no. 5 (August 2004): 54–57.

23. Pew Center on the States, *Ten Steps Corrections Directors Can Take to Strengthen Performance* (Washington, DC: The Pew Charitable Trusts, May 2008).

24. Alaska Department of Corrections Press Release, *Department of Corrections Actively Recruiting Alaskans for Correctional Officer Positions* (Juneau, Alaska: Department of Corrections, January 26, 2005).

25. Brian E. Cronin, Ralph Klessig, and William D. Sprenkle, "Recruiting and Retaining Staff through Culture Change," *Corrections Today* 70 no. 4 (August 2008): 48–51.

26. Gary C. Mohr, "Samberg Program Improves Leadership and Addresses Turnover," *Corrections Today* 71 no. 2 (April 2009): 56–58.

27. Tracy L. Reveal, "Structured On-the-Job Training Addresses Turnover in Ohio," *Corrections Today* 71 no. 2 (April 2009): 38–40.

28. Catherine C. McVey and Randolph T. McVey, "Responding to Today's Workforce: Attracting, Retaining, and Developing the New Generation of Workers," *Corrections Today* 67 no. 7 (December 2005): 80–82, 109.

29. A good discussion of this can be found in Kevin P. Coyne and Shawn T. Coyne, "The Baby Boom Retirement Fallacy and What it Means to You," *Harvard Business Review Blog*, May 16, 2008, http://blogs.harvardbusiness.org/cs/2008/05/the_baby_boomer_retirement_fal.html (accessed December 23, 2009).

30. Camp and Camp, *The Corrections Yearbook*, p. 147.

31. Ibid., p. 201.

32. American Correctional Association, p. 27.

33. David G. Keenhold, "What Do Managers Get Paid to Do?," *American Jails* 22 no. 3 (July/August 2008): 66.

34. Jeanne Gomez, "Correctional Coaching: Teaching Managers to be Coaches," *Corrections Today* 69 no. 1 (February 2007): 43.

35. Peter Perroncello, "Succession Planning in American Jails," *American Jails* 20 no. 1 (March/April 2006): 9–14.

36. Succession Planning, from Wikipedia, the Free Encyclopedia, http://en.wikipedia.org/wiki/Succession_planning (accessed December 23, 2009).

37. Rick Ruddell and Lisa Cecil, "Ten Steps to Developing Effective Leadership Training," *Corrections Today* 72 no. 1 (February 2010): 80–83.

38. Robert W. Eckles, Ronald L. Carmichael, and Bernard R. Sarchet, *Essentials of Management and First-Line Supervision* (New York: Wiley, 1974), pp. 494–495.

39. William F. Dowling, Jr., and Leonard R. Sayles, *How Managers Motivate: The Imperatives of Supervision* (New York: McGraw-Hill, 1971), pp. 129–131.

40. John M. Wynne, Jr., "Unions and Bargaining Among Employees of State Prisons," *Monthly Labor Review* 101 (March 1978): 10–16.

41. M. Robert Montilla, *Prison Employee Unionism: Management Guide for Correctional Administrators* (Washington, DC: U.S. Department of Justice, National Institute of Law Enforcement and Criminal Justice, 1978), p. 2.

42. For an overview of the positions regarding seniority in correctional negotiation, see Lynn Zimmer, "Seniority Job Bidding in the Prisons," Society for the Study of Social Problems, association paper 85S17096, Sociological Abstracts, Inc., 1985.

43. James B. Jacobs and Norma Meacham Crotty, *Guard Unions and the Future of Prisons* (Ithaca, NY: Institute of Public Employment, 1978), p. 41.

44. Andrew A. Peterson, "Deterring Strikes by Public Employees: New York's Two-for-One Salary Penalty and the 1979 Prison Guard Strike," *Industrial and Labor Relations Review* 34 no. 4 (July 1981): 545–562.

45. Lynn Zimmer and James B. Jacobs, "Challenging the Taylor Law: Prison Guards on Strike," *Industrial Labor Relations Review* 43 no. 4 (July 1981): 531–544.

7

Staff Organization and Functions

Introduction

What should now be apparent to you is that correctional administration has become very complex. The correctional mission has broadened in scope, and, therefore, the functions that must be performed by staff have increased and are much more intricate. First, the traditional boundaries of corrections have expanded. Historically, corrections began after sentencing. However, jails hold presentenced offenders. There are many community bail supervision and other diversion programs. Restorative justice is often the responsibility of correctional officials and includes the sentencing process. Prisoner reentry includes the integration of many community, criminal justice, and correctional activities. Even the long-established role of a prison is not the same as it was a few decades ago. Prisons are expected to do more than hold inmates, and thankfully, the era of "lock them up, work them, and feed them" has passed. Expansion of inmate rights, rehabilitative programs, and many more prison service options have broadened the internal management puzzle for administrators to piece together.

In addition, correctional organizations have changed dramatically as a result of prisons moving from "closed systems" to "open systems." Closed systems were impacted and focused only on the internal environment, and for prisons or jails, that meant what happened within the walls or fences, under the direct control of the wardens. The organization of a closed system, often with autocratic leadership, was usually very simple, and the mission and goals of the organization were determined, and compliance was enforced, by the leader. However, the civil rights movement, the Vietnam conflict, and an era of prison riots changed the way society perceived corrections and prisons. As external influences began to impact correctional management, open systems soon replaced the closed systems. Snarr described the open system of correctional management as having numerous inputs and outputs with external government units.[1] This evolution is presented in the following diagram, which represents how external factors influence the activities of a prison. An open system is the result of frequent interactions of an organization with other groups in order to obtain resources, gain support, and accomplish goals.

Second, there has been a major change in the number and types of offenders under correctional supervision over the past two decades. There were only 1.8 million adults on probation and parole and in jails and prisons in 1980. This number had doubled in only eight years by 1988, and by 2007, there were more than 7.3 million adults under the

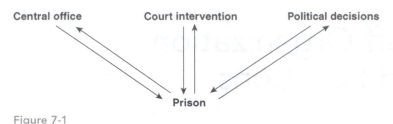

Figure 7-1
Impact of external factors on prison management.

supervision of correctional agencies in the United States.[2] A significant part of the growth in the number of adults under correctional supervision comes from growth in the prison population. In 1980, the rate of sentenced inmates incarcerated per 100,000 population was only 139, but increased to 762 per 100,000 population by 2008.[3]

In addition to growth in the numbers, there has been a change in the makeup of offenders under correctional supervision. In terms of gender, the rate for females has grown more rapidly than the number of males under supervision. In 1999, "Women represent about 21% of those on probation, 11% of those in local jails, just under 6% of those in prisons, and 12% of those on parole."[4] By mid-2008, females were 7.2 percent of the prison population and the average growth from 2000 to 2006 was 3.4 percent compared to an annual growth of 2.1 percent for male inmates.[5] In 2007, 12 percent of the 799,058 parolees in the United States were females, and of the 4.2 million U.S. probationers, 23 percent were females.[6]

Similarly, there has been a shift in the racial makeup of adults under correctional supervision. Whites made up a majority (65 percent) of the correctional population in 1986. However, by 1997, whites represented only 60 percent of all adult offenders under supervision.[7] There is considerable concern for racial disparity regarding offenders under supervision, as a majority of the prison population is minorities. In mid-2008, the population of prisons was 34.9 percent white, 39.5 percent black, 19.9 percent Hispanic, and 6 percent other races.[8] Of the 4,262,000 individuals under probation supervision in 2007, 56 percent were white, 30 percent were black, and 12 percent were Hispanic.[9] The fact that white offenders make up 56 percent of probationers, yet only 36.6 percent of prisoners raises further concern. And the state and federal prison or local jail population on June 30, 2008, included more black males (846,000) than white males (712,500) and Hispanic males (427,000), and 1 in every 9 black men and 1 in every 103 white men aged 20–24 were behind bars.[10]

Finally, the role of correctional administrators in dealing with the external environment (the public, the media, elected officials, and other government agencies) has increased the number of activities to which administrators must attend. Finally, the political and public interest of corrections puts additional demands on administrators, both on their time and on their sensitivity as to what they do and how they do it. Perhaps the biggest challenge to successful correctional administrators is navigating these "shark infested" waters, whereby errors of judgment or taking a position not supported by the public can end what had been a successful administrator's career. In order to respond to these increased activities, correctional organization have changed in focus and become very complex.

How are staff organized to carry out the expanded mission of corrections? What are the various functions that must be accomplished by correctional staff? What are the different levels of correctional staff, and what is the chain of command? What organizational entities have been created to respond to the external demands on correctional administrators? How are staff supplemented by volunteers or contractors to carry out their functions? All of these questions are addressed in this chapter. Included are sample agency, prison or jail, and community corrections organizational charts, with presentations of how various sections, divisions, and departments all work together to complete tasks both internal and external to the management of corrections.

Correctional Organizations

Over the past several years, the organization of correctional agencies has experienced a somewhat slow, but deliberate, transformation. There were few statewide correctional agencies until the 1970s. Until then, many wardens of state prisons were appointed by governors, and there was often not even a cabinet-level agency that oversaw prison operations. Prisons were organizationally within an umbrella agency that may include other law enforcement agencies or perhaps other social service agencies. Community corrections options were few, and probation supervision was fragmented and usually organized by county. It was not until the complexities of managing correctional operations created many issues that required a centralized and consistent approach that states formed departments of corrections to oversee activities in both facilities and the community.

The need for more centralization and consistency was driven by challenges facing contemporary prisons. As internal operations of prisons became more complex, prisons became more bureaucratic. Freeman characterizes this development as the **era of bureaucratic wardens,** in which wardens take responsibility for maintaining a safe, secure, and humane prison environment in accordance with accepted standards (the U.S. Constitution, sound management practices, applicable court decisions, etc.). In this regard, Freeman suggests the following specific activities for the bureaucratic warden:

1. Development of the mission statement for the organization.
2. Coordination of the budget process.
3. Strategic evaluation and emergency planning.
4. Management of daily activities.
5. Management of labor relations.
6. The formulation of policy.
7. The supervision and professional development of staff.[11]

Another way to describe the development of a bureaucratic approach to correctional management and organization is by its linkage of mission and goals to written policy and procedures. Prior to centralized control, there were few written policies and procedures that were consistently applied across all community or institutional functions. Mann notes that a bureaucracy is "an organization whose structure and operation are governed to a high degree by written rules."[12] Community correction functions and prisons began to organize around their mission by developing written policy and procedure to complete goals that would contribute to the mission. Goals were assigned to specific organizational entities, such as departments or divisions, to accomplish.

The centralization of authority also greatly influenced how correctional agencies were organized and managed. With pressures and influences from many external forces (courts, politicians, and the media), it was imperative that there be consistency among prisons, probation, or parole agencies within the same governmental jurisdiction. With the increasing intervention of courts, and as corrections became more in the public eye, many states formed departments specifically to oversee the community corrections and state prisons. Riveland notes, "Today, 32 states are organized with separate Departments of Corrections reporting to the Executive; 11 as separate departments reporting to boards or commissions; 5 under a Department of Public Safety umbrella, and 1 under a social services umbrella. Twenty-four of the separate departments have been so organized since 1979."[13]

Principles of Organizations

Before examining actual organizational structures of a few correctional agencies, it is important to understand some terminologies, basic principles, and the function and operation of a correctional agency. There are many basic principles of good management and organization that can be applied to corrections. However, correctional agencies, apart from other private or public organizations, experience certain pressures and influences that impact these principles. The following discussion considers such issues as how centralized an agency should be and whether there should be regional divisions to oversee field operations. How should work be divided, and what organizational divisions or departments should be created in prisons and headquarters? How much authority should various levels of the organization have and how should authority be aligned with responsibility? And finally, what is the chain of command and span of control?

Centralization and Regionalization

Centralization usually has two meanings when it is discussed in terms of management and correctional agencies. First, the typical definition of **centralization** has to do with the degree to which control and decision making is consolidated in one person in an organization. For instance, can prison staff make a decision without first consulting the warden? Can parole offices change the way they supervise offenders without approval of the central headquarters? Autocratic organizations usually have much power vested in one person: the leader. Traditionally, that was the way prisons operated, and there are still vestiges of that approach in corrections today. The degree of centralization of authority, today, usually has more to do with the personality of the leader and his or her willingness to trust staff and share decision making.

The second definition of centralization for a correctional agency involves the degree to which the headquarters or central office provides oversight and control over field operations. As is discussed later in the chapter, with the increase in complexities and of political and public interest in correctional operations, central headquarters have broadened their role and function regarding prisons and other field activities. Today, most correctional agencies have a rather large headquarters staff that develop budgets, manage human resource issues, create policy, deal with external interest groups, and direct field operations. Although central office staff provide services designed to assist and add consistency to prisons and field offices across their jurisdictions, many wardens and field office supervisors would suggest that the central office reach well beyond a service function to the point at which they unnecessarily dictate activities at the field level.

Regionalization involves geographically breaking down field operations into smaller and, therefore, more manageable components. Because the number of offenders under supervision and the number of staff have grown in nearly every jurisdiction, it has become almost impossible for a central correctional headquarters to stay abreast of all the activities taking place throughout the agency. As a result, many correctional agencies have created regions to oversee prisons and other field operations in a particular geographic area. These regions then create additional layers of staff to support and coordinate activities of the field operations. Regional supervisors must have service staff to assist them in directing and guiding the budget, human resources, policy, and operations. Therefore, correctional agencies that regionalize end up with three levels of organization with parallel, and oftentimes overlapping, functions. The true challenge for an organization that has a strong centralized headquarters as well as regions is to avoid duplication of staff and services, which can result in inefficiency and micromanagement of facilities and community corrections.

Division of Labor and Departmentalization

The first principle that must be considered in organizing an agency is **division of labor**, or specialization of work. There are many tasks that must be accomplished in a correctional environment, such as tracking gang members, classifying inmates, conducting community investigations, and providing medical treatment. Tasks are broken down into steps that can be completed by one person, and the tasks are then grouped into job specifications for each position. For example, a headquarters gang management specialist will collect information from prisons on inmate gang activities, review and approve recommendations to validate an inmate as a gang member, and issue reports on the latest gang activities and threats. A prison nurse will conduct medical screenings of new inmates, do a triage examination of inmates reporting for sick call, and instruct inmates on prescribed medication or rehabilitative exercises. A probation officer will check on offenders work performance and ensure they are participating in required programs. The division of labor results in like tasks being assigned to individuals who can be trained to perform them.

Once a group of specialists is identified by division of labor, they are usually organized into a coordinated group assigned like duties. The group may be made up of several individuals who do the same functions, such as correctional or probation officers. Or, it may be made up of individuals doing similar functions that support one another. For example, medical staff may have a nurse assigned to screen inmates at sick call and schedule them to see a physician, the physician does an examination and prescribes treatment, and a pharmacist prepares and delivers the medication to the inmates. These types of grouping are called **departmentalization**. Departmentalization allows for like activities to be coordinated in a way to efficiently carry out the required work, and is usually facilitated and supervised by a single manager. In prisons or jails, examples of departments include security, medical services, mental health, food services, and the business office. In probation or parole offices, there are departments that supervise offenders, those that provide substance abuse programs, job developers, and electronic monitoring specialists.

Responsibility and Authority

One of the most important principles of management is that responsibility and authority must be aligned and assigned for every role or position. Responsibility is the expectation and obligation to carry out assigned duties. In a probation office, the chief probation officer is responsible for managing the office and assuring offenders complete all the conditions of their probation. Likewise, probation officers are held responsible for carrying out their assigned functions, such as conducting office visits with probationers, doing home visits, or confirming employment and program participation. When tasks are assigned, it is essential that staff take responsibility to complete these tasks in the prescribed manner. Authority is the right of workers to give orders and have an expectation that those receiving the orders will comply with them. In a typical private company or public agency, authority usually is only vested in management and supervisory-level employees. However, in a correctional agency, all staff members supervise offenders and must have the authority to get compliance with policies that impact offender behavior.

How do responsibility and authority coincide? For each task assigned to an individual, there are certain actions that must be carried out to complete the task. When correctional officers conduct counts, they must ensure that inmates are in the proper cell during the count. Imagine inmates not being in their cells, the officer ordering them to the proper cells, and the inmates responding, "The unit manager said we did not have to be counted in our cells." If line correctional officers do not have the authority to require that counts be conducted in the prescribed manner, they cannot be responsible if the count is not right. Similarly, a probation officer responsible for inmate compliance to their conditions of supervision must have the authority to write violation notices, bring an offender into court for a case review, and issue an arrest warrant when they disappear from supervision.

Chain of Command and Span of Control

Chain of command and unity of command are critical to every organization, especially a "paramilitary" organization such as a correctional agency. The chain of command is most familiar to military operations, where ranks of individuals (private, sergeant, or captain) relate to their position in the chain of command. Chain of command is the vertical hierarchy in an organization, identified in terms of authority. Persons receive orders from the person immediately above them, who in turn issues orders to the people immediately below them. Figure 7-2 illustrates a simplified prison chain of command from a warden to a correctional officer.

Unity of command involves the principle that a subordinate should report to only one supervisor. For a worker to take orders from more than one person is not only inefficient but can also lead to conflict and chaos. Obviously, workers may receive orders from someone in their chain of command above their immediate supervisor.

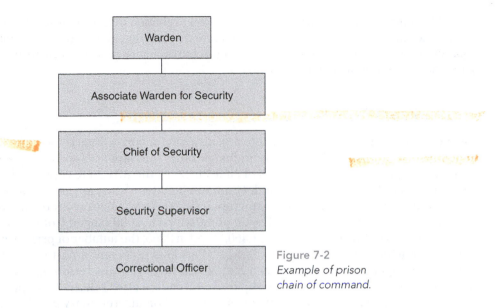

Figure 7-2
Example of prison chain of command.

A warden may see a security concern that needs attention (a door unlocked that should be locked), tell a correctional officer to take care of it (immediately lock the door), and there is usually no need to channel the order back through the chain of command. However, if the security concern is a broader issue, such as a change in procedures or need to reinforce current procedures (e.g., too many inmates moving across the compound during nonmovement times in a prison that uses "controlled movement"), then the warden would officially issue the order through the chain of command; the order (to limit inmate movement during nonmovement times) may be passed through the chain of command so that all in the chain, and all correctional officers, are made aware of the change.

Span of control is the reverse of unity of command. Just as subordinates should only report to one supervisor, supervisors should only supervise the number of staff they can effectively direct. The designated span of control for an organization dictates the number of vertical levels in the organizational hierarchy, and the number of managers and supervisors needed to carry out the organizational objectives. There is no magic number of persons a supervisor can effectively direct. It depends on the complexity of the functions and tasks and how much direction the workers need. A chief probation officer may determine that a probation supervisor can effectively direct twenty probation officers and still give them guidance and intermittently observe the performance of their duties. However, the chief probation officer may also determine that the substance abuse coordinator can only effectively direct the work of eight substance abuse counselors, as their work is clinical, their record keeping must meet prescribed protocols, and they must make judgments when probationers are ready to move from one level to another or have successfully completed the program.

These management principles are keys to understanding how correctional agencies are organized. In the following sections, three tables of organization are presented: for a central headquarters, for a prison or jail, and for a probation or parole office. In order to clarify roles in each organization and to illustrate the function and influences driving the organizational structure, each division and department is described in terms of its personnel, organization, and functions.

Centralized Headquarters Organization

The most usual centralized headquarters organization for corrections is the state department of corrections, which usually includes both the supervision of prisons and community corrections functions. As of June 30, 2008, the fifty states operated almost 1,250 prisons holding approximately 1.41 million inmates.[14] Just as the states are very different in terms of the size and demographics of their populations, the state prison systems vary dramatically as well. Prison populations in 2008 ranged from Texas with 173,232 inmates to North Dakota with 1,450,[15] and in 2005, the number of prisons ranged from 5 in Washington D.C. to 132 in Texas.[16] Parole is no longer a part of most state correctional agencies, as only fifteen states still have full discretionary parole for inmates. However, almost all states supervise offenders after release from prison. In 2006, while only 33 percent of inmates were released on discretionary parole, another 48 percent were released on mandatory parole with supervision, 9 percent were reinstated on parole after a brief prison stay, and 11 percent were released under other parole arrangements.[17]

In contrast to the reduction of parole within correctional organizations, although there are over 2,000 local agencies delivering probation services, there has been an increase in the centralization of probation. Although probation began as a service to the judiciary and an arm of the court, today, in more than half of the states, probation operations are centralized in the state department of corrections. This move toward centralization stems from the need for training, professionalism, and uniformity of standards, which can be better accomplished in larger administrative systems; there can also be better coordination with other correctional services. In approximately eight states and the federal government, probation and parole services are provided by the same state agency that supervises both probationers and parolees.

The Organization of State Correctional Systems

Over the past decades, state correctional agencies have gone through a slow but deliberate transformation. As noted, until recently, there was no central control of prisons and legislatures allocated budgets and personnel directly to each individual prison. State prison wardens were often said to have their own individual "fiefdoms," with complete control over the hiring and firing of staff and the management and discipline of inmates. As late as the first half of the twentieth century, many wardens of state prisons were appointed by governors, with no cabinet-level agency to oversee prison operations.

However, as prison systems became larger, their missions became more complex, there was increasing intervention by the federal courts, and as corrections became more visible and politically sensitive to the public, many states formed cabinet-level departments specifically to oversee the state prisons and community field operations. By 1997, Riveland reported that "Thirty-two states are organized with separate Departments of Corrections reporting to the Executive; 11 as separate departments reporting to boards or commissions; 5 under a Department of Public Safety umbrella, and 1 under a social services umbrella. Twenty-four of the separate departments have been so organized since 1979."[18] Nine of the fifty state adult correctional systems are also responsible for juvenile corrections, twenty-seven have some probation responsibility, thirty-three supervise parole or other supervised release functions, and twenty-nine manage community corrections programs.[19]

The most common organizational model (in twenty-four states) has the director, commissioner, or secretary of corrections as a cabinet-level officer, appointed by and reporting directly to the governor. This framework seems to have many positive advantages, especially by giving governors direct authority to operate the state prisons as they see fit. With crime and corrections often an issue in statewide political elections, candidates for governor usually take a policy position on correctional issues, and want to be in a position to influence the correctional agencies in a direct and immediate manner. This framework, however, often results in a change in correctional leadership with each new governor.

In eleven states, the chief of the corrections agency reports to a board or commission appointed by the governor, made up of individuals from different political parties, and have overlapping terms. The purpose behind this type of organizational model is to have some separation between politics and correctional policy. Therefore, governors are not able to immediately replace the board or commission with their own appointees, having to wait until terms end to replace members. The boards and commissions are relatively stable as a result, maintaining consistency of policy and leadership in the correctional agency.

The benefit of boards and commissions is that they somewhat insulate the corrections agency from political influence. This is believed to have at least two advantages. First, as noted previously, there is more likelihood of continuity of leadership in the correctional agency. In those states in which the corrections director serves at the direct pleasure of the governor, it is not unusual to have a new director appointed at each turnover of governor, regardless of how good a job the director did or how issue-free the department was. Second, there is likely to be continuity of policy and less political pressure to adopt politically popular, but poor, public policy. Even though the board or commission is a result of a political appointment, the members serve a fairly long term and become educated about the operations of a corrections agency. They are, therefore, able to make informed judgments about the value of a specific policy and weigh it against the political positions regarding the policy.

At the federal level, the Bureau of Prisons (BOP) is an agency of the U.S. Department of Justice, and the director is appointed by and reports to the Attorney General. Because of the size of the federal government, corrections is not as important politically as it is at the state level of government. Presidential candidates seldom campaign around an issue regarding the operation of federal prisons. However, with the BOP director reporting to a presidential cabinet secretary, the desires of the chief executive (the president) can easily be implemented. Historically, there has seldom been a change in the director of the BOP as a result of a political change of leadership. However, many people believe that this may change as corrections continues to become a larger federal budget item and a more important domestic policy issue.

Even with the advantages of the board and commission format, many directors of corrections favor working directly for the elected official. They believe they are capable and persuasive enough to educate the governor and the governor's staff about correctional policy, so that their professional input will be sought on policies that could impact prison operations. By working directly for the governor, the directors find they are better able to get the support of the executive branch agencies for positions and finances needed to meet a continually growing client demand. Even with corrections becoming a very political issue, most governors support good public policy once they are elected and become responsible for the operations of an agency. It is not unusual for gubernatorial candidates to modify their positions regarding correctional policy, if they find their positions have some negative consequences.

As a result of the rapid growth of corrections over the past twenty years, the complexities and expansion of correctional missions, and the growing interest of politics, states have moved to centralized functions overseeing corrections and created cabinet-level departments of corrections. Beyond this, the interest and continuous influence of external factors (politics, legislative oversight committees, the media, and public interest groups) on correctional operations have impacted the organization of the centralized agency. Most agencies find that there are great demands for information from the governor's staff, the media, and the legislature. To meet these demands, agencies create organizational entities to respond to requests and keep external interest groups informed of changes in correctional policy.

Figure 7-3 illustrates three models of correctional agencies. In the first, the corrections director reports directly to a governor. In the second, the director reports to a board or commission. The third is the federal model, in which the BOP director is appointed by and reports to the attorney general of the United States. And following the model is a real case study that illustrates how corrections has become more complex and more political, and displays the conflict that can come between policy and politics.

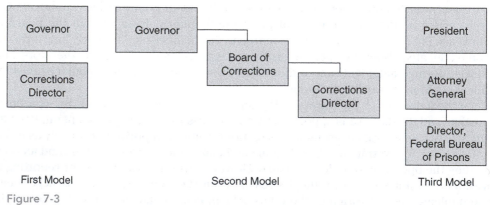

First Model   Second Model   Third Model

Figure 7-3
Three models of correctional agency relationships to the chief executive.

Practical Perspectives

When Policy Confronts Politics

The following case study describes the situation around a very experienced director of corrections having to deal with the political implications of implementing certain "tough on crime" correctional policies. The director began working in state government in 1962, became the warden of a maximum security prison in 1971, and progressed to director of corrections in that state. He served in that position on two occasions, leaving most recently in 1996. He was also director of corrections in two other states, chairman of the criminal justice department at a large state university, and president of a private planning and design firm that did consulting in forty-four different states. As is obvious, he was well qualified to lead a major state department of corrections.

He became the director of corrections for his home state for the second time in the 1990s. In the state, as in many other states, the politics of corrections drastically changed to a more conservative approach after the 1994 elections. The director, however, felt very comfortable in this position as director, working directly for the governor. The governor had worked in corrections, taught public policy at a university, and understood the nuances of correctional policies. However, the public was stirred up by the rhetoric of the 1994 campaign, and the governor listened to the public. There was a public cry for a harsher prison system, with fewer amenities, and policies that made it appear that inmates were being punished and would not enjoy their period of confinement. One poll had the public 85 percent in favor of chain gangs in the state.

The governor was listening to the voters and was very politically astute. He suggested that the director put some of these politically popular programs in place. However, the director was focusing on other things than implementing popular correctional policies, such as trying to implement effective programs to reduce the 39 percent recidivism rate in the state. He believed that if the corrections department was really going to safeguard the public, this needed to be done. He knew the state had good discipline, control, and a safe system, and was ready to move forward with the next step in program development. When the director did not implement the programs the public wanted, the governor sent the director a letter that was also for public consumption which outlined steps to reduce privileges and programs, and to make state prisons a harsher environment. In essence, the governor was making the director look bad publically, and was showing the public he was forcing the department of corrections to make changes in their operations. The director chose to resign instead of implementing the tough on crime policies in which he did not believe. The governor then appointed a former state legislator, with no experience whatsoever in corrections, to be the director of corrections.

The former director admitted that in retrospect, he was listening to the public, but did not react appropriately. He did not do the necessary market research to subsequently develop a program that made policy sense, and could offer the governor operations that would appear to meet the goals of public safety. The director does not feel that correctional leaders should cave in and implement correctional programs that are unsafe and destructive. But they need to be innovative enough to develop a package that is both effective and politically saleable. He stated that no corrections director can win a fight that forces the governor to choose between him and the public sentiment. He still believes in the things that the department was doing, but recognizes they were not acceptable at that point in time to the public and by the voters. The advice the director would give to others in his position would be to be proactive and read the concerns of the public and political leaders. He would put some programs in place that did appear to be tough on inmates, yet not undermine the most important functions of a safe and secure prison. In that way, correctional agencies can be both professional in implementing effective policy, and wise politically.

The Organization of the Central Office

The central organization that oversees the state and federal correctional systems is often called the "central office" or "headquarters." These organizations have grown dramatically with the increasing number of inmates, and the increasing demand for central control and consistency. As an example, Ohio created a cabinet-level correction agency (the Department of Rehabilitation and Correction) in 1971. Prior to that, the Department of Mental Hygiene and Corrections was the agency that oversaw the state prisons and parole operations. At that time, there were only six prisons and less than twenty corrections staff in the department's central office. There was little opportunity for strong leadership, guidance for the state prisons, or central policy coming from the headquarters.

Currently, Ohio is the sixth largest state correctional agency in the United States. The five largest (in order of size) are California, Texas, the Federal Bureau of Prisons, New York, and Florida. By the end of 2009, Ohio had 34 state prisons, almost 51,000 prison inmates, 36,500 offenders under community supervision, and 13,250 staff.[20] To oversee these activities, Ohio has approximately 327 staff working in the headquarters office in the state capital of Columbus. The table of organization of the central office of the Ohio Department of Rehabilitation and Correction (Figure 7-4) represents the complexity required to run an agency with an annual budget of $900 million and the expansive services it delivers across the state.

The headquarters tables of organization for major departments of corrections are similar, and those in Figure 7-4 represent how they are organized to meet the complex challenges faced by a correctional agency. One interesting note is that the head of the agency is called a *director, secretary, commissioner, or executive director*. While the titles are different, the role is the same to oversee the operations of the department and provide public safety through the supervision of criminal offenders. The following describes these organizational functions and the issues with which they must deal.

Office of the director.

Most central correctional agencies organizationally locate the external management functions close to the director, and they report either to the director or assistant director. There are two reasons for this. First, by dealing with these issues at the director level, it frees the rest of the organization to focus on accomplishing the mission (managing criminal offenders). Second, correctional agencies have found that external issues are so sensitive and can so quickly become political or media crises that there should be immediate access and no screening of the issues between the staff dealing with the issues and the director. The worst thing that can happen to a correctional agency is for an issue that is potentially sensitive (e.g., a community offender committing a serious and very public crime and victim groups becoming outraged) to be misrepresented by lower-level staff who have not been provided input from the person in charge of the agency. When public sentiment goes against the decisions made by the corrections agency, the head of that agency can quickly lose the confidence of their elected supervisor and lose their jobs. In fact, most heads of correctional agencies are fired because of how the agency handled external and public issues rather than due to a failure in the internal management of the agency. Therefore, directors of corrections do not want any surprises when it comes to developments around sensitive external communications.

Common organizational entities in the office of the director include communications (public or media affairs), legislative liaison, legal advisors, and internal affairs. State or large county correctional agencies are usually one of the largest state agencies (in terms of budget and employees), and there is a tremendous demand on them for public information and responding to the media. When minor items are of media interest only at a single prison or community corrections office, staff at that location will usually handle

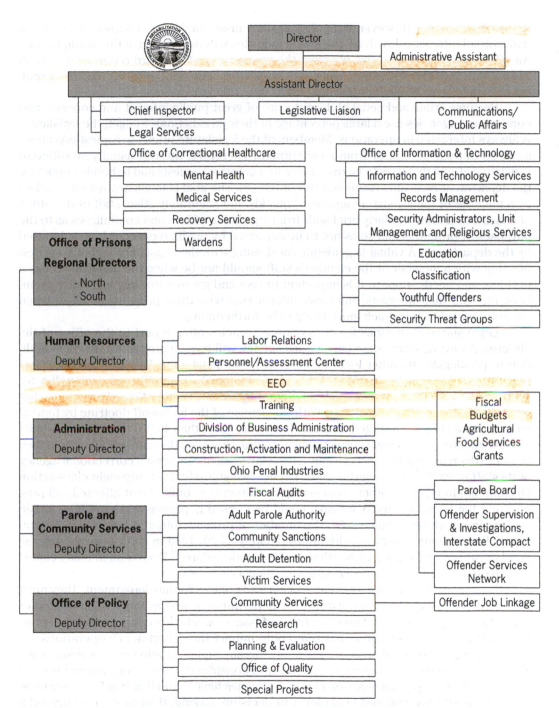

Figure 7-4

Table of organization for the central office of the Ohio Department of Rehabilitation and Correction.
Source: *Ohio Department of Rehabilitation and Correction. Reprinted with permission.*

the media requests. However, if a policy issue, a major incident, or something that has widespread interest is involved, the media inquiries will be handled at the headquarters. An office of public affairs also oversees the preparation of standard reports, such as an annual review of the department and its status or information regarding a program or project in which there is much public interest.

Because crime and penal philosophy are of great public interest and concern, and correctional agencies use a large percentage of their jurisdictions' budget, the legislature is always interested in operations. Members of the legislature often have questions about a prison in their district or from a constituent. Therefore, there is usually an office of legislative affairs that tries to be responsive to legislative requests and to build support for the department regarding resources and programs. The goal is to get any question asked by a member of the legislature answered quickly and accurately. Also, staff of the office of legislative affairs regularly brief staff from legislative offices and committees as to the purposes of programs and so as not to be surprised by media reports or bills submitted by the department. A valuable guideline for dealing with the legislature is that your first meeting with a member or the member's staff should not be when the department has a problem and needs support. It is important to visit and get to know key legislative members, find out their interests, and share information with them proactively. Then, when support is needed, it is much more likely to be forthcoming.

Legal services divisions for correctional agencies often report to the office of the director. An average size state corrections agency will have six to ten attorneys in addition to paralegals and other legal support staff. The legal work falls into three general categories: (1) responding to offender (primarily inmate) lawsuits; (2) reviewing policy for its legal impact; and (3) general advice regarding the implementation of programs that are in line with past legal decisions. With the demise of the hands-off doctrine by federal courts, inmate litigation surged. In 1995, there were more than 40,000 civil rights lawsuits filed by inmates against state correctional agencies. However, the number of lawsuits then began to decrease, and there were only 24,463 lawsuits filed against a correctional agency or its staff in 2000.[21] On January 1, 2002, twenty-two states had seventy-eight class-action lawsuits in effect; court orders concerning conditions of confinement affected 143 prisons; and limits on how many inmates could be housed in prisons were in effect at 135 prisons in ten states.[22] Since 2000, the number of prisoner-initiated lawsuits in federal courts has continued to drop, with approximately 25,000 filed in 2006, even though the number of inmates is much higher than in the decade before.[23] Even though many claims are frivolous, each requires processing and filing a response.

Legal staff also give advice on new or revised policies for the department. They must be aware of all cases decided regarding the department as well as those regarding other correctional agencies. They know the types of issues on which a court has taken a position, and where a precedent exists that could impact the department's operations. As changes in operations and procedure or new program implementation are discussed, legal staff offer advice on how the courts are likely to consider the new operation or program in light of the legal precedents. Correctional agencies have found that it is far better to be aware of prior case law, and consider it in decision making, than to have to defend a change in operations or a new program in court at a later time.

Finally, the office of the director usually has an inspector or internal affairs division as a part of the organization. Ethics in government is a high priority, and the opportunity for unethical, or even illegal, behavior is great when staff are in daily contact with manipulative inmates. Staff may be enticed to bring contraband into the prison, overlook a violation of community supervision, or they may be physically abusive to inmates. Whenever there is a complaint of staff misconduct by anyone (offenders or their families, other staff, or the general public), the allegation is investigated. An objective look by trained investigators is the best defense for staff against untrue allegations. Correctional staff know that offenders are likely to be unhappy with them, and may allege misconduct to cause them problems. Knowing that every allegation will be investigated and, if not sustained, the staff member will be cleared is comforting to correctional staff. However, staff also know that if they do become involved in unethical behavior, it will likely be reported and investigated. If sustained, they also know that there will be disciplinary or criminal charges filed against them. This reminder is a deterrent to staff who may be tempted to violate the agency's standards of ethics.

Administration division.
These divisions often end up with a combination of many areas. Two major responsibilities of the administrative division are budget development and new prison construction. Prisons and community correctional offices keep track of their spending and do required accounting and bookkeeping. However, the development of the annual budget is very complex and is done centrally by department staff in conjunction with the overall state budget office. The administration division collects information from the prisons, community offices, other divisions, and the governor's office to create a budget that represents desired programs, growth (or sometimes retraction), and continued operations. Once approved by the governor's office, the administration division begins to educate and explain the budget request to the legislative budget committee, which reviews the request and makes a recommendation for funding to the full legislative body.

Corrections spends lots of money and therefore gets intense scrutiny of the budget, and expenditures for correctional agencies have grown significantly. As indicated in Figure 7-5, expenditures for the police, judiciary, and corrections have all expanded from 1982 to 2006. However, corrections expenditures grew at the greatest rate of 660 percent during that period. In fiscal year 1991, state and federal adult correctional agencies' budgets totaled $18.1 billion,[24] but by fiscal year 2006, these budgets, with the inclusion of local jails, more than tripled to $68.7 billion.[25] In 2007, state correctional agencies consumed 6.8 percent of state general funds,[26] and by 2011, continued prison growth is expected to cost an additional $25 billion.[27] Figures vary widely, but the average per prisoner operating cost was $28,816 ($78.95 per day) in 2008.[28]

Usually included in a budget request are funds to construct new prisons. The administrative division is usually charged with overseeing design and construction of the new and renovated facilities. This includes hiring architects, coordinating their design with the department correctional experts, overseeing construction, and preparing to activate the new facilities. The number of inmates increased dramatically over the 1990s, and most correctional agencies were given new dollars to expand capacity by building new prisons. For example, in 1997, 31 new prisons were opened in the United States at a cost of $1.16 billion; 60 new prisons were under construction and 130 existing ones were expanding capacity at a cost of $3.8 billion; and funding for capital construction for budget year 1998 was $2.6 billion.[29] From 1993 to 2000, 288 new prisons were constructed and

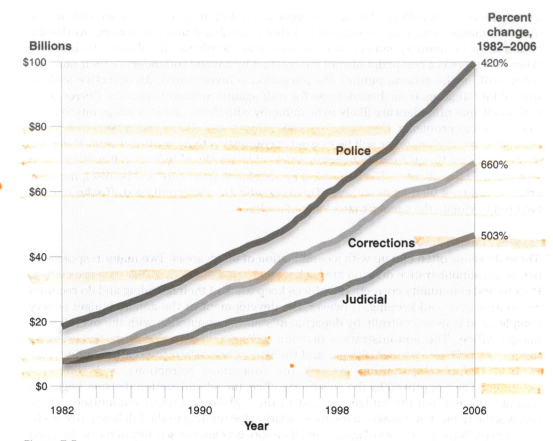

Figure 7-5

Direct Expenditures by Criminal Justice Function, 1982–2007

Source: *Bureau of Justice Statistics, Expenditure Facts at a Glance, www.ojp.usdoj.gov/bjs/glance/exptyp.htm (accessed January 30, 2010).*

opened,[30] from June 30, 2000 to December 30, 2005, 153 new state and federal prisons and 151 new private prisons were constructed and opened.[31]

Other functions within the administrative division include technology and prison industries. Technology has become increasingly important as correctional agencies look to use technologies to improve their efficiency or effectiveness. There are many standard technology applications that are used in the business world such as data storage or generation, electronic medical records, office applications to order supplies and pay bills in a paperless fashion, computerized time clocks that automatically create payroll, and identification systems to allow and record employee access. Law enforcement agencies are developing the ability to collect and share criminal or gang intelligence. Correctional agencies use technology to prevent or detect prison contraband, improve staff safety, and aid in supervising offenders in the community. Fabelo suggests that a correctional agency taking advantage of new technologies to reduce the costs of supervising criminal offenders and minimizing the risk they pose to society is called "technocorrections."[32]

Prison industries (addressed in Chapter 13) also fall into this division. Prison industries programs produce goods in prison that are then sold to other government agencies or sometimes within the private sector. They must be as much like private businesses as possible, in that they have to produce goods of high quality and at a price that makes them no more costly than could be bought elsewhere. In addition, most states require that they be self-supporting, or able to cover their costs by the sale of goods.

Correctional operations division.
A correctional agency will usually have a central office division that oversees prison operation and the policy development for functional areas such as security, education, religion, mental health, and unit management. In the Ohio headquarters table of organization, the supervision of the prisons is divided into the North and South geographic regions. The regional directors supervise the wardens and their principle roles are to ensure quality and consistency across all the prisons within their region. These regions have staff who develop policy, monitor operations, and advise prison staff in these functional areas. These individuals are subject matter experts in their functional areas and provide guidance to the prison department head who oversees that function in the prison. The headquarters staff may also create an audit checklist that must be accomplished in each prison and then conduct audits against the checklist. The audit checklist is policy based, in that it gives specific steps that must be completed to comply with policy.

Medical or health care division.
One of the most complicated and expensive functions within a prison is health care (presented in detail in Chapter 14). Quality medical care for inmates is a challenge, as most offenders have not had proper medical care throughout their lives, and often have serious medical problems. When inmates do not believe they have received the quality or scope of care they want, they often sue the prison and its administrators. Therefore, there is a central office division that develops policy, oversees quality assurance, and looks for ways to make more efficient and less expensive health care to inmates. Correctional health care has developed into a specialty within itself, unique because it deals with the practice of medicine for a high-risk, incarcerated population. As such, it is critical to recruit staff for this division who understand both health care and prison medical services.

Human resource management division.
Included under the human resource management division are the usual personnel functions of recruitment, hiring, evaluations, and retirement. In addition, most correctional agencies have groups to deal with affirmative action or equal employment opportunity (EEO), labor relations, and staff training. Workforce diversity is important for correctional agencies, particularly because of a high percentage of minority (African American and Hispanic) offenders and a growing number of women offenders. Most states have a unionized correctional workforce, and negotiating contracts and management of labor issues is critical and very time consuming. Therefore, the central office usually has staff with expertise in labor relations who do the negotiations and advise managers on labor contract issues. As noted earlier, these divisions are usually responsible for staff training. Some training is completed at prisons and community corrections offices. However, almost all states now operate a central training academy to prepare new prison and community staff for their duties.

Community corrections division.

Finally, central offices have a division that oversees and supervises community field operations. State correctional agencies can have responsibility for probation, parole, or postrelease supervision of offenders; they may operate community-based facilities such as halfway houses; and may have some responsibility for local jail inspections. In the Ohio example, there is a division to supervise parole and other community service functions. Even though prison operations have the majority of the staff and budget dollars directed to them, more offenders are supervised in the community than are held in prison. And with the concern for public safety and reduction of recidivism, community correctional operations and techniques for carrying them out have gotten a renewed focus. Statewide parole and probation functions are organized into geographic regions, districts, or city offices to supervise offenders, while headquarters staff are assigned to oversee the day-to-day operations of these field offices. In addition to probation and parole supervision, community corrections divisions sometimes include a section for victim services. Today, there is a much greater concern with the victim of crimes and their need for information and to be a part of the decision-making process. Victim services departments usually keep victims informed of parole hearings, invite their comments on the parole decision, and let them know of changes in prison assignment or in which community a released offender will be living.

Another area important to the community corrections division is a new and national focus on prisoner reentry. With over 1.6 million prisoners in federal and state prisons, until recently little attention has been paid to the fact that many more offenders are also leaving prison and returning to the community than at any prior time in history. During 2007, 725,402 prisoners were released by adult prisons, an increase from 120,544 in 2000.[33] These inmates are often released from prisons to the community with little preparation for the challenges they will face. In a study by the Vera Institute of Justice, it was found that prisoners reentering society encounter issues such as finding housing, lack of ties with family and friends, finding a job, alcohol and drug abuse, and avoiding continued involvement in crime.[34] Petersilia also identified six collateral consequences of imprisonment: (1) community cohesion; (2) employment and economic well-being; (3) democratic participation and political alienation; (4) family stabilization and childhood development; (5) mental and physical health; and (6) homelessness.[35] Therefore, most correctional agencies have a focus on how to overcome these reentry problems and help the transition from prison to community.

The role of the central office, particularly during times of intense scrutiny, has increasingly become one of dealing with external interest groups and ensuring consistency and quality in the operation of prisons and community corrections. The sections below present the way both prisons and community corrections offices are organized. Carlson notes, "The critical and dangerous task of running prisons requires uniformity within each specific facility (fairness and equity—the perception that all inmates receive the same treatment) and precision of control."[36] With this in mind, we turn to the organization of individual prisons.

The Organization of Prisons

Today, the organization of prisons is as complicated as that of the central headquarters. Although the mission of prisons has changed little over the past fifty years, the organizational structure has changed considerably. As an example, prison organizations usually include functions such as an inspector of institutional services, an institutional investigator, labor relations, and affirmative action or EEO activities. These are today critical to a prison operation, yet none of these functions were part of a prison table of organization a few decades ago. The organizational entities that control the internal management of staff and inmates are very similar to the past. There is still the hierarchal chain of command to oversee the day-to-day operations of the prison. For example, the table of organization for the Lebanon (Ohio) Correctional Institution is presented as Figure 7-6.

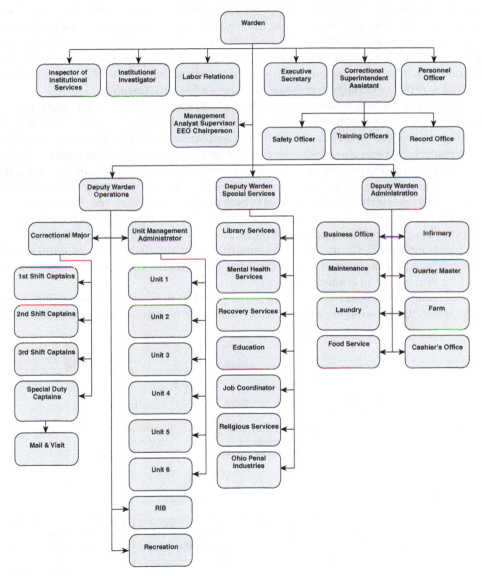

Figure 7-6
Table of organization for the Lebanon (Ohio) Correctional Institution.

It is interesting to compare a central office organization with a prison. Most, if not all, of the essential functions are replicated. This, however, does not mean that central office staff responsible for a function supervise those who deliver the same service in a prison. For example, the education administrator in the headquarters organization usually does not directly supervise the education supervisor in the prison. The role of headquarters staff is to be the technical expert who stays abreast of and develops policy to meet what are often changing issues in the delivery of any prison service, and to audit the prison to ensure compliance and offer advice and assistance. The prison supervisor is responsible for the execution of the policy or for bringing it to life in the real world of the prison. Also, prison administrators believe that the warden must be responsible for all functions within a prison, so that there is only one mission and no interference from those not responsible for the mission of the prison. When there is more than one set of directives that prison staff have to respond to, it can confuse and make less efficient an environment that is difficult enough to manage in a safe and secure fashion.

The direct reports to the warden often illustrate the priority or importance of a function. Some of the functions in the Lebanon model illustrate this point. The inspector of institutional services and the institutional investigator deal with inmate complaints against staff. Since Ohio allows collective bargaining for state employees, each Ohio prison has a full-time position to coordinate compliance with labor contracts and provide a first-line communication link with prison union officers. There is constantly a need for information and to review the effectiveness of prison programs and services. The management analyst supervisor collects and provides this information to central headquarters that can be used to answer public, media, and legislative questions, and be the foundation for budget preparation in future years. As mentioned in the discussion of central office organization, equal employment opportunity and affirmative action for staff are critically important and visible in contemporary prisons.

The table of organization for the warden's staff at the Federal Correctional Institution in Greenville, Illinois (Figure 7-7), illustrates some additional functions, including an

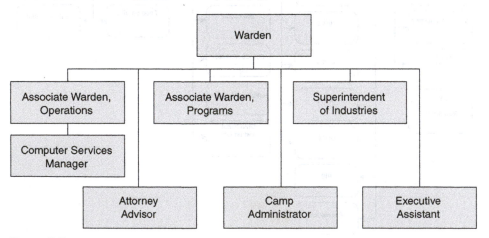

Figure 7-7

Table of organization for the warden's staff at the Federal Correctional Institution in Greenville, Illinois.

attorney advisor. Many federal prisons have full-time attorneys or paralegals as a part of the prison staff, and some larger or higher-security federal prisons may have a legal staff of two or three people. Their role is to handle the volume of information needed by headquarters legal staff and offices of U.S. attorneys, who provide legal representation for federal prison staff sued by inmates.

Also reporting to the warden are deputy, assistant, or associate wardens (jurisdictions use different terms). The general functions supervised by these individuals usually fall into three categories:

1. **Custody**—all the functions that come under the security activities within a prison; includes all uniformed employees, such as correctional officers and correctional supervisors

2. **Treatment**—all the rehabilitative functions focused on keeping inmates productively engaged and preparing them for release, including counseling, religious services, substance abuse programs, or education

3. **Services**—all the functions that are required to operate the prison, such as budget and finance, maintenance of the facility, human resources management, and those that provide basic services to inmates, such as food and health services, work programs, commissary, and laundry operations

In the Lebanon, Ohio, table of organization, there are three deputy wardens, for operations, special services, and administration. The deputy warden for operations supervises correctional security (correctional supervisors and officers), unit management, the inmate disciplinary committee (Rules Infraction Board [RIB]), and recreation. The deputy warden for special services supervises the library, mental health, recovery services (alcohol and drug abuse), education, prison job assignments, religious services, and prison industries (Ohio Penal Industries [OPI]). The deputy warden for administration supervises the business office, prison maintenance, laundry, food service, the infirmary (medical services), quartermaster (issuer of clothing), the farm, and the cashier.

In the Greenville, Illinois, federal prison, there are only two associate wardens (AWs), one for operations and the other for programs. The AW for operations (see Figure 7-8) is

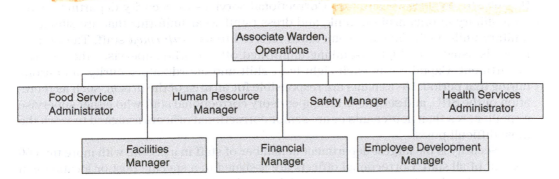

Figure 7-8

Table of organization for departments reporting to the association warden for operations at the Federal Correctional Institution in Greenville, Illinois.

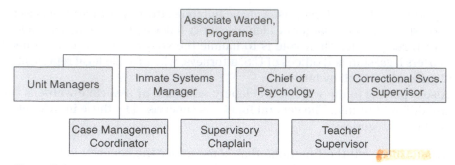

Figure 7-9

Table of organization for departments reporting to the association warden for programs at the Federal Correctional Institution in Greenville, Illinois.

similar to the Ohio deputy warden for administration and supervises food service, health services, facilities (maintenance), and finances (the business office). In addition, this AW also supervises human resources, safety, and employee development (training). The AW for programs supervises many of the same functions as the Ohio deputy wardens for operations and special services. These include (see Figure 7-9) unit management, psychology (mental health), correctional services (security), chaplain (religious services), teacher supervisor (education), and inmate systems (records). Although the titles of organization differ somewhat, these represent the basic functions required to operate and meet the mission of a prison. Several of these operational departments are described in Chapter 13. A general summary of the organization of the three major functions within a prison is presented below.

Custody and Security Functions

The custody and security component is often referred to as *correctional services* and encompasses all the security activities within a prison, including the duties of the security staff, the operations of the special housing unit (SHU), inmate transportation, and the inmate disciplinary process. Correctional services or security departments are paramilitary in organization, rank, and dress (staff wear uniforms that are similar to military uniforms). They are sometimes referred to as *uniformed* staff. The rank of major is usually the highest-ranking uniformed officer, who supervises the security department. Captains run each eight-hour shift and coordinate security operations during that period. Lieutenants are responsible for an area of the prison, such as recreation or the SHU, and sergeants are supervisory correctional staff who either supervise a smaller area than lieutenants or are senior correctional officers assigned to work the most difficult posts.

Security is the largest department in number of staff in a prison, with more than 50 percent of all staff. Correctional officers are assigned to a specific post or location in a prison such as housing in the dorms or cell houses in which inmates live, recreation areas such as the gym or yard, program or service areas such as the kitchen or education, or they may direct inmates on a job to do sanitation or work in the yard.

Treatment Functions

Treatment or programs include education and vocational training, recreation, mental health, religious services, and substance abuse or recovery services. These functions are critical to prepare inmates for reentry to the community by providing rehabilitative activities within a prison. Staff who work in these departments are sometimes referred to as *professional staff,* because most of the jobs within these disciplines require a college education and specific preparation or certification to perform.

Education departments operate academic teaching, vocational training, library services, and sometimes recreation programs for inmates. These departments are managed similar to a community elementary or high school. Teachers must be certified, but teach a general topic (math, English, or science), rather than a grade. As inmates enter prison, they are tested for academic competence and work toward completion of a GED (general equivalency diploma) at their own pace under the guidance of a teacher, who usually has a class of fifteen to twenty inmates. Vocational programs include carpentry or general building maintenance, landscape or horticulture, food service, and office skills. Recreation is sometimes a part of the education department, and recreation staff are assigned to areas such as the gymnasium or the recreation yard and not only supervise the area, but also plan and schedule leisure-time activities to try to involve the largest possible number of inmates.

Mental health programs are essential to be provided in every prison, since approximately 16 percent of prison and jail inmates are mentally ill.[37] Mental health departments usually employ one or two licensed psychologists to assess and counsel inmates. Few prisons have a full-time psychiatrist, but usually contract with one for a few hours per week to see the most ill patients who require psychotropic medication. There are also substance abuse or recovery programs that provide counseling for alcohol and drug abuse. Another critical treatment area within a prison is religious services. Prisons usually employ one or two full-time chaplains (often a Catholic priest and a Protestant minister) who hold religious services and coordinate other programs. Since all inmates have a right to practice the true tenets of their religious faith, prisons contract with clergy of other faiths (Muslim, Buddhist, Native American, or Jewish) to provide religious services and counseling to these inmates.

Service Functions

Service functions within a prison are those that deal with staff or facility issues (budget and finance, maintenance, and human resources management) and those that provide services to inmates such as food and health services, work programs, commissary, and laundry operations. Business office and human resources department are very similar to those of other government organizations. The budget office maintains control and records budget allocations, purchases necessary supplies and equipment, and prepares budget needs and does budget projections. The human resources department uses government requirements for selecting and hiring staff, and trains new employees for work in the prison. This department also oversees the evaluation of staff by supervisors each year, and the labor relations program to monitor compliance with collective-bargaining contracts and respond to labor union issues.

The components of the organization that provide services to inmates include food service, health care, laundry, commissary, and maintenance of the facility. Staff roles in the food and health care areas are described in Chapter 14. Services also include inmate work programs. Work programs benefit inmates as a rehabilitative tool, as inmates learn how to work for a supervisor, follow instructions, and develop positive work habits. These programs also benefit prison administrators by keeping inmates busy and assisting in maintaining control of the prison environment. And prison industry work programs also benefit the public, as by manufacturing and selling prison products, the cost of incarceration is reduced.

Unit Management

Another critical organizational entity in many prisons is unit management. Unit management was first established by the Federal Bureau of Prisons at the National Training School for Boys in 1966, and it was expanded throughout most federal prisons by the early 1970s. Since that time, almost every state has adopted **unit management** to assist in controlling their prisons. The BOP defines a unit as a "small, self-contained, inmate living and staff office area that operates semi-autonomously within the larger institution."[38] The purpose of establishing unit management was twofold. First, it decentralized the management of the prison, and second, it enhanced communication among staff and between staff and inmates.[39]

The average size of prisons has grown over the past three decades; there are few prisons designed to hold fewer than 1,000 inmates, and many hold 3,000 inmates or more. Recognizing that effective centralized management of such large prisons would be difficult, unit management breaks the prison into more manageable units based on housing assignments; assignment of staff to a particular unit; and giving the staff adequate authority to make decisions, manage the unit, and deal directly with inmates. Units usually comprise 300–500 inmates. The second advantage of unit management is that it enhances communication. Staff are not only assigned to units but also their offices are located in the housing unit, making them accessible to inmates and providing staff the opportunity to monitor inmate activities and behavior on a daily basis. Accessibility of staff provides, "each [unit] with a sense of group identity, and increases the frequency of employee–staff contacts [with inmates] so that small problems can be addressed before they become large problems."[40]

In addition to enhancing staff and inmate communication, unit management improves communications among staff from various departments. As illustrated in Figure 7-10, a table of organization for a functional unit includes staff from many disciplines and departments.

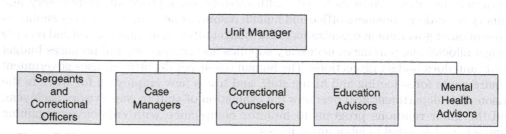

Figure 7-10
Table of organization for unit management.

A unit is directed by a unit manager. In most jurisdictions, unit managers are selected from a variety of disciplines, which may include security, case management, education, or psychology. The rest of the unit staff make up the "unit team," which jointly reviews inmates' backgrounds, evaluates needs, and determines program and job assignments. On arrival, new inmates meet with their team to outline their program activities and usually meet with their team every six months thereafter.

Directly reporting to the unit manager are case managers and correctional counselors. **Case managers** (sometimes called social workers or case workers in some states) have a caseload of from 100 to 150 inmates. They are responsible for developing the program of work and rehabilitation for each inmate and writing progress reports that can be used by release (parole) authorities or classification staff when considering an inmate for a program or transfer to another prison. **Correctional counselors** are selected from the ranks of correctional officers and wear officer uniforms. Their role is to work with inmates on the daily issues that confront inmates while in prison, such as creating a visiting or telephone list, correcting an error on their account of finances held by the prison, learning how to find a prison job, or getting along with other inmates. The wearing of a uniform reduces the perception that all security personnel do regarding inmates is enforce rules and give orders. Counselors assist inmates, and inmates begin to see that every staff who wears a uniform is not out to harass them.

Less clear is the supervision of correctional staff (sergeants and officers) who work in the housing unit. In some jurisdictions, these staff report to and are evaluated by the unit manager. In others, they still report to their security supervisors, but the unit manager provides input on their performance for their evaluation. Although they are not a direct reporting link, yet a part of the unit team, are educational and mental health specialists. These staff evaluate inmates and provide the unit team with information to help create a program of education, vocational training, substance abuse counseling, or psychological assistance that best fits the inmates needs. They may actually attend unit team meetings regarding inmates, or they may simply issue reports and recommendations to the team for each inmate.

The Organization of Community Correction

Community corrections departments are all similarly organized, whether they are a part of a state corrections department or an independent county operated department. While parole is a state function, probation is administered at the federal, state, and local level by more than 2,000 separate agencies; there is considerable diversity of operations and no uniform structure. Even though thought of as an arm of the court, in all but eleven of the states, adult probation is located in the executive branch of government. In more than half of the states, probation operations are centralized in the state department of corrections. And in approximately eight states and the federal government, probation and parole services are provided by the same state agency that supervises both probationers and parolees.

Figure 7-11 illustrates the table of organization for the Adult Field Services Bureau of the Los Angeles County Probation Department. As illustrated, there are four major sections in the Bureau, to include pretrial services, adult investigations, adult supervision, and

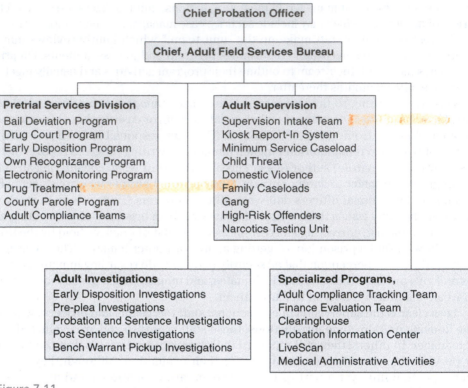

Figure 7-11
The Los Angeles County Probation Department, table of organization for the adult field services bureau.
Source: *Adapted from the Los Angeles County Probation Department website http://probation.co.la.ca.us/templates/default.asp (accessed January 31, 2010).*

specialized programs. This organization shows the scope of probation activities: reducing jail populations through pretrial services, investigations for judges to aid in sentencing, and actual supervision of those granted probation.

Pretrial services.

In Los Angeles County, the Pretrial Services Division includes many ways to avoid pretrial detention in a jail or to divert offenders from formal and traditional criminal sentencing. Program and units in the division include the drug court program, release on recognizance program, electronic monitoring, drug treatment, and adult compliance teams. Pretrial diversion programs are sometimes referred to as deferred prosecution or probation without adjudication. Many probation departments have bail and diversion staff who interview suspects in jail and then recommend to the court whether they should get bail or release on recognizance or whether they are good candidates for diversion. If offenders are charged with a nonviolent crime, have a limited prior criminal record, and possibly have a treatment need, such as for drug or alcohol abuse, the pretrial staff are likely to recommend that the judge grant the offender the opportunity for diversion. Pretrial conditions are very similar to those for probationers (avoiding additional criminality, reporting to the supervising officer as required, maintaining employment, and participating in the identified treatment program). Pretrial services staff then supervise the diverted offender in the community while making periodic reports to the court.

Probation departments often also supervise a release from jail or detention program to allow charged individuals who pose little threat to the community to be released from jail. Many individuals are released from jail on their own recognizance (ROR) or simply with their promise to appear for later court action. However, as many felony offenders were not granted this level of trust, by the middle of the twentieth century jails were becoming increasingly overcrowded with unsentenced offenders. The Vera Institute of Justice in New York City created the Manhattan Bail Project (MBP) in the 1960s to help judges identify individuals who were good candidates to be released on their own recognizance without commercial or monetary bond. This model has been followed in almost every jurisdiction since then.

Pretrial diversion staff interview defendants in jail and do community investigations to verify interview statements. They look for offenders with strong community ties who are likely to appear for trial and recommend to judges those who they believe are most suitable for release on recognizance. The goal is to decrease the number of offenders detained in jail awaiting trial while providing a more equitable form of release than simple bail. Since all these offenders are not truly "trust worthy," there are often supervised pretrial release (SPTR) programs for individuals who are considered poor risks for ROR but believed not a danger to the community and likely to show up for trial if supervised in the community. Under pretrial supervision, offenders must follow certain conditions (no criminal activity, no drug use, and steady employment), must report to a pretrial supervision officer, and can be violated (returned to jail) if they do not follow the conditions.[41] In some counties, such as Los Angeles, electronic monitoring can also be used to aid in supervision.

Adult investigations.
Before courts sentence an offender, they ask probation officers to conduct an investigation to provide information critical to an informed decision on a criminal sanction. This investigation is called a presentence investigation (PSI). The PSI details the criminal history, social background, education, employment, mental and physical health, and other factors regarding the criminal offender. Most states require a PSI to be completed for felony cases that allow the possibility of probation. When the court asks probation officers to make a recommendation within the PSI, that recommendation is followed 80–90 percent of the time. As in Los Angeles County, many probation departments have separate organizational groups that only do investigations and write PSIs. Others departments combine the investigative and the supervision divisions, and probation officers do a combination of both.

Adult supervision.
When offenders are granted probation, probation officers supervise them and get them to comply with conditions of their probation. The primary purpose of probation supervision is to maintain surveillance, enforce conditions of probation, and guide offenders into treatment to protect the public from further crimes. Officers monitor probationers' activities through a combination of office visits (probationers report to the officer at the probation office), verification of probationers' activities by visiting

their homes and contacting their employers or program providers, and monitoring activities such as drug testing of probationers. Supervision also includes helping offenders be placed into treatment and other social service programs to address their needs for education, mental health counseling, vocational training, or substance abuse programming.

Probation agencies generally organize caseloads into three types. Regular caseloads are used for probationers who may have a significant risk of reoffending or several program needs but do not warrant assignment to one of the other two types of caseloads. Intensive-supervision caseloads are for offenders with too high a risk or a need to be on regular supervision and are a final opportunity for offenders to avoid going to prison. Examples are high-risk offenders, sex offenders, or those with a history of violating probation conditions. These caseloads have fewer numbers and more required contacts between officers and probationers. Most jurisdictions also use special caseloads, whereby an officer's entire caseload is made up of probationers with a specific type of problem, such as substance abuse or mental illness. Such specialization allows the officer to become knowledgeable and proficient in dealing with this particular problem. In a 2002 survey, it was reported that 89.5 percent of probationers were on regular caseloads, 15.68 percent were on special caseloads, 4.2 percent were on intensive caseloads, and 0.7 percent were on a caseload using electronic monitoring.[42]

Specialized programs.

The function of the specialized programs within Los Angeles County is to enhance the department's collection of restitution, improve communications and information within and among other agencies, and to oversee the collection of DNA from offenders. In some ways, this is like the Administrative Division of a state corrections department as it covers many administrative functions that do not fall within the basic mission of conducting investigations and supervising offenders. The LiveScan unit does criminal identification and enters the information into a national database so that records of criminal activity are not limited to within jurisdictional boundaries.

SUMMARY

This chapter has illustrated how the organization of correctional agencies, prisons, and community corrections offices has evolved and changed as influences and demands on them have evolved and changed. A few decades ago, correctional central headquarters and their field operations were almost totally concerned with internal management, and there was little need or expectation for accountability, consistency between prisons, or interest from outside the organization. The functional organizational hierarchy was very simple and reflected the need for control and clarity in the chain of command without organizational entities to manage functions such as labor relations, affirmative action, legislative liaison, legal services, or media relations.

Today, there are several staff devoted to these functions, and correctional administrators spend as much of their time dealing with external as they do internal management activities. Organizational functions have staff and assigned duties that are focused on responding to external management requirements such as media relations, investigators for inmate complaints against staff, technology and information development, legislative communications, and legal coordinators. At the same time, the internal functions of prisons have become more complex, and the organizational hierarchies have evolved in response.

Prisons are much like other public agencies, as their organization is designed to most effectively complete tasks and carry out their mission. For prisons to provide safe and secure environments, with rehabilitative program opportunities for inmates, they must have several departments, clustered under the supervision of associate, assistant, or deputy wardens. Each department has goals and objectives that contribute to the overall prison mission. Staff within each department are similarly organized, with each job completing tasks that help to accomplish the departmental goals and objectives.

And community field officers or community correctional agencies have also expanded their organizational scope with the demands placed on them. Supervising offenders in the community is much more complex today than it was thirty years ago. Today, probation departments must help relieve jail overcrowding by designing and operating both diversion and expanded bail release programs. Investigations are critical for sound sentencing decisions by judges. And supervision styles and types have expanded beyond the traditional office visit and community checks for compliance. As the mission and responsibility of all these entities have become more complex and expanded, so have the types and functions of the organizations that oversee them.

KEY TERMS

Era of bureaucratic wardens
Centralization
Division of labor
Departmentalization

Responsibility
Authority
Chain of command
Unity of command

Span of control
Unit management
Case managers
Correctional counselors

YOU'RE THE CORRECTIONAL ADMINISTRATOR

1. You are the chief of program services in the central office of a medium-size state correctional agency. Your agency has not implemented unit management in the state prisons. The state director of corrections has asked you to review unit management and make a recommendation as to whether the state should adopt it as a management approach. Do not make a recommendation, but describe the process you would go through to consider whether it should be adopted. What are the key factors that you would look at within your state in your analysis? What are the key pieces of information you would like to find out from states who have implemented unit management? How would you blend these two types of information into a recommendation to the director?

2. You are the human resource manager for a county probation agency organized similar to the Los Angeles (CA) County Probation Department. The Chief Probation Officer has asked you to do an analysis of the organization and consider any need for a reorganization, in

order to improve efficiency or clarify lines of authority. Describe the process you would go through to analyze the most efficient organization you would recommend for the department. What type of information would be important, and how would you get the information?

WEB LINK EXERCISES

Go to the Ohio Department of Rehabilitation and Corrections (ODRC)—www.drc.ohio.gov
Find the community corrections components of the ODRC and identify how those components are organized. Based on this chapter's discussion of the principles of organizations, analyze how the community corrections components deal with centralization and regionalization, division of labor and departmentalization, chain of command, and span of control.

This exercise will require you to go to the Web sites of two state departments of corrections.

Go to http://www.doc.state.al.us/orgchart/htm

Print the one-page organizational chart of the Alabama Department of Corrections. Then go to http://www.oregon.gov/doc and print the organizational chart of the Oregon Department of Corrections found on the home page of the Web site. Examine these two organizational charts. These departments of corrections have very similar responsibilities, but as you can see, the organizational charts have some vast differences. What are the primary similarities and differences? Why do these differences exist? Which one is likely to be more expensive to operate, and why? Note that the organizational chart for Oregon contains names of persons in each position. Is this a good idea? Think in terms of turnover rate of positions, but also think of being responsive to public inquiry. How do these organizational charts compare with the one in your state's department of corrections?

GROUP EXERCISES

Each group will be assigned one of the following correctional organizations and must develop a comprehensive organizational chart with the titles of all the necessary positions: community correctional center, medium security prison, probation and parole department, correctional training academy, local jail.

ENDNOTES

1. Richard W. Snarr, *Introduction to Corrections*, 3rd ed. (Madison, WI: Brown & Benchmark Publishers, 1996), p. 179.

2. Bureau of Justice Statistics, Correctional Populations, *Key Facts at a Glance*, http://www.ojp.usdoj.gov/bjs/glance/tables/corr2tab.htm (accessed January 18, 2010).

3. Heather C. West and William J. Sabol, *Prison Inmates at Midyear 2008-Statistical Tables*, (Washington, DC: U.S. Department of Justice, Bureau of Justice Statistics, March 2009), p. 2.

4. Lawrence A. Greenfeld and Tracy L. Snell, *Women Offenders* (Washington, DC: U.S. Department of Justice, Bureau of Justice Statistics, 1999), p. 6.

5. West and Sabol, *Prison Inmates at Midyear 2008-Statistical Tables*, p. 2, and Heather C. West and William J. Sabol, "Prisoners in 2007," *Bureau of Justice Statistics Bulletin* (Washington, DC: U.S. Department of Justice, December 2008), p. 3.

6. Lauren E. Glaze and Thomas P. Bonczar, *Probation and Parole in the United States, 2007 Statistical Tables* (Washington, DC: U.S. Department of Justice, December 2008), pp. 1–6.

7. Bureau of Justice Statistics Correctional Surveys (*National Probation Data Survey, National Prisoner Statistics, Survey of Jails,* and *National Parole Data Survey*) as presented in *Correctional Populations in the United States, 1997* (Washington, DC: U.S. Department of Justice, 1998).

8. West and Sabol, *Prison Inmates at Midyear 2008-Statistical Tables*, p. 18.

9. Lauren E. Glaze and Seri Palla, *Probation and Parole in the United States, 2004* (Washington, DC: U.S. Department of Justice, Bureau of Justice Statistics Bulletin, November 2005), p. 6.

10. The Pew Center on the States, Public Safety Performance Project, *One in 31: The Long Reach of American Corrections* (Washington, DC: The Pew Charitable Trusts, March 2009), p. 34.

11. Robert Freeman, "Management and Administrative Issues," in *Prisons: Today and Tomorrow,* edited by Jocelyn M. Pollock (Gaithersburg, MD: Aspen Publishers, 1997), p. 279.

12. Michael Mann, *The International Encyclopedia of Sociology* (New York: Continuum, 1984), p. 28.

13. Chase Riveland, "The Correctional Leader and Public Policy Skills," *Corrections Management Quarterly* 1 no. 3 (1997): 23.

14. West and Sabol, *Prison Inmates at Midyear 2008-Statistical Tables*, p. 2.

15. Ibid., p. 3.

16. James J. Stephan, *Census of State and Federal Correctional Facilities* (Washington, DC: U.S. Department of Justice, 2008), Appendix Table 1.

17. Lauren E. Glaze and Thomas P. Bonczar, *Probation and Parole in the United States, 2006* (Washington, DC: U.S. Department of Justice, Bureau of Justice Statistics, December 2007), p. 6.

18. Chase Riveland, "The Correctional Leader and Public Policy Skills," *Corrections Management Quarterly* 1 no. 3 (1997): 23.

19. Camille Graham Camp and George M. Camp, *The 2002 Corrections Yearbook: Adult Corrections* (Middletown, CT: Criminal Justice Institute, 2003), p. 5.

20. Ohio Department of Rehabilitation and Correction Web site, *DRC Data Source Reports— Monthly Fact Sheet,* December 31, 2009, http://www.drc.ohio.gov/web/Reports/FactSheet/December%202009.pdf (accessed January 18, 2010).

21. John Scalia, "Prisoner Petitions Filed in U.S. District Courts, 2000, with Trends 1980–2000," *Bureau of Justice Statistics Special Report* (Washington, DC: U.S. Department of Justice, January 2002).

22. Camp and Camp, *The 2002 Corrections Yearbook*, pp. 72–73.

23. David Crary, "Law Curbing Inmates' Lawsuits Questioned," *USA Today,* February 13, 2008, http://www.usatoday.com/news/nation/2008-02-13-3685431048_x.htm (accessed August 16, 2009).

24. Bureau of Justice Statistics, *Expenditure Facts at a Glance*, www.ojp.usdoj.gov/bjs/glance/tables/exptyptab.htm (accessed January 17, 2006).

25. Camp and Camp, *The 2002 Corrections Yearbook*, p. 92.

26. National Association of State Budget Officers, "State Expenditure Report FY 2006," December 2007, http://www.nasbo.org/Publications/PDFs/fy2006er.pdf (accessed August 16, 2009).

27. *Public Safety, Public Spending: Forecasting America's Prison Population, 2007–2011*, Public Safety Performance Project (Washington, DC: The Pew Charitable Trust, February 2007), p. ii.

28. Pew Center of the States, *One in 31: The Long Reach of American Corrections* (Washington, DC: Pew Charitable Trusts, March 2009), p. 2.

29. Ibid., pp. 74, 76, and 87.

30. Camp and Camp, *The 2002 Corrections Yearbook*, pp. 82–83, 84, 97, 98, 118.

31. James J. Stephan, "Census of State and Federal Correctional Facilities, 2005," *National Prisoner Statistics Program*, (Washington, DC: U.S. Department of Justice, 2008), pp. 1–2.

32. Tony Fabelo, "Technocorrections: The Promises, the Uncertain Threats," *Sentencing & Corrections: Issues for the 21st Century*, Papers from the Executive Sessions on Sentencing and Corrections, No. 5 (Washington, DC: U.S. Department of Justice, May 2000).

33. Heather C. West and William J. Sabol, *Prisoner in 2007* (Washington, DC: U.S. Department of Justice, Bureau of Justice Statistics, December 2008), p. 3.

34. Nelson, Deess, and Allen, "First Month Out," 1999.

35. G. G. Gaes, T. J. Flanagan, L. L. Motiuk, and L. Stewart, "Adult Correctional Treatment," in *Prisons*, edited by Michael Tonry and Joan Petersilia (Chicago: University of Chicago Press, 1999), pp. 361–426.

36. Peter M. Carlson, "The Organization of the Institution," in *Prison and Jail Administration: Practice and Theory*, edited by Peter M. Carlson and Judith Simon Garrett (Gaithersburg, MD: Aspen, 1999), p. 28.

37. Doris J. James and Lauren E. Glaze, *Mental Health Problems of Prison and Jail Inmates* (Washington, DC: U.S. Department of Justice, Bureau of Justice Statistics, 2006).

38. United States Bureau of Prisons, *Unit Management Manual* (Washington, DC: U.S. Bureau of Prisons, 1977), p. 6.

39. For a discussion of the history of unit management within the Federal Bureau of Prisons, see Robert Levinson and Roy Gerard, "Functional Units: A Different Correctional Approach," *Federal Probation* 37, no. 4 (1973): 8–16.

40. Freeman, "Management and Administrative Issues," p. 300.

41. For a good description of pretrial supervision programs, see Thomas J. Wolf, "What United States Pretrial Service Officers Do," *Federal Probation* 61, no. 1 (March 1997): 19–24.

42. Ibid., p. 191.

8

Supervising and Empowering Employees

Introduction

Corrections staff doing their jobs in a professional manner will make the difference between success and failure to accomplish the correctional mission. In Chapter 6, we discussed how correctional agencies recruit, train, and prepare staff to do the difficult jobs in a prison or community correctional setting. This chapter presents another key element in making sure that the people of the corrections business perform their jobs as well as they are capable. This chapter discusses **supervision** of line staff and the importance of supervision in accomplishing the correctional mission.

When many people think of supervision or a supervisor, they may jump to the extreme and envision a Dilbert-style boss who is abusive and cares little about the employees they supervise. A more reasonable but still inaccurate vision would be of someone who simply tells employees what to do and criticizes them if they fail to do it. Supervision, however, is much more complex than either of these two examples, and includes training, coaching and mentoring, assisting, encouraging, sometimes disciplining, and seldom finding that "one style fits all" circumstances that they need to address. Supervision is extremely difficult to do well, and a poor job of supervising employees, particularly when it occurs in a stressful and dangerous correctional environment, can undermine morale, efficiency, and effectiveness. Being a good supervisor is not easy, and requires training and preparation, in addition to a mature, thoughtful, and conscientious approach. In this author's opinion formed from my over thirty years of working in corrections, supervision is the *most important element* in a correctional operation. All the security, programs, equipment, and financial resources can be deemed inconsequential, if staff supervision is poor. Outstanding recruiting and training of line staff can be undermined by negative supervision. Yet good supervision that motivates employees and helps them perform better can enhance the quality and operation of any organization, particularly quasi-military organizations and those that face dangerous situations such as corrections. What supervisors actually do is guide staff in the specific duties necessary to accomplish the agency mission. Excellent supervision is where "the rubber meets the road" in a correctional agency.

In this chapter, the role of supervision is defined, explained, and differentiated from leadership and management. The key components of supervision, including effective communications, clear expectations, delegation and directing of work, and giving feedback are also identified and discussed. Some of the challenges to effective supervision, including dealing with a problem employee, using the disciplinary process, and the preparation necessary to be a good supervisor, and the stressful situations that can accompany supervision are presented. Finally, the importance of "empowering" staff is introduced. Empowerment has become the buzzword in organizational leadership and supervision, and can particularly improve the effectiveness of a correctional operation. Developing an empowered workplace is not the same as developing effective supervision. And, empowerment does not replace the need for competent supervision. By the end of this chapter, you will have a clear understanding of why it is suggested that supervision is the most important element in a correctional operation.

The Supervisory Role

Historically, supervision has been seen as getting the job done through others or overseeing that work gets done. Supervisors must play many roles, including boss, manager, leader, advisor, counselor, mentor, coach, trainer, and motivator, and agent of discipline. The simple organizational chart (Figure 8-1) helps in understanding and defining some functions within the organization. However, the roles listed are not as clearly delineated within most organizations as they appear in this hierarchy. In fact, most employees do not delineate the levels of their organization as the leader, manager, supervisor, or coworker, but for the sake of explaining these roles, this delineation can be instructive.

For purposes of this discussion, leaders are those in an organization that create a vision and set direction, establish policy, manage the external environment, encourage and empower staff, shape organizational culture, and provide resources for the organization. Managers organize departments and the work they are to do, plan and develop goals and objectives, and oversee the efficient use of resources. Supervisors direct work activities, assign tasks, provide employees feedback, and serve as technical experts for the staff reporting to them. Line employees execute the functions assigned to them and delivery of services included in the mission of the organization. They not only complete tasks as assigned but are also encouraged to suggest improvements in the process of completion of tasks. Broadwell suggests, the higher the level of management, the more time is spent on long-range planning, giving direction to the organization and working on problems that have to do with setting up the structure of the organization . . . lower down the ladder of levels we should find people concerning themselves with short-range problems, such as, directing people and checking on how well the work is done.[1]

Supervision is difficult and almost impossible when supervisors have to play all these roles, sometimes simultaneously. However, staff do perceive their supervisors as leaders. Even in a prison, where the warden is the acknowledged leader of the organization, supervisors can support or undermine the warden's leadership when they do not follow the principles of the organization nor the priorities for work to be accomplished. Staff expect their direct supervisors to lead them by supporting them and showing understanding, courage, and conviction in their role. Supervisors are sometimes also responsible for managing a department or section, and must complete management tasks such as budget and policy development, as well as supervise other employees. And, supervisors often have to carry out functions just as line employees. Sometimes, supervisors have actual line staff duties (for instance, correctional sergeants in a prison that cover a post or a probation supervisor that also has an offender caseload). In these circumstances, their work must be accomplished at the same time they supervise employees.

Figure 8-1
The hierarchy of supervision.

Another way to look at this is that supervisors sometimes have to wear two hats: those of both worker and supervisor, or as a "functional specialist" and "management generalist." Phillips and McConnell describe a functional specialist as "the worker who is responsible for doing some of the basic work of the department . . . the specialist is ordinarily concerned with some function that is unique or nearly unique to that department. The management generalist, on the other hand, is concerned with activities that are common to many departments and to most situations in which someone must guide and direct the work of others."[2] Line employees are almost always functional specialists, and in large departments, the manager is almost always a management generalist. However, the supervisor's role falls between the two, and often, particularly in a department with a small number of staff, they end up performing both specialist and generalist roles.

Although the following discussion presents the key elements of the supervisory role, it should be clear that supervision does not have a distinct role and the boundaries of line worker, supervisor, manager, and leader can shift and are not distinct. This presents another challenge for those in a supervisory role, as they have to be "all things to all people." They are always in the limelight and seldom have the opportunity to not perform their best. Employees are always seeking direction and feedback and judging their effectiveness. Supervisors are very visible, and they are constantly watched and modeled for leadership style. They have to balance completion of tasks with available resources. Bartollas and Miller aptly describe the challenge of supervision in a prison below.

Supervisors have one of the most demanding positions in correctional institutions. They are cast in the role of interpreting top management's policies and must do so in a manner convincing to their subordinates. They must be able to coordinate the activities of many below them who may not agree with the philosophy of top management. Middle managers, perhaps even more than top executives, are responsible for developing effective communication networks throughout the organization.

Supervisors must be generalists and systems managers in much the same manner as their superiors. Even though they do not make policy decisions, they should be aware of how broad policy decisions affect their actions. They should also know how personnel above, under, and on their same level do their jobs.[3]

While supervision is difficult, it can also be very rewarding. Before moving to further discussions of various aspects of supervision, the accompanying illustration of a few hours in the life of a correctional (security) supervisor in a prison gives the reader some idea of supervision in a correctional environment.

Practical Perspectives

Second Shift—Federal Maximum Security Prison

Lieutenant Melody Rodriguez is a GS-11 lieutenant at a federal maximum security prison. She has worked with the Federal Bureau of Prisons for eight years, and been in her current assignment for eighteen months. As a GS-11 lieutenant, she acts as a shift supervisor. During the second shift (from 4:00 P.M. until midnight), she is usually the highest ranking staff member at the prison. She has twenty-three correctional officers assigned to the shift, with one GS-9 activities lieutenant, who works until 9:00 P.M. and covers the recreation yard, commissary, and other high-activity areas during the shift. In addition to the correctional services staff, there are also a few unit management staff, and four education and recreation staff who work until 9:00 P.M.

"Lieutenant Rod," as she is called by other staff, is thought of as a good lieutenant. She gets out of the office, visits most of the areas and posts where officers are assigned nightly, is direct yet pleasant with officers, and accessible to inmates. Her day usually begins by 3:00 P.M., because she likes to get to work early, talk to the day-shift lieutenants, get the feel for the institution, and be sure she has coverage for all posts if anyone has called in sick or there are special activities that require additional coverage.

A few minutes before 4:00, she holds a roll call for officers, briefing them on the activities of the day and what to expect during the evening. She also covers any special functions (e.g., volunteers in for a religious program) that are happening that evening. Today was pretty typical, with no unusual incidents or tensions among inmate groups. At 4:00 P.M. the most important institution count of inmates takes place because they have not been counted since early morning. It is also important to do it quickly, because inmates are anxious to go to dinner and begin evening recreation and educational activities.

A new officer in one of the units seems to be having trouble with the count and has called in a wrong number. Lieutenant Rod suspects the new officer has simply missed someone and asks the activities lieutenant to go support the officer and help if he is having problems with the count procedure. The next count is accurate, because the officer simply needed a reminder to make sure all inmates are out of bed and standing in easy view of the door of the cell. Inmates are then released to dinner, and Lieutenant Rod goes to the dining room to watch the meal.

She realizes that there are only three correctional officers in the dining room during the feeding of more than 1,000 inmates and uses the radio to ask available unit management, educational, and recreation staff to come to the dining room for additional support. That's a good move, because during the meal two inmates got into a shoving match, but they are quickly separated. Lieutenant Rod has the inmates handcuffed and instructs one officer and a recreation staff member to take one of the inmates to SHU, and another officer and a case manager to take the other one to the lieutenant's office. She wants them to be separate, in case emotions get hot again. She also instructs the officers to find out from the inmates what the problem was about and to inform her right away if it seems like more than simply a dispute between two individual inmates.

After the meal, Lieutenant Rod begins to go through paperwork in her office. There are overtime approval slips to sign and a memo noting it is time to conduct an audit of the SHU procedures for recreating inmates in the evening. She decides to do the audit tonight, because with only one special activity (the religious volunteers), she knows she can use a senior correctional officer who is working the main compound to conduct the audit.

The senior officer has a lot of ability and wants to be a lieutenant someday. Conducting the audit will be an excellent learning opportunity for him. She radios him to tell him he will be doing it and to meet her at 7:00 at SHU, where she will give him the format and instructions to do the audit.

At 6:15 P.M., Lieutenant Rod visits the recreation yard, which usually has 350–400 inmates jogging, playing basketball, or lifting weights on a nice evening. She talks to recreation staff, as well as the correctional officers working the yard. She notices a group of inmates recognized as members of the Mexikanemi, a Hispanic prison gang. She instructs the officers to keep an eye on them, list any inmates they recognize in the group, and submit a memo with the names at the end of the shift. On the way to SHU, an inmate stops her and explains he is being pressured to bring drugs into the institution by a group of inmates and is fearful for his safety if he does not do it. Lieutenant Rod tells the inmate she will arrange to have him placed on the "call out" to receive some legal material at the inmate records office in the next few days. One of the investigative lieutenants will meet him there and interview him in private, so that no attention will be drawn to the inmate talking to staff.

When she arrives at SHU, she delegates the audit to the senior officer, makes sure he knows how to do the job and understands the purpose, and explains that it is an excellent training opportunity for him. She tells him where she w in case he has any questions and tells the SHU staff that th senior officer will be doing the audit and to cooperate in any way necessary for him to get it done. She then decides to go to Unit 1 to talk to Officer Brady. Brady was ten minutes late tonight and that is the second tardiness in the past week.

She gets to the unit and chats with Brady, suggesting they walk through the unit as is usual when she makes her rounds. This makes it appear there is nothing out of the ordinary to inmates and that she is not "calling Brady on the carpet." She asks Brady about the tardiness and gets a poor excuse. Therefore, she informs Brady of the importance of being on time and how she cannot let it continue without taking some type of formal disciplinary action. She informs Brady that this should be considered an informal counseling session and that no formal action will be taken unless the tardiness continues.

It is now 8:00 P.M., and Lieutenant Rod's shift is half over. She goes to the officer's lounge to eat her dinner. She is not far from her office or anyone who needs her. This fifteen minutes to relax and reflect is all the break she gets. She thinks about the past four hours, feels good that all has gone well, thinks about how much she likes her job, and then heads out on the compound to be visible when the inmates are called to return to the units at 8:30 P.M.

The case study represents a typical four hours for a correctional supervisor in a prison. Lieutenant Rodriguez has done even more than it seems. She has reviewed the assignment of work to be accomplished by checking to see that she has adequate staff resources to operate the shift safely and securely and she found replacements for those officers who will be absent. She has shared information with her staff so they know what to expect during their shift. She has responded quickly to a potential problem (the wrong inmate count), without overreacting. Her sending the activities lieutenant as support was a learning opportunity for the new officer without making the officer feel incompetent and without everyone realizing the count was being conducted incorrectly. She has used her correctional knowledge and experience to make a good decision in handling the shoving match in the dining room, taking assertive action, and thinking ahead to keep the problem from escalating further.

Lieutenant Rod also decides that the audit can be done immediately, not putting it off until later. She does a good job of delegating the audit task as a learning experience to a senior officer, who has the interest and potential to become a lieutenant at some point. She uses her knowledge of the inmates to monitor the Mexikanemi activity and finds a way to get information from the inmate being pressured without putting him in danger. She also, in a direct, yet nonthreatening manner, advises Brady to get to work on time. Even when taking her break, Lieutenant Rod thinks about her job, her staff, and the next four hours.

Elements in Supervision

What kinds of things does a good supervisor have to do? What are the activities that must be performed for supervision to be as effective as possible? The following sections present the activities commonly recognized as important in supervising employees.

1. Communications
2. Clarifying expectations
3. Delegating and giving directions
4. Understanding behavior
5. Training and coaching
6. Giving feedback

While each of these elements is important to supervision, there is no single approach to accomplish them in the most effective way possible. No two people are the same, and no two supervisors do their jobs exactly the same way. The key is to understand each element and to blend each to one's own personality and supervision style.

Communications

Why is communications so important to supervision? Because the only way that managers and supervisors get things done is through others. A supervisor must constantly communicate by seeking input, giving direction, listening to what others have to say, and sharing

Training for Supervision. This trainer is illustrating the characteristics of a good leader. (Courtesy of Corrections Corporation of America).

information. In the case study of Lieutenant Rod, it is obvious that she communicates almost continuously. She asks questions, listens to concerns, gives instructions, and makes clear the outcome of failure to comply with directions. The higher up the organizational ladder one climbs, the more the job depends on communications. A rather dated, but still accurate, study discovered that first-line supervisors spend 74 percent of their time communicating, second-level supervisors spend 81 percent, and third-level supervisors spend 87 percent of their time communicating.[4]

Directions of Supervisory Communications

Supervisors communicate with everyone and in every direction. Not only must they communicate downward with the employees who work directly for them but must also communicate upward with their supervisors, managers, and executives within the organization. Information must flow both up and down in an organization. In a correctional organization, it is critical that information be transferred quickly to line staff so they are prepared to deal with incidents that may occur. One of the first things Lieutenant Rod did when the shift started was to give a shift briefing. If information had been obtained that day from a confidential informant (inmate) that there was trouble brewing between the Mexikanemi (EMI) and the Texas Syndicate (two Hispanic gangs often at odds in prison), the grouping of the EMI on the recreation yard would possibly have much more meaning than it would otherwise. Staff give feedback up the chain of command as well. Using the gang example, as intelligence is collected, it goes up to the managers who collect gang intelligence, "connect the dots," and search for trends or increasing risk of gang activity.

Supervisors also communicate horizontally with other supervisors and with other departments. In corrections, a complex task can seldom be accomplished with only one person or with only one division or department involved. As simple a task as Lieutenant Rod trying to get more staff into the dining room during the evening meal needed horizontal communications. Few correctional officers can leave their assigned posts, because they must stay in that position to monitor inmates and security. Other departmental staff, such as the unit management, education, or recreation staff are more likely to be available; however, Lieutenant Rod cannot simply issue an order for them to come to the dining room as these staff do not work for her. However, she explains the need to have more people in the dining room, and she would probably expect cooperation. If the lack of staff in the dining room was a continuing problem, Lieutenant Rod should communicate the concern to her supervisors, who can put a policy or procedure in place to ensure adequate staff are available, rather than force the lieutenant on duty to deal with this problem every evening.

In most correctional organizations, supervisors also communicate with labor union membership and union stewards. A large percentage of government line employees are members of labor unions and, as discussed in Chapter 6, have a negotiated contract that provides rules for the workplace. Although it is hoped that these rules provide clarity in acceptable relationships between supervisors and employees, there are always questions that arise and concerns that need to be communicated. Officer Brady may not like the fact that Lieutenant Rod said that no more tardiness would be tolerated and that formal disciplinary action could follow. If Brady complained to a union steward, the steward may ask Lieutenant Rod for some background regarding Brady's tardiness. The steward may point out that the contract requires Lieutenant Rod to give Brady a written memo of the discussion before she can take disciplinary action. Supervisor and union steward communications do

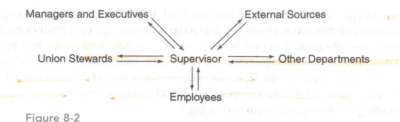

Figure 8-2
Information flow within an organization.

not have to be adversarial, and it is helpful to remind all parties of what is in the contract so that controversy can be avoided in the future. From her perspective, Lieutenant Rod had told the steward that Brady had been tardy twice this week. More than likely, the steward would support Lieutenant Rod and remind Brady of the responsibility to be on time.

Finally, supervisors may also communicate with external sources. Probation officers work as a hub of much communications with the probationer, the court, the offender family, and many social service or law enforcement agencies that serve or have an interest in the offender. Criminal justice organizations have recognized the value of sharing information and data across the boundaries of law enforcement, courts, and corrections. Community corrections staff spend more of their time communicating with other agencies than they do with their own.

Figure 8-2 presents a simple illustration of the directional flow of information between the supervisor and other groups within the organization. As is obvious, it is important for supervisors to communicate upward, downward, and horizontally. Communications is two-way and requires the supervisor both to speak and to listen. The next section deals with the supervisor–employee relationship and the critical skills required for effective communications.

Communication: A Two-Way Street

Although it would not seem necessary to remind people that communication is a two-way street, one-way communications still happen all too often. This can be because in the hectic pace of a day, supervisors sometimes become rushed and do not take time to make sure communications flow in both directions. Some supervisors are insecure in themselves and their position, and do not want feedback. Some supervisors believe they are both speaking and listening, but they do not really understand how to seek feedback. And sometimes, supervisors in a paramilitary organization simply develop bad habits and are not even aware that their communications have evolved into a one-way pattern. There are times when one-way communications are acceptable and effective, such as during a crisis. During a prison riot, staff expect to hear one-way directions and orders. There has been much training and planning for this type of situation, and staff know their roles and the types of directives that will be given in an emergency. In these cases, preplanned activities have already been developed with a give and take method, and staff know what information they are to provide in such a situation. Therefore, a discussion about the pros and cons of an action is usually not necessary. However, the situations in which this is acceptable are very few.

The importance of listening is discussed later in the chapter. Before supervisors can practice good listening skills, they must create an environment that shows they desire feedback and want communications to be two-way. Many times employees, when receiving directions, do not understand and have to ask a question to clarify the order. However, if supervisors make snide remarks, frown, or use body language that shows they think the question shows a lack of understanding on the part of the employee, employees will quickly learn not to ask questions. The employee then has to guess or ask a coworker how the supervisor wants the job done, which wastes other's time and often ends up with the task being performed in an unsatisfactory manner.

Some supervisors may also discourage feedback from employees about the effectiveness of a policy or procedure. As staff go about their duties, they often recognize that there may be a better way of carrying out an assignment. However, if supervisors give the impression that they do not want feedback, staff will quickly learn to not give it and will simply do the job the way the supervisor wants it done. Again, this results in inefficiency and a failure to ever improve on processes and procedures. It is the responsibility of the supervisor to create an atmosphere where communications are truly "two-way." Good supervisors will even set the tone for feedback by asking, "Have you done that task before, and do you know how it is to be performed?" Or, they may even seek feedback by requesting, "Do you have any suggestions on a good way to accomplish that task?"

Positive Verbal Communications

Through supervisory communications, many things are transmitted, including facts, opinions, feelings, and importance of the message. It is critical that supervisors think about what they want to communicate and how they want employees to hear it. The following steps can help supervisors avoid confusion during the communication process.

1. Know the subject.
2. Make sure the facts are complete and correct.
3. Organize remarks.
4. Know the background of the message recipient.
5. Use language the receiver understands.
6. Avoid generalities by being specific.
7. Consider the situation in which the message is delivered.
8. Communicate the purpose and importance of the message.
9. Seek feedback.

While supervisors are expected to know the elements of the duties they supervise, they cannot know everything and sometimes just lack necessary knowledge. Lieutenant Rod may not have known anything about the requirement of a regular audit of SHU or how that audit was to be performed. She could still have decided to delegate responsibility to do the audit, which, in this situation, would have meant delegating responsibility to determine the requirements of the audit. If supervisors try to communicate something they do not understand, the communication will often end up being unclear, particularly if the supervisor wants to give the false impression they do understand. Supervisors should know what they are talking about before they try to deliver a message, both for the sake of understanding and for their own credibility.

A related key step to communications involves getting the facts before communicating. When a person is uncertain about what needs to be communicated, it usually means there are unknown facts or information. If there is tension between two prison gangs, and a supervisor wants correctional officers to be aware of this and look for unusual activities, it is valuable to share what has caused the tension or what evidence of tension has been detected. Instead of a simple, "Watch for any signs of tension between the Mexikanemi and Texas Syndicate," the listener of the message gets much more understanding of what to do if the supervisor includes facts and information. The following would be much more helpful, "There was a fight between a Mexikanemi (EMI) and Texas Syndicate member yesterday. At lunch today, there seemed to be a lot of grouping of the gangs and movement between tables to pass messages. A credible inmate has said that there will be a meeting of the EMI tonight in the recreation yard to decide if they want to retaliate. Watch for groupings anywhere, the recreation yard, dining room, or library, and report them to the Lieutenant's Office immediately."

We all speak "off the cuff," without much thought or preparation of our message. However, the more important the communication, the more important it is to organize one's thoughts. In the preceding example about gang tension, the supervisor would have thought through the information to be conveyed, including the background, what to watch for, and how to report any findings. Organizing thoughts about simple messages usually does not take much time or require written notes. However, if the message is complex, and if it is important to communicate many facts and be specific with information, it may require more preparation and making of notes to use in communication.

It is also important for the communicator to consider the receiver of the message. Who will receive the message—what is their background, will they understand certain words or expressions I will use? If a probation supervisor is discussing a change in the risk assessment instrument the agency has adopted, a new probation officer will need a more extensive explanation than an experienced one. They may need some background on the current assessment instrument so they know how the change will affect the past process. Supervisors must consider the recipient of the information, and use language and terminology the receiver understands. Many employees will not ask questions, thinking they will sound "stupid" in front of their boss or coworkers if they do.

When they are in a hurry, or if they are not fully aware of the facts, supervisors may simply communicate generalities rather than the specifics of an assignment or information to be communicated. When Lieutenant Rod asked the senior officer to conduct the SHU audit, she took the time to go over the assignment rather than simply asking the officer to conduct the audit. Specifics include what is to be done, what guidelines to use, what authority the receiver will have, when the task is to be completed, and what outcome is expected. Without these specifics, all these elements are left to chance, and supervisors cannot be upset with employees who fail to carry out an assignment in the desired way if they did not communicate the specifics when giving the assignment.

The situation also dictates how communications are delivered and received. Is it in a training session to get into detail on a new process or duty? In the midst of a prison riot? Is it to advise probation officers of a new social service agency that can be used to aid offenders? Are inmates or probationers listening? Is it a part of an employee evaluation? Or, can the failure to follow through have dire consequences for the person or the organization? Supervisors must share the importance of the communications. When Lieutenant Rod told Brady that repeated tardiness would not be tolerated, she made it clear that formal disciplinary action would be taken if there was another incident of tardiness. That should have gotten Brady's attention, indicating that tardiness was unacceptable and would be personally costly if not corrected.

Finally, good communications should seek feedback. Supervisors can tell from the look on an employee's face or from body language whether the employee understands a message. The best supervisors regularly ask, "Are there any questions?" and give employees time to respond at the end of each communication. A message delivered without the opportunity for feedback is an incomplete message. It may have been misunderstood, some critical facts may have been left out, or the employee may not be aware of the authority and responsibility that go along with the assignment or message. It is the supervisors' responsibility to seek feedback and then move to the listening stage of the communications process.

The Listening Process

Even if a supervisor has asked for feedback, effective listening is still required. After communicating a message, supervisors have to thoughtfully move to a listening stage to complete the two-way communication. Many people are not good listeners, and it is a skill like many others that must be developed. It is important to supervisors' ability to do their jobs to be good listeners. Supervisors are ultimately held responsible for completion (or failure) of tasks by their staff. If supervisors fail to make clear an assignment and it is done incompletely or unsatisfactorily, they will not only have to take more time to correct it but will also be held accountable for the failure.

Sometimes people hear but do not listen. They may be distracted, be thinking of something else, or be thinking of what they want to say next instead of really listening. When the feedback is not what someone wants to hear, they often "turn off" their listening skills and begin to think negatively of the person speaking, wondering, "Why does this person always make it difficult to give him or her an assignment." The American Correctional Association has published a series of workbooks to promote professionalism and improve leadership skills in the workplace. In their supervision handbook, they identify seven steps to effective listening:

1. **Ask questions**. If something is unclear or seems to contradict your own personal sense of logic, ask questions. Asking questions shows that you're interested in understanding what's being said.

2. **Concentrate**. Don't let your mind wander. People think at the rate of about 500 words per minute, but people talk at a rate of only about 150 words per minute. Stay focused on what is being said, or you will risk missing key points.

3. **Listen for the main idea(s)**. It's not uncommon for people to develop ideas as they talk, to be somewhat vague when discussing sensitive issues, or to have trouble coming to the point. Make sure that you determine what the person's key issues are. Restate the other person's main ideas in your own words and ask him or her if you've understood correctly.

4. **Listen for the rationale behind what the other person is saying**. This is especially important if what he or she is saying doesn't seem to make sense to you. A staff member may be making a request on the basis of erroneous information about the organization. Be sensitive and make sure that you understand why the person is saying what he or she is saying.

5. **Listen for key words**. Key words can become your own internal cue or memory stimulator to help you retain what you hear.

6. **Organize what you hear in your own mind in a way that is logical for you**. Your way of organizing information may differ from the way the information was presented, but it is critical for you to use what you hear.

7. **Take notes if the issue or request is complex**. It is worthwhile to get your thoughts down in writing.[5]

Clarifying Expectations

A very important function of supervision is to set expectations for the acceptable quality of work performed. Supervisors give feedback to employees about how well they have done a job. As they do this, they are communicating a level of expectations. There are two important principles regarding setting expectations. First, staff want to achieve and will work hard to perform at the level of expectation. It is valuable for supervisors to set high yet achievable standards and encourage and reward staff who perform at those levels. Second, if these standards are compromised and less accepted, it lowers the standard for the future. Supervisors cannot say they expect a certain level but then ignore failure to reach that level. Consistency in holding accountable and expecting a stated standard is important, because the standard then becomes the lowest noted level of performance accepted rather than the highest. The following are examples of these two principles.

One function of a correctional supervisor in a prison is to do "quality assurance" checks of how well correctional officers perform their jobs. Lieutenant Rod, in making her rounds to the various posts, may stop to spend time with a housing unit officer. The officer is to perform many security checks during the shift, including checking windows for tampering, searching areas where contraband may be hidden, making sure all doors are locked, and "tapping" bars to make sure they have not been cut. Lieutenant Rod has the officer go through each of the checks with her, both as a review of the officer's technique and also to confirm it is being accomplished as required. She notices that the officer only "taps" every other bar. When questioned about it, the officer states that another officer told him this was acceptable practice, because it saved time and all the bars would be tapped over a few days. Lieutenant Rod can accept this (it seems reasonable), but instead she informs the officer that the post orders require tapping *every* bar, *every* night, and *nothing less* is acceptable. It is valuable to take time to explain why this is important, but what she has communicated is that nothing less than full compliance with post orders is acceptable. If correctional workers get in the habit of taking shortcuts or making compromises, they begin to perform every task with this same attitude. However, if staff understand the standard will not be compromised, they will get into the habit of performing at that level, and an organizational culture will develop for doing jobs at full compliance.

An illustration of the second principle is the following example. Lieutenant Rod is making rounds in the housing unit. There is a prohibition against smoking in the television rooms, because smoking is only permitted in inmate cells. Lieutenant Rod goes into a television room, and there are cigarette butts and the smell of smoke, but no inmates are there to indicate who has been smoking. If she does not say anything, the officer will accept that the rule against smoking in the television rooms is "not that important." However, Lieutenant Rod knows that the warden has emphasized enforcing this rule and stated that any evidence of smoking will result in the television rooms being closed for the day. She also knows this message has been communicated to inmates. She, therefore, instructs the officer to lock the television rooms, tells inmates that she ordered the locking because of the smoking policy violation, and that television rooms will be closed every time there is a violation. This takes the pressure off the correctional officer and confirms the high standard of no smoking in the television rooms. When this is understood by officers and inmates, it is much easier to enforce.

Supervisors set standards and expectations by every action they take or do not take. Not responding to something sets a standard. Ignoring minor violations of policy or procedure sets a standard. Trying to be a nice guy or gal sets a standard. The role of good supervisors is to make standards clear, hold staff who do not conform to the standard accountable, and reward or recognize those who do meet expectations. Supervisors cannot try to be liked by letting failure to conform be accepted. This type of supervisor is seldom liked and never respected. By accepting less than full compliance, they make it unlikely to ever occur. Also, accepting less than full compliance by staff makes it more difficult (if not impossible) for another supervisor who tries to enforce the rules and maintain the expected standard.

Delegating and Giving Directions

Much of supervisors' communications are orders or delegation of duties. **Delegation is the assignment of a task to someone.** In corrections, there are many procedures that must become a part of the regular routine, and staff are trained to perform their duties in a specific manner. However, there are also many special projects or activities outside the scope of normal duties. And these special projects or activities must be assigned or delegated to a correctional worker. Effective delegation is the key to successful completion of an assignment. When the assignment is not completed satisfactory, it is often due to poor delegation on the part of the supervisor.

Why do supervisors delegate, and who benefits from such delegation? There are three reasons and three primary beneficiaries. First, supervisors delegate to help themselves accomplish work. They cannot do all the work that passes down the chain of command and becomes their responsibility. Therefore, they delegate to get others to do the work, while they maintain control over the work to ensure it is done in a timely and quality manner. Second, supervisors delegate for organizational efficiency. Tasks should be assigned to staff best suited to complete them. Matching tasks with employees who have time and skill to effectively perform the duties results in a good product, therefore, benefiting the organization. Finally, delegation benefits employees. By assigning employees special projects or unusual duties, the employees improve their skills and become better prepared for promotion and advancement. Most public correctional agencies promote staff on a competitive basis, and proving competence at a task improves their competitive score and chance for promotion. And employees recognize that by being delegated an important task, "they are contributing to the organization and achieve greater job satisfaction as a result."[6]

An important part of delegation is the clear transfer of authority and responsibility. **Authority** involves the recognition by the organization and other employees that a particular employee has been delegated a task, and that employee can use agency resources and call on others to cooperate in or support the assignment. When supervisors delegate, they should give employees an adequate level of authority to get the job done, and communicate within the organization of the delegation. In the assignment of the senior officer to conduct the SHU audit, Lieutenant Rod informed the staff working in SHU of the senior officer's assignment, creating credibility in the senior officer's authority to ask for their cooperation.

Somewhat different, but often confused with authority, is responsibility. **Responsibility means that the delegation has passed to another the obligation to complete the work.** Persons who are delegated assignments understand that they are responsible for its completion, and if the assignment is not completed, they can legitimately be blamed for the lack of performance. Supervisors do not delegate to pass the blame for failure. However, it is important for employees who are delegated an assignment to realize that they are accountable for the completion of the task.

The Delegation Process

There are several key steps to effective delegation. Some supervisors believe that simply because they have told someone to do something, they have effectively delegated the assignment. In their mind, they believe they have delegated the task, and perhaps even in the mind of the employee, they have received the delegation. However, effective delegation involves much more than merely telling someone to do something and someone acknowledging that they are responsible to get it done. The following steps are essential to effective delegation, which results in a task being completed as expected.

1. Select, define, clarify, and organize the task.
2. Select the person for the delegation.
3. Instruct and motivate the person.
4. Gain consent for the delegation.
5. Establish limits of authority.
6. Maintain control and monitor the project.

These steps in the delegation process are further described and clarified below.

1. Select, define, clarify, and organize the task. Supervisors must determine what tasks they cannot complete and therefore should be delegated. Obviously, supervisors cannot delegate every task but must delegate some. In determining which tasks should be delegated, supervisors consider the importance, need for any special skill, learning opportunity for staff, and time frame for accomplishing a task. If they decide to delegate it, they must then clarify and define the task. For example, a probation supervisor wants a report of the percentage of drug use by probationers compared to the amount of time under supervision and decides to ask a probation officer to compile the report. The delegation should include a definition of "use," such as testing positive on a urine analysis. In addition, there should be a clarification of how to examine the number of months during supervision. For instance, the time may be per month or it may be categorized into three- or six-month intervals.

2. Select the person for the delegation. A delegation is doomed to failure if the supervisor does not think through the selection of the right person for a job. Phillips and McConnell suggest, "Pick the employee you will delegate to by matching the qualifications of available employees with the requirements of the task to be delegated."[7]

And Hecht notes that "In delegation, the supervisor must recognize that selecting the right individual is paramount to the delegated task."[8] The supervisor should consider several things: (1) Does the employee have the time, or can that employee's regular duties be reassigned to others to create the time; (2) does the employee have the skill and background necessary to complete the task; (3) have other employees of like status been given assignments so that developmental opportunities are equally shared; and (4) will there be ample opportunity to monitor and check on the assignment with this employee?

3. Instruct and motivate the person. Some of the important considerations in giving instructions for delegation are the same ones noted previously under positive verbal communications. The directions should be complete, organized, and specific. The time frame for accomplishing the task should be provided, as should the authority delegated to the employee. The supervisor should emphasize the importance of the delegation, and communicate its purpose and value to the organization. When the probation supervisor delegated the development of a report of the percentage of drug use by probationers compared to the amount of time under supervision, the value of this report was emphasized. In tight budget times, the probation agency was considering whether they could reduce the amount of supervision for offenders after a period of time without increasing the likelihood of further drug use. Another key instruction is simply to make clear that the supervisor is available for questions, and the employee does not have to figure everything from that point onward. Finally, persons receiving a delegation should be informed of possible positive and negative consequences of failing to complete the assignment, and let the employee opt out of the assignment if desired.

4. Gain consent for the delegation. Even though supervisors have the authority to delegate tasks to employees, it is important to gain the employee's consent for the assignment. An employee may not believe he or she is capable of completing a task, or may have other job responsibilities that prohibit him or her from accepting another. And some employees just do not want to take on any extra work, even if there is a potential benefit. The situation in which an employee does not want to accept the delegation is an excellent opportunity to have two-way communications, as the reason for not accepting the assignment and what that means for future assignments should be discussed. After that discussion, the supervisor has to decide whether to force the employee to accept it or to find someone else to whom to assign the task.

5. Establish limits of authority. When authority is vaguely defined, it can be abused or misrepresented, and often then resented by other employees. The supervisor should communicate with both the employee receiving the assignment and other employees the authority for completion of the task, so employees understand and cooperate as necessary with the person assigned the task. It should be clarified that when the task is complete, the delegated authority ends. Although few employees will take advantage of or abuse authority, clearly establishing limits avoids any potential for problems.

6. Maintain control and monitor the project. Even when a project is delegated, it is important for supervisors to monitor the progress of the project. A too common error by supervisors is to delegate and forget the project. It is not wise to assume that the person to whom the work is delegated is getting it done in a timely fashion, and just because it is delegated, the supervisor will still ultimately be responsible if not completed. Vokoun suggests setting clear timetables and reporting guidelines, while keeping a communications channel for questions that naturally come up along the way. The reporting guidelines should include periodic monitoring meetings with clear timeframes for completion of the steps in the project.[9]

During a delegation, employees should be informed of the type of feedback the supervisor expects. For instance, a supervisor may state, "Give me an update on your progress every Wednesday afternoon." This motivates the employee to keep on schedule and also allows for the opportunity to make adjustments, if the direction or method of completing the project is different than the supervisor expected. It is also valuable to visually inspect progress. Employees are not always candid in reporting on their progress, and supervisors should visit the work site or look at data collected or draft reports written to see what has been accomplished. If they do not, supervisors will, all too often, find that progress is not exactly as has been verbally reported.

Delegation of tasks is an extremely critical function for supervisors, and it can benefit supervisors, employees, and organizations. However, effective delegation requires thoughtful planning, good communications, and thorough follow-up. When delegation is done poorly, it wastes time and results in frustration by supervisors and employees. However, well-delegated assignments and successful outcomes are positive motivators for employees, provide encouragement for staff to take on extra tasks, and increase potential for future promotional opportunities.

Understanding Behavior

Most articles and books regarding supervision extensively describe the process, systems, and steps for effective supervision. However, few present the "human" side of supervision in any organization. Manufacturing companies have assembly lines and production equipment created by engineers. Technology companies have computers, processors, and the Internet. And most service companies have policies and procedures. But every organization has people who work for, and with, other people. Understanding the human side of supervision cannot be underestimated in its importance in making supervisors and their employees effective.

The value of understanding behavior, as it relates to the supervision process is not new. In a book on supervision published more than forty years ago but still true today, the authors write

> Recognizing that there is a cause behind each act is the first basic step toward understanding human behavior. It is also a fundamental principle for intelligent motivation of others. When the supervisor really knows the worker and when he explores and analyzes each situation and reaction, he is on the way to understanding the cause responsible for the reaction or behavior. He is then in a better position to know what will happen when an order is given and to understand the reason for what may appear to be insubordination or just plain stubbornness.[10]

The first step in understanding the behavior of others is to understand one's own behavior. Most people want to believe they are "close to perfect," do their jobs well, and are supportive of their employees, there is always that nagging feeling when they know they were wrong or did not do as good a job as possible. We are all our own best critics. Similarly, it is very important that supervisors recognize their own skills and weaknesses, their personality strengths and faults, and their tendencies to become stubborn and refuse to listen to good advice. Humans are not perfect, and understanding how these imperfections impact one's ability to supervise others increases the potential for effective supervision.

The second step is to understand employees, what motivates them, their personality and behavior, and the type of supervision to which they best respond. Some supervisors believe that employees should adjust to the supervisor's style. They believe that if they are impatient or brusque, "So what. Let them get used to it." However, effective supervisors understand the makeup of their employees and adapt their style to most effectively lead, direct, and guide them. And employees must recognize that supervisors are human and have weaknesses as well, and they should do their best to accommodate their style or behaviors. However, supervisors are responsible for getting tasks accomplished, and they have more to lose by not understanding their employees and what it takes to effectively lead them. By considering the characteristics of their employees (both as a group and as individuals) and tailoring communications and style around these characteristics, it will improve moral, save time, and enhance performance.

For example, consider the situation of Lieutenant Rod counseling Brady about being tardy. If she knows that Brady is a hardworking employee who tries to do the best job possible, she will probably spend more time trying to determine whether there is an issue or problem behind the tardiness, and she may try to help resolve the problem. However, if she knows Brady is not very dedicated and committed to the organization, shirks responsibility whenever possible, and seems to respond more to avoid disciplinary action than to seek encouragement, she will probably be more direct, ask if there is a problem, accept no excuse, and get quickly to the bottom line, "If tardiness continues, there will be formal action taken."

On-the-Job Training and Coaching

The process of training staff to work in the field of corrections was covered in detail in Chapter 6. In addition to formal training, supervisors are constantly coaching, instructing, and informally training employees. This instruction usually takes place without a lesson plan, is not in a classroom, and occurs without any official documentation. To clarify the teaching roles of supervisors, on-the-job training and coaching are differentiated. **On-the-job training** involves demonstrating to an employee the correct way to do a job, and is sometimes a formal element of preservice training. After classroom training sessions, employees often go to the job site and perform their duties for a specified period of time while being watched by their supervisor. Supervisors correct performance, and certify when employees have mastered the duties for which they are responsible. **Coaching**, however, is less official than on-the-job training and involves guiding, suggesting, mentoring, or prompting. Supervisors coach employees constantly. As probation supervisors review presentence reports written by new officers, they give them feedback as to further investigating an incomplete area or how to write in the style desired by the court. Supervisors will also check in with new officers to ensure they don't have questions or see if they are confused about anything as they begin their probation responsibilities.

Whether it is on-the-job training, coaching, or whatever it is called, good supervisors spend an enormous amount of time training and coaching staff. In fact, there is perhaps nothing more important for them to spend their time doing. Ineffective supervisors believe they do not have the time to train or coach, or that employees will learn more and remember things longer if they have to discover things relating to their job through trial and error. Good supervisors recognize that, in the long run, training and coaching saves both their time and employees' time, tasks are more likely to have better results, employees will probably have a better experience, and staff will look forward to the next assignment with enthusiasm.

There are several reasons why supervisors train and coach. The bottom line is that they want their employees to accomplish the job the way it is expected to be done. When expectations are not met, the problem is not that employees do not want to please their supervisors. A survey of 4,000 managers asked, "Why don't subordinates do what they are supposed to do?" The responses were as follows:

1. They don't know what they are supposed to do.
2. They don't know how to do it.
3. They don't know why they should do it.
4. There are obstacles beyond their control.
5. They don't think it will work.
6. They think their way is better.
7. Not motivated—poor attitude.
8. Personally incapable of doing it (personal limits).
9. Not enough time for them to do it.
10. They are working on wrong priority items.
11. They think they are doing it (no feedback).
12. Poor management.
13. Personal problems.[11]

If (item 8) the employee is, "personally incapable of doing it," the supervisor should refer the employee to the training department to receive remedial training. However, for all the other reasons on the list, performance can be improved by the supervisor acting as a trainer or coach. Sometimes, supervisors have to build confidence in employees that they can do a job, that it is worth doing, or that the procedure suggested is the best way to accomplish the task. Sometimes, supervisors have to counsel employees on how to manage their time or what tasks have the most priority. Other times, supervisors have to support employees by removing obstacles or co-opting other managers. And at times (particularly when dealing with employees with poor attitudes), supervisors have to be direct, make clear that employees are to do the task, and complete it the way the organization expects it to be done. Always, supervisors must provide feedback, inform employees of how they are doing, and tell them whether they are accomplishing what is expected.

Another reason that supervisors train and coach employees is to reduce turnover. Correctional agencies have high turnover. A 2003 survey by the American Correctional Association found that the average national turnover of correctional officers was 16.1 percent, and noncompetitive compensation was the most frequently cited reason for recruitment difficulty and the second most cited reason for retention. Demanding work hours, stress and burnout, and employees not understanding and finding that they were not suited for the job were other factors in turnover.[12] As problematic as these issues seem, they appear to be improving, as correctional agencies are addressing the most serious issues to recruitment and retention, and the recession and rising unemployment rates are making more people consider working as correctional officers. Many states have improved recruitment and increased pay for correctional staff.[13]

Another way by which correctional agencies are improving recruitment and retention is through positively changing the culture of their organizations. In a case study of Florida and Pennsylvania departments of corrections, it was noted that assessing and enhancing the workplace could reduce staff turnover.[14] And Corrections Corporation of America, the largest private prison company with over 17,000 staff, conducted interviews with staff to determine workplace satisfaction, and identified that the way correctional officers were treated by their first-line supervisors had a major impact on turnover. As a result, the company implemented a values-based training program for supervisors and has seen their retention rates improve as a result.[15] Since the initiation of this training for supervisors, the turnover rate has been reduced by 50 percent. The traits identified as essential for supervisors to lead others include:

- Strong sense of values
- Embracing diversity
- Self-awareness
- Humility
- Integrity
- Loyalty
- Trustworthiness.

Giving Feedback

Feedback provides employees an understanding of how well they are doing a job, and can be given either through a formal written evaluation process or through informal verbal comments. Supervisors cannot expect employees to perform as desired if the employees are not told about how well they are doing and what they need to improve. Giving feedback may be as simple as telling employees that they did a good job or giving constructive criticism regarding how to do a job better the next time. It may also be more complex, using agency evaluations, and influence decisions regarding retention, pay, and promotion. No matter how formal or informal it may be, giving feedback is a critical element of effective supervision.

As simple as this seems, many supervisors do a poor job of providing feedback to their employees. Some say, "they will know if I am not happy with their performance." Others are uncomfortable telling employees how they are performing and find it hard to give praise or provide constructive criticism. Some supervisors may not be familiar with the procedures of the formal evaluation process and avoid it because they don't understand it and know they will not do it well. Others think anything negative they tell employees will result in a complaint to the union. But supervisors who give regular feedback (a pat on the back, immediate correction of errors, and performance evaluations that are fair and follow the agency guidelines) find that their effectiveness as supervisors increases significantly.

Positive feedback is the easiest and most pleasant for supervisors to give. It is satisfying to tell people that they did a good job and that their efforts are appreciated. It can be argued that there is nothing that has more impact on morale than positive feedback. Conversely, the most negative impact on morale is a failure to give feedback or giving the same feedback to both staff who perform at a high level and those who perform at a low level. A good analogy is how some parents never pay attention to their children except to discipline them. Children crave attention and, therefore, misbehave simply to get some recognition. Similarly, good employees who get no feedback may question why they are working so hard and may end up performing at a lower level, or even performing poorly simply to get some feedback. When supervisors do not differentiate between good and poor employees, fail to give praise, fail to give constructive criticism, or give everyone the same evaluation, employees find little reason to maintain good performance.

Every agency has a formal evaluation procedure. The supervisor's role in the process is perhaps the most important.[16] Supervisors write evaluations and discuss them with employees. The evaluation process is delicate for both employees and supervisors; it is designed to encourage improved performance. However, if it is not done well, the evaluation process leaves no one satisfied, can have a negative affect on morale, and can have the opposite effect on performance. Following are tips for supervisors regarding their role in evaluating employees:

- Take the evaluation process seriously. If a supervisor gives the impression that the evaluation is not important, it will not serve as an incentive for employees to maintain good or improve bad performance.

- Give all employees the level of evaluation they deserve. By failing to differentiate between good and bad employees, the process has no credibility and will be ineffective.

- Do not "inflate" evaluation levels. Some supervisors do not want to hurt any employees' feelings, so they rate everyone highly. When good employees see poor employees get above adequate ratings, the good employees' own ratings mean less to them.

- Be candid in discussing performance. If a supervisor is not comfortable being direct and is not candid about the need for improvement by employees, the evaluation will not help them to improve.

- Spend the proportionate amount of time praising as well as correcting employees as they deserve. Many supervisors may not tell a good employee all the things they do right. They say, "You are doing a really good job, but I would like to see you improve on these items." If a supervisor thinks an employee is doing 90 percent of the job well, the evaluation discussion should reflect that, and the supervisor should spend 90 percent of the time saying how much he or she appreciates the way the employee performs certain tasks.

Preparing for Supervision

The old adage of the "born leader" has long been believed to be true. However, today the idea of born leaders is in question, especially with the emphasis on transformational over transactional leadership described in Chapter 3. As described, transformational leaders communicate values and principles, they create strategies to share information, and they push authority for decision making to the lowest possible level. A transformational leader of a correctional agency noted that once the staff became empowered, they grew tremendously in their willingness and skill at taking actions consistent with the organizational goals. The administrator even joked that he had nothing to do anymore, as staff were not constantly coming to him to ask what to do. Instead, they were constantly progressing and improving the agency performance in line with the principles desired without prompting or directing.

The same is true for supervisors. The contemporary challenge for supervision is not to learn how to give orders clearly but how to learn to develop staff through training, coaching, and creating opportunities for staff to experience and learn new things. Learning how to be a good supervisor and use your skills to motivate and encourage staff takes time and attention. Some staff believe all they have to do is wait their turn to become supervisors. However, successful supervisors are those who have taken advantage of their time by understanding the skills needed for supervision, candidly analyzing their strengths and weaknesses, and taking initiatives to improve and prepare themselves. The American Correctional Association has developed a certification for correctional supervisors that requires online training and passing a test.[17] A recent article in *American Jails* emphasizes how "We will never perfect or master the art and science of leadership, but only improve on it through a commitment of lifelong study of it."[18]

What are the skills and traits necessary for supervision? The American Correctional Association handbook on supervision lists the following personality traits or characteristics to be successful as a supervisor.[19]

- Patience
- Tolerance
- Sensitivity
- Empathy
- Punctuality
- Decisiveness

The authors suggest that prospective supervisors consider their own characteristics against this list of traits and consider how to improve their own abilities in these areas. Individuals do not have to accept that they are impatient or lack tolerance. They can recognize the need to make changes and can improve themselves in the area of valued supervisory traits.

One of the most important activities that line staff can take to prepare for being supervisors is to do their current jobs well. Sometimes, staff think so much about the job they want to have, they fail to concentrate on performing at a high level in their current assignment. When staff are considered for promotion to supervisory positions, the most important factor considered is how they perform their present jobs. Staff are usually evaluated for their potential as supervisors on how well they handle the technical aspects of their current jobs.

An important trait for supervisors is effective time management. Some people seem to get more done than others, and it is not clear why. While working hard is helpful, it is not the only and perhaps not the best solution. It is more important for employees to organize their workload and complete a task once it is started. In supervision, especially in a fluid correctional environment, there are many distractions that interrupt the accomplishment of an ongoing task. Effective supervisors know how to focus on a task and how to manage resources to complete assignments. Every employee has a variety of work tasks that must be organized and competed. Understanding and improving one's ability to organize work and manage time is excellent preparation for taking on supervisory responsibilities.

Another way to prepare for supervision is to develop skills to effectively manage stress. Correctional jobs by their nature are prone to a tremendous amount of stress. They can be dangerous, and fear of physical injury increases personal stress. As correctional staff climb the organizational ladder, they quickly realize they feel responsible for incidents such as fights, riots, prison escapes, or new crimes committed by probationers or parolees. Add to the usual stresses of supervising people, correcting performance, giving evaluations, or responding to bad attitudes or lack of motivation, and correctional supervision is a formula for high anxiety. Staff who do not learn how to manage stress have a difficult time as correctional supervisors. Phillips and McConnell provide the following five suggestions for supervisors to reduce job related stress.[20]

- Learn to say no, or at least to speak up, when the last request or demand (from your boss) finally becomes too much.
- Do not let work accumulate until it becomes uncontrollable.
- Delegate before the level of work gets out of control.
- Vary your pace by interspersing short, quiet tasks among the more hectic, tension-producing contacts required.
- When the going gets rough, take a few minutes to relax. There are methods to reduce the physical response to stress through stretching, breathing exercises, or walking to clear your head.

Good communication skills are essential for supervision. Supervisors must regularly communicate to individuals and to groups. They must have both good verbal and good written communication skills. Staff who do not have strong skills in these areas can improve their abilities. Individuals with inadequate writing skills should take writing courses. Most correctional agencies recognize the importance of written communications and provide self-study courses to improve these skills. Similarly, there are training programs to improve verbal communications. For individuals who are uncomfortable speaking to groups of people, the best way to reduce their anxiety is for them to practice public speaking. Employees who believe that their public speaking needs work should seek opportunities to speak to groups, for example, by briefing other employees or volunteering as trainers. The more one does public speaking, the easier it becomes.

Preparation for supervision includes the following. First, employees should candidly analyze their strengths and weakness. No one is perfect, and ignoring a weakness will only make it that much more of a weakness as employees increase their level of responsibility. Second, employees should develop a plan for their personal improvement. All required supervisory traits can be strengthened, and all weaknesses can be improved. Finally, employees must take initiatives to improve. Some employees make the mistake of waiting for their supervisors or the agency to recognize their training and development needs to place them in a program. However, the best and quickest way to improve and prepare for supervision is for employees to take action themselves. They should take self-study courses, enroll in college courses, avail themselves of opportunities to use and practice supervisory skills, and ask for training they believe will prepare them for supervision. As employees take these three steps, they will find they are prepared when the time comes for them to move into a supervisory role.

Empowering Employees: The Key to Success

The first section of this chapter addressed the methods and techniques to supervise employees. In the past two decades there has been a broader focus on creating a culture within an organization whereby staff are "empowered," understand the principles and goals of the agency, and can make decisions without being directed in line with the principles and goals of their organization. What is staff empowerment, and is there something different in today's organizational environment that makes it the right thing to do? Real employee empowerment is not easy to implement, although many managers believe they do it. Empowerment is especially difficult to implement in correctional agencies, in which issues such as crimes committed by community offenders or prison escapes and riots are feared by both agency and political leadership. Correctional leaders and managers often believe they have to personally attend to the activities in a prison or community correctional program in order to avoid problems and risk embarrassment.

In its pure sense, **empowerment** is an approach that is broader than supervising or delegating. It is more concerned about the overall culture of an organization. It is more than asking employees their opinions about policies and procedures. It extends beyond involving employees in creating solutions to problems. Empowerment involves pushing decision-making down to the lowest possible level and letting them manage themselves and make decisions. Empowerment involves giving employees the authority to create new approaches when they believe a new way improves the old. Empowerment involves providing employees with the principles and values of the organization, along with the desired outcomes (vision and mission), and encouraging them to make decisions and respond to situations that are consistent with accepted principles and values, while moving the organization toward its desired outcomes. Foy describes empowerment as follows:

> In empowering organizations, people know what the organization expects from them, and how well they are meeting their targets. More than that, in the ultimate empowering, they are able to help develop the objectives, and their experience feeds into the development of credible strategies. That kind of organization will be good for its members, and they will be good for the organization.[21]

Empowerment of employees and organizations is important in correctional organizations for several reasons. First, corrections is no longer a relatively stable environment, but is one that has to be flexible and adapt quickly to change. In fact, change is so rapid that correctional agencies sometimes have difficulty developing routine procedures that can be counted on to work over time. Second, because of such change, there are many situations that have never before been encountered. There can be no standardized policy or expected response if the issue or situation has never before had to be dealt with. Third, employees are better educated today than they were in the past and have grown up in an environment of rapid change. These employees are therefore prepared to meet never-before confronted challenges. Finally, today's employees demand to be involved in the organization and cringe at a rigid bureaucracy in which they are only expected to follow orders and carry out prescribed functions. They do not tolerate the old adages of "we have always done it this way" or "if it ain't broke, don't fix it." If they know a better way to carry out their duties, they will expect to have the authority to implement it.

For these reasons, empowering employees is extremely important in a correctional environment. Change is continuous and rapid, as new inmates, updated technology, changing community supervision standards, and tremendous growth in the number of clients require new approaches and the ability for staff to react quickly to whatever they confront. Correctional administrators cannot personally stay ahead of all the changes and revise policy and procedure manuals and train staff in what to expect. They must rely on their staff to deal daily with issues and incidents within the correctional environment to understand the vision and principles of the organization and respond appropriately to issues or emergencies. In dealing with probationers, probation officers have dozens of interactions every month that cannot be covered by policy and procedure, and officers must use their judgment to respond in a way consistent with the philosophy of their agencies.

Contemporary correctional staff are professional, experienced, trained, and educated. They have grown up in a computer and information age, have learned how to face new challenges, and are comfortable without routine, prescribed methods and procedures. The current generation of employees does not accept orders without wanting to know why. They require understanding how the organization developed a specified responses to situations. These staff are more committed to an organization outcome or procedure that they were involved in creating. Over the past two decades, the inability to influence their workplace has been a key reason for staff turnover. Prison staff, in noting reasons why they terminated their employment, listed two issues: the quality of the work environment and the inability to influence prison policy.[22] In a study of prison climate, with more than 3,000 staff responses, it was found that staff with greater input into decision making had higher job satisfaction and believed they were more effective in their roles.[23] And in a study of the Florida and Pennsylvania departments of corrections, it was noted that assessing and enhancing the workplace could reduce staff turnover.[24]

Therefore, empowerment is not only acceptable but is also almost a requirement for the effective and efficient management of a modern correctional agency. The question is not whether to empower staff, rather it is how to empower staff without giving up authority and without failing to provide leadership. It may seem that empowering staff to make decisions acknowledges that employees will learn by making mistakes. However, in correctional organizations, mistakes can result in a very serious negative outcome, and leaders do not simply let staff do what they want to do, and experiment with a variety of procedures. By involving staff, forewarning them of information about offenders and offender groups, and training them about the risks and potential dangers regarding responses to problems, staff can then use sound professional judgment to make decisions. This is not "trial and error." It is using informed, professional judgment at all staff levels within a correctional organization. To see how this can be accomplished, the next few sections present the practices and processes to effective empowerment.

Leadership and Empowerment

As noted previously, leadership in the complex world in which correctional administrators operate today requires a very different style of interacting with employees than the traditional models of correctional leadership. Transactional leaders were the experts who sent commands down the chain of command, through layers of bureaucracy, and when an issue needed resolved, everything stopped until the boss could be consulted. Today, as the work environment continuously faces new issues that have not been experienced before, the future-oriented, transformational leader, by creating a vision and empowering employees to fulfill that vision, is the preferred leadership style. By providing staff the principles guiding decisions and the desired outcome, employees make decisions and operate in a manner consistent with those principles.

One way to structure transformational leadership in the roles, functions, and decision making by leaders, managers, and line staff is illustrated in the leadership and empowerment triangle in Figure 8-3. The triangle is not the same as an organizational chart with an increasing number of employees from top to bottom, and it does not indicate lines of reporting or authority among staff. It relates to the type and scope of tasks that each layer of the triangle should perform. As described below, leaders focus on only a handful of key organizational responsibilities, and line staff execute dozens of policies and procedures on a daily basis.

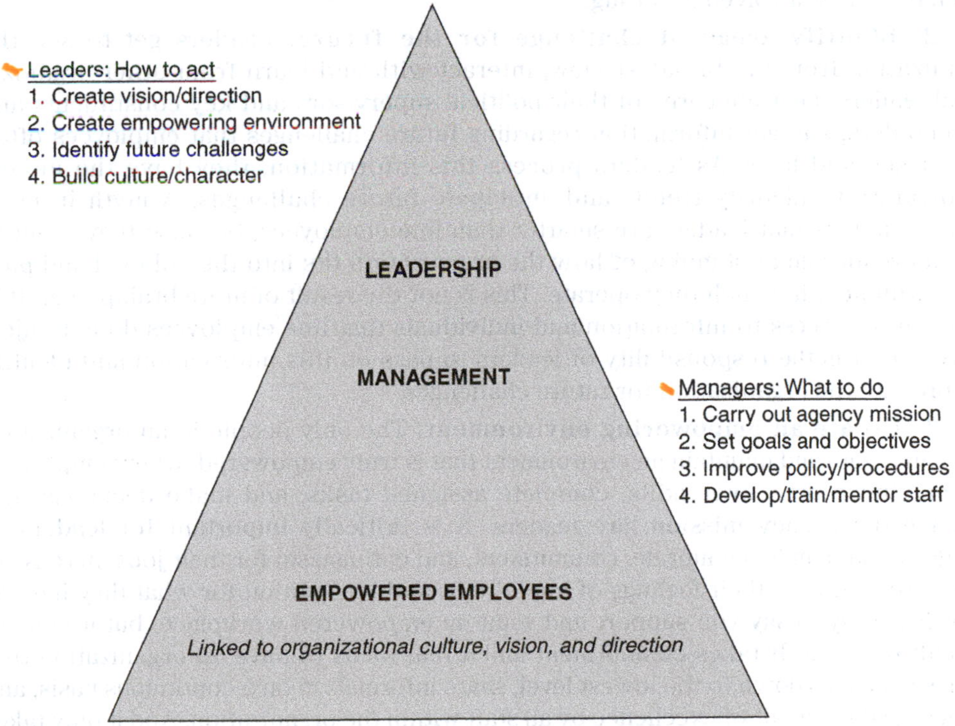

Leaders: How to act
1. Create vision/direction
2. Create empowering environment
3. Identify future challenges
4. Build culture/character

LEADERSHIP

MANAGEMENT

Managers: What to do
1. Carry out agency mission
2. Set goals and objectives
3. Improve policy/procedures
4. Develop/train/mentor staff

EMPOWERED EMPLOYEES

Linked to organizational culture, vision, and direction

Figure 8-3
Leadership and empowerment triangle.

At the top of the triangle are the tasks that should be carried out by leaders in order to create an empowered correctional environment. These tasks focus on providing staff with tools and opportunities to better manage and operate the agency. As is apparent, leaders' roles have changed considerably over time, from directing specific actions to empowering employees to take the actions they recognize are necessary. Instead of telling employees "what to do," leaders shape "how employees act." Following are the four key functions that are recommended for correctional leadership to create an empowered and involved workplace.

1. Create a vision and set the direction for the organization. As noted in Chapter 4, agencies and organizations must have a vision, a road map or understanding, of where they want to go and what they want to be. It is the responsibility of leaders to create this vision for their agencies. This does not mean that leaders sit alone in their office and write the vision for the organization. Instead, leaders should involve employees as much as possible in setting the vision. Leaders do not have a monopoly on understanding where the agency should go or what the agency should be. But they are well positioned to act as a primary resource for information and help guide the process of establishing the vision. It can be argued that employees are sometimes even more vested in the future of the organization than leadership. The leaders are usually older, and will retire or move to another position before the typical line correctional employee. And employees are much more likely to support and work to accomplish a vision in which they were involved in setting.

2. Identify areas of challenge for the future. Leaders get to see the organization from the broadest view, interact with and learn from other organizational leaders, hear concerns of their political supervisors and key constituents and stakeholders, and get information regarding future challenges that employees often do not see and hear. As leaders process this information, they have the unique opportunity to identify trends and anticipate future challenges. A myth in most organizations is that leaders are smarter than line employees, because they seem to have a broader understanding of how the organization fits into the political and public environment in which they operate. This is not the result of more brainpower. It is the result of access to information and individuals that line employees do not enjoy. Therefore, it is the responsibility of leaders to pass on this information and identify and prepare the organization for future challenges.

3. Create an empowering environment. The only people in an organization who can create and maintain an environment that is truly empowered, where employees can maximize their own skills, complete assigned tasks, and make decisions that enhance the agency mission, are leaders. It is critically important for leaders to recognize that employee morale, commitment, and enthusiasm for their jobs increase in direct proportion to their feelings of importance and recognition for what they have to offer. It is easy to say you support and want an empowered workplace, but it is more difficult to live it. It takes commitment and a real focus to have an organization that pushes decisions down to the lowest level, share information on a continuous basis, and encourage the pursuit of excellence by all staff within the organization. And it only takes a few acts of bringing decisions back to the leaders circle of influence and show you do not trust employees to undermine the creation of an empowered workplace.

4. Build (or reinforce) the organization culture and character. Organizational culture includes the shared values, purposes, and behaviors that carry on in an organization. You often hear about organizations having a "culture of excellence" that emanates throughout the workforce and employees just always strive to do and be their best. Most agencies have a culture, and hopefully one that encourages professionalism and dedication to the mission. However, negative cultures can also develop, and it is a true test of leadership to change a negative into a positive agency culture. Integrity often is thought to be carried on by culture in criminal justice organizations. In a study of police integrity, the behavior of officers was often found more likely to be influenced by the culture of the department than other factors such as who they hired.[25] Leaders must determine the type of culture they desire for their organization, and then take consistent and continuous steps and actions to insert or reinforce that culture.

The second level of the leadership and empowerment triangle is the management level. Managers are those who make sure things are done the right way. Just as the role of leaders has moved beyond traditional tasks, the role of managers has also increased in the level of sophistication required to take over some of these functions. Managers are the people who ensure that the agency mission is accomplished. They do this by working within their divisions or departments to set goals and objectives, to refine and improve policies and procedures, to develop staff through training and mentoring, and to continually reinforce the agency mission in employees' minds. They often do this through setting goals, measuring performance against those goals, and recognizing and rewarding staff for their accomplishment.

The biggest change in roles illustrated in the leadership and management triangle comes in the actions of line employees. Supervision has always emphasized the importance of clearly describing tasks for employees, overseeing their work, and holding them accountable for completing those tasks. However, every line correctional employee makes dozens of decisions during an eight-hour day. How do they respond to a community-supervised offender committing minor violations of their supervision? How do they deal with a somewhat noncompliant offender? How do they handle a minor security breach? How do they counsel an offender who has an issue that needs immediate attention? How do they respond when they see a coworker being less than professional?

The end result of leadership in an organization is to empower employees to make decisions and respond to situations in a manner consistent with the culture, principles, ethics, and values desirable within an agency. When the leaders of all levels successfully carry out their activities already described, employees will adapt their behavior to conform to the culture, organizational direction, and professional approach desired. Leaders and managers cannot be everywhere to observe operations and cannot advise and direct staff on every interaction or work activity. By creating the proper empowering environment and ensuring employees understand the vision and direction of the agency, employees are better prepared to make appropriate decisions and function in a professional manner.

The Empowerment Process

As noted earlier, creating an empowering work environment does not come easy, and takes a great deal of care and attention by leaders. Just as with any other change, correctional administrators must plan an implementation strategy for creating an empowered environment.

It is never simple to change "how we manage," and is much easier to change "what we manage." However, with a clear focus and planning, an empowered environment can be created. The following steps are important to the implementation of an empowering organization environment.

1. Tell staff they are going to be empowered.
2. Explain what empowerment means.
3. Generate commitment by top managers.
4. Realign responsibilities.
5. Provide staff direction and a vision for guidance.
6. Involve staff in the creation of a strategic plan, including empowerment strategies.
7. Simplify the organization, and remove any unnecessary levels.
8. Create a focus on performance and outcome.
9. Establish a communications strategy.
10. Initiate a mechanism for feedback.

1. Tell staff they are going to be empowered. It may seem simple, but it is very important to tell staff they are going to be empowered. Organizational leaders must inform staff that there is going to be a change in the way the organization is managed. Staff hear about changes in the organization all the time, to the point that they often tend to ignore them until the changes actually occur and affect the way they perform their day-to-day jobs. By telling staff of plans for empowerment, correctional administrators commit to the change and put their credibility at risk. Staff know this, and respect leaders who are willing to take this risk. Also, announcing the plan begins the process of staff understanding that they must accept some responsibility in return.

2. Explain what empowerment means. The next step is to educate staff on what empowerment means and what will be expected of them. Staff at first will think, "Oh, great, I won't have a boss looking over my shoulder at everything I do from now on." However, once they realize that a tremendous amount of responsibility comes with empowerment, it will be threatening to them. The biggest change with empowerment is that staff can't simply do their jobs and avoid taking responsibility for improving processes. Instead of only being concerned with "process," every staff member becomes responsible for "outcome." Staff must continually look for ways to improve both themselves and the organization.

3. Generate commitment by top managers. Perhaps most hesitant to accept empowerment are mid- and upper-level managers in an organization who believe they are losing the most. And, they are in many ways losing something. For managers who relish and protect information to maintain their organizational importance, providing information to employees and allowing them the authority to make decisions at the lowest level, empowerment can be threatening. Sometimes, these managers must themselves be convinced that empowerment is right for the organization. It is critical for correctional administrators to tend to the concerns, fears, and needs of these managers by explaining their new roles as mentors and coaches for line staff. Creating an empowered workplace will not be successful unless managers support the philosophy.

4. Realign responsibilities. To implement an empowering environment, almost everyone in the organization must change what they do and how much time they spend on various functions. As described in the leadership and empowerment triangle, leaders should focus on their four activities. Managers must emphasize the setting and completion of goals and objectives, refine and improve policies and procedures, develop staff through training and mentoring, and continually reinforce the agency mission in employees' minds. And line employees must recognize and accept that they are empowered to respond to situations and make decisions in a manner consistent with the culture, principles, ethics, and values desirable within the organization.

5. Provide staff direction and a vision for guidance. For staff to be successful in an empowered environment, they must know what the organization values, wants to be, and the types of behaviors that contribute to this outcome. These elements are captured in an organization's vision, and as staff understand and buy into the vision, they perform in a manner consistent with it. In Chapter 4, the vision of the federal prison in Greenville, Illinois was presented as "We envision FCI Greenville as a safe, pleasant, and empowered workplace." To implement an empowered workplace, Greenville leaders presented and constantly reinforced this vision statement to convey to staff the values, principles, and expected outcomes of the organization. Staff then began to repeat and use this vision as guidance and direction for their behavior.

6. Involve staff in the creation of a strategic plan, including empowerment strategies. The next step is to plan to implement empowerment strategies. Key strategies focus on communications, performance and outcome, and continuous feedback. However, these activities simply do not occur without considerable planning and thought. Implementation requires considerable effort by all staff until empowering activities become habit and part of the routine way of doing business. An implementation plan should be developed that identifies specific strategic activities and dates they will be implemented. Staff from all levels of the organization should be involved, and should participate as peers, rather than superiors and subordinates.

7. Simplify the organization, and remove any unnecessary levels. Many organizations, especially public agencies, become increasingly bureaucratic over time, and they create organizational layers and departments to respond to new issues and challenges. Too many levels within an organization chart become an obstacle to effective empowerment. It is important to simplify communications and avoid redundant layers through which information passes. While implementing empowering strategies, organizations should examine themselves to determine whether they have created unnecessary layers that exacerbate the ability to share information and empower staff. If so, the organization should eliminate unnecessary and overly bureaucratic layers of management.

8. Create a focus on performance and outcome. Too often, public organizations measure input and process rather than output. This comes almost naturally from the public sector budget process requiring funding for programs, number of staff, number of clients, or number of forms processed. In correctional agencies, budgets are primarily for the number of staff employed. Few public agencies have an effective outcome oriented budget process and seldom require measurement of outcomes. In *Reinventing Government*, a book recommending a redesign of government to make it more efficient and responsive to tax payers, the authors suggest, "Organizations that measure the results of their work—even if they do not link funding or rewards to those results—find that the information transforms them."[26] For example, a probation agency can go a long way toward empowering probation officers and improving performance by simply collecting information and rewarding staff on the number of probationers who find and maintain productive employment, rather than the number of probationers on the officers' caseload.

9. Establish a communications strategy. A communications strategy to continuously share information throughout the organization about the success of the empowerment implementation is extremely important. As noted earlier, bureaucratic and strict hierarchical approaches of passing information up and down the chain of command make it difficult to have a fully empowered environment. However, communication strategies must ensure that managers and supervisors are not "jumped over" with the flow of information to line staff. Therefore, it is important to develop strategies that work for the entire organization and to share information quickly and continuously. With today's technology, there are many ways to have information "immersion" whereby updates or outcomes can immediately be transmitted to all staff. Phone systems can be programmed to call all staff phones with a recorded message of breaking information. Or, there can be a "dial in" message center (with staff-only access) with a recorded message about what occurred and possible follow-up incidents of which to be aware. Computer systems can transmit "flash" messages to all staff at the same time. A certain radio code or signal on the prison loud speaker system can alert staff to use a planned system for information sharing. Although face-to-face communications remain important, it is even more important to have quick and widespread access to information.

An example of how this can work within a prison illustrates the ability to link the chain of command and immersion of information successfully. As incidents occur and information develops (e.g., a fight in the recreation yard between two gang members that may lead to additional fights between gang members), those in possession of the information (e.g., the warden or the chief of security) can do an information immersion and then conduct a briefing for all available staff. This allows for questions, interchange of information, and even collecting ideas for strategies if further incidents occur. As other staff report for work, they can be briefed with information updates by their supervisors. A similar situation could work for an incident by a probationer or parolee who committed a serious crime and there is a need for quick information collection and a change in supervision procedures. The many opportunities for immediate and continuous sharing of information provide a key to successfully empowering staff, allowing them to make sound decisions based on the situation and the impact it will have on the overall correctional environment.

10. Initiate a mechanism for feedback. Finally, there should be opportunities for line employees to discuss their ideas, propose solutions or changes in procedures, and share proposals with correctional administrators. In most situations, staff cannot change procedures on their own without resulting in inconsistency in operations. If an employee idea for a change in procedures has merit, it should be discussed and considered throughout the organization. One way ideas have been considered in a correctional agency is through creating a Line Staff Advisory Committee. The administrator meets with the committee and listens to suggestions from line staff. Decisions to make changes in procedures are not made at these meetings. However, if the committee agrees an issue needed attention, committee members are assigned responsibility to talk to other staff, identify some options for responding to the issue, and discuss the suggestions with the responsible department head. The process can initially seem threatening to department heads who are concerned that line staff have more authority to create policies or procedures. They soon realize that the committee merely identified problems and works with them to find the best solutions. Department heads still have the final decision, but they get line staff to submit ideas and do much of the communications work for them. Through this process, line staff have an outlet for feedback, rather than grumbling and complaining among themselves that problems are never addressed. Department heads still have the authority to make decisions about procedures under their control. As both line staff and mid-level managers recognize the opportunity to make positive change in the organization, they become enthusiastic about looking for ways to improve procedures.

Empowerment of staff is important for correctional agencies, but efforts to empower must be well planned to be successfully implemented. It is easy to say staff are empowered, but actions speak much louder than words. Staff throughout the organization must be committed to the empowerment process, and definitive steps must be taken to change both actual behavior and staff taking up responsibility for improvement. If empowerment is successfully implemented, the improvement in efficiency, morale, and operations can be dramatic.

SUMMARY

Supervision is perhaps the most difficult, yet the most critical function within a correctional agency. Failure to effectively supervise employees can very quickly undermine the ability to operate a safe and secure prison, to efficiently manage a community corrections program, or to prepare offenders for success in the community. Correctional line employees carry out the day-to-day functions of corrections, and require support, coaching, and guidance from their supervisors. Regardless of facilities, technology, or financial resources, if line staff do not do their jobs well, correctional goals will not be fulfilled. Correctional supervisors play a critical role in accomplishing the mission through the staff they supervise.

Poor supervision wastes resources, discredits the agency, damages morale, and undermines staff loyalty and dedication. Good communications, clarifying expectations, proper delegation, understanding behavior, on-the-job training and coaching staff, and giving feedback to employees are all essential tasks for supervisors. These activities cannot be taken for granted. They require specific skills to be carried out effectively. Beyond these basic supervisory functions, contemporary supervisors must learn to empower staff, enlighten them with the organizational vision, and trust them to take responsibility and make decisions that conform to the organization's principles and values. It can be the most rewarding function for those staff who perform supervision well. It is gratifying to watch staff you have developed perform at a high level, take responsibility, and mature into effective staff who contribute to the organization.

KEY TERMS

Supervision   Responsibility   Feedback
Delegation   On-the-job training   Empowerment
Authority   Coaching

YOU'RE THE CORRECTIONAL ADMINISTRATOR

1. You are a unit manager in a prison, supervising two case managers, two correctional officers, two correctional counselors, and one secretary. You have a very good, dedicated team with generally positive morale. However, one of your case managers has been performing very poorly for the past three months. This case manager has missed several days of work, does not get required tasks completed on time, and regularly complains about more work than is possible to do. The other staff are becoming unhappy about the situation. They regularly have to adjust their schedules to cover in the case manager's absence. They often have to help perform tasks the case manager doesn't complete or to redo them. How do you handle this as the supervisor? Describe the steps you would take to ensure that the case manager performs at expected standards and that the rest of the team continues to perform at a high level.

2. You are a very talented probation officer who is ambitious in your desire for rapid promotion. You want to get ahead as fast as possible; you want your bosses to recognize your talent and consider you for the next probation supervisor job. You are not the most senior officer. There are at least five other officers who have more experience. What can you do to enhance your potential to receive this promotion? Be as specific as possible in creating a list of activities you could take to prepare yourself and come to the attention of the probation administrators who decide on the promotion.

WEB LINK EXERCISES

Go to http://humanresources.about.com/od/retention/a/more_retention_2.htm

Scroll down and look to the left side for Related Articles and click on *Top Ten Ways to Make Employee Empowerment Fail* (2 pages). Read the ten ways that are not recommended for a good empowerment program. Try to relate to the ten ways as if you were a jail supervisor and were supervising a group of correction officers. Empowering employees is an important and continuous function and these tips may give you some guidance on performing this task.

Go to www.danpink.com/drive.html

You should take the quick quiz to determine what type of person you are. Dan Pink, the author of the bestselling *Drive*, indicates that type I persons value the intrinsic meaning of work and are motivated by the joy of the job, while type X persons are motivated by extrinsic incentives primarily. His belief is that organizations should attempt to develop and hire more type I persons as they inherently enjoy their jobs more. What type of person are you?

GROUP EXERCISES

Each group will be assigned one of the following important elements in staff supervision. Groups are to present their topic by describing the role of the element, why it is important to quality supervision, how it is carried out in a correctional environment, and provide at least one realistic scenario that fully explains the element: communicating, coaching, delegating, performance evaluating, and empowering.

ENDNOTES

1. Martin M. Broadwell, *Moving Up to Supervision* (Boston, MA: CBI Publishing Company, 1979), p. 3.

2. Richard L. Phillips and Charles R. McConnell, *The Effective Corrections Manager: Corrections Supervision for the Future* (Sudbury, MA: Jones and Bartlett Publishers, Second Edition, 2005), p. 27.

3. Clem Bartollas and Stuart J. Miller, *Correctional Administration: Theory and Practice* (New York: McGraw-Hill Book Company, 1978), p. 143.

4. Keith Davis, *Human Relations at Work: The Dynamics of Organizational Behavior*, 3rd ed. (New York: McGraw-Hill Book Company, 1967), p. 326.

5. Bruce B. Tepper, adapted for the American Correctional Association by Ida M. Halasz, *Supervision: A Handbook for Success* (Lanham, MD: American Correctional Association, 1998), pp. 59–60.

6. Frank Hecht, "The Art of Delegation," *American Jails* (September/October, 2006), p. 51.

7. Phillips and McConnell, *The Effective Corrections Manager*, p. 76.

8. Hecht, "The Art of Delegation."

9. Melissa Vokoun, "Delegation with Confidence: Five Essential Steps," *ManagerWise* (2008), http://www.articlesbase.com/organizational-articles/delegation-with-confidence-five-essential-steps-389989.html (accessed April 23, 2010).

10. Willard E. Parker, Robert W. Kleemeier, and Beyer V. Parker, *Front-Line Leadership* (New York: McGraw-Hill Book Company, 1969), p. 249.

11. Ferdinand F. Fournies, *Coaching for Improved Work Performance* (New York: Van Nostrand Reinhold Company, 1978), p. 77.

12. Jane Lommel, "Turning Around Turnover," *Corrections Today* 66 no. 5 (August 2004): 54–57.

13. For a description of what states are doing to improve recruitment and retention, see Richard P. Seiter, *Corrections An Introduction* (Columbus, OH: Pearson Education, 2011), pp. 399–400.

14. Brian E. Cronin, Ralph Klessig, and William D. Sprenkle, "Recruiting and Retaining Staff Through Culture Change," *Corrections Today* 70 no. 4 (August 2008): 48–51.

15. Gary C. Mohr, "Samberg Program Improves Leadership and Addresses Turnover," *Corrections Today* 71 (April 2009): 56–58.

16. For a discussion on conducting employee evaluations, see Chapter 6, How to Conduct Employee Performance Evaluations," in *Staff Supervision Made Easy*, edited by Scott Hutton (Lanham, MD: American Correctional Association, 1998), pp. 51–60.

17. To learn more about the ACA Professional Certification program for Correctional Supervisors (as well as officers, managers and executives), go to the ACA Web site at http://aca.org/certification.

18. Lynn Franklin Nehring, "Living Leadership," *American Jails* 22 no. 1 (March/April 2008): 10.

19. Tepper, Supervision, p. 7.

20. Phillips and McConnell, *The Effective Corrections Manager*, pp. 111–112.

21. Nancy Foy, *Empowering People at Work* (Brookfield, VT: Gower Publishing Limited, 1994), p. 7.

22. Nancy C. Jurik and Russell Winn, "Describing Correctional Security Dropouts and Rejects—An Individual and Organizational Profile," *Criminal Justice and Behavior* 14 (1987): 5–25.

23. William G. Saylor and Kevin N. Wright, "A Comparative Study of the Relationship of Status and Longevity in Determining Perceptions of Work Environment Among Federal Employees," *Journal of Offender Rehabilitation* 17 (1992): 133–160.

24. Brian E. Cronin, Ralph Klessig, and William D. Sprenkle, "Recruiting and Retaining Staff Through Culture Change" *Corrections Today* 70 no. 4 (August 2008): 48–51.

25. Carl B. Klockars, Sanja Kutnjak Ivkovick, and Maria R. Haberfeld, "Enhancing Police Integrity," *NIJ Research for Practice* (Washington, DC: U.S. Department of Justice, 2005).

26. David Osborne and Ted Gaebler, *Reinventing Government: How the Entrepreneurial Spirit Is Transforming the Public Sector* (Reading, MA: Addison-Wesley, 1992), p. 146.

9

Fiscal Management and the Challenge of Cost Containment

Introduction

One of the most significant challenges for correctional administrators and other officials responsible for public budgets is the ever-increasing cost of correctional operations. With the increasing number of offenders under correctional supervision and with many factors driving up the per capita costs of operations, the amount of public funds that must be directed toward corrections reduces the dollars available for other public purposes, and even the fiscal solvency of some state and local governments. The increased funding requirements for correctional agencies bring attention and pressures to elected officials to encourage correctional administrators to find ways to reduce budget requirements and brings into question many policies and practices that the public believes create unnecessary expenditures.

The economic downturn over the past few years has resulted in reduced tax receipts by states and the federal government. When the economy was strong and governments were experiencing budget surpluses, no one worried about expanding prison space and other correctional services to meet the burgeoning population under supervision. However, with the difficult budget challenges faced by governments, it is now a complicated decision as to whether to increase taxes, reduce the correctional population, or eliminate some services or supervision to meet budget shortfalls. Correctional administrators are being called on to find solutions to the budget dilemma. They are often given more offenders to manage, and these offenders may be higher risks to recidivate, have more program needs, and have a more serious history of violence and gang involvement. However, they still have to reduce overall budget costs, and the public and elected officials do not want to hear excuses of the challenges and demands placed on their agencies. They have to examine ways to "do more with less" and become more efficient in their operations. They look for ways to reduce demand for correctional services by finding alternatives to incarceration or by shortening supervision times. They look for ways to create revenue and to offset some of the increasing spending demands. And they look at nontraditional approaches to providing services, such as contracting with the private sector to reduce costs.

Over the past twenty years, the number of clients served by adult correctional agencies has grown significantly. At the end of 2008, over 7.3 million individuals were under correctional supervision of probation, prison, jail, or parole.[1] Correspondingly, expenditures for correctional agencies have also grown, as corrections budgets nationwide increased by 529 percent from 1992 to 2006.[2] In fiscal year 1991, state and federal adult correctional agencies' budgets totaled $18.1 billion.[3] By fiscal year 2006, these budgets, with the inclusion of local jails, more than tripled to $68.7 billion.[4] As prison budgets have increased, so have budgets for probation and parole. The average budget for state probation and parole agencies more than doubled from $34.3 million in 1992 to $82.9 million in 2002, and it was estimated that over $9 billion will be spent to supervise offenders in the community in 2007.[5] In 2007, these state agencies supervised 5.12 million offenders on probation or parole[6] at an average cost of $3.42 per day of community supervision.[7]

And correctional agency spending is expected to continue to increase for the next several years. There were 41,368 new prison beds under construction in 1999, 47,476 in 2000, 58,422 in 2001, and 26,869 in 2002.[8] From June 30, 2000, to December 30, 2005, there were 153 new state and federal prisons and 151 new private prisons constructed and opened.[9] As these new beds were put to use at an average cost of over $78.95 per inmate per day in 2008, the budget figures will continue to climb dramatically. State correctional agencies consumed 6.8 percent of state general funds in 2007,[10] and by 2011, continued prison growth is expected to cost an additional $25 billion.[11] State and local budgets have never had such a dire situation. In January 2009, states reported over $50 billion shortfalls in revenue to fund their 2009 budgets; the gap widened in 2010 budgets to $84.3 billion,[12] and while the drop in state revenues is beginning to subside, it is estimated there will be a cumulative state budget gap of $89 billion in FY 2011, $73.5 billion for FY 2012, and at least $64.7 billion gap as far out as FY 2013.[13]

This chapter examines all of these as potential solutions to the increasing costs for corrections. First, the causes of increased correctional demands and budgets are examined. Second, the expenditures that are currently being committed to correctional agencies and the past trends in dollars for corrections are reviewed. Third, the methods by which agencies develop and monitor correctional budgets are investigated. Fourth, the alternatives available to correctional administrators to meet budget challenges are considered. Finally, the use of the private sector to provide correctional services and the potential for increased cost efficiency through this approach are examined.

The Budgetary Process for Corrections

Increased oversight by elected officials and a critical appraisal of how correctional agencies operate and spend their funds by the many interest groups that are affected by how much money is devoted to corrections or how much money is diverted from other public agencies can be expected from the dramatic increase in correctional agency budgets. Correctional agencies have operated and budgeted in very much the same manner throughout the entire history of corrections in the United States. Even with a number of different systems of public budgeting (line item budgeting, performance budgeting, planning–programming budgeting, and zero-based budgeting),[14] correctional budget development has basically been expense based and incremental.

With **expense-based budgets**, corrections agencies calculate how much it costs them for salaries, programs, and services and develop a budget based on these expenses. It is not "outcome" based or "value" based, in that it does not question or propose what is to be accomplished nor does it put a value to society on the amount of dollars that are being expended. Correctional agencies are merely asked to estimate the cost of their operations for the next or future fiscal years and ask the legislative body for that amount of money. If the correctional agency has 10 prisons to operate, 10,000 inmates to feed and clothe, supervises 15,000 offenders in the community, and employs 3,000 staff, administrators calculate the cost of these items, which becomes the budget request. The expectation is that they will continue to do business next year as they did in the past, and the budget provides for dollars required to conduct this business.

Correctional budgets are also **incremental**, in that the agency begins budget calculations by looking at the costs of operations last year and the increase in cost that new staff or new prison beds will create for the coming year. The budget process seldom is designed to take any major policy issues into consideration. Years ago when correctional budgets were relatively small, before they began to get so big that they required funds that elected officials would have liked to put into education, mental health, child care programs, or even tax cuts, elected officials paid little attention to them. Today, every budget process is a battle of politics, philosophy, and dollars. There are never enough dollars to do what everyone wants and to take the safest political position to not release prisoners early or fail to supervise them intensively in the community. However, we are reaching a point where economics may triumph over politics, and the dollars to continue to supervise the large number of offenders may force a reconsideration of correctional and sentencing policy.

Reasons for Increases in Correctional Budgets

Correctional budgets have increased tremendously over the past two decades, primarily because of toughening policies and attitudes about the need to get tough and punish criminal offenders. Elected officials have become tougher on crime, even where there is little evidence of their effectiveness and with the knowledge that they are extremely expensive in relation to community alternative sanctions. Perhaps the watershed political event regarding politics and criminal justice policy occurred during the 1988 presidential campaign, when Vice President George Bush successfully used the public's fear of crime as a campaign tool against his opponent, Governor Michael Dukakis of Massachusetts. Bush used campaign ads presenting Dukakis as soft on crime for allowing a Massachusetts **furlough** program and suggesting that it led to the commission of a tragic murder by Willie Horton, a furloughed inmate, while he lived in a halfway house.

Other candidates for public office saw the danger of being labeled "soft on crime," and campaigns everywhere promised to keep dangerous offenders in prison longer. Another example is the nation's war on drugs, in which President Ronald Reagan pushed through legislation to toughen drug laws and require mandatory prison terms for federal drug offenders. The dramatic increase in the federal prison population resulted in almost two-thirds of the federal prison population as drug offenders. Once politics forces correctional policy to move in this direction, it is difficult to turn back the clock, and increasing costs of corrections take money from other public services. The National Conference of State Legislatures reported that state spending on higher education experienced the highest reduction in its history during the 1990s, during which state correctional spending had its fastest growth.[15] Addressing this dilemma, Irwin and Austin argue that society must turn away from the excessive use of prisons, which is diverting money from education, child care, mental health, and medical services, all of which have a greater impact on reducing crime than does building more prisons.[16]

It is interesting to note that the public is not nearly as strongly in favor of "get tough" policies as elected officials believe. One change in sentencing policy has been the implementation of sentencing guidelines, determinate sentencing without parole, and mandatory sentencing. All these reduce discretion by judges and correctional professionals, and result in an inability to treat offenders by their risk and chance for successful rehabilitation. As Petersilia writes, "One of the most distinguishing characteristics of U.S. crime policy since the 1980s has been the gradual chipping away on individualized decision making and its replacement with one-size-fits-all laws and policies."[17] The primary interest of the public is to be protected and they do not support sanctions perceived as merely punishing offenders without protecting society. In an Ohio survey, when informed that prison space is scarce and expensive, the public supported the use of community corrections instead of paying for new prison construction.[18] A National Opinion Survey on Crime and Justice (NOSCJ) survey also found support for community correctional programs: Seventy-three percent of those surveyed indicated that intensive probation supervision was either "very effective" or "somewhat effective," 55 percent similarly supported house arrest, 73 percent supported electronic monitoring of offenders, and 78 percent supported the use of boot camps as alternatives to traditional prison sentences.[19]

Tight Budgets and Challenges to Corrections

In mid-2002, the population of the nation's prisons and jails for the first time reached 2 million, and as of June 30, 2008, there were 2,396,120 offenders incarcerated in the fifty states, the District of Columbia, federal prisons, and local jails. One-third of these were in jails (785,556) and two-thirds were in prisons (1,610,584).[20] Even though both prison and jail numbers have continued to grow over the past decade, there has been a declining rate of growth in the number of people incarcerated. During the 1990s, the inmate population grew an average of 8.7 percent per year,[21] and from 2000 to 2006, the incarcerated population increased 2.6 percent per year. However, during the six months ending June 30, 2008, the prison population increased by only 0.8 percent compared to a 1.6 percent increase during the same six months in 2007, and the jail populations increased only 0.7 percent over twelve months ending June 30, 2008, the lowest growth in jail populations in twenty-seven years. Sixteen states actually had a decline in their prison population during the first half of 2008.[22] While the slowdown of the increase has not been a result of a dramatic change in sentencing or incarceration policy, there are considerations for reducing the inmate population and save money.

Many jurisdictions now have to confront the expense of sentencing policies that mandate certain offenders go to prison and lengthen sentences for others. A recent report by the Pew Center notes that "Some policy makers are questioning the wisdom of devoting an increasingly large slice of the budget pie to incarceration, especially when recidivism rates have remained discouragingly high."[23] As a result, many policy makers are looking to lower correctional costs by considering both the opportunity to divert lawbreakers guilty of nonviolent or less serious crimes and to restructure sentencing to reduce the overall length of stay for a large proportion of the prison population. In a recent report summarizing how states are dealing with the fiscal crisis they face, three areas of activity were highlighted:

1. **Operating Efficiencies:** States are trying to reduce budget expenditures through reducing healthcare services, joining purchasing coops to lower medical and other supplies, reducing the number of staff by instituting hiring freezes, reducing salaries and benefits, consolidating facilities, and reducing offender programs.

2. **Recidivism Reduction:** States are strengthening community corrections programs to reduce parole and probation violations and improving reentry services.

3. **Release Policies:** States are trying to reduce both the number of offenders entering prison and their length of stay in prison. Many states identify groups of people who can be safely released after serving shorter sentences.[24]

As finding the money to fund increasing correctional budgets has become a serious dilemma, there are many considerations for ways to reduce the overall costs or at least slow down the increases in the future. The following sections describe many of these options that are being considered. Some seem to have promise, are politically attractive and supported, and may result in lowering correctional costs. Others may seem effective but have little political support. Or, they may be politically attractive but have little effect on reducing the cost of correctional operations in a jurisdiction. Some of the alternative policies include the following:

- Developing community alternatives and diverting offenders from prison.
- Restructuring sentencing to reduce the number of inmates.
- Reducing the cost of correctional operations.
- Reducing the cost of prison construction.
- Creating revenues in the correctional operations.
- Privatizing services or operations.

Diverting Offenders From Prison

There are two ways to divert offenders from prison. The first is to reduce the number of prisoners on the "front end of sentencing" by using more community diversion programs to keep offenders in the community rather than in prisons. The second approach is "on the back end" by reducing the revocation rate of offenders on parole or supervision after serving their prison terms. The following examples are what many states are doing to create community alternatives to prison so that offenders can stay in the community rather than being sentenced to prison.

Texas plans to divert thousands of inmates from prison to rehabilitation facilities designed to help them reenter society and has funded new treatment facilities for offenders sentenced for driving while intoxicated (DWI) at which they are provided substance abuse treatment. They have also expanded drug treatment diversion beds in lieu of sending offenders to prison. The goal of this is to reduce the need for construction of costly new prisons. "We have changed the course of the ship substantially in the state of Texas," said

Representative Jerry Madden, chairman of the House Corrections Committee and an engineer of the prison plan.[25] Texas estimates they have avoided spending $523 million in building more prison beds by expanding drug treatment and diversion beds, many of them in secure facilities.

An accepted target for diversion is nonviolent offenders with drug addictions. Since 2004, at least thirteen states have adopted legislation creating or expanding community corrections options for nonviolent offenders, including the use of drug courts.[26] In 2009, New York repealed the 1970s Rockefeller drug laws that required mandatory prison terms for low-level drug felons, and gave judges more authority to send nonviolent drug offenders to community treatment instead of prison. This is seen as an opportunity "to focus on treatment rather than punishment to end the cycle of addiction."[27] Although the treatment programs will cost $80 million per year, in the long run, the repeal is expected to save money as it will be less expensive than the $45,000 it costs per year to confine a prisoner in New York.

Kansas has also enhanced their efforts to save money by diverting offenders from prisons to less expensive community alternatives. The governor for Kansas, Kathleen Sebelius, signed into law a plan to reduce prison admissions by providing counties with financial incentives to create community correctional systems and to provide opportunities for low-risk inmates to reduce their sentences by participating in prison programs. If counties reduce their recidivism rates of probationers and parolees by 20 percent or more, they qualify for grants from the state. The law also allows early release of up to sixty days for qualified offenders who successfully complete education and counseling programs that are expected to decrease their chances of returning to prison.[28]

Instead of increasing the cost of its prison system, Hawaii decided to deal with its offenders on probation, as judges were sentencing inmates to ten years in prison because they missed appointments with their probation officers. Judge Steven Alm has created a new approach and sends probation violators from his court immediately to jail, but only for a few days. As they comply with their probation expectations, they get more freedom and have fewer check-ins with their probation officer. A four-year study of the program found that there are more than 80 percent fewer violations, and more importantly, the number of new crimes committed by the people on probation has been cut in half.[29] And Wisconsin is using dollars from the 2009 Recovery Act funds (the stimulus bill passed by the Obama administration) to divert offenders from prison, keeping the most serious offenders in prison while increasing supervision for nonviolent and lower-risk offenders in the community. Governor Doyle believes that additional focus on reentry, community treatment, and diversion programs will reduce recidivism and the number of offenders that must be held in prisons.[30]

Keeping Offenders Out of Prison

On the "back end," some states are considering changing how to deal with those who violate rules of probation and parole. In 2005, parole violators accounted for more than one-third of all prison admissions.[31] And in 2006, 44 percent of parolees were successfully terminated from supervision, whereas 39 percent were returned to incarceration.[32] The success rate among those discharged from parole dropped from 50 percent in 1990.[33] During 2006, 179,259 parole violators were returned to prison, however, only about 5 percent were returned as a result of a new offense, a figure unchanged since 1998.[34] In 2007, 248,923 admissions to prison were parole violators, representing about 36 percent of all admissions.[35]

Over the past decade, there has been less tolerance for technical violations of parole (such as failing a drug test or missing an appointment with their parole officer), and parole failures now constitute a growing proportion of all new prison admissions. Parole agencies are hesitant to take the risk of continuing offenders on parole who are not following the conditions of the release, in case they later commit a crime and the parole agency is blamed for not violating them for the technical violation.

To reduce the number of prison admissions, jurisdictions are opting to punish technical parole violators with community-based sanctions, such as day reporting centers, electronic monitoring systems, and community service. A good example is California, which has a parolee return to prison rate of 66 percent (compared to the national average of 40 percent), representing two-thirds of all admissions to the state prisons. California recognized that they are recycling their inmates, as violators can be returned by the Board of Parole Hearings for no more than twelve months. In a report analyzing this problem, the authors suggested the development of a range of intermediate, community-based sanctions (especially for parolees with substance abuse problems) instead of a return to prison.[36]

The Washington Institute for Public Policy in 2006 published a very important work that reviewed 571 evaluations of correctional programs that had rigorous methodologies and could be used to determine what worked to reduce crime and save taxpayers money.[37] Their work identified categories of programs that were determined to be "evidence based" in that there were sufficient data to prove that they were effective in reducing crime and were therefore cost effective. Programs found effective included vocational training and education, cognitive behavioral therapy, prison industries, sex offender treatment, and drug treatment for prison inmates. In the community, drug courts, employment training, drug treatment, and intensive supervision with treatment are effective. The conclusion was that states should implement these evidence-based programs to save money while not endangering public safety.

Restructuring Sentencing to Reduce the Number of Inmates

A second approach jurisdictions are taking to reduce the number of prisoners is to restructure sentencing codes so that prisoners do not stay longer than is necessary for punishment and the opportunity for rehabilitation. How many of the proposals being discussed will become a reality and how significantly the changes in policy or law will reduce prison populations is still a question. Several times in the past three decades, there have been modest efforts to restructure sentences to either reduce costs or create a system that seems to provide more equity and fairness. However, political reaction has always been strongly negative, and the sponsors of such legislation have backed down with few changes and very little change in policy or budgets. If the current recession deepens and continues, the likelihood that these efforts will this time lead to more significant and longer-lasting change increases.

However, some states are giving inmates the chance to earn more good time in order to reduce the length of sentence served. In California, Governor Arnold Schwarzenegger proposed to release 22,000 nonviolent inmates early and place them on unsupervised parole. In Rhode Island, lawmakers expanded good time to move more offenders from prison to postprison supervision. In Kentucky, nonviolent offenders were allowed to serve up to 180 days of their prison sentence at home. In Mississippi, Governor Haley Barbour signed into law a measure to make nonviolent inmates eligible for release after serving 25 percent of their sentences. In South Carolina, there was a proposal to abolish parole to slow down the return of parole violators to prison.[38]

The issue of cost is not a yes–no question of whether offenders should be sanctioned by imprisonment or community supervision, but for how long and in what combination of prison and community sanctions. As a result of the tough on crime mentality of many policy makers, sentences for imprisonment have lengthened, more offenders receive mandatory prison terms rather than probation, three-strikes law sends repeat criminals to prison for life, opportunities for inmates to earn good time are reduced, there is longer postincarceration supervision, and both probation and parole are more likely to add to the costs of supervision with electronic monitoring or intensive supervision. The result of lengthening prison sentences and "stacking" community supervision has not been worth the increase in cost, nor has it resulted in a proportionate reduction of crime and increased safety to society. The accompanying Practical Perspectives case illustrates some of the dilemmas facing those trying to find options for reducing costs and the impact of even minor sentence modifications. As the example suggests, a lot of money can be saved by reducing sentences minimally, with little impact on public safety.

Practical Perspectives

Small Modifications Can Have Large Budget Implications

A state experiencing a rapid increase in the number of offenders in prison received a grant from the National Institute of Corrections to fund a prison overcrowding program. This program brought together legislators, judges, prosecutors, citizen groups, and correctional administrators to discuss the causes of the increase in prison population, to look for opportunities to reduce overcrowding, and to consider the need for more prison space while reducing the overall cost of the state correctional system. Many recommendations were suggested by the committee, one of which was a proposal to allow inmates to earn more good time for completion of drug abuse, educational, and vocational programs.

The state director of corrections began talking to legislators to explain the proposals and to urge their passage. One of the arguments was that if all inmates earned enough extra good time to reduce their sentences by only ninety days, it would save the state $500 million over thirty years. Legislators were shocked by these figures, but the director explained how they were calculated. The state held approximately 20,000 inmates, and reducing the sentence served by each for three months would, over time, reduce the population by 500 inmates. To build a 500-bed prison would cost approximately $50 million, and it is estimated that construction costs represent only 10 percent of the overall operating costs of a prison over 30 years, or a total of $500 million. This represents how minor adjustments in time served can save massive amounts of dollars for state governments.

Reducing the Cost of Correctional Operations

As expenditures increase for correctional agencies and difficult choices must be made to not fund other preferred government operations, elected officials and the public express opinions on reducing the cost of current correctional operations. In a tough on crime climate with tough on criminals attitudes and rhetoric, it is not surprising that many people believe the costs of incarceration should be reduced by eliminating any programs or services that they see as not essential or that may detract from the punitive aspect of the sentence. In addition, correctional administrators know that they must do more with less and that their budgets will not continue to increase in direct proportion to the inmate population.

States have perhaps been hit the hardest in terms of the need to cut budgets. Governor Jim Douglas of Vermont, who is chair of the National Governors Association, reported that "43 states cut $31 billion from their budgets in 2009. For fiscal year 2010, even with nearly $30 billion in new revenue, 36 states have been forced to cut $55 billion. Thirty states have cut elementary, secondary and higher education."[39] In a tight budget climate, legislative bodies sometimes pass specific legislation to require the elimination of some programs or services, or they may refuse to provide funds for correctional activities they do not support.

There have been times when the involvement of the legislature lets politics get in the way of good policy. For instance, in the 1990s, California tried to save money by reducing the number of correctional officers. The correctional officer union is very strong in that state, and after some negotiations between the legislature and the union, it was agreed to eliminate some correctional officer positions if gun ports were built inside of the prison in areas such as the dining room and cell houses so that the officers would be protected. The policy allowed staff to shoot inmates to break up serious fights, so as not to put staff at risk by breaking up fights. Unfortunately, this policy resulted in regular shooting incidents within California prisons, with correctional officers killing 36 inmates and wounding 207 others from 1989 until 1998.[40] From 1994 until 1998, only six inmates were fatally shot by staff in all other states, with all involved inmates trying to escape.[41]

A typical prison budget will be 60–65 percent salaries and benefits for staff, 10 percent for medical care, 5 percent for food, 5 percent or more for utilities, and another 5 percent or more for buying goods and supplies. With the largest cost for staff, targeting reduction in personnel costs can save the most money. Raises for staff may be eliminated or freezes on the hiring of new positions may be invoked. Jurisdictions have also put in place furlough programs for staff, whereby they may have to take 10–12 days per year off without pay. And other jurisdictions have increased the percent of insurance paid by the employee rather than by the government.

Another high cost item is for medical care, although it is difficult to reduce costs without limiting medical care or reducing the quality. Instead, states have stopped doing what they consider optional or cosmetic types of care, such as doing nonemergent dental care or removing tattoos. Food is very important to inmates and most jurisdictions are very careful in trying to save money through food reductions. However, some jurisdictions have reviewed and reduced the daily calorie counts when they believe they are too high (most run in the range of diets and menus that provide 3000–3500 calories a day). In addition, some have opted to serve only two meals per day on the weekend, and this usually is acceptable as less than half the inmates get up when they do not need to and go to breakfast.

With utility costs being a large part of prison and jail budgets, correctional agencies have targeted how to save on the consumption by turning down heat in the winter or air conditioning in the summer. Water usage is high in a correctional facility, so flush valves to reduce water use in toilets or reduced flow water heads in showers can save on water use and gas for hot water. And a few states have even cancelled or renegotiated all contracts for services, and in 2009, California even began issuing "vouchers" instead of making payments to vendors.

One of the easiest targets for legislators has been to reduce inmate recreation or educational programs. Over the past fifteen years, several states have banned weight lifting in prisons, believing it was a security risk because inmates strengthening themselves may make it difficult for staff to physically control the inmates. The issue, however, was really the negative image of inmates lifting weights in prison when they were supposed to be punished. In the late 1990s, the U.S. Congress did not ban weight lifting in federal prisons but added an amendment to the budget bills that no funds could be spent on inmate weight lifting and many other recreational activities.

Historically, many state prison agencies used **Pell grants** to fund inmate college programs. Pell grants began in the 1970s as a way for "disadvantaged populations" to receive funds for college courses. Inmates met the requirements for these grants, and most prisons had active college programs to motivate and improve inmate morale. In 1994, Congress specifically eliminated inmates from receiving Pell grants, and many active and proven college programs in prisons were eliminated.[42] Some jurisdictions kept college-level programs on a limited basis. However, in 2000, the Federal Bureau of Prisons proposed modifying their own rules to make inmates responsible for all college degree tuition costs.[43]

Unfortunately, many jurisdictions are reducing spending for programs that both help reduce idleness among inmates and can aid in rehabilitation and reduce recidivism. In 2010, the state of California decided to reduce their prison program budgets by $250 million and lay off 850 staff who deliver education and substance abuse classes. The cuts will result in 17,000 inmates who enroll in academic and vocational programs and 3,500 who are in substance abuse programs being idled. Critics have noted that with California's 70 percent recidivism rate (the highest in the nation), it is unwise to reduce programs that make a difference in whether offenders reoffend after release.[44] Other states (Florida, Ohio, Georgia, and Texas to list a few) have also planned to reduce programs to make up budget shortages.

Savings for correctional operations does not end with prisons and jails, and community corrections budgets have also been examined for cost savings. The largest opportunities come in two ways. The first is to reduce the contracts for transitional care, such as halfway houses. Halfway houses are used both for probationers and inmates returning to the community and provide a combination of supervision, structure, accountability, and programming to aid in community supervision. Most jurisdictions contract with not-for-profit organizations such as church groups or the Salvation Army that run halfway houses. Even though they are less expensive than the operation of a prison (average cost per inmate per day was $78.95 in 2008[45]) compared to the 2001 average cost of $43.41 for contracted halfway houses,[46] they are often an added rather than alternative cost to correctional agencies. This means the contract for a service in addition to their normal probation supervision or release to the community. By reducing the budget for halfway house contract beds, fewer offenders will receive service. For example, the Texas

Department of Criminal Justice (Corrections) proposed in their 2011 budget to reduce funding for halfway houses by $1.6 million, resulting in 400 fewer inmates released from prison and placed in a halfway house as a transition to the community.[47]

Another way to save money in community corrections is to reduce the number of offenders under supervision and then reduce the number of probation or parole officers. Probation and parole officers classify offenders according to risk to reoffend (scored on the number of prior convictions, employment status, age, and present offense) and use this classification to determine the supervision level. The risk level can result in multiple levels of supervision. Intensive supervision is for offenders posing a significant risk of committing a new offense; they are assigned to smaller caseloads, must report at least once per week to the supervising officer, and are visited two to three times per month at home or at work. Most probationers are placed on regular supervision, with larger caseloads and fewer reporting requirements. For offenders who pose little risk to the community, minimum supervision is satisfactory, and these offenders have contact with their probation officer only every few months. Some jurisdictions are eliminating any supervision for minimum risk offenders, saving the number of staff necessary for this role. Also, they believe no supervision will result in fewer technical violations and fewer probationers and parolees returning to prison.

Overall, there are many ways to reduce the costs of correctional operations, but as is obvious, these come with risks and potential unintended consequences. While not desired, these challenging budget times are forcing correctional administrators to find ways to reduce costs. Many believe that these are not good long-term solutions, but hope that as the recession ends, employment improves, and tax revenues return to prior levels, these cuts can be restored and effective practices can be renewed.

Reducing the Cost of Prison Construction

Correctional administrators are continually pressured to find ways to reduce the cost of building prisons. There is no doubt that it is expensive to construct facilities that safely and securely house criminals; have sufficient space for operational needs such as food and medical services; and have program opportunities such as education, vocational training, and recreation. All of these activities require considerable space, and prison construction is not inexpensive.

As an example of prison architecture, the last facility I worked in as a warden was the Federal Correctional Institution (FCI) in Greenville, Illinois, opened in 1994. The facility includes approximately 357,000 square feet of space at the main medium security facility, 74,000 square feet at the minimum security camp, and 42,000 square feet of shared facility space such as the warehouse and central utility plant. The prison was constructed with 512 medium security cells and 128 minimum security inmate cubicles.[48] The cost of construction was approximately $62 million. With the Federal Bureau of Prisons calculating the **design capacity** of this prison at 768 medium security and 256 minimum security inmates, the combined total cost per inmate bed was more than $60,000. It must be understood, however, that the cost per bed includes the overall cost for constructing the prison as well as all the space other than that used for cell or cubicle construction.

As correctional populations continued to rise over the 1990s, new prisons were needed, and from 1993 to 2000, 288 new prisons were constructed and opened,[49] and from

June 30, 2000 to December 30, 2005, 153 new state and federal prisons and 151 new private prisons were constructed and opened.[50] With this added bedspace, the issue of how much it costs to build a prison became a target for elected officials. The desire was to bring down these costs and make adding bedspace as economical as possible. As a result, several approaches to saving money on prison construction were considered and adopted, helping to keep costs down for a while, as construction costs rose during the first few years of the 1990s and then declined in 1996 and 1997. In both maximum and medium security prisons, the 1997 cost was actually less than that in 1990.[51] However, a 2006 report noted that, "a typical new prison [2000 beds] costs about $250 million to build and $45 million a year to operate."[52] This calculates to $125,000 per bed.

There are many approaches to reducing construction costs. The biggest savings for prison construction are associated with space and type of security. The housing units make up far less than 50 percent of the total square footage at FCI, Greenville. If a jurisdiction decides they could do without space for education, prison industries, religious programming, drug abuse, and recreation, then considerable funds would be saved on construction. In addition, if a jurisdiction determined that inmates with security designations above minimum (medium or even maximum) could safely be held in open dormitory space (cubicles) instead of cells, there would also be considerable construction savings. Apart from these questionable philosophical and policy considerations, jurisdictions look for other methods and opportunities to reduce construction costs, and several approaches have been successful, including the use of inmate labor for portions of the construction, design/build construction techniques, and the use of prototype prison design and construction.

All states use inmate labor to renovate space or even do small construction projects within existing prisons. This is a cost-effective way to renovate prisons, as well as excellent experience and training for the inmates. One reason it saves considerable dollars is because it is not necessary to bring outside construction crews and equipment into the prison, and develop what turns out to be expensive approaches to providing security for the construction project. If inmates do the work and correctional staff supervise their efforts, there is less need to provide security and to keep inmates away from the construction area.

However, a few states have tried to use inmate labor to reduce construction costs of new prisons. In the early 1990s, the Federal Bureau of Prisons contracted with private construction companies to build housing units and key operational areas such as food service and medical areas. The private contractors also built the outer shell of the program and activities buildings. The shells included the foundations, roofs, and unfinished walls. Inmates were then moved into the prison and completed the interiors of these buildings, including installing electrical wiring, heating and ventilation systems, and drywall ceilings and walls.

The size of a facility has much to do with the cost of construction, and many jurisdictions try to take advantage of economies of scale by building prison complexes that place a number of facilities in the same location. There may be three facilities sharing an administration building: warehouse, water treatment systems, and training building.[53] And **fast-track construction** methods have also been shown to save money by reducing the time of construction. Fast-track methods involve a collaborative process with the architect, contractor, and client working together throughout the process to begin some construction even before all of the design is completed. While opponents note the risks of this, most projects have been completed without major problems and are believed to save money.[54]

Design/build is a rather new approach for government and prison construction. **Design/build** basically tries to consolidate responsibility for design and construction of a facility to "meet very tight construction schedules, guarantee budgets in the early phases of construction and simplify construction administration.[55] Design/build is an alternative to "design–bid–build," in which an architect designs the prison, bids are accepted for many portions of the prison from construction firms, and the winning bidders build the portion of the prison for which they received the bid. Each step is completed in sequence, and the average time of design and construction is 30–36 months. With design/build, "the entire scope of work—architectural and engineering design, construction, project management, cost management and quality control—[is] shared as a single-source responsibility by the designer and the builder under one individual contract.[56]

The belief is that design/build will reduce the construction schedule, because construction actually can begin on early phases (such as site preparation and underground utilities) even before the entire architectural and engineering designs are completed. It also has the advantage of providing a known fixed cost, because the entire project is bid to one contractor for a set price, rather than having 20–30 bids for small pieces of the construction pie. Although there are risks with this approach, both construction time and costs are usually reduced. In describing the use of a design/build for the U.S. Penitentiary in Coleman, Florida, Mary S. Galey, construction project administrator for the Bureau of Prisons, writes,

> The result was a design that more than meets the minimum needs of the BOP and still allows the contractor to construct the institution in an economical and efficient manner. Approximately 50 percent of the contract time has passed, the design is complete and the contractor is working with a schedule that has a construction completion date two months prior to the contract completion date.[57]

Finally, governments have been using **prototype prison construction** as a cost savings approach. The fact that many jurisdictions are building more than one prison of similar size and security level allows a single design to be used for more than one prison.[58] Correctional agencies can use the prototype designs in a variety of ways. They can select one architect to develop a prison design for several different sites. This reduces the cost and time for architectural planning. The Federal Correctional Institutions at Greenville and Pekin, Illinois, are identical designs, with the only variations being a few color changes and slight adaptations for varying gradations between the two sites. Another prototypical approach is to use the same architectural design for certain portions of a prison, such as housing units, food service, or a program building.

Whatever approaches are used to reduce construction costs, there is ample opportunity to save money. The sheer volume of construction over the next several years will be significant. The *1999 Corrections Yearbook* reports that on January 1, 1999, there were in total 41,368 beds to be added to state and federal prisons at a cost of more than $1.9 billion.[59] Correctional agencies can select a variety of security and operations philosophies that have a meaningful impact on construction costs. And there are several approaches to construction that can reduce costs, including the use of inmate labor, design/build, and prototypical prison designs. And with a large amount of correctional budgets going toward prison construction, these cost reduction efforts can have significant monetary impact.

Precast cells for prison construction. Precast cells are constructed with doors, windows, toilets, and sinks already installed. When brought to the construction site, they are stacked into place and are a way to reduce construction costs.
(Courtesy of Corrections Corporation of America)

Creating Revenues in Corrections

Seldom does one think of creating revenues when it comes to operating a correctional agency. However, many jurisdictions have become quite innovative in finding opportunities for creating revenue, and there are possibly many others that, although perhaps somewhat controversial, may be sources of income. In a chapter entitled "Enterprising Government: Earning Rather than Spending," the authors of *Reinventing Government* write,

> Our (government's) budget systems drive people to spend money, not to make it. And our employees oblige. We have 15 million trained spenders in American government, but few people who are trained to make money. . . . But can you imagine the creativity they would turn loose if they thought as much about how to *make* money as they do about how to *spend* it?[60]

Since Osborne and Gaebler wrote about the need and ways to reinvent government, there has been much more attention paid to creating revenue by public agencies. The government often has unused products and services that could be sold to the private sector or even other government agencies. There is often the opportunity for government agencies to charge individuals fees for services, for example, to play on a recreational softball team, to use a public camp ground, or to tour a public building. With a bit of creativity, there are many ways that correctional agencies could create revenue. Agencies are charging offenders for supervision or for services, and are using offenders to produce products that can be sold for income or at least to reduce the cost of correctional operations.

Charging offenders for some aspects of their supervision has been going on for some time, particularly with community corrections. As a condition of probation, offenders have regularly been charged a fine or had to pay victim restitution, and many probation agencies charge offenders for services such as drug counseling, halfway house stays, or participation in work release programs, as well as for their supervision costs of electronic monitoring, intensive supervision, or drug testing. Forty-one states and almost all county probation departments report using such fees.[61]

Another approach with much political appeal has been to charge inmates for the cost of their incarceration, and over the past ten years, many jurisdictions have approved **cost of incarceration fees** for prisoners housed in local jails or state and federal prisons. These fees require inmates to pay the cost of their incarceration, if they have the financial resources. However, few offenders have the means to pay these fees, and there have been few instances in which a significant amount of money has been collected from an inmate to cover his or her cost of confinement.

Many jurisdictions charge inmates a fee for medical care while in prison or jail. By the early 2000s, forty states and the U.S. Bureau of Prisons were charging inmates a small **copayment** of $2–$5 when they requested medical care, just as most citizens pay a copayment when they see a family physician.[62] While this copayment may generate a small amount of revenue, the primary purpose is to reduce the demand for medical services. Private medical insurance companies know that a copay is considered by individuals and they will not go to a doctor for minor colds or illnesses they do not consider serious. As a corrections example, Nevada was one of the first states to begin to use copayments, and in the first two years after implementing a copayment, inmate medical utilization was reduced by 50 percent.[63]

Another program that results in generating revenues and reducing the cost of incarceration is prison industries, in which inmates produce products that are sold to generate revenue and, in many cases, make a profit to help cover the cost of prison operation. On January 1, 2002, there were 78,881 inmates (7.8 percent of the prison population) working in prison industries in the fifty states, the District of Columbia, and the Federal Bureau of Prisons. In 2001, these programs had sales of $1.7 billion and profits of nearly $19 million.[64] All costs of the work program are covered to include industrial supervisors who train and supervise inmates, avoiding the cost to taxpayers for other inmate training programs. Also, inmates are paid between $2.63 and $7.64 per day,[65] and these earnings are often used to pay for their cost of incarceration or for fines and victim restitution.

A form of prison industry program is the **PIE Program**, in which private companies hire inmates to produce goods inside the prisons. In 2001, there were 5,103 inmates employed in over 200 PIE industry programs. A requirement of PIE programs is that inmates must be paid wages comparable to private-sector workers, and the daily wage as of January 1, 2002, for inmates working in PIE ranged from $21.43 to $36.50.[66] PIE inmates are required to have deductions for fines, victim compensation, room and board, support of families, and payment of taxes from their pay. From the beginning of the PIE Program until June 2003, on wages of $264 million, more than $146 million was withheld from pay, of which 48 percent was for room and board, 24 percent for taxes, 17 percent for victim restitution, and 11 percent for family support.[67]

Prison industry programs keep inmates busy and produce products that can be sold to cover their operational and staff costs.
(Courtesy of Corrections Corporation of America)

Creation of revenues by correctional agencies is still very small, particularly in terms of the millions of offenders under the supervision of correctional agencies on any given day. However, these difficult budget times are forcing public agencies to consider opportunities to create revenues that they may not have done in the past. Opportunities will always be limited, but the entrepreneurship and creativity that will result from trying to find revenues should be a skill that will benefit correctional administrators far into the future.

Privatizing Services or Operations

Another way that jurisdictions have attempted to save money is to contract with the private sector so that the service can be provided cheaper than by the public correctional agency. The private sector has been involved in the administration of various correctional aspects almost since the origination of penal codes. When countries transported offenders to penal colonies, the offenders were often required to serve as indentured servants to individuals and businesses that had contractual agreements with the governments. Early prisons allowed businesses to contract for the use of prisoners as a labor source, with the funds offsetting the cost of prison operations. These contracts were ripe for abuse and led to federal legislation limiting the products of prison labor being sold on the open market. Since the 1950s, halfway houses have served as a transition from prison to the community. Most halfway houses are privately operated, although most are owned by faith-based or not-for-profit charitable organizations. By the 1980s, almost every state had contracts with privately operated halfway houses to provide residential services, supervision, and transitional programs for inmates leaving prison and returning to the community.[68] Also, many states with very small juvenile offender populations have often found it cost effective to contract with privately operated facilities, rather than to open state-run juvenile facilities. In 1984, it was reported that 65 percent of all juvenile facilities were private, housing approximately 32,000 offenders.[69] During the 1980s, prisons began to contract with private companies to provide food services, medical and mental health care, educational programming, and substance abuse counseling, and by the turn of the century, there were 126 state and federal prisons contracting for food services and 397 for medical care for inmates.[70] Another 300 prisons had private contractors providing mental health services, and 226 prisons contracted for substance abuse services.[71]

These uses of the private sector in corrections have not been controversial. However, when agencies began to contract to house adult prisoners in private for-profit prisons, many ethical and practical questions were raised. The use of private prisons as a cost-saving mechanism is herein described and discussed. A **private prison** is any secure correctional facility operated by an organization other than a governmental agency and usually in a for-profit manner that contracts with the government to provide security, housing, and programs for adult offenders. In a private prison, staff are employees of the company that owns and operates the prison. Such prisons can be administered without cumbersome governmental purchasing and personnel policies, although they are still held to the same constitutional standard for treatment of inmates as a public prison.

The first private contract to house adult offenders was in 1984, for a small, 250-bed facility operated by Corrections Corporation of America under contract with Hamilton County, Tennessee. Soon thereafter, additional contracts with the private sector to house illegal aliens (contracted with the U.S. Immigration and Naturalization Service) and youthful offenders (with the Federal Bureau of Prisons) were established. The growth over the next few decades in the privatization of correctional facilities was spurred by the increasing number of inmates and the rapid need to build new prisons, the budgetary challenges required to fund these new prisons, and the Reagan-era support of using the private sector to help downsize the scope of government. Welch notes,

> At that time, the prevailing political and economic philosophy encouraged government officials to turn to the private sector to administer public services, such as sanitation, health care, security, fire protection, and education. As a result of the introduction of free-market principles into the administration of public services, . . . the privatization of corrections appeared to be a new and novel approach to some old problems (i.e., overcrowding and mounting costs).[72]

By 1990, Logan reported that private prisons held just over 9,000 adult inmates,[73] but by June 30, 2008, there were 126,249 state and federal prisoners held in private prisons, accounting for 7.8 percent of all prisoners.[74] At an average cost of $53.38 per day, these contracts equate to almost $2.5 billion per year.[75] Table 9-1 illustrates the numbers and percentage of all state and federal inmates held in private prisons.

Table 9-1
NUMBER OF PRISONERS HELD IN PRIVATE FACILITIES, DECEMBER 31, 2000–2007, AND JUNE 30, 2007 AND 2008

Year	Number of Prisoners			Percent of all Prisoners
	Total	Federal	State	
2000	90,542	15,524	75,018	6.5%
2001	91,053	19,251	72,702	6.5
2002	93,912	20,274	73,638	6.5
2003	95,707	21,865	73,842	6.5
2004	98,628	24,768	73,860	6.6
2005	107,940	27,046	80,894	7.1
2006	113,697	27,726	85,971	7.2
2007				
June 30	118,239	30,379	87,860	7.4%
December 31	125,997	31,310	94,687	7.9
2008		32,712	93,537	7.8%
June 30	126,249			
Annual change				
Average annual change, 12/31/2000–12/31/2007	4.8%	10.5%	3.4%	
Percent change, 06/30/2007–06/30/2008	6.8	7.7	6.5	

Note: Includes estimates for Illinois for 2006, 2007, and 2008 and Nevada for December 31, 2007. Not Calculated
Source: Heather C. West and William J. Sabol, *Prison Inmates at Midyear 2008–Statistical Tables* (Washington, DC: U.S. Department of Justice, Bureau of Justice Statistics, March 2009), p. 12.

How Private Prisons Function

When a jurisdiction decides to attempt to contract the placement of prisoners in a private prison, a formal legal and contractual process must begin. The first step is to determine the need for housing of inmates, both in terms of the number of inmates and security level required. Second, the correctional agency develops a **request for proposal (RFP)**, which outlines in detail the requirements, expectations, and standards to be met by the bidding companies. In the RFP, the agency will usually clarify the geographic area for which they will consider contracting for bed space. It is usually not necessary for the private prison to be located in the same jurisdiction as the correctional agency. It is not unusual for states to contract for bed space in a state some distance away.[76]

For a private company to own and operate a prison and contract for prisoners with a governmental agency there must be **enabling statutes** by the state in which the private prison is located. Several states do not allow private prisons to operate within the state or limit the operation to contract with and house only prisoners from that state and not bring in prisoners from other states. Also, the state must pass legislation allowing the state to delegate by contract its correctional authority. In order to clarify responsibilities and avoid legal challenges,

> This statute must specifically address rules, regulations, licensing, policies, and procedures pertinent to the operation of private correctional facilities, as well as designate staff, facilities, budgets, and responsible agencies for the oversight of those rules, regulations, licensing, policies, and procedures. Enabling statues must grant judges authority to sentence defendants to private institutions; without such legislation, any sentence to a private prison would be subject to a jurisdictional challenge.[77]

The agency makes public the RFP, and any private company that meets the minimum requirements of experience and capabilities may submit a bid. Bids are usually evaluated on both cost and quality of service delivery, often rated by the company's past record and description of how they would operate the prison. The governmental jurisdiction then awards the contract, transports prisoners to the facility, and monitors compliance with contract provisions. These provisions are usually both general in nature, such as requiring the company to comply with American Correctional Association standards, and very specific, such as directing the availability of sick call for inmates or the number of calories per day in meals served.

There are several variations of operations by private companies as they comply with RFPs. First, the RFP may require a private company to own (already or build) a prison to house the inmates. Many times, a private company will build a large prison and then respond to RFPs from many jurisdictions to fill it. Very few problems result from having inmates from a variety of jurisdictions in the same facility. Second, a jurisdiction may already have a prison and may seek a private operator to manage the facility. Some jurisdictions prefer this approach, fearing that if contractual problems result with the private company, they can find another manager. However, if the company owns the prison, they must find available space elsewhere if the contract ends.

Finally, there are some governmental agencies that operate as private firms and respond to RFPs from other jurisdictions. Sechrest and Shichor refer to these as **public proprietary facilities** operated by "small jurisdictions without a strong economic base, thus making the (facilities) a potential source of income and employment."[78] These municipalities or counties pass bonds and build prisons specifically for contracting with other governmental jurisdictions. They often contract with one of the large private prison companies to manage them. However, the fact that they are owned by a governmental agency makes the contracts less bureaucratic to develop, and a response to an RFP can usually be avoided and a "direct award" to the public proprietary facility is legally allowable.

Issues in Prison Privatization

As noted, privatizing the operation of prisons has been controversial, and there are arguments both for and against private involvement in corrections. These arguments include two general areas of issues: philosophical and pragmatic. The philosophical issues center on the distinction of roles between the private sector profit-making enterprises and government, ethics and corruption, and the larger public interest. The pragmatic arguments include cost effectiveness, quality of service, security and public protection, and liability.

Logan identified the following ten issues that are key to any deliberations regarding the use of private prisons:

1. **The propriety of proprietary prisons**—Can the punishment of offenders be delegated to nonpublic agencies?

2. **Cost and efficiency**—Are private prisons operated less expensively than public prisons?

3. **Quality**—Does the profit motive diminish the drive for delivery of quality services and programs to inmates?

4. **Quantity**—Does the involvement of the private sector to make a profit encourage the expansion of imprisonment beyond what is in the public interest?

5. **Flexibility**—Does the fact that the private sector does not have to follow bureaucratic government policies for purchasing and personnel management increase efficiency?

6. **Security**—Does the fact that an emphasis on profits and cost cutting undermine security for inmates, staff, and the community?

7. **Liability**—What impact does a government contracting with a private firm for housing inmates have on the liability of the government for violation of inmates' constitutional rights?

8. **Accountability and monitoring**—How will the private contractor be monitored to fulfill requirements and be held responsible if they do not?

9. **Corruption**—Without the restraints inherent in government to reduce the likelihood of corruption, will there be an increase in private prisons?

10. **Dependence**—Will the public sector become dependent on the private sector contract, and if so, how does this affect decision making?[79]

Some of these issues are addressed at this point. The basic issue is the philosophical issue of whether private companies should be allowed to make a profit out of incarcerating criminal offenders. Many individuals and groups (such as the American Civil Liberties Union [ACLU]) argue that taking away an individual's freedom is the responsibility of the government and should not be abdicated to the lowest bidder. At this point, the U.S. Supreme Court has not clearly established whether government can transfer correctional functions to the private sector.[80] Logan notes, however, that the authority of government is derived from the consent of the governed and, therefore, may be delegated further with similar consent.[81] Although this question continues to be raised in every discussion of private prisons, it has generally been decided by the dozens of state and local governmental agencies that make use of the private sector to incarcerate inmates.

The issue of whether or to what extent a government agency that contracts with the private sector is able to pass on liability is complex and not yet clearly established through case law. It is generally accepted that the state or local government does not escape liability by simply contracting with a private provider for housing criminal offenders. The government maintains responsibility for the constitutional rights of all citizens, including prisoners. Private prisons under contract with government agencies act "under the color of the law," or with the power of the government. In general, pertinent case law indicates that governmental liability under the Federal Civil Rights Act (42 USC Section 1983) would most likely not be reduced by contracting with the private sector.[82]

In *Lugar v. Edmonson Oil Co.*, the U.S. Supreme Court determined that a party alleging a violation of its constitutional rights must first show that the violating party was acting under the color of law.[83] When this has been established, both private contracts and the governmental agency can be held liable. (See *Medina v. O'Neill*[84]) In *Medina*, the Immigration and Naturalization Service detained stowaways on a vessel, placed some in a local jail, and placed others in the custody of a private company. When the illegal aliens attempted to escape, a private guard accidentally killed one of them. The Court found both the government and the private company liable for damages in the death.

If it is determined that it is legally and ethically acceptable to contract with the private sector to incarcerate inmates, the next key issue is that of cost efficiency. Several studies have compared the cost of privately operated prisons. The earliest review of the Hamilton County, Tennessee, private prison suggested that it saved from 4 to 15 percent annually over county-operated penal farm costs.[85] A 1992 study comparing costs for public and private facilities housing parole violators in California found a lower cost per day for private facilities.[86] A study initially funded by private prisons determined that between 1999 and 2004, "states that have some of their prisoners in privately-owned or -operated prisons experience lower growth in the cost of housing their public prisoners."[87] A *Harvard Law Review* article concluded that "what imperfect empirical evidence there is suggests that private prisons cost less than public prisons and that their quality is no worse."[88] A literature review in 2002 by the Reason Foundation identified seventeen studies that measure quality of operations by government and private prisons, and fifteen of those conclude that "the quality at the private facilities is as good or better than at government-run facilities."[89] However, Segal and Moore, in a review of the costs of outsourcing correctional services, conclude that "Policymakers should be wary of over-reliance on cost-comparison data in making privatization decisions, and be certain that cost analysts do not take it upon themselves to make policy assumptions in determining cost figures."[90] Further, there are still many concerns with states contracting with for-profit companies to incarcerate offenders. Dolovich questions the legitimacy of this approach, even if private prisons can operate for less money without a drop in quality.[91]

Another reason why correctional agencies turn to privatization is to eliminate having to appropriate funds for the enormous capital outlay required to build prisons. During the period of tremendous growth in the inmate population from the late 1980s through the early 2000s, the private sector was able to fund, build, and provide prison beds more rapidly than the public sector. Austin and Coventry note that, because private companies are not subject to government regulations regarding construction of buildings, the private sector can build prisons for nearly 25 percent less and in half the time compared to the public sector.[92] Culp also notes that some states were approaching their debt ceilings or did not have the time to issue bonds to fund new prison construction.[93] A 2004 analysis of Oklahoma's use of private prisons found that the state succeeded in housing a substantial number of offenders without spending a penny on building new facilities.[94]

There have also been reviews of quality with mixed results. A study comparing costs of public and private prisons in Kentucky and Massachusetts found that private prisons appeared to be better managed than public prisons.[95] Results from a Florida study comparing recidivism of releasees from private and public prisons favored the private prisons. Recidivism of releasees from the private prisons was lower than for those released from public prisons, and of those who reoffended; the crimes were less serious for the private prison releasees.[96] When the General Accounting Office (GAO) conducted a comprehensive review of five outcome studies of private prisons completed since 1991 in Texas, New Mexico, California, Tennessee, and Louisiana, analysts did not believe that three of these studies were sufficiently designed to use results, but found that outcomes from the remaining two indicated minimal or no differences between the public and private prison operations.[97]

Other studies have also failed to find any significant differences between the outcomes of offenders released from public versus private prisons.[98] In a national survey to compare private and public prison operations that analyzed the types of inmates, inmate misconduct, and general characteristics of prisons and their staff, Camp and Gaes concluded that private prisons had higher escape rates and more positive results from drug tests and did not enhance staff or community safety.[99] There has not yet been a sufficient number of "apples to apples" comparisons of quality and cost between public and privately operated prisons to draw decisive conclusions. The most recent and perhaps most comprehensive is a review of the Taft, California, private prison, which found that inmates and staff were provided a safe living and working environment and the private facility cost less to operate, but it had lower rates of assault, more escapes, higher rates of drug use, and higher rates of inmate grievances.[100]

Perhaps the most difficult issue to address is the one of "quantity." Essentially, the question is whether the involvement of the private sector as a profit-making entity in control of the imprisonment of offenders may somehow push for more, rather than less, incarceration. Sentencing policies and the increasing number of prisoners are always areas of public debate and dispute, and it is reasonable to examine the interest of private prison operators regarding these issues. In a recent article, David Shichor identified the issues and discussed problems of the free-market model in providing human services and the symbolic references of private prisons and corporate ethics.[101]

Earlier, Lilly and Knepper investigated the developing private correctional enterprise and compared the commercial pressures for expansion to those that exist in the "military-industrial complex."[102] There is no doubt that successful private correctional companies have spent millions of dollars lobbying and educating elected officials in their role and performance. Although it is doubtful that private correctional companies would intentionally push for changes in sentencing that would end up sending more offenders to prison simply for the potential business, the private companies certainly could benefit from such laws. However, this issue is more of a perception than reality. There is no evidence that the involvement of private corrections influences overall sentencing policy.

Warden in housing unit with extra bunks in day room. Some private prison companies argue that contracting with the private sector can increase capacity, reduce overcrowding, and bring down the cost of incarceration.
(Courtesy of the Federal Bureau of Prisons)

The Future of Private Corrections

Although the growth in the number of state and federal prisoners has slowed down over the past two to three years, significant increases in the number of inmates are still expected, and with state and federal revenues down due to the 2008 through 2010 recession continuing, very few jurisdictions are constructing new prisons. Tightening government budgets force public officials to increasingly look for alternatives to the traditional approaches. And the continued lack of public confidence in the public sector leads many citizens to support giving the private sector a chance. Gowdy notes

> Nonetheless, the public's unsatisfactory view of today's penal system in terms of its costs and high recidivism rates are two factors that are likely to encourage further expansion of the private sector's role.[103]

Although the growth of the prison population has slowed down and even declined in 2010, it is estimated that approximately one-half of the growth during the past decade has gone into private prisons. The tight budget situation may make this even more likely in the future. There is little if any construction by public correctional agencies during the recession, and they are looking to reduce their population through other approaches mentioned earlier. This could mean that at some point, these relief valves will be exhausted and the growth will come without any capacity ready to receive it. If this is the case, it is likely that the future of privatization will be even stronger in the next decade than it has been in the past ten years.

SUMMARY

Why have correctional budgets increased so rapidly, and is there anything that can be done to slow down this increase? What are the pressures on correctional administrators as government budgets tighten, and what alternatives to increased spending are available to them? What is the role of correctional administrators in developing alternatives to incarceration, and what risks do they face by encouraging such alternatives? What nontraditional approaches can correctional administrators consider, and how much flexibility do they have in experimenting with or implementing these approaches? And, if they attempt to contract with the private sector to provide historically public correctional services, what are the issues that must be addressed in the contract award and monitoring?

All these questions have been addressed in this chapter, and they have prompted an examination and consideration of the complex administrative and political challenges that confront today and tomorrow's correctional administrator. The recession has resulted in lower than expected tax revenues, and state and local governments have had to look for ways to reduce spending. Since corrections has become one of the largest users of taxpayer dollars, it is targeted for reductions and correctional administrators are forced to find ways to reduce their costs.

The most obvious way to reduce costs is to reduce demand by reducing the number of incarcerated offenders, as prisons and jails make up most of the cost for corrections. However, even with budget pressures, it is very difficult to get political support to divert offenders or shorten the time they serve. The past few years has seen the slowing of inmate growth, and even a reduction in the total number of inmates in several states in 2009. However, this change in population has had minimal effect on budgets to date, and government officials continue to search for other measures to reduce spending.

The most likely options for correctional administrators in responding to the challenges of tight budgets is to reduce their own daily costs of operation, to reduce costs of prison construction, and to privatize those services and needs for additional beds that are likely to be cost effective. There is a move to eliminate all prison "amenities," from prisons and jails and even to reduce spending for inmate programs that may reduce recidivism. This may seem shortsighted; however, many decisions are being made to reduce costs in the short term and worry about the long-term impact later. Reducing construction costs does offer a potential budget savings; correctional administrators can consider some of the techniques identified in this chapter as proven cost-reduction techniques. However, construction costs represent only a small percentage of the commitment of funds when a new prison is built when compared with the outlook of growth for a correctional agency.

Finally, correctional administrators are turning more often to the private sector to provide various services for offenders, including the construction and operation of prisons. With thoughtful contracting, enhanced competition before the acceptance of a bid for the service, specific requirements for quality of service delivery, and clear and constant evaluation and monitoring of performance, the private sector can take some of the burden off correctional administrators in planning how to meet growth needs and maintain budget accountability. While this practice will continue to generate controversy, it is likely to continue and grow in use in the future.

The future for correctional administrators in meeting budgetary challenges is cloudy and far from resolved. Although there are many alternatives that are being, and need to continue to be, explored, there is no panacea for resolving this issue. Although this creates stresses for, and taxes the abilities of, today's correctional administrators, future correctional administrators who want challenges are almost guaranteed them as well. There will be no quick end to the recession nor significant improvement in the revenues of state and local governments.

KEY TERMS

Expense-based budgets	Fast-track construction	PIE Program
Incremental	Design/build	Private prison
Furlough	Prototype prison construction	Request for proposal (RFP)
Pell grants	Cost of incarceration fees	Enabling statutes
Design capacity	Copayment	Public proprietary facilities

YOU'RE THE CORRECTIONAL ADMINISTRATOR

1. You are the director of a state department of corrections, responsible for operating the state prisons, parole and probation supervision, and a variety of community sanctions that are alternatives to incarceration. Your prison inmate count has increased by 25 percent over the past four years, the prisons are very overcrowded, and you are building new institutions to help with the overcrowding. However, your agency budget increases have not kept up with demand, and you have a higher inmate to staff ratio, meaning you have fewer staff available to manage the prisons. Legislative budget committees are asking you to reduce the costs of operation, because they do not want to have a tax increase to fund the increasing corrections budget. How do you develop a proactive plan to reduce the increased budget needs yet still operate all of the state correctional functions in a safe and effective manner? Describe the plan you would put in place over the next three years.

2. You are the contract administrator for a county correctional agency. The jail is filled well beyond capacity, and the increases are expected to continue, at least for the next three years. Instead of building a new jail, the county commissioners have decided to contract with a private corrections company to house the overflow of prisoners. There are already two companies that operate jails and have space within a 100 mile radius of the county. They ask you to prepare a request for proposal (RFP). How do you go about developing the RFP? What do you put into the RFP to make sure you are getting the best price and that you are getting the services needed to meet your responsibility to house inmates in a manner that meets the constitutional requirements for incarceration?

WEB LINK EXERCISES

Go to The Bureau of Justice Statistics (http://www.bjs.ojp.usdoj.gov)

Click on the left side at Employment and Expenditure. Upon opening this window, scroll to the graph entitled, *Direct Expenditure by Criminal Justice Function, 1982–2006.* Click directly on the graph. See the figures for expenditures for police, judicial, and corrections for 1982–2006. Note that in 1986 the corrections expenditures were about half that of the police, but in 1985 the ratio began to change. By 1998, corrections was just one-third of the police expenditures and remains nearly that today. Why is that and is the ratio likely to change by 2015?

Go to Corrections Corporation of America www.correctionscorp.com

Or to Geo Group, Inc www. thegeogroupinc.com

Go to the Web site for either of these two private sector companies that operate private prisons. Describe the purpose or mission for the company and list the benefits they suggest are available by the private sector involvement in public corrections. Which two or three of these benefits do you believe are the most realistic? Explain why.

GROUP EXERCISES

Each group will be provided with a blank line-item prison budget document and will be required to get appropriate information from their local jail on realistic figures for a comparative analysis among groups.

ENDNOTES

1. Bureau of Justice Statistics, *Key Facts at a Glance: Correctional Populations*, http://bjs.ojp.usdoj.gov/content/glance/tables/corr2tab.cfm (accessed April 23, 2010).

2. Bureau of Justice Statistics, *Expenditure Facts at a Glance*, www.ojp.usdoj.gov/bjs.glance/exptyp.htm (accessed February 15, 2010).

3. Bureau of Justice Statistics, *Expenditure Facts at a Glance*, www.ojp.usdoj.gov/bjs/glance/tables/exptyptab.htm (accessed January 17, 2010).

4. Camille Graham Camp and George M. Camp, *The 2002 Corrections Yearbook: Adult Corrections* (Middletown, CT: Criminal Justice Institute, 2003), p. 92.

5. Pew Center on the States, Public Safety Performance Project, *One in 31: The Long Reach of American Corrections* (Washington, DC: The Pew Charitable Trusts, March 2009), p. 11.

6. Lauren E. Glaze and Thomas P. Bonczar, *Probation and Parole in the United States, 2006* (Washington, DC: U.S. Department of Justice, Bureau of Justice Statistics, 2007), p. 2.

7. Pew Center on the States, *One in 31*, p. 12.

8. Camille Graham Camp and George M. Camp, *The 1999 Corrections Yearbook: Adult Corrections* (Middletown, CT: Criminal Justice Institute, 2000), pp. 76; Camille Graham

Camp and George M. Camp, *The 2000 Corrections Yearbook: Adult* Corrections (Middletown, CT: Criminal Justice Institute, 2001), p. 89; and Camille Graham Camp and George M. Camp, *The 2001 Corrections Yearbook* (Middletown, CT: The Criminal Justice Institute, 2002), p. 89; Camp and Camp, 2003, p. 84.

9. James J. Stephan, "Census of State and Federal Correctional Facilities, 2005," *National Prisoner Statistics Program* (Washington, DC: U.S. Department of Justice, Bureau of Justice Statistics, October 2008), pp. 1 and 2.

10. National Association of State Budget Officers, "State Expenditure Report FY 2006," December 2007, http://www.nasbo.org/Publications/PDFs/fy2006er.pdf (accessed August 16, 2009).

11. *Public Safety, Public Spending: Forecasting America's Prison Population, 2007–2011,* Public Safety Performance Project (Washington, DC: The Pew Charitable Trust, February 2007), p. ii.

12. National Conference of State Legislatures, *Update on State Budget Gaps: FY 2009 & FY 2010* (Denver, CO: National Conference of State Legislatures, January 2009).

13. National Conference of State Legislatures, *State Budget Update: March 2010* (Washington, DC: National Conference of State Legislatures, April 2010).

14. For a description of these budget processes and corrections, see James G. Houston, *Correctional Management: Functions, Skills, and Systems,* 2nd ed. (Chicago, IL: Nelson-Hall Publishers, 1999), pp. 125–130.

15. Sam C. Proband, "Corrections Leads State Budget Increases in FY 1997," *Overcrowded Times* 8 no. 4 (1997): 4.

16. John Irwin and James Austin, *It's About Time: America's Imprisonment Binge* (Belmont, CA: Wadsworth, 1994).

17. Joan Petersilia, *When Prisoners Come Home: Parole and Prisoner Reentry* (New York: Oxford University Press, 2003), p. 221.

18. As cited in Peter D. Hart Research Associates, *Changing Public Attitudes toward the Criminal Justice System* (New York: Open Society, February 2002).

   S.E. Skovan, J.E. Scott, and E.T. Cullen, "Prison Crowding: Public Attitudes toward Strategies of Population Control," *Journal of Research in Crime and Delinquency* 25 no. 2 (1988): 150–169.

19. As cited in Peter D. Hart Research Associates, *Changing Public Attitudes toward the Criminal Justice System* (New York: Open Society, February 2002).

20. Bureau of Justice Statistics, Press Release, *Growth in Prison and Jail Populations Slowing: 16 States Report Declines in the Number of Prisoners* (Washington, DC: U.S. Department of Justice, released March 31, 2009), http://www.ojp.usdoj.gov/bjs /pub/press/pimjim08stpr.htm (accessed August 16, 2009).

21. See *Prisoners in 2000, Bureau of Justice Statistics Bulletin* (Washington, DC: U.S. Department of Justice, 2001).

22. Bureau of Justice Statistics, Press Release.

23. Ibid., p. 15.

24. Christine S. Scott-Hayward, *The Fiscal Crisis in Corrections: Rethinking Policies and Practices* (New York: Vera Institute of Justice, 2009).

25. Ibid., p. 3.

26. Vera Institute of Justice, *Managing State Prison Growth: Key Trends in Sentencing Policy* (New York: Vera Institute of Justice, January 2008).

27. Jeremy W. Peters, "Albany Reaches Deal to Repeal '70s Drug Laws," *The New York Times* March 26, 2009, p. A21.

28. John Gramlich, "States Seek Alternatives to More Prisons," Stateline.org, June 18, 2007, http://www.stateline.org/live/details/story?contentId=217204 (accessed August 16, 2009).

29. Laura Sullivan, "Shrinking State Budgets May Spring Some Inmates," *National Public Radio Legal Affairs Report*, April 1, 2009, http://www.npr.org/templates/story/story. php?storyId=102536945 (accessed August 16, 2009).

30. "$30 million in Stimulus for Public Safety," a report WKOW television in Madison, Wisconsin, April 9, 2009, www.wkowtv.com/Gloval/story.asp?S=10157862 (accessed August 16, 2009).

31. William J. Sabor, et al., *Prison and Jail Inmates at Midyear 2006* (Washington, DC: U.S Department of Justice, Bureau of Justice Statistics, June 2007).

32. Lauren E. Glaze and Thomas P. Bonczar, *Probation and Parole in the United States, 2006* (Washington, DC: U.S. Department of Justice, Bureau of Justice Statistics, December 2007), p. 7.

33. Glaze and Bonczar, *Probation and Parole in the United States, 2006*, p. 7.

34. Ibid., p. 8.

35. Heather C. West and William J. Sabol, *Prisoners in 2007* (Washington, DC: U.S. Department of Justice, Bureau of Justice Statistics, December 2008), p. 3.

36. As cited in Janet Mandelstam, "California Study Looks at Factors Leading to Parole Revocation," *Corrections Today* 71 no. 5 (October 2009), pp. 122–123.

37. Steve Aos, Marna Miller, and Elizabeth Drake, *Evidence-Based Public Policy Options to Reduce Future Prison Construction, Criminal Justice Costs, and Crime Rates* (Olympia, WA: Washington State Institute for Public Policy, 2006).

38. All of these examples were taken from Keith B. Richburg and Ashley Surdin, "Fiscal Pressures Lead Some States to Free Inmates Early," *Washington Post*, May 5, 2008, p. A01.

39. Robert Pear, "States Have Not Seen the Worst of Economic Times, Governors at Meeting Say," *New York Times*, February 21, 2010, National Section, p. C-3.

40. *Los Angeles Times*, "California Uses Deadly Force" *Los Angeles Times*, October 19, 1998, p. 1.

41. Ibid.

42. John Linton, "Inmate Education Makes Sense," *Corrections Today* 60 no. 3 (1998): 18.

43. Steve Peacock, "BOP Proposes Inmates Pay All Tuition Costs for College," *Corrections Journal* 4 no. 10 (2000): 7.

44. Marisa Lagos, "Cuts in Programs to Help Inmates Questioned," *The San Francisco Chronicle*, February 16, 2010, p. A-1, http://sfgate.com/cgi-bin/article.cgi?f=/c/a/2010/02/16/MNR21BSOIE.DTL (accessed April 18, 2010).

45. Pew Center on the States, *One in 31*, p. 2.

46. Ibid., p. 145.

47. Letter from Brad Livingston, Executive Director of the Texas Department of Criminal Justice, to Ms. Mary Katherine Stout, Director, Governor's Office of Budget, Planning

and Policy and Mr. John O'Brien, Director, Legislative Budget Board, dated February 15, 2010.

48. Federal Bureau of Prisons, *Greenville Federal Correctional Institution*, unpublished document (Washington, DC: U.S. Department of Justice).

49. Camp and Camp, 2002, p. 87.

50. James J. Stephan, "Census of State and Federal Correctional Facilities, 2005," *National Prisoner Statistics Program* (Washington, DC: U.S. Department of Justice, 2008), pp. 1–2.

51. Camille Graham Camp and George M. Camp, *The Corrections Yearbook, 1998* (Middletown, CT: Criminal Justice Institute, 1999), p. 79.

52. Washington State Institute for Public Policy, *Evidence-Based Public Policy Options to Reduce Future Prison Construction, Criminal Justice Costs, and Crime Rates* (Olympia, WA: Washington State Institute for Public Policy, 2006), p. 1.

53. Stan Bates, "Planning Ahead: Reducing Operating Costs in Prison Construction," *Prison Review International* no. 1 (July 2001), pp. 23–26.

54. Emily Waltz and Mike Montgomery, "Fast-Track Construction," *Corrections Today* (April 2003), pp. 104–107.

55. Mark Reilly and Jim Grothoff, "Packaging the Process," *Corrections Today* 59 no. 2 (1997): 75.

56. James R. Conley, "Design/Build: The Future of Contracting," *Corrections Today* 62 no. 2 (2000): 118.

57. Mary S. Galey, "Design/Build: The BOP's View," *Corrections Today* 62 no. 2 (2000): 119.

58. For a description of the use of prototype prison or jail construction, see Thomas Beilen and Peter Krasnow, "Jail Prototype Leads to Faster Construction, Lower Costs," *Corrections Today* 58 no. 2 (1996): 128–131. See also Bates, "Planning Ahead."

59. Camp and Camp, 2000, p. 76.

60. David Osborne and Ted Gaebler, *Reinventing Government: How the Entrepreneurial Spirit is Transforming the Public Sector* (Reading, MA: Addison-Wesley, 1992), pp. 195–196.

61. C. S. Baird, D. A. Holien, and J. A. Bakke, *Fees for Probation Services* (Washington, DC: U.S. Department of Justice, National Institute for Justice, 1986).

62. Camp and Camp, *2002 Corrections Yearbook*, pp. 105–106.

63. M. Nolan, "Medical Co-Payment System: Nevada Department of Prisons," Paper presented at the annual conference of the American Correctional Health Services Association, Salt Lake City, Utah, April 1992.

64. Camp and Camp, *The 2001 Corrections Yearbook*, pp. 118 and 124.

65. Ibid., p. 120.

66. Camp and Camp, *2001 Corrections Yearbook*, p. 120.

67. Bureau of Justice Assistance, "Prison Industry Enhancement Certification Program," *Bureau of Justice Assistance: Program Brief* (Washington, DC: U.S. Department of Justice, March 2004).

68. Harry Allen, Evelyn Parks, Eric Carlson, and Richard Seiter, *Program Models, Halfway Houses* (Washington, DC: U.S. Department of Justice, 1978).

69. Edmund R. McGarrell and Timothy Flanagan, *Sourcebook of Criminal Justice Statistics, 1984* (Washington, DC: U.S. Department of Justice, 1985).

70. Camp and Camp, *2002 Corrections Yearbook*, pp. 100 and 101.

71. Ibid., pp. 103 and 104.

72. Michael Welch, *Corrections: A Critical Approach* (New York: McGraw-Hill, 1996), p. 416.

73. Charles Logan, *Private Prisons: Cons and Pros* (New York: Oxford University Press, 1990), p. 20.

74. West and Sabol, *Prison Inmates at Midyear 2008*, p. 12.

75. Average revenue per working day was calculated from the annual reports of the three publicly traded companies (CCA, GEO, and Cornell).

76. Hawaii, for example, contracts for the housing of approximately 800 inmates with the Correctional Corporation of America in a prison located in Minnesota. Although this is inconvenient for administrators and inmate families, inmates do not have a right to be imprisoned close to their home state.

77. Ronald Becker, "The Privatization of Prisons," in *Prisons: Today and Tomorrow*, edited by Joycelyn M. Pollock (Gaithersburg, MD: Aspen Publishers, Inc., 1997), p. 395.

78. Dale K. Sechrest and David Shichor, "Comparing Public and Private Correctional Facilities in California: An Exploratory Study," in *Privatization and the Provision of Correctional Services: Context and Consequences*, edited by G. Larry Mays and Tara Gray (Cincinnati, OH: Anderson Publishing, Co., 1996), p. 135.

79. Logan, *Private Prisons*.

80. Ira P. Robbins, "Privatization of Corrections: Defining the Issues," in *The Dilemmas of Corrections: Contemporary Readings*, 3rd ed., edited by Kenneth C. Haas and Geoffrey P. Alpert (Prospect Heights, IL: Waveland Press, 1995), pp. 592–594.

81. Logan, *Private Prisons*, pp. 52–54.

82. Ira P. Robbins, "Privatization of Corrections: Defining the Issues," *Judicature* 69 no. 6 (April–May 1986): 325–331.

83. *Lugar v. Edmonson Oil Co.*, 457 US 922 (1982).

84. *Medina v. O'Neill*, 589, F. Supp. 1028 (1984).

85. Charles Logan, *Looking at Hidden Costs: Public and Private Corrections* (Washington, DC, U.S. Department of Justice, 1989), pp. 52–54.

86. Dale K. Sechrest and David Shichor, "Comparing Public and Private Correctional Facilities in California: An Exploratory Study," in *Privatization and the Provision of Nashville, TN: Correctional Services: Context and Consequences*, edited by G. Larry Mays and Tara Gray (Cincinnati, OH: Anderson, 1996), p. 135.

87. James F. Blumstein, Mark A. Cohen, and Suman Seth, "Do Government Agencies Respond to Market Pressures? Evidence from Private Prisons," *Virginia Journal of Social Policy & the Law* 15 no. 3 (Spring 2008): p. 466.

88. James F. Blumstein and Mark A. Cohen, "Developments in the Law of Prisons: A Tale of Two Systems: Cost, Quality, and Accountability in Private Prisons," *Harvard Law Review* 115 no. 7 (May 2002): 1891.

89. Geoffrey F. Segal, *Comparing Public and Private Prisons on Quality* (Los Angeles: The Reason Foundation, 2005), http://www.reason.org/ps290.pdf (accessed August 16, 2009).

90. Geoffrey F. Segal and Adrian T. Moore, *Weighing the Watchmen: Evaluating the Costs and Benefits of Outsourcing Correctional Services* (Los Angeles: Reason Public Policy Institute, January 2002), p. 17.

91. Sharon Dolovich, "State Punishment and Private Prisons," *Duke Law Journal* 55 no. 3 (2005): 439–546.

92. J. Austin and G. Coventry, *Emerging Issues on Privatized Prisons* (San Francisco: National Council of Crime and Delinquency, March 1999).

93. Culp, "Rise and Stall."

94. Douglas McDonald and Carl Patten, *Governments' Management of Private Prisons* (Washington, DC: U.S. Department of Justice, January 2004), p. 102.

95. J. Hackett and H. Hatry, *Issues in Contracting for the Private Operation of Prisons and Jails* (Washington, DC: U.S. Department of Justice, 1987).

96. Lonn Lanza-Kaduce, Karen F. Parker, and Charles W. Thomas, "A Comparative Recidivism Analysis of Releasees from Private and Public Prisons," *Crime and Delinquency* 45 no. 1 (1999): 28–47.

97. U.S. General Accounting Office, *Private and Public Prisons: Studies Comparing Operational Costs and/or Quality of Service* (Washington, DC: GAO, 1996).

98. Studies showing little evidence of cost savings include A. Cheung, *Prison Privatization and the Use of Incarceration* (Washington, DC: Sentencing Project, January 2002); P. Mattera and M. Khan, *Jail Breaks: Economic Development Subsidies Given to Private Prisons* (Washington, DC: Institute on Taxation and Economic Policy, October 2001).

99. Scott D. Camp and Gerald G. Gaes, "Growth and Quality of U.S. Private Prisons: Evidence from a National Survey," *Criminology and Public Policy* 1 no. 3 (July 2002): 427–449.

100. Douglas C. McDonald and Kenneth Carlson, *Contracting for Imprisonment in the Federal Prison System: Cost and Performance of the Privately Operated Taft Correctional Institution* (Washington, DC: U.S. Department of Justice, November 2005).

101. David Shichor, "Private Prisons in Perspective: Some Conceptual Issues," *Howard Journal of Criminal Justice* 37 no. 1 (February 1998): 82–100.

102. Robert J. Lilly and Paul Knepper, "The Corrections-Commercial Complex," *Crime and Delinquency* 39 no. 2 (April 1993): 150–166.

103. Voncile B. Gowdy, "Should We Privatize Our Prisons? The Pros and Cons," *Corrections Management Quarterly* 1 no. 2 (1997): 61.

10

Managing Risk Through Offender Classification

Introduction

What is offender classification, and how does risk assessment contribute to it? What does it have to do with correctional administration? And, how do each of these assist in the management of offenders and of correctional agencies? These questions are answered in this chapter. Both of these concepts are defined and presented in detail in this chapter. In general terms, classification is a process that is used throughout the criminal justice decision-making process to identify and match offender needs with correctional resources, resulting in the assignment of offenders into groups of individuals with similar traits or characteristics. Risk assessment, to some extent, is a subcomponent of offender classification. Risk assessment is an attempt to predict an offender's future behavior, especially the potential for or likelihood of future criminal violations. Therefore, risk assessment provides information useful to offender classification decisions and helps guide the placement of offenders into homogeneous management categories.

Classification is a technique that has been used by correctional administrators for several years. The earliest classification of prisoners was the separation of women from men, and of youths from adults. Systems and groupings have become extremely sophisticated, and a variety of approaches are available for correctional administrators to categorize offender groups for housing, program assignments, security, and management purposes. Margaret Pugh, previously the commissioner of the Alaska Department of Corrections, notes, "I still believe in that old correctional ideal that classification is the cornerstone of good management."[1] Classification is used in almost every type of correctional setting and, as Pugh notes, is the beginning of policy and practices for how to staff, fund, and manage a particular group of offenders.

Early uses of classification helped identify treatment needs in response to the medical model of corrections. Over the years, however, classification has evolved in response to the changing priorities for correctional goals. As the medical model lost support and public sentiment began to favor offender accountability and public safety, classification models began to change focus from treatment purposes to predicting the potential for escapes, violence, and recidivism. This chapter includes the historical evolution of risk assessment as an aid to classification, its purposes and practical uses, and its applications for the administration of correctional agencies.

Actually, risk assessment is not a new development; it has been used by correctional administrators since John Augustus, the father of probation, began bailing criminals out of jail who indicated a willingness to change their ways and commit no further crimes. Historically, risk assessment was a subjective or, later, clinical, appraisal of how likely an offender was to commit crimes after release or to create a risk for violence or escape while in prison. Over the past few decades, risk assessment has become increasingly objective, using actuarial methods. **Actuarial methods** involve identifying factors that are linked to future behavior and determining the strength of the relationship between those factors and behavioral outcomes of past offenders to create formulas to predict an offender's expected future behavior. As correctional administrators have become fearful of negative publicity around criminal acts by offenders under their supervision, they have turned to these actuarial risk assessment instruments to aid in decision making regarding prison assignment, release on parole, and level of supervision while in the community.

In this chapter, you examine the many uses of classification for correctional administrators. Classification is used for making decisions about sentences and placement of offenders in community or institutional settings, to determine the level of supervision required to monitor an offender's behavior, and to decide on the types of programs or services needed by a group of offenders. You also review risk prediction as a refinement to and a philosophical change in classifying offenders. The actual process for classifying offenders is described for both prison inmates and offenders in the community. Finally, you consider some of the issues surrounding risk assessment and classification, including the impact of changing sentences and the relationship of race and gender with classification and risk assessment.

Current Uses of Classification Systems

Most people with little knowledge of correctional processes have a fairly limited idea of how classification systems are used by correctional administrators. Some uses of classification systems have not changed throughout the history of corrections. However, the development of actuarial risk assessment methods to aid classification decisions has expanded the potential use of this information for correctional administrators. The following illustrate some of the most common uses of classification and risk assessment.

1. To ensure that the high-risk offenders supervised in the community receive an appropriate level of supervision and treatment services. Historically, offenders in the community under parole or probation supervision were assessed using a clinical model. With this approach, an experienced officer interviewed the offender and used professional judgment to determine the best level of supervision and any required treatment. Although the clinical model of assessment is still popular, risk assessment using actuarial methods has been implemented in many jurisdictions throughout the 1990s. The actuarial predictive models have become popular among probation and parole officers both to set supervision levels and to add monitoring through intensive supervision or electronic monitoring. Also, these models can be used to predict risk when considering whether to violate community supervised offenders after technical violations. Although some studies indicate that actuarial methods are superior to clinical methods,[2] many practitioners believe the best results are achieved through a combination of the two approaches.

2. To determine the appropriate security level of a prison to which an inmate should be assigned. Most states now use some level of actuarial risk assessment to determine an inmate's initial assignment to a prison. Many states have a reception center, where newly received inmates are processed into the correctional system, and decisions are made regarding their prison placement and treatment needs. One of these reviews is to determine their initial classification to a certain security-level prison. This initial classification is based predominantly on offense history and sentence length. The goal of the initial assignment is to ensure that inmates are placed in institutions with an appropriate level of physical security to prevent escapes and provide them a safe and controlled environment.

Prison security levels range from minimum to maximum. According to the *Corrections Yearbook*, as of January 1, 1998, 11.7 percent of all prison inmates were assigned to maximum security prisons, 13.3 percent were assigned to close/high security prisons, 34.6 percent were assigned to medium security prisons, 30.6 percent were assigned to minimum security prisons, 4.1 percent were assigned to community security prisons, and 5.7 percent were unclassified.[3] It is interesting to note how classification assignments to certain security prisons have changed over time. In 1978, 51 percent of prisoners were in maximum security, 38 percent in medium, and 11 percent in minimum security prisons.[4] Using clinical rather than modern actuarial classification methods resulted in a tendency to overclassify inmates, taking a conservative approach in assuming dangerousness and propensity for escape unless there was some evidence that they do not exist. In reporting on this tendency, which results in lower-security inmates being assigned to higher-security prisons, Duffee notes that "Few correctional administrators would admit that this distribution is consistent with the security rating of the inmates . . . prison administrators try to accommodate this situation by creating more desirable subunits within an otherwise undesirable fortress-prison."[5] The new inmate classification system based on actuarial methods rather than clinical approaches is called an **objective classification system.**

A major benefit of using objective classification systems is the realistic matching of an inmate's need for security to available physical security of a prison. There is no need to have minimum security inmates housed in a maximum security prison. Maximum security prison beds are expensive to build and operate, and it is wasteful to overclassify and assign inmates to this level of prison when their security needs do not require it. With objective classification systems providing actuarial information to staff who assign inmates to prisons, it is much less likely that overclassification will occur, and the system can make better use of its expensive high-security bed space. Much of the downward trend in classification (comparing 1978, when 51 percent of inmates were in maximum security prisons to 1998 when less than 25 percent were in maximum or close/high security prisons) can be credited to the implementation of risk assessment and objective classification systems.

3. To determine which type of housing assignment within a prison (internal management classification) is most suitable for each inmate. Once they have been assigned to an institution, inmates must then be placed in an appropriate housing situation. This decision is important for two reasons. First, many prisons have a variety of housing areas for inmates, which may be either individual or multiperson cells or dormitory style housing with several (possibly hundreds) inmates in an open area without physical security to separate them from each other or from staff. Second, certain housing areas may be designated for particular groups of offenders (the mentally ill, sex offenders, or aggressive and violent offenders). As reported in 1994, only ten states and the Federal Bureau of Prisons (BOP) have implemented a formal internal classification system, independent from the external classification used for initial prison assignment.[6] Internal classification systems are tools to assign inmates to housing or programs after they are placed in a particular prison. Most agencies still make these decisions based on "clinical" judgments, or they make housing assignments based primarily on the availability of space.

The most widely used internal classification system is the Adult Internal Management System (AIMS) developed by Dr. Herbert Quay. AIMS classifies inmates based on two inventories: the analysis of life history records and a correctional adjustment checklist. The resultant classification identifies the likelihood that inmates will be violent and aggressive, or whether they are likely to be victimized, and it allows staff to separate likely victims from likely aggressors. Different states have designed their own systems. Illinois, for example, uses an internal classification system to make assignments within its maximum security prisons. The Illinois system uses some of the criteria regarding past criminal behavior from the external classification system, but adds prison disciplinary conduct and history of gang activities to predict a level of institutional aggression, which becomes the basis for assignments of housing, work, and inmate programs.

4. To guide interinstitutional transfers because of security or treatment purposes. Once offenders are assigned to particular institutions, they usually will not stay at that prison during their entire term of incarceration. Over their time served, inmates' risk of violence and escape and their program needs almost always change. Therefore, correctional agencies regularly move them to other (higher- or lower-security level) prisons based on these changes. The two factors most often used to determine changes are time served on the current sentence (often calculated in percentage of sentence served) and institutional conduct.

As inmates serve a portion of their sentence, it is natural to assume that they will adjust and be less likely to attempt escape. Correlations of time served to risk of escape have proven to be positive, because inmates, after serving significant portions of their sentence, understand that the chance of escape is low and the risk of an attempt usually results in additional prosecution and time added to a sentence. Therefore, inmates who have served a large part of their sentence usually decide to get out of prison the legal way, by finishing their sentence. In addition, past prison conduct is a valid predictor of future prison behavior, and using an inmate's disciplinary record as an added score to the external classification instrument indicates whether there is a need for changing the security level. Inmates with serious or violent misconduct receive scores that add to their security needs, and they are likely to be transferred to higher-security prisons. Inmates who serve a portion of their sentence with little or no misconduct reduce their security need scores and are likely to be reassigned to a less secure prison.

5. To match offenders to appropriate treatment and services. Matching offenders to appropriate treatment and services, sometimes using risk assessment, is valuable for both community and institutional placements. Although it is more commonly expected to be used in a clinical classification process under the medical model of corrections, contemporary objective classification systems also contribute to this purpose. This can occur in two ways. First, through the process of determining security needs of offenders, objective classification instruments also help align appropriate program and service activities. In each prison, there are some programs and services that are unique to the security level of facilities. For instance, in extremely high security prisons (sometimes called "supermax"), in which inmates spend most of their time in their cells, many educational or self-improvement programs are presented via videotape presentation in the inmates' cells, without the need for an instructor or group settings. In minimum security prisons, there are often community service programs whereby inmates can assist the community by cleaning up of community areas such as parks or highways. These programs are not available for high-security inmates.

Just as the security level dictates types of programs, it is common to find like program needs clustered around inmates with like security requirements. Inmates serving long periods of time are more likely to be in high-security prisons. Also, inmates serving long periods of time have needs for basic education, active recreation programs, and psychological counseling. Inmates serving short sentences, who are usually assigned to minimum or low security institutions, are more in need of prerelease preparation, substance abuse counseling, and work-related training. Therefore, as inmates are matched to required security levels, programs and services are likely to be matched to prisons that serve a certain security level of inmate.

6. To begin the process of positive interaction between staff and offenders. Just as any new relationship is uncomfortable until common ground is found for discussion, the relationship between offenders and staff charged with their supervision and management can be uncomfortable to a heightened degree. However, the classification process facilitates the beginning of a process of positive interaction. With both clinical and actuarial approaches to classification, inmates and staff participate in an interview and discussion to clarify certain background factors and identify present needs. The requirement of a structured discussion to determine these issues forces inmates to be honest with staff and gives staff the opportunity to explain the process and how information will be used.

With objective classification instruments, the process "depersonalizes" the staff member's judgment of the inmate. First, staff do not make professional judgments regarding the inmate's placement that are, perhaps, difficult for them to explain and the inmate to understand. The staff member can share the objective scoring sheet with the inmate, illustrating how factors are weighted and how the final score is determined. With the possibility of later reassignment and a move from one security level to another, staff can even show an inmate how (and sometimes when) certain factors will be reduced if the inmate's behavior is good, thereby facilitating the inmate's placement in a lower-security prison. The processes are also depersonalized, because staff do not have to threaten any type of action. Inmates do not have to try to convince staff that they have been doing a good job and deserve special treatment. The staff member simply explains how the system works, how certain factors and behaviors are weighted, and what will occur if an inmate behaves in a good or bad way.

The initial classification process also usually includes a discussion of an offender's needs for certain programs. As the staff and offender discuss these needs, they agree on goals and program assignments that are designed to benefit the offender. These discussions exhibit a concern by staff for offenders to resolve issues and improve the inmates' chances for success both while under supervision and after release. The program plan developed serves as the road map for monitoring the offender's progress throughout the period of incarceration or community supervision.

7. To match assignment of staff and financial resources to offender security and program needs. There is a significant difference in the numbers and categories of staff required to manage an offender population at various security levels, both in an institutional and in a community setting. As noted previously, it is possible to identify certain program needs (and related staff resources) of offenders based on a security classification system. Security classification systems also identify the need for supervision and control that offenders require, whether in an institution or in the community. These requirements for supervision and programs dictate the corresponding requirements for staff as well.

In a prison, inmates always outnumber staff. The key to controlling the inmate population is to have the right number of staff available to supervise inmates. For staff safety reasons, one would never want to have too few staff. Yet, for cost reasons, it would be expensive to have too many. A typical minimum security prison for 1,000 inmates may have a staff complement of 250, whereas a maximum security prison for the same number of inmates would have double the number of staff. Although costs for food and clothing would be the same for inmates in the two facilities, the staff costs (estimating $40,000 for salaries and benefits) would require an additional $10 million per year in personnel costs. A probation officer supervising an intensive caseload may be responsible for twenty-five probationers, while an officer supervising a regular caseload may be responsible for over one hundred probationers. These examples indicate how much cost is linked to staff salaries and how critical it is to have the right amount and type of staff for prison operations or for supervision in the community.

8. To use in planning for future prison bed space needs. In the ten-year period from 1986 to 1996, the number of prisoners in adult state correctional facilities in the United States grew from just more than 500,000 to more than one million inmates. Housing these 500,000 new inmates required almost 500 new prisons to be designed, constructed, and opened. The first requirement in planning a new prison is to determine the security level of the prison. As noted previously, the level of security has a dramatic effect on staff numbers and operational costs. In addition, the cost of construction varies greatly by security level. As reported in the *1998 Corrections Yearbook*, the average construction cost per bed by security level for prisons under construction in 1998 was $70,909 for maximum security, $49,853 for medium security, and $29,311 for minimum security.[7]

These costs indicate how critical it is to correctly plan bed space needs by security level. Under the clinical approach to classification, it is much more difficult to anticipate the need for security level of the required expansion. However, objective classification systems can predict the future needs for bed space at each security level. The increase in prisoners is because of two factors. First, sentenced inmates are serving longer periods of time in prison. Second, as a result of increased law enforcement and court prosecution emphasis on certain crimes (drug offenses, for example), more offenders are entering prison. Predicting the growth in the number of inmates has become a fine art; however, most states have become very accurate in the process. The state agency planners use past break downs of the percentages of inmates who were assigned to various security levels to predict incoming inmates' security needs. Objective classification systems have increased the accuracy of these predictions, and, as a result, have saved states millions of dollars by not building higher-security prisons than will be necessary.

History of Risk Assessment in Classifying Offenders

As noted previously, classification has been a critical element of corrections for many years. In a 1947 document published by the American Prison Association (the precursor to the American Correctional Association), it is noted that, "Classification is a term that has been used with increasing frequency in the field of correctional administration during the past two decades. . . . The field of criminal treatment is in the stage of development. Classification methods and techniques are in their formative stages."[8]

The report on classification also included a discussion of the purposes of classification: "Increasing emphasis [is] given to the concept that the fundamental purpose of prisons is the protection of the public welfare," and "Not all offenders needed all of the constructive services which were being developed. Not all required vocational training or academic education or psychiatric treatment."[9] The earliest uses of classification were to determine what programs were needed and which inmates needed treatments. Although public safety has always been considered a critical goal of correctional institutions, at the time of this report, it was believed that the public could best be protected by effectively treating and preparing offenders for release. The report noted, "the necessity for an institution program which will have a constructive effect upon prisoners is based upon the inescapable fact that over 95 percent of all prisoners committed to prison are sooner or later returned to the community."[10]

In the earliest days of corrections and prisons, offenders were classified by a team of correctional officials who interviewed the offenders and discussed their needs for housing and program assignments. An interesting side note was the methods used to identify inmates prior to fingerprinting and even DNA testing. Prisons used the "Bertillon" method, which was named after its creator, Alphonse Bertillon. With this method, illustrated by the accompanying 1905 Bertillon information sheets for a federal prison inmate, a photograph and specific body measurements were the primary means of criminal offender identification.

Prison Classification Team in the 1940s. Prior to the use of risk assessment instruments and objective classification, a team of several professionals met with each inmate to determine their needs and create a treatment plan. (Courtesy of the Federal Bureau of Prisons)

As the medical model became more widely accepted and practiced by correctional administrators during the 1950s and 1960s, clinical decisions by trained professional staff were more extensively used for classification decisions. Diagnoses of offenders' problems using psychological and medical examinations, social investigations, and educational and vocational studies were made. After data were collected on an offender, a staff conference would be held to discuss the case and develop a treatment and training program. The treatment team ensured that the offender's program was carried out, and the team would observe the offender's progress as a result of program participation and make changes in the program as necessary. The entire classification process is based on the way medical personnel diagnose and staff a case, carry out treatment, monitor progress, and make changes and adjustments as necessary. Decisions were subjective, arrived at by using the professional judgment of treatment team members, and there was no formula to weight factors.

Little changed in the classification process until the mid-1970s, when correctional agencies began to reexamine the subjective methods they used to classify offenders. As a result of a changing public view of the goals of corrections, which emphasized accountability and public safety, correctional administrators reconsidered the purposes of the classification process, and looked to research for identifying factors predictive of success and failure of criminal offenders. As described in earlier chapters, with the Martinson report indicating nothing works, the movement away from the medical model of corrections and toward a repositioning of the use of risk assessments for classifying inmates in order to reduce their risk of reoffending began.[11]

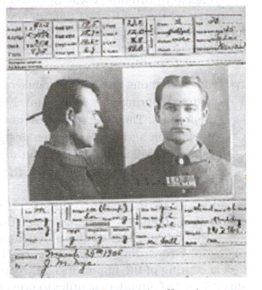

Bertillon Method of Identifying Inmates. Prior to the use of fingerprint, prison staff took exact measurements of inmates' bodies, noting scars, marks, and moles for purposes of identification. This method is demonstrated in the 1905 Bertillon method of inmate John Arnold at the U.S. Penitentiary in Atlanta, Georgia.
(Courtesy of the Corrections Corporation of America.)

At the same time the medical model was being questioned, several alternative correctional approaches and philosophies began to emerge that impacted the classification and risk predictions of offenders. For one, Fogel suggested the "justice model," with less emphasis on rehabilitation, elimination of discretionary parole board decision making, and surveillance of offenders after release by law enforcement rather than parole officials.[12] Andrew von Hirsch also argued against the continued use of discretionary parole release, suggesting that sentencing should be simple and consistent for offenders committing the same types of crimes. He advocated a "just desserts" form of sentencing, with rehabilitation irrelevant to the parole decision, substituting instead a determinate sentence based on the severity of the crime.[13] Noted criminologist James Q. Wilson maintained that without scientific evidence to support the medical model, sentencing should consider deterrence and incapacitation as primary goals. In arguing for isolation and punishment, he noted that society must protect itself from dangerous offenders, because "society really does not know how to do much else."[14]

These arguments against the continued use of the medical model helped to push the emphasis of corrections away from rehabilitation and toward punishment, deterrence, and incapacitation. Protection of society became the most important function of the criminal justice system, and methods and mechanisms to implement this policy change began to develop. The predictive capabilities of certain traits in criminals had been identified as early as the 1920s, but they were used little by prison officials to classify offenders or by parole boards to consider release decisions. Although the medical model and offenders' readiness for release were the dominant approaches in corrections, expert clinical judgments about treatment, management, and release of offenders was believed to be most important. As rehabilitation lost support and the public lost confidence in correctional officials' ability to treat and manage offenders, it was only a matter of time before more objective measures were developed for predictive purposes. According to Daniel Glaser,

> "An accelerating rate of acceptance of statistical tables for risk classification has occurred during the 1970s and 1980s because of a change in stance by researchers. They began to present their prediction tables as purely advisory information and in many cases designed tables to deal with other problems besides classification for risk. But most important for the acceptance of these tables, the officials who would use them were involved in designing the tables."[15]

In addition to the use of classification systems for separating inmates within correctional facilities, there have been three other developments using risk prediction since the 1970s. Each of these developments was prompted by a changing public philosophy regarding the role of corrections. Public mood and expectation became less accepting of the importance of treatment and more in favor of the importance of surveillance of offenders in order to prevent further criminal behavior. First, predictions of risk concerned release decision making by parole boards was initiated. Risk prediction also began to be used to identify the level and intensity of community supervision required for parolees and probationers. Finally, risk prediction provided a foundation for the use of sentencing guidelines by courts in determining appropriate criminal sanctions.

Risk Management and Classification of Prison Inmates

Prison classification systems are an important management device for controlling inmate behavior. Prison classification systems help control inmate behavior in three ways. First, classification is used to determine the appropriate prison security level to which an inmate should be assigned. When inmates are initially sentenced, the correctional agency does an assessment to determine their risk of escape and potential for violence. By matching inmates' risk of escape and violence to prison physical security, security policies and procedures, and staff allocations, the potential for escape or violence is reduced. Second, once inmates are assigned to a prison, internal classification systems are used (in some states) to determine the type of housing assignment within a prison (single cell, multiple-inmate cell, or dormitory) that is most suitable for each inmate. Finally, the reclassification of inmates after they are assigned to a prison acts as a motivator for good behavior. Inmates' behavior is regularly reviewed and can lead to a reassignment to a higher-security prison with tighter restrictions and fewer privileges or to a lower-security prison.

Initial Classification Process

Until the 1970s, most states used a clinical classification process, in which a team of experienced correctional staff interviewed inmates and reviewed their criminal, medical, psychological, and social histories. They would then decide what type of prison housing, work assignment, and treatment programs would be best for the inmate. Currently, most states use an objective classification system—an actuarial risk assessment—to determine an inmate's initial assignment to a prison. This initial classification is based predominantly on offense history and sentence length. In describing the need for these actuarial systems, Dallao writes, "Instead of assigning offenders to certain security levels based on gut reaction and subjective discussion, this new system provided an orderly and objective way of separating violent from nonviolent inmates."[16]

During the 1970s, correctional agencies attempted to identify factors in an inmate's background and prison behavior that were predictive of violence or escape. Objective classification systems were developed that could assign weighted scores to various background, sentence, and behavioral factors. The first objective classification systems were developed by the Federal Bureau of Prisons, California, and New York. The National Institute of Corrections (NIC) then developed a model system of classification.[17] The development of objective classification instrument by the BOP illustrates how such systems came about. The BOP assigned a team of specialists to design a classification system that was more predictive of behavior than the early clinical approaches. The team initially identified ninety-six factors that were considered important for classification purposes and sought the opinion of correctional professionals across the country on these factors. The original list was pared to forty-seven factors, and later to six: history of escape or attempted escape, detainers, types of prior commitments, history of violence, severity of offense, and length of sentence. These factors focus on public risk by using acts that occurred prior to sentencing. Brennan suggests that these security classifications emphasize "legal variables, history of criminality, seriousness of current offense, and past escape attempts."[18]

These factors have also been noted to contribute to the predictive strength of a classification instrument, with length of sentence often having the most influence on determining an inmate's custody level.[19]

The goal of initial classification is to have similar-risk inmates assigned to appropriate security-level prisons, and the goal of reclassification is to maintain homogeneity of inmates by security level. Both overclassifying and underclassifying inmates can cause problems: Housing high-security inmates in a low- or minimum-security facility increases the potential for escape, predatory behavior, or other types of violence, whereas housing low- or minimum-security inmates in high-security prisons places them in danger of violence and intimidation and wastes correctional resources, because high-security prisons cost three to four times as much to build and operate as do minimum-security prisons.

Since the adoption of these early systems, almost every state has developed objective classification systems to assign the levels of prison security for inmates. As of December 30, 2005, 20.4 percent of all prisons were classified for maximum-security inmates, 26.3 percent of all prisons were classified for medium-security inmates, and 53.2 percent of all prisons were classified for minimum-security inmates.[20] Objective classifications reduce the tendency to overclassify, which often resulted from clinical systems. For example, in 1978, 51 percent of prisoners were in maximum-security, 38 percent in medium-security, and 11 percent in minimum-security prisons.[21]

Most correctional agencies use a similar process to classify inmates which includes reception and initial classification, reclassification or interim classification, and prerelease classification. Most states have prison reception centers, where all inmates are initially placed until their security and program needs are determined. Shortly after they are sentenced, offenders are transferred to the state reception center for processing. During this time, they may take psychological, educational, or vocational tests; their records are reviewed, and any previously unknown information is collected. The reception process can take from 60 to 90 days. However, because of overcrowding at the prison where the inmate will be assigned, an inmate may have to wait in reception until space is available, even after completing the classification process.

Some states and the BOP do these assessments right after sentencing, while the offender is in jail or on bond pending the beginning of a sentence. On sentencing, the correctional agency is formally notified and given a copy of the sentence order, and it begins the classification process. The sentencing court is then notified (usually within a matter of days) of the prison assignment, and the court makes arrangements for the inmate to be transferred to the prison by jail staff, or (if they pose a very low security risk and are on bond) an offender may be allowed to report independently to the assigned prison on the date the sentence is to begin. In both situations, the presentence investigation (PSI) is the key document for determining risk and program needs. If there is information required that is not in the PSI, correctional staff may need to conduct interviews with the offender at the reception center or the local jail. On occasion, correctional staff will have to collect some information themselves, either because there is no PSI or because it does not have all the elements required by the correctional agency. When a PSI is not available, a **postsentence investigation** is completed, which then becomes the basis for the initial classification process.

The BOP's current security levels of prisons are minimum, low, medium, and high. Just after sentencing, a staff person responsible for inmate designations reviews the background of the offender and assigns a score for each of the six areas. Figure 10-1

INMATE LOAD AND SECURITY DESIGNATION FORM—MALE (BP-337)

INMATE LOAD DATA	1. REG NO		2. LAST NAME		

3. FIRST NAME	4. MIDDLE	5. SUFFIX

6. RACE	7. SEX	8. ETHNIC ORIGIN	9. DATE OF BIRTH

10. OFFENSE/SENTENCE

11. FBI NUMBER	12. SOCIAL SECURITY NUMBER

13. STATE OF BIRTH	14. OR COUNTRY OF BIRTH	15. CITIZENSHIP

16. ADDRESS-STREET	17. CITY

18. STATE	19. ZIP CODE	20. OR FOREIGN COUNTRY

21. HEIGHT—FT: IN:	22. WEIGHT	23. HAIR	24. EYES

25. ARS ASSIGNMENT

SECURITY DESIGNATION DATA

1. PUBLIC SAFETY FACTORS
   A—NONE   F—SEX OFFENDER   I—SENTENCE LENGTH
   B—DISRUPTIVE GROUP   G—THREAT GOVT OFFICIAL   L—SERIOUS ESCAPE
   C—GREATEST SEVERITY OFFENSE H—DEPORTABLE ALIEN   M—PRISON DISTURBANCE

2. USM OFFICE	3. JUDGE	4. REC FACILITY	5. REC PROGRAM

6. TYPE OF DETAINER	0—NONE 1—LOWEST/LOW MODERATE	3—MODERATE 7—GREATEST 5—HIGH

7. SEVERITY OF CURRENT OFFENSE	0—LOWEST 1—LOW MODERATE	3—MODERATE 7—GREATEST 5—HIGH

8. MONTHS TO RELEASE _____

9. TYPE OF PRIOR COMMITMENT	0 = NONE	1 = MINOR	3 = SERIOUS

10. HISTORY OF ESCAPE OR ATTEMPTS		NONE	>15 YEARS	10–15 YEARS	5–10 YEARS	<5 YEARS
	MINOR	0	1	1	2	3
	SERIOUS	0	3 (S)	3 (S)	3 (S)	3 (S)

11. HISTORY OF VIOLENCE		NONE	>15 YEARS	10–15 YEARS	5–10 YEARS	<5 YEARS
	MINOR	0	1	1	3	5
	SERIOUS	0	2	4	6	7

12. PRECOMMITMENT STATUS	0 = NOT APPLICABLE −3 (R) = OWN RECOGNIZANCE −3 (V) = VOLUNTARY SURRENDER

13. VOLUNTARY SURRENDER DATE	14. VOLUNTARY SURRENDER LOCATION

15. CRIM HX PTS _____	16. SECURITY POINT TOTAL

17. OMDT REFER (Y/N) _____

18. REMARKS

Figure 10-1

Inmate security classification form.

Source: Federal Bureau of Prisons, *Security Designation and Custody Classification Manual*, (Washington, DC: U.S. Department of Justice, 1990, Chapter 5, p. 1).

Table 10-1

SECURITY DESIGNATION TABLE FOR DETERMINING PLACEMENT IN A SPECIFIC SECURITY LEVEL OF FEDERAL PRISON FOR MALE INMATES

Classification Score	Public Safety Factors	Inmate Security Level
0–5	**No public safety factors**	**Minimum**
	Deportable alien	Low
	Greatest severity offense	Low
	Sex offender	Low
	Threat to government officials	Low
	Sentence length	
	Time remaining > 10 years	Low
	Time remaining > 20 years	Medium
	Time remaining > 30 years (includes nonparolable life or death penalty cases)	High
	Serious escape	Medium
	Disruptive group	High
	Prison disturbance	High
6–8	**No public safety factors**	**Low**
	Serious escape	Medium
	Sentence length	
	Time remaining > 20 years	Medium
	Time remaining > 30 years (includes nonparolable life or death penalty cases)	High
	Disruptive group	High
	Prison disturbance	High
9–14	**No public safety factors**	**Medium**
	Disruptive group	High
	Prison disturbance	High
	Sentence length	
	Time remaining > 30 years (includes nonparolable life or death penalty cases)	High
15+		**High**

Source: Federal Bureau of Prisons, *Security Designation and Custody Classification Manual* (Washington, DC: U.S. Department of Justice, 1999), Chapter 7, p. 7.

shows the form used to determine security designations for each inmate. An offender's total security point is then the basis for assignment to a federal prison. As indicated in Table 10-1, there is a range of point totals that determines the security assignment when there is no public safety factor. **Public safety factors**, such as being a member of a disruptive group (prison gang) or a sex offender, are special factors the BOP uses to override the standard security-level assignment and usually result in placement in a higher-security-level prison. As noted in Table 10-1, with no public safety factor, the following security point totals result in placement in the corresponding security level of federal prison:

Security Point Totals	Prison Security Level
0–5	Minimum
6–8	Low
9–14	Medium
15+	High

Reclassification of Inmates

For correctional agencies that have multiple institutions at varying security levels (and, therefore, varying costs of operation), there is an effort to continuously review inmates' progress and move them to a different security level when their needs warrant a change. Therefore, a **reclassification** review is scheduled at regular intervals (often three or six months) to modify the original classification and possibly reassign the inmate to a different prison. Reclassification has three basic purposes: (1) to consider changes in program needs, mental health, or medical condition; (2) as an incentive for good behavior by dropping the security level of inmates who conform and follow prison rules; and (3) to identify the need to increase inmates security level because of misconduct and resultant disciplinary action.

At the regular reclassification review, staff and the inmate interact, reviewing the progress toward intended program goals in preparation for release. These goals can include educational participation, substance abuse programming, or psychological counseling. Because various prisons have different program offerings, an inmate may need to be transferred to a prison where programs better match the inmate's needs. There is also a review of mental health and medical status. Any change in these conditions could warrant a transfer to another prison better equipped to deal with the inmate's condition. Between regular reviews, if an inmate's mental health or medical condition suddenly and unexpectedly changes, there will be an immediate consideration of the need to transfer to another prison.

Reclassification is also an incentive for good behavior. At the reclassification review, an inmate's behavior and the percentage of the sentence served is combined into the classification score system. If behavior is good, and as the inmate reaches certain stages in the sentence (so many months served or a certain percentage of the sentence completed), it may result in a lowering of the security score and resultant prison assignment. Because most prison systems want to use their highest security bed space in the most efficient manner, it is cost effective to move an inmate who warrants a lower classification to a less secure (and less costly) prison. Inmates become well aware of the scoring system and know what will make them eligible for reassignment to a lower-security prison. Less security generally increases an inmate's privileges and results in a less stressful and less dangerous environment. Therefore, inmates strive to reach these levels to be considered for a reduced security level.

Reclassification can also be initiated by serious inmate misconduct, illustrating that the inmate cannot be controlled in the current security level and must be placed at a higher level (such as moving from medium to maximum security). When an inmate commits a serious disciplinary infraction or continues to commit minor infractions, the inmate receives extra points on the security instrument, which may warrant an upgrade to a higher-security-level prison. With increased security come fewer privileges, more control, less freedom of movement, often fewer program opportunities, and housing with other inmates who have shown a propensity for misconduct.

In California, there is a four-level system of prison security. Using more common terminology, level I is similar to minimum security and, in California, includes facilities and camps that consist of primarily open dormitories with a low security perimeter. Level II is similar to low security and includes facilities that consist primarily of open dormitories with a secure perimeter, which may include armed coverage. Level III is similar to a medium security prison, with a secure perimeter with armed coverage, and housing units with cells adjacent to exterior walls. Level IV facilities are maximum security, with a secure perimeter with internal and external armed coverage, and housing units as in level III facilities or cell block housing with cells nonadjacent to exterior walls.[22] Inmates who receive the following number of points on the classification score sheet are assigned to the matching level of prison:

0 to 18 points	Level I
19 to 27 points	Level II
28 to 51 points	Level III
52 or more points	Level IV

After initial assignment to a prison, inmates' behavior continues to be monitored, and they may be reassigned to another prison based on either good or bad conduct. Figure 10-2 is the California Department of Corrections reclassification score sheet. Unfavorable and favorable behavior scores are combined to recalculate an inmate's classification score. Unfavorable factors include serious rule violations, escapes, assaults on staff or inmates, drug smuggling, weapon possession, or inciting a disturbance. Favorable behaviors include maintenance of minimum custody, continuous living in dormitory type housing, no serious rule violations, and good program performance. For

Inmates who violate prison rules are disciplined and can lose privileges and be assigned a higher classification level.
(Courtesy of Corrections Corporation of America)

reclassification purposes, inmates are usually reassessed every six months or when there is a serious rule violation that may trigger an increase in the number of security level points.

The overall goal of both classification and reclassification is to maintain homogeneity of inmates by risk and stability and to ensure they are placed in prison facilities that are physically designed to meet their potential for violence and escape. Housing high-security inmates in a facility that is low or minimum security only invites escape, predatory behavior, violence, and other management problems. Yet housing inmates with low or minimum security classifications in high-security prisons has equally serious, yet not so obvious, results. Placing lower-security inmates in danger of violence and intimidation is a waste of correctional resources. It cost three to four times as much to build and operate a high-security than a minimum security prison, and these costs are not necessary for the risks associated with low-security inmates. In the next section, we examine the physical security issues that coincide with the risk factors presented by various security levels of inmates.

Although it is often dealt with informally rather than as a discrete stage in the classification process, **prerelease classification** is usually conducted within the last year of an inmate's incarceration, and it can serve three functions. First, as staff begin

STATE OF CALIFORNIA CDC Reclassification Score Sheet DEPARTMENT OF CORRECTIONS

II. RECALCULATION OF SCORE

A. UNFAVORABLE BEHAVIOR SINCE LAST REVIEW

Last Review Date

☐☐ – ☐☐ – ☐☐ 24
mo   day   year

1. Number of serious disciplinaries
   dates: _____ _____ x 6 = ☐☐ 30

2. Number of escapes during current period
   date: _____ x 8 = ☐☐ 32

3. Number of physical assaults on staff
   date: _____ x 8 = ☐☐ 34

4. Number of physical assaults on inmates
   date: _____ x 4 = ☐☐ 36

5. Number of smuggling/trafficking in drugs
   date: _____ x 4 = ☐☐ 38

6. Number of deadly weapon possessions
   date: _____ x 16 = ☐☐ 40

7. Number of inciting disturbance
   date: _____ x 4 = ☐☐ 42

8. Number of assaults that caused serious injury
   date: _____ x 16 = ☐☐ 44

9. TOTAL UNFAVORABLE POINTS = + _____

B. FAVORABLE BEHAVIOR SINCE LAST REVIEW

Number of Six Month Periods

1. Continuous minimum custody
   _____ x 4 = ☐☐ 46

2. Continuous dorm living
   _____ x 2 = ☐☐ 48

3. No serious 115's
   _____ x 2 = ☐☐ 50

4. Average or above performance in work, school, or vocational program
   _____ x 2 = ☐☐ 52

5. TOTAL FAVORABLE CREDITS = – _____

C. COMPUTATION OF CLASSIFICATION SCORE

1. Prior Classification Score = ☐☐☐ 54

2. Net Change in Behavior Score (A.9 minus B.5) = ☐☐☐ 57
   (+ or –)

3. Change in term points = ☐☐ 60
   (+ or –)

4. Current Classification Score = ☐☐☐ 63

III. PLACEMENT

A. SPECIAL CASE FACTORS

1. Placement Concerns
   a) Hold (enter A, P, or #)   b) Restricted Custody Suffix (enter R or *)   c) Medical Restriction (enter FULL, REST, UNAS, or *)
   Felony INS
   ☐ 66 ☐ 67   ☐ 68   ☐☐☐☐ 69

2. Other Placement Concerns
   a) (*)   b) (*)
   ☐☐☐☐ 73   ☐☐☐☐ 77

3. Caseworkers
   a) Counselor
   ☐☐☐☐☐☐☐ ☐ 81
   Last Name   FI

   b) Supervisor
   ☐☐☐☐☐☐☐ ☐ 90
   Last Name   FI

4. Current Custody
   ☐☐ – ☐ – ☐☐ 99

5. Current Institution and Facility
   ☐☐☐ – ☐☐☐ 107

B. CLASSIFICATION STAFF REPRESENTATIVE ACTION

1. Classification Staff Representative
   ☐☐☐☐☐☐☐☐ 114
   Last Name

2. Date of CSR Action
   ☐☐ – ☐☐ – ☐☐ 122
   mo   day   year

3. Administrative Determinants
   a) (*)   PRIMARY
   ☐   ☐☐☐ 128
   b) (*)   c) (*)
   ☐☐☐ 132   ☐☐☐ 136

4. Placement Approved   a) Cat.
   ☐
   b) Institution and Facility
   ☐☐☐ – ☐☐☐ 141

5. Reason for Administrative or Irregular Placement
   ☐☐ 148

I. IDENTIFYING INFORMATION

A. CDC NUMBER
☐ ☐☐☐☐☐ 1

B. INMATE'S LAST NAME
☐☐☐☐☐☐ 7

C. Date of Current Review
☐☐ – ☐☐ – ☐☐ 15 –
mo   day   year

D. PAROLE VIOLATOR ADMISSION TYPE (enter RTC or WNT)
☐☐☐ 21

Figure 10-2

The California Department of Corrections Reclassification Sheet.
Source: State of California, *Code of Regulations*, Title 15, Crime Prevention and Corrections, Division 3, updated December 31, 2004, p. 156.

to prepare the inmate for transition to the community, they may reexamine program needs and create a continuum of suggested services that can be found in the community. Inmates will be monitored by a parole or other postrelease supervision officer after release from prison. Many institutions conduct a specific prerelease program to educate inmates on services available to them on release and the requirements of any mandatory supervision.

The second function of prerelease classification is to use some of the same criteria used in the security classification process for the parole or other type of discretionary release decision. Parole boards often use actuarial guidelines to assist in their decision making, and parole staff may review this material and prepare guideline recommendations prior to the formal parole board deliberation. Third, a prerelease classification may be used to determine whether the inmate is in need of a residential transition from the prison to the community.

Every state and the Federal Prison System uses halfway houses to transition some inmates to the community. Prison staff often weigh the need for assistance against the risk to the community. Not all inmates have a need for a placement in a halfway house, but those with no definite place to live and few financial resources are usually considered candidates for halfway houses. Even if inmates have little need, if there is a high likelihood to recidivate, they may still be placed in halfway houses to maximize the level of supervision and restrictions on the offender's movements. Prison officials, during the prerelease classification process, weigh the combination of needs and risk to determine whether and for how long inmates will receive a halfway house placement. For most jurisdictions, halfway house placements last from 60 to 180 days.

The accompanying case study presents a good example of how a state moved from a subjective to an objective classification system.

Risk Assessment in Parole Decision Making

During the 1970s and 1980s, there was a public outcry for reform and reduction of the seemingly total discretion of parole boards. There had been many high profile cases of offenders paroled from prison who later committed heinous crimes, and there was much second-guessing of the decision to release them from prison. Indeterminate sentencing and release via **discretionary parole** had been the predominant sentencing approach from the 1950s. By 1977, the use of parole reached its peak as more than 70 percent of prisoners were released on discretionary parole.[23] However, due to the outcry to reform parole, fifteen states and the federal government ended the use of indeterminate sentencing and parole, and twenty other states severely limited the parole-eligible population. A common reform to counter the arguments against using discretionary decision making was to use formal risk prediction instruments, or **parole guidelines**, to help structure parole decisions, reduce disparity, and make decisions more understandable to the public and inmates. Parole guidelines, like sentencing guidelines, use predictive factors to determine the offenders' risk to the community and chance for success. Guidelines suggest a projected parole date after the inmate has served a set number of months, assuming good behavior during the prison term.

Practical Perspectives

Creating an Objective Classification System

In the early 1980s, a new director of corrections had been appointed to lead a fairly large state prison system, a system that was considered outdated in terms of modern professional correctional practices. The director was chosen from outside the state, partly because of his experience, but also because he had worked in other jurisdictions and had had the opportunity to witness the most current developments in correctional management and practices throughout the United States.

On arrival in the state and beginning his new job as director, he began to identify the areas that needed upgrading and change. In terms of classification, the state still used a model of inmate classification and assignment to institutions from the 1950s. The state had approximately ten prisons: one maximum security prison, one female institution, one for youthful offenders, and the rest medium security with small minimum security satellite prisons. While offenders were still in reception status, a central office classification committee reviewed the cases and assigned them to one of the prisons. The most serious offenders were sent to maximum security, females to the female prison, those under twenty-five to the youthful offender prison, and others to whichever prison had bed space available.

After arrival at the designated prison, an inmate would meet with the "classification committee," which was composed of the assistant warden of treatment, the chief psychologist, and the head of social services. Their job was to discuss the needs and problems of the inmate and to create a treatment plan for the inmate. The committee would meet regularly to review the inmate's progress to determine whether new programs were needed or whether the inmate could be reassigned to the satellite minimum security facility (or, in the case of a maximum security prison, to a medium security prison). There was very little movement between facilities, because each prison was very much the same in terms of security and programs, and females and youths, of course, stayed at their respective assigned prisons. All decisions were subjective and reflected the culmination of expertise of the committee members, who knew best how to handle offenders.

The new director was aware of the expanding use of objective classification systems and the benefits that could result. Not only could inmates be better separated by risk of escape and risk of violence but also they could be moved up or down in security as time passed and as their behavior and length of sentence served would warrant a move down (or up) in security level.

Inmates would be aware of the factors in this decision, and the system would seem fairer and more consistent to them. Staff and other resources could be appropriately assigned to institutions based on the types of inmates the facility housed. And with a statewide problem of prison overcrowding, objective classification based on risk factors could maximize the efficient use of bed space.

Another interesting benefit of an objective classification system was the ability to explain inmates' assignments to certain prisons. The director found that he was getting requests from advocates of certain inmates to consider moving them from one prison to another, often for ease of visitation with their families. Although it was easy to explain that there were different security levels of prisons, it was difficult to explain the factors that go into deciding the security level of an inmate or when an inmate would be considered eligible for a security reduction. In an objective classification system, inmates and their families knew why they were placed at one institution, what an inmate could do to earn a security reduction (such as good behavior), and at what point in the sentence risk factors were reduced.

The director asked the NIC to support the review of an objective classification system to determine whether it would be good to implement such a system in the state. If the decision were made to implement, NIC would then fund two national experts to come to the state and guide the staff in its implementation. NIC funded state staff to travel to another similar state that had an objective classification system. Visiting staff liked the approach, and on return to their home state, recommended implementation of such a system. Two national experts (Dr. Robert Levinson, who had developed the system for the BOP, and Dr. Allen Ault, a national expert on inmate management and previously the director of corrections in three different states) were recruited to help the state implement an objective classification system.

The first step was to conduct a research study of the state's inmates to identify factors (similar to those noted in the BOP system previously discussed) that were predictive of risk of violence and risk of escape. This resulted in many of the same factors already being used. Staff were trained on how to use the classification system and how to rate the predictive factors. Inmates were given written notice of how the system would work and how their behavior contributed to their institutional assignments. Rating forms were printed and distributed throughout the institutions. Institutions were realigned in security levels from minimum, medium, and maximum to a four-level system of minimum, medium, close, and maximum security. This four-level system better facilitated separation of inmates by risk and efficient use of bed space.

The new system was implemented and used successfully for more than ten years. Thereafter, another review of the factors was completed, adjustments were made, and the system continues today, almost twenty years later. It was determined to be more fair by staff and inmates; it allowed for better utilization of bed space; institutions were realigned by security level, and staff and resources were assigned based on security needs; and it provided much better background checking, data gathering, and follow-up on success than the previous subjective system. Overall, the implementation was deemed a success and an important management advancement by the state.

The U.S. Parole Commission was the first release agency required to use guidelines beginning in 1976 by the Parole Commission and Reorganization Act (Public Law 94-233). To develop the guidelines, the commission hired a group of researchers to identify the factors that are most salient to success on parole. These six most predictive factors (Figure 10-3) are used to create the salient factor score for inmates.

The salient factor score is then inserted into the guidelines table (see Figure 10-4) with categories of offenses listed as to the severity of the crime. The combination of the offense severity and salient factor score gives a guideline range for the number

Table 10-2 ABOLITION OF DISCRETIONARY PAROLE	
Jurisdiction Abolishing Parole	Year Abolished
Maine	1975
Indiana	1977
Illinois	1978
Minnesota	1980
Florida	1983
Washington	1984
Federal government	1984
Oregon	1989
Delaware	1990
Kansas	1993
Arizona	1994
North Carolina	1994
Mississippi	1995
Virginia	1995
Ohio	1996
Wisconsin	1999

SALIENT FACTOR SCORE (SFS 98)

Item A.   PRIOR CONVICTIONS/ADJUDICATIONS *(ADULT OR JUVENILE)* . . . .
None = 3; One = 2; Two or three = 1; Four or more = 0

Item B.   PRIOR COMMITMENT(S) OF MORE THAN 30 DAYS *(ADULT/JUVENILE)* . . . .
None = 2; One or two = 1; Three or more = 0

Item C.   AGE AT CURRENT OFFENSE/PRIOR COMMITMENTS . . . .

26 years or more	Three or fewer prior commitments = 3
	Four prior commitments = 2
	Five or more commitments = 1
22–25 years	Three or fewer prior commitments = 2
	Four prior commitments = 1
	Five or more commitments = 0
20–21 years	Three or fewer prior commitments = 1
	Four prior commitments = 0
19 years or less	Any number of prior commitments = 0

Item D.   RECENT COMMITMENT FREE PERIOD *(THREE YEARS)* . . . .
No prior commitment of more than 30 days (adult or juvenile) or released to the community from last such commitment at least 3 years prior to the commencement of the current offense = 1; Otherwise = 0

Item E.   PROBATION/PAROLE/CONFINEMENT/ESCAPE STATUS VIOLATOR THIS TIME . . .
Neither on probation, parole, confinement, or escape status at the time of the current offense; nor committed as a probation, parole, confinement, or escape status violator this time = 1; Otherwise = 0

Item F.   OLDER OFFENDERS . . . .
If the offender was 41 years of age or more at the commencement of the current offense (and the total score from Items A–E above is 9 or less) = 1; Otherwise = 0

TOTAL SCORE . . . .

Figure 10-3
U.S. Parole Commission salient factor score sheet.
Source: U.S. Parole Commission, *Rules and Procedures Manual*, (Washington, DC: U.S. Parole Commission, 1998).

of months that should be served before release. As an example, for an offender in Category Five (which includes bank robbery and intent to sell hard drugs) who had a salient factor score of six, the guidelines suggest thirty-six to forty-eight months to be served before release. The parole board can consider other mitigating or aggravating circumstances of the offense or offender to set the release date within the guideline range.

After the federal government developed and began using guidelines, many states adopted similar guidelines for their parole decision making. These objective instruments have been found to be accurate in predicting the range of risks for reoffending by inmates

GUIDELINES FOR DECISION MAKING

**[Guidelines for Decision Making, Customary Total Time
to Be Served Before Release (Including Jail Time)]**

OFFENSE CHARACTERISTICS	OFFENDER CHARACTERISTICS: Parole Prognosis (Salient Factor Score 1998)			
Severity of Offense Behavior	**Very Good (10–8)**	**Good (7–6)**	**Fair (5–4)**	**Poor (3–0)**
	Guideline Range			
Category One	<=4 months	<=8 months	8–12 months	12–16 months
	Guideline Range			
Category Two	<=6 months	<=10 months	12–16 months	16–22 months
	Guideline Range			
Category Three	<=10 months	12–16 months	18–24 months	24–32 months
	Guideline Range			
Category Four	12–18 months	20–26 months	26–34 months	34–44 months
	Guideline Range			
Category Five	24–36 months	36–48 months	48–60 months	60–72 months
	Guideline Range			
Category Six	40–52 months	52–64 months	64–78 months	78–100 months
	Guideline Range			
Category Seven	52–80 months	64–92 months	78–110 months	100–148 months
	Guideline Range			
Category Eight*	100+ months	120+ months	150+ months	180+ months

*Note: For Category Eight, no upper limits are specified due to the extreme variability of the cases within this category.

Figure 10-4

U.S. Parole Commission guidelines for decision making.
Source: U.S. Parole Commission, *Rules and Procedures Manual* (Washington, DC: U.S. Parole Commission, 1998).

released on parole.[24] The use of parole guidelines became popular and by the mid-1990s, almost all of the states that still had discretionary parole used a formal risk assessment instrument for the parole decision process.[25]

Risk Management and Classification of Community Offenders

Risk management of offenders in the community is also important and offenders are often classified for risk to the community and need for treatment programs. The identification of offender risks guides assignment of supervision levels and the distribution of resources. The use of actuarial instruments became popular during the 1980s,[26] although risk assessment for case management of community supervision was originally developed in Wisconsin in 1975. The Wisconsin Client Management Classification (CMC) system helped to identify the required level of surveillance for each offender and also determined the specific needs of the offender and the resources that would be needed by the offender. The NIC then suggested the Wisconsin system as a model, and it was adopted in many jurisdictions throughout the United States. In 1976, the U.S. Comptroller General tested the predictive power of community risk-prediction models and concluded that "probation prediction models could improve probation systems operations by allocating resources to offenders who most need help. . . . Model sources appeared to be useful in determining supervision levels and more successfully selected probationers for early release."[27] A NIC report titled *Directions for Community Corrections in the 1990s* noted, "In general, one effective way to increase decision reliability is to make visible the criteria for decisions. For that reason, we advocate the use of statistically based devices to classify offenders according to relative risk."[28]

Community classification systems score offenders based on their offense background and personal characteristics. Figure 10-5 illustrates the current Missouri model used to determine levels of community supervision. Probation and parole officers initially complete the Client Analysis Scale-Risk for the offender. Each case is scored on the number of prior convictions, employment status, age, present offense, and whether the present offense is a felony. The scores are combined to determine the permanent risk score, which is used to determine the classification of risk and the supervision level.

Offenders receiving probation are released from prison on parole, if under the supervision of an agency using statistical risk assessment, are scored based on their offense background and personal characteristics. Again, similar to institutional classification, community classification can be described as initial, reclassification, and prerelease classification. At the initial classification, once scored for risk, offenders are assigned a supervision level. Usually, the higher the risk score the greater the level of supervision. The highest level is called intensive supervision. Intensive supervision offenders are classified as posing a significant risk of committing a new offense and are assigned to a small caseload (usually about 25). They must report at least once a week to the supervising officer, and they are visited two to three times per month at home or at work. There may also be additional random contacts as the officer believes necessary.

Those offenders not posing as serious or immediate a risk to the public, yet who require substantial to moderate levels of supervision and have significant problems

STATE OF MISSOURI DEPARTMENT OF CORRECTIONS **CLIENT ANALYSIS SCALE-RISK**		OFFICER CODE
NAME	NUMBER	DATE

PRIOR CONVICTIONS (ADULT-FELONY, MISDEMEANOR, CRIMINAL ORDINANCE INCLUDING SIS)

☐ 1	☐ 2	☐ 3
NONE	1 OR 2 PRIORS	3 OR MORE

EMPLOYMENT/VOCATION

☐ 0	☐ 1	☐ 2
FULL TIME WORK	PART TIME WORK	UNEMPLOYED

AGE (AT ASSIGNMENT)

☐ 0	☐ 1	☐ 2
30 YEARS OR OVER	22 TO 29 YEARS	21 YEARS OR YOUNGER

PRESENT OFFENSE (CHARGE FOR WHICH CONVICTED) (ROBBERY, BURGLARY, STEALING, FORGERY, SEXUAL ASSAULT AS PER RSMo 589.015)

☐ 0	☐ 1
NO	YES

PRESENT OFFENSE A FELONY (OFFICIAL CHARGE)

☐ 0	☐ 1	
NO	YES	
		RISK SCORE

Figure 10-5
Missouri client analysis scale-risk for probationers and parolees.
Source: Missouri Department of Corrections.

needing assistance, are assigned to **regular supervision**. Under regular supervision, officers supervise approximately fifty offenders. Officers serve the dual function of monitoring behavior and assisting offenders through substance abuse programs or employment counseling. Most jurisdictions also have specialized caseloads, whereby an officer's entire caseload is made up of offenders with a particular type of problem, such as substance abuse or a history of sex offenses. Such specialization allows the officer to become knowledgeable and proficient in dealing with this particular problem.

Those offenders who pose little risk to the community may be placed on **minimum supervision**, with caseloads as high as 300 offenders. These offenders often have contact with a parole or probation officer only for very few months and are basically themselves responsible for following the conditions of their supervision. These offenders have few needs and are likely to have committed white-collar crimes. They are aware that their community supervision can be revoked and that they can be sent to prison. That threat is enough of a deterrent for them to follow supervision conditions and avoid further criminal acts. Some jurisdictions also have a category called **administrative supervision**. Offenders under administrative supervision have no contact with a parole or probation officer. However, they are still under conditional release, and if they commit another crime, their original parole or probation will be revoked. Administrative supervision is not likely to be used on initial classification. However, after low-risk offenders demonstrate a good adjustment to supervision, this status may be assigned.

In addition to the degree of supervision, community offenders with a special treatment need, such as mental health, substance abuse, or sex offenses can be placed on a special caseload. In addition, some states use electronic monitoring for a small portion of their community offenders who are at high risk. On January 1, 2002, 87.0 percent of parolees were on regular caseloads, 5.3 percent on intensive caseloads, 5.0 percent on special caseloads, and 0.8 percent on electronic monitoring.[29] Table 10-3 lists the average size for parolees on four types of caseloads. These parole caseload sizes are about the same as probation caseload sizes for intensive, special, and electronic monitoring caseloads. However, while the average parole caseload for regular supervision was 63, it was 133 for probation.

Table 10-3
AVERAGE CASELOAD PER OFFICER DURING 2001 BY TYPE OF CASELOAD

Type of Caseload	Average Size of Caseload
Regular	63
Intensive	18
Special	35
Electronic	28

Source: Adapted from Camille Graham Camp and George M. Camp, *The 2002 Corrections Yearbook: Adult Systems* (Middletown, CN: Criminal Justice Institute, 2003), p. 195.

Another example of how offenders risk levels are linked to supervision is illustrated in Figure 10-6. In this Ohio supervision instrument, a variety of characteristics regarding history of crime, employment, and alcohol or drug use results in a classification score used to determine the classification level. A serious history of substance abuse, mental illness, or some other treatment need may result in an immediate designation to an intensive caseload.[30] Otherwise, the supervision level is based on the assessment score as follows:

Basic high	Risk score of 28 and above
Basic medium	Risk score of 11 to 27
Basic low	Risk score of 10 or below

Based on the classification level, supervision policy often requires a certain minimum frequency of contacts, but additional contacts can be required if they are deemed necessary to meet the supervision needs of the individual offender:

Intensive: Five contacts per month, with at least one positive contact. For substance abusers, there should also be four drug tests per month.

Basic High: Three contacts per month with at least one positive contact. Substance abusers should be tested three times per month.

Basic Medium: One contact per month. Substance abusers should be tested twice per month.

Basic Low: No contacts required, but the offender completes and submits a form listing his or her activities related to jobs, residences, and so on. For substance abusers, there is one drug test per month.[31]

A **positive contact** is a face-to-face contact with the offender by the officer, and other contacts are those in which significant information is collected (from the offender or an ancillary service such as a treatment provider or employer). Currently, however, many parole agencies no longer specify a set number of contacts per risk level. Instead, the parole officer develops a supervision plan unique to the individual needs of the offender. In 2007, agencies reported that 84 percent of parolees were on active supervision, with weekly or monthly face-to-face contact with their supervision officer.[32]

Throughout community supervision, there are regular reviews of status, and a reclassification, in which the risk factors are rescored based on behavior and time spent under supervision. The purpose of reclassification is to ensure proper matching of resources and placement of offenders at a supervision level. As supervision time goes on without a violation, it becomes evident that an offender is at a reduced risk, and a lower level of supervision is usually warranted sufficient to monitor behavior and meet offender needs.

In the Missouri policy, after the initial classification of risk, each offender is scored on the Monthly Supervision Report (Figure 10-7) to review the status of the supervision and determine the need for changes. Offenders with a risk score of ten or more and a need score of eleven or more are automatically assigned to intensive supervision or another special-supervision caseload. If the review indicates that considerable supervision time has

ASSESSMENT OF OFFENDER RISK

Offender Name:		Offender #:
Date:	F.U. Date:	Unit Location:
Officer (Last, First):		

Select the appropriate answer and enter the associated weight in the score column. Total all scores to arrive at the risk assessment score.

SCORE

Number of Prior Felony Convictions: . . . . (or Juvenile Adjudications)	0 None 2 One 4 Two or more	_____
Arrested Within Five (5) Years Prior to Arrest . . . . for Current Offense (Exclude Traffic):	0 None 4 Yes	_____
Age at Arrest Leading to First Felony Conviction: . . . . (or Juvenile Adjudications)	0 24 and over 2 20–23 4 19 and under	_____
Amount of Time Employed in the Last 12 Months: (Prior to Incarceration for Parolees/PRC Offenders)	0 More than 7 months 1 5 to 7 months 2 Less than 5 months 0 Not applicable	_____

Alcohol Usage Problems (Prior to Incarceration for Parolees/PRC Offenders):	0 No interference
	  with functioning
	2 Occasional abuse;
	  some disruption
	  of functioning
	4 Frequent abuse;
	  serious disruption;
	  needs treatment
		_____

Other Drug Usage Problems (Prior to Incarceration for Parolees/PRC Offenders):	0 No interference
	  with functioning
	2 Occasional abuse;
	  some disruption
	  of functioning
	4 Frequent abuse;
	  serious disruption;
	  needs treatment
		_____

Number of Prior Adult Incarcerations in a State or Federal Institution:	0 0 3 1–2 6 3 and above	_____
Age at Admission to Institution or Probation/Community Control for Current Offense:	0 30 and over 3 18–29 6 17 and under	_____
Number of Prior *Adult* Supervisions:	0 None 4 One or more	_____
Number of Prior Probation/Community Control/Parole/ PRC Revocations Resulting in Imprisonment (Adult or Juvenile):	0 None 4 One or more	_____

TOTAL: _____

CLASSIFICATION CODE:

_____

1 INTENSIVE
2 BASIC HIGH (28 & above)
3 BASIC MEDIUM (11–27)
4 BASIC LOW (10 & below)
5 MONITORED TIME

OVERRIDE CODE:

_____

1 HIGHER
2 LOWER
3 NONE

IF OVERRIDE, SUPERVISOR'S INITIALS:

DRC 3001 (7/97)   DISTRIBUTION: WHITE–Central Records   CANARY–District File

Figure 10-6

Assessment of offender risk.

Source: Ohio Department of Rehabilitation and Corrections, Policy Manual 3019, revised July 1997.

STATE OF MISSOURI DEPARTMENT OF CORRECTIONS BOARD OF PROBATION AND PAROLE **SUPERVISION REPORT FORM**	OFFICE USE ONLY ☐ INITIAL SCALE ☐ ENTER	Officer Name & Number DOC Number

Name	Home Telephone	Cell Phone

Address	City	State	Zip Code

Mailing Address (if different than above)	City	State	Zip Code

With whom do you reside? (Include names and relationships)

Emergency Contact (Include name, relationship)

Emergency Contact address	Telephone Number	Cell Phone Number

Name of Present Employer	Employer's Phone Number

Present Employer Address	City	State	Zip Code

Name of Employment Supervisor	Is your employer aware you are on probation/parole? ☐ No ☐ Yes	Total income for the past 30 days

Do you own a vehicle? Make ☐ Yes ☐ No	Model	Year	License Plate Number	Vehicle Color/Description

Have you been arrested in the past 30 days? ☐ No ☐ Yes - Date of arrest:	Arresting Police Department	Charge(s)

Signature	Accepted by	Date	Time ☐ A.M. ☐ P.M.

DO NOT WRITE BELOW THIS LINE

___ **EMPLOYMENT/EDUCATIONAL/VOCATIONAL**
0 = Full time for the past 3 months
1 = Part time; school; training; full time for less than 3 months;
    Unemployment Compensation
2 = Unemployed; underemployed (less than 20 hours per week)
Date employed/unemployed _____

___ **TECHNICAL VIOLATIONS**
1 = No technical VR/mandatory citation in the past 6 months
2 = Technical VR/mandatory citation in the past 4-6 months
3 = Technical VR/mandatory citation in the past 3 months or
    pending revocation
Date of last technical violation/mandatory citation_____
Conditions cited _____

___ **SOCIAL**
0 = No problems
1 = Problem not requiring intervention*
2 = Problem requiring intervention*
Date of last occurrence _____

A corresponding social category must be marked

___ **LEGAL** (Excludes present offense)
1 = No arrests in the past 3 months
2 = No convictions, 1 arrest in the past 3 months
3 = 2 or more arrests, pending charge, or conviction in past 3 months
Date of arrest/conviction _____

___ **SUBSTANCE ABUSE**
1 = No drug use/alcohol abuse in the past 6 months
2 = Drug use/alcohol abuse in the past 4-6 months
3 = Drug use/alcohol abuse in the past 3 months
Date of last use/problem _____

PROBLEM CODES: 1=No Problem   2=Identified History
                 3=Problem past 4-6 months   4=Problem past 3 months

SUBSTANCE ABUSE	SOCIAL	
___ Alcohol	___ Mental Problems	___ # UAs
___ Marijuana/Hashish	___ Family Problems	
___ Opiates	___ Financial	___ # Positive UAs
___ Stimulants/Cocaine	___ Assault/Aggressive	
___ Depressants	___ Physical	___ # Pending UA
___ Inhalants/Solvents	___ Reporting	Results
___ Hallucinogens		

Need Score	Risk Score	Supervision Level

☐ Dangerous Felon   ☐ Sex Offender (Not Eligible for Intervention Level I)

Notes:

MO 931-3698 (01-2009)

Figure 10-7
Missouri Probation and Parole Monthly Supervision Report.
Source: Board of Probation and Parole, Missouri Department of Corrections, 1991.

passed without a violation, a lower level of supervision will likely be assigned. Classification processes are extremely valuable to match resources to offenders' risk and needs and help officers make decisions regarding supervision level, revocation, or successful termination of supervision.

Finally, risk prediction can be useful for consideration of termination from supervision (both for positive and negative reasons). When offenders meet all their supervision requirements, they can be considered for early termination of their supervision, a form of prerelease classification. Almost every jurisdiction provides offenders the opportunity to be released from community supervision before the maximum period, if their behavior has been good and they have met all of the special conditions of their supervision. Although there are usually no formal criteria for an early release from probation or parole supervision, risk assessments provide guidance regarding the likelihood of the offender reoffending. Offenders with high scores usually continue under supervision, whereas those with low risk scores may receive an early termination.

On the negative side, when offenders commit technical violations (rather than commit new crimes), it is difficult to decide if their supervision should be revoked and imprisoned or if they can remain in the community. In this situation, Fry suggests the use of a "utility model" to both protect the public and provide maximum opportunity for rehabilitation.[33] In this model, the question is whether the offender poses such an unacceptable risk to public safety to not continue community supervision, or is there a risk level that is manageable. However, even though recognizing the value of actuarial models to aid in this risk analysis, Fry cautions that since actuarial assessments are predictive probabilities of eventual recidivism, they "do not provide near-real-time recidivism predictions adjusted for violation responses."[34]

Principles of Effective Intervention and Risk Reduction

A very useful report in finding ways to reduce risk of community offenders was completed by the NIC in 2009. *Implementing Evidence-Based Policy and Practice in Community Corrections* includes results of research conducted to determine the most effective evidence-based practices to reduce offender risk. The report includes eight principles that, when taken together, improve the likelihood of reducing risk.[35] These include the following:

1. Assess actuarial risk/needs. Offenders should be assessed using a valid actuarial instrument as an ongoing process rather than a single event. But the informal assessment through routine interactions and observations by officers and offenders is also important and can help to guide the assignment of treatment programs.

2. Enhance intrinsic motivation. It is believed that offenders are more likely to change behavior if they have an intrinsic motivation. These motivations are most positively influenced by respectful and constructive interactions with officers, treatment providers, and institutional employees.

3. Target interventions. There are several principles that serve as ways to target treatment (see below). These include individual characteristics of offenders (risk, need, motivation, gender, etc.) as well as treatment characteristics (the intensity and timing as well as the evidence of effectiveness with specific groups).

4. **Skill train with directed practice.** Evidence indicates that cognitive and behavioral treatment methods are most effective when delivered by well-trained providers. The expected skills and behaviors are not just taught to offenders, but are practiced and role-modeled throughout the treatment.

5. **Increase positive reinforcement.** It is recommended that a much higher ratio of positive to negative reinforcement be used as a part of supervision. The increased use of positive reinforcement does not reduce or replace the need for consistent and swift application of negative reinforcement when necessary. However, negative reinforcement as the primary driver of behavior is found to be ineffective.

6. **Engage ongoing support in natural communities.** The most important place to search for pro-social support is in the community in which offenders live. Engaging family members, spouses, and others who can be supportive increased the likelihood of success.

7. **Measure relevant processes/practices.** Evidence-based practices highlight the importance of measuring progress and outcomes. Intermediate measures of cognitive and behavioral change as well as increase in skills are important guideposts along the way to success.

8. **Provide measurement feedback.** The measures of success must be fed back to offenders to hold them accountable and reinforce positive change. And regular performance audits of how well officers and agencies are following these evidence-based principles have been found to positively reduce recidivism.

The target interventions fall into five principles.

- The *Risk Principle* is to target and prioritize supervision and treatment resources for high-risk offenders. Targeting resources to low-risk offenders produces little if any positive results.

- *Need Principle* emphasizes focusing the resources toward the criminogenic needs which correlate to the likelihood of committing new crimes (antisocial behavior, antisocial personality, criminal thinking, criminal associates, dysfunctional family, employment and education, leisure and recreation, and substance abuse).

- *Dosage* recognizes the first six to nine months of postrelease supervision as the highest risk for reoffending. It is recommended that for high-risk offenders, 40 to 70 percent of their time during this period should be structured and occupied with routines such as outpatient treatment, employment assistance, and education programming.

- *Treatment Principle* is to make the treatment plan (particularly cognitive-behavioral treatment) an integrated component of the full sentence and sanction requirements. Making these types of treatment a part of the sentence or sanction ensures that all individuals involved in the case and treatment plan are supportive and coordinated in their efforts.

An important step for implementing these principles is that they are reflected in the policies, procedures, and day-to-day work of the supervision agency, officers, and treatment providers. And the supervision style of officers also impacts effectiveness. Supervision is most successful and change most likely to occur when officers, "strike a balance between an enforcement and intervention role; clarify their role with the client; model pro-social behaviors, show empathy without diminishing accountability; and focus interactions on problem solving and addressing criminogenic needs."[36]

Risk Assessment in Sentencing

The final development in the use of risk assessment concerns sentencing guidelines. **Sentencing guidelines** are procedures designed to structure sentencing decisions based on measures of offense severity and criminal history. Minnesota was one of the first states to implement a sentencing guidelines process in the early 1980s. Figure 10-8 illustrates the current Minnesota sentencing guideline grid. The left side of the grid is a list of crime categories in order of increasing severity. Across the top, offenders' criminal histories are scored on factors such as the number of prior offenses, age at first offense, history of violence, or escape from a prison or absconding from community supervision.

There are several reasons why states adopt sentencing guidelines. First, it was believed that judges might not be harsh enough on certain criminals and required guidelines to ensure that dangerous criminals are sent to prison. Second, sentencing guidelines provide uniformity, ensuring that offenders who commit similar crimes receive similar sentences. Third, sentencing guidelines can help project the need for prison space when used with projections of crime rates and the number of inmates in prison or offenders under probation supervision. Most important, sentencing guidelines (by combining factors of offense severity and criminal history) provide a rational approach to determining a sentence.[37] In some states, judges have very little discretion and cannot vary from the guidelines. In other states, the guidelines are just "guidelines," and judges are not required to follow them.

Guidelines must be adopted by the state legislature before being used by the courts. There is usually some limited discretion allowed to sentencing judges, but they often must include their reasons for varying from the guidelines if warranted. The guidelines provide a narrow range of sentences for each type of offense, increasing the sentence with the severity. As in the Minnesota model, many states include a prediction of risk for the offender to be factored into the sentencing decision. Factors, such as the number of prior convictions, history of incarceration, absconding from community supervision or escape from prison, history of violent offenses, or age at first arrest, are often included as risk predictors. Once the score for these items is developed using information from the presentence investigation, the offender is assigned a severity score.

Risk assessment has become an often-used and important part of the criminal justice system and particularly the correction system. Many correctional agencies use risk assessment in some capacity, substituting actuarial tables for discretion and professional judgments. Some argue that we have gone too far in implementing actuarial methods and that the loss of discretion and the judgment of experts makes the system too insensitive to individual situations, disallowing innovation in sentencing and handling of offenders. Since there is no proof that subjective decision making was effective and met the goals of sentencing and offender decision making, there is general consensus that risk assessment is a notable improvement. However, there is room for both predictive instruments

IV. SENTENCING GUIDELINES GRID
Presumptive Sentence Lengths in Months

Italicized numbers within the grid denote the range within which a judge may sentence without the sentence being deemed a departure. Offenders with non-imprisonment felony sentences are subject to jail time according to law.

CRIMINAL HISTORY SCORE

SEVERITY LEVEL OF CONVICTION OFFENSE (Common offenses listed in italics)		0	1	2	3	4	5	6 or more
Murder, 2nd Degree (intentional murder, drive-by-shootings)	XI	306 *261–367*	326 *278–391*	346 *295–415*	366 *312–439*	386 *329–463*	406 *346–480[2]*	426 *363–480[2]*
Murder, 3rd Degree Murder, 2nd Degree (unintentional murder)	X	150 *128–180*	165 *141–198*	180 *153–216*	195 *166–234*	210 *179–252*	225 *192–270*	240 *204–288*
Assault, 1st Degree Controlled Substance Crime, 1st Degree	IX	86 *74–103*	98 *84–117*	110 *94–132*	122 *104–146*	134 *114–160*	146 *125–175*	158 *135–189*
Aggravated Robbery, 1st Degree Controlled Substance Crime, 2nd Degree	VIII	48 *41–57*	58 *50–69*	68 *58–81*	78 *67–93*	88 *75–105*	98 *84–117*	108 *92–129*
Felony DWI	VII	36	42	48	54 *46–64*	60 *51–72*	66 *57–79*	72 *62–84[2]*
Controlled Substance Crime, 3rd Degree	VI	21	27	33	39 *34–46*	45 *39–54*	51 *44–61*	57 *49–68*
Residential Burglary Simple Robbery	V	18	23	28	33 *29–39*	38 *33–45*	43 *37–51*	48 *41–57*
Nonresidential Burglary	IV	12[1]	15	18	21	24 *21–28*	27 *23–32*	30 *26–36*
Theft Crimes (Over $5,000)	III	12[1]	13	15	17	19 *17–22*	21 *18–25*	23 *20–27*
Theft Crimes ($5,000 or less) Check Forgery ($251–$2,500)	II	12[1]	12[1]	13	15	17	19	21 *18–25*
Sale of Simulated Controlled Substance	I	12[1]	12[1]	12[1]	13	15	17	19 *17–22*

Presumptive commitment to state imprisonment. First-degree murder has a mandatory life sentence and is excluded from the guidelines by law. See Guidelines Section II.E. Mandatory Sentences, for policy regarding those sentences controlled by law.

Presumptive stayed sentence; at the discretion of the judge, up to a year in jail and/or other non-jail sanctions can be imposed as conditions of probation. However, certain offenses in this section of the grid always carry a presumptive commitment to state prison. See, Guidelines Sections II.C. Presumptive Sentence and II.E. Mandatory Sentences.

[1] One year and one day

[2] M.S § 244.09 requires the Sentencing Guidelines to provide a range for sentences which are presumptive commitment to state imprisonment of 15% lower and 20% higher than the fixed duration displayed, provided that the minimum sentence is not less than one year and one day and the maximum sentence is not more than the statutory maximum. See, Guidelines Sections II.H. Presumptive Sentence Durations that Exceed the Statutory Maximum Sentence and II.I. Sentence Ranges for Presumptive Commitment Offences in Shaded Areas of Grids.

Effective August 1, 2009

Figure 10-8
Minnesota Sentencing Guideline Grid.
Source: Minnesota Sentencing Guidelines Commission, *Sentencing Guidelines Grid,* effective August 1, 2009, http://www.msgc.state.mn.us/guidelines/grids/grid_2009.pdf, (accessed April 29, 2010).

and professional judgments in correctional administration. Those agencies that acknowledge this, and create procedures that encourage and allow for both have the best of both worlds. Predictive instruments can provide information and be guidelines useful to knowledgeable professionals in the formulation of their judgments and decisions.

Issues in Risk Assessment and Classification

The use of actuarial risk assessments in correctional decision making has created several issues that must be addressed. These issues include the use of classification in jails; the impact of longer sentences on early objective classification systems; the influence of race, gender, and age on offender classification; the effect of prison overcrowding on classification; and the lack of resources devoted to classification and risk assessment.

Jail Classification Systems

Some jail systems are larger than all but a few state prison systems, and some are extremely small (four or five beds). Jails face unique issues, such as dealing with unknown offenders, managing detoxification and medical problems, and serving the court with security and prisoner transportation. In mid-2008, the nation's 3,376[38] local jails held 785,556 inmates, up from 765,819 in mid-2006 and 780,174 in mid-2007.[39] Each year between the full censuses of jails, the Bureau of Justice Statistics does a sample survey of jails to estimate baseline characteristics of the jails and the inmates housed in them. From 2006 to 2007, it was estimated that there were more than 13 million new admissions to jails or about seventeen times the size of the jail inmate population.[40]

Although prison systems have historically used some type of classification, the use of classification in jails is less used and more recent. Even now, many jails still only classify (in reality, separate) males from females, adults from juveniles, and sentenced from unsentenced prisoners. There are very few jails that use more sophisticated systems to separate inmates by risk or dangerousness. However, over the past decade, the NIC has been assisting jails to implement objective classification systems.[41]

More recently, **objective classification systems** have been used to replace these subjective classification processes. Similar to prisons, jail objective systems identify offenders' criminal history and personal characteristics (number of violent offenses, history of violence, age, marital status) that have been found to be statistically linked to dangerousness or escape potential; they result in an actuarial assessment of risk that is used in assigning inmates to a type of housing unit or recommending certain mental health or substance abuse programs.

There are several problems and operational restraints that confront the implementation of classification systems in jails. First, jails hold a very diverse population, such as offenders in every pretrial stage, offenders serving short sentences, offenders being held or detained for another jurisdiction, and those sentenced and awaiting transfer to a prison system. Second, jails have limited information regarding offenders on which to base classification decisions. Jails receive offenders immediately after arrest, and the only verified information available is the crime for which they are charged. Jail staff conduct interviews with offenders to collect self-reported information, such as medical histories, suicide potential, and the need for separation from other inmates in the jail. And, because most jail inmates are released within seventy-two hours of confinement, there is little time to collect any official criminal history. Third, jails (in comparison to prisons) have an extremely large number of admissions, and without a large staff, it would be overwhelming to attempt to do as thorough a classification as is done in prisons.

In addition to these operational constraints, Brennan suggests that jail classification has "suffered from benign neglect. Unlike prison administrators, jail administrators traditionally have not accorded classification a central role in management."[42] It is not unusual for jail inmates, who have little criminal history and have been arrested for minor crimes, to be assaulted by other inmates who have lengthy and violent criminal histories. In these cases, it is now common for assaulted inmates to sue the jail for failure to separate and protect them from higher-risk inmates. The increasing number of legal challenges from jail inmates for failure to protect them from more dangerous offenders is forcing additional jails to implement some form of basic classification system.

Even with these problems, there are several reasons for having effective jail classification systems:

1. They provide a guide for separating violent, predatory inmates from potential inmate victims. One of the most challenging problems for jails is to protect inmates who could be preyed on by dangerous inmates. With little prior information and many housing arrangements in which numerous inmates live together, it is critical to try to separate inmates by risk of assault against one another.
2. They provide a guide for identifying and managing differently inmates with special needs, such as the emotionally disturbed or those at risk for suicide.
3. They provide a guide for identifying inmates with a high risk of escape and housing them in more secure settings than those with a low risk of escape. Such systems allow jails to have a variety of housing assignments, rather than all maximum-security areas that are very expensive to build and operate.

Jail staff use classification systems to make decisions on the housing assignment for inmates, the types of programs they should participate in, the number of staff assigned to various housing areas, the type of supervision to provide inmates, and whether inmates should be allowed to work or participate in diversion programs. In this regard, classification is an important and valuable tool in jail management. With the legal and operational issues, it is expected that classification will continue to be developed and used extensively in jail systems.

Changing Sentence Structures and Classification

Over the past two decades, the United States has been experiencing a more punitive approach to sentencing. As a result, there have been several changes in sentences, including the implementation of mandatory minimum sentences, the lengthening of sentences, three strikes legislation, and truth-in-sentencing laws. **Mandatory minimum sentences** limit judicial discretion and require a set minimum sentence in prison for certain crimes. **Three strikes legislation** is similar to prior "habitual offender" statutes, requiring that offenders who are convicted of three felonies (in some jurisdictions, violent felonies) serve a long sentence, usually life without parole. Finally, **truth-in-sentencing** laws are a federal initiative passed in the 1994 Federal Omnibus Crime Bill to reward states that move to determinant sentences and require offenders to serve 85 percent of their sentences prior to release. The initiative started as a result of prosecutors and other public officials complaining of parole of inmates well before their mandatory maximum sentence. If a criminal received a sentence range of three to ten years, the officials believed that the public expected the offender would serve close to ten years. As a reward for implementing the truth-in-sentencing, the federal government gives states financial grants to build new prisons in order to house the increased prison population as a result of the truth-in-sentencing laws.

The result of these changes in sentencing laws is that the makeup of the inmate population within a prison system changes, because a larger proportion of the inmate population is serving long sentences. With objective classification systems weighing heavily on the length of the sentence and time left to serve to predict risk, there is an upward movement in terms of the percentage of inmates requiring placement at medium- and high-security institutions. As these inmates serve longer sentences, their age and their propensity for violence is reduced, balancing out the importance of the length of sentence. As noted by Austin, "unless these and other states take steps to adjust their instruments and policies, inmates will be over classified and the types of facilities being constructed will not mirror the security needs of an older and less aggressive inmate population."[43] Austin suggests that states rework their classification systems to take these new factors into account or conduct an "administrative override" and reduce the level of security that results from changes in criminal statutes.

The Influence of Race, Gender, and Age on Classification

Race, gender, and age are three characteristics of offenders that are not considered by most objective classification systems. Yet, all seem to have some definitive correlation and influence the classification process in some manner. Race, in itself, is not thought to be a predictor of criminal behavior or a predictor of risk to reoffend. However, almost one-half of all inmates in state and federal prisons as of January 1, 1999, are African American,[44] approximately four times the percentage of the general population of the United States.

Many factors (low economic status, lack of education, low availability of jobs, and high concentration of drug use in low-economic status) are most often mentioned as the cause of high rates of crime among African American citizens. Although some studies have found little evidence to support systematic discrimination against African Americans,[45] the fact is that African Americans are arrested, prosecuted, convicted, and incarcerated in numbers far disproportionate to their percentage in the population. High crime rates and the fact that typical African American offenders have a more extensive history of crime and violence than white offenders cause African Americans to be more concentrated in high- than low-security prisons. Therefore, there is a high correlation between risk and race.[46] Even with an understanding of the apparent overclassification of security level for African American offenders, there have been no efforts to date to try to adjust for this factor.

Concerning gender, some jurisdictions are reexamining and making adjustments in their objective classification systems. In the late 1980s, the BOP reviewed their classification system and made adjustments based on gender. The BOP found that female inmates, when classified using the same instrument as male inmates, were being placed at a much higher level of physical security prisons than their risk to escape or tendency for violence warranted. To correct the problem, the BOP administratively reduced the number of points assigned for certain types of crimes (such as crimes of violence or use of a weapon during the offense). They found that, in most cases, women were accomplices with men, and the male offenders were the ones who actually handled the weapons or resorted to violence. In addition, the BOP realized that female inmates often had children and close ties in the community, factors important in predicting escape. By making adjustments, the BOP was able to move a high percentage of their female inmate population to less secure, and less expensive to build and operate, prisons.

Finally, age is another factor that is correlated with risk of escape and violence, and risk to reoffend, and results in youthful offenders being placed in high-security prisons.[47] As noted earlier, as sentence lengths increase, the average age of prisoners also increases. The implementation of mandatory minimum sentences and the use of sentencing guidelines also require judges to sentence elderly criminals to prison without considering their age. Therefore, there is an aging population in prison, which results in some prisons resembling nursing homes more than correctional institutions. In the largest maximum security prison in the United States, the Louisiana State Prison in Angola, it is estimated that more than 80 percent of the prisoners will die before they are released. About one-half of the inmates are serving life sentences and not eligible for parole, and another one-third of the prisoners have such long sentences that they are not likely to survive.[48]

Most states now have prisons for older inmates and, to a point, ignore the objective risk assessments, using instead common sense to determine who should be assigned to them. It makes no sense to place feeble and elderly inmates in a high-security prison, with the latest technology and secure fences around the perimeter. Most of these inmates do not have the physical capabilities to climb a fence or run away from staff while trying to escape. Age is also negatively correlated with recidivism: The older an offender is at release, the lower the rate of recidivism. Therefore, risk assessments to determine community supervision levels also must be adjusted to take age into account in determining intensity of supervision.

Prison Overcrowding and Classification

One obstacle in the use of risk assessments and objective classification is the ability to maintain effective classification systems in times of severe prison overcrowding. Throughout correctional jurisdictions in the United States, the greater the overcrowding, the higher the security of the prison. Many high-security inmates get held over in a reception center until an appropriate security-level bed is available, "or they may be placed in any bed that's open. This can create security risks, not to mention a host of other problems throughout the system."[49]

There is no simple solution to this problem. Although reception centers are usually designed to house high-security inmates, they are not designed to house offenders for long periods, and the lack of programs and recreational opportunities can cause tension among an inmate population "held in limbo." Placing offenders in a lower-security prison than their classification warrants is an even greater risk, because without the physical security and staff ratio to supervise and control inmates, the probability of escape and violence greatly increases.

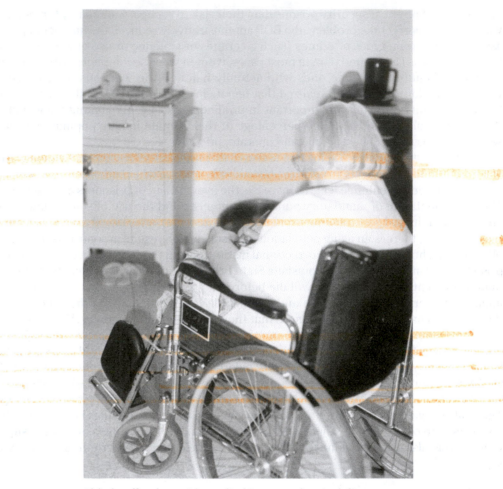

Elderly offenders with medical issues and an inability to move
freely create problems for prison administrators.
(Courtesy of the Corrections Corporation of America.)

The most common solution to the lack of available high-security space is to resort to
the old clinical model and make administrative "overrides" of the classification system. As
noted previously, age and gender are related to risk. Classification teams may be asked to take
these factors into account and identify inmates who they believe can be successfully placed
in a less secure prison. The classification teams are sometimes directed to review circumstances around the use of a weapon during the offense or the manner in which violence was
involved in the offense. Both of these factors drive up the security designation, yet, the
circumstances in many cases do not indicate a pattern of violence that warrants the high
level of security resulting from the objective classification process. When an agency requests
staff to review cases and make these judgments, the efforts usually do reduce security levels of inmates waiting assignment and temporarily relieve the problem of overcrowding by
placing inmates in lower-security prisons that are not overcrowded. If the overcrowding in

higher-security prisons persists, some agencies allow for clinical judgments and administrative overrides to be built into the classification instrument on a permanent basis.

Resources Committed to Classification

The final issue regarding classification of offenders is the general lack of resources devoted to the process. No correctional agencies ever seem to have as many staff as they need to complete their mission in the manner the agency leadership would like. When having to make a decision on how to extend staff in times of increasing demand, so-called "staff" rather than "line" positions are reduced or not increased. Line positions include those persons who directly deliver services, such as probation or correctional officers. Staff positions include those people who complete administrative functions, such as those who complete the classification process or determine when the classification system needs revision or updating. As a result, shortcuts in the classification process often occur, and continuous tests of relevancy and predictive value of certain criteria are not performed. The lack of these activities can undermine the effectiveness of a classification system and relegate such a system to a paper process, rather than as a predictor of behavior to match correctional resources with offender risk. Again, there is no simple solution to a lack of resources. Correctional administrators must be cautious of the dangers in ignoring staff functions, particularly those associated with a failure to monitor and revise a classification system as necessary. These are dangers of overspending and overclassifying rather than dangers of undermining safety and security. However, they are the errors of omission that trained leaders must avoid.

SUMMARY

Prison classification has been recognized as important for more than 100 years. However, sophisticated risk assessments to predict risks to public safety have only of late been implemented in prisons and community supervision. These objective classification instruments can be extremely useful to correctional administrators, because they help increase the safety of staff and inmates and help appropriately assign scarce resources where they are most needed. Currently, most states do use objective classification for prisons, and a growing number are implementing such systems for community supervision.

However, as far advanced as these systems have become, and as recognized as their benefits are, there remain many issues and concerns that must be addressed. Objective classification systems and actuarial methods are only successful if they reflect the changing population and demographics of the offenders they are supposed to evaluate. Although many prisons use systems developed by the NIC and other agencies, they must still train staff in system use, application, and underlying principles. As changes occur in sentencing laws, the makeup of the offender population, and offender characteristics, staff must make adjustments to keep the system current and functioning effectively. When the objective systems fail to meet agency needs, staff must resort to clinical and professional judgment to ensure that the system works efficiently and that offenders are placed under appropriate security and supervision levels.

KEY TERMS

Classification	Prerelease classification	Positive contact
Risk assessment	Discretionary parole	Sentencing guidelines
Actuarial methods	Parole guidelines	Objective classification
Objective classification	Salient factor score	systems
system	Community classification	Mandatory minimum
Postsentence investigation	systems	sentences
Public safety factors	Intensive supervision	Three strikes legislation
Internal classification system	Regular supervision	Truth-in-sentencing
Postsentence classification	Minimum supervision	
Reclassification	Administrative supervision	

YOU'RE THE CORRECTIONAL ADMINISTRATOR

1. You are the chief of classification for a large prison system that has had an objective classification system in place for almost twenty years. You are experiencing extreme overcrowding in the high-security prisons. The director of corrections has asked you to assess the situation and see if you are "overclassifying" offenders to a higher security level than they need. Where do you start? What questions do you want answered? How would you go about identifying whether the classification system is doing what it should be or adding to the overcrowding problem?

2. You are the chief of probation in a county with more than 5,000 offenders on probation. You do not use any type of classification system. Everyone who is placed on probation starts under regular probation supervision, and each probation officer can recommend a reduction in an offender's supervision level. You also have an intensive probation supervision (IPS) and an electronic monitoring house arrest program, both of which offenders can be assigned to with the recommendation of probation officers. Your probation caseload sizes have been increasing, and you cannot get support from the courts or county commissioners for any new positions. What can you do to stretch your current resources to meet the growth needs?

WEB LINK EXERCISES

Go to http://www.assessments.com/assessments_documentation/LSI-R%20report.PDF.

For this chapter we will examine a commonly used classification instrument, the LSI-R (Level of Service Inventory—Revised). Examine the various questions of this instrument for a person being considered for pretrial release. Do the questions appear to be relevant in determining an offender's risk of reoffending? Note the *Probability of Recidivism* score. This score is the primary indicator of an offender's likelihood of recidivating.

Go to National Institute of Corrections (NIC) site www.nicic.org.

This is the Web site for the National Institute of Corrections. Read the general mission and role that NIC plays for adult correctional agencies. One of the principle activities of NIC is to provide technical assistance. Describe what technical assistance is, the issues it can be used to address, the types of assistance available, and the process for applying for technical assistance. Then, identify one issue in correctional administration that would benefit from receiving technical assistance.

GROUP EXERCISES

Each group will be assigned one of the following inmate groups and will explain in a competitive manner with the other groups on the critical importance and how difficult it is to properly classify the inmate group: sex offenders, the mentally ill, elderly offenders, gang members, and juveniles in adult prisons.

ENDNOTES

1. Mary Dallao, "Keeping Classification Current," *Corrections Today* 59 no. 4 (July 1997): 86.

2. See R. M. Dawes, D. Faust, and P. E. Meehl, "Clinical Versus Actuarial Judgment," *Science* 243 (1989): 1668–1674. Also, C. E. Goggin, *Clinical Versus Actuarial Prediction: A Meta-Analysis*, unpublished manuscript (Saint John, NB: University of New Brunswick, 1994).

3. Camille Graham Camp and George M. Camp, *The Corrections Yearbook: 1998* (Middletown, CT: Criminal Justice Institute, Inc., 1998), pp. 18–19.

4. Joan Mullen, *American Prisons and Jails*, Volume I: Summary and Policy Implications of a National Survey (Washington, DC: U.S. Department of Justice, 1980), p. 57.

5. David E. Duffee, *Corrections: Practice and Policy* (New York: Random House, 1989), p. 334.

6. James Austin and Luiza Chan, *Survey Report on Internal Offender Classification System* (San Francisco: National Council on Crime and Delinquency, April 1994).

7. Camp and Camp, *The Corrections Yearbook*, p. 79.

8. The Committee on Classification and Case Work of the American Prison Association, *Handbook on Classification in Correctional Institutions* (New York: American Prison Association, 1947), p. iii.

9. Ibid., p. 1.

10. Ibid.

11. Douglas Lipton, Robert Martinson, and Judith Wilks, *The Effectiveness of Correctional Treatment and What Works: A Survey of Treatment Evaluation Studies* (New York: Praeger, 1975).

12. David Fogel, *We Are the Living Proof* (Cincinnati, OH: Anderson, 1975).

13. Andrew von Hirsch, *Doing Justice: The Choice of Punishments* (New York: Hill and Wang, 1976).

14. James Q. Wilson, *Thinking About Crime* (New York: Basic Books, 1985).

15. Daniel Glaser, "Classification for Risk," in *Prediction and Classification: Criminal Justice Decision Making*, edited by Don M. Gottfredson and Michael Tonry (Chicago: University of Chicago Press, 1987), pp. 266–267.

16. Mary Dallao, "Keeping Classification Current," *Corrections Today* 59 no. 4 (July 1997): 87.

17. For a review of these models, see James Austin, "Special Edition: Prison Classification Systems," *Crime and Delinquency* 32 no. 3 (July, 1986): 272–290.

18. Tim Brennan, "Classification for Control in Jail and Prison," in *Prediction and Classification: Criminal Justice Decision Making*, edited by Don M. Gottfredson and Michael Tonry (Chicago, IL: University of Chicago Press, 1987), p. 343.

19. Norman Holt, *Inmate Classification: A Validation Study of the California System* (Sacramento, CA: California Department of Corrections, June, 1996).

20. Mullen, *American Prisons and Jails, Volume I*

21. Brennan, "Classification for Control in Jail and Prisons."

22. These definitions are taken from the classification manual of the California Department of Corrections (Sacramento, CA: California Department of Corrections, 1998).

23. Bureau of Justice Statistics, *National Prisoner Statistics*.

24. Norman Holt, "The Current State of Parole in America," in *Community Corrections: Probation, Parole, and Intermediate Sanctions*, edited by Joan Petersilia (New York: Oxford University Press, 1998), pp. 28–41.

25. John Runda, Edward Rhine, and Robert Wetter, *The Practice of Parole Boards* (Lexington, KY: Association of Paroling Authorities, International, 1994).

26. Todd R. Clear and K. W. Gallagher, "Probation and Parole Supervision: A Review of Current Classification Practices," *Crime and Delinquency* 31 (1985): 423–444.

27. General Accounting Office, *State and County Probation Systems in Crisis* (Washington, DC: U.S. Government Printing Office, 1976), p. 53.

28. Vincent O'Leary and Todd R. Clear, *Directions for Community Corrections in the 1990s* (Washington, DC: U.S. Department of Justice, June 1984), p. 11.

29. Camille Graham Camp and George M. Camp, *The 2002 Corrections Yearbook: Adult Systems* (Middletown, CT: Criminal Justice Institute), p. 191.

30. Ohio Department of Rehabilitation and Correction, "APA Offender Classification," Policy Section 501, no. 28, February 15, 2001, p. 3.

31. Ibid., pp. 5–6.

32. Lauren E. Glaze and Thomas P. Bonczar, *Probation and Parole in the United States, 2006* (Washington, DC: U.S. Department of Justice, 2007), p. 4.

33. Russ Fry, "Community Corrections: Dealing with Violations in the 21st Century," *Corrections Today*, 72 no. 1 (February 2010): 15–17.

34. Ibid., p. 16.

35. Meghan Guevara and Enver Solomon, *Implementing Evidence Based Policy and Practice in Community Corrections*, 2nd ed. (Washington, DC: U.S. Department of Justice, October 2009).

36. Ibid., p. xi.

37. For a discussion of sentencing guidelines, see Bureau of Justice Statistics, *Report to the Nation on Crime and Justice*, 2nd ed. (Washington, DC: U.S. Department of Justice, 1988), p. 92.

38. There were 3,376 jails in the United States on June 30, 1999, according to Bureau of Justice Statistics, *Sourcebook of Criminal Justice Statistics, 2003* (Washington, DC: U.S. Department of Justice, 2003), p. 91.

39. Todd D. Minton and William J. Sabol, *Jail Inmates at Midyear 2008—Statistical Tables* (Washington, DC: U.S. Department of Justice, Bureau of Justice Statistics, March 2009), p. 2.

40. William J. Sabol, Todd D. Minton, and Paige M. Harrison, "Prison and Jail Inmates, Midyear 2006," *Bureau of Justice Statistics Bulletin* (Washington, DC: U.S. Department of Justice, January 2007), pp. 2–3.

41. See National Institute of Corrections, *Objective Jail Classification Orientation Workshop* (Longmont, CO: National Institute of Corrections, 1990).

42. Tim Brennan, "Implementing Organizational Change in Criminal Justice: Some Lessons from Jail Classification Systems," *Corrections Management Quarterly* 3 no. 2 (1999): 14.

43. James Austin, "The Impact of Truth in Sentencing on Prison Classification Systems," *Corrections Management Quarterly* 1 no. 3 (1997): 55.

44. Camp and Camp, *The 2002 Corrections Yearbook*, p. 13.

45. M. DeLisi and B. Regoli, "Race, Conventional Crime, and Criminal Justice: The Declining Importance of Skin Color," *Journal of Criminal Justice* 27 no. 6 (November–December, 1999): 549–557.

46. Stephen D. Gottfredson and G. Roger Jarjoura, "Race, Gender, and Guidelines-Based Decision Making," *Journal of Research in Crime and Delinquency* 33 no. 1 (1996): 49–70.

47. Ibid.

48. Jurgen Neffe, "The Old Folk's Slammer: Aging Prison Population in the U.S.," *World Press Review* 44 no. 6 (June 1997): 30–32, reprinted from *Der Spiegel* (10, March 1997).

49. Dallao, "Keeping Classification Current," p. 86.

11

Managing the External Environment

Introduction

Up to this point in this textbook, we have presented many of the things that correctional administrators must manage within their internal environment. They have to plan, create a mission and vision, and set the tone for their agency. They have to construct effective methods to recruit and develop their workforce, while efficiently organizing work functions into segments that can be carried out by professional staff. They have to find the most successful ways to supervise and empower their employees. And key for a public administrator is to thoroughly understand the budget process, and particularly during the difficult budget times during the recession, they have to find ways to deliver a quality correctional product within their budget limits.

Next however, we move to the need to manage the **external environment**. Correctional administrators have effectively "honed" their skills in internal management. However, they have not spent as much time developing their talents in management of the external environment. In these times, we find that failure to properly and proactively manage the external environment is what undermines programs and initiatives and gets correctional administrators into trouble. Contemporary correctional administrators operate in a fishbowl, and the success of their agencies and themselves often is more dependent on the influence of external sources (public opinion, political decisions, and media coverage) than on the efficiency and effectiveness of accomplishing their correctional mission. In describing talents correctional administrators need, Hickman writes, "They need political acumen and the backing and input of peers, employees, policy-makers, and the public."[1]

Throughout the history of the United States, the American public and their elected officials have paid little attention to corrections. Few people cared about what went on in jails or prisons or even about how offenders were supervised in the community. But with increasing media coverage of crime, people began to fear for their safety and worried about the potential of victimization. In turn, in the 1980s, crime became the most important domestic issue on the public's mind, and there were demands that government take action to make communities safer. Elected officials responded by creating policies and passing legislation that directed (and possibly micromanages) correctional agencies to take specific actions. Some of these are not good public policy and many have been shortsighted.

As a result, correctional leaders must find ways to manage proactively in the public arena. If they do not, they lose control of an issue, mindsets become firm, people form opinions, and policy gets implemented without the ability of correctional administrators to make logical arguments about the effects or outcomes. When this occurs, correctional administrators are often not consulted for their professional judgments; or if they offer them too late, they are seen as not sharing a level of concern for public safety that they should have. By learning to better manage the external environment, correctional administrators are more likely to be involved in the discussions of such issues of correctional policy.

There are several proactive activities that can facilitate correctional administrators becoming involved in the external decision making related to correctional policy.[2] First, correctional administrators must understand the factors that shape public opinion. Public reaction to crime and corrections policies is important in terms of both support and political decision making. Administrators must respond to public opinion and put in place programs important to the general public and political leaders. Second, correctional administrators must fully understand and be involved in the political decision-making process. If administrators just sit on the sidelines and watch idly as hearings are held, positions are taken, and legislation passed, they will fail in their responsibility to lead and contribute to the quality of decisions and correctional policy. They must understand and work within the points of view of elected officials.

Third, correctional administrators must communicate their own messages about the importance of what they do. Although the media is not the only way to do this, it is the key way. They can influence media coverage through education and sharing of information to media members. Finally, correctional administrators must know the results of correctional programs, and where there are none, create them. This is an age of accountability, and without data to show success, it is difficult to convince those outside of corrections that you are being a good steward of both public safety and the taxpayer's money.

A key skill for correctional administrators is to practice compromise. We as correctional administrators who grew up in a paramilitary organization sometimes have a difficult time not getting things done the way we envision they should be. However, the public policy-making process does not always result in getting things exactly like you want, and effective compromise is getting the key things you know will lead to success and be willing to give up others for the sake of what is important to others.

This chapter describes four key elements for correctional administrators to manage the external environment. These include understanding public opinion, how it is shaped, and how it influences correctional policy. The second is understanding the political process, the role of correctional administrators in it, and how politics shapes correctional policy. Third is the importance of media relations, how correctional administrators must guide their agencies' response to media questions and issues, and more importantly how to develop relationships with the media to avoid education during a crisis. And finally, the value of measuring and communicating outcomes is discussed. While this chapter is in many ways very different from the others, it is the same in that managing the external environment is a key skill for correctional administrators that can significantly impact their success or failure.

Public Opinion and Correctional Policy

An important feature in crime and corrections policy development is the opinion of the public. We live in a democracy, in which our elected leaders take into account the will of the people while forming a policy. **Public opinion** is the collection of individual preferences on any given issue. Opinions are formed in many ways, including media reports, the political process, and presentations by knowledgeable insiders at community organizations. Correctional administrators have both proactive and reactive responsibilities in managing externally in regard to public opinion. First, correctional administrators create and use opportunities to educate the public about specific issues or initiatives. This can be as simple as speaking to community groups such as service clubs or neighborhood associations. Or it can be doing interviews with media outlets or issuing press releases about new programs or policies. And through testifying at legislative hearings that are reported in the media, correctional administrators get their side of an issue into the public domain.

It is the responsibility of leaders to shape public opinion and build confidence in corrections. By reaching out to the public, the media, and elected officials, increased trust, support, and understanding of what corrections does can be built, even if there is not total agreement about how it is accomplished. To this point, former U.S. Senator Mike DeWine advises that correctional administrators not sit back and let public opinion be shaped by sensational media coverage of extreme cases, offender failures, and stories that the news media find interesting.[3] The following are some examples of public opinion on crime and correctional issues. How correctional administrators respond to public opinion in shaping correctional policy is discussed in a later section.

Perhaps the best beginning in an examination of public opinion is a discussion of whether people believe the crime problem is getting better. Crime (particularly violent crime) has gone down significantly since 1993. In that year, 87 percent of the public answered "more" to the question of whether there is more or less crime in the United States than a year ago. And in 2009, there has been only a small change, as 74 percent of those surveyed answered "more" to the same question.[4]

It is interesting to note that public opinion is not nearly as strongly in favor of "get tough" policies as elected officials believe. The political mentality is that the public demands to be safe and we must be tough on crime and criminals to get this result. But public attitudes are becoming less punitive in what they believe is the most effective way to handle criminal offenders. In 1994, only 48 percent of Americans favored addressing root causes of crime and 42 percent preferred a punitive approach. By 2002, a poll conducted by Peter D. Hart Research Associates found that the public favored addressing causes of crime over strict sentencing, by 65 percent to 32 percent, and respondents favored a more rational sentencing for offenders. Only 28 percent of Americans in the poll results believed that the most effective way to reduce crime is to keep offenders off the street as long as possible, and nearly two-thirds believed that the most effective way to reduce crime is to rehabilitate prisoners by providing education and job training.[5] A 2006 Gallup Poll found that 65 percent of those surveyed believe crime can best be lowered by "attacking social problems," while 31 percent responded with "more law enforcement." A 2006 poll conducted by the National Council on Crime and Delinquency found that 87 percent of the

U.S. voting public favored rehabilitative services for inmates as opposed to a punitive approach to sentencing.[6]

There have also been disagreements with the punitive approach we take in dealing with drug offenders. In the Hart survey, respondents recognized drug abuse as a medical problem, with 63 percent favoring providing counseling and treatment and only 31 percent believing that it is a serious crime that should be handled through the courts and prisons. Respondents also showed a lack of support for the three-strikes law, with 56 percent favoring elimination of these and other mandatory sentencing laws, while returning discretion to judges to decide appropriate sentences. Only 35 percent supported the general direction we are taking in response to crime and 54 percent believed we are on the wrong track.[7]

What the public wants is to be protected. If they believe that community sanctions effectively protect them, the public supports the use of community sanctions over imprisonment. When informed that prison space is scarce and expensive, an Ohio poll showed the public supported the use of community corrections instead of paying for new prison construction.[8] A National Opinion Survey on Crime and Justice (NOSCJ) survey also found support for community correctional programs as 73 percent indicated that intensive probation supervision was either "very effective" or "somewhat effective," 55 percent similarly supported house arrest, 73 percent supported electronic monitoring of offenders, and 78 percent supported the use of boot camps as alternatives to traditional prison sentences.[9]

The most serious problem facing government agencies today is a shortage of budget funds. With corrections taking a large portion of budget dollars (as described in Chapter 9), the effort to find less expensive alternatives is supported by the public and elected officials, especially when there is independent evidence that it is good policy. A 2009 report by the National Conference of State Legislatures (NCLS) examined the use of earned credits to reduce time served by inmates in thirty-one states. The review of several studies concluded that the use of such policies can save substantial funds while maintaining or reducing recidivism rates.[10]

Elected officials continuously evaluate public opinion in their consideration of support or opposition for correctional policies. In an interview on this topic with former U.S. senator Mike DeWine, there were several points made about how elected officials look at correctional policies and programs. He notes that the public support programs like **community service**, whereby offenders have to "payback" society for their crimes, correctional agencies focus on the victims as well as offenders, and rehabilitative programs can be used to give offenders the tools they need to make a living and deal with problems that contributed to their criminality.[11]

A key to effective management of the external environment is for correctional administrators to be sensitive to the issues important to the public and be proactive in implementing such programs. All too often, correctional administrators wait until there is a demand by the public (soon thereafter by elected officials) to take some action. By putting programs in place that are supported by the public, before being asked or having the programs legislated into law, correctional officials can create confidence that they are acting in the public's best interest. And in turn, it is expected that elected officials will trust and more often support positions important to correctional administrators.

Practical Perspectives

Public Opinion and Repositioning Rehabilitation

To many peoples' satisfaction, corrections is now moving past the era of punishment into one of implementing programs that twenty-five years ago would have been labeled as "treatment" even though we have not revived the medical model of corrections. Today, these activities are called "programming," and the emphasis is not toward "helping" the offender, but toward providing public safety, through "forcing" offenders to deal with their problems that can reduce their likelihood of recidivism. In this era, offenders are considered responsible for their past and their future. They are not, as under the medical model, considered sick, but irresponsible and lacking respect for others and society.

This new era has been fed by several developments, most of which just occurred naturally, without correctional leadership strategically pushing the field in that direction. First, there is a new generation of correctional workers who did not experience the "rehabilitative" and "medical model" era. They entered corrections philosophically based in a more criminal justice and individual-offender responsibility mind-set. But they bring with them an interest in implementing programs that can improve offenders' chances for success and hopefully reduce recidivism. They have not been burdened by failure of the medical model, criticized by the media or the public for using community sanctions instead of focusing on incapacitation, or faced budget cuts for programs that could not be proved effective.

Second, while the principal interest of the public is to be protected, once they feel their safety concerns are met through incarceration of offenders, they support rehabilitative programs such as education and vocational training, drug abuse, work programs, and counseling for inmates. Public support can lead to funding, and funding and encouragement from political officials lead to innovation and enthusiasm by staff implementing such programs.

Third, correctional programs have been "repositioned" to better fit into the current philosophical approach to criminal justice and corrections. The repositioning is a shift toward holding offenders responsible for their criminal activity and for changing their own behavior to prepare for successful release to the community. There is no consideration of how society may have let these people down, how their lack of education and employment skills resulted in their inability to compete in society, or how their poor upbringing caused psychological problems that did not allow them to cope with challenges and problems. The focus is more toward acknowledging that people have free will, and that they make decisions for their lifestyle that move them toward work and law-abiding activities or toward a life of crime and violence.

In this repositioned era, correctional administrators can offer correctional programs, but within a philosophy and in a manner that puts responsibility on offenders, both for their crimes and for their correction. For purposes of discussion, this approach to correctional programs will be called the responsibility model.[12] Current correctional programs in the **"responsibility model"** are often mandatory, and offenders are expected to participate and comply with the program requirements. They must often go to school, participate in substance abuse counseling, work in a prison job, or do community service. The bottom line is, more is expected from offenders, and excuses for their past behavior are not accepted. The eras of "rehabilitation" and "reintegration" have almost naturally evolved into the era of "responsibility." This responsibility model is easy to support, by the correctional staff, the public, and elected officials.

Politics and Correctional Policy

Much of our public correctional policy is influenced by politics. Historically, correctional administrators were removed from the political side of policy and were ill-equipped to participate in a way that let their opinion be known and was sound enough to influence elected officials. However, it is impossible for them to avoid involvement in political decisions today. Rees underscores this point as follows, "Correctional administrators are very busy and, consequently, inclined to focus only on those things that are directly within their control. This is a mistake; the [administrator] who ignores the political realities of the external environment will fail."[13] Political decisions do not mean "partisan," but merely that they play out in the political arena of legislative bodies or via executive orders from the bosses of correctional administrators.

There are several examples of correctional policy that is not supported by the judgment of professional correctional administrators. In Chapter 13 there is a discussion of recreation programs and weight lifting in prisons. After an incident related to using weight bars to aid in a riot, Congress and many state legislatures enacted a prohibition against weight lifting in prisons, although few correctional administrators support it or think weight lifting is a problem. Similarly, there have been many statutes restricting "amenities" in prisons such as musical instruments or coffee pots. While few facilities do allow these, it seems like an overreach and micromanagement to correctional administrators.

There are several "tough on crime" sentencing statutes that require offenders to serve mandatory and sometimes extremely long prison terms, even though correctional administrators believe the sentences undermine rehabilitation, go beyond the time needed for punishment and deterrence, and make prisons more difficult to manage. What we do know is that politics does influence policy. Stucky, Heimer, and Lang examined politics and state policies regarding imprisonment rates. They found a relationship between an influence of party politics when factoring in time in control and the level of competition in state elections on admissions to prison.[14]

After legislative action to ban weight lifting in several prisons and jails, other types of exercise equipment such as "dip" bars were installed for inmates to use. (Photo by Richard P. Seiter)

There are two views on the proper role of correctional administrators in the politics of the policy-making process. Some authors argue that since correctional administrators serve the public and carry out the requirements of their political leaders, they should not try to influence policy. Garrett suggests,

> Institution administrators should not become involved in the political process. As experts in corrections, professional administrators are sometimes called upon to share such expertise and facilitate the consideration of proposed changes in the law. While senior institution staff should always welcome the opportunity to educate lawmakers, they must be cautious not to give the appearance that they are trying to influence the legislative process.[15]

Others suggest that correctional administrators are "experts" and have a responsibility to be involved in the process and to influence policy development. As experts, correctional administrators influence policy by giving opinions based on information and experience, and they argue for policy that best meets the overall purpose or mission of the agency. Important to this debate is the approach a correctional administrator takes to influence public policy. In a thoughtful and practical article, Riveland identifies the many ways that correctional leaders can be involved in public policy creation and suggests ways to be involved in the political process in the proper role of expert.[16] Some of his suggested steps for involvement in public policy include the following:

- Facts should drive the policy. However, it is often done backward, as ideas for policy are put forward and facts are then developed to justify them.
- Leaders have to sell every reason a policy makes sense and benefits the stakeholders, and when it doesn't, that should be explained.
- Take time (have patience) and let parties become comfortable with the ideas, issues, and solutions.
- Involve a diversity of opinions in big issues. Involving critics presents other sides of an issue and legitimizes the decision.
- Build constituencies for topics that do not have much political support. Issues such as overcrowding and inmate health care have few supporters until a crisis hits.
- Be honest and candid with the media. Explaining background information to the media, especially editorial boards, can go a long way toward influencing policy in a beneficial manner.

For correctional administrators to be successful (this is a relative term and some would suggest "survive" is more accurate) in the political process, they must understand the **first rule of politics**—elected officials want to get reelected. Even the most responsible and dedicated elected officials will make decisions counter to the professional judgment of correctional administrators if that judgment endangers their reelection. When elected officials believe they will not have to worry about correctional administrators implementing politically unpopular policies that could ultimately damage their chances for reelection, the professional judgments of correctional administrators will more likely be sought and valued.

There are several actions a correctional administrator can take to be proactive and improve the political policy making. These are educating their political leaders, using data and facts over philosophy or emotion, developing relationships of trust with elected officials, and making decisions in consideration of public opinion. The first of these is to educate political leaders. Every senior correctional administrator works for an elected official, be it a mayor, governor, or some other official. These elected officials often seem disinterested in what we do in corrections and it is easy to not keep them informed of the issues or policies involved in correctional operations. However, there will always come a time when an issue hits the front burner, and the official must take a position. Without a thoughtful and thorough education on why we do what we do in corrections, when the time comes for making a decision during a crisis, the official will often side with the position being supported by public opinion or other elected officials, since they cannot measure it against the value it serves. However, if there had been a continuous process that both provides information and evokes trust, the official would have dealt with it before the crisis and could have supported the position of the correctional administrator.

The second key activity is to use data and facts rather than emotion and get involved in philosophical arguments. For instance, a possible issue is a county administrator being pushed by a union to allow probation officers to be armed when the chief of probation does not support it. The union may argue staff safety and that the official is not support-ing probation officers if they are forced to go into some neighborhoods without a weapon. The best track for the chief to take is to use research of how often an officer is attacked or assaulted, how often being armed was a negative and reduced officer safety, and what the professional opinion of the American Probation and Parole Association is on the topic. If the chief merely argues against the union for philosophical reasons, it forces the county administrator to make a decision of who is more important to reelection. If the facts are presented, most responsible officials will weigh those and make a decision on that basis.

The third is developing relationships of trust with elected officials. An old adage for public administrators is, "Don't let the first time you go see a member of the legislature be when you need a favor." When I was the director of corrections in Ohio, a friend who often worked the political side of policy told me this and I spent considerable time visiting all the members of correctional oversight committees, updating them on issues and challenges in the department of corrections, and asking if they had any concerns with what we were doing. These visits led to positive feedback, especially by low-ranking members who often did not receive visits by cabinet members. And it is also important to include legislative staff. They carry a lot of power and influence with their bosses.

Using an investment analogy, we found that these "deposits of goodwill" paid interest many times over. It was said that Director Seiter was trusted and could get support for almost any correctional policy he wanted from the legislature (more on that topic later). But the point was that when correctional administrators take the time to visit elected officials when there is not an issue, when they share information with them, and when they show interest and concern for the position of the elected official (regardless of party line), trust builds that will continue and help get over difficult or contentious issues.

John Rees, who was director of corrections in Kentucky, similarly suggests the impor-tance of gaining credibility. He identifies four ways to do this: being honest even when it hurts; trying to help legislators when you can; being aware of the mood of the legislature and couching your program or budget needs in a package that fits into this direction; and being aware of other agendas besides yours that come into play.[17] Relationships are important in any business or organization. These do not have to be "friendly" relationships, but are built on sharing of information and an understanding of the role and challenges of both parties. Such relationships are an important beginning point of any discussion.

The final action correctional administrators can take to be proactive and improve policy making is to make decisions in consideration of public opinion. This does not mean that every decision correctional administrators make will be popular or that they will be guided by public opinion. However, as noted earlier in this chapter, correctional administrators must learn the art of compromise; almost every initiative or policy has its key elements without which it does not accomplish its purpose, and then there are elements that are on the margin or the periphery of the purpose and the approach loses little if they are not included. There are two points to make in this regard.

First, correctional administrators should understand the positions of others with every important initiative and modify those not critical to success or the purpose if they are controversial or there are strong beliefs by other. An important step is to understand how people feel about significant or controversial initiatives. Correctional administrators should take the time to communicate what they want to do and why and get feedback from key officials or interest groups. Then, if there are ways to make the initiative more palatable to them without undermining its purpose, they should do it. The second part of this point is to not begin a battle that cannot be won, unless losing the battle and possibly your job is worth it. There are times this is true, but these are few and far between. As noted above about Seiter and the Ohio legislature, the reason it was said he could get support for anything he proposed was that he did not propose anything the legislature could not support.

There are always many issues that individual members of the legislature cannot support either because of the impact on their constituents or a philosophical reason. And it is never possible to take an action without some opposition. However, it is important to talk to even adversaries, weigh their concerns, and see if there is a way to address them. If not, continue to present and point out why you believe in your position, and use data and trust to make your point. It is almost always the case that there are enough responsible elected officials who do the right thing and hence will support the best position even if some of their members do not. This seems unreal in the current partisan environment within the U.S. Congress and Administration. However, it is usually true of correctional policy considered outside of Washington, DC.

Elected officials always consider public opinion and often get their sense of what it is from media reports. The media can spur controversy and make it seem an issue more important to the public than it may really be. That is why it is very important for correctional administrators to understand and work proactively to build positive media relations. This is the topic of the next section.

Media Relations

As already noted, it is very important in these times for correctional administrators to develop positive and proactive **media relations**. Historically, we have thought of the media as newspaper, radio, and television. Today, there are "webcasts, podcasts, instant messaging, and the Internet, [making] traditional methods of communication . . . essentially obsolete."[18] Just as with so many other things that correctional administrators are involved in, media relations has evolved and changed dramatically, and old approaches are no longer as effective as they once were. The media is often the primary means by which information is shared about crime and corrections. Crime is a major part of any newscast or front page of the newspaper.

There has not always been the best relationship between the media and correctional agencies. Corrections has been a "closed system" in which the only focus was the internal environment, and there was little interest in what happen within corrections by those outside. The public and media had little interest in what happened within prison walls, and likewise prison administrators had no interest in the media coming into prisons, especially to interview inmates. A California prohibition of media conducting face-to-face interviews with inmates was challenged but upheld by the U.S. Supreme Court in the 1974 case of *Pell v. Procunier*.[19] The Court believed that inmates had the opportunity to communicate with the media and to express their concerns about their conditions of confinement through writing or visits by family and friends.

And in *Saxbe v. Washington Post*, the Court went even further and ruled that the First Amendment did not apply to the extent of providing the media access to information that is not available to the public.[20] The Federal Bureau of Prisons (BOP) argued that allowing individual inmates access to the media would make them "big wheels" in the prison and create tension between inmates and staff that could undermine security. However, after the decision, the BOP reconsidered their position, and decided they would create guidelines to allow interviews of inmates with the media. The standards used by most correctional agencies in their media policy contain the following:

- The media member requesting an interview must be affiliated with traditional media and have press credentials, such as a newspaper, radio, or television station.
- The media person cannot have a past personal relationship with the inmate.
- The media must request an interview through the inmate, who will then have to sign a form that they desire the interview. The inmates must also accept that they will give up their privacy rights by talking to the press.
- The media must sign a form that they acknowledge privacy requirements of the prison and not take pictures of or interview other inmates who have not agreed.
- There cannot be a significant demand of staff time to supervise the interview. Most are therefore done during regular visiting hours in the visiting room.
- There cannot be a negative impact on prison operations or security.

As is obvious, this history and even the current restrictions do not create a relationship of trust between correctional agencies and the media. This puts an administrator attempting to create a positive relationship with the media at a distinct disadvantage. In an article in the *Police Chief* regarding media relationships (many media relations issues within law enforcement are similar to those in corrections), Garner suggests that collaboration is more positive and rewarding than the police fighting with the media. He describes how good media relations include police leadership seeking common ground, having clear interview guidelines, handling bad news, and fostering positive media relationships.[21]

With the need to engage the media and be available for interviews during a crisis, many correctional agencies have started training programs for correctional administrators on conducting media interviews
(Courtesy of Corrections Corporation of America)

All these provide little specific guidance for correctional administrators in dealing with the press. However, there are several key elements that are commonly accepted as important. These include being transparent and totally open and willing to share information, being honest and never hiding news, understanding of media requirements for deadlines and reporting expectations, providing information on good as well as bad news, and encouraging media touring prisons and other correctional programs.

The accepted belief is that in today's world of twenty-four-hour media, there are lots of opportunity for the media to get information from offenders, their families, and even correctional staff. It makes no sense for correctional agencies to try to hide anything. They are much more successful if they get bad news out on their own and put the right background information on it. Correctional agencies all have public information officers (PIOs), many of whom have been reporters in their past and understand the value of good media relations. Therefore, there is seldom a lack of transparency among correctional agencies in dealing with the press. The second expectation goes along with this—being honest. Not only should correctional agencies be open and share information, the cardinal rule is never to lie about it. There is no way to hide the truth, so be open and honest from the beginning.

Media reporters have specific deadlines and good PIOs understand this and try to respond quickly so that the media can get their stories out in a timely fashion. And good PIOs recognize that although good news stories (the number of inmates that earned GEDs and an agency receiving ACA accreditation) may not be reported on by the press, you should continue to do press releases on these things. On a slow news day, they may be included in the media, but at a minimum they put the type of news coming from a correctional agency in perspective; there are good things as well as bad things that occur. And finally it is important to give media representatives access to prisons and other correctional programs. Just like every other citizen who has not seen a prison, they look and feel much better than envisioned. Doing media tours when there is nothing to report on helps them understand what you are trying to do and builds relationships that can be helpful in times of crisis.

The Importance of Evaluating Outcomes

A final point of focus for managing the external environment is the importance of evaluating outcomes. Chapters 15 and 16 discuss current evaluative findings and what this will mean in terms of support for rehabilitation. However, when it comes to managing the external environment accountability is as significant as outcome. As suggested in the introduction of this chapter, we are in an era of accountability, and especially as budget shortages increase, officials are searching for the most cost-effective outcomes to target resources. There will no longer be the idea of "trust the experts" that this will work and is a good use of taxpayer money. Today, people want results, and to build credibility and gain support, correctional administrators must know and themselves target resources toward programs that prove effective.

But this is also a time of a renewed interest in rehabilitation. Not only are people looking at the short term as to whether surveillance in the community or long sentences best protect them through a focus on deterrence and incapacitation. They now also want to know if rehabilitative programs work to protect them in the long term through offenders having skills and opportunities other than a return to crime. **Cost-benefit analysis** for all types of things (does increased pay reduce turnover for correctional employees and save money or does an investment in technology reduce the need for staff and provide an acceptable return on investment) are now important for correctional administrators.[22]

For years, corrections officials have been hampered in attempting to argue for programs without good research data to confirm that what they do is effective. Since the 1970s when Robert Martinson wrote about what worked and argued that "nothing works," correctional officials have been on the defensive.[23] Corrections is a big business, with billions of dollars directed to the operation of correctional agencies. Yet, there has been very little information to prove which programs are effective or which archaic programs, such as chain gangs, are ineffective. Allen Ault, former commissioner of corrections in three states and former chief of the NIC National Academy of Corrections noted,

I do not believe that we in corrections will ever be a "profession," or that we in it will ever be considered professionals or listened to by the public or the politicians, until we have our own body of knowledge—the distinction of a profession—that is backed by solid research. We have adapted other knowledge from many other professions and attempted to apply it in the correctional setting, but too often we did not have any research component to consider if it worked or not. It is hard to sell programs when you do not have facts to back up their effectiveness.[24]

We now have sound research studies that can show the effectiveness of correctional activities and programs. There is evidence that shows a relationship between drug programming, job readiness classes, and education that link program completion with reduced criminality.[25] We know that a focus only on surveillance does not improve the success or reduce the risk of community offenders reoffending. For correctional administrators to have credibility with the external environment, it is important to know and be able to describe the results of program effectiveness and to be able to use data to argue for correctional programs they believe improve their ability to manage or reduce recidivism.

SUMMARY

This chapter has dealt with an issue that was not even of interest to correctional administrators fifty years ago, managing the external environment. The outside world of the media, public, and elected officials had little concern for prisons and community corrections until only a few decades ago. This has intensified as public budgets have gotten more tight and public officials are looking at ways to reduce costs. And corrections is one of the major spenders of taxpayer money. This brings debate as to what are the most important policies and what value do they bring to public safety or rehabilitation of offenders.

In this chapter, we have discussed the key elements in the external environment, including public opinion, politics and correctional policy, and the news media. All these are intertwined and influence one another. And without the correctional administrator proactively involved and knowing how to work within each one, messages are sent; opinions made; and positions taken that cannot be changed later on. The message of this chapter for the correctional administrator is that you either need to know how and contribute to the shaping of opinions and policies or you will be left in the dust and the world you work in will go on without your involvement.

Yet, managing the external environment requires skills that most correctional administrators do not develop through their normal job duties. While these are important, there are often few training programs or formal developmental activities that administrators can sign up for. These require taking the initiative for self-development and building programs yourselves in many cases. There are many media relations courses, but few that provide good training on how to shape public opinion or influence the political process or policy making. Yet, individuals who do not build their skills to do these things will not succeed as a modern-day correctional administrator.

KEY TERMS

External environment	Responsibility model	Media relations
Public opinion	First rule of politics	Cost-benefit analysis
Community service		

YOU'RE THE CORRECTIONAL ADMINISTRATOR

1. You are the director of corrections for a state that has severe budget crisis and you have been asked to take many cuts without reducing quality. You believe you can do this to a certain extent, but expect it will not be the last request and you are afraid if the cuts go much deeper, you will not be able to continue to operate without reducing safety and security within your prisons. The governor's office has told you that you have to make the first rounds of cuts, but has given you permission to try to educate legislators as to the potential problems that could result if further cuts are required. What do you do to educate legislators? What is your key message, where do you start, who do you talk to, and what outcome do you expect to have? You will also be asked to testify before the Budget Committee of the legislature in three weeks. Outline the key points you will make in your testimony.

2. You are the Public Information Officer for a state department of corrections. You have had many incidents in the prisons and several high visibility crimes committed by offenders on parole. The reporters are becoming increasingly hostile when they call and question why so many things are going wrong. They have even suggested that perhaps your boss should be fired. What do you do to restore confidence in the department? Outline the way you would go about it to include actions you would take, messages you would communicate, and ways you would try to become more proactive.

WEB LINK EXERCISES

Go the Minnesota Department of Corrections media policy http://www.media-policy. org/law-enforcement.html

Scroll to the Minnesota Department of Corrections. See the MCOD policy on *Media Contacts*—read the policy. Does it meet your ideals of a public agency in dealing with the media? What is particularly good about the policy and what may be not so good? Do you think it complies with the ACA standards for a prison media policy? (Note near the top of the policy the reference to the ACA standard).

GROUP EXERCISES

Each group will be assigned one of the following external stakeholders and present how (good and bad) and to what degree they influence the operations of a correctional environment: media, state legislators, local citizens, inmate family members, and volunteers.

ENDNOTES

1. Roderick Q. Hickman, "Politics, Power, the Press and Prisons," *Corrections Today* 69 no. 1 (February 2007): pp. 46–48.

2. Richard P. Seiter, *Contemporary Issues in Corrections*, unpublished monograph prepared for the National Institute of Corrections (Washington, DC: U.S. Department of Justice, 2000).

3. An interview with Senator DeWine is in Richard P. Seiter, *Corrections: An Introduction* (Upper Saddle River, NJ: Pearson Education, 2011), pp. 507–508. In addition, see Mike DeWine, "Public Opinion and Corrections: A Need to Be Proactive," *Correctional Management Quarterly* 1 no. 3 (1997): 6–9.

4. Sourcebook of Criminal Justice Statistics, Table 2.33.2009, "Attitudes Toward Level of Crime in the United States." Adapted with permission from The Gallup Organization by SOURCEBOOK staff, http://www.gallup.com/poll/1603/Crime.aspx (accessed December 16, 2009).

5. Ibid.

6. Barry Krisberg and Susan Marchionna, "Attitudes of U.S. Voters Toward Prisoners Rehabilitation and Reentry Policies," *Focus: Views from the National Council on Crime and Delinquency* (San Francisco, CA: NCCD, April 2006).

7. Ibid.

8. S. E. Skovan, J. E. Scott, and E. T. Cullen, "Prison Crowding: Public Attitudes Toward Strategies of Population Control," *Journal of Research in Crime and Delinquency* 25 no. 2 (1988): 150–169.

9. Barbara A. Sims, "Questions of Corrections: Public Attitudes toward Prison and Community-Based Programs," *Corrections Management Quarterly* 1 no. 1 (1997): 54.

10. Alison Lawrence, *Cutting Corrections Costs: Earned Time Policies for State Prisoners*, (Washington, DC: National Conference of State Legislatures, 2009).

11. See this interview in Seiter, *Corrections*, 2011.

12. Richard P. Seiter, "A Rebirth of Rehabilitation: The Responsibility Model," *Corrections Management Quarterly* 2 no. 1 (1998): 89–92.

13. John D. Rees, "A Lesson in Political Reality," *A View from the Trenches: A Manual for Wardens by Wardens*, 2nd ed. (Annapolis Junction, MD: American Correctional Association, 2007), p. 4–10.

14. Thomas D. Stucky, Karen Heimer, and Joseph B. Lang, "Partisan Politics, Electoral Competition and Imprisonment: An Analysis of States Over Time," *Criminology* 43 no. 1 (February 1005): 211–248.

15. Judith Simon Garrett, "Political Involvement in Penal Operations," in *Prison and Jail Administration: Practice and Theory*, edited by Peter M. Carlson and Judith Simon Garrett (Gaithersburg, MD: Aspen Publishers, 1999), p. 440.

16. Chase Riveland, "The Correctional Leader and Public Policy Skills" *Corrections Management Quarterly* 1 no. 3 (1997): 22–25.

17. John D. Rees, "Working with the Legislative Process," *A View from the Trenches: A Manual for Wardens by Wardens*, 2nd ed. (Annapolis Junction, MD: American Correctional Association, 2007), pp. 4-11–4-12.

18. Hickman, "Politics, Power, the Press and Prisons," pp. 47–48.

19. *Pell v. Procunier*, 417 U.S. 817 (1974).

20. *Saxbe v. Washington Post*, 417 U.S. 843 (1974).

21. Gerald W. Garner, "Surviving the Circus: How Effective Leaders Work Well with the Media," *Police Chief* 76 no. 3 (March 2009): pp. 52, 54, 57.

22. A good article discussing cost-benefit analysis can be found in James Austin, "Myths and Realities in Correctional Cost-Benefit Analysis," *Corrections Today* 72 no. 1 (February 2010): 54–57.

23. Douglas S. Lipton, Robert Martinson, and Judith Wilds, *The Effectiveness of Correctional Treatment: A Survey of Treatment Evaluation Studies* (New York: Praeger, 1975).

24. Richard P. Seiter. "Managing Within Political Comfort Zones: An Interview with Allen Ault," *Corrections Management Quarterly* 1 no. 1 (1997): 74–75.

25. For a good overview of the results of correctional treatment in reducing recidivism, see Gerald G. Gaes, Timothy F. Flanagan, Laurence L. Motiuk, and Lynn Stewart, "Adult Correctional Treatment," in *Prisons*, edited by Michael Tonry and Joan Petersilia (Chicago, IL: The University of Chicago Press, 1999), pp. 361–426.

12

Managing Security in Prisons

Introduction

What, in a prison, can be more basic and essential than maintaining security? An often stated saying in a prison is "24–7," referring to the fact that prisons are operational twenty-four hours per day, seven days per week. Inmates must live in the prison and endure the environment twenty-four hours per day, seven days per week. Staff usually work only forty hours per week, but still relate to 24–7 as they understand that the environment during the time they are there is impacted by events that occur in the prison at any other time. If there is a breakdown in security or a conflict between two inmate groups on a Sunday at 8:00 P.M., the staff working the "day-watch" on Monday may have to deal with the results of that breakdown or conflict. In every sense, maintaining prison security is a 24–7 responsibility.

What are the key elements for managing security within a prison? There are no simple solutions to how to maintain safety and security, and it is getting more difficult to do so. Inmates are serving longer sentences, often have little hope for quick release, and may have few incentives for positive behavior. Long sentences can also create frustration and a sense of bitterness among inmates toward staff. The increasing percentage of the inmate population that are youthful, impulsive, and gang affiliated heightens the likelihood of violence,[1] and increased violence and fighting by inmates not only undermines a safe environment but also contributes to the development of a violent inmate subculture, which results in a downward spiral of fear and danger for staff and inmates.[2]

Maintaining a safe and secure prison involves the integration of several elements within the prison. As noted in a National Institute of Corrections (NIC) document, "Good sight lines, integrated with sound security hardware and reliable technology have become the hallmarks of efficient, safe, secure, and humane correctional housing and they serve to balance cost effectiveness, ease of maintenance, and efficient use of staff resources."[3] Yet, this alone is not enough to ensure a successful security program. The NIC document continues,

> The most innovative design and advanced technology cannot substitute for well-trained staff and good security practices that are based in comprehensive security policies, procedures, regulations, and rules that are clearly written, standardized, and fully implemented. And even then, without a well-planned, comprehensive monitoring program, effective security practices cannot be sustained over the long term.[4]

In this chapter, there is extensive discussion of the elements necessary for prison safety and security. It is first essential to design a prison that provides sound physical security and a management style that aids in promoting security. And, there is the opportunity to use technology to complement physical security and enhance security. Second, prisons must have appropriate written policies and procedures that are fully implemented and monitored. Third, inmate accountability involves knowing where inmates are supposed to be at any given time of the day and ensuring they are where they are supposed to be. Next, there must be control of contraband, those items that pose a risk for escape or undermine prison security. For managing inmates, there must be a fair inmate disciplinary system, and staff must constantly monitor and suppress gang activity. Finally, there must be preparation for the worst, and although prison administrators hope they never have to call on them, there must be preparation for and emergency response teams to manage prison riots or disturbances.

The Design of Prisons

The importance of the architectural design of prisons cannot be overstated. When planning the architecture for a new prison, the management philosophy of the correctional agency should dictate the way the prison is designed. Once the prison is built, correctional administrators have to manage in a way consistent with the layout of the prison. Although some minor modifications may be possible, the type or design of housing units, the location of the buildings within the secure perimeter, and even the perimeter itself mandate certain operational and staffing patterns.

Prison architecture has evolved slowly over the past 150 years. There have been few major changes since the first prisons were built in the United States in the early 1800s. The first U.S. prison was the Walnut Street Jail in Philadelphia, Pennsylvania, which was not designed as a prison. An existing wing of the jail was converted to house the first offenders receiving a term of incarceration as punishment for their crimes. The philosophy of the Walnut Street Jail was toward prisoner reformation, and the main activities were for inmates to read the Bible, work, and reflect on their behavior, all done alone in their cells. In fact, the Walnut Street Jail maintained a totally **separate system**, with single cells and total isolation of prisoners from one another. Therefore, the design and operation of the facility was focused on preventing contact between prisoners.

This emphasis on a "separate system" continued as Pennsylvania built the Western State Penitentiary in Pittsburgh, which opened in 1826. In planning for the facility, there was to be little movement out of cells by prisoners; cells were very small and designed on the "inside" of the cell blocks so that inmates would not face each other. However, the small and dark inside cells were quickly found lacking, because inmates could perform little work. The state legislature quickly modified the operational plan and approved changes to allow inmates to perform labor. The original cells were torn down in 1833 and replaced with larger "outside" cells.

In the early days of prison design, both inside and outside cell designs were "linear"; the cells were arranged side-by-side in one long row. With inside cell design, the cells back up to one another, with a corridor for staff movement around the cells, between the cell fronts and the cell block walls. With **outside cells**, the staff corridor is between the two rows of cells, which face each other and are abutted to the wall. The **inside cells** are considered more secure, because inmates attempting escape would have to both get out of their cells and get through the cell block walls. With outside cell arrangements, each cell usually has its own window, and there is only one barrier between the inmate and breaking out of the cell block.

Learning from the mistakes of the Western Penitentiary, Pennsylvania later built the Eastern Penitentiary outside of Philadelphia. The design included larger outside cells, so inmates could perform work in their cells, yet the separate system with no communication between inmates was maintained. The Eastern Penitentiary was constructed using the **radial design,** in which the cell blocks extended from a central hub, although there was still a linear array of cells within the blocks. Figure 12-1 illustrates inside cell, outside cell, and radial designs.

The state of New York, in planning its own construction and operation of prisons, was impressed with the reported success of the Pennsylvania system of separate confinement. In 1816, the state legislature authorized the construction of a prison in Auburn, New York, based on the Pennsylvania design and operations. Initially opened in 1819 using the Pennsylvania silent and separate model, the prison was marked by inmate idleness, sickness, insanity, and suicide, and it was quickly determined a failure. By 1822, the Auburn administrators created a new approach to operations. Inmates remained in their cells at night, but during the day, they worked with other inmates in common areas. They continued the emphasis on silence to prevent contamination between inmates, however, and enforced strict discipline through use of the whip and solitary confinement. The **congregate system** of the Auburn prison became the model for many other states; it was copied by almost thirty prisons built and opened before 1850.

A more modern prison design is campus style. Campus style prisons were initiated by the Federal Bureau of Prisons (BOP) and were first used at the Federal Correctional Institutions in Morgantown, West Virginia; Pleasanton (now called Dublin), California; and Miami, Florida. In campus designs, the buildings are separated and spread out within the secure perimeter. It is believed that forcing inmates to move from one building to another, walking outside instead of within a corridor, has a positive effect on the environment of the prison. Also, with the decentralized location of the buildings, there is little inmate congestion as they move through the prison, reducing the likelihood of tension.

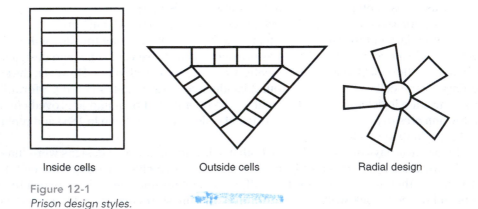

Inside cells   Outside cells   Radial design

Figure 12-1
Prison design styles.

As the benefits of the campus style of prisons became better known, this model was adopted by several states. The following case study is an excellent description of an administrator's challenge in moving from the old style of prison design to a campus style design, incorporating the benefits, and having prison design consistent with the desired operational philosophy.

Practical Perspectives

In with the New, Out with the Old

A new director of corrections was appointed in a fairly large state; she knew the state needed to become more progressive and modern in its correctional philosophy. The Department of Corrections was facing many challenges, among them a rapidly growing inmate population and the need for significant prison expansion. The state legislature had approved a $550 million prison construction program, and the outgoing administration had hired architects and initiated designs for the first two prisons.

The state had not built a new prison in almost twenty years, and the last prison (a maximum security prison) was a telephone-pole design with a linear array of cells in the cell blocks. When the new director arrived at the department, she was quickly visited by the architects for the first prison, which was a 1,250-bed, medium security prison with a budget of $60 million. This new facility had already been designed in a telephone-pole style, very much like the last prison constructed in the state. The state was very traditional and conservative in their style of prison management, and every prison in the state was in a telephone-pole design. The director wanted to change to a campus style design, but in meetings with the architects, was told how they could not make the modifications to the design work that was already completed. She was told that the design work (with a $2 million fee) was almost complete. The dilemma was how to get the type of design consistent with the management approach that the director wanted to instill in the department without wasting the $2 million already spent on design work.

The director sought the advice of associates who had designed campus style prisons in other states and the BOP. She asked these associates if they thought the completed design could be modified, and what the additional design and construction costs might be. She was told that a change from the current design to campus style would be almost impossible, and the changes still would not have the overall benefit

of campus style management she desired. So the director asked the associates for their cost estimates for design and construction if the entire plan was started from scratch, incorporating a campus style.

The rough estimates were that the design costs would again be close to $2 million, but the prison could probably be constructed for $54 million. Even with starting over, the total cost would be approximately $58 million, which included the original $2 million for the first design, the second design of another $2 million, and construction cost of $54 million. Although it was both a financial (depending on whether bids were received to construct the prison for $54 million) and public relations risk, the new director decided to scrap the first design and commission a new design for a campus style prison. The original architects were committed to the telephone-pole design (the same architects also designed the last prison built in the state) and were not supportive of the decision. They even complained to friends in the governor's office and state legislature about the director's decision to "throw out $2 million of design fees."

However, the director was determined and convinced the governor to let her proceed with the new design. Finally, the new prison was built for $54 million, both saving money and resulting in the style of prison consistent with direct supervision and unit management as was planned to be implemented by the new director. When the decision was final, the entire department staff welcomed it, knowing that the new director could handle pressure from politically influential groups and that the campus design would allow for progressive changes in how the state managed their prisons. The rest of the new prisons were built based on this campus model. Fifteen years later, the Department of Corrections considers this change in design and philosophy a turning point in their administration and management, from a very traditional to a more progressive and professional style.

As the campus design was used more regularly, a further refinement came into being. As illustrated in Figure 12-2, the campus design was modified to take advantage of potential cost savings. Instead of each area of the prison being a separate building, some buildings are put together to use common walls and a common roof. An example of this style of architecture is the Federal Correctional Institution (FCI) in Greenville, Illinois. At FCI Greenville, one large programs and operations building includes space for maintenance, food/inmate services, vocational training, education, Unicor (industries), and passive recreation. As the "footprint" of FCI Greenville illustrates, the prison is still a campus style, even with these several activities sharing a common roof and walls.

Another development in prison design that is often used in campus designs is **podular designs**, which are considered to have several advantages over linear designs. They provide common areas in the center of the unit (called dayrooms), in which inmates

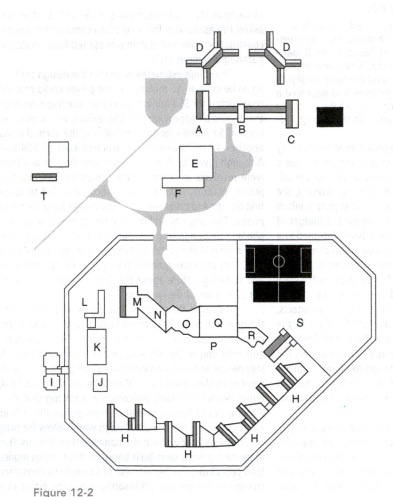

LEGEND

PRISON CAMP
A - Administration/Visiting
B - Food Service/Medical/
    Education
C - Active Recreation
D - Housing Building

SHARED FACILITIES
E - Central Warehouse
F - Vehicle Maintenance
T - Staff Training Facility

MEDIUM SECURITY FACILITY
H - Housing Units
I - Administration Building
J - Visiting Area
K - Medical Facilities
L - Special Housing
M - Institution Maintenance
N - Food Service/
    Inmate Services
O - Vocational
P - Educational
Q - Unicor Factory
R - Passive Recreation
S - Active Recreation

Figure 12-2
The design of FCI Greenville.
Source: Federal Bureau of Prisons, *Greenville Federal Correctional Institution* (Washington, DC: U.S. Department of Justice, no date), p. 3.

can watch television or play table games during the day, thus getting out of their cells and reducing idleness and tension. Podular designs also make it easier for officers to view inmate activity in the cells as well as the dayroom from one central location. And podular designs easily lend themselves to the use of direct supervision of inmates. Podular housing units often use a "triangle" design, and two triangles can be connected by central staff offices and record storage areas, creating a "bow tie," as illustrated in the housing building in Figure 12-3.

Direct Supervision

A very positive development in prison design is the use of **direct supervision** in inmate housing buildings. Direct supervision is both physical, in that it improves the lines of site for inmate monitoring, and philosophical, in that it puts staff in direct contact with inmates during most of the day. In a direct supervision design, inmate cells are situated around the outside of the building, with staff offices, showers, and quiet recreation rooms interspersed among the cells. During the day, cell doors are kept unlocked, and inmates may move from their cells into the open, central day room space where there may be televisions,

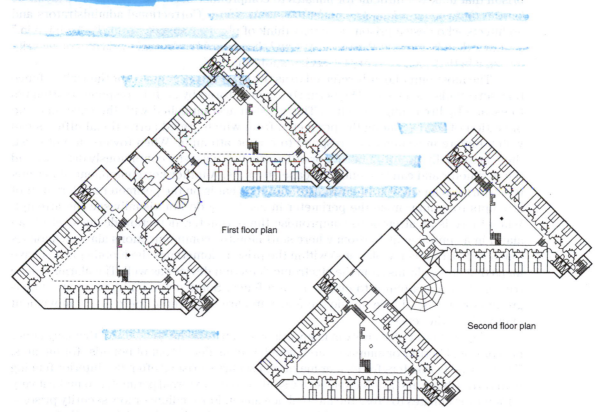

First floor plan

Second floor plan

Figure 12-3
Podular design of prison housing units.
Source: Federal Bureau of Prisons, *Greenville Federal Correctional Institution* (Washington, DC: U.S. Department of Justice, no date), p. 8.

tables for writing, and cards or other games. Correctional officers move freely with inmates in the day room and can easily see into cells. The cells seldom are more than two tiers high to facilitate supervision and inmate movement. This design is ideal for unit management, because staff offices are located among the cell locations and make staff easily accessible to inmates.

The design of a prison greatly contributes to the management style desired by administrators. Most contemporary prisons use the campus style of design, because it is compatible with unit management and disperses inmates across a large area within the secure perimeter. Once administrators have decided on the architecture of a new prison, they can then create programs and operations that compliment the design and contribute to the secure and safe management of the prison.

Physical Security of Prisons

Prison physical security results from the inclusion of certain physical features within a prison that makes it difficult for inmates to compromise security. Prisons have layers of barriers between the inmate population and freedom. Correctional administrators and architects who design prisons generally think of physical security from the "outside in," meaning they begin with the perimeter, and then consider the various layers of security working in that are necessary for each institution.

The most outer layer is referred to as the **perimeter security** or the wall or fence that surrounds the prison. The perimeter is monitored by staff to respond to attempts to escape by breaching the fence. This is often accomplished with the existence and operation of **towers** along the perimeter, from which armed correctional officers can watch inmate movement and respond to escape attempts. When towers do not exist, there are usually **mobile patrols**, or officers in vehicles who continuously drive around the perimeter and can respond to escape attempts. Another key component of perimeter security is an **electronic detection device** that is on the perimeter to alert staff of attempts to compromise the perimeter in case they do not visually see the attempt. When there is an attempt to compromise the perimeter, detection devices set off an alarm in a central control room where staff monitor communications alarm responses (such as fire or fence violations) within the prison. Sometimes the mobile patrols have maps that show alarms from the electronic detection devices as well. The alarms can be triggered by any attempt to climb or cut a fence. Some detection devices are underground or at ground level inside the fence and are triggered if there is any movement encroaching the fence.

The next layer of security in many prisons is an **internal perimeter** that may either be a physical barrier or simply an area which is considered "out of bounds" for inmates. The internal perimeters for high or maximum security prisons often use interior fencing with razor ribbon and a detection device similar to the external perimeter to make it very difficult for inmates to cross the internal perimeter. For medium or low security prisons, the internal perimeter acts more like a boundary, with "slow down" fences that are not physically imposing or difficult to cross. Both inmates and staff know inmates are not to cross the internal perimeter, and it is a violation of the rules for them to do so and would be considered an attempt to escape.

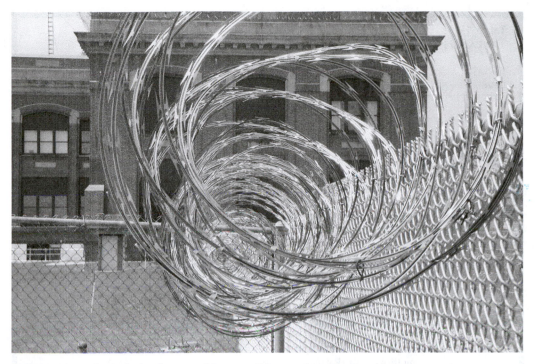

Perimeter security includes fences with razor ribbon to keep inmates from attempting to cross over or climb it.
(Courtesy of the Corrections Corporation of America.)

Finally, prison housing buildings for inmates include a **secure envelop,** which is designed to hold inmates in a building or cell, both to make escape difficult and to isolate them from other inmates or staff during certain periods of the day. Housing is either **dormitory style**, with several beds (often double bunk beds) lined up in one room, or cells in which one or two inmates live. In addition to the layering of physical security, other security considerations for a prison include the type and amount of lighting after dark, the type of building materials that make up walls and other barriers, whether there are interior corridors for inmate movement or whether inmates move freely in an outside area, the location and design of posts for staff supervision, and how technology (such as camera detection or electronic cell and other door-opening devices) is integrated into the physical design of the prison. Table 12-1 illustrates the coordination of various elements of physical security to security levels assigned to prisons.

Technology can be a valuable element of physical security. There are high-tech systems that use global positioning satellite (GPS) systems and can identify where all inmates in a prison are at any time. There are systems that conduct retina scans to ensure proper identification of inmates or staff. There are also electrified fences that deliver a lethal charge of current to anyone coming in contact with the fence. All of California's high-security prisons use this type of perimeter fence to help reduce escape attempts.

Table 12-1
TYPICAL DESIGN FEATURES OF FACILITY SECURITY

Security Levels	I	II	III	IV	V
Perimeter	None	Single fence	Double fence and/or unarmed "posts"	Double fence secure entrance/exits	Same as IV and/or wall and secure entry/exits
Towers[1]	None	None[1]	Combination	Combination of intermittent tower and/or patrol surveillance	Same as IV with tower and/or patrol surveillance
External patrol	None	Intermittent	Yes	Yes	Yes
Detection devices	None	Optional	Yes, at least one type	Yes, more than one type	Yes, extensive
Housing	Single rooms and/or multiple rooms or dorms	Single rooms and/or multiple rooms or dorms	Single cells or rooms	Single outside or inside cells	Single inside cells
Lighting	Minimal	Some lights on perimeter and interior	Entire perimeter and interior compound illuminated	High-intensity illumination of all perimeter and interior areas	High-intensity illumination of all perimeter and interior areas

[1]Towers may be used for control of traffic and/or pedestrian movement.
Source: James D. Henderson, W. Hardy Rauch, and Richard L. Phillips, *Guidelines for the Development of a Security Program*, 2nd ed. (Lanham, MD: American Correctional Association, 1997), p. 21.

Perhaps the most commonly used and useful technology is the integration of camera surveillance with inmate movement, the design of buildings, and the availability of staff supervision. Camera surveillance can aid in the supervision and monitoring of sensitive and high-risk areas of the prison, such as the pharmacy, special housing units (SHU), and entrance and exit gates. Cameras may also be used to assist in surveillance of high-density inmate activity, such as the recreation yard, dining room, or housing units. Most camera systems also provide continuous videotaping, and the videotapes can be reviewed to identify inmates and help investigate particular incidents.

A popular use of technology is to make prison staff safer. The National Institute of Justice reported that technology can make corrections work safer with body armor to protect staff from stabbings, devises to detect drugs in the mail, and technology to monitor inmate behavior.[5] An example is Staff Alarm and Inmate Tracking (SAINT), which pinpoints the location and nature of problems such as an assault on an officer within seconds of its occurrence. There are also duress alarms that can be worn by officers, which can be triggered by the officer or automatically goes off if the officer is knocked down. When triggered, it not only sends an alarm but also identifies the location on a map of the prison and can direct a pan-and-tilt camera to automatically focus on that spot and begin recording.[6] These types of systems are believed to be a deterrent to assault by inmates and provide a stronger perception of safety by staff working in a prison.

Physical Security by Level of Prison

Physical security is matched to the classification level, as noted in Table 12-1. No state is exactly the same in their definition of security level or in their specific guidelines as to what physical security should be used with each level, but the following examples indicate some common approaches. Terminology of security levels varies, and some states will have as few as three or as many as six categories of security. For purposes of illustration, the following five categories are used: Level I (minimum), Level II (low), Level III (medium), Level IV (close), and Level V (maximum).

Level I, or **minimum security,** prisons are used to house those offenders who pose no serious risk for violence or escape; if they do escape (walk away), there is little risk to or concern by the community about their being at large. Such offenders are usually nonviolent, first offenders, white-collar offenders, or those who have spent most of their sentence at a higher-security level with good behavior. As such, they have an "investment" on their sentences and they would not choose to escape and face additional charges and an additional sentence. Therefore, at Level I prisons there is usually no perimeter fence of any kind; the only thing keeping inmates in the prison is their knowledge that violating the privilege of being in minimum security will cause an additional sentence or movement to a higher-security prison.

Without a concern for escape, physical security is almost totally absent, because it would be inefficient to spend much money on expensive and secure construction. Walls, even in housing units, are of commercial or residential construction to keep costs down. Housing styles are usually multiple room or open dormitory, which are much less expensive to construct than cells. There is little use of security, and if there are cameras, they are to monitor traffic, and sometimes to keep "outsiders" from entering the prison grounds. The most significant risk at this level of prison is the likelihood that inmates will have someone bring prohibited substances (such as drugs or alcohol) into the prison.

Level II, or **low security,** prisons hold inmates who have committed more serious crimes and who may have a minor history of violence. Like minimum security, there may also be inmates who have demonstrated good behavior at a higher-security prison or those who have violated the rules at a minimum security facility and have been reassigned to low. This level of security will have a single, or sometimes double, fence, sometimes with a detection device and mobile patrols. The perimeter security is often not enough to prevent serious and well-planned escape attempts but is enough to avoid the impulsive act of walking away that can occur at minimum security prisons. Housing in low security prisons is usually either dormitory or multiple-occupancy rooms similar to minimum security. The walls of the housing units may use security construction features such as reinforced concrete and windows with bars.

Level III, or **medium security**, prisons are those that house inmates who are violent and escape risks. In many states and the federal correctional system, inmates in medium security prisons may be serving average sentences of ten to twelve years and often may have prior sentences of incarceration. The perimeter security at medium prisons is designed to stop escape attempts or at least make them very difficult. The standard perimeter has two twelve-foot-high fences with several rolls of **razor ribbon** hanging from the fences and stacked between the fences. Razor ribbon can be described as high-technology barbed wire made of stainless steel in a ribbon design with sharp barbs at frequent intervals along the ribbon. When rolled into approximate twenty-four-inch circles and stacked or hung on a fence, individuals who come in contact with razor ribbon will receive many cuts and often their clothes or even their skin becomes entangled in the barbs. Inmates have quickly learned to avoid the razor ribbon, knowing the peril of coming in contact with it. There are detection devices along the perimeter, and mobile patrols and (in some states) towers to monitor the perimeter.

Housing for medium security is usually external cells, adjacent to the outside wall of the housing unit. There is always a preference to have single cells, but many states accept multiple-occupancy cells for medium security prisons. Construction of the housing unit uses reinforced concrete and barred windows, making escape through walls or windows difficult without tools to cut bars or chip away concrete. Cameras are often used to enhance supervision of inmates and monitor areas of the prison that are more important for the overall security operation. Inmate movement is usually across an open area (rather than in corridors), but movement is limited and steel doors keep buildings locked when there is no scheduled movement of inmates.

Level IV, or **close security**, prisons are for the more dangerous and escape prone inmates. The physical security aspects of a close security prison are often the same as a maximum security facility, but it allows for a larger inmate population and, therefore, a greater economy of scale. The larger the population, the more danger there is that a riot could get out of control and the more staff that would be assigned to monitor and supervise inmates. Therefore, only the smallest percentage of the most dangerous and violent inmates are reserved for **maximum security** prisons. The perimeters for both close and maximum will have double fences or walls, with armed gun towers, continuously staffed to monitor movement and prevent escapes. Often there are also mobile patrols and extensive detection devices on the perimeter in case one is not working or inmates are able to avoid detection.

Housing at both levels consists of single cells. Close security might use external cells, whereas maximum security always has internal cells for an extra physical barrier to prevent escape. These security-level prisons may have remote officer stations that are protected and separated from inmates with bars and glass. From these isolated posts, staff observe inmate movement and control electronic door opening and closing. In a few states, some of these inside secure posts are armed, and staff are instructed to use deadly force if violence erupts that threatens staff or other inmates. Inmate movement is often through corridors with several grill gates at intervals along the corridor that can be closed electronically if there is a disturbance. These corridors reduce the freedom of movement by inmates, and if there is a riot, the gates help isolate small groups of inmates who can then be brought under control. Cameras and other high-technology systems are extensively used to monitor inmates. Cameras often have continuous videotaping of activities,

Guard towers on a perimeter have armed staff that oversee the perimeter and will use deadly force if an inmate tries to climb the fence to escape.
(Courtesy of the Corrections Corporation of America.)

so that any rule violations or violence can be reviewed on tape to aid in identifying involved inmates and assisting with prosecution or inmate discipline for the violations or crimes.

As is obvious, physical security is designed to match the risk of violence and escape, and the highest security prisons use extensive layers of physical security to prevent escapes and keep staff and other inmates safe from violent predators. This level of security is very expensive, however, and should not be provided to those inmates who do not need it. In addition, as extensive as some of the physical security may seem, it alone is not enough to create a safe and secure prison environment. There must also be well-developed policies and procedures that are consistently followed and enforced by professional correctional staff.

Security Policy and Procedure

The common vision of a secure prison is "steel and concrete" or the physical security of prisons. Yet, no matter how expensive, how high-tech, or how overlapping the layers of physical security, they can all be compromised if not properly used and monitored. That is where the value of well-written, clearly communicated, and consistently enforced security policies and procedures becomes evident. Inmates can overcome or break through any physical security if given the time and tools. They can find ways to get dangerous and prohibited items (such as weapons and drugs) into a prison if there are not satisfactory checks of packages and individuals who enter a prison. And they can threaten, intimidate, and coerce other inmates if there are not adequate procedures for inmate accountability and control by staff.

There are three key elements to ensure that policy and procedure contribute fully to a safe and secure prison environment. First, policies must be consistent with professional standards. The American Correctional Association (ACA) is the major professional organization for corrections in the United States and publishes standards for all types of correctional practices. Similar to the American Medical Association or the American Bar Association, ACA standards are created by practicing professionals in the field, and are considered best practices for quality prison operations.

All prisons and jails establish their own policy and procedure manual of operations and there is no requirement they meet ACA standards. While it seems trite to suggest that policies and procedures should be written, written policy manuals were not universal in corrections even thirty years ago, and today many practices are passed on by word-of-mouth or informal memos. However, it is critically important to formalize policy in writing and have an official sign and authorize the policy for implementation throughout the facility. By formalizing policy in this manner, it begins the process of communicating it to staff and inmates and facilitates training and discipline of staff and inmates.

The second element of effective policy and procedure is that it should be clearly communicated to staff and inmates. However, there are some policies that are only available for staff. For instance, inmates should not know the tactics staff will use to respond to a disturbance or a riot. However, most nonsensitive policies are available to inmates, so they know what is expected of them and of staff. A failure in policy implementation often occurs when it is assumed that once a policy is adopted, written, and authorized, it will be followed by staff. Policies are used as the basis for training of staff, so that they both know and can perform the duties required by policy.

The third element of effective security policy is to ensure procedures are consistently carried out. Just issuing a policy does not mean that every staff member will follow it, and it is important to monitor its compliance. For instance, many prisons have policies prohibiting smoking in common areas, such as in television rooms. If one correctional officer lets inmates smoke in the television room, it makes enforcement of the policy much more difficult for those who do not allow smoking. It can also cause tensions and fights between inmates who want to smoke and those who do not want to be bothered by smoke. Security policies often relate to issues where inmates should not have a choice, and staff have to make a decision and enforce it. To ensure policy is carried out, there are several methods to monitor compliance. The next section describes some of the quality-assurance practices used in policy monitoring.

Monitoring Policy Compliance

A challenge for correctional administrators is how to ensure compliance with policy. The method most commonly used to monitor policy compliance is through "security audits," a process to determine the extent to which a policy is effectively carried out and contributes to maintaining security in a prison. There are three types of audits of correctional facilities to monitor security operations: an audit of ACA standards, a policy audit, and a security operations audit.[7] As already noted, ACA standards are not required of any jurisdiction. However, if the jurisdiction decides to apply them, they can contract with the American Correctional Association to audit their correctional facilities. With an ACA audit, a team of objective auditors comes to the prison, reviews written policy, and observes procedures. If all standards identified as "life safety" and 90 percent of others are met,

ACA will "accredit" the prison, meaning that it meets standards of professional operations. ACA standards and audits cover the full operation of the prison and not just security standards.

The second type of audit is a policy audit, which ascertains whether broad agency policy is in place at the prison. In most states, the central headquarters of a correctional agency dictates broad policy that must be complied with by each prison. An example of a statewide security policy is that "all vehicles, carts, and equipment must be thoroughly inspected before being allowed to enter or exit a prison." The policy audit would check to see if there was a facility policy in place to implement the statewide policy. A policy audit is valuable to begin an overall review of security operations, but it only identifies whether there are the required scope of written, authorized, and mandated policies at the prison. It does not determine whether the policy is being carried out consistently and in a quality manner.

That type of intensive review is the role of the security operations audit. The security audit identifies whether and how the policies are actually being carried out by correctional staff. While a policy audit is a review of written documents, the security audit is a review of actual operations. It is usually completed by a team of knowledgeable security professionals who can observe the methods by which correctional staff carry out their assignments and identify if there is any lack of compliance with established policy. Even though staff are aware their behavior is being observed during a security audit, such an audit procedure can identify a lack of quality that can result from failure to train staff, use of improper procedures, or misunderstandings about the policy requirements.

A good program of policy and procedure will meet acceptable professional standards, such as those pronounced by ACA, will clearly communicate policy to staff and train them in its implementation, and will audit procedures on a regular basis to ensure compliance. To reiterate, policy and procedure should be well written, clearly communicated, and consistently carried out. With these elements in place, policy and procedure are an integral part of creating a safe and secure prison environment.

Inmate Accountability

Inmate accountability is the ability to know that inmates are following routines and movements and are where they are expected to be at any given time of the day. With inmates out of their cells for almost eighteen hours on a normal day, it is essential to have systems to maintain accountability of where they are supposed to be and to confirm that they are there. In *Guidelines for the Development of a Security Program*, the authors write, "Inmate accountability, the staff's ability to locate and identify inmates at any point in time, is the very heart of institution security, from minimum-security camps to maximum-security penitentiaries."[8] For this textbook, inmate accountability will be more broadly defined, with several categories of activities:

- The availability of program and work opportunities and a process to assign inmates to these opportunities in order to have them under the supervision of staff responsible for that program or work activity.
- A system of movement that reduces the likelihood that inmates may go to other than their assigned locations.

- Both casual and direct inmate supervision during all out-of-cell times.
- Inmate counts at regular and random times to ensure the correct number is in custody and in the location within the prison as assigned.

Program and Work Assignments

In addition to the rehabilitative potential of programs for inmates, they also aid in security by keeping inmates active, providing opportunities for positive interaction between staff and inmates, and helping to pass the time. However, the most important security outcome of inmate assignments is that they result in supervision by staff as inmates are kept under watch throughout the program day.

In most prisons, inmates have work or program assignments for five days per week. Some work activities (such as food service) involve work on the weekends and may not follow the normal Monday through Friday schedule. Each work and program assignment is supervised by a staff member. For example, inmates assigned to participate in an educational program will be assigned to the classroom of a specific teacher, who checks them in at the beginning of the activity and is responsible for them until the end of the assignment. Similarly, inmates working in the maintenance department are assigned to a staff member, who supervises their work as the inmates remain under his or her supervision until the assignment ends for the day. The benefit for inmate accountability is that there are specific correctional staff responsible for inmates who are assigned to them, and the staff maintains continuous supervision of the inmates during that period of time.

Inmate Movements

Inmates do not stay in one location throughout the day. They move in large groups from their housing units to work, to meals, or to educational or recreation programs. As an alternative to total individual movement or unregulated mass movement, many institutions use a "controlled" system of inmate moves. Controlled movement is based on the daily schedule and provides for all inmates to move at the specified time. For example, when the 7:30 A.M. work call is announced, the doors to the housing unit and the program work activity areas will be concurrently unlocked, staff stand at the doors and watch inmates come and go, and inmates have a certain amount of time (usually ten minutes) to go from one location to another. At the end of the ten minutes, the doors are all relocked and inmates must be at their assigned area or be subject to disciplinary action.

The advantage of a controlled movement system is that it limits the times that inmates may be moving or walking around the prison and when they must be monitored. With everyone moving at once, security doors within the prison can remain locked most of the time, allowing for inmates to be isolated in smaller groups if a disturbance breaks out. With a relatively short period of time for a move, inmates cannot stand and talk to other inmates (perhaps to organize gang activities or pass information), and they do not have time to go to an unauthorized area and still get to their designated location. A prison that has an effective controlled movement system is a model of efficiency as doors are unlocked and locked exactly on time. Inmates know they cannot move slowly and miss the movement without getting in trouble for violating a rule. Efficient controlled movement gives staff both real and perceived control over inmates, because they, through subtle and relaxed means, require inmate compliance and obedience to rules.

Controlled movements are when inmates move at a specified time from one prison location to another and then all doors are locked and inmate movement stops.
(Courtesy of Federal Bureau of Prisons)

There are instances when inmates must move individually and may not be able to move at the exact time of a mass movement. For example, they may have a visit from family or an attorney, they may have an appointment with the prison physician, or they may be required to meet with a staff member who is not their work or program supervisor. These individual movements can also be controlled in a variety of ways. Usually, prisons require these institutional appointments to be scheduled at least a day in advance. A **call out** schedule is prepared and distributed to staff with a list of all inmates who have times they are authorized to move to a location other than their usual assignment.

Instead of, or sometimes in addition to a call out, some institutions also use a "pass system" to authorize movement. A prison **pass system** is a form of movement in which an inmate is issued a pass by the work or program supervisor to go to a scheduled appointment. It is similar to that used in many high schools when a teacher issues a pass to a student to leave class and go somewhere. The pass indicates the time an inmate leaves the supervision of the releasing staff, and it is signed by the receiving staff who notes the time the inmate arrives and leaves the appointment. On return to the work or program supervisor, the pass is returned to the staff member, who completes the process by noting the return time. Staff are aware of the time it takes to move from one area of the prison to another and quickly recognize any discrepancy in the times noted on the pass. Staff who see inmates moving ask to see their pass allowing the movement, proving they are authorized to go where they are headed.

Direct and Casual Supervision of Inmates

Another element of inmate accountability is the direct and casual supervision of inmates. As noted, work and program supervisors are responsible for inmates during the times they are assigned to a particular activity, and directly supervise them during these times. Also, inmate accountability is enhanced through casual, as well as direct, supervision. **Casual supervision** is supervision by staff that are not responsible for the inmate but still have the opportunity to watch inmate movement and activity. Well designed prisons take advantage of the benefit for casual supervision. The location of staff offices and windows, and the use of windows in walls between areas of the prison, allow staff to watch inmates as they perform other duties.

The design of a prison educational area is an example of how casual supervision works. Educational administrators have offices with windows that view the prison center yard or compound area, across which inmates move from one location to another. The administrators also have large windows into adjacent classrooms or the library area, so they may casually supervise inmates in those locations and support the supervising staff in case of any confrontations. Classrooms have large windows from the classroom to the interior corridor, adjacent classrooms, and the outside of the building. Teaching staff can watch other inmates, and other staff can see if the teachers are in trouble and need assistance. This ability to see in and out keeps staff from feeling isolated and insecure, as well as providing opportunities for casual supervision of inmates throughout the prison.

Inmate Counts

The final "piece of the puzzle" for inmate accountability is a procedure of counting inmates at varying locations and times of the day. Counts are done to determine that all inmates are where they should be and that no inmates either are out of bounds (in an unauthorized area) or have escaped. There are three types of **prison counts**: regular, census, and random. Regular counts are the scheduled counting of inmates in their housing units to ensure they are in the prison and have not escaped. Because counting is done several times during the day, inmates know they will be quickly discovered missing. ACA standards require a minimum of one count per eight-hour correctional shift; however, most agencies have at least five scheduled counts during a day. These counts usually take place at midnight and 3:00 A.M. when inmates are asleep in their cells, before work call at approximately 7:00 A.M., after return from work for the day (approximately 4:00 P.M.), and when inmates are required to return to their housing units after evening programs or recreation (approximately 9:00 P.M.). These counts not only note the number of inmates to ensure all are present but also identify the inmates (sometimes using cards with pictures of the inmates during the count).

In addition, census counts are less formal counts, conducted by work and program supervisors. They are held at the beginning and end of each work period to ensure that all inmates are in attendance with each work or program detail. A third type of count is the random count, which can be done at any time. Because inmates know when the regular and census counts are held, random counts "keep them honest," so they cannot plan on trying to leave their assigned area right after a count. A warden or other prison executive can call for a random count at any time. When called, all inmates must "freeze" where they are and it can be determined if they are where they are supposed to be.

Control of Contraband

Another essential element of prison security is to control contraband. **Contraband is defined as any item that inmates are not allowed to possess.** Contraband includes those items that can assist in an escape (ladders or ropes), are dangerous (weapons or drugs), can sabotage or subvert prison physical security (chewing gum that can damage locking devices or wire cutters that can cut a security fence), or nuisance items that can promote unhealthy or unsanitary conditions (clothing beyond the issued amount or unsealed food that could spoil in an inmate's cell). All of these categories of contraband can undermine the maintenance of a safe and secure prison environment. Many prison policies and procedures and much staff time is directed toward the control of contraband.

All prisons have policies that identify contraband items that are not allowed in an inmate's possession, or those items that are allowed in certain amounts and the limits for an inmate's possession (e.g., one pair of personally owned athletic shoes or four sets of prison-issued work clothing). In addition, the policies often categorize the risk of certain contraband items, and how they should be handled and stored. Tools used in the maintenance and repair of the prison are often included in such categories. One guideline suggests using a minimum of two categories:

- Class A tools are those, such as files, knives, saw blades, ladders, ropes, extension cords, lift devices, grinders, and others, presenting inherent safety or security risks. Class A tools should be used only under the direct supervision of staff and are always placed in a secure tool storage area when not in use. Poisonous chemicals, dangerous drugs, acids, and hypodermic needles should be controlled with the Class A methods.

- Class B tools, such as light pliers, short power cords, and others, constitute a lower-level of risk. They may be stored, issued, and used under less stringent conditions, but the institution or department must still account for them.[9]

Institution policy also identifies procedures to keep inmates from possessing contraband items and methods to search for contraband. Contraband may end up in the possession of inmates in many ways. First, they may receive prohibited items through the usual mail and package procedures. Second, visitors may bring items into the prison. Third, items that are in the prison, but that should not be in the possession of inmates without staff supervision, may be smuggled by inmates out of the area of use or storage. And finally, unethical staff may provide inmates with prohibited items.

Prisons encourage correspondence by inmates with family and friends, and inmates may usually send and receive an unlimited number of letters. Prisons require inmates to pay for their own postage, unless they are indigent, in which case they will be provided with a small number of stamps per month. Mail received in a prison is not read, but it is opened and searched for contraband items. This process takes a tremendous amount of staff time, yet it is critical to keep small items such as drugs from being mailed to a prison.

Many prisons prohibit receiving packages (with food or personal clothing items) from family or friends, because items cannot be searched well enough to find anything that could be concealed in them. Hardback books and magazines may only be ordered and mailed to the inmate directly from the publisher, reducing the opportunity for anyone to hide a small item in the publication.

The visiting area is highest in risk for introducing contraband into a prison setting. Visiting is considered by prison officials as important in order to maintain inmates' ties to their community contacts and in order to accomplish successful reintegration on release. The visiting room is designed to allow as relaxed as possible contact and conversation between inmates and visitors. Only inmates who have proven to be a serious risk for escape or committing violent acts are not accorded contact visiting. Therefore, in the usual visiting setting, it is difficult to control the introduction of contraband such as drugs. Visitors have been known to put drugs in small balloons and pass them to the inmate who swallows the balloon. At a later time, the inmate retrieves the drugs in the balloon when they defecate. As unthinkable as this seems, the value of drugs in a prison make this a method that inmates are willing to endure.

Prisons initially require inmates to list the persons they want to include on their visiting list, and if a proposed visitor has a criminal record, they may be denied the right to visit. Visitors must pass through a metal detector on entry to the prison, and they are permitted to take only limited personal items into the visiting room, such as money and unopened packages of cigarettes. The prisons provide lockers for storage of other personal items such as purses. During the visit, correctional staff (often using camera surveillance for assistance) watch the visiting room and the conduct of inmates and visitors. When the visit is over, inmates are "strip searched" before reentering the prison area. When all visiting is over, the visiting room is searched before any more inmates enter the area.

In local jails and for violent and escape-prone inmates, visiting is "noncontact" and is afforded through glass and telephones. Even in these situations, drugs have been smuggled in, often by inserting a drug-filled straw through the hole where the telephone handset cord enters the wall. A relatively new technology to avoid this is video visitation, allowing inmates to converse with visitors without leaving their housing areas.[10] In these circumstances in which noncontact visiting is an acceptable practice, video visitation reduces the smuggling of drugs and other small items. Video visiting can also reduce staff time. "Prior to the installation of video visitation, Brevard County (Florida) Jail was using four staff members to conduct visitation. Today, only one staff member is assigned to that task."[11]

Inmates often attempt to smuggle items already in the prison out of the allowed area of supervision. An example of contraband that can cause health and sanitation problems is food that is served in the dining room. Inmates may try to get extra food, sell it to others, or keep it for their own use at a later time. More serious contraband includes tools, such as those described as Class A, that are a serious risk to safety and security. Inmates who work in food service often must be issued knives to prepare food. Those who work in a maintenance shop may sometimes be issued pliers that can cut wires. Prison procedures call for several actions to reduce the chance of tools that can aid in escapes or be used in violent acts from falling into an inmate's unauthorized possession.

Class A tools are usually hung on a "shadow board," a light colored background with the outline of the tool painted on it. It is quickly obvious to staff when a tool is missing. When they are issued to inmates, there is a record of which staff issued what tool and the inmate to whom it was issued. As a double check, inmates who work in these areas often have "chits," or small metal or plastic tokens with their names engraved on them, and the chits are hung on the shadow board in place of the tool when it is checked out. Before the end of the work period, all tools must be accounted for and should be placed back on the shadow board before inmates are allowed to leave. And finally, before inmates are released from a work area, they are searched and may have to walk through a metal detector.

Finally, and unfortunately, unethical staff may provide contraband items to inmates. Some staff may do this to make money. Inmates will arrange payment to the staff member by someone in the community if they bring drugs or possibly weapons into the prison. Other naive staff may do it "to be nice," bringing an inmate only nuisance items such as food or cigarettes that an inmate cannot get in prison. After a staff member has agreed to do this, however, manipulative inmates then threaten to tell prison officials about the staff's violation of rules, knowing that the staff member will be punished for violating rules, unless the staff member agrees to bring more serious and dangerous contraband into the prison in exchange for the inmate's silence.

To deter such actions by staff, some prisons search their staff or require them to walk through metal detectors as they come to work. Since staff are well aware of these procedures and can easily avoid detection of bringing contraband into a prison, many prisons do not even attempt such searches. Instead, they rely on hiring the right kind of people and treating staff as trusted professionals, while encouraging all staff to share in the responsibility of identifying staff who may be smuggling items into the prison. Prison training programs for new staff present the dangers of providing contraband to inmates and how it undermines the safety of all staff. Although these efforts work for most staff, there is always a staff member who fails to heed the warning and, whether for money or because of poor judgment, is a target for inmates who try to get them to bring contraband into the prison.

Prison officials not only take many precautions to prevent contraband from getting into the hands of inmates but also require regular efforts to search for contraband that an inmate may have acquired. Every day a considerable amount of time is devoted to searching areas of the prison or shaking down inmates to find contraband and deter its possession. Correctional officers assigned to housing units have postorder requirements to search a certain number of cells every day, and teams of staff may be assigned to an area (such as prison industries or a recreation building) for a complete search. Inmates are randomly selected for shakedowns or frisk searches of their bodies (similar to the standard pat downs performed by police officers on criminal suspects) as they move across the compound. And all inmates leaving work areas where Class A tools are used (food services, maintenance, or industries) are patted down and may have to walk through a metal detector.

Inmate Disciplinary Systems

What does a prison administrator do to encourage inmates to follow the rules? Although it may seem easy to suggest that staff simply "make them do it," this issue requires a complicated system of enforcing discipline among an inmate population. An **inmate disciplinary system** is the process by which correctional staff respond once they become aware of violations of prison rules by inmates. There must be a written policy

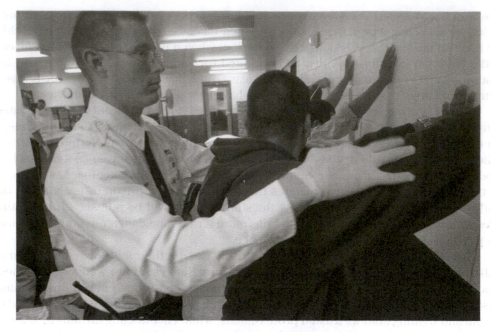

These two photos show staff actions to control contraband. One is performing a "pat down" of inmates and the other is searching property in an inmate cell.
(Courtesy of the Federal Bureau of Prisons and Corrections Corporation of America)

describing behavior that is prohibited and a corresponding list of sanctions based on the rule violation. This policy is communicated and made available to inmates. If a violation is believed to occur, the process includes an accusation of the violation, investigation of the incident, a hearing to determine guilt, and the pronouncement of a sanction if guilt is determined.

Inmate disciplinary processes and policies are guided by the Fourteenth Amendment to the U.S. Constitution, which provides that, "No State shall make or enforce any law which shall abridge the privileges or immunities of citizens of the United States; nor shall any State deprive any person of life, liberty, or property, without due process of law, nor deny any person within its jurisdiction the equal protection of the laws." For inmates, the 1974 case of *Wolff v. McDonnell* created the standards that are still used by most correctional agencies to guide their disciplinary processes.[12] In this case, the Supreme Court differentiated between due process required by a defendant at trial and that of a prison inmate, and identified the following as required prisoner due process rights:

- The right to receive advance written notice of the alleged infraction
- The right to have sufficient time (at least twenty-four hours) to prepare a defense
- The right to present documentary evidence and to call witnesses on his or her behalf, unless permitting this would be unduly hazardous
- The right to have assistance (by an inmate or staff representative) when the circumstances of the case are complex or if the prisoner is illiterate
- The right to a written statement of the findings of an impartial disciplinary committee of the evidence relied on to support the finding of fact and the reasons the disciplinary action was taken

Inmate Discipline Policy and Process

The first component of an inmate disciplinary system is a written policy that documents the specific behavior that is prohibited. This documentation usually explains the process for considering guilt and determining punishments, and the range of punishments that usually result from rule violations. The purpose and scope of the Federal Bureau of Prisons' policy regarding inmate discipline is stated as follows:

> So that inmates may live in a safe and orderly environment, it is necessary for institution authorities to impose discipline on those inmates whose behavior is not in compliance with Bureau of Prisons rules. The provisions of this rule apply to all persons committed to the care, custody, and control (direct or constructive) of the Bureau of Prisons.[13]

The policy lists all prohibited acts by inmates, such as assaulting any person, escaping from custody, possession of weapons, introduction or possession of any narcotic or drug, stealing, and a general statement prohibiting any conduct that disrupts the secure running of an institution. A copy of the policy is provided to every inmate on arrival at a prison, and in most correctional agencies, the inmates sign it indicating that they have received, read, and understood the policy. If the inmate is illiterate or does not speak or read English, the policy is translated. Because many correctional agencies have a large number of Spanish-speaking inmates, inmate disciplinary policies are usually also available in Spanish. The purpose of providing and having inmates sign the policy is to send a clear message that they are responsible for their actions and that sanctions will be taken against rule violators. The fact that inmates were fully informed of prohibited acts also reduces the potential for successful appeals of inmate disciplinary actions before a federal court.

In most correctional systems, the prohibited acts are categorized by severity. In the BOP policy, there are four categories of prohibited acts: greatest, high, moderate, and low moderate.[14] A specific range of sanctions is authorized for each category if the inmate is found to have committed the prohibited act. There is a two-stage disciplinary process, allowing minor violations to be handled in a less formal manner. The policy process also spells out the time frames associated with each step, so inmates know the time available for collecting evidence or seeking assistance (see Figure 12-4).

In the BOP policy, once staff become aware of the inmates' involvement in the violation, they have twenty-four hours to give the inmate written notice (an incident report) of the charges. During this period, there is an investigation of the incident. If, during the investigation, it becomes likely that the incident may result in criminal prosecution for the

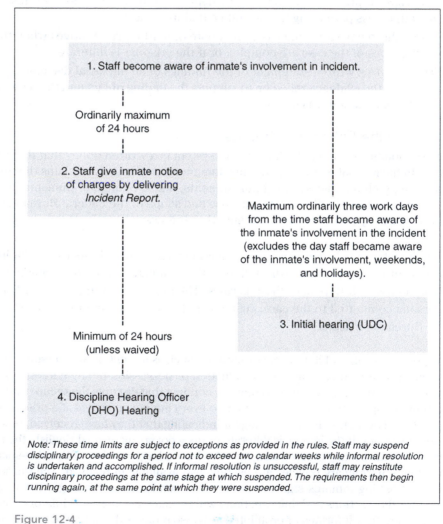

Figure 12-4

Time limits in the inmate disciplinary process.

act, the prison's investigation is suspended, and law enforcement officials are notified to complete the investigation, providing the inmate full due process rights as a criminal offender. When the infraction is minor, the bureau and many other jurisdictions allow correctional officials to use an informal resolution, such as assigning the inmate extra work. On completion of the assignment, the incident report is expunged, and there is no mention of the infraction on the inmate's prison record.

When an incident report is issued to the inmate, there must be an initial hearing within three work days. At this hearing, if the infraction is not serious, the hearing panel (the Unit Disciplinary Committee [UDC] in the BOP; Infractions Board in some states) can determine guilt and impose minor sanctions, such as a loss of privileges. The inmate may be present during the hearing (except during deliberations), may make a statement, and may present documentary evidence. If the violation is more serious and could result in other than minor sanctions (such as a loss of good time, therefore, lengthening the overall time served in prison, disciplinary transfer to another prison, or disciplinary isolation from the general inmate population), the lower panel will refer the case to an upper-level hearing panel, a Discipline Hearing Officer (DHO) in the Bureau of Prisons.[15] In some jurisdictions, this level of hearing panel will not be a staff member of the prison in which the incident took place in order to assure impartiality.

On referral to the DHO, inmates are advised of the rights they will be afforded based on the *Wolff v. McDonnell* standards. A 1995 U.S. Supreme Court case clarified and gave new guidance to circumstances requiring inmate due process. In *Sandin v. Conner*, the Court acknowledged that the purpose of prison disciplinary action is to maintain good prison management and achieve prisoner rehabilitative goals.[16] The Court determined that disciplinary actions in pursuit of those goals that do not add on to the sentence being served or change the conditions contemplated in the sentence being served do not create a liberty interest and do not require due process. Thus, under *Sandin*, placement in disciplinary segregation for a temporary period does not trigger the need for due process, whereas loss of good time extending the sentence does. However, even after the *Sandin* decision, most prisons continued to provide the full *Wolff* due process rights for handling inmate discipline.

Prisons do not allow inmates to use attorneys to assist them in disciplinary hearings but will provide a staff representative to ensure that the inmate understands the process and their rights. Staff may also assist in gathering evidence or speaking to witnesses.[17] The inmate may be present for the hearing, request witnesses who have information directly relevant to the charges, and present evidence.

The DHO considers all evidence presented at the hearing and may find that the inmate either committed or did not commit the prohibited act. A record is made of the proceedings, including the advisement of the inmate rights, the findings, the decision and evidence relied on in the decision, and a statement of the reasons for the sanctions imposed. The inmate is given a copy of the decision shortly after the hearing. The sanctions imposed, if there is a finding of guilt, are carried out immediately, even if the inmate appeals the decision. It would be overly burdensome to delay a sanction of disciplinary segregation or transfer simply because an inmate indicated a plan to appeal. The next section describes the types of punishments available for various degrees of disciplinary infractions.

Punishing Inmates for Rule Violations

To enforce rules and provide a disincentive for commission of prohibited acts, prisons have several sanctions that may be taken against misbehaving inmates. Sanctions can be minor, such as restriction from privileges, or may be serious, such as transfer to a "supermax" prison in which inmates have no freedom of movement and very limited time out of their cells. Table 12-2 lists the types of sanctions (in increasing levels of severity) that are often used to discipline inmates.

Once there is a finding of guilt and imposition of a sanction, the inmate has the opportunity to appeal the disposition. Correctional agencies usually provide an **administrative appeals process**, and federal courts often require inmates to exhaust their administrative remedies before filing for consideration before the court. These administrative appeals are usually at least two levels: The first is for reconsideration by the warden, and if the inmate is not successful, a second level of review is available at the headquarters or central office level of the agency. Because inmates are seldom accepting of any disciplinary sanction and because the appeal procedure is simple and not burdensome, most serious disciplinary sanctions are appealed by inmates.

In most correctional agencies, the appeal cannot dispute a finding of fact and is limited to a complaint regarding the procedure and due process rights. Inmates have a time

Table 12-2
POSSIBLE SANCTIONS RESULTING FROM INMATE DISCIPLINE

Warning

Reprimand

Assignment of extra duty

Restriction to quarters

Impounding of personal property

Loss of job

Removal from program or group activity

Change of quarters

Loss of privileges (recreation or commissary)

Monetary restitution

Withholding good time

Disciplinary segregation

Disciplinary transfer

Placement in supermax prison

limit to appeal, usually thirty days after notice of the decision. In describing the review process, Cripe provides the following description:

> The records (the disciplinary offense report, the investigation report, and the written report of the hearing officer or committee) are examined, to be sure that the procedures required by the agency's disciplinary policy have been followed. The facts of the case and the sanction imposed are summarily reviewed. There must be some evidence to support the finding of the disciplinary authority. The reviewer ensures that the sanction imposed is within the range of punishments authorized for that offense. There is a legal requirement that the hearing officer or committee record the evidence relied on to support the conclusion reached, and that the reasons for the sanction(s) imposed be given.[18]

Although few disciplinary decisions are overturned in the review process, this process is important to maintain credibility and fairness in the system. In some cases, federal courts will review the appeal process and ensure that appeals are examined as suggested. The courts may examine if, in those instances in which the prison staff did not provide appropriate due process or have sufficient evidence to support the finding of guilt, the appeal process does overturn the decision. If the appeals do not overturn decisions in which there are errors, the courts are likely to accept inmate appeals for consideration. An impartial appeal process promotes acceptance by inmates and prevents expensive and burdensome reviews of disciplinary decisions by federal courts. It also provides an avenue to relieve inmate frustrations and tensions.

Special Housing Units of a Prison

An essential tool for a prison administrator is the ability to temporarily separate inmates believed to be a danger to prison security, or in danger themselves, from the general inmate population. Therefore, prisons have a separate housing area, often referred to as a **special housing unit(SHU)**, which serves a similar function to jails in the community. Like a jail, an SHU holds inmates in two general situations: when they are under investigation as a result of an incident or potential incident (administrative detention) and when they are serving a sentence for violating prison rules (disciplinary segregation). An SHU should only be a temporary housing assignment, even though the length of stay could be as long as twelve months. If there is a need for a longer separation from a prison's inmate population, the inmate will usually be moved to another prison.

Administrative detention is a "non-punitive confinement used to house inmates whose continued presence in the general population may pose a serious threat to life, property, self, staff, or other inmates, or to the security or orderly running of the institution."[19] Before inmates can be placed in administrative detention, they must be provided notice of the reasons for placement, with a reasonable degree of detail to facilitate their understanding of those reasons. There are at least three specific categories of placement in administrative detention.

First, inmates may be charged with violating serious rules in the prison, and allowing the inmates to remain in the general prison population threatens prison security or order. Second, if staff have a reasonable suspicion that an inmate was involved in the

A standard SHU cell is very secure with a steel toilet, sink, and mirror with a metal bed bolted to the wall and floor. The cell and furnishings are resistant to inmates breaking them or using them for weapons.
(Ohio Dept. of Rehabilitation and Corrections)

incident but need more time to determine what occurred, they will hold that inmate in administrative detention until an investigation is completed. Third, inmates may be placed in administrative detention for their own safety. If inmates believe they are in danger, they will usually be placed in administrative detention while the seriousness of the threat is determined and a decision made as to protecting them.

The other SHU placement is for **disciplinary segregation**. This is a punitive status, as a result of the finding of guilt for a serious prison rule violation. Disciplinary segregation is for a set amount of time established by the disciplinary officer or committee, and inmates cannot be held in this status beyond the time specified. In the Bureau of Prisons disciplinary policy, infractions of "greatest" severity can result in disciplinary segregation of up to sixty days, infractions of "high" severity can result in up to thirty days, and those of "moderate" severity can result in up to fifteen days.[20]

Managing Prison Gangs

A key to managing prison security is to manage prison gangs, which contribute greatly to acts of violence and the resulting tension. A recent report indicated that according to crime victims, 6 percent of violent crimes (or 373,000 per year) were committed by gang members between 1993 and 2003.[21] These criminals get sent to prison and continue their predatory, violent ways. In addition, the 2009 National Gang Threat Assessment estimates that there are approximately 1 million gang members belonging to more than 2,000 gangs active in crimes in the United States.[22] Gang members stick together to intimidate other inmates, control drug sales and prostitution, and gain power and influence. In a study of the relationship between gang affiliation and violent acts, researchers found that both specific and generic gang indicators were statistically related to violence and misconduct[23] and concluded that controlling gang activities has great potential to reduce tension and violence within prisons.

Prison gangs were first identified in California in the early 1960s. A Department of Justice report on the early development of gangs and their prison activities notes, "Their organization was so firmly entrenched (in California) before authorities understood the danger confronting them that control of the institutions was seriously threatened. This phenomenon has been repeated in numerous jurisdictions as the presence and influence of gangs have spread throughout the country."[24] Gangs have continued to grow in number and influence in the nations' prisons. A national survey in 1985 identified more than a hundred gangs, with a total membership of approximately 13,000.[25] But by 2002, state and federal correctional agencies reported a total of 61,353 gang members in prisons, making up 4.9 percent of the prison population.[26] Fleisher and Decker suggest, "Motivated by a desire to make money and be at the top of an institution's inmate power structure, prison gangs exploit the inherent weaknesses resulting from overcrowded, understaffed mega-prisons."[27]

Correctional administrators have become more sophisticated in understanding the operation, membership, and organization of prison gangs. In an issue of *Correctional Management Quarterly* devoted entirely to the threat of prison gangs, Seiter writes, "Correctional administrators can never hesitate, stop gathering intelligence, or fail to stay ahead of the gangs' operations. . . . For the individual correctional staff involved, their will to further the correctional mission—to provide a safe environment for staff and inmates—cannot waiver."[28]

Many prison gangs started as an extension of street gangs. When such groups as Bloods and Crips found that many of their street gang members ended up in prison, it was only natural that they continue their criminal activities while recruiting members, intimidating other inmates, and attempting to control the drug dealing in prison. Other gangs, such as the Mexican Mafia, Dirty White Boys, and Black Guerilla Family, originated in prison as ethnic and racial groups of inmates began to band together for strength and support. They discovered that such alliances could lead to control over other prisoners, create funds, and provide members power to gain advantages in prisons they might otherwise not have. Some of the current major prison gangs include the Aryan Brotherhood (AB), Mexican Mafia (MM), Black Guerilla Family (BGF), La Nuestra Familia (NF), Mexikanemi (EME), and Texas Syndicate (TS).[29]

Prison Gang Control Strategies

To control the activities and violence of gangs, correctional staff focus on a variety of strategies. Perhaps the most important action that prison staff can take to control gangs is early detection of gangs and their leaders. Correctional agencies collect and maintain detailed records of gang membership, often divided into leaders, hard-core members, and marginal members.[30] Other terms to identify levels of gang involvement are *member*, *associate,* or *suspect.* A **gang validation process** allows specific validating factors to categorize inmates into one of these three levels of involvement. Factors include

- Self-admission: An inmate may admit that he is a gang member. This inmate should be asked to sign a self-admission statement. Self-admission should not be the sole source of membership validation since an inmate may lie in order to intimidate others or for personal advantage.
- Presentence investigation report: This document may contain information about an inmate's street gang affiliation and activities.
- Staff information: An inmate's central file may include staff reports that substantiate gang affiliation.
- Confiscated gang-related documents: These materials may provide membership lists or notes and letters from confirmed gang members. An inmate may also possess items (e.g., photographs, insignias, correspondence) that establish gang membership.
- Disciplinary records: An inmate's disciplinary file may reveal involvement in illegal activities associated with prison gangs (e.g., drug trafficking, gambling, homicide). Such involvement may substantiate gang affiliation.
- Records of previous incarceration: Facilities operated by the federal government, county jails, or other states may have information pertaining to an inmate's gang affiliation or activities.
- Known associates: Gang members typically associate only with one another. An inmate who fraternizes with known or suspected gang members or who was a codefendant with confirmed members may also be a gang member.[31]

As gang members are identified, the next strategy is surveillance of their activities. After gang members are identified, their activities are closely monitored and recorded. The National Major Gang Task Force of the U.S. Department of Justice recommends the following actions to monitor gang members:

- *Posted picture file:* A centralized photo and data file on significant gang members, suspects, and associates.
- *Confidential reports:* All staff report gang-related grouping activity on the daily confidential reports.
- *Gang communications:* There should be a priority with prison staff to intercept notes passed between gang members.
- *Identify gang visitors:* Visitors of gang members should be identified and their names shared with other prisons. Often visitors of gang inmates at multiple institutions pass along gang information and "hit contracts."
- *Gang control efforts:* Staff should watch for efforts by gangs to dominate any physical area of the institution or access to any inmate program.[32]

Another important activity to control prison gangs is to deny them signs of influence and perceived power. Gangs like to show their strength to recruit members, tout themselves as controlling activities or areas, and show willingness to be violent against their enemies. Gangs will try to flaunt colors, hand-signs, and symbols, and stake out turf to give them an image greater than their real numbers. Colors mean certain things to different gangs. For instance, Bloods and the La Neustra Familia favor red, while Crips and the Mexican Mafia favor blue. Prisons avoid providing clothing or selling items in the commissary that have these colors. There are many National Football League or National Basketball Association teams whose logos are used by certain gangs. Chicago Bulls clothing is preferred by the Bloods, as "BULLS" means Bloods Usually Live Longer and Smarter. The Latin Kings favors the Los Angeles Kings team clothing. The People favor the Dallas Cowboys clothing, because the five-point star represents the People's Nation.

Inmates also give each other gang tattoos. The Mexican Mafia likes to use a large letter "M," and the Aryan Brotherhood prefers two parallel lightning bolts or the number 666. Inmates will also get specific haircuts that identify them as gang members, such as hash marks on their left or right eyebrow (left representing Folks and right representing People). Even the way inmates wear clothing can identify them as a gang. Some gangs will roll up a specific pant leg, or wear caps to a certain side. The Crips and Bloods like to "rag and sag," by wearing their trousers very low on their hips and often partially open.

Some jurisdictions isolate gang members by moving them to a high-security prison. The BOP policy requires that validated members (not associates or suspects) be assigned to a maximum-security prison. In the 1990s, Connecticut developed a unique gang control strategy in which they moved gang members and leaders to a high-security prison in lockdown status, similar to disciplinary segregation or a supermax prison. The only way for members to get out of the lockdown situation is to renounce their membership and **debrief** or tell correctional officials everything they know about the gang operations and membership. Once inmates debrief, they can never be accepted back into the gang and, in fact, become an enemy of the gang.

Recently, the California Department of Corrections (CDC) began to racially segregate prisoners for up to sixty days when they arrive at a new prison, asserting that this prevents violence caused by racial gangs. However, inmates alleged the policy violated their Fourteenth Amendment right to equal protection. The district court initially granted the CDC summary judgment on grounds that they were entitled to qualified immunity. However, the U.S. Supreme Court heard and decided *Johnson v. California* in 2005, and reversed and remanded the decision. While not deciding if the policy violates the right to equal protection, the Court required the district court to rehear the case and use a test that must narrowly tailor any racial segregation and prove that it serves a compelling state interest.[33]

Gangs are a danger to staff and other inmates within a prison, and correctional staff spend considerable time and effort to identify gang members and control their activity. If they do not, the gangs gain power, other inmates feel compelled to join a gang for their own protection, and prisons become a "war zone" rather than a secure and safe place in which inmates who desire to participate in self-improvement programs can do so. To break the cycle of crime and have any chance of returning prisoners to their communities as law-abiding citizens, prisons must control gang activities and limit potential violence.

Inmate Riots and Disturbances

No matter how well the best practices in security are followed, emergency situations such as riots, escapes, hostage taking, and nonviolent food or work strikes can occur. Throughout the history of prison administration, there have been several serious riots.[34] One of the most memorable was the 1971 riot at the state prison in Attica, New York.[35] A large proportion of the Attica inmates were African Americans from New York City, whereas staff members were predominantly whites from rural upstate New York. In September 1971, inmates took control of much of the prison and held several staff members hostage. Negotiations between correctional officials and inmates continued for four days until the governor of New York and the director of corrections decided it was time to end the siege. The New York State Police were authorized to use deadly force to regain control. After they retook the prison, thirty-two inmates and eleven staff members were found killed. The investigation discovered that the state police killed thirty-nine of those during the retaking of the prison.

Another serious riot occurred in February 1980, when prisoners took over the entire prison in Santa Fe, New Mexico. Inmates held twelve staff members as hostages, controlled the prison for thirty-six hours, and caused more than $100 million in damage.[36] Inmates were able to get records of which other inmates had acted as informants, and tortured and killed thirty-three inmates of those believed to have aided staff.

Another serious riot took place in 1993 at the Southern Ohio Correctional Facility in Lucasville, Ohio.

On Easter Sunday 1993, inmates returning to L-block from recreation at the maximum security Southern Ohio Correctional Facility in rural Lucasville assaulted the entry officer. Minutes later, L-block was overrun, and the longest prison siege in U.S. history where lives were lost was underway. Eleven days later the riot ended. Corrections Officer Robert Vallandingham and nine inmates had been murdered. Thirteen corrections officers had been taken hostage. Five were held for the duration of the disturbance. L-block was virtually destroyed.[37]

Most inmate riots and disturbances are not planned and initiated by inmate leaders. Disturbances more often result from the coalescing of two types of factors and events. **Environmental factors** create tension and an underlying unrest among inmates. They can include hot weather, reduction in budgets for recreation equipment, prison crowding, poor food service or medical care, a perceived pattern of unfairness in prison management, or poor security procedures that allow inmates to create an unsafe environment. **Precipitating events**, the "spark in the haystack," then set off a riot. In most cases, the riot results from the mix of environmental factors and a precipitating event.

The "Practical Perspectives" box gives an example of a riot that occurred while the author was the warden of the Federal Correctional Institution in Greenville, Illinois. It illustrates how environmental factors and a precipitating event can combine to result in a serious riot culminating in staff injury and major destruction of a prison.

A burned-out U.S. Penitentiary in Atlanta, Georgia. In 1987, Cuban detainees took control of the prison and held over 100 staff hostage for several days. By the time the government regained control, the Cubans had destroyed almost the entire prison and completely burned down the prison factory.
(Courtesy of the Federal Bureau of Prisons)

Planning for Emergency Situations

While not all riots can be prevented, there are several actions that prison administrators can take to reduce inmate unrest and lessen the chance that a single precipitating event will result in a riot. These include the following:

- Understanding the importance to both staff and inmates of managerial visibility and approachability
- Using security audits to discover security deficiencies so they can be corrected before inmates exploit them
- Enforcing all rules and regulations
- Maintaining effective communications between inmates and staff, among staff, and particularly between line and supervisory personnel
- Providing appropriate programs and services (food, medical care, and so forth)
- Implementing effective management systems, such as sanitation, safety and security inspections, contraband deterrence and detection, tool and key control, and inmate accountability

Practical Perspectives

Causes of a Riot

In October 1995, the Federal Correctional Institution in Greenville, Illinois, was a new federal prison. It was constructed using BOP standard medium-security guidelines, with solid wood cell doors and card tables and folding chairs used by inmates in the housing units' common areas. The prison had just over 500 cells, but because of severe overcrowding in other federal prisons, it rapidly filled to twice that capacity to more than 1,000 inmates, with two inmates in every cell and even three inmates in some cells. Many inmates were transferred to Greenville from Southeast and West Coast federal prisons, which were experiencing the most overcrowding. These inmates were moved away from their families and friends, could not receive visits, and strongly objected to being in southern Illinois. While some experienced staff members were transferred to Greenville, the majority of line staff had no prison experience. Newly hired correctional officers were learning to deal with medium-security inmates who knew how to try to take advantage of new staff and procedures.

Throughout 1995, there was considerable public discussion about changing the federal drug laws regarding crack cocaine. There was a ten-to-one ratio of crack to powder cocaine, meaning that to receive a mandatory ten-year prison sentence, crack cocaine offenders had to possess only one-tenth the amount required for powder cocaine offenders. This became a perceived issue of racial injustice as crack cocaine was primarily used in African American communities, and 95 percent of the crack cocaine offenders at Greenville were African American. The U.S. Sentencing Commission was considering this inequality, and in the summer of 1995, recommended to Congress that the two drugs should be equalized in their weight and corresponding sentence. Through rumor, African American inmates convicted of crack cocaine trafficking believed that a change would be made, it would be retroactive, and many would receive an immediate reduction of their sentences.

Also, a fall 1995 report issued by the U.S. Department of Justice, Bureau of Justice Statistics, noted that black men between ages nineteen and thirty were incarcerated at a much greater rate compared to their percentage in the overall U.S. population. Over the summer and fall of 1995, there was also considerable media attention on the upcoming "Million Man March" to be led by Minister Louis Farrakhan, the controversial leader of the Nation of Islam. The Million Man March organizers called on African American men to take responsibility for their families. However, it also emphasized, especially in the minds of inmates, the issue of racial injustice regarding the disparity between crack and powder cocaine sentencing.

The Million Man March occurred on Monday of the third week of October. On Wednesday evening of the same week, Congress rejected the recommendation by the Sentencing Commission to reduce the disparity between crack and powder cocaine sentences. The next day riots broke out in federal prisons in Alabama, Tennessee, and Pennsylvania. There was national media coverage of the fires and destruction from these riots, and inmates in Greenville watched these events unfold on television news coverage.

On Friday of that week, the Bureau of Prisons took peremptory action to prevent more riots, ordering a national lockdown of all federal prisons. At Greenville, inmates were called back to their housing units around 3:00 P.M., about one hour earlier than usual, and were told to go to their cells to be locked down. Several inmates refused and began assaulting staff. A riot ensued and resulted in injury of thirteen staff members and massive destruction of two housing units. Four or five other federal prisons also experienced smaller disturbances during the next few weeks.

Environmental factors in this riot included inexperienced staff implementing new procedures. Many inmates were extremely unhappy about being in Greenville. Feelings of racial injustice were heightened by the Million Man March. There were expectations that some of these would be rectified by congressional action regarding the disparity of crack and cocaine sentences. The congressional action to maintain current sentences was unexpected by prison officials and was disappointing to inmates. The precipitating event was the attempted lockdown, in a time when external (societal) tensions were high. The inmates were extremely upset because they did not know the duration or reasons for the lockdown or even if this action was warranted.

- Developing sensitivity to changes in inmate actions or the institution atmosphere
- Using risk-assessment programs to identify trouble spots and correcting them as soon as possible. Useful data include the use of objective indicators (tests, review of incident data, and sick call data) or more subjective elements (staff and inmate interviews) to assign levels of risk to a situation or institution[38]

To prepare for emergency situations, prisons develop plans to identify the responses and procedures to be put in place in case of a disturbance. Plans include key ways to prevent disturbances and in the event of a riot, the initial reactions, communications, staff response, potential use of firearms and crowd control ordinances, managing the media, and postemergency actions. Emergency plans are a critical guide for actions in a time when emotions are high, staff and inmates may be in danger or already injured, things seem chaotic and out of control, and the warden and top prison officials may be out of the prison. Staff are trained in the implementation of the plan in the event of an emergency. Well-coordinated, appropriate, and timely reaction at the beginning of a disturbance is critical. Boin and Van Duin write, "As prison authorities find themselves confronted with a riot, . . . [they] will have to take some sort of action in order to cope with the threat and restore a state of normalcy. It is in this stage that the actions of prison authorities may make the difference between a food strike in an isolated cell block (a riot you will never hear about) and the overtaking of an entire institution (a riot you might never forget)."[39]

Emergency Response Teams

Emergency plans require creation, staffing, and training of at least three teams to prepare for hostage negotiation, disturbance control, and use of deadly force. These three teams give decision makers options to decide which team to use and how to react. It has been suggested that "negotiation, the option involving the least amount of force, is the preferred option when time permits . . . "[40]

Hostage negotiation teams (HNTs) are trained to deal with staff members being taken hostage, a very difficult and stressful situation that eliminates or delays many of the activities that could be used to respond to a nonhostage emergency. The HNT is made up of eight to ten prison employees with excellent communication skills and ability to perform under stress. The team's principal role is to open lines of communication with the captors as quickly as possible so that inmates see an option to injuring the hostage and begin to consider how to resolve the situation. Through this, the HNT hopes to preserve life and regain control of the prison and inmates. Once they open communication lines, they attempt to "reduce stress and tension with the hostage takers, build rapport, obtain intelligence, stall for time, allow hostage takers to express emotion and ventilate, and establish a problem-solving atmosphere."[41] Over the period of negotiations, a common occurrence is that a rapport builds between the negotiators and the captors. Referred to as the Stockholm Syndrome, it is believed that the hostages and captors begin to identify with each other; as captors see the hostages as people rather than just objects and are therefore less likely to physically harm or kill them.

Disturbance control teams (DCT) have a primary mission of controlling inmates during riot situations by using defensive tactics and equipment to move them, isolate them, and get them to give up and stop the disturbance. The team wears helmets, ballistic-resistant vests, and baseball-catcher-style shin guards and carries riot batons, gas masks, handcuffs, chemical agents such as tear and pepper gas, and ordnance such as smoke grenades, stun and flash rounds, and Sting-Ball grenades. The DCT responds to a riot with a deliberate, orderly, and disciplined approach. Through this "show of force," inmates often end the confrontation, recognizing that the DCT is well trained and the inmates are likely to be hurt if they do not capitulate.

Unfortunately, some riots and hostage situations do not end successfully through negotiation or the use of the DCT. In these cases, the third type of team, the **special emergency response team** (SERT), may be called upon. SERT is similar to a police SWAT team, and is trained in the use of weapons, explosives, entry procedures, and snipers. They will be authorized to use lethal force when all else fails to resolve an emergency situation. The most difficult decision for correctional officials is to commit to the use of a SERT assault with deadly force. Captors always give deadlines and threaten to kill hostages if their demands are not met. It is good strategy to have the negotiating team try to talk hostage takers past deadlines, while hoping that they will not injure hostages. Yet hostage takers may reach a point at which they are about to kill or injure hostages, and the order must be given and the SERT prepared to begin an assault.

SERT prepares a detailed plan that must receive the approval of the emergency decision maker. Once approved, the team moves into position and stays ready to begin the assault upon receiving the "go" order. If force is necessary, it must be overwhelming, but only in the amount necessary to restore order. Prison officials' goal is to develop a tactical action that ensures total control of the inmates as the final outcome so that inmates cannot take the weapons and have SERT members as more hostages.

SERT members training with weapons. If called upon, SERT members may have to use lethal force to rescue hostages or resolve an emergency situation. *(Photo Reprinted with permission of the American Correctional Association.)*

These teams must be well trained and prepared to act at any time. Prison administrators know their capabilities and the type of situations they can most effectively handle. All prison staff must know and be trained in their roles in a disturbance or hostage situation. And staff must be aware of the risk of working in a prison and discuss this risk and the types of responses available to prison officials with their families. In this way, families can understand what is happening if their family member is taken hostage. Although inmate disturbances are dangerous and can cause great property damage, proper preparation by prison staff greatly increases the chance to regain control while minimizing the likelihood of harm to persons or destruction of property.

SUMMARY

This chapter described the activities that are critical to managing security and creating a safe and secure environment in prisons. The overlapping and integration of certain security elements (layers of physical security, use of technology, methods of inmate accountability, emergency planning) seems very complex. Yet, there are many basics to effective prison security (good communications, doing what you say you will do, consistency in practices, and so on) that seem rather simple. In reality, managing prison security results from a combination of some very complex and some very simple components. The simpler task for an administrator is to construct the needed concepts in the creation of a security program. The most difficult task is to execute and maintain that program at a consistent and acceptable level of performance.

A good prison security program begins with the proper facility design and effective physical security. Professionally accepted policies and procedures are then used to guide staff in sound security practices. Policies include ways to maintain inmate accountability and prevent inmate access to contraband. Inmate disciplinary systems hold inmates accountable for their actions and provide punishments as disincentives for misbehavior. Prison gangs have grown tremendously during the past decades and actively seek to further their own power and control. Only through aggressive strategies that identify and manage prison gang members can correctional officials keep their activities in check. Finally, inmate collective actions, such as riots and hostage taking, can occur because of conditions at a prison or conditions totally out of the control of prison administrators. Although administrators try to balance and maintain effective programs and operations as well as security, the potential of violence by inmates must never be underestimated, and preparation by staff must never be shortchanged.

Professional life in the public sector, especially when it requires accomplishing complex tasks through other people, is a very tenuous situation. Even when all the proactive systems of security are implemented in perfect fashion, and everything is going smoothly in a prison, the one thing that is sure is that things will change. People are different and act differently from day to day. The racial makeup of inmates or the number of gang members can cause conflicts that disrupt stability. Factors outside the prison (legislative adoption of new laws or budget cuts) can change the mood of the inmate population. And the success of prison security can be undermined by one staff member failing to perform as per policy or in the manner and at the level of quality that is expected. The challenge for prison administrators is a bit of art and a bit of science, and this chapter provides the science of prison security, but the art is an issue of leadership as addressed in Chapters 2, 3, and 4.

KEY TERMS

Separate system	Low security	Special housing unit (SHU)
Outside cells	Medium security	Administrative detention
Inside cells	Razor ribbon	Disciplinary segregation
Radial design	Close security	Prison gangs
Congregate system	Maximum security	Gang validation process
Podular designs	Inmate accountability	Debrief
Direct supervision	Controlled movement	Environmental factors
Perimeter security	Call out	Precipitating events
Towers	Pass system	Hostage negotiation team
Mobile patrol	Casual supervision	(HNT)
Electronic detection device	Prison counts	Disturbance control team
Internal perimeter	Contraband	Special emergency response
Secure envelop	Inmate disciplinary system	team (SERT)
Dormitory style	Administrative appeals	
Minimum security	process	

YOU'RE THE CORRECTIONAL ADMINISTRATOR

1. You are the chief of prison design for a large state correctional agency. The state has not built a prison for more than twenty years, but a new prison construction bill has just been passed that authorizes and funds the construction of seven new prisons. You are charged with determining the type of prisons (security level, location, etc.) that are needed and the style in which they will be designed. How do you go about the process of making these decisions? What information do you seek? Who do you involve in the process? How do you test and confirm your decisions are right before they are literally "set in stone"?

2. You are the gang intelligence officer for a large maximum security prison. There has been an increase in gang violence and from all the information you are getting, this could just be the beginning, as the tension between racial gangs is increasing and a few more incidents could cause an all-out gang war. You have briefed the warden and leadership team, and they asked you to come back within forty-eight hours with a plan of action. They said you can muster all the resources you need to find a solution. What do you do? Where do you start? Outline the plan you would take to include the major steps, types of information you need and how you will get it, and the actions that need to be taken in the short and long term to reduce gang activity and violence.

WEB LINK EXERCISES

Go to http://prisondesign.org/category/design-concepts/

In this Web exercise, we will examine prison design. This is a British Web site which thoroughly examines the issue of prison design. Scroll down to the ultra-modern double cell design and examine the features. Do you see the bunks and the chairs? Note the extensive use of glass on the front of the cells. Continue scrolling and read the short introduction to prison design. To learn more, continue scrolling through the various topics relevant to prison design. Do you see how the design of a prison can affect the entire prison experience?

Go to http://www.fotosearch.com/photos-images/prison-cell.html

This Web site will provide many pictures of older and newer cells. Some have barred doors and some have solid doors with windows for observation. You should keep this Web site in your favorites as these photos are good for your PowerPoint presentations. What are the advantages and disadvantages of having a door constructed of steel bars as opposed to having a solid door with a window and food pass door?

GROUP EXERCISES

The design of an inmate housing unit is critical as an element in providing a safe and secure environment in a prison or jail. Each group is to design a forty-eight-bed maximum-security housing unit in a jail that will provide the highest degree of security without being a supermax unit. Groups will present their unit by explaining how certain design concepts affect the level of security. Be certain to include the cell arrangement, dayroom, shower area, offices, control room, treatment space, mop closets, stairways (if multiple tiers), and other spaces the group decides to include (visitation?).

ENDNOTES

1. R. Montgomery, "American Prison Riots: 1774–1991," in *Prison Violence in America*, 2nd ed., edited by M. Braswell, R. Montgomery, and L. Lombardo. (Cincinnati, OH: Anderson Publishing, 1994), pp. 224–252.

2. M. Silberman, "Violence as Social Control in Prison," *Virginia Review of Sociology* 1 (1992): 77–97. Another good overview of violence in prisons is found in Matthew Silberman, *A World of Violence: Corrections in America* (Belmont, CA: Wadsworth, 1995).

3. No author, "The Security Audit Program: A 'How To' Guide and Model Instrument for Adaptation to Local Standards, Policies, and Procedures," a work in progress document by the National Institute of Corrections (Washington, DC: U.S. Department of Justice, November, 1999), p. 1.

4. Ibid.

5. NIJ Staff, "Making Corrections Safer with Technology," *Corrections Today* 70 no. 1 (February 2008): 62–63.

6. Office of Justice Programs, "Duress Systems in Correctional Facilities," in *Short: Toward Criminal Justice Solutions* (Washington, DC: U.S. Department of Justice, June 2006), http://www.ncjrs.gov/App/Publications/abstract.aspx?ID=236482 (accessed March 15, 2010).

7. "The Security Audit Program," p. 2.

8. James D. Henderson, W. Hardy Rauch, and Richard L. Phillips, *Guidelines for the Development of a Security Program*, 2nd ed. (Lanham, MD: American Correctional Association, 1997), p. 65.

9. Ibid., pp. 143–144.

10. Harry S. Sands Jr. and Anthony H. Johnson, "Visitation in Absentia: New Technology Allows Inmates to Receive Visitor Without Leaving Cells," *Corrections Today* 59 no. 2 (April 1997): 96–98.

11. Ibid., p. 97

12. *Wolff v. McDonnell*, 418 US 539, 94 S.Ct. 2963, 41 L.Ed.2d 935, 71 O.O.2d 336 (1974).

13. Federal Bureau of Prisons, policy statement number 5270.07, *Inmate Discipline and Special Housing Units* (Washington, DC: U.S. Department of Justice, December 29, 1987), Chapter 1, p. 1.

14. Ibid., Chapter 4, p. 4.

15. Ibid., Chapter 2, p. 3.

16. *Sandin v. Conner*, 515 US 472 (1995).

17. In *Baxter v. Pahnigiano*, 425 US 308 (1976), the U.S. Supreme Court reiterated its ruling that inmates are not entitled to attorneys in the disciplinary process.

18. Clair A. Cripe, "Inmate Disciplinary Procedures," in *Prison and Jail Administration: Practice and Theory*, edited by Peter M. Carlson and Judith Simon Garrett (Gaithersburg, MD: Aspen Publishers, 1999), Chapter 29, p. 214.

19. Henderson et al., *Guidelines for the Development of a Security Program*, p. 129.

20. Federal Bureau of Prisons, *Inmate Discipline and Special Housing Units*, Chapter 4, pp. 4–10.

21. Erika Harrell, "Violence by Gang Members, 1993–2002," *Bureau of Justice Statistics Crime Data Brief* (Washington, DC: U.S. Department of Justice, June 2005), p. 1.

22. National Gang Intelligence Center and the National Drug Intelligence Center, *2009 National Gang Threat Assessment*, http://www.fbi.gov/pressrel09/ngta020209.htm (accessed April 16, 2009).

23. Gerald G. Gaes, Susan Wallace, Evan Gilman, Jody Klein-Saffran, and Sharon Suppa, "Influence of Prison Gang Affiliation on Violence and Other Prison Misconduct," *Prison Journal* 82 no. 3 (2002): 359–385.

24. National Institute of Corrections, *Management Strategies in Disturbances and with Gangs/Disruptive Groups* (Washington, DC: U.S. Department of Justice, 1991), p. 2.

25. George M. Camp and Camille Graham Camp, *Prison Gangs: Their Extent, Nature, and Impact on Prisons* (Washington, DC: U.S. Government Printing Office, 1985).

26. Camille Graham Camp and George M. Camp, *The 2002 Corrections Yearbook*, (Middletown, CT: The Criminal Justice Institute, 2003), p. 37.

27. Mark S. Fleisher and Scott H. Decker, "An Overview of the Challenge of Prison Gangs," *Corrections Management Quarterly* 5 no. 1 (2001): 5.

28. Richard P. Seiter, "Winning a Battle of Wills: Correctional Administrators and Prison Gangs," *Corrections Management Quarterly* 5 no. 1 (2001): iv.

29. For a description of these gangs, see Richard P. Seiter, *Corrections: An Introduction*, 3rd ed. (Upper Saddle River, NJ: Pearson Education/Prentice Hall, 2011), Chapter 11.

30. National Institute of Corrections, *Management Strategies* (Washington, DC: U.S. Department of Justice, 1991), p. 2.

31. Ibid., pp. 5–6.

32. Intelligence Section, Federal Bureau of Prisons, *Gang Interdiction Strategies Briefing Guide* (Washington, DC: U.S. Department of Justice, April 29, 1996), p. 17.

33. *Johnson v. California*, 321 F.3d 791 (2005).

34. For a good historical overview, see Reid H. Montgomery, Jr. and Gordon A. Crews, *A History of Correctional Violence: An Examination of Reported Causes of Riots and Disturbances* (Lanham, MD.: American Correctional Association, 1998).

35. There are several official and government reports on this riot. However, a source of interesting reading is Tom Wicker, *A Time to Die* (New York: Quadrangle/New York Times Book Company, 1975).

36. Attorney General's Office, *Report of the Attorney General on the February 2 and 3, 1980 Riot at the Penitentiary of New Mexico* (Santa Fe, NM: Office of the Attorney General, 1980).

37. Reginald A. Wilkinson and Thomas J. Stickrath, "After the Storm: Anatomy of a Riot's Aftermath," *Corrections Management Quarterly* 1 no. 1 (1996): 16.

38. Henderson et al., *Guidelines for the Development of a Security Program*, pp. 180–181.

39. R. Arjen Boin and Menno J. Van Duin, "Prison Riots as Organized Failures: A Managerial Perspective," *Prison Journal* 75 no. 3 (1995): 365.

40. Earnest A. Stepp, "Preparing for Chaos: Emergency Management," in *Prison and Jail Administration: Practice and Theory*, edited by Peter M. Carlson and Judith Simon Garrett (Gaithersburg, MD: Aspen, 1999), p. 371.

41. Gothriel Lafleur, Louis Stender, and Jim Lyons, "Hostage Situations in Correctional Facilities," in *Prison and Jail Administration: Practice and Theory*, edited by Peter M. Carlson and Judith Simon Garrett (Gaithersburg, MD: Aspen, 1999), p. 376.

13

Managing Programs in Prisons

Introduction

Another key issue for prison administrators is the management of inmate programs. It is often said that "good programs are good security." And so, it is appropriate to address the administrative challenges regarding the provision of programs in prisons. Prisons are expected to provide inmates the opportunity to participate in programs that can help in their **rehabilitation** and successful reentry to the community. Although rehabilitation has always been acknowledged as a correctional goal, support for it has ebbed and flowed over the history of U.S. corrections. However, the public continues to support and correctional officials continue to encourage programs that improve offenders' deficiencies that may have contributed to their past criminality. This chapter discusses programs for offenders in an institutional setting, including educational and vocational preparation, mental health issues for inmates, substance abuse programs, prison work programs, religious, and recreational programs.

Rehabilitation as a goal reached its peak during the 1960s and early 1970s, when the medical model was predominant in corrections. Under the medical model, crime was believed to result from an underlying pathology of offenders, which could be diagnosed and treated. Offenders were thought of as "sick" and in need of treatment. Society was blamed for many of the afflictions of offenders, and the lack of education, widespread unemployment, disintegration of social institutions, poverty, discrimination, and drug addiction were often believed to be the core causes of criminality. Offenders were seen almost as "victims" of the system, unable to avoid their involvement in criminal behavior. As a result, corrections focused on implementing a variety of treatment programs to improve offenders and to provide them with the tools necessary to be successful members of society.

Over the past two decades, there has been a decline in public support of rehabilitation, partly the result of a 1970s study of the effectiveness of correctional treatment. In a review of findings from 231 correctional treatment programs, Lipton and colleagues found no common themes in correctional interventions that consistently reduce recidivism.[1] Citing this study, Martinson stated that "with few and isolated exceptions, the rehabilitative efforts that have been reported so far have had no appreciable effect on recidivism."[2] As a result, an era of "nothing works" began.

More recently, correctional philosophy reverted to Darwinism and the "classical model," whereby offenders are believed to be rational individuals with free will who chose to commit, and are personally accountable for, their crimes. Swift, certain, and severe sanctions are thought to be effective crime prevention strategies. Punishment and deterrence are the dominant goals of corrections. Even in this era focused on holding offenders accountable, society has not given up on the importance of rehabilitation and providing offenders opportunities and tools to change.

Rehabilitative programs continue in prisons although terms such as *rehabilitation* and *treatment* are less likely to be used to describe the purpose of such programs. Correctional "programming" is now provided for many practical reasons: to keep offenders productively occupied, to upgrade skills, or to deal with drug abuse or psychological disorders. In this regard, instead of correctional agencies "treating" offenders, inmates themselves must commit to program involvement and are responsible for successfully completing and benefiting from participation.

Although the public expects criminals to be punished, they support rehabilitation programs for inmates. Innes found "no evidence in the available survey data that the general public shares the view that there is any necessary incompatibility among the goals of justice in society, punishment of criminals, and teaching or training programs for inmates."[3] A 2006 public opinion survey indicated that 87 percent of those surveyed favor rehabilitative services for prisoners as opposed to a punishment-only system,[4] and greater than 90 percent of those surveyed rated as "important" that prison inmates receive job training, drug treatment, mental health services, family support, and housing assistance.[5]

The following sections describe the processes and programs that are ordinarily provided within prisons, which include assessing the program needs of inmates and creating a plan for them to follow during their period of incarceration. These programs can include education and vocational, recreational, substance abuse, mental health, and work programs.

The Importance of Prison Programs

Today, a wide variety of programs are offered in prisons. The importance of rehabilitative programs continues for many reasons. First, it is recognized that most offenders do have problems that need to be addressed. Few are well educated, or have marketable vocational skills or successful work histories. Approximately 70 percent of offenders have a history of alcohol or drug abuse. Many offenders suffer from low self-concepts, do not deal well with frustration or control their anger, and have an assortment of other interpersonal or emotional problems. Although many offenders are parents, they often have suffered from abuse and neglect as children, and do not know how to be appropriate role models and parents for their own children. And very few take responsibility for the situations that got them in trouble or learn how to avoid these situations in the future.

Second, an increasing number of programs have been evaluated and are showing a positive impact on recidivism.[6] Although there is no panacea of programs that work with everyone to reduce their likelihood of future criminality, many correctional programs have been found effective. Although correctional administrators cannot predict future success for specific participants, providing evidence-based programs that will make a difference with some offenders almost requires that they be continued. It takes only a small number of successes, resulting in a reduction of crimes and victims, a financial savings for processing through the criminal justice system, and an increase in the productivity and societal contribution by exoffenders, to make program efforts worthwhile. And, quite frankly, even without statistical proof that prison programs will reduce recidivism, it is very difficult to give up on the belief that offenders can and will change.

Finally, it is important to provide programs to inmates as involvement in positive programs reduces idleness and gives hope to offenders. We have to only look at the idleness that resulted in U.S. prisons during the 1940s and 1950s, because the large prisons designed for factory operations had to drastically reduce prison work as a result of complaints by labor unions and passage of anti-prison labor bills by the U.S. Congress. Resultant idleness and an increasing emphasis on security and control to try to manage large inmate populations created tensions and led to prison unrest and disturbances. Productive programs are a key tool for prison administrators to manage inmates who face increasingly long sentences, with reduced prison amenities and an ever-hardening public attitude regarding offenders and crime.

Types of Correctional Programs

Inmates have a variety of needs, and every inmate has unique problems that need to be addressed. However, some program areas that respond to needs of a high percentage of inmates are education and training, mental illness, substance abuse, and a lack of work skills. Only about one-half of inmates entering prison have graduated from high school. Nearly 70 percent of state prison inmates have a drug or alcohol problem. Very few inmates have an extensive work history or marketable vocational skills. And approximately 16 percent of incarcerated offenders are mentally ill. Prisons, therefore, attempt to create programs to meet the general needs of inmates and deal with individual requirements within these programs. Educational and vocational, mental health, substance abuse, work, religious, and recreational programs within prisons are presented next.

Educational and Vocational Programs

In describing the educational and vocational programs available to offenders, it is important to first consider the value of educational and vocational training in reducing adult incarceration. The United States is unique, in that all children, regardless of race, ethnic background, or economic status, are provided the opportunity for free education at the primary and secondary levels. Therefore, it would be reasonable to believe that most children receive the benefits of education and are equally prepared for the opportunities and challenges as adults of making a living. Unfortunately, this is not the case. Although 77.6 percent of whites graduate from high school, only 55.3 percent of African Americans, and 57.8 percent of Latinos graduate from high school in the standard four years.[7] Many young people still drop out of school and are ill equipped for the world of work. "If high schools and colleges were able to raise the graduation rates of Hispanic, African American, and Native American students to the levels of white students by 2020, the potential increase in personal income across the nation would add, conservatively, more than $310 billion to the U.S. economy."[8]

There is also a correlation between high school experience and the likelihood of adult incarceration. In a study of high school experience and the risk of adult incarceration, Amos concluded that,

> Dropping out of school does not automatically result in a life of crime, of course. Indeed, the vast majority of individuals who leave high school without diplomas are, and remain, law-abiding citizens. High school dropouts are, however, more likely than others to be arrested or incarcerated.[9]

In a 2003 publication of the Bureau of Justice Statistics, it was reported that only 18.4 percent of the general population had not completed high school or received a GED, whereas 39.7 percent of state prison inmates, 26.5 percent of federal prison inmates, 46.5 percent of jail inmates, and 30.6 percent of probationers had only some high school or less.[10] Although the percentages of inmates entering prison who have not completed high school or earned a GED remained about the same between 1991 (40 percent) and 1997 (41 percent), the number of such inmates entering state prisons increased from 293,000 in 1991 to 420,000 in 1997.[11]

Correctional education has long been accepted as important in prisons. Zebulan R. Brockway first advocated it at the American Prison Association conference in Cincinnati, Ohio, in 1870. Brockway argued that law-abiding behavior was attainable through legitimate industry and education. As a result, almost all prisons have complete educational and vocational training opportunities, and community corrections agencies usually direct offenders with needs to programs within the community. The American Correctional Association has adopted the following as a standard for correctional educational programs:

> . . . written policy, procedure, and practice provide for a comprehensive educa-tion program, available to all inmates who are eligible, that includes the following: educational philosophy and goals, communications skills, general education, basic academic skills, GED preparation, special education, vocational education, postsecondary education, and other education programs as dictated by the needs of the institutional population.[12]

When inmates enter a prison, there is usually a record of their educational and vocational history. However, to assess their actual level of literacy, inmates are tested, and assigned to an educational program comparable to their level. Education programs generally target improving literacy and preparing inmates to take the GED. A recent survey of adult correctional facilities found that about nine in ten state prisons and all federal prisons provided educational programs for inmates.[13] As indicated in Table 13-1, a variety of education programs are offered, with secondary education programs to prepare inmates to take the GED, the most prevalent during 2000.

There are just over one-half of the inmate population (52 percent of state and 57 percent of federal inmates) that has taken education classes since their most recent admis-sion (Table 13-2). Although the percentages of inmates participating in such programs decreased from 1991 to 1997, the actual number of inmates who were educated in prison

Table 13-1
EDUCATIONAL PROGRAMS OFFERED IN STATE, FEDERAL, AND PRIVATE PRISONS, 2000 AND 1995, AND LOCAL JAILS, 1999

Educational Programs	State Prisons		Federal Prisons		Private Prisons		Local Jails
	2000	1995	2000	1995	2000	1995	1999
With an education program	91.2%	88.0%	100.0%	100.0%	87.6%	71.8%	60.3%
Basic adult education	80.4	76.0	97.4	92.0	61.6	40.0	24.7
Secondary education	83.6	80.3	98.7	100.0	70.7	51.8	54.8
College courses	26.7	31.4	80.5	68.8	27.3	18.2	3.4
Special education	39.6	33.4	59.7	34.8	21.9	27.3	10.8
Vocational training	55.7	54.5	93.5	73.2	44.2	25.5	6.5
Study release programs	7.7	9.3	6.5	5.4	28.9	32.7	9.3
Without an education program	8.8	12.0	0.0	0.0	12.4	28.2	39.7
Number of facilities	1,307	1,278	*	*	242	110	2,819

Source: Caroline Wolf Harlow, *Education and Correctional Populations* (Washington, DC: U.S. Department of Justice, Bureau of Justice Statistics, January 2003), p. 4.
Note: Detail may not add to total because facilities may have more than one educational program.
*Changed definitions prevent meaningful comparisons of the numbers of federal facilities, 1995 and 2000.

increased during this period from 402,500 to 550,000.[14] As noted in Table 13-2, vocational programs and high school or GED programs were the most popular among inmates, with about one-third participating in vocational programs and one-fourth participating in high school classes.

While most prison educational programs are voluntary, many states and the Federal Bureau of Prisons (BOP) have **mandatory prison educational programs**. In 1983, the BOP was the first agency to implement a mandatory literacy program for inmates who functioned at less than a sixth-grade educational level. This was increased to an eighth-grade level in 1986, and in 1991, the *Crime Control Act of 1990* (Public Law 101-647) directed the BOP to have a mandatory functional literacy program for all mentally capable inmates, and the BOP raised their educational standard to the twelfth grade.

Research has resulted in mixed results concerning the impact of correctional education on recidivism. Several studies have indicated a positive relationship between participating in prison education programs and lower recidivism.[15] A study of recidivism of inmates released from Texas prisons during 1991 and 1992 found that inmates at the lowest levels of educational achievement benefited most from participation in academic programs as indicated by lower recidivism rates.[16] Vito and Tewksbury evaluated a program in Kentucky to increase the literacy levels of state and local inmates and to reduce recidivism. Although

Table 13-2
PARTICIPATION IN EDUCATIONAL PROGRAMS SINCE MOST RECENT INCARCERATION OR SENTENCE, FOR STATE AND FEDERAL PRISON INMATES, 1997 AND 1991, FOR LOCAL JAIL INMATES, 1996, AND FOR PROBATIONERS, 1995

| | Prison Inmates | | | | Local Jail Inmates | Probationers |
| | State | | Federal | | | |
Educational Program	1997	1991	1997	1991	1996	1995
Total	51.9%	56.6%	56.4%	67.0%	14.1%	22.9%
Basic	3.1	5.3	1.9	10.4	0.8	0.4
GED/high school	23.4	27.3	23.0	27.3	8.6	7.8
College courses	9.9	13.9	12.9	18.9	1.0	6.1
English as a second language	1.2	. . .	5.7	. . .	. . .	. . .
Vocational	32.2	31.2	31.0	29.4	4.8	7.0
Other	2.6	2.6	5.6	8.4	2.1	3.4
Number of inmates	1,046,136	709,042	87,624	53,753	501,159	2,055,942

Source: Caroline Wolf Harlow, *Education and Correctional Populations* (Washington, DC: U.S. Department of Justice, Bureau of Justice Statistics, January 2003), p. 4.
Note: Detail may not add to total due to rounding or inmates' participation in more than one educational program.

graduates of the program increased their reading and math competencies by up to three grade levels, the educational component did not seem to have any effect on their recidivism rates when compared to nongraduates measured twelve to fifteen months after program involvement.[17]

Most prisons also offer vocational training programs to improve inmates' vocational skills. **Vocational training** is specific training in a trade area such as carpentry, electronics, welding, office equipment and word processing, food services, or horticulture and landscaping. These programs are often certified by and meet the same requirements as a technical school, and offenders receive a certificate of completion of the same curriculum that other nonprison students receive. Completion qualifies inmate students for entry-level positions in the vocational area they have chosen.

In two studies, recidivism was found to be significantly lower for those offenders who complete vocational training programs. In a study that examined the impact of industrial work experience and vocational or apprenticeship training in federal prisons, Saylor and Gaes found that "prison programs can have an effect on post-release employment and post-release arrest in the short run and recommitment in the long run."[18] Specifically, the authors found that the study group of inmates who had industrial work, vocational training, or apprenticeship training was "more likely to be employed than

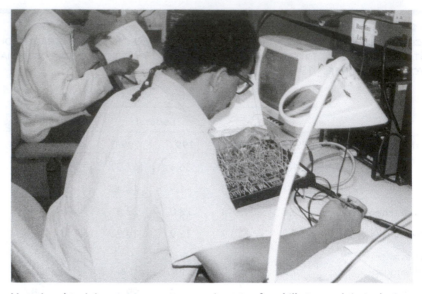

Vocational training programs prepare inmates for skills to work in today's workforce. In this photo, an inmate is receiving training to work on electronic circuit boards.
(Courtesy of the Ohio Department of Rehabilitation and Correction)

comparison group members. By the twelfth month, study group members were 14 percent more likely (71.7 percent versus 63.1 percent) to be employed."[19] As regards long-term recidivism, "those who participated in either vocational or apprenticeship training were 33 percent less likely to recidivate through the observation period,"[20] which was as long as twelve years and as few as eight years.

In a second study, Lattimore, Witte, and Baker also found a reduction in recidivism rates by vocational training participants.[21] The authors evaluated the effectiveness of vocational rehabilitation programs offered at two North Carolina prisons for young offenders. The vocational program included working individually with inmates to identify vocational interests and aptitudes, developing individual plans of study for improving vocational skills, providing vocational training, and helping inmates secure postrelease employment. The evaluation of the Vocational Delivery System (VDS) was unusual, in that a true experimental design was used to randomly assign subjects to experimental and control groups that differed in their exposure to the VDS program. Findings were that the inmates who participated in the VDS program were less likely (36 percent) to be arrested following release from prison than the control groups (46 percent). The results of these two studies indicate that vocational training for inmates does effectively reduce recidivism, and lend support to correctional administrators' efforts, to continue or expand funding for such programs.

Currently, few prisons have extensive postsecondary education programs, even though several thousand inmates took college classes and earned college degrees in the past. State and federal prisons previously used **Pell grants** to fund inmate college programs. Pell grants were enacted and funded by Congress in the 1970s as a way for "disadvantaged populations" to receive funds to take college courses. Inmates met the definition of *disadvantaged*, and most prisons arranged with local colleges to offer courses in the prison and qualify inmates to receive Pell grant funds to pay their tuition. These college programs were considered a productive use of inmate time and were found to motivate inmates and improve morale.

However, in 1994, after complaints that inmates should not get a "free" college education in prison, Congress specifically eliminated inmates from receiving Pell grants, and many active and proven college programs in prisons were eliminated.[22] Very few states were able to provide funding and keep college-level programs going on a minimal basis. Most did as the BOP, who modified its rules in 2000 to make inmates responsible for all college-degree tuition costs.[23] Prison educational staff provide assistance to help inmates arrange to take correspondence courses, but all costs must be borne by the inmate. Even fifteen years after the end of the Pell grants, most correctional educators still bemoan their loss as a step back in correctional education and the ability to encourage inmates to maximize their education potential, at a time when they have little else to do.

Substance Abuse Programs

Substance abuse programs are critical activities within prisons because such a high proportion of inmates have a history of drug or alcohol abuse. In a recent survey of the drug and alcohol abuse patterns of incarcerated offenders, the Bureau of Justice Statistics categorized inmates based on their substance abuse involvement (see Table 13-3).

Table 13-3
PREVALENCE OF DRUG DEPENDENCE OR ABUSE AMONG STATE AND FEDERAL PRISONERS, 2004

Diagnostic Criteria	Percent of Prison Inmates—	
	State	Federal
Any dependence or abuse	53.4%	45.5%
Dependence and abuse	34.9	27.5
Dependence only	1.2	1.2
Abuse only	17.3	16.8
No dependence or abuse*	46.6	54.5

*Includes inmates who did not use drugs.
Source: Christopher J. Mumola and Jennifer C. Karberg, "Drug Use and Dependence, State and Federal Prisoners, 2004," *Bureau of Justice Statistics Special Report* (Washington, DC: U.S. Department of Justice, October 2006), p. 7.

Fifty-three percent of state and 45.5 percent of federal prison inmates were classified as having any dependence or abuse. Of these, most (56 percent of those in state prisons and 50 percent of those in federal prisons) were regular drug users in the month prior to their arrest.[24] In addition, 9 percent of state and 5 percent of federal inmates were determined to have been involved in alcohol abuse at the time of their offense.

The link between substance abuse and crime is well recognized, and the general public believes correctional agencies have a responsibility to offer programs to address these problems. In reality, explaining the relationship between substance abuse and crime is complex and lacks a cohesive conclusion. The *National Survey on Drug Use and Health (NSDUH)* has tracked patterns of licit and illicit drug use among Americans twelve years old and older since 1975. Findings indicate that illegal drug use, as measured by the number of people using an illicit drug in the previous month, has steadily declined from 1979 to 1992, with a leveling off of the decline at that time. "However, from 2004 to 2009, lifetime use of illicit drugs among 10th and 12th graders fell by about 10 and 9 percent respectively."[25] Although this seems to indicate that drug abuse is substantially less of a problem today than it was two decades ago, research has consistently shown a high degree of correlation between drug use and criminal behavior.

The U.S. Department of Justice has found evidence of a strong relationship between drug use and crime, as summarized in the following three relationships:

- Drug-defined offenses: Violations of laws prohibiting or regulating the possession, distribution, or manufacture of illegal drugs.
- Drug-related offenses in which drugs' pharmacologic effects contribute: Offenses are motivated by the user's need of money to support continued use; and offenses connected to drug distribution itself.
- Drug-using lifestyle: Drug use and crime are common aspects of a deviant lifestyle. The likelihood and frequency of involvement in illegal activity is increased because drug users may not participate in the legitimate economy to situations that encourage crime.[26]

This information makes it clear that alcohol and drug abuse programs must be a part of all correctional programs. Most agencies recognize that many offenders abuse both alcohol and drugs, and provide a combined "substance" abuse treatment program. Table 13-4 illustrates the types of drug abuse treatment that are provided to state and federal prisoners, and in 2004, about 39 percent of state prisoners and 45 percent of federal prisoners those who were drug dependent or abusing in the year before their admission to prison took part in a drug abuse program.[27]

Residential treatment is the most intensive program, where inmates live together in a housing unit entirely focused on a substance abuse milieu. This type of program has also been found to be effective. In a study of BOP residential treatment programs, only 3.3 percent of those receiving treatment (compared to 12.1 percent of a similar group that did not receive treatment) were rearrested in the first six months after release.[28] While proven effective, residential programs are staff intensive and expensive. That perhaps explains why (as indicated in Table 13-4) only 9.2 percent of state and 8.7 percent of federal inmates participate in residential programs.

Table 13-4

DRUG TREATMENT OR PROGRAM PARTICIPATION SINCE ADMISSION AMONG STATE AND FEDERAL PRISONERS WHO USED DRUGS IN THE MONTH BEFORE THE OFFENSE, 1997 AND 2004

| Type of Drug Treatment or Program Since Admission | Percent of Prisoners Who Used Drugs in the Month Before the Offense— | | | |
| | State | | Federal | |
	2004	1997	2004	1997
Any drug treatment or programs	39.2%	34.3%	45.3%	38.8%
Treatment	4.1%	14.6%	15.2%	15.4%
Residential facility or unit	9.2	8.8	8.7	10.9
Counselling by a professional	6.0	6.0	6.8	5.5
Detoxification unit	0.9	1.0	0.8	0.3
Maintenance drug	0.3	0.3	0.2	0.4
Other programs	33.7%	28.3%	38.8%	31.7%
Self-help group/peer counseling	26.9	23.1	20.8	15.8
Education program	17.0	14.1	28.1	23.8

Source: Christopher J. Mumola and Jennifer C. Karberg, "Drug Use and Dependence, State and Federal Prisoners, 2004," *Bureau of Justice Statistics Special Report* (Washington, DC: U.S. Department of Justice, October 2006), p. 9.

An example of a residential substance abuse program is the Federal Bureau of Prisons' Drug Abuse Programs (DAP), a 500-hour program, during which inmates reside in a treatment unit separate from the prison general inmate population. The program operates with a philosophy that offenders must assume personal responsibility for their behavior and, despite the influence of environmental conditions and circumstances, the individual must make a conscious decision to avoid engaging in drug-taking and criminal behavior. The treatment model is bio-psycho-social and emphasizes comprehensive lifestyle change, with issues of physical well-being, family relationships, and criminality, all targeted for change while acquiring positive life skills as a vehicle to avoid future drug use.[29] The five-part treatment strategy includes (1) orientation screening and referral, (2) drug abuse education, (3) nonresidential drug abuse treatment services, (4) residential drug abuse treatment, and (5) transitional services. Although effective, residential programs are also the most expensive.

Many prisons create residential treatment programs with a mission to address issues other than substance abuse. The following Practical Perspectives describes the steps taken to create a "residential values" program in a medium security prison.

Practical Perspectives

Creating a Residential Values Program

A residential program initiated at the Federal Correctional Institution in Greenville, Illinois is the Residential Values Program (RVP). The RVP is perceived to have produced excellent results within the institution, because it improved relations between staff and inmates and reduced the number of incident reports of negative inmate behavior.

The Federal Correctional Institution (FCI) in Greenville, Illinois, was opened as a 750-bed medium-security institution with a 250-bed minimum-security satellite camp. The institution has four separate units. During activation, institution management decided that one of these units should have a specialized program focus. They believed this important program would add productive activities to keep inmates busy and, at the same time, create a culture of positive programming and professional staff–inmate interaction. The BOP had developed a short, twenty-hour program (called "Living Free") that focused on the four basic values of honesty, tolerance, respect, and responsibility. The Greenville staff believed that these values were a good foundation for the type of program they desired and expanded the twenty -hour Living Free program into a six-month, residential program. The RVP was based on the understanding that healthy living is comprised of positive values, physical health, and an individual sense of purpose. By reinforcing such qualities, the RVP serves to develop the safety and security of the institution.

No funds or staff positions were available to the institution to start the RVP. Therefore, the plan was to use existing staff from a variety of departments to teach/coach in the program and recruit community volunteers to contribute with special presentations and with small group programming. The unit manager responsible for the unit in which the RVP is located is responsible for the operation of the unit, and the program coordinator, a staff psychologist, is responsible for overseeing the delivery of the program content.

The original twenty-hour Living Free program is first presented to begin to get participants to consider the value of a prosocial lifestyle. Courses address such topics as the costs and benefits of criminality, an examination of personal values, the identification of destructive thinking patterns, an introduction to changing personal habits, a review of the relapse process, the influence of family and values, and effective goal setting. A unique health promotion and disease prevention element provides inmates with an understanding of how to develop healthy living practices. Participants undergo health evaluation both at the beginning and at end of the program, and determine improvements in cholesterol levels, heart rate, muscular endurance and fitness, and body fat composition.

The curriculum also includes classes in anger management, financial responsibility, and decision making based on values and morals. The Personal Power program designed by Anthony Robbins exposes participants to the primary motivators that can create long-lasting change and ways to develop peak performance. Inmate participants can also teach topics of interest on items such as travel and foreign culture, both for general interest and for inmates to be fully involved in the program design and delivery.

The 300-hour program takes approximately six months to complete. Inmates attend classes for a half day and go to a work assignment the other half of the day. Inmates are also required to get involved in other institutional programs in addition to the RVP curriculum. As the program concludes, inmates review the information presented over the previous few months and are given new issues and ideas to enhance prosocial living. A formal graduation ceremony for current and past RVP graduates brings an end to the 300-hour program.

The RVP is considered to be an excellent program at FCI Greenville. Staff enjoy working in the unit and believe inmates in the program take more responsibility for their behavior. RVP inmates have fewer misconduct violations than other Greenville inmates. And, the inclusion of community volunteers builds positive relations with citizens and develops support for rehabilitative programs. Since its inception, the RVP has become acclaimed throughout the BOP, and many other federal prisons have modeled after it, creating similar residential programs. In addition, in 2000, the RVP unit manager received one of the highest awards in the BOP, the Assistant Director Award for Correctional Programs, for her work in supervising the RVP. The program has become the positive and successful program that its originators desired.

Mental Health Programs

Mental health treatment programs are very important in prisons as a high percentage of inmates have mental health problems. Also, mentally ill inmates can create serious security challenges and destabilize the environment. And correctional agencies were not created with a mission to provide mental health programs to the same extent as mental health agencies. In many states, there is a mixed responsibility between correctional and mental health agencies. In some states the mental health department provides all services (even in the state correctional facilities), but unfortunately, it is sometimes not as high a priority of that agency as it should be.

A 2006 survey by the Bureau of Justice Statistics estimated that more than half of all prison and jail inmates experienced a mental health problem within the past twelve months.[30] And, 15 percent of state prisoners and 24 percent of jail inmates reported symptoms classified as psychotic disorders.[31] This is consistent with an earlier estimate that 16.2 percent of all prisoners were identified as mentally ill.[32] Beck and Maruschak found that as of June 30, 2000, 1,394 of the nation's 1,558 public and private adult prisons provided mental health services to inmates, yet, only one in eight prisoners were receiving mental health therapy or counseling services.[33] Although still too low, this appears to have marginally improved. A 2006 review indicated that 34 percent of state inmates, 24 percent of federal inmates, and 17 percent of jail inmates received mental heath treatment since their admission.[34]

While almost every prison provides mentally ill inmates with outpatient treatment, a 2000 census reported that there were 155 prisons that were specifically designed for and had an operational mission to provide mental health programming for inmates.[35] Some of these facilities house mentally ill inmates for long periods or throughout their incarceration. Others are used to house and treat inmates who have experienced acute episodes of mental illness for short terms, stabilize them with medication and treatment, and then return them to the general-population prison. In some states, there are agreements with the state mental health agencies to transfer the most severely mentally ill inmates to secure psychiatric hospitals for long-term treatment. However, this usually requires a probate hearing by a court to determine that the inmate's illness is so acute that he or she must be hospitalized in such a facility.

Table 13-5 illustrates the number of inmates who were receiving mental health treatment while confined in state correctional facilities. Three categories of treatment are provided: twenty-four-hour care, therapy/counseling, and the provision of psychotropic medication. There are 16,986 state prisoners that receive twenty-four hour care through being housed in a unit with a program mission to deliver mental health care. Almost 13 percent of state inmates (about 79 percent of those identified as mentally ill) receive mental health therapy or counseling services on a regular basis. A higher percentage of female inmates received therapy than male inmates. And nearly 10 percent of all state inmates were receiving psychotropic medications such as antidepressants, stimulants, sedatives, or tranquilizers.

In the provision of mental health care, it is important that there be a continuum of care both while inmates are incarcerated and after release. While in prison, inmate needs may require varying levels of treatment. The most intensive level of care is an inpatient prison hospital, in which inmates with acute needs who represent a risk to themselves or others

Table 13-5
INMATES RECEIVING MENTAL HEALTH TREATMENT IN STATE CONFINEMENT FACILITIES, BY FACILITY CHARACTERISTIC, JUNE 30, 2000

| | Number of Inmates Receiving— | | | | | |
| | 24-hour Mental Health Care | | Therapy/ Counseling | | Psychotropic Medications | |
Facility Characteristic	Number	Percent	Number	Percent	Number	Percent
Total*	16,986	1.8%	122,376	12.9%	95,114	9.8%
Facility operation						
Public	16,270	1.8%	116,296	13.0%	90,721	10.0%
Private	716	1.3	6,080	10.8	4,393	7.7
Authority to house						
Males only	13,064	1.5%	100,371	11.9%	74,736	8.7%
Females only	830	1.5	14,744	27.1	12,119	22.1
Both	3,092	5.9	7,261	14.3	8,259	15.2
Security level						
Maximum/high	6,928	2.4%	44,637	14.9%	35,069	11.5%
Medium	9,608	1.8	65,726	12.6	52,208	9.8
Minimum/low	448	0.4	11,593	9.3	7,355	5.8
Facility size**						
1,500 or more	6,298	1.4%	59,970	12.8%	45,283	9.3%
750–1,499	5,140	1.6	41,953	13.0	31,816	9.9
250–749	4,582	3.5	16,831	13.4	14,866	11.6
100–249	888	3.3	3,309	12.4	2,867	10.9
Fewer than 100	78	2.3	313	11.0	282	8.8

*Excludes inmates in mental health treatment in Florida for whom only statewide totals were reported.
**Based on the average daily population between July 1, 1999, and June 30, 2000.
Source: Allen J. Beck and Laura J. Maruschak, *Mental Health Treatment in State Prisons, 2000* (Washington, DC: U.S. Department of Justice, Bureau of Justice Statistics, July 2001), p. 3.

can receive aggressive treatment. As a step-down to hospitalization, there are short-term crisis units to stabilize inmates' symptoms and then return them to the prison's general population. The next level of treatment is a residential unit within a general-population prison, in which mentally ill inmates live and receive treatment in a therapeutic milieu, yet interact with other inmates for work, food services, and other program participation. And finally, regular prisons provide outpatient therapy and counseling for mentally ill inmates who can live and function in a general-population prison.

Mental health programs within prisons are critical to accomplishing the mission of a correctional facility. Mentally ill offenders deserve to be treated and stabilized so that they can live as normal a life as possible while incarcerated. And without the types of programs described, mentally ill inmates will become disruptive and undermine the safe and secure operation of a prison. The final step in an effective correctional mental health program is transition to the community. Yet, without treatment, inmates may not be prepared for release and reenter to the community. The continuum of care must then continue into the community. As preparation for release, prisons work with parole and postrelease staff to create a transition program to continue mental health treatment in the community and encourage (or require) the offender to seek care following release.

Prison Work Programs

In addition to typical inmate programs already described, inmates are also assigned to work while in prison. Some would not label work as a "program." However, prisons usually create a work environment that is similar to that in the free-world, and inmates develop skills such as working for a supervisor, understanding quality performance or production of a quality product, and learning to work cooperatively with coworkers. These skills are as necessary for success as many of the treatment results from substance abuse or mental health care. Work has been an important part of prisons since the Walnut Street Jail opened in 1790 in Philadelphia. The Quakers who found the Walnut Street Jail believed in hard work, and work by prisoners became a key component of the operation of the first prison in the United States, and subsequent early prisons opened under a philosophy with work as an important component of redemption. Inmates were expected to labor in individual cells at spinning wheels, small textile looms, and shoemaking.[36]

As the separate system with inmates working alone in their cells failed, the Auburn system was welcomed, which allowed inmates to work in groups and was more productive for the manufacture of goods that could be sold to help cover the costs of prison operations. In the early 1800s, prisons tried to find other ways to create revenues, and began to lease prisoners for work in the private sector. The company winning a bid for the lease would essentially become the leaseholder and have control of the prison and its labor. The leaseholder could work the inmates in their industrial operations, spending as little as possible to house and feed the inmates, and try to earn as much as possible through the unpaid inmate work. The use of inmate labor by the private sector continued into the twentieth century, when abuses of the lease system caused most of them to end, and states returned to operating their own prison industries to both keep inmates busy and create a profit from the production and sale of goods.

During the first forty years of the twentieth century, the prison population grew by 174 percent.[37] The Industrial Era of prisons lasting from approximately 1910 to 1935 resulted in large prisons being built on a model of work with the main function of the prison being the production of goods to be sold on the open market.[38] Unfortunately, these prison industries became so efficient that organized labor began to complain about the unfair competition resulting from free prison labor's production of goods. Lobbying before the U.S. Congress resulted in the passage of the Hawes–Cooper Act in 1929, which required that prison products be subject to the laws of any state to which they were shipped. Subsequent legislation, the Ashurst–Sumners Act of 1935, required that prison products be clearly marked as prison-made goods. This act was amended in 1940 to fully prohibit the interstate shipment of prison goods. This series of legislation effectively ended the sale of prison products on the open market.

Since then, goods produced in prisons began to be sold for use only by the state and federal governments. Under the "state-use" system, prison industries produced products such as inmate clothing and furniture, grew food for their own consumption, and made office furniture and products for other government agencies. Work programs in prisons now are a combination of work to support the prison operations and, to a smaller extent, work in prison industries. The following describes these two types of prison work programs.

Work to Support Prison Operations

Most inmates work in assignments that are essential for operating the prison and providing services to the inmate population. This includes the operation of prison laundries, food services, and maintenance departments; cutting grass and maintaining the grounds; and cleaning and doing janitorial services for the general sanitation of the prison. In addition, prisoners work in almost every other aspect of prison operations, including assisting staff in recreation services, typing and doing clerical work, tutoring in educational classes, and even working in the prison law library.

Every prison has a laundry, washing the tons of sheets, blankets, and inmate clothing on a daily basis. These are usually unskilled jobs, such as sorting laundry, loading washing machines, transferring clean laundry to dryers, and folding and preparing laundry to be returned to the inmate population. However, inmates do learn to understand the technical requirements for operating an industrial laundry (sanitation, mix of chemicals, and maintenance of equipment). Food service operations require many inmates. As in the laundry, inmates work under the supervision of staff to store food, prepare it for cooking, read recipes and cook food, serve food to the inmate population, and clean dishes and cooking equipment for the next meal. Think of the food preparation requirements for a prison with 1,000 inmates serving three meals per day, 365 days per year, for a total of more than 1 million meals per year. With this amount of work, it would not be unusual to have 25 percent of the inmates assigned to the food service operation in a prison of this size. While many jobs in food service are unskilled (washing dishes, cleaning tables, serving from the food line, and so on), other jobs include food operations knowledge similar to a restaurant or commercial food preparation business. Inmates learn and practice how to read recipes, prepare food, and present it in an attractive and efficient manner. There are many food jobs available to inmates after release and these skills can easily lead to a position after release.

Another service area in a prison requiring inmate labor is to maintain the prison. Inmates do plumbing, electrical maintenance, heating and air conditioning upkeep, carpentry, and general maintenance of a prison. Just as in other jobs, some require little

Prison laundry. Prisons have an enormous amount of laundry to be cleaned.
Sheets, blankets, and inmate clothing must be regularly cleaned, creating many
jobs for inmate workers.
(Courtesy of the Federal Bureau of Prisons)

training, but inmate workers may also lay brick and concrete blocks, install electrical wiring, build finish carpentry products, and run heating ducts. And finally, there are many sanitation and cleaning jobs. Most people envision an inmate pushing a broom. However, commercial cleaning approaches are used, and inmates learn how to mix cleaning chemicals, wax and buff a floor, and sanitize areas for disease prevention.

Prison Industries

Even with the restrictions placed on the sale in the open market of prison-made goods, inmate work activities in prison industries continue to be an important element in prison operations. Prison industries have several benefits for the institution, its management, and the inmates:

1. Industrial work assignments that are similar to private sector operations provide inmates realistic work experience and instill positive work habits.
2. Work experience can provide valuable training and skill development that inmates can use after release.
3. Inmate earnings can be used to support families, pay fines and restitution, and provide inmates with money to purchase personal items allowed in prison.
4. Earnings by the industry can be used to offset the cost of incarceration.
5. Industrial work assignments are a positive way to reduce idleness, and they serve as an incentive for good behavior, which is valuable for inmate management.

Every state prison, and many local jails, operates **prison industries**. Industry work assignments differ from other prison work programs in that the products or services are sold, and the industry creates income to cover the cost of operations, staff salaries, and (in almost every state) minimal reimbursement for inmate workers. Even after the congressional acts of the 1930s, prison industry programs have grown significantly. On January 1, 2002, there were 78,881 inmates (7.8 percent of the prison population) working in prison industries in the fifty states, the District of Columbia, and the BOP. In 2001, these programs had sales of $1.7 billion and profits of nearly $19 million.[39] Inmates work under the supervision of staff, who must maintain a close watch over security and quality. Some of the most common products produced and sold for state use include garments and textile products, wood furniture, printing services, metal products, and other services such as laundry, warehousing, data entry, and construction. Inmates are paid between $2.63 and $7.64 per day.[40]

In addition to the state-use programs of prison industries, Congress expanded the available markets for goods in 1979 when it passed the Private Sector Prison Industry Enhancement Certification Program, referred to as the PIE program. Under the **PIE program**, if states meet certain conditions, they can be certified to sell their goods on the open market. These requirements include the following:

1. Paying the inmates wages comparable to similar jobs in the community.
2. Consulting with representatives of private industry and organized labor.
3. Certifying that the PIE industry does not displace employed workers in the community.
4. Collecting funds for a victim assistance program.
5. Providing inmates with benefits in the event of injury in the course of employment.
6. Ensuring that inmate participation is voluntary.
7. Providing a substantial role for the private sector.[41]

PIE programs are operated by private companies that create production factories in prisons. The private organizations fund the purchase of equipment and pay the salaries of their staff and the inmates they hire. Almost two-thirds of the states are involved in the PIE programs, and in 2001, there were 5,103 inmates employed in over 200 PIE industry programs. Since they must pay inmates wages comparable to private-sector workers, the daily wage as of January 1, 2002, for inmates working in PIE ranged from $21.43 to $36.50.[42] Another requirement is that a share of the inmates' salary is withheld for fines, victim compensation, room and board, support of families, and payment of taxes. From the beginning of the PIE program until June 2003, on wages of $264 million, more than $146 million was withheld from pay, of which 48 percent was for room and board, 24 percent for taxes, 17 percent for victim restitution, and 11 percent for family support.[43]

Prison industry programs are not only an asset to prison operations but they also have been found to reduce recidivism. Saylor and Gaes studied the outcome of prison industries by collecting data on more than 7,000 federal offenders for a four-year period, and comparing those participating in prison industries work programs with similar offenders who did not participate in such programs. The results demonstrated significant and substantive effects on both in-prison (misconduct reports) and employment and arrest

A textile factory in a prison. Prison industries are important to train and keep inmates productively busy. They provide the skills necessary to get and retain jobs after release.
(Courtesy of the Ohio Department of Rehabilitation and Correction)

rates following release.[44] As beneficial and successful as prison industries are to a prison operation, it is unfortunate that the limits of **state use** and the requirements of the PIE program result in a low percentage of inmates being able to participate in these programs.

Other Prison Programs

Because prisons are, in a sense, microcosms of the larger society and operate similar to a small city, they must provide a wide variety of programs and activities. In addition to the treatment and work programs described earlier, prisons also include religious programming, recreation, and other leisure-time activities. Prisons were created as places for religious reformation, so it is not surprising that religious programs within prisons have always been important to administrators and inmates. Providing religious programs for any group or individual that wants to worship as they truly believe is much more difficult than would be imagined. Although most inmates are Muslim, Jewish, Protestant, or Catholic, there are dozens of other religious sects and worship groups. Prisons attempt to allow inmates to worship in whatever manner is a valid tenet of their religious belief, if it does not undermine security.

Although religious activity has always been an important part of prison operations, the issue of what type of practices should be allowed has resulted in considerable judicial intervention. In the 1964 landmark case of *Cooper v. Pate*,[45] the U.S. Supreme Court ended the "hands-off doctrine," and heard a case regarding religious freedom in prison.[46] Black Muslim inmates were not being allowed to congregate, eat their prescribed religious diet, or wear distinctive items of clothing. The Supreme Court noted the constitutional right to worship even while in prison and gave guidance that if inmates wanted to practice an established religion, they could. This decision gave direction to allowing the practice of religion within a correctional institution. Today, the courts allow restrictions when there is a "reasonable and substantial justification," but they often put the burden of proof on correctional administrators to show they cannot make accommodations and to prove why the administrators must impose restrictions.[47]

Religious services are a critical part of prison programs.
(Courtesy of the Federal Bureau of Prisons)

Most inmates are Muslim, Jewish, Protestant, or Catholic, yet there are dozens of other religious sects and worship groups. In most prisons, religious services and activities are coordinated by one or two full-time chaplains who contract with ministers of other sects to hold services and provide religious guidance for prisoners of those faith groups. In addition to regular services, activities may include Bible study or religious discussion groups. With usually fifteen to twenty different religious groups, the schedule for religious programs is usually very tight, and there are often two or three faith groups meeting on any given night. Volunteers play a particularly important role in providing religious programs; they are used to lead study or discussion groups.

Another area of prison programming involves recreation. Idle time is a prison administrator's worst enemy, and wardens continuously challenge recreation staff to create and supervise activities that engage and keep a large proportion of the inmate population busy. Most prison systems require inmates to work or participate in programs approximately six hours per day, five days per week. Even if inmates participate in evening programs such as counseling or religious activities, there are still many hours of idleness if the time is not absorbed with productive leisure time programs. To reduce the amount of idle time, prisons have recreation programs, including outside sports, such as soccer, basketball, or softball; less active recreation, such as table games, card playing, billiards, or ping pong; arts and craft activities, such as painting; and fitness programs, such as running or calisthenics. Organized athletic activities such as intramural teams can have positive rehabilitative benefits, in that they require inmates to work together, develop teamwork, and follow rules and procedures. Recreational programs are also an incentive for good behavior, because inmates can be disciplined by restriction of their participation in such activities.

Perhaps the most controversial recreational activity is weight lifting. Over the past two decades, there has been a debate over weight lifting that has resulted in many state prisons and local jails eliminating all weight-lifting equipment. Philosophically, some do not like the image of people who have victimized others spending their time working out with weights and getting stronger. Practically, it can be argued that inmates who get stronger represent a danger to correctional and law enforcement officials. And weight bars and plates have been used as weapons against inmates and staff. For example, in the 1993 riot at the Southern Ohio Correctional Facility, rioting inmates used weight-lifting equipment to break into an area and take staff hostages. As a result of this incident, the first legislative action to ban weight lifting in prisons was the initiative of an Ohio congresswoman, who heard about the incident and believed that eliminating weights would protect staff from harm. Many other similar legislative acts took place, and many of these legislative acts also banned the use of electronic musical instruments, paid programming such as HBO movies, and leisure activities such as pool and billiards.

However, few correctional agencies or officials are against the use of weight equipment in prisons. Although they understand the political sensitivity, they have not seen many instances in which an inmate used brute strength to overpower staff, as staff are trained not to attempt to break up fights and not to get into physical confrontations in situations in which they do not have a definite physical advantage or in which staff do not greatly outnumber inmates. Also, inmates who are serious weight lifters seldom get into trouble, because they are usually disciplined and self-controlled. These inmates also do not want to lose the privilege and opportunity to continue to exercise.

Over the past decade, and partially as a result of the ban on weight lifting in many juris-dictions, prisons have started recreation programs focusing on educating inmates regarding health and diet to encourage them to develop healthy lifestyles. Offenders enter prison with histories of poor medical care, nutrition, and eating habits and a lack of understanding of the importance of exercise and aerobic activities to reduce fat and improve heart function-ing. Long prison sentences have increased the costs of inmate medical care significantly. Health education programs are a negligible investment in improving the long-term health of offenders and thereby reducing health care costs for inmates in the future.

Recreation programs for inmates will continue to be an important part of prison programs. There is no alternative to increased idleness if inmates have nothing to do with the time they are not at work or participating in a self-improvement program. Prison admin-istrators fear idleness as a precursor of violence and inmate unrest, especially in today's overcrowded prisons, and forcibly argue this point to elected officials, and prisons will continue to have active recreational programs to encourage good behavior and maintain order. Inmates value the opportunity to exercise and respect the privilege. Prisons without recreation would be dangerous and tense environments and would reduce the chance for rehabilitation upon an inmate's release.

Does Correctional Treatment Work?

This chapter describes many current correctional programs designed to improve the likelihood of offenders returning to society as productive and law-abiding citizens. These programs have a variety of goals. First, they reduce idleness and keep offenders positively engaged. Second, they create opportunities for inmates to learn how to work in a group and open channels for communications with staff. Third, they can increase the confidence and self-esteem of offenders, and encourage them to accept challenges and strive for success. And, finally, these programs can increase the skills of inmates (through educa-tion, vocational training, and work experiences) that can be used as they compete for jobs and success in the community.

However, the key question is whether these programs effectively reduce recidivism. Latessa and Holsinger argue for measuring the quality of programs, yet point out that "Recidi-vism cannot be ignored."[48] Although the public supports rehabilitative programs for offend-ers, there is the expectation that such programs will have a cost-effective outcome of reducing crime and recidivism. If not, corrections is merely repeating the rehabilitative era of the 1960s and early 1970s, which ended with the Martinson conclusion that nothing works.

What is different today from the early 1970s when the evidence indicated that there was little benefit from treatment programs? For one, Martinson, whose earlier study initiated the concern with prison rehabilitation, did a further review of 555 studies of correctional programs and reconsidered the conclusion that nothing worked. He found evidence of effective treatments, noting that correctional interventions have differential effects, and concluded that "those treatments that are helpful must be carefully discerned and increased, those that are harmful or impotent eliminated."[49]

In a recent review of the effectiveness of correctional treatment, Cullen and Gendreau point out several limitations in the review by Martinson.[50] First, since the initial study, there have been developments in researchers' abilities to quantitatively synthesize and assess the impact of research findings, particularly through the use of meta-analysis. Meta-analysis statistically measures the average effect an intervention has on recidivism across all studies, while identifying and controlling for various conditions such as the characteristics of the offenders treated, the type of setting, and the study methodology. Second, although the review by Lipton and colleagues was comprehensive for that time, there were a limited number of studies per treatment category: "7 for casework/individual counseling; 15 for skill development; 12 for individual psychotherapy; 19 for group methods; and 20 for milieu therapy."[51] Third, the Lipton review did not include cognitive-behavioral therapy programs, which have been found to be successful treatment approaches for offenders.[52] Finally, the review did not consider any impact or outcome other than recidivism, such as prison behavior or educational achievement.

In what was referred to as the Carleton University Meta-Analysis, Andrews, Zinger, and others reviewed 124 studies of correctional interventions, and the difference in recidivism between the control and treatment group. Overall, they found that these interventions reduced recidivism by an average of 15 percent.[53] Although this reduction in recidivism is significant, it is even more impressive to review the further analyses of these studies. The authors categorized studies using three principles: risk, need, and responsivity. First, they wanted to determine whether the treatment provided was appropriate, unspecified, or inappropriate for the learning styles of offenders. Second, they wanted to determine whether the treatment impacted intermediate targets (changing antisocial attitudes, promoting familial affection, or increasing self-control). In the fifty-four studies identified as providing "appropriate" treatment, there was a 30 percent reduction in recidivism.[54] In contrast, this study also included thirty studies of the impact of enhanced criminal sanctions, and found that "more versus less" punishment actually increased recidivism by 7 percent.[55]

In a 1993 analysis of the impact of correctional treatment, Lipsey and Wilson reviewed ten meta-analyses and identified a 25 percent reduction of recidivism by psychological, educational, and behavioral correctional treatment programs.[56] And, in 1995, Losel reviewed thirteen meta-analyses and found that the average impact from the treatment intervention would result in a recidivism rate of 45 percent for the treatment group and 55 percent for the control group.[57]

In another review of correctional rehabilitative programs, Gibbons first describes many studies completed over the past decade that indicate positive outcomes; then he deliberates the question of what we have learned over the past thirty years in developing and delivering rehabilitative programs. Gibbons expresses surprise on the volume of material that has been developed regarding correctional treatment. He summarizes his review by noting,

> However, although still fairly weak, there are signs of reviewed interest on the part of both politicians and ordinary citizens in correctional treatment and intervention or, in other words, positive efforts to divert delinquents and criminals away from lawbreaking paths.[58]

These findings make one reconsider the 1972 Martinson conclusion that "nothing works." Fortunately for those who support the correctional goal to rehabilitate offenders, there has been resurgence in support for rehabilitation programs. Partly due to tightening budgets and partly due to the belief that we cannot continue to "recycle" offenders through correctional programs only to have them continue to fail when returned to the community or once leaving parole or probation supervision, many jurisdictions search for and implement programs that are "evidence based." This means there is evidence of success, generally defined as reducing recidivism. Over the past decade, there has been a renewed focus on determining whether a program works or not.

An excellent example of how focusing on program evaluation can lead to better policy decisions and savings has been in Washington State. The state faced forecasts that they would need to construct several new prisons in the coming decades, and in 2005, the Washington legislature directed the Washington State Institute for Public Policy to find "evidence-based" options that could reduce recidivism and avoid the need for expensive prison construction. The institute conducted a review of 571 program evaluations within corrections, estimated their benefits and costs, and created an alternative policy of putting money into effective programs rather than new prison construction. The findings are being implemented, and the estimated savings for avoiding prison construction in the state is approximately $2 billion.[59] In this era of tightening budgets, a critical question for the future is whether positive research findings and fiscal challenges will result in increased funding for rehabilitative programs in other jurisdictions.

SUMMARY

This chapter has presented an overview of the reasons for and the operations of rehabilitative programs. Even in an era demanding punishment, retribution, and offender accountability, there is still a critical need for treatment and skill-building correctional programs. These programs benefit inmates. They benefit correctional administrators, who struggle with how to keep inmates productively occupied. And, they benefit the general public, because there is significant evidence that they can reduce recidivism. For all of these reasons, it is important to provide programs for offenders.

Prison programs such as education, substance abuse treatment, counseling for mental illness, religious activities, recreation, and work all help create an environment of productivity and, even more importantly, hope. These programs reduce idleness, teach inmates to live and work in groups, open staff–inmate channels of communication, increase the confidence and self-esteem of offenders, encourage them to accept challenges and strive for success, and increase the educational and vocational skills of inmates. Prisons can easily drift into a dire and depressing climate, which impacts negatively on staff and inmates. While these circumstances can result in tension and inmate unrest, prisons that can actively promote and provide programs will build an atmosphere of optimism without undermining punishment and deterrence. The result is a much better situation for taxpayers as well as offenders and the staff who must govern prisons.

Many correctional programs have proved effective in reducing recidivism, as there have been several studies that have affirmed the value of prison rehabilitation programs.[60] Although the public wants offenders to be punished, they also expect them to receive treatment to better prepare them to return to the community as law-abiding citizens. Rehabilitative programs are a reasonable investment in saving money associated with continued offender criminality. We know that simply enhancing criminal sanctions and increasing the level of punishment do not reduce recidivism. However, correctly classifying offenders and providing them with quality treatment interventions result in a significant reduction in recidivism.

KEY TERMS

Rehabilitation
Mandatory prison education
 programs

Vocational programs
Pell grants
Prison industries

State use
PIE program

YOU'RE THE CORRECTIONAL ADMINISTRATOR

1. You are the warden at a medium security prison with 1,000 inmates. The director of the department of corrections has decided it would benefit the department, and corrections nationally, if the state had a few "model" prison programs that could be shown to meet offender needs, be cost effective, and reduce recidivism. The director has asked you to create a model program at your prison, any type of program. You cannot increase staff; you must reassign current staff to meet any staffing needs. What program would you pick, how would you build it, and how would you make it as successful as possible? Describe why you decided to create this model program.

2. You are the chief budget analyst for a state department of corrections. The state legislature wants to cut the budget for the department and suggests reducing by 50 percent all funding for community and prison treatment programs. Create an argument that is as convincing as possible that this money should not be cut from the department budget.

WEB LINK EXERCISES

Go to Sourcebook of Criminal Justice Statistics at http://www.albany.edu/sourcebook.

Click on Public Opinion on the left side of the page. Examine all the categories of public opinions related to the criminal justice system. Scroll down to the category, *Social and Other Issues* and click on Rehabilitation. See the topic *Attitudes towards whether the criminal justice system should try to rehabilitate offenders.* . . . Click the pdf file format to bring up the data. While this opinion is somewhat dated, note the level of agreement that citizens have about rehabilitating offenders. So why don't we spend more correctional dollars in this area?

Go to Correctional Industries Association (CIA) at http://www.nationalcia.org.

Identify what the CIA is and the role it plays. Then, find information on the Prison Industries Enhancement (PIE) Program and identify the requirements for a private company and a correctional industry to enter the PIE program. Which requirements provide the major impediments to forming a successful PIE partnership?

GROUP EXERCISES

Each group will be assigned to develop one of the following treatment programs and describe how they may rehabilitate offenders by changing thinking patterns and behavior, and their likelihood of having an impact on recidivism: education, religion, pre-release programming, substance abuse therapy, and sex offender therapy.

ENDNOTES

1. Douglas Lipton, Robert Martinson, and Judith Wilks, *The Effectiveness of Correctional Treatment* (New York: Praeger, 1975).

2. Robert Martinson, "What Works? Questions and Answers about Prison Reform," *The Public Interest* 35 (1974): 25.

3. Christopher A. Innes, "Recent Public Opinion in the United States Toward Punishment and Corrections," *Prison Journal* 73 no. 3 (1993): 232.

4. Barry Krisberg and Susan Marchionna, "Attitudes of US Voters toward Prisoners Rehabilitation and Reentry Policies," *Focus: Views from the National Council on Crime and Delinquency* (Washington, DC: National Council on Crime and Delinquency, April 2006).

5. Ibid.

6. For a recent summary of the effectiveness of treatment programs, see Richard P. Seiter, *Corrections: An Introduction* (Upper Saddle River, NJ: Pearson Learning, 2011), Chapter 15. Another less recent but still valuable source is Gerald G. Gaes, Timothy J. Flanagan, Laurence L. Motiuk, and Lynn Sterart, "Adult Correctional Treatment," in *Prisons*, edited by Michael Tonry and Joan Petersilia (Chicago: The University of Chicago Press, 1999), pp. 361–426.

7. Jason Amos, *Dropouts, Diplomas, and Dollars: U.S. High Schools and the Nation's Economy* (Washington, DC: Alliance for Excellent Education, 2008), p. 2.

8. Ibid., p. 2.

9. Ibid., p. 12.

10. Caroline Wolf Harlow, *Education and Correctional Populations* (Washington, DC: U.S. Department of Justice, Bureau of Justice Statistics, January 2003), p. 1.

11. Ibid.

12. Commission on Accreditation for Corrections, "Comprehensive Education Program, Standard 3-4410," in *Standards for Adult Correctional Institutions* (College Park, MD: The American Correctional Association, 1990), p. 141.

13. Ibid., p. 4.

14. Ibid., p. 5.

15. See J. Gerber and E. J. Fritsch, "Adult Academic and Vocational Correctional Education Programs: A Review of Recent Research," *Journal of Offender Rehabilitation* 22 (1995): 199–242; M. D. Harer, "Recidivism among Federal Prisoners Released in 1987," *Journal of Correctional Education* 46 no. 3 (1995): 98–128; and M. Jancic, "Does Correctional Education Have an Effect on Recidivism?," *Journal of Correctional Education* 49 no. 4 (1998): 152–161.

16. K. Adams, K. J. Bennett, T. J. Flanagan, J. W. Marquart, S. J. Cuvelier, E. Fritsch, J. Gerber, D. R. Longmire, and V. S. Burton, Jr., "Large-Scale Multidimensional Test of the Effect of Prison Education Programs on Offenders' Behavior," *Prison Journal* 74 no. 4 (December 1994): 433–449.

17. G. F. Vito and R. Tewksbury, "Improving the Educational Skills of Inmates: The Results of an Impact Evaluation," *Corrections Compendium* 24 no. 10 (1999): 1–17.

18. William G. Saylor and Gerald G. Gaes, "Training Inmates Through Industrial Work Participation and Vocational and Apprenticeship Instruction," *Corrections Management Quarterly* 1 no. 2, (1997): 42.

19. Ibid., p. 40.

20. Ibid., p. 42.

21. Pamela K. Lattimore, Ann Dryden Witte, and Joanna R. Baker, " Experimental Assessment of the Effect of Vocational Training on Youthful Property Offenders," *Evaluation Review* 14 no. 2 (1990): 115–133.

22. John Linton, "Inmate Education Makes Sense," *Corrections Today* 60 no. 3 (1998): 18.

23. Steve Peacock, "BOP Proposes Inmates Pay All Tuition Costs for College," *Corrections Journal* 4 no. 10 (2000): 7.

24. Christopher J. Mumola and Jennifer C. Karberg, *Drug Use and Dependence, State and Federal Prisoners, 2004* (Washington, DC: U.S. Department of Justice, Bureau of Justice Statistics, October 2006), p. 1.

25. U.S. Department of Health and Human Services, National Institutes of Health, National Institute on Drug Abuse, NIDA Info Facts, *Nationwide Trends*, http://www.drugabuse.gov (accessed April 20, 2010).

26. U.S. Department of Justice, Bureau of Justice Statistics, *Drug use and crime*, http://bjs.ojp.usdoj.gov/index/cfm?ty=tp&tid=352 (accessed April 20, 2010).

27. Mumola and Karberg, *Drug Use and Dependence, State and Federal Prisoners, 2004*, p. 9.

28. Federal Bureau of Prisons, *TRIAD Drug Treatment Evaluation Six-Month Report: Executive Summary* (Washington, DC: U.S. Department of Justice, 1998).

29. Federal Bureau of Prisons, "Drug Treatment Programs in Federal Prisons, in *Best Practices: Excellence in Corrections*, edited by Edward E. Rhine (Lanham, MD: American Correctional Association, 1998), pp. 427–430.

30. Doris J. James and Lauren E. Glaze, "Mental Health Problems of Prison and Jail Inmates," *Bureau of Justice Statistics Special Report* (Washington, DC: U.S. Department of Justice, September 2006), p. 1.

31. Ibid.

32. Paula M. Ditton, *Mental Health and Treatment of Inmates and Probationers* (Washington, DC: U.S. Department of Justice, Bureau of Justice Statistics, 1999).

33. Allen J. Beck and Laura J. Maruschak, *Mental Health Treatment in State Prisons, 2000* (Washington, DC: U.S. Department of Justice, Bureau of Justice Statistics, July 2001).

34. James and Glaze, "Mental Health Problems of Prison and Jail Inmates," p. 9.

35. Ibid.

36. For a description of the work programs in early prisons, see Enoch C. Wines and T. W. Dwight, *Report on the Prisons and Reformatories of the United States and Canada* (Albany, NY: Van Benthuysen & Sons, 1973).

37. Margaret Calahan, *Historical Corrections Statistics in the United States: 1850–1984* (Washington, DC: U.S. Department of Justice, 1986), p. 36.

38. For a description of the Industrial Era, see Seiter, *Corrections*, Chapter 1.

39. Camille Graham Camp and George M. Camp, *The 2001 Corrections Yearbook* (Middletown, CT: The Criminal Justice Institute, 2002), pp. 118 and 124.

40. Ibid., p. 120.

41. National Institute of Justice, *Developing Private Sector Prison Industries: From Concept to Start Up* (Washington, DC: Government Printing Office, 1990), p. 22.

42. Camp and Camp, *2001 Corrections Yearbook*, p. 120.

43. Bureau of Justice Assistance, "Prison Industry Enhancement Certification Program," *Bureau of Justice Assistance: Program Brief* (Washington, DC: U.S. Department of Justice, March 2004).

44. William G. Saylor and Gerald G. Gaes, "The Post-Release Employment Project: Prison Work Has Measurable Effects on Post-Release Success," *Federal Prisons Journal* 2 no. 4 (1992): 33–36.

45. *Cooper v. Pate*, 378 U.S. 546 (1964).

46. For a description of the development and end of the "hands-off" doctrine, see Seiter, *Corrections*, Chapter 14.

47. The standard for correctional institutions limiting religious practices was modified to "reasonable and substantial justification" in *Brown v. Johnson*, 743 F.2d 408 (6th Cir. 1985).

48. Edward J. Latessa and Alexander Holsinger, "The Importance of Evaluating Correctional Programs: Assessing Outcome and Quality," *Corrections Management Quarterly*, 2 no. 4 (1998): 28.

49. Robert Martinson, "Reaffirming Rehabilitation, New Findings, New Views: A Note of Caution Regarding Sentencing Reform," in *Offender Rehabilitation: Effective Correctional Intervention*, edited by Francis T. Cullen and Brandon K. Applegate (Dartmouth: Ashgate, 1998), p. 90.

50. Francis T. Cullen and Paul Gendreau, "Assessing Correctional Rehabilitation: Policy, Practice, and Prospects," in *Policies, Processes, and Decisions of the Criminal Justice System*, edited by Julie Horney (Washington, DC: U.S. Department of Justice, National Institute of Justice, 2000), pp. 109–175.

51. Ibid., p. 127.

52. See D. A. Andrews, Ivan Zinger, Robert D. Hoge, James Bonta, Paul Gendreau, and Francis D. Cullen, "Does Correctional Treatment Work? A Clinically Relevant and Psychologically Informed Meta-Analysis," *Criminology* 28 (August 1990): 369–404; and D. A. Andrews and James Bonta, *The Psychology of Criminal Conduct*, 2nd ed. (Cincinnati, OH: Anderson, 1998).

53. D. S. Andrews, I. Zinger, R. D. Hoge, J. Bonta, P. Gendreau, and F. T. Cullen, "Does Correctional Treatment Work? A Psychologically Informed Meta-Analysis," *Criminology* 28 (1990): 369–404.

54. Ibid., p. 382.

55. Ibid., p. 398.

56. Mark W. Lipsey and David B. Wilson, "The Efficacy of Psychological, Educational, and Behavioral Treatment," *American Psychologist* 48 no. 12 (1993): 1181–1209.

57. Friedrich Losel, "The Efficacy of Correctional Treatment: A Review and Synthesis of Meta-Evaluations," in *What Works: Reducing Reoffending*, edited by James McGuire (West Sussex, UK: Wiley, 1995).

58. Don C. Gibbons, "Review Essay: Changing Lawbreakers—What Have We Learned Since the 1950s?," *Crime and Delinquency* 45 no. 2 (April, 1999): 272.

59. Steve Aos, Marna Miller, and Elizabeth Drake, *Evidence-Based Public Policy Options to Reduce Future Prison Construction, Criminal Justice Costs, and Crime Rates* (Olympia: Washington State Institute for Public Policy, 2006).

60. Robert Martinson, *Offender Rehabilitation: Effective Correctional Intervention*, edited by Francis T. Cullen and Brandon K. Applegate (Aldershot, UK: Ashgate, Dartmouth, 1998), Chapter 4; D. A. Andrews and J. Bonta, *The Psychology of Criminal Conduct* (Cincinnati, OH: Anderson, 1994); Paul Gendreau, "The Principles of Effective Intervention with Offenders," in *Choosing Correctional Options That Work: Defining the Demand and Evaluating the Supply*, edited by A. Harland (Thousand Oaks, CA: Sage, 1996), pp. 117–130; M. W. Lipsey, "Juvenile Delinquency Treatment: A Meta-Analytic Inquiry into the Variability of Effects," in *Meta-Analysis for Explanation*, edited by T. D. Cook, H. Cooper, D. S. Cordray, H. Hartmann, L. V. Hedges, R. J. Light, T. A. Louis, and F. Mosteller (New York: Russell Sage, 1992), pp. 83–127; and D. S. Andrews, I. Zinger, R. D. Hoge, J. Bonta, P. Gendreau, and F. T. Cullen, "Does Correctional Treatment Work? A Psychologically Informed Meta-Analysis," *Criminology* 28 (1990): 369–404.

14

Managing Basic Services in Prisons

Doing the Basics

In looking at the management of contemporary prison operations in this section of the textbook, we have examined how prisons manage both security and programs, and balance these two seemingly conflicting components of prisons. However, there is a third leg to this stool of balanced operations, and that is the management of basic services that must be provided in a prison setting. The final chapter of the section on the prisons provides an overview of some of the key services, including medical care, food service, laundry, mail, visiting, and commissary operations.

Most correctional administrators would agree that one of the most important activities for successful management of a prison is to "take care of the basics." One of the results of incarceration is that inmates do not have the right to choose the many services they receive, such as food, medical care, clothing and laundry service, or the purchase of personal items. They have to eat whatever is served in the dining room at meals. They receive medical care from prison medical staff or contracted medical personnel, but cannot choose their doctor or request a second opinion. They wear the clothing that is issued, and they may not alter or personalize it to fit their own taste or cultural style. They can receive mail and visits from family and friends; however, these services are restricted and must conform to prison policy. And, although they are allowed to buy limited personal items such as athletic clothing and shoes, snack foods, and toiletries, they must buy the brands and pay the prices offered at the prison commissary.

It is not unusual to hear citizens and public officials suggest that prisoners should not complain and should feel lucky they even get these services; most at taxpayer's expense. The issue is much more complicated in prisons, however, as the courts have generally required that these types of services be provided and be at a certain standard of quality. And these services are very important to inmates, whose daily lives often hinge around going to the dining room for meals; they are sensitive about the medical care they receive, and the days they can buy commissary items is important and even exciting. When people do not have a complete choice in how they receive these services, they naturally believe the services are inferior and they deserve better, so they often complain about the quality and timely delivery of service. Therefore, it is important for the morale and orderly running of a prison that these basic services are provided professionally and at a level of quality that meets acceptable community standards.

Although there are legitimate concerns among the public about the policy of how these services are provided and offered in prisons, once an expectation for a certain level of service is established, it must be maintained. If prison policy dictates that services will be provided in a certain manner and inmates perceive the policy is not being met, that failure undermines security and safety. Correctional administrators understand that inmates will accept many things and conditions of their incarceration if they believe the service follows the policy, staff perform professionally and show empathy, and there is consistency in the quality of the services. Inmates know they are in prison, and if staff are honest and communicate with inmates regarding issues and why they do certain things, inmates will generally accept it.

Medical Care for Inmates

One of the most challenging operations within a prison is the delivery of medical care. There are many challenges to quality care as described here. But in addition, there are very few prison administrators with backgrounds in medicine, and it is difficult to sort out the complex medical issues that arise, so they must rely on the substantive expertise of their medical staff. The courts are very willing to respond to inmate suits regarding medical care, and there is no area of prison management that results in more inmate grievances or lawsuits filed. And the problems for delivering quality medical care in prisons continue to increase. An aging inmate population, an increasing number of inmates with AIDS and other infectious diseases, rapid increases in cost of care, and difficulty recruiting staff all make the continued delivery of quality medical care a considerable challenge.

At the same time, there are unanswered philosophical questions about the quality and quantity of medical care that should be provided to incarcerated felons. As the cost of inmate health care continues to rise and there is pressure on administrators to reduce medical spending, the scope of medical care to be provided is often questioned. Prisons have never been an attractive recruiting ground for medical personnel, and competition for providers has intensified over the past decade. All of these issues require prison administrators to look for new ways to solve serious problems. Yet, there are few states that would suggest they have found the answers and are comfortable with the cost and quality of the medical care provided in their prisons.

Yet, great progress has been made and there are many new approaches that hold promise for the future. Some states have looked at the private sector approach of "managed care" to determine whether they can limit the delivery of nonessential health care. Prisons are now contracting with private providers to deliver medical care in prisons, and although some appear very successful, others are questionable. The use of technology such as telemedicine has many advantages and can enhance quality while providing cost savings. And prison administrators are trying to be more proactive, by providing health promotion and disease prevention programs that may reduce the long-term medical needs of inmates, a large proportion of whom are serving extremely long or even life sentences.

Background of Prison Medical Care

During the first 150 years of the United States, there was little concern about the quality of medical care provided to inmates. Prisons delivered limited medical care to inmates, and few trained medical personnel were part of the staff. In many cases, inmates themselves even delivered what little care was provided. However, beginning in the late 1960s, the need for improved medical care in prisons came to the public eye. Federal courts began to accept prisoner complaints about inadequate treatment. In addition, the uprisings in many prisons during the 1970s brought attention to the dilemmas of prison health care administration.

When forty-three inmates and staff lost their lives in the riot at New York's Attica Correctional Facility, many of the problems in the nation's prisons became apparent. One of the reasons attributed for the riot was the administration's failure to address a variety of longstanding inmates' grievances, including medical care.[1] This lack of adequate medical care was a problem not only in New York but also in many other places. As suggested by Prout and Ross, "In the 1970s, . . . 95 percent of the inmates of most prisons needed medical attention, two-thirds had never had a medical examination in their lives, more than one-half were drug abusers, and at least 15 percent had diagnosable psychiatric disturbances."[2]

Questionable medical care also resulted in the federal courts reviewing these alleged issues. Prior to the 1960s, the U.S. Supreme Court had accepted a "hands-off" doctrine regarding prison operations. Under the doctrine, the Court recognized it had no expertise in corrections and should show deference to prison administrators, while worrying that accepting prison cases would "open the floodgates" to further litigation.[3] It was not until the 1964 case of *Cooper v. Pate* that the Court changed its policy and agreed to hear a case regarding religious freedom in prison.[4] In the 1970 case of *Holt v. Sarver*, the court looked at conditions throughout the Arkansas prison system, including medical care, and created a **test of cruel and unusual punishment** within the Eighth Amendment. Instead of only including the concept of torture or physical punishment, the Court found that if people of reasonable sensitivity found the treatment shocking or disgusting, it would also be considered cruel and unusual.[5]

After the *Holt* decision, there were many other significant Supreme Court decisions that clarified the constitutional standards for the delivery of prison medical care. In *Estelle v. Gamble*, the Court determined that because inmates are dependent on prison authorities to provide treatment for their medical needs, the authorities have a duty to provide that treatment. As such, the Court prohibited "**deliberate indifference**," in that neither the medical staff in responding to needs, nor correctional staff in denying, interfering with, or delaying access to medical care can be deliberately indifferent to such needs without the unnecessary or wanton infliction of pain.[6] The Court went further in *Ramos v. Lamm* when it suggested that deliberate indifference can also result from "repeated examples of negligent acts which disclose a pattern of conduct" by the correctional and medical staff.[7] And in *Fernandez v. United States*, the court established that medical care in prisons must be "reasonably commensurate with modern medical science and of a quality acceptable within prudent professional standards."[8] Currently, both inmates and staff are aware of and attempt to meet the standards prescribed by the courts.

The Development of Professional Standards for Prison Medicine

These legal cases provided guidelines for the required level and quality of medical care for incarcerated offenders. At the same time, corrections as a discipline was becoming more professional, and the American Correctional Association (ACA), the American Bar Association (ABA), and other professional organizations were developing standards for the operation of prisons and jails in the United States.[9] In the ACA standard's document, a justification for provision of proper medical care is included:

> The delivery of medical and health care is expensive. However, compensatory costs for employees and inmates injured, disabled or killed far exceed the cost of an adequate health care program. Recent judicial rulings and jury awards in health care related cases often have been staggering blows to the financial plans for correctional agencies. For these reasons, coupled with the universal concern to alleviate suffering, all correctional programmers must direct increasing attention toward the management, planning and supervision of the health care program.[10]

In the most recent update of correctional standards regarding health care by the ACA, there are fifty-four standards,[11] under the stated principle that "The institution provides comprehensive health care services by qualified personnel to protect the health and well-being of inmates."[12] ACA standards are valuable for many reasons. One of the first things that a federal court considers when an inmate claims inadequate medical care is whether the prison is "accredited"[13] by the ACA or meets other professional standards for health care delivery. In addition, with correctional administrators lacking substantive knowledge of medical care, they can use these standards as a barometer of the quality of prison medical services. Many prisons, in fact, make the ACA standards available in the library, so that inmates can see the standards and expectations accepted by the prison for health care. When inmates compare and recognize that the prison is meeting these standards, they often, although reluctantly, acknowledge that the level of care provided is adequate. However, they may still believe they personally have not received the services that their illness or injury warrants.

Another association that has developed standards and assisted correctional agencies in improving their delivery of health care is the National Commission on Correctional Health Care (NCCHC). Having roots within the American Medical Association, the NCCHC was initiated in 1983 to improve correctional health care. The NCCHC created a series of standards and "is the only accrediting agency that uses medical, dental, and mental health professionals to maintain its accreditation program."[14] NCCHC is recognized and supported by both the ACA and the American Jail Association (AJA) for their work with correctional agencies and correctional medical staff.

Since the federal courts became involved and professional standards were created, the delivery of prison health care has improved dramatically. Although health care is still an area of prison operations that results in many inmate complaints and lawsuits, most correctional agencies believe they meet a level of care consistent with "community standards," the term used to describe the level of care established in the *Fernandez* decision. In describing this progress, McDonald writes,

> Since the intervention of the federal courts and the emergence of professional standards pertaining to medical care, correctional authorities have moved away from relying on untrained inmates and unlicenced physicians for primary care.

Now, primary care is generally delivered by medical professionals, principally physicians, physicians' assistants, nurses, and pharmacists.[15]

Issues in the Delivery of Correctional Health Care

As noted previously, there are many issues that challenge the effective delivery of quality medical care in a prison. Moore suggests that "Problems in providing care to the incarcerated fall into two broad categories: health status of the inmate population and deficiencies in the delivery of medical care."[16] Moore also identifies six factors inherent in correctional settings that hamper the provision of health services:

1. not a priority of the correctional institution;
2. limited financial resources;
3. difficulties in staff recruitment;
4. absence of a current manual of health care policies and procedures;
5. isolation of the institution from community health care; and
6. lack of a constituency for inmate health services.[17]

Several issues that complicate the delivery of health care in prisons are presented and described here. How do you determine the quality and quantity of care that should be provided? Inmates have extensive medical needs and the costs for delivering care continue to rise. There must be ways to contain costs without reducing quality. Inmate medical problems are getting more serious, with an aging prison population suffering from years of unhealthy life experiences. The problem of infectious diseases has reached epidemic proportions in certain instances, and inmates historically have a higher rate of these diseases than the general population of citizens in the community. And it remains a problem to recruit and retain qualified medical staff to work in prisons.

How Much Medical Care Should Be Provided?

A common complaint by the public is that inmates get more extensive and better medical care than many law-abiding citizens, especially the millions of Americans who are without medical insurance. This complaint often pressures state legislatures and correctional agencies to try to limit the availability of care provided. Studies that have examined the amount of health care services by inmates are inconclusive, even though they do document a relatively high level of service.[18] Inmates have little ability to get over-the-counter medications and treat themselves, because they are more reliant on medical professionals than are citizens in the community.

While the courts have prescribed the minimum levels of care to be provided to incarcerated inmates, there are no guidelines for maximum levels. Questions such as the following persist: Should death row inmates receive organ transplants? Should AIDS-infected inmates receive some of the very expensive medication, even without conclusive evidence that it cures the disease? Should cosmetic surgery be performed when it is believed that it will make a significant difference in inmates' self-esteem and chance of future success? It is difficult to create limits on what type of care should be delivered, and inmates become very difficult to manage when they believe they are not being adequately treated for obvious ailments. In the community, there are health care providers, patients rights groups, and governmental agencies who inspect, license, certify, and regulate the type of care provided. However, in the prison setting, inmate patients have no powerful voice and cannot bargain for improvements or guidelines. Without some limits and guidelines on quality and quantity of care, it is almost impossible for correctional agencies to both keep up with health care demands of inmate populations and contain costs in any viable manner.

Inmates Have Extensive Medical Needs

It is generally acknowledged that prison inmates have a higher level of medical needs than the general population of free citizens, and it is expected that these needs will continue to increase. However, there have been few research studies that compare the needs of long-term prison inmates with community citizens. A 1975 study of inmates admitted to New York City jails did not find that these inmates had more health problems than private citizens but concluded that "prisoners are not a healthy population, but have a high frequency of medical complaints, problems and prior hospitalizations, largely associated with substance abuse, psychiatric disorder, and trauma."[19]

It is believed that inmates present more difficult health problems than the nonincarcerated because of increases in the length of sentences and exposure of inmates for longer periods of time to the stress and dangers inherent in prison, the extensive drug use by offenders, the rising proportion of elderly offenders in prison, and the relatively high number of offenders with infectious diseases. According to a 2002 report by the Bureau of Justice Statistics, more than two-thirds of jail inmates were determined to be dependent on or to abuse alcohol or drugs. In 2004, 32 percent of state and 26 percent of federal prisoners reported drug use at the time of their offense.[20] In addition, 17 percent of state prisoners and 18 percent of federal inmates in 2004 said they committed their current offense to obtain money for drugs.[21]

Fifteen years ago, Silverman wrote that "The number of inmates age 55 years and older more than doubled from 1981 to 1990."[22] And since then, there have been many statutory enhancements of prison sentences for almost every crime, so that once offenders are sentenced to prison, they stay there for a longer time. Also, three-strikes and habitual-offender laws often require offenders to go to prison for life without parole. These factors increase the average age of the U.S. prison population. In 1995, only 6.1 percent of the inmates in state and federal prisons were age fifty or older,[23] and on December 31, 2007, there were 156,600 inmates older than age fifty, representing 10.2 percent of the prison population.[24]

Inmates are more likely to have infectious diseases, requiring extensive medical care and the prescription of expensive drugs. Reviews have identified that the populations of our nation's jails and prisons account for a higher percentage of the total population who are infected with HIV or AIDS, hepatitis C, and tuberculosis than would be expected.[25] Therefore, the problems of infectious diseases in inmates are often greater than that in the general U.S. population, and management by correctional officials of infected offenders causes more serious problems in handling offenders and keeping diseases from spreading. Infectious diseases most common to and most problematic with correctional populations include HIV/AIDS, tuberculosis, and hepatitis C. The challenge of infectious diseases in prisons is further described later in this chapter.

The Cost of Inmate Health Care

Health care for inmates is one of the largest expenditures (other than staff salaries and benefits) in the operation of prisons. State correctional agencies consumed 6.8 percent of state general funds in 2007,[26] and by 2011, continued prison growth is expected to cost an additional $25 billion.[27] Figures vary widely, but the average operating cost per prisoner was $28,816 ($78.95 per day) in 2008.[28] And medical care has been found to be approximately 12 percent of state prison operating expenses ($9.47 per day).[29] What can prison administrators do to try to keep down the increasing cost of inmate health care? There are some promising alternatives, reviewed later in this chapter, such as managed care, the use of technology, and contracting with the private sector. One question involves whether it is possible to simply reduce the level of health care provided to inmates because of a lack of financial resources. To some extent, this question has already been answered. The federal courts will not accept limited budgets as an excuse for reducing the level of inmate health care provided. In *Jackson v. Bishop*, Judge Blackman writes, "Humane considerations and constitutional requirements are not to be measured or limited by dollar considerations."[30]

There are many problems that complicate cost-containment strategies in providing medical care for inmates. One is the fact that it is difficult to recruit quality health care providers to prisons, and institutions often have to pay a premium price to induce specialty physicians and other providers to treat inmates. Another problem is the fact that most prisons are located in rural areas, and there is very little (if any) competition in contracting for hospitalization or specialty treatment to keep prices low. Finally, it is likely that inmates do have more complicated and serious medical problems than a comparable age group of nonoffenders. As these offenders continue to serve longer sentences and rely on prisons for the provision of their health care needs, per capita medical costs for prisons are likely to continue to rise.

Recruiting and Retaining Medical Staff

Although the perceptions may not be true, there is a common perception among medical professionals that the working conditions in a prison would be unpleasant and they do not consider prison health care as a career choice. In describing staffing challenges, McDonald writes,

> But there are a number of difficulties in recruiting well-trained professionals, including physicians, because of the prisons' remote locations and generally unappealing conditions, the absence of formally organized health care systems distinct from other functional divisions, inadequate facilities, and inadequate medical record-keeping systems.[31]

There are many reasons medical staff hesitate to consider employment in a correctional institution. First, they believe that the facilities are inadequate. Most people have a perception of prisons as dark, dungeonlike buildings and a prison hospital as little more than a dreary room with an examination table. Second, there are concerns that inmates are difficult patients who sue the medical staff for any care that the inmates believe is inadequate. Prisoners can be difficult patients, but in reality are probably no different in attitude than many others in the general public.

Third, prison routines and security precautions can be frustrating to medical personnel who do not want to be burdened with the inflexible schedules and security procedures necessary to prison operations. In addition, some medical personnel do not consider prison work because they fear for their safety, and there is a potential (although it seldom occurs) for assault by an inmate. Finally, it is probably a fact that the salaries for public sector medical persons is lower than many options available to health care providers in the community. However, with today's emphasis on managed care and efficiency in treating patients, the gap in pay and working conditions between a prison and the community is closing.

Prison administrators have to work hard to counter the negative image that medical staff have about prisons. In reality, there are many benefits to working in a prison environment. The facilities are often new and are certainly comparable to those in any physicians' office or community clinic. Prison physicians usually do not have to carry malpractice insurance, because they are government employees and are not personally liable (the government agency has to cover legal fees and lost claims) if they practice according to accepted professional standards. Some medical personnel find prison medical care fascinating work, because they see a wide variety of medical problems in a population of prisoners. And pay and benefits (especially retirement) are not as bad as most people perceive. As government agencies found that they could not compete for medical staff, many adjusted their pay scales to be able to hire and retain medical staff.

Current Medical Operations in a Prison Setting

Medical care for prisoners is usually provided with a combination of prison and community resources. Care is typically provided through four levels: the standard prison infirmary, contracts with community specialists, the use of community hospitals for serious problems or surgical needs, and prison hospitals for inmates with long-term or continuous medical needs. Correctional agencies have their own staff of full-time medical personnel and have part-time contracts with specialty providers. Individual prisons usually have contracts with many local hospitals to meet the more serious needs that cannot be met at the prison. The next sections describe these four levels of prison medical care.

Prison Infirmaries

The first level of medical needs within a prison is for the day-to-day minor illnesses and injuries, similar to the needs of the general public who go to a family practice physician's office. Inmates with colds, influenza, sprained ankles, and other routine medical conditions are seen and treated at the **prison infirmary**. The infirmaries are a combination of doctor's office, dentist's office, and pharmacy. There is usually staff coverage of the infirmary twenty-four hours every day, and physicians or other midlevel practitioners are typically in the infirmary on week days. Most prison infirmaries have an x-ray machine, a laboratory, and an emergency or trauma room for injuries and illnesses requiring immediate attention. The standard staffing pattern for a prison infirmary includes one or two physicians (sometimes a physician and a nurse practitioner), a dentist and dental assistant, several nurses (a combination of RNs and LPNs), and a pharmacist.

Most inmate medical needs can be met in the infirmary, and services include preliminary medical screening when inmates are received at a prison, daily sick call, referrals to specialists, and continuous treatment for inmates with chronic illnesses. At the preliminary screening, inmates receive a physical examination, there is an inquiry into current illnesses and health problems (which include dental and mental health needs), and a treatment plan is developed for meeting these needs during the period of imprisonment. Every day, prisons hold **sick call**, at which inmates with a medical need can come to the infirmary and be examined by a nurse, who can either provide necessary treatment or schedule the inmate for an appointment with the physician. If the physician prescribes medication, the prescription is given to the prison pharmacy to fill. Inmates are not allowed to have prescription drugs in their possession, because they may not take them as prescribed or may abuse them in some way. Therefore, they must come to the "pill line," which is held several times per day, and receive and take their dosage. Pill line is simply that. Inmates line up at the pharmacy window or counter, are given their dosage of medication, and must take it in front of a medical staff member. Most over-the-counter medicines may be kept by inmates, and although some prisons provide it, others require inmates to purchase these medicines at the inmate commissary.

If the prison physician determines that an illness or injury must be referred to a specialist, the referral is made and an appointment scheduled by prison medical staff. Many inmates have chronic medical problems that require long-term treatment plans. If the plans do not require hospitalization, the inmate may stay at the prison under the care of the prison physician or a contract specialist. The treatment plans may include certain exercises, a special diet, physical therapy, and regular doctor visits and checkups. All of

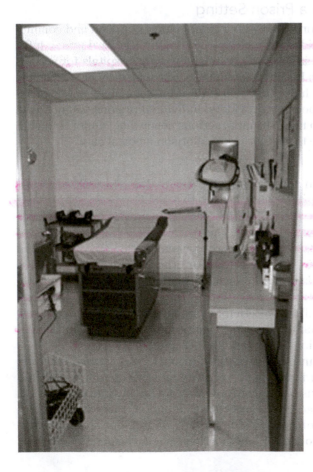

Typical examination room in a prison infirmary. Inmates are seen by healthcare providers in examination rooms that are very similar to those in a community physician's office. *(Ohio Dept. of Rehabilitation & Correction.)*

these activities can be provided in most prisons, and the medical staff coordinate exercise or dietary requirements with other departments within the prison.

Specialty Medical Care

If an inmate suffers from medical needs that cannot be met by the full-time staff, they are referred to a community medical specialist. Prisons usually contract with special medical providers in the community, including orthopedic surgeons, heart specialists, psychiatrists, dermatologists, and eye care providers. This care is delivered in one of two ways. The method preferred by the prison administration is to have the specialist visit the prison and see patients for as many hours per month as required. Most infirmaries are equipped to provide examination areas for these specialists to see and treat patients. If there is a need for specialized testing, inmates may be transported to the physicians' office or a hospital for the testing.

If the contracted medical specialist cannot or will not come to the prison infirmary to see patients, the inmates will be transported to the hospital or physicians' office for examination and treatment. This requires extensive security precautions, including escort by two or three armed correctional officers, restraining the inmate with handcuffs and leg irons (chains), and secrecy regarding the time and route of transportation so that the inmate will not know the exact time or location of the appointment. Because of the security and staffing requirements, transporting an inmate to a local hospital or physician's office for a visit ends up being expensive.

Local Hospitalization of Inmates

When an inmate requires surgery or other treatment that must be provided in a hospital, the prison uses a local hospital through a contract for services. Each prison establishes a contract with local hospitals to provide services that are beyond the scope of care available at the infirmary but that do not require transfer to the state prison hospital. The process for admitting an inmate is no different than that for community citizens. A physician admits the inmate for hospitalization and performs the tests, treatment, or surgery during the hospital stay. After completion of treatment, inmates stay in the hospital long enough for recovery and to be seen by the attending physician. Once the physician discharges an inmate from the hospital, the inmate returns to the prison and receives any follow-up care by prison medical staff or further visits with the specialist.

Security of the inmate is always difficult during hospital stays. Even though the inmate is sick and the chance of escape is reduced, the prison administrators must take all available security precautions. Depending on the security level of the inmate and potential for violence or escape, there will be from one to three armed correctional officers constantly guarding the inmate. Officers usually work eight-hour shifts, and then another group of officers relieve them in the hospital. Inmates are not handcuffed while they are in the hospital, but they usually do have leg irons (cuffs for the ankles) attached to one leg and to the hospital bed. Inmates are not allowed visits from family or friends while they are in the hospital, because there are no facilities to ensure that visitors do not bring weapons or drugs to the inmate. Movement of inmates to a hospital is a dangerous situation for staff. A few years ago, correctional officers from the U.S. Penitentiary in Lewisburg, Pennsylvania, were escorting an inmate to a local hospital. Associates of the inmate found out about the time of the hospital trip, ambushed the escort team in an escape attempt, and murdered one of the officers.

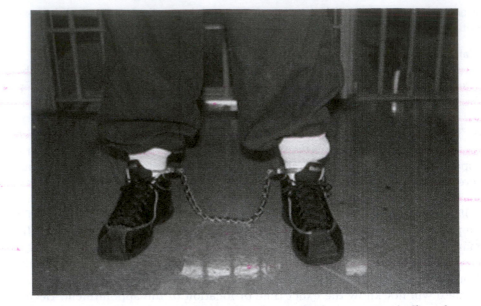

Leg irons. Even though inmates are under the watch of a correctional officer, for security of inmates while hospitalized, they have leg irons that are attached to their ankles and the other end attached to a secure place on the hospital bed. This does not interfere with care but keeps them from running away. *(Photo by Deborah L. O'Brien)*

Prison Hospitals

Every state and the Federal Bureau of Prisons operate at least one **prison hospital**. The role of these hospitals it to house and treat inmates with serious chronic care needs over a long period of incarceration, or whose medical problems are so serious that they cannot be met in a regular prison infirmary. Prison hospitals are used instead of local contract community hospitals when the length of stay in a hospital makes it more cost efficient to transport the inmate to the prison hospital. These prison hospitals are a combination of standard prison housing and in-patient hospital beds. Inmates with in-patient needs are housed in rooms that look very much like regular hospital rooms at the prison, with medical staffing and equipment similar to any community hospital. When these inmates are able to be released from the hospital, they may be returned to a regular prison or stay in the regular housing status at the prison hospital. The following is a description of the function of a prison hospital as published in the inmate handbook for the Federal Medical Center at Rochester, Minnesota:

> FMC, Rochester has long established a tradition of excellence in correctional health care. We are frequently relied upon to provide health care to offenders with complex mental and physical illnesses. Inmates are sent to us directly from the U.S. Courts, as well as from other Bureau of Prison facilities throughout the country. The expertise and knowledge of our many correctional and health care professionals will assist in many avenues during the tenure of your confinement

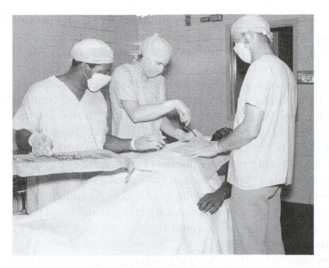

Surgery in prisons. Few prison doctors do surgery in prisons today; however, it was common practice until the 1960s. Inmates were even used as medical assistants. *(Courtesy of the Ohio Department of Rehabilitation and Correction)*

to include release preparation, a most important component, and the successful treatment of any illnesses. FMC, Rochester's health care delivery system has become a trademark model within the agency.[32]

Historically, these prison hospitals have provided all types of treatment, including complicated surgeries. However, most states have found that they cannot afford to keep up with modern technology and equipment required for such surgical procedures, nor can they recruit surgeons as full-time staff. Therefore, current prison hospitals more commonly use local community hospitals and contract surgeons, performing required surgical procedures in the community. Following the surgery, inmates are housed at the prison hospital for postoperative treatment and recovery.

Challenges and Approaches to Providing Medical Care for Inmates

There is no question that the delivery of health care to prison inmates has improved dramatically over the past few decades. The involvement of federal courts and the implementation of correctional health care standards are two factors that have most influenced this improvement. However, there are still many issues regarding increasing need for inmate care and the resulting cost of care that must be addressed. Therefore, correctional administrators are experimenting with a variety of new approaches for the delivery of medical care for inmates. These include dealing with the problem of infectious diseases; cost containment initiatives, such as requiring inmate copayment for services; the implementation of managed care procedures; contracting with the private sector; the increased use of available technology; and inmate health educational programs.

The Challenge of Infectious Diseases in Prisons

Prisons face problems of infectious diseases often greater than in the general U.S. population. Infectious diseases most common to and most problematic with correctional populations include HIV/AIDS, tuberculosis, and hepatitis C (HCV). In 2007, a health and academic policy conference on correctional health care examined the research and prevention of infectious diseases in prisons and jails and agreed that the focus should be on HIV and HCV infections due to the prevalence of both in incarcerated populations.[33]

Human immunodeficiency virus (HIV) attacks the body's immune system, increasing the chance of infection and other diseases. The HIV virus can develop into acquired immune deficiency syndrome (AIDS), which usually proves fatal after some time. It is estimated that between 800,000 and 900,000 Americans are infected with the HIV virus. The overall rate of confirmed AIDS cases among the U.S. prison population (0.50 percent) was approximately three times the rate in the general U.S. population. On December 31, 2004, there were 21,336 state prison inmates (1.9 percent of the state prison population) and 1,680 federal inmates (1.1 percent of the population) known to be HIV-positive, and 6,027 were confirmed to have developed AIDS.[34] As indicated in Table 14-1, the percentage of the prison population infected with HIV has declined from 2.3 percent of the prison population in 1995 to 1.8 percent in 2004. During 2004, 203 inmates died from HIV-related causes.[35]

To determine whether inmates have HIV/AIDS, many states require inmates to have an HIV test. In a 2005 survey, 33 percent of state and federal prison systems reported that they conduct mandatory HIV testing of inmates.[36] All prison systems provide educational information to inmates to inform them of the potential for inmates in population to have HIV/AIDS, describe the types of behaviors that can lead to infection, and reduce the fear of infection from other inmates. Once inmates are determined to be positive for HIV, prisons take different approaches to the management of this population. In a survey

Table 14-1
PERCENTAGE OF HIV-POSITIVE PRISON INMATES BY YEAR

Year-End	Number	Percent of Population
1995	24,256	2.3%
1996	23,881	2.2
1997	23,886	2.1
1998	25,680	2.2
1999	25,801	2.1
2000	25,333	2.0
2001	24,147	1.9
2002	23,864	1.9
2003	23,663	1.9
2004	23,046	1.8

Source: Laura M. Maruschak, *HIV in Prisons, 2004.* Bureau of Justice Statistics Bulletin (Washington, DC: U.S. Department of Justice, November 2006), p. 1.

conducted by the Criminal Justice Institute during 2005, thirty-eight states reported that they did not separate inmates testing positive for AIDS, whereas twelve reported that they did separate these inmates from the general inmate population.[37]

A controversial issue is to what extent HIV is transmitted inside of prisons. In a recent study, Krebs found that in a sample of 5,265 male inmates incarcerated as of 1978 and released from prison before 2000, thirty-three inmates (0.63 percent) contracted HIV while in the sampled state prison system.[38] Another 238 inmates released were positive for HIV, but there was no evidence they contracted HIV while in prison. These findings are consistent with other studies indicating that most inmates who have HIV are probably infected in the community prior to their incarceration.[39] Hammett notes that "although transmission within correctional facilities has been documented, it does not occur often enough to justify the all-too-commonly used metaphor of correctional facilities as 'breeding grounds' for HIV/Aids."[40]

Tuberculosis (TB) was a serious medical problem during the early 1900s in the United States; it declined and then resurged in the 1980s and 1990s. It is particularly a problem in prisons and jails, as inmates have high rates and risk of TB because of their background of poverty, poor living conditions, substance abuse, and a higher level of HIV/AIDS than the general U.S. population. Also, overcrowded conditions in correctional facilities increase the potential for transmission of TB among inmates. Early in the 1990s, particular concern was raised by various outbreaks of multidrug-resistant TB in New York State and other jurisdictions. During 2003, there were a total of 14,355 tuberculosis cases among the noninmate population and 475 cases (3.8 percent) among the federal, state, and local prisoner population.[41]

An inmate found to have active TB is immediately isolated from the rest of the inmate population, and all effort is made to prevent any staff or inmate from breathing the contaminated air around him or her. Most prisons now have negative pressure isolation rooms in their medical areas and prison hospitals, in which the ventilation system for that room is contained and does not flow into the general ventilation system for the prison. Inmates are placed in these rooms and treated with medication until they prove no longer contagious. They will be regularly screened to detect whether they have returned to an active state.

Hepatitis C virus (HCV) is the most common blood-borne illness in the United States and is a serious problem among criminal offenders. It is a serious viral disease that attacks the liver and can result in lifelong infections of the liver, cancer, liver failure, or death. The disease is most commonly spread through the bloodstream as a result of drug users sharing needles. In a 2004 publication, a survey with 1,209 prisons responding indicated that almost all facilities test for the disease and of all inmates tested, 17,911 (31 percent) were positive for hepatitis C.[42] It is estimated that 39 percent of all Americans infected with the disease are in prison.

Hepatitis C was not identified until the mid-1990s, and it is widely accepted that 15 to 20 percent of those who contract the disease will require no treatment, but in the remainder, the disease will lead to a chronic infection.[43] State and federal prisons struggle with how to care for inmates with this serious disease, and the Centers for Disease Control in 2003 sponsored a meeting for correctional health care workers to share experiences and improve the delivery of treatment options in a correctional setting.[44] The ability to identify, diagnose, and treat hepatitis C has improved, but it is often complicated by the simultaneous problems of drug abuse and mental illness among those infected.

During 2009, another infectious disease that had a major impact on almost every state and federal prison was the pandemic flu. At that time, the "swine flu" or H1N1 virus was spread throughout America and caused several deaths. The Centers for Disease Control and Prevention estimated that approximately 59 million people were infected with the swine flu and there were between 8,520 and 17,620 2009 H1N1-related deaths between April 2009 and February 13, 2010.[45] The midlevel in this range is about 12,000 H1N1-related deaths in 2009. There were many professional conferences, medical meetings, and publications about the best way to prevent and treat H1N1 in a correctional setting. The flu was treated similar to seasonal flu, but could have a more serious impact on those inflicted who already had a health problem such as another infectious disease or were chronic care inmates. In a recent article,[46] the following steps were suggested to control the spread of H1N1 in a correctional environment:

- Medical screenings: Thorough screening as inmates enter a facility can detect symptoms of the disease and keep it from spreading to others. If detected, inmates are isolated and tested to confirm if they are contagious.

- Housing area medical restrictions: When a case or cases are discovered in a housing unit, the entire unit is put on restriction. Restricted movement keeps those infected from passing it to others and care is given to all who showed symptoms in the housing unit.[47]

- Sanitation: Extra cleaning takes place throughout a facility, to include sanitation with disinfectant solutions.

- Staff protection: Staff working in direct contact with infected inmates are issued appropriate masks and gloves and are educated about the disease and how to protect themselves from it.

Cost Containment Initiatives

One of the ways correctional agencies are trying to contain cost increases for prison health care is through managed care strategies, similar to those implemented in the community. The major components of community managed care include universal access, limited scope of services, limited choice of providers, minimal copayments, selective contracts with a network of providers for specialized treatment, and the use of negotiated fixed fees for service providers. All these practices are usually associated with health maintenance organizations (HMOs), which (although not universally accepted as successful) have shown success in containing the cost of health care delivery.

It has been suggested that correctional agencies provide favorable settings for this type of managed care, and several agencies have been using it for some time. Texas has established a Correctional Managed Health Care Committee to provide cost effective health care for the inmates housed within the Texas Department of Criminal Justice. The mission of this committee is as follows:

- Providing TDCJ offenders with timely access to care consistent with constitutional standards

- Maintaining a quality of care that meets accepted standards of care

- Managing the costs of delivering comprehensive health care services to a growing and aging offender population.[48]

Although this statement is true, there are many factors that have worked against prisons using this mission to the fullest to contain cost.

With the rural location of most prisons and lack of competition among prospective medical providers, prisons many times cannot develop networks or medical contracts using fixed costs for services. In many cases, prison managers believe that they are fortunate to get anyone to provide medical services, even if it costs a premium. Security, not cost-efficiency, concerns must also be the dominant decision-making factor in the delivery of medical care. McDonald identifies three strategies that can be used by correctional agencies to implement managed care principles and contain costs, including "reducing the costs of purchased goods and services, containing costs by limiting or dissuading prisoners' use of services, and contracting with full-service firms to deliver health care."[49] One common approach by states is to attempt to use their state university medical schools as a resource for providing health services to inmates.

A large portion of a correctional medical budget goes toward prescription drugs. A very successful way to save money without reducing quality of care is through the use of a drug formulary. A formulary is a listing of the drugs authorized to be used, which includes a wide range of medications to allow health professionals to prescribe needed treatment. To develop the formulary, medical providers provide input on the types of drugs they prescribe for common medical issues they see. A committee of health care professionals reviews and picks a list of drugs to be used for each care. If all providers use the same drugs (and generic when possible), much better bulk buying can occur rather than filling and purchasing each prescription separately. The Kentucky Department of

A prison pharmacy. Inmates who require prescription drugs have the prescription filled from the pharmacy located within the prison. Drug formularies are a good way to keep down the cost of prescription drugs. *(Photo by Deborah L. O'Brien)*

Corrections (KDOC) notes that in 2008, they spent over $46 million for health care to inmates and $5.7 million for pharmaceuticals. Through use of a formulary, KDOC is realizing savings of nearly $500,000 per year.[50]

One of the most interesting approaches in delivery of prison medical care has been the requirement of a copayment from inmates. By the early 2000s, forty states, the U.S. Bureau of Prisons, and hundreds of county jails were charging inmates a small copayment of between two and five dollars when they requested medical care, just as most citizens pay a copayment when they see a family physician.[51] The primary purpose of the copayment is not to generate revenues, but to reduce the demand for medical services, under the assumption that some inmates come to sick call even when it is not required. This unnecessary use drives up the overall cost of providing prison health care and diverts staff resources from where they can better be used.

In order to make copay fair, without denying access to medical care, the California Medical Association's Corrections and Detention Committee developed guidelines for its use. These guidelines include the communication of the policy and fee schedules to inmates, a possibility to waive fees for indigent inmates, a grievance process for inmates to challenge a billed service, and the importance of evaluating the effectiveness of a copay system.[52] Most correctional agencies believe that their copay policies have been effective. For example, an Alabama jail director of nursing reports that the jail had cut its sick call to see a nurse, doctor, or dentist by 50 percent.[53] Nevada was one of the first states to begin to use these copayments, and reported that in the first two years after implementing a copayment, inmate medical utilization was reduced by 50 percent.[54]

A rapidly growing approach to providing health care to inmates is through contracting for its delivery with the private sector. Moore describes the state of private sector involvement in prison health care as follows:

> The first jail system to contract for a wholly provided inmate health system by a private vendor was Rikers Island in June of 1973. . . . Today, there are 14 private sector firms that provide inmate health care on a national or regional basis, and 20 states have privatized all or part of their inmate health care services.[55]

Under a full-service contract, the private vendor operates the prison infirmary and provides all health care and prescription medications to inmates. The private vendor hires and pays the salaries of all the medical staff, contracts for specialty services or hospitalization in the community, and makes medical decisions regarding inmate needs. The contract with the private provider usually lists the types of services that must be provided, such as initial health screening, daily sick call, specialty care clinics, radiology services, physical therapy, and treatment of infectious diseases such as TB and HIV/AIDS. Contracts are usually a fixed price for each inmate per day, although they may specify a maximum spent on any one inmate per year.

There are many advantages and disadvantages of contracting with a private provider. Advantages can include lower costs through use of utilization reviews or pharmacy formularies, improved quality of service delivery, and enhanced recruitment of health care staff. Disadvantages can be union or public staff resistance, or the profit motive undermining quality care.[56] The request for proposal must be very detailed and the contracts with private providers must be closely monitored and evaluated. The government agency does not contract its overall responsibility for the delivery and quality of the health care, but can still be liable for failure to provide adequate health care for inmates.

The Use of Technology

The most widely used technology to respond to current challenges in the delivery of prison health care has been the use of "telemedicine." Simply stated, **telemedicine** is "the use

Practical Perspectives

Reducing the Cost of Prison Health Care

A state department of corrections was suffering from extremely rapid increases in health care costs. The inmate population was aging, it seemed like they had more inmates with infectious diseases, and they could not control their costs for inmates sent out of the prisons to specialists, for tests, and for hospitalization. They decided to look at all other departments of corrections to see if there were practices they could adopt and they looked for ways other industries were keeping their health care costs under control. Several good ideas were evaluated and many of them were implemented.

First, they considered the implementation of electronic medical records. This would be time consuming, very costly, and they would have to get their medical providers to change the way they practiced medicine. Instead of a physician having a nurse to take notes in the medical record, they had to do it themselves in laptop computers in each exam room. They believed the payoff was worth it, but decided to do further study and implement other more short-term savings ideas before they attempted to go to paperless records.

They next looked at their utilization rates. Like most correctional agencies, it was difficult to recruit physicians and nurse practitioners, and they often had several contractors working part time who never became proficient at the practice of correctional medicine. Therefore, they sent a large number of inmates to specialists outside the prison, just because they did not understand the security challenge of this and they did not want to take the risk of getting sued if they took a more conservative treatment. The department put several initiatives into place. First, they wrote sound medical protocols to guide decisions of medical professionals who may not be familiar with the way to treat certain types of illnesses. They did more training of providers on common medical issues and dealing with inmates. They formed a peer review committee so that other physicians could look at the types of tests and

outside referrals each provider ordered, and when one seemed way out of line, they would have peer physicians meet and discuss alternatives that were within a standard of care but could be tried before ordering more tests. They also hired an orthopedic surgeon to give opinions to primary physicians as an alternative to sending lots of inmates out for x-rays or to see a physician for back pain. All these reduced some of the unnecessary utilization.

They then realized that they were paying "retail" rates at each local hospital the prisons used. Since inmates do not have any insurance, there were no negotiated or Medicare rates they could follow. They reached out to two sources: the state university hospital and several insurance companies. They asked the university if they would provide all the medical care for state inmates and give them a discount on rates. At the same time they asked insurance companies if they could "buy in" to their provider network and get their client rates if they paid an up front fee to join. They compared the two of these and while both would have saved them money, they chose to use the university medical staff and hospital for services.

Finally, they created a drug formulary and required all their providers to use it. Through this, they not only used less expensive generic drugs that met their needs but they were also then able to combine purchases of these drugs through competitive bidding and received much better rates. All together, they saved over $3 million per year on delivering medical care to inmates. And they had no inmate complaints, as they did not reduce the quality of care. They "banked" some of the savings to fund the purchase of the technology to use to create electronic medical records. They estimated that at this rate, they can afford the electronic record system in three years and then be able to save even more money on their medical delivery to inmates.

of telecommunications technologies to offer health care or clinical information, across geographic, time or cultural barriers."[57] Telemedicine works by using live video conferencing that enables a health care provider at another location to examine an inmate. A medical staff member with the inmate "presents" the patient, summarizing the medical history and current problem. The camera illustrates the symptoms, and the physician at the remote location can ask questions of the patient and request other camera views of the affliction. It is also possible to use a "document" camera to share medical information and data such as x-rays and EKG results. With this technology, many specialty examinations can be completed without the physician being at the same location as the patient. Equipment has become more sophisticated over time, and telemedicine machines are now more than video conferencing, and can include testing equipment as a part of the system that allows the remote provider to conduct additional tests as he or she sees the patient.

Telemedicine can help solve many of the problems facing correctional health care. As noted, with the rural location of many prisons, there are few specialty providers who are available or willing to see inmates. Because telemedicine does not require the specialist to be located near the facility, the availability of specialty clinics is expanding and contracting can become more competitive. Also, it solves the issue of recruitment of medical staff to remote location, as providers can be anywhere in the country and still deliver care. In addition, the high cost for security to take inmates outside the prison for examinations is eliminated. No extra staff cost is incurred, because inmates simply report to the prison infirmary for video conferencing examinations. While the costs for the newest version of the equipment can be expensive (approximately $30,000 per site), this cost is soon recovered with the reduction of the costs for inmate transport outside the prison.

Health Educational Programs

One of the most promising strategies for reducing the demand for inmate health care is the implementation of health promotion and disease prevention programs. Prison administrators, recognizing that they will have custody of many offenders for long periods of time, have realized the potential financial and service-avoidance benefits of such programs. Few offenders have lived a very healthy lifestyle prior to their incarceration. Although there is no verifiable evidence, it is assumed that improved habits in diet and exercise, along with reducing high-risk activities, such as intravenous drug use or homosexual activities, can reduce the frequency of inmate illnesses in the future.

Although most of the health educational programs are preventative, some also educate inmates in better managing their own illnesses, thereby lessening the severity of the problem and the need for medical care. For instance, inmates with lower-back problems are educated about the importance of stretching before exercise, how to perform their own physical therapy, and activities to avoid. This conservative treatment can reduce pain, allow inmates to continue their normal activities, and lessen the potential need for back surgery. Similarly, inmates with diabetes or heart disease receive education on the benefits of proper diet and exercise, which can reduce the potential for a heart attack or death. Almost every prison educates inmates on the danger of infectious diseases, such as HIV/AIDS or TB, and how to avoid activities that can lead to infection of these diseases.

Other areas often included in health educational programs are changes in recreation and diet by inmates. Instead of offering only traditional recreation programs targeting young and healthy inmates, many prisons are now providing moderate exercise programs for all segments of the population (including the elderly or handicapped) to encourage them to increase their activity and improve their long-range health. And prison medical staff work closely with food service staff to offer heart healthy meals. In 2000, the Federal Bureau of Prisons announced that they will even provide a "meatless" diet for interested inmates. All of these activities are believed to provide excellent opportunities to reduce the long-term health problems of incarcerated offenders.

As has been illustrated, medical services to inmates represent a difficult problem for prison administrators: Costs for medical care are rising dramatically, it is difficult to recruit qualified staff, inmates regularly sue prison administrators for failure to provide adequate medical care, and offenders with long prison terms are aging and have even more medical needs. However, prison administrators are experimenting with a variety of new approaches to meet these challenges. Although many cost reduction and disease prevention strategies are expected to prove successful, there are still many controversial issues in the use of private providers to deliver medical care. The next decade should prove whether these strategies are successful.

Food Service Programs in Prisons

The history of food service in prisons in many ways mirrors the history of prison medical care. In the early years of prison operations, food was poorly prepared, met few nutritional standards, and was not served in a professional or attractive style. The vision of "slopping" unrecognizable food on a tray for inmates was not too far from reality in the 1800s and early 1900s. However, just as with medical care, another causal factor behind many prison riots (including Attica) in the 1970s was poor food service operations. Federal courts also started looking into food service and other areas of prison operations. As a result, prison administrators turned to organizations such as the ACA for guidance in the development of professional standards.

In the ACA *Standards for Adult Correctional Institutions*, the principle guiding food service standards is that, "Meals are nutritionally balanced, well-planned, and prepared and served in a manner that meets established governmental health and safety codes."[58] The standards that follow this principle include the need to plan food menus well in advance to meet nutritional needs, maintain stored and prepared foods at appropriate temperatures to avoid food-borne illnesses, and serve food in a relaxed and normal cafeteria setting whenever possible. Another organization that works to assure quality prison food service operations is the American Correctional Food Service Association (ACFSA). The ACFSA was formed in 1969 and currently states that their mission is to "develop and promote educational programs and networking activities to improve professionalism and provide an opportunity for broadening knowledge."[59]

Food service in a correctional institution is extremely important to inmates, and there are few other services that impact the morale and undermine control quicker than poor food service. Much of this has to do with the fact that, unlike citizens in the community, inmates have limited choices in what is available to eat. In most prisons, inmates can buy a few snack items in the commissary. However, prisons do not want inmates eating exclusively from commissary purchases, and, therefore, the amount and selection is limited. With three meals each day, food service is experienced by all inmates at every meal, and it plays a key role in their daily routine. Therefore, it is understandable why some authors suggest that prison food service "is no doubt the most personal service provided in a correctional setting . . . if personnel do not do their jobs correctly and on time, negative reactions from the inmate population are likely to occur."[60]

The challenge for prison administrators is to provide tasty and nutritional meals at a reasonable cost. It is estimated that in 2008, prison food service costs were approximately 4 percent of state prison operating expenditures or $3.16 per inmate per day for food costs.[61] There are several measures used by prisons to keep these costs relatively low. First, state prisons often combine their food ordering needs, and because they purchase extremely large quantities of food, they often get a very good price. In addition, many correctional agencies operate farms and can provide for some of their own food needs. Food is prepared by inmates, and, therefore, labor costs for food preparation and serving are very low. However, even with these advantages, it is a continuous challenge for menu planners and food administrators to provide good food service and stay within the relatively low food service budgets.

Food Service Operations

There are several key areas of prison food service, including menu planning, food preparation, serving options, and special diets. For an idea of the challenges of correctional food service, the following description in the California Department of Corrections is enlightening.

Imagine you're the team of California Department of Corrections' (CDC) food managers. It's Thanksgiving Day, and 150,000-plus inmates are wondering, "Where's the turkey?" What do you do? For starters, you order 77,000 pounds of turkey. Then stuff the turkeys with 51,000 pounds of dressing, and start them baking. Next, whip up 38,000 pounds of salad, 51,000 pounds each of potatoes and yams, and top it off with 300,000 dinner rolls. That's a Traditional Thanksgiving, CDC-style. And that's pretty typical for a holiday menu in a California prison. While this is more sumptuous than on average days, inmates receive heart-healthy, well-balanced, tasty meals three times a day, seven days a week, 52 weeks a year. "As your food service program goes, so goes your institution," said CDC Food Administrator Don Barker.[62]

The first key for prison food service administrators is menu planning. Most correctional agencies develop agencywide menus that can be modified and supplemented by each prison. The menu is developed by a food dietitian to ensure that the meals are well-balanced and meet daily health needs and requirements. Most states create menus to provide between 2,700 and 3,500 calories a day. With the menu providing the prison food administrator the types of food combinations and portions to meet nutritional needs, the local prison staff can then mix the serving order and supplement the menu to meet the specific needs and likes of their inmate population, as long as they stay within their budget allowances.

An "old style" prison dining room in the Leavenworth Federal Penitentiary. This style of dining room, with steel tables lined up in a row, was used until the 1970s. (Courtesy of the Ohio Dept. of Rehabilitation & Corrections.)

The next key to successful food service is preparation and service. Prisons usually keep a thirty-day food products supply, just to ensure they do not run out because of unexpected problems with wholesale sellers or transportation of food products. To prepare food, prisons employ a core of staff who supervise inmates in preparation and cooking. The inmate cooks follow standard recipes, such as the Armed Forces Recipe Cards, that are designed for food preparation for large numbers of people. Once prepared, there are several ways in which food is served to the inmate population, including cafeteria style and feeding on the units.

Cafeteria style feeding is done in two ways. The first is the "open line," similar to buffet restaurants in the community, where customers take a tray and move along a line of foods, selecting those they want to purchase. In a prison cafeteria, inmates come to the dining room in groups, either from housing units or from their work assignments. They form a line and move along the serving line with their trays. With the open line style, inmate servers put food on the trays, or inmates may be allowed to serve themselves certain items (perhaps potatoes or bread) if there is no limit on serving portions. Some prisons use "blind lines" in which inmates cannot see who is serving, and servers cannot see who will receive the tray. This reduces complaints of the size of portions inmates receive, because they simply get the next full tray on the line. Unlike a community cafeteria restaurant, inmates have few choices from the prison menu, but they can choose not to take an item on the menu. There are, however, usually religious or medical diet options, such as nonpork options for Muslims, or nonsalt or heart-healthy servings for medical reasons.

When they reach the end of the food line, most prisons allow inmates to sit wherever they want in the dining room. Dining rooms are usually large and optimally seat about one-third of the entire prison population at a time. Inmates are allowed to talk to friends at the table, but they are not usually allowed to move around the dining room to talk to other inmates. Allowing inmates to move around the dining room from table to table creates a minor security concern, because large numbers of inmates are together in one location. However, the more important concern is the need to quickly move inmates through the dining room, so that all inmates can be fed in a reasonably short (usually one hour) period of time.

Modern prison dining room. This style of dining is more relaxed than the old style and attempts to create an environment more like a school.
(Photo by Richard P. Seiter)

The second food service option is to bring the food to the inmates in the unit in which they are housed. With **unit dining**, the food is prepared in a central kitchen and then transported in hot and cold carts or in insulated trays (to maintain proper food temperatures) to the units. Unit dining is primarily used in jails or detention facilities, or in prison special housing units (SHUs) in which the inmates seldom leave their cells. If the institution uses insulated trays, the food is put on the trays ahead of time and delivered to each inmate in the cell or in a small unit dining area. If the food comes in a bulk hot/cold cart, it is usually placed on the trays at the housing unit by inmate servers under the supervision of staff to maintain portion control.

Many states use a "cook chill" process for feeding.[63] In the cook chill process, food is prepared in a central kitchen, and quickly chilled to thirty-four degrees, just above freezing, and maintained in walk-in coolers for up to three days. For serving, it is delivered to satellite kitchens near the housing units in the institution, where it is "rethermed," or heated to the proper temperature for serving. California has found this to be a convenient and efficient method of preparing and serving food. Many of the California prisons house more than 4,000 inmates, and it would be impossible to bring that many inmates to a central dining area.

An important element to successful food service is the inmate workforce. With a few core staff to supervise, inmate workers read recipes, cook food, and serve it to the rest of the population. Inmates must be trained and focus on quality so as to make food service in prisons satisfactory. One incentive for these inmate workers is that they know they can develop this work into a trade and potential job opportunity. In a survey from

1999 to 2003 of where exoffenders found jobs, "accommodation and food services" was the third highest ranking industry in terms of the number of exoffenders hired.[64] While working in the prison kitchen, they quickly learn that while restaurant work is not easy, it can be a good vocation.

Food service operations in a prison are a key to inmate morale and order. Food service staff must be knowledgeable of nutritional requirements, food purchasing, cost containment, food preparation, health and safety issues, and attractive service practices. Many correctional administrators believe food service staff have one of the most challenging jobs in a prison. They must supervise a large inmate workforce; they must maintain security of food, equipment, and utensils; and they must ensure that tasty and nutritional meals are prepared and served three times every day. And unfortunately, as Scott Fisher, a former food administrator for the Federal Bureau of Prisons, says, "You are only as good as your last meal."

Visiting, Mail, and Commissary Operations

Other prison services critical to inmates and prison administrators are visiting, mail, and commissary operations. Each of these is important to inmates in terms of their maintaining ties to their family and communities, and in terms of their overall quality of life in a prison. All these can not only create a problem of inmate morale if not managed well but also present a serious security risk. For these reasons, much time and attention is paid to these service areas.

The First Amendment of the Constitution prohibits Congress from "abridging the freedom of speech, or of the press, or the right of the people peaceably to assemble. . . ." Yet, there are some restrictions to the common citizen's rights to free speech, and it is easy to imagine that many such restrictions would apply to free speech, access to the press, or freedom to assemble in a prison environment. The balancing test created in *Pell v. Procunier* is the guideline used in determining the reasonableness of restricting First Amendment rights to inmates. This balancing test is a challenge with inmate mail. Mail is recognized as important in communicating with family and friends outside prison, and such contact aids in rehabilitation and success after release. In the case of *Procunier v. Martinez* (1974), the U.S. Supreme Court acknowledged that there was a valid security interest in prison officials reading inmate mail, but determined that they could not censor it.[65] Prison officials also cannot prevent inmates from writing letters that are vulgar or disparaging about prison staff (*McNamara v. Moody*, 1979).[66] In *Turner v. Safley* (1987), the Supreme Court also allowed prison officials to continue to ban inmates from writing to inmates in other correctional institutions.[67] And in regard to restricting the right of assembly, the Supreme Court in 1977 supported the ban on inmates soliciting other inmates to join an inmate union, having union meetings, and doing bulk mailings regarding the union (*Jones v. North Carolina Prisoners' Labor Union, Inc.*).[68]

With these restrictions, prisons attempt to let inmates communicate regularly and as much as they want through the mail with those outside of prison. Inmates may send out as many letters as they like, but must pay for their own postage, unless they are deemed indigent, and then will be given a small number of stamps (often ten) per month. Letters must not be sealed, and prison staff are allowed to read them before they are sent out.

Inmates have been known to mail threats to others or to include powders or other suspicious substances.[69] For these reasons, inmate mail is considered the property of the institution until it is handed over to the U.S. Postal Service.

Other than from other inmates, they can receive letters from anyone. Incoming mail is opened and searched (usually just unfolding the letters and shaking them out) for contraband such as drugs, but is then delivered to inmates. There have been efforts to find technologies that could help detect drugs in corrections mail. Ion mobility spectrometry scanners were tested under the supervision of the National Institute of Justice. However, there were false positives from the tests, and these technologies are expensive and are used by very few correctional institutions.[70]

Another important and high-risk service within prisons is the visiting of inmates by family and friends. Inmates suffer from the separation from their family and friends, and visiting is the key way they can maintain contact and their ties to the community.[71] Separation from children is difficult for inmates and there is no way to maintain some type of normal parental relationship even through visits. This is particularly true for female inmates. Approximately 62 percent of women held in state prisons have children under age eighteen, and about two-thirds of these women (compared to 42 percent of male inmates) lived with their young children before entering prison.[72] Most children of female offenders end up with their maternal grandmothers. In contrast, almost 90 percent of children of male inmates live with the children's mothers.

With such a large proportion of inmates having children, visiting in prison is particularly important. Visits are problematic for female inmates and their children due to the long distance between the inmates' homes and the prisons in which they are incarcerated, as female prisoners are a small portion of total inmates and with fewer female prisons, women are often placed farther from their homes than men. While wives of male inmates regularly bring children to visit their fathers, when mothers end up in prison, they receive fewer visits with children due to the distances and the logistical problems those giving child care have in making visits.[73]

Prison visiting areas usually provide seating similar to that in an airport waiting area, and inmates and their visitors just sit next to or across from each other and talk or play table games. Even for adults to visit, it is difficult to sit for more than an hour or two and just talk with little else to pass the time. Prisons allow visiting several times per week, and visitors can usually come without an appointment if they have been preapproved as a visitor. Visitors may not bring anything into the visiting room, and there are vending machines for them to purchase food items so they can stay through a meal time. The set up of visiting rooms is not conducive to visits from children, although many prisons provide a small room or area of the larger visiting room for small children with a television, videos, and books or toys for children to play with.

The potential for smuggling contraband into the prison during visits is high, and prison administrators devise procedures for preventing this from occurring. Drugs are the most likely contraband smuggled in, as it is very small and can often be passed to the inmate without detection. To prevent this, staff are positioned in the visiting room and there are usually cameras to videotape the interactions between inmates and visitors. Visitors must go through a metal detector, but are not pat searched. Inmates leaving the visiting room, however, are strip searched to keep them from smuggling drugs back into the prison compound.

This is a good example of a prison that created a room for children to visit their parents in a setting that is fun and relaxing for them.
(Courtesy of the Ohio Department of Rehabilitation and Correction)

One approach to prevent contraband from coming into a prison is video visitation, which is "noncontact" and the visitor does not enter the prison to visit in person with the inmate. The visitor and inmate sit in front of a video monitor and talk over the video. It saves time in processing visitors into the visiting room and by not searching inmates. It has also been shown to decrease contraband (75 percent in one Texas jail).[74] However, it is more often used in jails in which inmates are housed for short duration only. For prisons with inmates serving long sentences, it does not satisfy a need and opportunity for maintaining strong relationships and preparing for release.

An unusual approach to normalize visiting is to allow **conjugal visiting**, sometimes referred to as family visiting. Conjugal visiting is private visiting between inmates and their spouses (sometimes entire families), and there is no prohibition against engaging in sexual relations. Only six states (California, Connecticut, Mississippi, New Mexico, New York, and Washington) permit conjugal visits.[75] While most allow only a few hours of privacy, California inmates may have an entire weekend. Immediate family (spouse and children) can come, bring food, and have a weekend in a trailer on the prison grounds. They can watch television or movies, and cook their own meals. Supporters of conjugal visiting argue that it provides a normal release of sexual tension, is an incentive for good behavior (only inmates with good records earn such a visit), and reduces homosexual activity in prison. Opponents believe it can only be provided to a small number of inmates and therefore has little impact on homosexual activity. Also, it creates issues such as discriminating against inmates who are not legally married and degrades women in that the visit becomes more sexually oriented than family or social oriented.

The final key area of services is how inmates buy snacks, toiletries, and even some clothing items (tennis shoes or exercise clothes) through the prison commissary. Prisons allow inmates to maintain bank accounts (just holding their money but not paying interest) at the prison, from which they can make purchases at the commissary. Inmates are usually paid a minimal amount for working at the prison ($10 to $30 per month) or they can have family members send money into their account. With their funds, they can use the commissary, which is stocked similarly to a small convenience store. There is usually a limit on how much an inmate can spend per month (often around $100) for other than clothing items.

Once a week, inmates may make purchases in one of two ways. The first is for them to actually go to the commissary and fill out a shopping form, give it to the staff member working the counter who will tally the cost and deduct funds from their account. Inmate workers then fill a bag with the purchased items and a staff member checks to be sure it has all and no extra items. The inmates are also required to check to see they have all their items before leaving the commissary. A complaint that they did not receive everything will not be honored after they leave the physical area where the shortage can be confirmed. The second way inmates shop is to fill out a form that is then transmitted to a commissary (which may be remote from the prison). The order is filled and bagged, and the bag is delivered to the inmate in his or her housing area. This "bag and drop" approach keeps every prison from having to operate a commissary, is more efficient, and does not require the prison to stock items that may not be purchased.

Prison mail, visiting, and commissary operations are important to inmates, and prison administrators work hard to carry out these functions in an efficient and high quality manner. While each has security concerns, they also have many benefits. Inmate visiting and mail are key to their maintaining ties to the community that are important in their successful rehabilitation after release. Prison commissaries allow inmates to have some choice over what they eat and allowing them to purchase their own toiletries saves the prison money if they had to provide it all. Again, it provides choice as inmates want to choose the type of shampoo or shaving cream they use.

SUMMARY

In Part IV of this text, we described the management of prisons, including managing security, programs, and prison services. Key to prison security is the design of the facility, using professionally accepted policies and procedures to guide operations, inmate accountability, and control of contraband. Even in the provision of programs and services, it was obvious that security features such as control of contraband cross over operational lines and can impact every function within a prison. Also essential for prison security is how inmates are disciplined for violating rules, the ability of administrators to control prison gangs, and how they prepare for emergencies.

In the chapter on managing prison programs, the reasons why programs are important were discussed. A variety of programs (education and vocation training, mental health counseling, substance abuse treatment, recreation, and religious programming) were described and challenges to administrators presented. Another key program is prison work, and in addition to work to operate the facility, prison industry programs were described. Finally and importantly, the effectiveness of prison programming was offered, so that students could form their own opinion as to the value both for prison operations and for reduction of recidivism.

The final focus of Part IV was on some of the service operations within a prison. Two basic services in a prison are medical care and food service. Both share a not-too-proud history, one in which the provision of these services was done poorly and unprofessionally. Unfortunately, it took prison riots and the intervention of the federal courts to bring attention to the need for upgrading these areas. However, prison staff who manage these areas in modern prisons should be commended for the excellent jobs they do in very difficult situations. While there are many challenges to the delivery of high-quality, yet cost-effective, prison health care and food service, new techniques and experimenting with new procedures provide promise for a much brighter future. In addition, the use of mail, visiting, and commissary services in prisons was described, and the benefits and challenges addressed.

In the final section of this textbook, we look at current and future issues that prison administrators must address. The future issues are complicated by the lack of knowledge of the expected numbers of offenders who will be incarcerated and/or supervised in the community and the challenge of government budgets to the provision of quality correctional operations. Politics will always enter into corrections, as there is much debate and controversy over sentencing practices, philosophy of operations, and safety of the community from various sanctions. These issues ensure that correctional administrators will continue to be challenged in the future even more than they have been challenged in the past.

KEY TERMS

Test of cruel and unusual
  punishment
Deliberate indifference
Prison infirmary
Sick call

Prison hospital
Managed care
Copayment
Telemedicine
Health education programs

Cafeteria style feeding
Unit dining
Conjugal visiting

YOU'RE THE CORRECTIONAL ADMINISTRATOR

1. You are the chief of medical services for the state department of corrections. The department budget planners have come to you for advice. They show you figures on how the medical services budget has increased by almost 18 percent a year for the past four years. They are concerned because the budget is getting tighter, the number of inmates is increasing, and you have been projecting that certain developments within the department may increase medical costs by an even greater percentage. They ask you to estimate the

increase and come up with several solutions that can be implemented to reduce costs or at least slow the increases. What are some of the types of issues that must be considered when calculating medical costs for prisoners, and how do you first identify issues? Also, mention some techniques that you can implement statewide to reduce the cost of medical care, and the steps you would take to implement these techniques.

2. You are the food service administrator for a large department of corrections. The department is building a new prison and thinking about the best way to serve food. Of the current prisons, some have a dining room with cafeteria style service and others take food to and serve on the housing units. There are pros and cons for each, but you prefer the dining room option. However, building a dining room will add space and therefore cost to the construction. Think through what things you would consider in terms of quality, potential cost savings, and any other factors that should be considered before you make your recommendation to the architectural committee designing the new prison. Then make a decision and justify what you would recommend.

WEB LINK EXERCISES

Go to National Commission on Correctional Health Care (NCCHC) http://www.ncchc.org

First, read the mission statement and the short introduction to the Standards for Health Services. Then, go to the right side of the page and click on Journal of Correctional Health Care. Click on *Current Issue*. Look at the peer-reviewed articles and click on one that interests you (click on pdf). If your university subscribes to a service which contains this journal, you can go to the proper resource and open it for free.

Next at the same Web site, you will find a discussion of certification for individuals who work in correctional health care. Process description, eligibility, and cost are included in the discussion. Read this section, and identify what you think are the benefits of becoming certified by NCCHC. Then, recommend whether you think the cost and time required to become certified make it worthwhile.

GROUP EXERCISES

Each group will be assigned to construct a contract for private operation for one of the following services: medical care, food service, commissary operation, maintenance, and the laundry for your local jail. Groups must determine what provisions and conditions must be included, along with how the contract provisions will be monitored for compliance.

ENDNOTES

1. John DiIulio, *Governing Prisons* (New York: The Free Press, 1987), p. 29.
2. Curtis Prout and Robert Ross, *Care and Punishment* (Pittsburgh: Pittsburgh Press, 1988), p. 5.

3. See *Ruffin v. Commonwealth of Virginia*, 62 Va (21 Gratt.) 790, 796 (1871).

4. *Cooper v. Pate*, 378 US 546 (1964).

5. *Holt v. Sarver*, 309 F. Supp. 362 [E.D. Ark. 1970], *aff'd* 442 F.2d 304 98th Cir. (1971).

6. *Estelle v. Gamble*, 429 US 97 (1976).

7. *Ramos v. Lamm*, 639 F.2d 559, 576 (10th Cir., 1980).

8. *Fernandez v. United States*, 941 F.2d 1488 (11th Cir. 1991).

9. For a review of the earlier developed standards for correctional facilities, see American Correctional Association, *Sample Guidelines for the Development of Policies and Procedures for Use in Adult Correctional Institutions and Adult Local Detention Facilities* (College Park, MD: American Correctional Association, 1987); American Bar Association, *Medical and Health Care in Jails, Prisons, and Other Correctional Facilities: A Compilation of Standards and Materials* (Washington, DC: American Bar Association, 1974); and American Public Health Association, *Standards for Health Services in Correctional Institutions* (Washington, DC: American Public Health Association, 1976).

10. American Correctional Association, *Sample Guidelines for the Development of Policies and Procedures for Use in Adult Correctional Institutions and Adult Local Detention Facilities*, p. 277.

11. American Correctional Association, *Standards for Adult Correctional Institutions: Third Edition* (Lanham, MD: American Correctional Association, 1990), pp. 109–128.

12. Ibid., p. 109.

13. The ACA (through the Commission on Accreditation for Corrections) has a process whereby prisons can be inspected by independent correctional professionals to determine whether they meet the standards at a level that allows them to be "accredited" and recognized as meeting the professional standards for operating a prison.

14. Kenneth E. Kerle, *American Jails: Looking to the Future* (Boston, MA: Butterworth-Heinemann, 1988), p. 121.

15. Douglas C. McDonald, "Medical Care in Prisons," in *Prisons*, edited by Michael Tonry and Joan Petersilia (Chicago: University of Chicago Press, 1999), p. 428.

16. Jacqueline M. Moore, "Privatization of Inmate Health Care: A New Approach to an Old Problem," *Corrections Management Quarterly* 2 no. 2 (1998): 46.

17. Ibid., p. 47.

18. For a summary of the question of whether inmates receive too much medical care, see McDonald, "Medical Care in Prisons," pp. 445–446.

19. Lloyd R. Novick, R. Della Penna, M. S. Schwartz, E. Remmlinger, and R. Lowenstein, "Health Status of the New York City Prison Population," *Medical Care* 15 no. 3 (1977): 215.

20. Christopher J. Mumola and Jennifer C. Karberg, "Drug Use and Dependence, State and Federal Prisoners, 2004," *Bureau of Justice Statistics Special Report* (Washington, DC: U.S. Department of Justice, October 2006), p. 5.

21. Ibid., p. 6.

22. Charles Silverman, "Geriatric Inmates—Design and Health Care Considerations," *The State of Corrections: Proceedings of the ACA Annual Conferences in 1993* (Lanham, MD: American Correctional Association, 1994), p. 145.

23. Camille Graham Camp and George M. Camp, *Corrections Yearbook: Adult Corrections, 2002* (Middletown, CN: Criminal Justice Institute, 2003), pp. 32, 33.

24. Heather C. West and William J. Sabol, *Prisoners in 2007* (Washington, DC: U.S. Department of Justice, 2008), p. 19.

25. Theodore M. Hammett, Cheryl Roberts, and Sofia Kennedy, "Health Related Issues in Prisoner Reentry," *Crime & Delinquency* 47 no. 3 (July 2001): 390–409.

26. National Association of State Budget Officers, "State Expenditure Report FY 2006," December 2007, http://www.nasbo.org/Publications/PDFs/fy2006er.pdf (accessed August 16, 2009).

27. Public Safety Performance Project, *Public Safety, Public Spending: Forecasting America's Prison Population, 2007–2011* (Washington, DC: The Pew Charitable Trust, February 2007), p. ii.

28. Pew Center of the States, *One in 31: The Long Reach of American Corrections* (Washington, DC: Pew Charitable Trusts, March 2009), p. 2.

29. The 12 percent figure is in James J. Stephan, "State Prison Expenditures, 2001," *Bureau of Justice Statistics Special Report* (Washington, DC: U.S. Department of Justice, June 2004).

30. *Jackson v. Bishop*, 404 F.2d 572 CA (1968).

31. McDonald, "Medical Care in Prisons," p. 438.

32. Federal Medical Center, *Admission and Orientation Handbook* (Rochester, MN: U.S. Bureau of Prisons, September 2007), p. 1.

33. David Paar, Carol Bova, Jacques Baillargeon, William Mazur, and Larry Boly, "Infectious Disease in Correctional Health Care: Pursuing a Research Agenda," *Journal of Correctional Health Care* 14 no. 4 (October 2008): 263–268.

34. Laura M. Maruschak, *HIV in Prisons, 2004* (Washington, DC: Bureau of Justice Statistics, November 2006), p. 1.

35. Ibid.

36. Theodore M. Hammett, Sofia Kennedy, and Sarah Kuck, *National Survey of Infectious Diseases in Correctional Facilities: HIV and Sexually Transmitted Diseases* (Washington, DC: National Institute of Justice, March 2007).

37. Ibid.

38. Christopher P. Krebs, "Inmate Factors Associated with HIV Transmission in Prison," *Criminology and Public Policy* 5 no. 1 (February 2006): 113–136.

39. Theodore M. Hammett, M. P. Harmon, and W. Rhodes, "The Burden of Infectious Disease among Inmates of and Releasees from U.S. Correctional Facilities," *American Journal of Public Health* 92 (1997): 189–194.

40. Theodore Hammett, "Editorial Introduction: HIV in Prisons," *Criminology and Public Policy* 5 no. 1 (February 2006): 108.

41. Jessica R. MacNeil, Mark N. Lobato, and Marisa Moore, "An Unanswered Health Disparity: Tuberculosis among Correctional Inmates, 1993 through 2003," *American Journal of Public Health* 95 no. 10 (2005): 1800–1805.

42. Allen J. Beck and Laura Maruschak, "Hepatitis Testing and Treatment in State Prisons," *Bureau of Justice Statistics Special Report* (Washington, DC: U.S. Department of Justice, April 2004).

43. H. J. Alter and L. B. Seeff, "Recovery, Persistence, and Sequelae in Hepatitis C Viral Infection: A Perspective on Long-Term Outcome," *Seminars in Liver Disease* 20 no. 1 (2000): 17–35.

44. S. A. Allen, A. C. Spaulding, and A. M. Osei, "Treatment of Chronic Hepatitis C in a State Correctional Facility," *Annals of Internal Medicine* 138 (2003): 187–190.

45. Center for Disease Control and Prevention, *Questions and Answers: H1N1 Flu in the News*, http://www.cdc.gov/h1n1flu/in_the_news/updated_cdc_estimates.htm (accessed March 12, 2010).

46. Erik Berliner, "Responding to an H1N1 Outbreak in an Urban Jail Setting: The NYC Experience," *Corrections Today* 71 no. 5 (October 2009): 26–29.

47. For a description of how correctional agencies responded to H1N1, see A. C. Spaulding, V. A. McCallum, D. Walker, A. Reeves, C. Drenzek, S. Lewis, E. Bailey, J. W. Buehler, E. A. Spotts Whitney, R. L. Berkelman, "How Public Health and Prisons Can Partner for Pandemic Influenza Preparedness: A Report from Georgia," *Journal of Correctional Health* 15 no. 2 (April 2009): 118–128.

48. Texas Correctional Managed Health Care Committee, *Self Evaluation Report* (Austin, TX: Sunset Advisory Commission, August 19, 2005).

49. McDonald, "Medical Care in Prisons," pp. 459–471.

50. Scott Haas, "Formulary Management: What Is It and Why Do We Do It?" *Corrections Today* 71 no. 5 (October 2009): 34–36.

51. Camp and Camp, *Corrections Yearbook*, pp. 105–106.

52. For a full description of the California guidelines, see John Clark, "Guidelines for Implementing Inmate Medical Fees," *Corrections Today* 59 no. 6 (October 1997): 106–107.

53. Kerle, *American Jails*, p. 130.

54. M. Nolan, "Medical Co-Payment System: Nevada Department of Prisons," Paper presented at the annual conference of the American Correctional Health Services Association, Salt Lake City, Utah, April 1992.

55. Moore, "Privatization of Inmate Health Care," p. 48.

56. Ibid., p. 51.

57. Michelle Gailiun, "Telemedicine Takes Off: Correctional Systems Across Country Embrace Cost-Saving Technology," *Corrections Today* 59 no. 4 (July 1997): 68.

58. American Correctional Association, *Standards for Adult Correctional Institutions*, p. 99.

59. From the ACFSA website at http://www.acfsa.org/index.php (accessed March 21, 2010).

60. Lavinia B. Johnson, "Food Service," *Prison and Jail Administration: Practice and Theory*, edited by Peter M. Carlson and Judith Simon Garrett (Sudbury, MA: Jones and Bartlett Publishers, 2008), p. 149.

61. The 4 percent figure is in James J. Stephan, "State Prison Expenditures, 2001," *Bureau of Justice Statistics Special Report* (Washington, DC: U.S. Department of Justice, June 2004). The 2008 average per day cost is in Pew Center of the States, *One in 31: The Long Reach of American Corrections* (Washington, DC: Pew Charitable Trusts, March 2009), p. 2.

62. California Department of Corrections, "Corrections' Dedicated Food Service Team Plans Menus a Year in Advance" (Sacramento: California Department of Corrections, 1997), unpublished document, p. 1.

63. For a description of how cook/chill systems work, see Dale Stockton, "Space-Age Food Service: Jail Takes a Page out of NASA's Cook/Chill Methods," *CTM-Corrections Technology & Management* 5 no. 4 (July/August 2001): 16–19.

64. Eric Lichtenberger, "Where Do Ex-Offenders Find Jobs? An Industrial Profile of Employers of Ex-Offenders in Virginia," *Journal of Correctional Education* 57 no. 4 (December 2006): 297–311.

65. *Procunier v. Martinez*, 416 U.S. 396 (1974).

66. *McNamara v. Moody*, 606 F. Supp. 2d 621 (5th Cir. 1979).

67. *Turner v. Safley*, 482 U.S. 78 (1987).

68. *Jones v. North Carolina Prisoners' Labor Union, Inc.*, 433 U.S. 119 (1977).

69. Tripp Brinkley, "Screening Inmate Mail for Threatening or Dangerous Materials," *Corrections Today* 67 no. 4 (July 2005): 88–102.

70. Allan Turner and Becky Lewis, *Stopping Drugs in the Mail* (Washington, DC: U.S. Department of Justice, 2002).

71. A good description of the dynamics of maintaining ties through visiting is found in Johnna Christian, "Riding the Bus: Barriers to Prison Visitation and Family Management Strategies," *Journal of Contemporary Criminal Justice* 21 no. 1 (February 2005): 31–48.

72. Lauren E. Glaze and Laura M. Maruschak, *Parents in Prison and Their Minor Children* (Washington, DC: U. S. Department of Justice, 2008), pp. 3, 4, 16.

73. Karen Casey-Acevedo and Tim Bakken, "Visiting Women in Prison: Who Visits and Who Cares?" *Journal of Offender Rehabilitation* 34 no. 3 (2002): 67–83.

74. Donna Rogers, "Visiting Via Video," *Law Enforcement Technology* 31 no. 6 (June 2004): 112, 114, 117.

75. Camp and Camp, *Corrections Yearbook*, p. 149.

15

Critical Issues for Correcti Administration

Introduction

Throughout this textbook, several issues facing today's correctional administrator were noted. These issues were categorized into three areas: substantive, administrative, and policy and philosophy. Examples of substantive correctional issues include dealing with prison overcrowding, managing offenders serving long periods of time, controlling young and violent offenders, and prisoner transition to community supervision. Administrative issues include maintaining budget growth to meet an increasing number of offenders, recruiting an increasing number of staff and training and developing them for the future, and planning for a rapidly changing and uncertain future. Issues of policy and philosophy include the appropriate balance between punishment and rehabilitation, the appropriate use of risk assessment instruments, and whether the private sector should operate correctional programs for a profit.

These general topics seem daunting enough for even the most experienced and capable correctional administrators. However, this chapter is more specific and presents additional issues that face administrators and tax their organizations and personal abilities. Most of these issues are not new but have become more critical over the past few years or are expected to intensify even more going forward. Everyone has heard the comic retort when someone is asked if they have been keeping busy. "Busier than a one-armed paper hanger!" Although simple and perhaps not funny to some, one can envision this person running back and forth, trying to get paper on the wall, applying adhesive, and not ending up with total chaos. After reading about the many issues facing correctional administrators in this chapter, you will have a similar vision of an administrator running from one issue to the next, trying to keep them each from faltering, and trying to continue to move the organization forward.

Unfortunately, that image is too often the life of the modern correctional administrator. There is seldom a boring day, never a lack of issues that need attention, and always an opportunity to create new policy and practices in response to these issues. The successful administrator is one who can juggle many balls at the same time without dropping any. For individuals who like activity and thrive under challenges, correctional administration is the career for them. For those who want a more mundane and slow-paced professional life, stay away from corrections. The pace is going to increase before it slows down.

Following are only a few of the many issues that present serious challenges for those who manage and lead correctional agencies, or those who are politically charged with setting policy or allocating budget and personnel resources. There are issues about sentencing, such as prison versus community alternatives, the impact of the many legislative initiatives that drive up the prison count, and the political debates that go on about public safety and cost. There are issues regarding the changing makeup of offenders, such as juveniles sentenced as adults, aging offenders, women offenders, and those who commit sex crimes. A long-term issue that is receiving more attention is the importance of and new approaches to recruiting correctional staff. Another issue that needs to be addressed is evaluating correctional options and programs for impact on recidivism and the link between policy and effectiveness. Finally, the issue that emerged within the last decade has to do with the reentry of a large number of prisoners from correctional supervision back to society. Although reentry issues have been around for as long as criminal sanctions, the increase in the number of offenders that leave prison and return to their communities each year has created challenges regarding community services, offender families, victims, and the community in general. As we present current correctional issues, this also sets the stage for looking forward and examining what this means for the future in Chapter 16.

Sentencing Issues

Over the past twenty-five years, sentencing has changed considerably and has had a tremendous impact on both the prison population and the number of offenders under supervision in the community. Over the decade of the 1990s, the one thing that was clear, both in policy and practice, was that criminal offenders were being sentenced to longer periods in prison than previously for the same crimes. Regardless of whether this was good policy, the end result was that the prison population increased dramatically, resulting in a changed makeup of inmates in terms of age, length of sentence, gang affiliation, and needs. As of January 1, 1990, the nation's prisons held 750,000 inmates. This number increased steadily from 6 to 8 percent per year, until it reached 1.32 million on January 1, 1999.[1] During the 1990s, the inmate population grew an average of 8.7 percent per year[2] (Bureau of Justice Statistics, 2001).

Less than ten years later (on December 31, 2008), 2,424,279 offenders were incarcerated in the fifty states, the District of Columbia, and federal government's prisons and local jails. One-third of these were in jails and two-thirds were in prison.[3] However, the growth has slowed over the past decade. From 2000 to 2006, the incarcerated population increased by an average of nearly 3 percent per year.[4] However, growth slowed even more during the twelve months ending December 31, 2008, as the incarcerated population increased by only 0.2 percent. Also, nineteen states actually had a decline in their prison population during 2008.[5] The year thereafter witnessed another slowdown and a major change. Early estimates suggest that in 2009, the state prison population actually decreased for the first time in nearly forty years. The Pew Center for the States collected data that indicate that as of January 1, 2010, there were 1,403,091 inmates in state prisons, thus suggesting a decrease of 5,739 from the number of inmates on December 31, 2008.[6] The following sections describe some of the policies, politics, and approaches that impacted sentencing over the past several years.

The Public Fear of Crime

Over the past two decades, the public fear of crime has increased, resulting in a demand for tougher sentencing. According to Gallup polls, 74 percent of citizens believed that there was more crime now than a year before (see Table 15-1), despite the fact that both violence and property crime have been on a continual decline since 1993.[7] This has been true for twenty years, and public fear of crime resulted in a demand to get tough on crime and on criminals. It did not matter that criminal sentences had already been significantly increased, the public wanted criminals sentenced for longer periods of time, and they did

Table 15-1
ATTITUDES TOWARD THE CRIME LEVEL IN THE UNITED STATES, 1989–2009: IS THERE MORE CRIME IN THE UNITED STATES THAN THERE WAS A YEAR AGO, OR LESS?

	More (%)	Less (%)	Same (%)	No Opinion (%)
2009 October 1–4	74	15	6	5
2008 October 3–5	67	15	9	9
2007 October 4–7	71	14	8	6
2006 October 9–12	68	16	8	8
2005 October 13–16	67	21	9	3
2004 October 11–14	53	28	14	5
2003 October 6–8	60	25	11	4
2002 October 14–17	62	21	11	6
2001 October 11–14	41	43	10	6
2000 August 29–September 5	47	41	7	5
1998 October 23–25	52	35	8	5
1997 August 22–25	64	25	6	5
1996 July 25–28	71	15	8	6
1993 October 13–18	87	4	5	4
1992 February 28–March 1	89	3	4	4
1990 September 10	84	3	7	6
1989 January 24–28	84	5	5	6

Source: The Gallup Organization, *The Gallup Poll* (Online), http://www.gallup.com/poll/1603/Crime.aspx (accessed April 27, 2010).

not want prisons to be places where criminals could spend idle hours watching television or working out with weights.

In an effort to respond to this fear of crime, elected officials vowed to "lock 'em up and throw away the key" for any criminal that commits serious crimes or continues a pattern of criminality. As a result, the average length of incarceration of 23.7 months in 1990 increased to 30.0 months in 1996[8] and to 29.2 months in 2001.[9] More than 300,000 inmates were serving sentences of twenty years or more or life on January 1, 2002.[10]

Even with the "tough on crime" approaches resulting in more prison sentences for longer periods of time for many offenders, the largest proportion of offenders remain on probation or are supervised in the community. As indicated in Figure 15-1, the estimated number of people under correctional supervision increased from 1.84 million in 1980 to 7.3 million by 2008. Of these, 4.27 million (58 percent) were on probation, 785,500 (10.7 percent) were in jail, 1.52 million (20.7 percent) were in prison, and 828,000 (11.3 percent) were on parole.[11]

Partisan Politics and the Lack of Policy Alternatives

One reason the U.S. prison population has increased so much over the past twenty years is the influence of politics on sentencing policy. In examining the use of incarceration as a sanction for criminal offending, changes in sentencing policies had significantly more impact than other changes. Blumstein and Beck examined the growth of imprisonment between 1980 and 1996 and concluded that 88 percent was due to changes in policy, including sentencing to prison rather than probation (51 percent) and lengthening time served by offenders (37 percent). Only 12 percent of the growth was the result of changes in the crime rate or the makeup of criminal offenders.[12]

As noted above, elected officials have aggressively embraced "tough on crime" policies, because they believe they are good politics. The watershed political event regarding politics and sentencing policy occurred during the 1988 presidential campaign, when Vice President George Bush successfully used the public's fear of crime as a campaign tool against his opponent, Governor Michael Dukakis of Massachusetts. Bush used campaign ads presenting Dukakis as soft on crime for allowing a Massachusetts furlough program

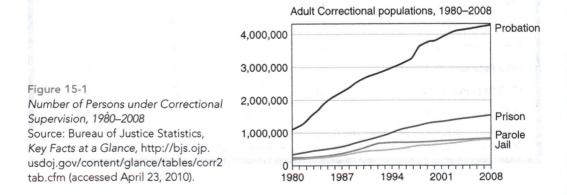

Figure 15-1
Number of Persons under Correctional Supervision, 1980–2008
Source: Bureau of Justice Statistics, *Key Facts at a Glance*, http://bjs.ojp. usdoj.gov/content/glance/tables/corr2 tab.cfm (accessed April 23, 2010).

that allowed the commission of a tragic murder by Willie Horton, a furloughed inmate, while he lived in a halfway house.

Other candidates saw the effectiveness and feared that they would be labeled "soft on crime" if they did not make similar campaign promises to keep dangerous offenders in prison for longer periods of time. As a result, we have seen legislation such as the California three-strikes law, which was passed after a similar public campaign to toughen laws. A twelve-year-old girl named Polly Klaas was murdered by Richard Allen Davis, who was on parole after serving only eight years of a sixteen-year sentence for kidnapping. These laws required any criminal with three felonies to serve the rest of their life in prison with no opportunity for parole.

Another major impact on sentencing policy came about with the nation's war on drugs, in which President Ronald Reagan pushed through legislation to toughen drug laws, allocate more resources to investigating and prosecuting drug laws, and require mandatory prison terms for federal drug offenders. Even first-time offenders, if they are involved in the sale of drugs, will be sentenced to either a five- or ten-year term depending on the volume of drugs in the conspiracy of sale and distribution. The dramatic increase in the federal prison population resulted primarily from these policies, to the point that over one-half of the federal prison population is currently drug offenders.

Unfortunately, once political rhetoric forces correctional policy to move in this direction, it is difficult to change the direction and turn back the clock. Increasing costs of correctional budgets usually take money from other public services, such as education, social service programs, and improvement of deteriorating infrastructures. For example, the National Conference of State Legislatures reported that state spending on higher education experienced the highest reduction in its history during the 1990s, during which state correctional spending had its fastest growth.[13] Addressing this dilemma, Irwin and Austin argue that society must turn away from the excessive use of prisons, which is diverting money from education, child care, mental health, and medical services, all of which have a greater impact on reducing crime than does building more prisons.[14]

It is interesting to note that the public is not nearly as strongly in favor of "get tough" policies as elected officials believe. Public attitudes are becoming less punitive about the most effective way to handle criminal offenders than in the past. In 1994, only 48 percent of Americans favored addressing the causes of crime and 42 percent preferred the punitive approach. In 2002, a public opinion poll found the public favored addressing the root causes of crime over strict sentencing, by 65 percent to 32 percent. Poll respondents also favor a more rational sentencing for offenders. Only 28 percent of Americans surveyed believed that the most effective way to reduce crime is to keep offenders off the street as long as possible. Nearly two-thirds of those surveyed believed that the most effective way to reduce crime is to rehabilitate prisoners by providing education and job training.[15] And in 2006, a National Council on Crime and Delinquency poll found that 87 percent of the U.S. voting public favored rehabilitative services for inmates as opposed to a punitive approach to sentencing.[16]

Americans have also expressed concern with the punitive approach taken by the war on drugs. In the Hart survey, respondents recognized drug abuse as a medical problem, and 63 percent favored handling it primarily through counseling and treatment, whereas only 31 percent believed that it is a serious crime that should be handled mainly by the courts and prison system. Respondents also expressed concern with the overreach of three-strikes law; 56 percent favored elimination of these policies and other mandatory sentencing laws, and giving judges more discretion to choose the appropriate sentence. In general, only 35 percent supported the direction of the nation's crime approach, and 54 percent believed we are on the wrong track.[17]

The primary interest of the public is to be protected and they do not support sanctions they believe punish offenders but do not protect society. If they believe that community sanctions effectively protect them, the public supports the use of community sanctions over imprisonment. In an Ohio survey, when informed that prison space is scarce and expensive, the public supported the use of community corrections instead of paying for new prison construction.[18] A National Opinion Survey on Crime and Justice (NOSCJ) survey also found support for community correctional programs: 73 percent of those surveyed indicated that intensive probation supervision was either "very effective" or "somewhat effective," 55 percent similarly supported house arrest, 73 percent supported electronic monitoring of offenders, and 78 percent supported the use of boot camps as alternatives to traditional prison sentences.[19]

Perhaps most important to the politics of sentencing policy is the effectiveness of "tough on crime" approaches in making the public safer and reducing the crime rate. There has been much debate on this by researchers, with data on both sides. Several studies have suggested that significantly increasing the number of offenders in prison has reduced crime, and it is often cited that for every 10 percent increase in the number of prisoners, the crime rate declines by 2–4 percent.[20] This would be expected as it has long been understood that criminals commit several crimes before they are arrested and incarcerated. The pubic policy issue is whether the cost of the increase in incarceration is worth the decline in crime.

Impact on Correctional Administrators

This issue of sentencing that results in more offenders being sent to prison for longer periods of time has an impact far beyond cost and resources directed to law enforcement, courts, corrections, and other elements of the criminal justice system. Although it can be argued that sentencing policy is outside the scope of responsibility for correctional administrators, it still must be dealt with and responded to by those managing correctional agencies and environments. First, administrators must manage the problems that result from these sentencing practices, such as managing a prison population that will serve extremely long periods of time and have little motivation for good behavior, or how to provide a reasonable quality of health care within limited budgets for older offenders with extensive health care needs. Second, administrators have the opportunity to take a leadership position and encourage policies and practices that can either be put in place to reduce the negative effects of sentencing practices or can push for a reconsideration of these practices if they prove to be costly and ineffective in reducing crime.

One such policy to lessen the negative effects of long sentencing is to provide early intervention programs to support at-risk children, parents, and their families. Juvenile correctional administrators deal almost totally with at-risk children. Adult correctional agencies deal with parents who have at-risk children because of the parents' involvement

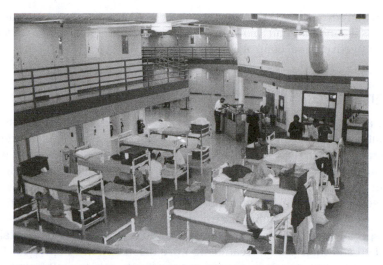

A major result of the "tough on crime" mentality is the overcrowding of prisons. This photo illustrates putting dorm bunks in the dayroom of a prison built with cells.
(Courtesy of the Ohio Department of Rehabilitation and Correction).

in the criminal justice system. Most correctional programs focus only on the offender and almost ignore the spouse and children. However, this does not have to be the case, and it is not a long journey to link family issues to these programs, or begin programs in parenting skills specifically aimed at intervening with children to reduce their likelihood of delinquency and criminal involvement. A similar proposal is to invest in at-risk children through programs such as Big Brothers/Sisters and other nonprofit community programs that target emotional and material resources toward children. Correctional officials can reach out to private and church-based volunteer intervention programs to form partnerships and expand the services and support they can potentially provide.

The third proposal is to reaffirm rehabilitation. Cullen and colleagues suggest that "One value of rehabilitation is that it is the only correctional philosophy that argues that the state should make an effort to support offenders both as an end in itself and as a means to the end of making society safer."[21] As noted in Chapter 13, there is now evidence of the effectiveness of rehabilitative programs in reducing recidivism, and public opinion polls indicate that citizens support rehabilitation as a concept and correctional goal.[22] There is no group better able to advocate the need for rehabilitation than correctional administrators directly involved in the delivery of these programs. In fact, if correctional administrators do not take the initiative and "reaffirm rehabilitation," then it is unlikely anyone else will do so.

This section regarding sentencing covers an issue that will confront correctional administrators for several years, and will have multiple effects on the operation of correctional activities and organizations. These sentencing approaches result in longer sentences, a changing makeup of the population under correctional supervision, and an "aging" of the supervised population. Administrators can reach beyond the traditional scope of their responsibility and consider proposals and implement programs that are more proactive than reactive. They can advocate and, therefore, influence policy makers regarding the importance of these proposals, and they can also suggest the importance of alternatives to longer prison sentences as effective crime control agendas.

Management of Special Offenders

Today, there are many groups of offenders serving sentences both in the community and in prison that require special management. These groups of inmates are referred to as **special offenders**, defined as offenders whose circumstances, conditions, or behaviors require management or treatment outside the normal approach to supervision. This may be the result of some physical problem, a history of sexual assaults, age (juvenile or elderly), or gender. All these circumstances required correctional officials to create special methods of managing, handling, or treating these offenders.

Other special offenders may have substance abuse problems or be mentally ill. These were described and their prison treatments were discussed in Chapter 13. This chapter describes the circumstances and management approaches that result from the individual needs of other groups of special offenders. Included are the needs and management of offenders under age eighteen who are waived from jurisdiction of the juvenile court to adult court and correctional systems, aging offenders (older than fifty), women offenders, and those convicted and sentenced for sexual offenses. This chapter provides you with an understanding of the challenges and difficulties in attempting to manage all these special populations within a correctional environment.

Aging Offenders

A *Time Magazine* article notes, "Picture an 86-year-old man clutching a walker as he shuffles down a prison hallway. This is not exactly the image of a dangerous killer locked up for the good of society. Chances are, it's not what the judge envisioned either when he sentenced John Bedarka, a Pennsylvania coal miner, to life without parole for shooting his wife's lover to death thirty years ago. But, Bedarka is still in prison . . . in frail health, severely depressed, and a threat to no one."[23] There are many John Bedarkas in prison today. The prison population in the United States is getting older, partly because the population of the United States is aging. Those ages sixty-five and older represent the fastest growing age group in the United States; their numbers reached 38 million in 2007.[24] Also, older offenders are being sent to prison due to changes in sentencing already described, with sentencing guidelines and mandatory sentencing taking away sentencing judges' discretion to consider age, health issues, and risk to the community.

And the simple longer sentences given for almost every crime over the past two decades results in inmates staying in prison a longer time. The three-strikes and habitual-offender laws often require offenders to go to prison for life without parole. These prisoners naturally age while serving their sentence and end up dying while in prison. In 1995, only 6.1 percent of the inmates in state and federal prisons were age 50 or older,[25] and on December 31, 2008, 149,900 inmates were older than age 50 (representing 10.5 percent of the prison population).[26]

This increase in the average age and number of older offenders creates many management, resource, and programmatic issues for correctional administrators.

Perhaps the most critical, expensive, and difficult issue is the increasing health care needs. With a history of risky lifestyle choices (tobacco, drug, and alcohol use, and high-risk sexual behavior) these individuals begin to experience medical problems that are more serious and at an earlier age than others. And prison medical clinics are usually not prepared to deal with the depression, sexually transmitted diseases, tuberculosis and other infectious diseases, heart problems, and reduced circulation that occur in older inmates.

There are also security, work opportunity, and program issues. Prisons were designed and operational processes created to hold young and physically active inmates. Prison architecture, recreation facilities, and types of housing were all designed without consideration for older inmates. Simple problems, such as difficulty in getting around in wheelchairs or inability to walk long distances, result from the campus-style prison architecture emphasizing space to spread out inmates over as much area as possible. Prison recreation programs such as basketball, jogging, and weight lifting do not meet the needs or interests of the elderly. Few work opportunities can be assigned to older inmates.

To respond to these problems, many prisons make policy allowances for cell and bed assignments, or even for inmate movement, and let older inmates begin moving from one building to another before younger inmates. Some correctional agencies even use entire prisons or housing units to house older inmates and create counseling programs and recreation that meet their needs. Prisons also try to create inmate jobs that can be done by older inmates and have recreation departments schedule leisure activities such as stretching classes or table-game tournaments to occupy these inmates and meet their special needs. These are all issues confronted by prison administrators to deal with older inmates sentenced to prison.

Juvenile Offenders Tried and Sentenced as Adults

Another result of the "get tough on criminals" movement has been a move to handle serious juvenile offenders as adults within the criminal justice system. The public has been led to fear juvenile offenders who they perceive as becoming more violent and dangerous. And juvenile crimes today are more serious than in the past. During the 1980s, murder arrests for juvenile offenders increased by 93 percent and arrests for aggravated assault increased by 72 percent.[27] The proportion of violent crimes cleared by juvenile arrests averaged about 9 percent of all violent crimes during the late 1980s, but climbed to 14 percent of all violent crimes in 1994. However, from 1997 to 2006, the percentage of violent crimes committed by juveniles declined by 20 percent.[28] Yet, the damage was done, the pubic was afraid of juvenile gangs victimizing innocent citizens, and laws were passed to treat some juveniles as adults.

Currently, all states allow juveniles who commit offenses to be waived from the jurisdiction of the juvenile court and be prosecuted in the adult criminal court system. There are various legal processes for transferring juveniles to the adult court system, primarily focusing on who has the discretion to make the transfer or waiver decision. There are three variations of how this can occur.

1. *Waiver*: The juvenile court judge is the decision maker and determines whether the offender is waived from the juvenile justice system to adult criminal court.

2. *Direct file*: Fifteen states have concurrent original jurisdiction, in that the prosecutor has the discretion to file charges in either the juvenile justice or criminal justice system. In these states, the prosecutors' discretion is limited by specific age and offense criteria.

3. *Statutory exclusion*: Twenty-eight states have mandatory waiver to adult courts for specific age and offense criteria. If a juvenile is above the minimum age specified and commits a serious offense designated by statute, judges and prosecutors have no discretion; the case must be prosecuted in adult criminal court.[29]

The question of whether serious juvenile offenders should be tried and sentenced in adult courts is certainly one for debate, and many correctional administrators oppose the process. The American Correctional Association (ACA) standards note that the juvenile justice system has significantly different processes, procedures, and objectives from adult corrections, and these require specialized services and programs. James A. Gondles, executive director of ACA, has suggested that, "We will never, in my view, solve our problems on the back end with punishments. . . . Treating kids as adults solves very little; it's another quick-fix solution to a complex problem that took years to reach and will take years to resolve."[30]

Yet, it is generally recognized that many juveniles age sixteen or seventeen are not "children," taking into account their physical maturity, willingness to commit violent acts, and danger to the public. Juvenile justice systems that try to protect and nurture them do not meet their needs and do not protect society from their potential violent acts; however, binding these youthful offenders over to the adult court system is not an ideal response either. Adult correctional administrators must now face philosophical, political, and operational issues as they try to put facilities and programs in place to handle these juvenile offenders.

Even with the concern for dealing with serious juvenile offenders in a punitive and public safety-oriented approach and with the expansion of authority to move juveniles into the adult court and correctional process, there have not been an overwhelming number of cases transferred to criminal courts. The number of delinquency cases judicially waived to criminal court peaked in 1994 with 12,100 cases, a 51 percent increase over the number of cases waived in 1989 (8,000). However, by 2005, the number of cases waived to criminal court declined to 7,000.[31] Cases most likely (almost 50 percent) to be waived to adult court in 2005 were crimes against persons.[32]

Over the past several years, the number of people under eighteen held in state prisons has increased, yet remained relatively constant as a proportion of the overall prison population. From 1985 to 1997, the number increased from 2,300 to 5,400,[33] yet by mid-2008, there were only 3,650 inmates under age eighteen held in state prisons. Of these, 3,531 were male and only 119 were female.[34] Nine states had more than a hundred juvenile prisoners, six states had fewer than ten, and nine states and the Federal Bureau of Prisons had no inmates under eighteen as of mid-2008.[35]

There are three approaches for housing offenders under eighteen in state correctional systems. First, six states allow **straight adult incarceration** that places juveniles in adult prisons, with no separate housing or differentiation in programming or job assignment. Second, twelve states use **graduated incarceration**, with the juvenile initially

The waiver of juveniles to serve time in adult prisons causes difficult problems for correctional administrators who have to keep them safe (often separate) and yet offer an adequate array of program opportunities.
(Photo by Richard P. Seiter)

placed in a juvenile facility. Once they are eighteen, they are transferred to an adult prison to complete their sentence. Finally, eight states use **segregated incarceration**, in which inmates under eighteen are housed in an adult prison but constantly separated from adult inmates.[36] A logistical problem of separation is that many states have only a handful of juvenile offenders, making it difficult to keep them separate from adults and yet provide a full range of program offerings. These issues make management of this problem difficult and there is evidence that treating juveniles as adults may not be working as desired. A recent study found that the prevalence and frequency of misconduct and violence among juveniles housed in adult prisons are far more likely than adult offenders to be involved in prison violence and misconduct.[37]

Women Offenders

Women offenders have been increasing as a percent of both prisoners and offenders under community supervision more rapidly than male offenders. In 2007, women made up about 24.5 percent of all arrests by law enforcement agencies, an increase from 8.3 percent in 2003. In 2007, women made up 3.2 percent of all arrests for violent offenses, 15.8 percent of arrests for property offenses, and 10.1 percent of arrests for drug offenses.[38] Women's involvement in crime has resulted in an increase in the number of female offenders under correctional supervision. In *Women Offenders*, a detailed study of female offenders by Greenfeld and Snell, it was reported that the number of women under correctional supervision increased 118 percent compared to 70 percent for males under supervision between 1986 and 1997, and in 1998, women constituted approximately 16 percent of the total correctional population, including 21 percent of the probation population, 11 percent of those in jails, 6 percent of prisoners, and 12 percent of parolees.[39] This trend continued into the 2000s, and by June 30, 2008, of the 1,610,584 prisoners in state and federal prisons, 115,779 (7.2 percent) were women.[40] An earlier review found that women in prison made up 4.5 percent of all convictions for violent crimes, 10 percent for property crimes, and 10 percent for drug offenses.[41]

Female offenders under correctional supervision have similar traits to male offenders. As reported by Greenfeld and Snell, although nearly two-thirds of women on probation are white, almost two-thirds of women in jail or prison are minorities.[42] Women in prison are older than those on probation or in jail. This indicates that when factoring criminal history into sentencing decisions, as offenders grow older and accumulate a more extensive offense history, they are more likely to receive a prison sentence. Women under correctional supervision are more likely than the general population to have never been married, and the majority of female offenders have completed high school.

An interesting point is that the average length of prison sentence served by women is considerably less than that served by men. On January 1, 2002, men in prison were serving an average sentence of 5.3 years, whereas women in prison were serving an average of 3.7 years.[43] But the question is whether women should be sentenced (often to prison) in the same manner as men. Some suggest that there should be consistency of how males and females are sentenced and the use of sentencing guidelines and mandatory sentences is as appropriate for women as for men. Others suggest the most effective way to prepare female offenders for success in the community is to maximize the use of alternative programs to incarceration. They hold out that most people consider women as less risk of further victimization and therefore are good candidates for community supervision. The alternative used by most states is work release, in which inmates either leave the prison during the day and go into the community and work or are moved to community residential centers (halfway houses) to find jobs and work in the community. When women are incarcerated, they also face many issues not problematic for male inmates.

Issues for Female Prisoners

Since females constitute only 7.2 percent of prisoners, there are fewer prisons for them and therefore the scope of facilities and programs is less than that for male inmates. This creates a challenge for prison administrators to provide the same quantity and quality of correctional programs for female prisoners as that provided for male prisoners. Federal courts began to look at this issue as early as 1974 in the case of *Barefield v. Leach*, which found that New Mexico was not providing parity in vocational training and work opportunity for female inmates and ruled that such disparity could not be justified just because the smaller number of female inmates made it more costly to provide parity in these programs.[44] In the 1995 case of *Pargo v. Elliott*, the Eighth Circuit Court found that just the fact that there are differences in programs between male and female prisons is not necessarily a violation of the equal protection clause of the Constitution, but that criteria used to examine whether differences in prison programs are discriminatory include the number of inmates in a prison, the prison security level, the crimes committed by inmates, the length of sentences being served by inmates, and any other special characteristics that could be identified by the prison as reasons for program differences.[45]

Much of the issue of disparity has been resolved due to the growth in the number of female inmates. Rafter reports that although only 1 to 3 new female prisons were opened every decade between 1930 and 1950, during the 1980s more than 34 new women's prisons were opened, by 1990 there were 71 women's prisons, and in 1995 there were 104 prisons designated for female offenders.[46] The increase in the number of prisons allows a broader offering of vocational training or other treatment programs for women inmates. Also, additional prisons scattered across states enable women to be more likely housed closer to their homes than when a state had only one female prison.

There are many unique issues that impact women prisoners. Some of these issues include their history of substance abuse and their need for medical care. Just as for men, a high percentage of women offenders have a serious history and problem with alcohol and substance abuse. Fifty-nine percent of female state prisoners in 2004 were using drugs within the month before their offense, 17 percent of females inmates (compared to 10 percent of men) used methamphetamines in the month before their offense,[47] and 40 percent of women (compared to 32 percent of men) were under the influence of drugs at the time of their crime.[48] And "[n]early 1 in 3 women serving time in State prisons said they had committed the offense which brought them to prison in order to obtain money to support their need for drugs."[49]

This problem is not being met satisfactorily, as although 74 percent of all prisons offered drug or alcohol counseling in 2005,[50] in 2002, only 12.9 percent of the prison populations participated in drug treatment programs.[51] Only 20 percent of women offenders report receiving drug or alcohol treatment during the period of their incarceration.[52] In addition, it has been noted that women's programs should focus on the specific issues around female drug abuse and what occurs after release. Chesney-Lind suggests

> Women's programs must . . . be gender-sensitive in additional ways: they must understand that most women take drugs as a form of self-medication, and they must be sensitive to women's unique circumstances (by providing such services as child care and transportation).[53]

It is believed that female inmates have more serious health problems than males. This results not only from the need for gynecological care but also from a history of poverty, drug and alcohol abuse, poor diet and nutrition, and past neglect and lack of health care.[54] Besides this, women have medical issues around pregnancy. Greenfeld and Snell report that 5 percent of women admitted to state prisons are pregnant, and although 90 percent of these had received a gynecological exam since their admission, only 4 percent had received prenatal care since their admission.[55]

Recidivism by Female Offenders

Recidivism rates for female offenders are high. In a 1983 study of 6,400 women released from prison in eleven states, 52 percent of them were rearrested, 39 percent were reconvicted, and 33 percent were returned to prison during a three-year follow-up.[56] Another review indicated that among women with only one arrest record, 21 percent were rearrested within three years. Of those with two to three prior arrests, 33 percent were rearrested; those with four to six prior arrests had a 47 percent rearrest rate; among those with seven to ten priors, 69 percent were rearrested; and nearly eight out of ten women with eleven or more priors were rearrested.[57]

Many factors influence the likelihood of recidivism among women. Before noting some of these, it is important to identify the factors called "gendered pathways" to criminality by women, such as victimization, economic marginalization, and substance abuse.[58] With this as a background, the most important factor in predicting recidivism for women is prior arrest history; the greater the number of prior arrests, the higher the rate of rearrest among women released from prison.[59] A recent multivariate analysis of recidivism among women also found that recidivism is closely related to age, as younger women were more likely to recidivate than older women, and to prior incarcerations, and women who completed high school or had stable mental health were less likely to fail on parole.[60]

Practical Perspectives

Real Life Issues for Female Inmates

The first job I had in a prison was as a case manager in a female prison. I was very nervous about the job as many friends warned me that working with women offenders was a challenge and much different than working with males. I really did not understand what they were saying, so I went to the library and checked out every book I could find on female offenders. I did find there to be a great difference, yet I found working with female offenders very rewarding in many ways. I recently interviewed a current case manager in a female facility who agreed with many of my observations and said not much had changed. The following are the differences we both agree you find with female compared to male offenders.

- Females need more contact with agencies outside of the prison. More women are filing for divorce and need contact with the family courts. More women have children issues and must contact the division of family services. These types of contacts often require telephone calls as they cannot be completed only through the mail.

- Sentences for women are overall less than for men, so the turnaround is greater. More women are referred to halfway houses, and staff have to move more quickly to get referrals completed.

- Medical and mental health issues are different and more intense. Female inmates are sometimes pregnant while in prison and need prenatal care. Mental health issues seem more pronounced for female inmates, they need more psychological services, and a higher percentage seem to be on antidepressants.

- Women stay much more attached to the community than men, who seem to psychologically separate themselves from their families and community ties. Female inmates take more responsibility with regard to their children and family, especially their parents, and are continually more stressed out about their problems in the community.

- Female inmates are very different in regard to their relationships with staff and other inmates. Women seem to need someone to talk to and will talk more freely than men to staff about their problems. They are also much more open about their sexual relationships (in prison) than men. They may have a girlfriend; they may have a breakup; and there is more fighting about these sexual relationships. A higher percentage of women seem to participate in homosexuality, or they hide it less. Men get involved in homosexual activity more for the sexual gratification, whereas women get involved for the emotional relationship.

- Women are more interested in being involved in programs. There is a high demand for drug programs, and they are more willing to confront their drug use as a problem that needs attention. They work better with staff and are more willing to take orders and follow instructions.

- One interesting issue concerns property. Men want food or snacks, but women try to accumulate hobby or craft items, to create more of a "homey" atmosphere in their cell or dormitory area than men. They try to get jewelry and often have visitors bring them things that are not allowed. They have different demands of the commissary; they desire hair dye, skin care products, and other personal cosmetic items.

- Race is not as much of an issue with women, but is a very important issue with men. Female inmates seem less concerned about race and do not self-segregate nearly as much. In male prisons, most gangs are related to race, and there is often conflict and violence between the groups.

■ Women have fewer disciplinary issues than men. They just seem to accept their incarceration without breaking the rules as much.

■ Female inmates, however, are far more manipulative with staff than male inmates. They are more likely to exaggerate or outright lie about a problem at home that requires immediate attention or a crisis phone call home.

■ In general, women have many more demands and take much more staff time than men. They realistically have more issues, particularly related to home, and desire immediate attention from staff. When case managers need to talk to male inmates to prepare a progress report, they almost have to order them to come in to talk and discuss their community plans. Women are lined up at the door to talk about issues at home.

Sex Offenders

Over the past twenty-five years, as a result of two major factors, the number of sex offenders under correctional supervision has risen significantly. **Sex offenders** are those who commit a legally prohibited sexual act or, in some states, any offender who commits any crime that is "sexually motivated." The term *sex offender* usually includes offenders convicted of rape or sexual assault (such as statutory rape, forcible sodomy, lewd acts with children, and other offenses relating to fondling, molestation, or indecent practices).

In 2005, sex offenders constituted approximately 4.7 percent of all offenders under correctional supervision. Most sex offenders are supervised in the community. In 2005, there were 491,720 offenders in state sex offender registries, a 47 percent increase from 1997.[61] However, the number of imprisoned sex offenders is growing. In 1980, only 20,500 sex offenders were in state prisons; by 1994, this number had climbed to 88,100,[62] and by 2005 to 164,600.[63] By 2007, 12.6 percent of all state prisoners were sex offenders.[64] Once in prison, sex offenders are serving longer periods of time. In 1990, offenders convicted of rape were serving an average of sixty-two months in jail or prison, and those convicted of other sexual offenses were serving thirty-six months. By 1999, this had increased to seventy-nine months for rape and forty-seven months for other sexual assaults.[65]

Sex offenders present a difficult challenge for correctional administrators in both community and institutional settings. A National Institute of Justice survey of state supervision of sex offenders in the community described a five-part **containment model** with a "triangle" of supervision: "treatment to teach sex offenders to develop internal control over deviant thoughts; supervision and surveillance to control offenders' external behaviors; and polygraph examinations to help design, and to monitor conformance to, treatment plans and supervision conditions."[66]

Successful treatment of sex offenders is difficult; however, recidivism rates for sex offenders are not as high as often expected. A review of sex offender inmates in state prisons in 1991 who were recidivists reveals that 24 percent of those serving time for rape and 19 percent of those serving time for sexual assault had been on probation or parole at the time of the offense for which they were incarcerated.[67] In a three-year follow-up study of recidivism by probationers, rapists on probation were found to have a lower rate of rearrest for new felonies (19.5 percent) than other violent probationers (41 percent).[68] Another three-year follow-up of offenders discharged from prison during 1994 had similar findings. Table 15-2 illustrates how ex-inmates who served a sentence for rape or sexual assault had lower rearrest, reconviction, and reincarceration rates than for those who served a sentence for all violent offenses.

Table 15-2
RECIDIVISM RATES OF VIOLENCE, RAPE, AND SEXUAL ASSAULT OFFENDERS, 1994

| | Percent of All Inmates | | | |
Offenders	Rearrested	Reconvicted	Reincarcerated with New Sentence	Reincarcerated without New Sentence
All violent offenses	61.7%	39.9%	20.4%	49.8%
Rape	46.0	27.4	12.6	43.5
Sexual assault	41.4	22.3	10.5	36.0

Source: Bureau of Justice Statistics, *Sourcebook of Criminal Justice Statistics, 2001* (Washington, DC: U.S. Department of Justice, 2003), p. 508.

The management of sex offenders creates significant challenges for correctional administrators. There are very few offenders who evoke a more strident response than sex offenders, yet correctional administrators must not respond emotionally and must professionally deal with these offenders in the same manner that they manage other offenders. There is little tolerance for sexual offenders under community supervision, as almost two of every five offenders are returned to prison, even when not committing a new crime. Intensive treatment and monitoring in the community, including the use of polygraph examinations to confirm compliance with treatment and supervision conditions, often lead to revoking supervision as a preventive approach to avoid further criminality.

Preventing Suicides

Another serious issue for correctional administrators is preventing suicides while offenders are in custody in jails and prisons. A 2005 Bureau of Justice Statistics report notes that suicide rates are reducing. Jail suicide rates declined from 129 per 100,000 inmates in 1983 to 47 per 100,000 in 2002, and rates are lower in prisons. They declined from 34 per 100,000 in 1980 to 14 per 100,000 in 2002. These suicide rates are much higher than the rate of suicide in the community (10 per 100,000 people).[69] Even with the decline in rates, however, there were 314 suicides in jails and 168 suicides in prisons in 2002.[70] It has consistently been the case that violent offenders in both prisons and jails have suicide rates twice that of nonviolent offenders. Forty-eight percent of all jail suicides occur during the first week following admission.[71]

Jails have higher rates for several reasons. First, they receive inmates right off the streets and little is known about their mental health status or propensity for suicide. Many jail inmates are unsure of what faces them in the future and are likely to take their lives due to the fear of the unknown, the potential of a long-term sentence, and the embarrassment of their crime causing depression and irrational behavior. With the high rates of suicide during the first week, it is important for jails to do a preliminary screening upon an offender's entry to the jail to determine whether there are immediate concerns about an attempted suicide. These screenings are interviews by medical or mental health staff asking questions about offenders past history of mental health or thoughts or attempts of suicide.

Second, both jails and prisons have initiated **suicide prevention programs**. Fewer than 3 percent of 2,866 jails surveyed reported that they did not have specific procedures for suicide prevention. Suicide prevention programs include risk assessment at admission, special staff training, counseling for inmates, and monitoring and observing high-risk inmates. Training includes observing for signs of potential suicide, including sleeping a lot, depression, staying by oneself, giving away property to other inmates, or confiding their thoughts to family or friends. Inmates identified as high risk for suicide as a result of the assessment or staff observation are closely monitored. Third, some may even be placed on a **suicide watch** in which inmates are placed in a cell without any material that can be used for a suicide attempt (blankets, sheets, belts, and shoestrings) or cell furnishings or places in the cell to hang something from. For example, beds are only a few inches above the floor and heating vents are too small to wrap a sheet or towel through. Suicide watch cells constantly observe either through a camera or through a person so that staff can quickly react if the inmate begins any dangerous activity. Even with all these programs, it is difficult to prevent suicides of inmates truly committed to ending their lives.

Suicide prevention cells have only a low mattress with no furnishings that could be used by inmates to harm themselves.
(Photo by Richard P. Seiter)

In addition to these approaches, correctional administrators believe that suicides are preventable and they do not accept that suicides just happen. They have found that the most important thing is to have a written suicide prevention policy. There are eight important prevention activities:

1. *Training of both correctional and mental health staff.* All staff should receive eight hours of suicide prevention training in their preservice training so that they understand the risk of suicide. Annually, staff should receive a refresher of two hours as a constant reminder that suicide prevention is an important issue to the jail and its management. It also serves as a reminder that every inmate is potentially suicidal.

2. *Intake screening and assessment.* Specific questions should be asked of every new admission to jail that address the risk of suicide. Are you thinking about committing suicide now? Have you considered it in the past? Have you recently experienced a serious loss? Is there any history of suicide in your family? Do you have a history of mental illness? Arresting or transporting officers should be asked if the inmate mentioned anything or showed any unusual behavior that might be a red flag for suicide.

3. *Communication.* The first level of communication is between the arresting or transporting officer and the jail staff. The second level is among the staff in the jail so that everyone knows if an inmate is likely suicidal and how he or she should be managed. The third level is between the staff and the suicidal inmate, watching and teaching the inmate how to deal with the urge.

4. *Housing.* Jails must provide suicide-resistant housing for inmates identified as suicidal. It is usually not practical for all jail cells to be suicide resistant, so jailers must identify and create cells that are protrusion free, that is, without things that inmates can use to hang themselves (95 percent of inmates commit suicide by hanging using clothing or sheets attached to a protrusion).

5. *Levels of observation provided to suicidal inmates.* Most standards recommend at least two levels. The most extreme is constant observation of an inmate who is acutely suicidal, who if not constantly watched will make an effort to commit suicide. The second level of observation is close supervision that results in observation at staggered fifteen-minute intervals (not so routine that inmates can anticipate how frequently the jailer will make the check). This level is appropriate for inmates who are at low to medium risk of committing suicide. They may be feeling distraught or suffering from mental illness or depression, or they may have made a suicide attempt in the past.

6. *Intervention in a suicide attempt.* This is similar to a medical emergency response and includes ensuring the responding officer is trained in first aid, has a suicide prevention kit that includes a special knife to cut down a hanging victim, and follows a protocol detailing the role of every staff member when responding to a suicide attempt. There should also be regular mock exercises for staff to practice an emergency situation.

7. *Reporting.* This is straightforward and includes writing a report by everyone involved in finding a suicide or anyone who had contact with the victim.

8. *Morbidity and mortality review process.* After any serious suicide attempt (requiring medical attention at the jail clinic or outside hospital), there should be a morbidity or mortality review. These include a multidisciplinary approach with both mental health and correctional staff involved. They look at the total event and not just how staff responded to it. They examine a time line of when the inmate arrived at the facility and look for any issues of mental health or medical issues that went undiscovered. This is not an investigation or internal affairs review, but a systemic review to address what happened and what we can learn from the opportunity for suicides in the future.

These indicate the most frequently used approaches to prevent suicides. In a 2008 article, Etter lists four important factors that managers can use to prevent suicides:

- Staff training.
- Frequent observation and contact with inmates.
- A capable, proactive administration and effective supervisors.
- Polices and procedures to prevent possible successful suicide attempts.[72]

Suicide is and will continue to be a challenge for correctional administrators. The positive aspect is that great progress has been made and the rate of suicides has decreased. All state prisons and the largest and most sophisticated of jails have adopted suicide prevention programs that have proven effective. All suicides cannot be prevented. There will always be offenders who desire to end their lives, have no history, and give no outward indication to give staff a reason to begin a suicide watch program for them. Perhaps the most positive development is that correctional administrators do not accept that suicides will happen and believe that with the implementation of programs, they can reduce suicides on their watch.

Recruiting Correctional Staff

Historically, corrections did very little to recruit quality staff. Positions were advertised through normal government processes, and the only recruitment may be an advertisement in the newspaper. The only other method of recruitment was informal by relatives or friends who worked at the correctional agency. There was no plan by which characteristics of successful employees could be identified, organizational needs considered, or a recruitment plan developed to target the types of workers the agency desired. An example in the state of Massachusetts notes, "corrections with its similar salary and benefits (to police and fire departments) was in reality a 'walk-in' job. Screening and selection were largely limited to investigation of possible criminal records of applicants. The prison officer recruit was largely self-selected."[73]

While there are many types of correctional jobs, most people enter the field in one of four job categories: probation officer, parole officer, correctional officer, or prison counselor. Once offenders are granted probation, probation officers supervise them and monitor their compliance with conditions of their probation. Officers have a dual role of supervising and helping. The primary functions of supervisors are to maintain surveillance and enforce conditions of probation. Officers monitor probationers' activities through a combination of office visits, verification of probationers' activities by visiting their homes and contacting their employers or program providers, and monitoring activities such as drug testing of probationers. Officers also help offenders succeed by determining program or treatment needs and placing probationers in social service programs that address their needs for education, mental health counseling, vocational training, or substance abuse programming. In a survey, officers responded that their primary role is to ensure public safety, to supervise and offer resources to help the client readjust to society, to prevent recidivism, to steer offenders in the right direction, to monitor offenders, and to hold offenders highly accountable for their actions and responsibilities.[74]

Parole officer roles are very similar to probation officers, and they supervise parolees from the time of their release until they either successfully leave supervision or have their parole revoked. Officers usually have two primary tasks, supervision and investigations, with supervision making up approximately 80 percent of their responsibilities. They conduct investigations to determine if their proposed release (where they will live, who they will leave with, and job possibilities) plans are satisfactory. In many jurisdictions, supervision of both parolees and probationers is done jointly by the same agency and many times by the same officers. On June 30, 2006, there were an estimated 14,000 full-time parole officers supervising nearly 528,000 parolees, which resulted in an average caseload of about thirty-eight persons on active parole supervision.[75]

Correctional officers (COs) make up the largest job category in prisons, jails, and other correctional facilities. Their basic responsibility is to maintain order and contribute to the secure operation of the institution. They control doors and grills and lock and unlock them to allow only approved inmate movement. They must search inmates and areas, being alert for contraband such as drugs and weapons that can endanger staff and inmates. They must also conduct inmate counts to maintain inmate accountability and prevent escapes. They make inmates obey the rules and initiate disciplinary action. They often oversee inmate work crews, such as those assigned sanitation responsibilities, and ensure that the inmate crew performs the work at the accepted standard.

In addition to these security routines, officers also mediate between inmates, educate inmates about rules and procedures, and are a link between the inmate culture and staff management of a prison. Correctional officers contribute to the rehabilitation of inmates by contributing to an environment of control without threats and tension, communicating with inmates in a relaxed and professional manner, and providing human services such as overseeing the feeding of inmates, referring sick inmates to medical staff, or assisting with recreational programs.

In 2005, there were 295,261 correctional officers working in state and federal prisons in the United States.[76] In a 2002 survey of officers, 78 percent were male, 70.4 percent were white, and 21.2 percent black. Seventy-seven percent of female COs and 3.5 percent of male COs worked in a prison with inmates of the opposite gender.[77] While most prison systems do not require a college education for officers, many require either experience or a two- or four-year degree. Many states and the federal prison system use correctional officer jobs as the entry level into the prison system; staff who are successful as officers gain communications and security skills that serve them well throughout their careers and often help them get promotions and additional career opportunities.

Another either entry level or promotional opportunity job is that of a prison counselor or caseworker. These professionals work directly with inmates, with the primary responsibility of classifying offenders and creating and monitoring plans for program and work participation. The plans continue throughout the period of confinement and build to the preparation for release. Some caseworkers actually perform counseling, but in most state and federal prisons, their principal role is to guide inmates through all aspects of their prison sentence, including the legal sanction and expectation for release, an understanding of their individual treatment needs, and the availability of prison programs to meet these needs. They also assist inmates with services outside the prison (job assistance, family counseling, or halfway house agencies) that will aid in their transition from prison to community.

There are two major challenges facing correctional administrators in recruiting quality staff. First, they must change the perception of the work as dangerous, low paid, and unpleasant. It is very difficult to recruit quality individuals as correctional workers who are interested in corrections as a career and committed to giving the job a fair trial to see if it works before quitting. Correctional jobs can be stressful, dangerous, and tedious, and there seems to be little recognition for the work they do. A New York state correctional officer noted, "Police and firefighters are recognized as heroes. It's not as glamorous to be a correctional officer."[78]

There is no question that working in corrections presents a unique challenge for employees. It is important to seriously consider the roles and specific duties of these jobs before applying for a job and committing to a career in corrections. Corrections is a people business, meaning it is the staff who make correctional organizations effective. Correctional agencies are responsible for protecting the public by limiting offenders' freedoms, and when correctional staff fail to effectively do their jobs, innocent citizens may be victims of crime. Correctional staff have considerable discretion in how they carry out their duties and take away offenders' individual freedoms. Therefore, staff members doing these difficult jobs must follow the highest of ethical standards.

Even with these challenges, recruiters still have many positive points that they can make to encourage people to enter the correctional workforce. First, there is an availability of jobs. The most recent report (May 2004) by the Bureau of Justice Statistics reported there were 747,061 correctional employees working at the federal, state, and local levels in the United States in 2001.[79] This is almost a 30 percent increase since 1992, when there were 556,500 correctional employees.[80] Second, these jobs are very stable, and there are many career opportunities. Talented staff with the proper educational requirements that work hard and do a good job will be promoted and given opportunities for advancement.

Third, the pay is better than most people believe, and the benefits are very good. In 2008, examples of annual salaries for correctional officers were $27,540 for Texas and $45,288 for California.[81] Public-sector correctional agencies usually have excellent vacations, days off, and health care coverage. Many have a special retirement system, similar to those of law enforcement agencies, in which employees can retire after twenty-five to thirty years of service at any age. And most people find a career in corrections to be interesting and enjoyable. Workers deal with people, face new challenges, and have the opportunity to make a difference in our society. Corrections is not for everyone, but it is a career for people who do not want to be desk-bound, who enjoy working with people, who are not afraid of challenges, and who want to serve the public. If recruiters use some of these positives and bring potential employees into the workplace to see it themselves, they often can overcome the negative impression many people have of corrections work.

A second challenge correctional agencies face is the extremely high turnover of staff. Recruiting, training, and then seeing staff exit the agency seems like a revolving door. Many people start a correctional job and then decide it is not the right type of position for them. Turnover rates for correctional officers between 1993 and 2001 increased from 11.6 percent to 16.6 percent.[82] Although many job-related functions lead to stress for correctional workers (understaffing, rotating shift work, inmate demands and manipulations, and poor public image), in a survey of correctional officers, the threat of violence was mentioned more frequently than any other single feature of their occupation.[83]

Examples of turnover during the past decade include the following. In 2005, Oklahoma starting pay for a correctional officer was $21,000, and the state prison system had 500 vacant positions. In New York, state correctional officers were paid between $30,000 and $50,000 per year, but this was not adequate to draw qualified applicants in counties near New York City.[84] During 2000, correctional officers in the North Carolina prison system were paid approximately $21,000 per year, the vacancy rate was approximately 11 percent, and turnover was approximately 37 percent per year. In 2001, the Texas prison system had 3,300 vacancies in its complement of 26,000 correctional officers.[85] A survey of those separating from correctional employment found that 68.5 percent left because they were dissatisfied with the salary, and 37 percent would have stayed if the salary and shift schedules could have improved.[86]

However, prompted by high turnover and the challenge of a growing workforce, correctional agencies became much more sophisticated in recruiting potential workers. Recruitment efforts targeted other criminal justice agencies, individuals leaving the military, public and private social service agencies, and community and four-year colleges. Staff vacancies and turnover seem to be improving, as correctional agencies are addressing the most serious issues to recruitment and retention and the recession and rising unemployment rates are making more people consider working in correctional agencies. Recently, Delaware, Louisiana, North Dakota, Vermont, Virginia, and West Virginia have raised pay for correctional officers to make them more comparable to law enforcement officers.[87] Alaska is attempting to improve hiring practices by shortening the time it takes to hire, as they have discovered that they lost many qualified candidates because of the long lag time between application and hiring.[88] In 2008, the Texas prison system increased correctional officer starting pay by 10 percent and within six months of hiring, officers were paid approximately $28,500. In 2009, Texas also provided a $1,500 recruiting bonus if an applicant agrees to work at one of four designated understaffed correctional institutions.

Correctional agencies are also improving recruitment and retention by improving the culture of their organizations. In Florida and Pennsylvania departments of corrections, case studies found that enhancing the workplace does reduce turnover.[89] And Corrections Corporation of America, the largest private prison company with over 17,000 staff, conducted interviews with staff to determine workplace satisfaction, and identified that the way correctional officers were treated by their first-line supervisors had a major impact on turnover. As a result, the company implemented a values-based training program for supervisors and has seen their retention rates improve as a result.[90]

Although recruitment and retention are improving among many correctional agencies as a result of thoughtful improvements in pay, culture, and working conditions, perhaps the biggest impact on turnover is the recession. With severe economic times come layoffs and high unemployment. During these times, individuals look for what they consider to be more stable employers, and correctional agencies are perceived to be "recession proof." What remains to be seen is if the improvements made by these agencies will help in retaining employees as the economy improves and jobs in noncorrectional agencies are again available.

Another way corrections improves its quality of staff and reduces turnover is through effective hiring practices that screen and select the most qualified individuals. The first step is for correctional agencies to identify the competencies they want in employees and create a screening process to rate applicants' abilities. As noted in Chapter 6, traits such as good interpersonal skills, making sound decisions, and ability to supervise others are some of the traits and abilities that make a successful correctional worker.

Similar to other employers, correctional agencies use a variety of rating mechanisms. In many cases, candidates must not only complete a fairly extensive application but also provide examples of how these past experiences are indicative of the required traits and abilities. The highest rated candidates then have personal interviews, at which interviewers present difficult and stressful scenarios, have candidates describe how they would handle them, and then rate the candidate's response. Since correctional staff are continually confronted with opportunities to personally benefit from giving offenders favored treatment, integrity interviews (or in some cases a screening instrument) are also used to determine whether candidates have issues such as financial problems, past employment problems, current drug or alcohol abuse, or other conditions that could put them in a compromising situation or make them more likely to accept a bribe to show favored treatment to an inmate. And finally, candidates often have to provide a writing sample to determine their ability to communicate in writing.

Evaluating Effectiveness

Over the past several years, there has been an increase in the expected "accountability" for correctional administrators. Accountability usually refers to "are you delivering the value you should for the money you spend." Even though there could be many measures of outcome, the most commonly asked question is whether the activities, initiatives, or programs make a difference in reducing recidivism. Although ideological arguments about the best way to punish, rehabilitate, and deter criminals will continue, the most important issue has become, "What are the most cost-effective approaches?" Correctional administrators must be prepared to answer this question. They must understand measures of outcome, must be able to use and cite relevant research, and in many cases oversee their own research and evaluation departments. With the latter, they must set the agenda for these departments to work, and guide their work to best answer the question of what delivers the most "bang for the buck."

Recidivism as a Measure of Outcome

Throughout the history of corrections, the expectation has always been that correctional activities should reduce **recidivism**. Although it is often argued that it is unrealistic to expect a correctional sanction or program to have a significant impact on the future criminality of offenders, it continues to be the measuring stick for effectiveness. It is common for legislators to ask a correctional administrator, "What impact does that program have on reducing crime?" The complex answer to how a program may make offenders more employable or may improve their self-image does not go far in the legislator's mind, unless those intermediate goals are associated with a reduction in recidivism.

There are many limits in the use of recidivism as an outcome measure. First, there are questions of how to define recidivism. Should it be defined as an offender committing any new crime, commission of a felony during the period of community supervision, or return to prison? The length of the follow-up is also a concern. Can a correctional sanction or program be expected to have an impact on an offender for three or even five years after the termination of the sanction or program? Is six months a more reasonable follow-up period? And finally, how does a research design control for the many external and internal factors that can affect recidivism rates?

Evaluations of correctional programs regularly use rates of arrest as the primary determination of whether a program or sanction is successful. The definition used has a lot to do with the level of perceived success of a program. With the possibility of wide variations in the definition, it becomes almost impossible to compare effectiveness of programs using recidivism rates. In fact, some researchers whimsically suggest that "the best way to ensure a low recidivism rate is to define it very narrowly (e.g., incarceration in a state penal institution) and to use a very short follow-up period."[91]

Over the past decade, there has been a resurgence of interest in the effectiveness of correctional programs, primarily because of tight budget dollars and consideration as to whether community versus institutional sanctions equally impact recidivism and protect society. In addition, the improvement of correctional outcome measures and more thoughtful evaluative designs have resulted in findings showing that certain programs do make a difference, encouraging a renewed interest in rehabilitation. One element of improved evaluative designs is the inclusion of a measure of "quality of the program" as a variable linked to success. One way to assess the quality of a correctional program is the Correctional Program Assessment Inventory (CPAI), developed by Gendreau and Andrews.[92] The CPAI examines six elements within a program to assign a quality score: implementation and leadership; offender assessment and classification; program characteristics; characteristics and practices of staff; quality control; and other items, such as ethical considerations and level of support. By controlling for the quality of a program, all programs that target a certain area (such as drug abuse or sex offender treatment) are not considered the same in their comparison of outcome.

A second enhancement of correctional research is the use of **meta-analysis**, which is a way to quantify research results. Meta-analysis allows correctional researchers to examine many different outcome studies of programs, identify their individual indicators of success, and link those success indicators in a way that provides answers to more general policy issues. Gendreau, Goggin, and Smith help clarify what meta-analysis is and how it can be used:

What is meta-analysis? Consider how one would assess an individual's academic performance in undergraduate courses. Grades, of course, would be recorded as well as numerous other facts about the individual (i.e., age, gender, race, aptitude, study habits, types of courses, how they were taught, methods of grading, etc.). One can speculate about the individual's performance. If the grades were poor, was it due to poor study habits, "tough" courses, and so on? In order to obtain a more accurate assessment of the magnitude of the results (i.e., average grade) and how they may vary by age, study habits, and so forth across all undergraduates, then the data could be assessed on a sample of 100 students. Essentially, this is what meta-analysis does, but in this case, the individual represents one "research study."[93]

The Effectiveness of Probation and Parole

Over the past three decades, there have been many studies of the effectiveness of probation, parole, or other community-based programs. A 1986 review of 79,000 felons sentenced to probation revealed that within three years of sentencing, while still on probation, 43 percent were rearrested for a felony.[94] A 1985 RAND study followed California adult felons on probation in Los Angeles and Alameda counties over a forty-month period. Of the sample of 1,672 probationers in 1980, 65 percent were rearrested, 51 percent were reconvicted, and 34 percent were reincarcerated.[95] According to the most recent report on probation in the United States, 57 percent of offenders exiting probation during 2006 were successful completions, and 18 percent were incarcerated.[96]

Although these outcomes question the effectiveness of probation, other studies show some success of probation in reducing recidivism. A review of seventeen evaluations of felony probation found rearrest rates as low as 12 percent and as high as 65 percent.[97] This review concluded that probation without adequate surveillance and treatment is not effective. However, well-managed and adequately funded probation programs do reduce recidivism. However, all of the evaluations only cite success rates without a comparison of alternative sentencing outcomes.

In some evaluations, when probation success rates are compared to the success of ex-inmates, probationers' recidivism is consistently lower. That, however, would be expected as offenders who receive probation are a less serious group than those who are sentenced to prison. However, in a study with groups of 511 probationers and 511 parolees matched to have an equal likelihood of recidivism, the results over a two-year follow-up indicated that probationers were more successful; 72 percent of parolees and 63 percent of probationers were rearrested, 53 percent of parolees and 38 percent of probationers had new charges filed, and 47 percent of parolees and 31 percent of probationers were incarcerated in jail or prison.[98]

Views on the effectiveness of parole vary, and there are many ways to examine success. In some studies, effectiveness is defined as what percentage of offenders successfully complete their terms of supervision. The U.S. Department of Justice reports that of the more than 519,200 parolees discharged from supervision in 2006, 44 percent had successfully met the conditions of their supervision, and 39 percent had been returned to incarceration because of either a rule violation or a new offense. An additional 11 percent had absconded and 2 percent failed to successfully meet the conditions of supervision but were discharged without incarceration.[99]

During 2006, 179,259 parole violators were admitted to adult prisons in the United States. It is interesting to note, however, that about 5 percent were returned to incarceration as a result of a new offense, a figure unchanged since 1998,[100] while the rest were returned for technical violations of parole. In 2000 the 203,569 parole violators represented about 35 percent of new admissions. By 2007, there were 248,923 violators, or about 36 percent of prison admissions.[101]

A second definition of effectiveness considers the percentage of offenders who recidivate by committing new crimes or are being returned to prison. A study of recidivism among released inmates by Langan and Levin in 2004 reports, "Of the two-thirds persons released from prisons in 15 states in 1994, an estimated 67.5% were rearrested for a felony or serious misdemeanor within 3 years, 46.9% were reconvicted, and 51.8% returned to prison or jail."[102] The highest recidivism occurred during the first six months after release.

The third measure of effectiveness is how parole and other supervision following release compare to release with no parole or supervision. Sacks and Logan compared court-ordered prison releasees who received no supervision to those with parole and found that after three years, the parole group recidivated at a rate of 77 percent, whereas the group receiving no supervision recidivated at a rate of 85 percent.[103] A similar federal study found that the average time offenders remained in the community before a return to prison was seventeen months for those receiving supervision and only thirteen months for those without supervision.[104] Table 15-3 shows successful discharge from parole by

Table 15-3
PERCENTAGE OF SUCCESSFUL STATE PAROLE DISCHARGES, BY METHOD OF RELEASE

| Year | All Discharges | Method of Release | |
		Discretionary Parole	Mandatory Parole
1990	44.6%	51.6%	23.8%
1991	46.8	52.6	24.9
1992	48.6	50.7	29.8
1993	46.9	54.8	33.5
1994	44.3	52.2	30.4
1995	44.3	54.3	28.0
1996	45.2	55.9	30.2
1997	43.4	55.8	30.8
1998	43.8	55.3	32.2
1999	41.9	54.1	33.1

Source: Timothy A. Hughes, Doris James Wilson, and Allen J. Beck, *Trends in State Parole, 1990–2000* (Washington, DC: U.S. Department of Justice, Bureau of Justice Statistics, October 2001), p. 11.

method of release by the Bureau of Justice Statistics from 1990 to 1999. Inmates released by the decision of a parole board were more successful than those under mandatory parole (those released after serving a determinate sentence with supervision to follow).

Such data are very important for correctional administrators at the present times, when governments are looking for ways to save money and considering whether they can reduce sentences, reduce probation and parole violations, or even eliminate supervision for certain parolees. While there is no clear answer as to the impact of some of these policies, correctional administrators must use relevant data and link them to potential policies regarding cost savings and public safety. Elected officials are looking to them to suggest alternative approaches that make sense. Their definition of "makes sense" is that it costs less but does not reduce public safety to a point in which citizens (voters) will respond negatively. In Chapter 9, we presented several examples of states modifying sentencing and community supervision to reduce the number of prisoners. It will be interesting to examine how many states that recently made changes stand firm even after isolated incidents that make some question the wisdom of reducing the number of people in prison. The result will depend not only on the political implications but also on the skill of correctional administrators who can use effectiveness and outcome data to put these incidents into proper perspective.

Prisoner Reentry

As has been well established, there has been a tremendous growth in the prison population with more than 1.6 million prisoners currently in federal and state prisons. However, just as significant an issue is the increase in the number of offenders leaving prison and returning to the community each year. During 2007, 725,402 prisoners were released by adult prisons, an increase from 120,544 in 2000.[105] In California, 178,161 prisoners left prisons after completing their sentences in 2007, more than ten times the number of releases only twenty years earlier.[106]

When there was only one-half of the number of releases per year, the issues surrounding the release of offenders were not overly challenging for communities. However, with the current number of offenders returning home, many without postrelease supervision, there has been a call for academics and correctional administrators to identify the impact of these phenomena on the offenders, their families, and their communities.[107] This focus on **prisoner reentry** has resulted in examining issues such as finding housing, lack of ties with family and friends, finding a job, alcohol and drug abuse, continued involvement in crime, and the impact of parole supervision.[108] Petersilia has listed six collateral consequences of imprisonment: (1) community cohesion; (2) employment and economic well-being; (3) democratic participation and political alienation; (4) family stabilization and childhood development; (5) mental and physical health; and (6) homelessness.[109] These issues and consequences increase the likelihood that offenders will return to crime, and therefore it is critical that programs be provided to assist in preparing inmates for and assisting in the transition to their communities.

Programs that are effective in improving prisoner reentry, such as work and prison industry programs, substance abuse counseling, sex offender programs, and release from prison through a halfway house,[110] are available only to small numbers of inmates. However, as of December 30, 2005, only 31 percent of all prisons offered prison industries, 28 percent offered work release, 36 percent offered sex offender programs, and 74 percent offered drug or alcohol dependency counseling.[111] On January 1, 2002, state and federal prisons reported only 117,945 inmates (12.9 percent) in drug treatment programs, a decline of more than 50,000 inmates since 2000.[112] On the same date, only 78,881 inmates (7.8 percent) were assigned to prison industries, which have been found to be extremely successful in improving work skills and reducing recidivism.[113] On January 1, 2002, only 12,192 inmates (2.6 percent) were enrolled in sex offender programs.[114] Only 31,390 inmates were placed in halfway houses during 2004, yet this represented only 4.7 percent of the 669,132 inmates released from state and federal prisons that year.[115] And, during 2001, a total of 59,180 inmates were placed in work or study release.[116]

On the community end, there are many sociological issues regarding the community's ability to handle the return of so many ex-inmates. One is the impact on social cohesion and community stability. Anderson identified how the attitudes and behaviors of ex-inmates are transmitted to those in the community on release and concluded that "family caretakers and role models disappear or decline in influence, and as unemployment and poverty become more persistent, the community, particularly its children, become vulnerable to a variety of social ills, including crime, drugs, family disorganization, generalized demoralization and unemployment."[117] Rose, Clear, and Scully found an increase in crime when large numbers of offenders returned to a concentrated area within communities and questioned the deterrent and rehabilitative effect of prison. They suggest that releasing a large number of parolees to a community in one year destabilizes the community's ability to exert informal control over its members, because there is little opportunity for integration, there is increased isolation and anonymity, and ultimately the crime rate increases.[118]

Recently, there has been progress in understanding reentry issues and developing programs to improve success. After many papers were published regarding reentry, a Re-Entry Policy Council (a bipartisan collection of nearly 100 elected officials, policymakers, and practitioners) was formed, and in 2005, they released a set of recommendations to reduce recidivism and help ex-offenders succeed in their communities.[119] In 2008, the Second Chance Act (H.R. 1593/S. 1060) passed Congress and was signed into law.[120] The act authorized $362 million for prisoner mentoring programs, job training, and rehabilitative treatment designed to protect public safety and reduce recidivism rates.

Another positive improvement is the development of specialized **reentry courts**. The purpose of these courts is to oversee a prisoner's reentry to the community, review their plans and progress, order (when necessary) participation in treatment and reintegration programs, use drug and alcohol testing to monitor compliance, and provide graduated sanctions in lieu of a violation and return to prison. It is suggested that by placing a reentry court judge into the role of reentry manager, a new relationship is developed between community services to inmates and the criminal justice system.[121] To test reentry courts, the U.S. Department of Justice Office of Justice Programs awarded grants to nine states to set up courts and track their success. The research is still inconclusive and has to date produced mixed results,[122] but continues to be studied and modified to improve operations.[123]

It is critical that continued focus and innovation continue in prisoner reentry. We cannot afford to simply recycle criminals from prison to the community and back to prison. We must invest in successful programs that have proven to work in prisoner reentry. Correctional administrators can examine programs that work for prisoner reentry and put those in place to improve successful transitions to the community. For example, in a review of research regarding prisoner reentry programs, Seiter and Kadela identified several programs that work to reduce the recidivism of released prisoners and found a positive result for vocational training and work release programs, for drug rehabilitation, to some extent for education programs, for halfway house programs, and for prerelease programs. In addition, there are promising results for sex and violent offender programs.[124] We spend billions of dollars in locking up offenders, but to some extent have created a revolving door of offenders who will be committed to prison again and again as they fail in the community. This is not only a failure by the inmates but also a failure of release and reentry policies. With billions of dollars focused on imprisonment, it is only fitting that a few million more be focused on their return to the community.

SUMMARY

There are many significant issues that confront correctional administrators that complicate their day-to-day tasks. Years ago, life for correctional administrators was much simpler. Today, however, there are issues of budget, changes in sentencing, special offenders, recruiting staff and reducing turnover, accountability and evaluating effectiveness, and enhancing prisoner reentry. There are very few days without some type of crisis for the correctional administrator, either with budgets, staff problems, or offender conflicts. Perhaps the most important trait for successful correctional administrators is to be flexible and be able to deal with change. Not only should correctional administrators be prepared to react quickly to issues as they develop but they must also think strategically to recognize the developing trends and issues and put initiatives in place that address these issues proactively.

Unfortunately, the number, scope, and intensity of these challenges and issues are only going to increase. Governments are looking for ways to create new paradigms for sentencing and corrections that cost less and can be sustained without undermining public safety. Changes in approaches such as these will result in unexpected consequences that must also be managed. The diversity of special offenders seems to get broader every year, and a larger percentage of the offender population requires some type of special management. During the recession, the number of job applicants has increased. Yet, correctional agencies must use this hiatus to build recruitment and hiring systems and change their work environment for staff so that new employees remain as the economy improves. Corrections is all about outcomes. Everything we do is expected to increase public safety and improve the chances of offenders becoming productive and law-abiding citizens. Correctional administrators must both understand research findings and know how to use them to develop policy, and they must improve the major challenge of prisoner reentry so we end the revolving door of prison exit and return.

KEY TERMS

Special offender	Sex offenders	Recidivism
Straight adult incarceration	Containment model	Meta-analysis
Graduated incarceration	Suicide prevention programs	Prisoner reentry
Segregated incarceration	Suicide watch	Reentry courts

YOU'RE THE CORRECTIONAL ADMINISTRATOR

1. You are the chief of correctional programs for a state correctional agency. A lawyer representing 200 inmates, all over age fifty, in the state prisons comes to see you. The lawyer shows you a lawsuit that he is about to file alleging improper treatment and inhumane conditions. The suit alleges that as a result of the campus layout of the prisons, elderly inmates have to walk several hundred yards to work, programs, and the dining room. It alleges a lack of medical care for the elderly. It includes an absence of work or recreation geared to their needs as well as many other allegations. He says instead of filing the suit, his clients will wait for sixty days to see if you develop any plans to improve their situation. Unfortunately, you have been hearing some of the same issues from the wardens and know that the agency has not addressed these problems. What do you do? How do you determine whether there are unmet needs? How do you modify operations to meet needs that should be addressed?

2. You are the chief of mental health services for a state department of corrections. The director is under pressure from the governor and mental health advocates, who say that the department has ignored the needs of mentally ill inmates. You know their points have some merit, because the department does not have many specialized mental health programs. This issue has been heightened by two mentally ill inmates committing suicide by hanging themselves in the prisons over the past sixty days. In addition, a mentally ill inmate was raped in another prison. And an inmate suffering from mental illness murdered a staff member last week. How do you design an effective mental health program for inmates, and what resources can you seek or consult to establish and implement the program?

WEB LINK EXERCISES

Go to a special report from the site of the Bureau of Justice Statistics—http://bjs.ojp. usdoj.gov/content/pub/pdf/sujfry09.pdf.

This is a special report on Sexual Victimization in Juvenile Facilities Reported by Youth, 2008–2009. This is an excellent report on a very serious problem. Scroll down and examine the many graphs and charts. Look at your state's data and discuss it in class.

Go to New Directions in Corrections: www.renewalinc.com

This is a Web site for Renewal, Inc. Find out about Renewal and what services they offer to assist offenders in reentering the community as law-abiding and productive citizens. Describe the services you think are most helpful to offenders, and explain why.

GROUP EXERCISES

Each group will be assigned one of the following inmate special populations to explain all special considerations for a successful reentry program: sex offenders, aging offenders, mentally ill offenders, women offenders, and juveniles in adult prisons.

ENDNOTES

1. Camille Graham Camp and George M. Camp, *The Corrections Yearbook, 1999: Adult Corrections* (Middletown, CT: The Criminal Justice Institute, 1999), p. 3.

2. Bureau of Justice Statistics, "Prisoners in 2000," *Bureau of Justice Statistics Bulletin,* (Washington, DC: U.S. Department of Justice, 2001).

3. William J. Sabol, Heather C. West, and Matthew Cooper, *Prisoners in 2008—Statistical Tables* (Washington, DC: U.S. Department of Justice, December 2009).

4. William J. Sabol, Heather Couture, and Paige M. Harrison, "Prisoners in 2006," *Bureau of Justice Statistics Bulletin* (Washington, DC: U.S. Department of Justice, 2007).

5. Sabol et al., *Prisoners in 2008.*

6. 2010 figures were compiled by the Pew Center for the States in partnership with the Association of State Correctional Administrators. Data reported in Pew Center for the States, *Prison Count 2010: State Population Declines for the First Time in 38 Years* (Washington, DC: Pew Charitable Trusts, March 2009). The 2008 figures come from William J. Sabol, Heather C. West, and Matthew Cooper, "Prisoners in 2008," *Bureau of Justice Statistics* (Washington, DC: U.S. Department of Justice, December 2009).

7. Sourcebook of Criminal Justice Statistics Online, *Table 2.36.2008, Attitudes toward Level of Crime in Own Area,* http://wwwalbany.edu/sourcebook/pdf/t2362008.pdf (accessed August 23, 2009).

8. Camille Graham Camp and George M. Camp, *Corrections Yearbook, 1998* (Middletown, CT: Criminal Justice Institute, 1999), p. 57.

9. Camille Graham Camp and George M. Camp, *Corrections Yearbook, Adult Corrections 2002* (Middletown, CN: Criminal Justice Institute, 2003), p. 39.

10. Ibid., p. 41.

11. Bureau of Justice Statistics, "Correctional Populations," *Key Facts at a Glance,* http://bjs.ojp.usdoj.gov/content/glance/tables/corr2tab.cfm, (accessed April 23, 2010).

12. Alfred Blumstein and Allen J. Beck, "Population Growth in U.S. Prisons: 1980–1996," in *Prisons: A Review of Research,* edited by Michael Tonry and Joan Petersilia (Chicago: University of Chicago Press, 1999), pp. 17–62.

13. Sam C. Proband, "Corrections Leads State Budget Increases in FY 1997," *Overcrowded Times* 8 no. 4 (1997): 4.

14. John Irwin and James Austin, *It's About Time: America's Imprisonment Binge* (Belmont, CA: Wadsworth, 1994).

15. Ibid.

16. Barry Krisberg and Susan Marchionna, "Attitudes of U.S. Voters toward Prisoners Rehabilitation and Reentry Policies," *Focus: Views from the National Council on Crime and Delinquency* (San Francisco, CA: NCCD, April 2006).

17. Ibid.

18. S. E. Skovan, J. E. Scott, and E. T. Cullen, "Prison Crowding: Public Attitudes toward Strategies of Population Control," *Journal of Research in Crime and Delinquency* 25 no. 2 (1988): 150–169.

19. Barbara A. Sims, "Questions of Corrections: Public Attitudes toward Prison and Community-Based Programs," *Corrections Management Quarterly* 1 no. 1 (1997): 54.

20. The following studies report that level of reduction of crime based on increased use of incarceration: W. Spelman, "What Recent Studies Do (and Don't) Tell Us about Imprisonment and Crime," *Crime and Justice: A Review of Research*, edited by Michael Tonry (Chicago: University of Chicago Press, 2000), pp. 419–494; S. Aos, *The Criminal Justice System in Washington State: Incarceration Rates, Taxpayer Costs, Crime Rates, and Prison Economics* (Olympia, WA: Washington State Institute of Public Policy, 2003); and W. Spelman, "Jobs or Jail? The Crime Drop in Texas," *Journal of Policy Analysis and Management* 24 no. 1 (2005): 133–165.

21. Ibid., p. 201.

22. Jody L. Sundt, Francis T. Cullen, Brandon K. Applegate, and Michael G. Turner, "The Tenacity of the Rehabilitative Ideal Revisited: Have Attitudes Toward Offender Treatment Changed?," *Criminal Justice and Behavior* 25 (1998): 426–442.

23. Tammerlin Drummond, "Cellblock Seniors: They Have Grown Old and Frail in Prison. Must They Still Be Locked Up?" *Time* 153 no. 24 (June 21, 1999): 60.

24. U.S. Census Bureau, "Quick Facts" (Washington, DC: U.S. Census Bureau), http://quickfacts.census.gov/qfd/states/00000.html (accessed April 11, 2009).

25. Camp and Camp, *Corrections Yearbook, Adult Corrections 2002* (Middletown, CN: Criminal Justice Institute, 2003), pp. 32, 33.

26. William J. Sabol, Heather C. West, and Matthew Cooper, "Prisoners in 2007," *Bureau of Justice Statistics Bulletin* (Washington, DC: U.S. Department of Justice, December 2009), p. 36.

27. John J. Wilson and James C. Howell, *Comprehensive Strategy for Serious, Violent, and Chronic Juvenile Offenders: Program Summary* (Washington, DC: U.S. Department of Justice, Office of Juvenile Justice and Delinquency Prevention, 1993), p. 2.

28. Snyder, *Juvenile Arrests 2006*, p. 4.

29. Patricia Griffin, Patricia Torbet, and Linda Szymanski, *Trying Juveniles as Adults in Criminal Courts: An Analysis of State Transfer Provisions* (Washington, DC: U.S. Department of Justice, Office of Juvenile Justice and Delinquency Prevention, December 1998), p. 1.

30. James A. Gondles, Jr., "Kids Are Kids, Not Adults," Editorial, *Corrections Today* 59 no. 3 (June, 1997): 3.

31. Charles M. Puzzanchera and Melissa Sickmund, *Juvenile Court Statistics 2005* (Washington, DC: U.S. Department of Justice, National Center for Juvenile Justice, July 2008), p. 40.

32. Ibid.

33. Kevin J. Strom, *Profile of State Prisoners under Age 18, 1985–97* (Washington, DC: U.S. Department of Justice, Bureau of Justice Statistics, February 2000), p. 1.

34. Heather C. West and William J. Sabol, *Prison Inmates at Midyear 2008—Statistical Tables, National Prisoner Statistics* (Washington, DC: U.S. Department of Justice, March 2009), p. 20.

35. Ibid.

36. Paige M. Harrison and Jennifer C. Karberg, *Prison and Jail Inmates at Mid-Year 2002* (Washington, DC: U.S. Department of Justice, Bureau of Justice Statistics Bulletin, April 2003), p. 10.

37. Attapol Kuanliang, Jon S. Sorensen, and Mark D. Cunningham, "Juvenile Inmates in an Adult Prison System: Rates of Disciplinary Misconduct and Violence," *Criminal Justice and Behavior: An International Journal* 35 no. 9 (September 2008): 1186–1201.

38. Federal Bureau of Investigation, *Crime in the United States, 2007*, Table 35, http://www.fbi.gov/ucr/cius2007/data/table_42.html (accessed April 2, 2009).

39. Lawrence A. Greenfeld and Tracy L. Snell, *Women Offenders* (Washington, DC: U.S. Department of Justice, Bureau of Justice Statistics, December 1999), p. 5.

40. West and Sabol, *Prison Inmates at Midyear 2008*, p. 2.

41. West and Sabol, *Prisoners in 2007*, p. 21.

42. Greenfeld and Snell, *Women Offenders*, p. 7.

43. Camp and Camp, *Corrections Yearbook, Adult Corrections 2002*, p. 38.

44. *Barefield v. Leach*, No. 10282 (D.N.M., 1974), 196.

45. *Pargo v. Elliott*, 49 F.3d 1355 (8th Cir. 1995), 196.

46. Nicole H. Rafter, *Partial Justice: Women, Prison, and Social Control*, 2nd ed. (New Brunswick, NJ: Transaction, 1990).

47. Christopher C. Mumola and Jennifer C. Karberg, "Drug Use and Dependence, State and Federal Prisoners, 2004," *Bureau of Justice Statistics Special Report* (Washington, DC: U.S. Department of Justice, October 2006), p. 3.

48. Greenfeld and Snell, *Women Offenders*, p. 8.

49. Ibid.

50. Stephan, Appendix Table 19.

51. Camp and Camp, *Corrections Yearbook, Adult Corrections 2002*, p. 136.

52. Jennifer C. Karberg and Doris J. James, *Substance Dependence, Abuse, and Treatment of Jail Inmates, 2002* (Washington, DC: U.S. Department of Justice, Bureau of Justice Statistics Bulletin, July 2005), p. 10.

53. Meda Chesney-Lind, "The Forgotten Offender, Women in Prison: From Partial Justice to Vengeful Equity," in *Exploring Corrections: A Book of Readings*, edited by Tara Gray (Boston, MA: Allyn & Bacon, 2002), p. 11.

54. Robert R. Ross and Elizabeth A. Fabiano, *Female Offenders: Correctional Afterthoughts* (Jefferson, NC: McFarland, 1986).

55. Greenfeld and Snell, *Women Offenders*, p. 8.

56. Reported in Greenfeld and Snell, *Women Offenders*, p. 11.

57. Ibid.

58. J. Belknap, *The Invisible Woman: Gender, Crime, and Justice* (Belmont, CN: Wadsworth Publishing, 2007).

59. Greenfeld and Snell, *Women Offenders*.

60. Beth M. Huebner, Christina DeJong, and Jennifer Cobbina, "Women Coming Home: Long-Term Patterns of Recidivism," *Justice Quarterly* 27 no. 2 (April 2010): 225–254.

61. National Alert Registry, http://www.registeredoffenderslists.org (accessed December 9, 2005).

62. Kim English, Suzanne Pullen, and Linda Jones, *Managing Adult Sex Offenders in the Community—A Containment Approach* (Washington, DC: U.S. Department of Justice, National Institute of Justice, January 1997).

63. West and Sabol, *Prisoners in 2007*, p. 21.

64. Ibid.

65. Bureau of Justice Statistics, *Sourcebook of Criminal Justice Statistics, Sourcebook 2003* (Washington, DC: U.S. Department of Justice, 2004), p. 511.

66. Ibid., p. 2.

67. Greenfeld, p. 25.

68. Ibid., pp. 25–26.

69. Christopher J. Mumola, *Suicide and Homicide in State Prisons and Local Jails* (Washington, DC: U.S. Department of Justice, Bureau of Justice Statistics, August 2005), p. 1.

70. Ibid., p. 1.

71. Ibid., p. 8.

72. Greg W. Etter, "Preventing Jail Inmate Suicides," *American Jails* 22 no. 5 (December 2008): 29–31.

73. Kelsey Kauffman, *Prison Officers and Their World* (Cambridge, MA: Harvard University Press, 1988), p. 167.

74. Richard P. Seiter and Angela D. West, "Supervision Styles in Probation and Parole: An Analysis of Activities," *Journal of Offender Rehabilitation* 38 no. 2 (2003): 57–75.

75. Lauren E. Glaze and Thomas P. Boncar, *Probation and Parole in the United States, 2006* (Washington, DC: U.S. Department of Justice, 2007), p. 3.

76. James J. Stephan, "Census of State and Federal Correctional Facilities, 2005," *National Prisoner Statistics Program* (Washington, DC: U.S. Department of Justice, October 2008), p. 4.

77. Camille Graham Camp and George M. Camp, *Corrections Yearbook, Adult Systems, 2002* (Middletown, CN: Criminal Justice Institute, 2003), pp. 158, 159, 165.

78. Quoting correctional officer Donna Verrastro in an AP National article by David Crary, "High Stress, Low Glamor: Correctional Officers Struggle with Workplace Strains," *PoliceOne.com News*, May 8, 2005, http://www.policeone.com/pc_print.asp?vid=100392 (accessed April 12, 2009).

79. Lynn Bauer and Steven D. Owens, "Justice Expenditure and Employment in the United States, 2001," *Bureau of Justice Statistics Bulletin* (Washington, DC: U.S. Department of Justice, May 2004), p. 5.

80. Bureau of Justice Statistics, *Sourcebook of Criminal Justice Statistics, 1994* (Washington, DC: U.S. Department of Justice, updated March 2003), p. 26.

81. Texas Department of Criminal Justice (Corrections), http://www.tdcj.state.tx.us/vacancy/coinfo/cosalary.htm and California Department of Corrections and Rehabilitation, http://www.cdcr.ca.gov/Career_Opportunities/POR/docs/payandbenefits.pdf (accessed August 17, 2009).

82. Camp and Camp, *Corrections Yearbook, Adult Systems, 2002*, pp. 170–171.

83. Ibid., p. 14.

84. Ibid.

85. Glen Castlebury, "Correctional Officer Recruitment and Retention in Texas," *Corrections Today* 64 no. 3 (June 2001): 80–83.

86. North Carolina Department of Corrections, "DOC Addresses Correctional Officer Recruitment and Retention Issues," (April 2000), http: www.doc.state.nc.us/NEWSZ/cnews/0007/recruit.htm (accessed April 12, 2009).

87. Pew Center on the States, *Ten Steps Corrections Directors Can Take to Strengthen Performance* (Washington, DC: The Pew Charitable Trusts, May 2008).

88. Alaska Department of Corrections Press Release, *Department of Corrections Actively Recruiting Alaskans for Correctional Officer Positions* (Juneau, Alaska: Department of Corrections, January 26, 2005).

89. Brian E. Cronin, Ralph Klessig, and William D. Sprenkle, "Recruiting and Retaining Staff Through Culture Change," *Corrections Today* 70 no. 4 (August 2008): 48–51.

90. Gary Mohr, "Samberg Program Improves Leadership and Addresses Turnover," *Corrections Today* 71 no. 2 (April 2009): 56–58.

91. Edward J. Latessa and Alexander Holsinger, "The Importance of Evaluating Correctional Programs: Assessing Outcome and Quality," *Corrections Management Quarterly* 2 no. 4 (1998): 23.

92. P. Gendreau and D. Andrews, *The Correctional Program Assessment Inventory*, 5th ed. (Saint John: University of New Brunswick, 1994).

93. Paul Gendreau, Claire Goggin, and Paula Smith, "Generating Rational Correctional Policies: An Introduction to Advances in Cumulating Knowledge," *Correctional Management Quarterly* 4 no. 2 (2000): 56–57.

94. *Bureau of Justice Statistics National Update* (Washington, DC: U.S. Department of Justice, 1994), p. 10.

95. Joan R. Petersilia, Susan Turner, James Kahan, and Joyce Peterson, *Executive Summary of Granting Felons Probation: Public Risks and Alternatives* (Santa Monica, CA: RAND, 1985), p. 1.

96. Glaze and Bonczar (December 2007), p. 2.

97. Michael Geerken and Hennessey D. Hayes, "Probation and Parole: Public Risk and the Future of Incarceration Alternatives," *Criminology* 31 no. 4 (1993): 549–564.

98. Joan R. Petersilia and Susan Turner, *Prison versus Probation in California: Implications for Crime and Offender Recidivism* (Santa Monica, CA: RAND, 1986): 27–33.

99. Glaze and Bonczar, "Probation and Parole," p. 7.

100. Ibid., p. 8.

101. Heather C. West and William J. Sabol, *Prisoners in 2007* (Washington, DC: U.S. Department of Justice, Bureau of Justice Statistics, December 2008), p. 3.

102. Patrick A. Langan and David J. Levin, "Recidivism of Prisoners Released in 1994," *Bureau of Justice Statistics Special Report* (Washington, DC: U.S. Department of Justice, June 2002), p. 1.

103. Howard R. Sacks and Charles H. Logan, "Does Parole Make a (Lasting) Difference?" in *Criminal Justice: Law and Politics*, 4th ed., edited by George F. Cole (Pacific Grove, CA: Brooks/Cole, 1984), pp. 362–378.

104. William J. Sabol, William P. Adams, Barbara Parthasarathy, and Yan Yuan, *Offenders Returning to Federal Prison, 1986–1997, Special Report* (Washington, DC: U.S. Department of Justice, Bureau of Justice Statistics, September 2000), p. 6.

105. West and Sabol, *Prisoners in 2007*, p. 3.

106. Joan Petersilia, *Challenges of Prisoner Reentry and Parole in California* (Berkeley, CA: California Policy Research Center, 2000), p. 1. Also, Glaze and Bonczar, "Probation and Parole," p. 26.

107. Joan Petersilia, "Parole and Prisoner Reentry in the United States," in *Prisons*, edited by Michael Tonry and Joan Petersilia (Chicago: University of Chicago Press, 1999), pp. 479–529.

108. Marta Nelson, Perry Deess, and Charlotte Allen, "First Month Out: Post Incarceration Experiences in New York City," (unpublished monograph, New York: The Vera Institute, 1999).

109. G. G. Gaes, T. J. Flanagan, L. L. Motiuk, and L. Stewart, "Adult Correctional Treatment," in *Prisons*, edited by Michael Tonry and Joan Petersilia (Chicago: University of Chicago Press, 1999), pp. 361–426.

110. These have been reported in Richard P. Seiter and Karen R. Kadela, "Prisoner Reentry: What Works, What Doesn't, and What's Promising," *Crime and Delinquency* 49 no. 3 (April 2003): 360–388.

111. James J. Stephan, "Census of State and Federal Correctional Facilities, 2005," *Bureau of Justice Statistics: National Prisoner Statistics Program* (Washington, DC: U.S. Department of Justice, October 2008), p. 5.

112. Camp and Camp, *Corrections Yearbook, Adult Systems, 2002*, pp. 136–137.

113. Ibid., p. 119.

114. Ibid., p. 134.

115. Ibid., pp. 71, 146.

116. Ibid., p. 144.

117. Elijah Anderson, *Streetwise: Race, Class, and Change in an Urban Community* (Chicago: University of Chicago Press, 1990), p. 4.

118. Dina R. Rose, Todd Clear, and Kristen Scully, "Coercive Mobility and Crime: Incarceration and Social Disorganization," unpublished paper presented at the American Society of Criminology, Toronto, November, 1999.

119. Council of State Governments, *Report of the Reentry Policy Council* (New York: The Justice Center, Council of State Governments, 2005).

120. In the Senate there are 33 cosponsors, including Senators Joseph Biden (D-DE), Arlen Specter (R-PA), Sam Brownback (R-KS), and Patrick Leahy (D-VT). In the House there are 92 cosponsors, including Representatives Danny Davis (D-IL), Chris Cannon (R-UT), John Conyers (D-MI), Lamar Smith (R-TX), Bobby Scott (D-VA), Randy Forbes (R-VA), Stephanie Tubbs Jones (D-OH), and James Sensenbrenner (R-WI).

121. Jeremy Travis, Anna Crayton, and Debbie A. Mukamai, "A New Era in Inmate Reentry," *Corrections Today* 71 no. 6 (December 2009): pp. 38–41.

122. Donald J. Farole, *Harlem Parole Reentry Court Evaluation: Implementation and Primary Impacts* (New York: Center for Court Innovation, 2003).

123. A good overview of these courts is available in Shadd Maruna and Thomas P. LeBel, "Welcome Home? Examining the 'Reentry Court' Concept from a Strengths-based Perspective," *Western Criminology Review* 4 no. 2 (2003): 91–107.

124. Seiter and Kadela, "Prisoner Reentry."

16

The Future and Correctional Administration

Introduction

In this textbook, correctional administration has been examined from both broad and narrow perspectives and also through administrative, substantive, and philosophical issues. From the broad perspective, the history, philosophical developments, and attitudes and perceptions surrounding corrections and its administration have been reviewed. Conversely, policies and practices required to carry out critical correctional functions such as staffing, managing prison security, and reducing correctional costs have also been described. Administrative activities such as strategic planning, management of human resources, and budget development and administration have been considered. Substantive correctional issues such as classification of offenders, provision of treatment programs, and the delivery of medical care to inmates were addressed. Also, the philosophical challenges within correctional administration such as the importance of balancing punishment and rehabilitation, the political and public policy perspectives of corrections, and the need for new styles of correctional leadership were assessed.

One thing should be clear to readers of this textbook: Corrections is not a static discipline. It is often suggested that the only thing correctional administrators can count on is that things will change. Consider the changes that have occurred regarding correctional issues over the past two decades. During the 1990s, the population of inmates in prisons and jails in the United States more than doubled, yet during the first decade of the 2000s, the population growth slowed and even declined in 2009. During the 1990s, there was tremendous growth in the budgets and staff resources directed toward correctional agencies, but by 2008, governments were broke and looking for ways to reduce the money spent on corrections. The makeup of the offender population has also changed; the population is getting older, minorities and women are increasingly represented, and there is a larger proportion of offenders who are members of prison or street gangs. There is an increasing specialization of how to manage these offenders in both prisons (special units and programs) and the community (specialized caseloads), and you see special programs for sex offenders, older inmates, and the mentally ill.

It is frightening to consider that the pace of change that must be confronted and managed by correctional administrators is unlikely to slow down. In fact, change will probably come even more rapidly, as some of the forces that have driven correctional change will continue to impact correctional agencies and other forces are intensifying. There are many new correctional concepts that are being considered and will have to be evaluated. Those that prove valuable will be incorporated into the landscape or agenda of correctional administration. The people who work in corrections today are very different than their predecessors, and agencies have become more sophisticated in how they recruit, develop, supervise, and empower staff. There is no question that corrections and the challenges for correctional administrators will continue to change.

Where Are We Today?

Unfortunately, many people have a fairly negative perception of corrections as lacking professionalism, effectiveness, and responsiveness to the public's interests and offenders' needs. A good example was what Vermont correctional officials found out during the 1990s when they kept getting feedback with dissatisfaction from offenders and offender groups, victims and victim's rights groups, the public and their elected officials, and even correctional administrators themselves. This situation prompted them to survey public opinion, and they were surprised and disappointed by what they found out.

> The upshot was that the criminal justice system was thoroughly disgusted with our inability to hold anyone to their minimum sentence release date. The media castigated us nightly as "the revolving door," using "corrections math," and the victims' community declared us to be the enemy. Our staff morale was shot. Quite clearly, the problem wasn't us. It was everybody else. It was their fault. They just didn't understand us.[1]

As a result, Vermont began to redefine the problem it faced and began to educate the public about how corrections really functioned, including approaches that could better meet the needs of victims, the public, and offenders. Their efforts are described in the discussion of restorative justice.

This example was true for many if not most correctional agencies. And many have become better at educating the public and casting their message into the flow of information that they do understand and appreciate what is expected of them and that they are really better at it than the public knows. Over the past twenty years, correctional administrators (as discussed in Chapter 11) have had to become better at working with the external environment and making adjustments to better reflect the public's desire for certain policies and approaches. Reforms and improved operations came in many areas of correctional administration. Several new prisons were constructed to reduce overcrowding and provide a safer environment. These prisons were more efficient than the older ones, and had enhanced security and the quality of the environment for staff and inmates. Treatment programs have expanded and often use evidence-based practices. There were improvements in service areas such as medical care and food service. Corrections leaped forward in professionalism, aided by the American Correctional Association (ACA) accreditation process. Risk assessment instruments improved decision making concerning inmate prison classification, release on parole, and supervision in the community. Correctional staff became better trained, better educated, and better represented by minorities and women.

As noted previously, one of the most important areas for the reform and improvement of correctional organizations and their administrations has been accreditation by the American Correctional Association (ACA). By March 2009, there were 612 of the 1,697 (36 percent) adult prisons accredited by ACA. At this time, there were also 254 community residential facilities (halfway houses) and 199 juvenile correctional facilities that were accredited.[2] Even though 64 percent of prisons are not accredited, this does not mean these prisons are not professionally operated or do not meet constitutional standards. In fact, with the active involvement of federal courts in reviewing complaints by inmates, correctional agencies have been proactive in meeting professional standards rather than fighting expensive lawsuits they may lose, resulting in the agency having to change operations anyway. Although it was not unusual to find correctional agencies operating prisons that were obviously unprofessional and inhumane in the 1950s and even 1960s, it is highly unusual to find such prisons today.

In Part IV of this text, we described the ways prisons accomplish safety and security, provide rehabilitative programs to inmates, and provide services such as health care, food, mail, and visiting. Podular designs of housing units, direct supervision, and unit management are all improvements that have helped security operations. Since the 1970s craze of Martinson's "nothing works," prison programs have proven effective at reducing recidivism, and education, vocational training, substance abuse, and many other prison programs are considered important to aid in prisoner reentry. Also, essential prison services to deliver health care and food to the inmate population have improved tremendously and are no longer an afterthought for prison administrators.

Staff professionalism has been aided through improved recruitment, training, and a focus on diversity. Part II of this book describes the management of correctional staff, including how correctional agencies have had to improve their methods to recruit qualified staff, train them professionally, and create an empowering environment in which they feel valuable, want to stay, and begin to think of corrections as a career and not just a job. Diversity of staff is important, and correctional agencies have expanded the makeup of their staffs; by January 1, 2002, of the total 435,688 staff employed by prisons and jails, 69.0 percent were white, 20.1 percent were black, and 7.6 percent were Hispanic.[3] Whites still represent a large percentage of the workforce; however, the percentage of nonwhite employees has increased from 28.8 percent in 1994 to 30.8 percent in 2002.[4] The improvement in probation and parole agencies is better, as a 2002 survey of 60 probation and parole agencies reported that of the 50,640 people employed, 66.7 percent were white, 23.5 percent were black, and 7.2 percent were Hispanic.[5]

The use of actuarial risk assessments (described in Chapter 10) also assist correctional administrators in sentencing, classifying, and supervising offenders in the community; identifying risk and assigning inmates to appropriate security level facilities; and making parole and release decisions. There is little dispute that these instruments have improved decision making within correctional agencies, yet it is also acknowledged that they are not a substitute for professional judgment. The instruments have also made correctional decisions understandable to offenders and to the general public. They have improved the ability to assign inmates to appropriate settings with physical security that reduces escapes and violence. They have also allowed community corrections administrators to align scarce resources with the offenders with the greatest risks and needs.

Although correctional reforms over the past few decades are impressive, they are likely to be insignificant compared with the change and restructuring that will be required by correctional agencies over the next decades. The issues that confront correctional administrators were presented in Chapter 15, and these are complicated by the serious budget crisis faced by most state and local governments today (discussed in Chapter 9). These issues regarding sentencing, aging offenders, juvenile offenders, women offenders, mentally ill offenders, effectiveness and accountability, technology, and prisoner reentry challenge even the most talented and experienced correctional administrators, and are getting more complex every year. The budget shortages brought on by the recession will not diminish any time soon, and correctional administrators are being pushed to find the most cost-effective alternatives to managing offenders without undermining public safety. Throughout the remainder of this chapter, we examine expectations for the future and developing concepts that will influence corrections and transform the work of correctional administrators.

Where Are We Going in the Future?

There are different opinions as to where corrections is headed in the future. On one hand, there are those who suggest the future of corrections is bleak, because the many problems that have confronted correctional administrators over the past decade are expected to intensify. On the other hand are those who believe the worst is past and that many problematic trends, such as the increase in the number of inmates and community offenders, are likely to decline. There are at least three complicating factors that will impact where corrections is going in the next five years. These are volume (the number of offenders under community or prison and jail supervision), budgets (the shortage of funds and search for ways to reduce expenditures), and politics (the argument between being tough on crime and emphasis on public safety versus the practical reality that we cannot incarcerate every offender who presents some risk to reoffend). In this section, we examine how these overlaying factors will intersect with some specific trends to paint a picture of where we are going in the future.

In terms of volume, there has been a changing trend in the number of offenders in prison or jail. Although the number of prisoners in adult and federal prisons has risen steadily over the past twenty years, there is evidence that this could be changing. As of January 1, 1990, the nation's prisons held 750,000 inmates, and during the next decade the number of prisoners increased an average of 8.7 percent per year, reaching 1.32 million on January 1, 1999.[6] On December 31, 2008, there were 2,424,279 offenders incarcerated in state and federal prisons and local jails (two-thirds in prisons and one-third in jails).[7] However, the growth has slowed from 2000 to 2006, when the incarcerated population increased by an average of only 3 percent per year,[8] and even more slowly over the twelve months ending December 31, 2008, as the population increased by only 0.2 percent. Nineteen states actually had a decline in their prison population during 2008.[9] And in 2009, the state prison population actually decreased for the first time in nearly forty years. The Pew Center for the States reported that as of January 1, 2010, there were 1,403,091 inmates in state prisons, a decrease of 5,739 from the number of inmates on December 31, 2008.[10]

Government budget shortages have certainly impacted these numbers. The states reported a gap in funding of budgets of $73 billion in 2009 and $113 billion in 2010.[11] With tightening budgets, it is now a much more complicated decision as to whether to increase taxes, reduce the correctional population, or eliminate some services or supervision to meet budget shortfalls. Corrections is the fifth largest budget category, and elected officials are struggling between continuing that spending in lieu of demands for education, infrastructure, and health care.[12] As states look for ways to reduce costs, they may attempt to reduce the number of inmates through community diversion programs, they may overcrowd their own prisons, or they may turn to privatization when it saves them money.

There are many who believe we have to seriously change how we decide who or how many need to be incarcerated at a very high cost to society. Innes suggests that "the American correctional system costs too much . . . [which] means either that it is more than what someone needs or that it is simply more than someone can afford."[13] In 2008, an initiative began to consider what it would take to reduce the correctional population by half in eight years. This would seem to dramatically change the paradigm of how we make sentencing, release, and violation decisions. The report *Reducing America's Correctional Population: A Strategic Plan* by Austin written for this initiative points out that the large increases in the correctional populations over the past twenty-five years have been the result of an increase in the number of prison admissions from both new crime convictions and parole violations and a significant increase in the average length of stay, and to reduce the correctional populations, these trends need to be reversed. However, Austin points out that meeting one-half the target in eight years is achievable and relatively small adjustments in key decision points can have a large cumulative effect on the total correctional population over a short period of time.[14] These types of activities lead us to the third factor of politics.

The politics of sentencing and diversion from prison has also changed considerably. For two decades, state legislatures have tried to outdo one another in reacting to heinous crimes and passing tough sentencing laws they think will prevent such crimes and make the public safer. Perhaps the classic case illustrating the "overreach" of mandatory prison terms was the 1995 sentencing of Jerry Williams under the 1994 California three-strikes law. Williams had two prior felony convictions involving violence; when he stole a piece of pizza from four children, it resulted in a mandatory life sentence under the California law. California passed the statute in order to keep habitual and dangerous offenders in prison forever. However, the costs to the state for Williams' incarceration will be $500,000. Budget shortages and a dramatic increase in the number of prison inmates have made elected officials question the efficacy of such tough sentencing statutes. And besides the costs and prison management problems resulting from lifetime mandatory prison terms, judges lament their loss of discretion to consider mitigating circumstances in sentencing offenders. In fact, in a speech at the Pepperdine (CA) School of Law in February 2010, U.S. Supreme Court Justice Anthony M. Kennedy lamented the resulting overcrowding of prisons and the poor state of rehabilitation in our nation's (and particularly in California) prisons. He noted that sentences in the United States are eight times longer than that for comparable crimes in Europe. Criticizing the mandatory life sentences for third-time criminals, Justice Kennedy said that "The three-strikes law sponsor is the correctional officers' union and that is sick!"[15]

With a focus on the economic crisis, several state legislatures reconsidered sentencing policies that better manage correctional populations. In 2009, states revised sentencing laws, expanded community-based diversion programs, and created programs to reduce recidivism. California, Delaware, Maryland, Montana, Oregon, and Washington increased the monetary thresholds for theft-related crimes resulting in less severe penalties, and New York amended the "Rockefeller Drug Laws" by decreasing mandatory minimums. Other states (Kentucky, Florida, and North Dakota) have expanded substance abuse treatment as an alternative to a return to prison for probation and parole violators. Furthermore, California, Colorado, Illinois, and Montana enacted performance incentive funding policies for counties who reduce probation revocations.[16] The Pew Center for the States in a March 2010 report on the decline of prison population suggested that while the budgetary crisis was driving reform, "states began to realize they could effectively reduce their prison populations, and save public funds, without sacrificing public safety."[17]

Although the punitive atmosphere dominated criminal sentencing for the past two decades, there is now a realization by many that "tough on crime" criminal sentencing may have gone too far. Supporters of long sentences (especially for repeat criminals) cite evidence that by significantly increasing the number of offenders in prison, we have reduced crime.[18] This would be expected if most of the habitual offenders who commit a large portion of crimes are already in prison. They argue that although prisons are expensive, they are worth the cost, and increasing the use of imprisonment reduces crime and saves money. Opponents of these sentencing practices suggest that rather than locking up more people, changing demographics, better economic times, and declining drug use and drug crimes have more to do with the reduction in crime rates.[19] There is no question that the extensive use of imprisonment as a sanction has certainly prevented the commission of several crimes. The important policy questions, however, are whether the cost of incarcerating this number of offenders for such long periods of time is worth the expense and at what point does society reach a "diminishing return" on the investment in more prisons.[20]

Now the question of where we are going in the future? We are at a crossroads. As noted above, many states have modified their sentencing and community diversion programs to reduce the number of inmates and save money. After several months of keeping offenders in the community or shortening sentences, there have been some high profile crimes and some stepping-back from full support to these approaches by many elected officials. However, it appears at this time that the economics of the issue will outweigh the politics of the issue. In other words, while many politicians would like to make political hay out of the sentencing modifications, they recognize that they will have to say how they will pay for it if they want a return to more offenders going to prison. The public is accepting of some risks to save money that can be used to fund education, social service, unemployment benefits, or heath care.

So at this point, the answer to the question is that as long as the recession continues, we will continue to reduce prison terms and divert more offenders and probation or parole violators from prison. Will the recession end soon? While there are signs in 2010 that unemployment may have bottomed out, there is still little increase in hiring by companies who have found they can live without the extra employees they laid off. The recession is likely to continue well into 2011. And even as things get better, state income and sales tax revenues will lag behind employment and it will be several more months before states and local governments get financially healthy again. By then, they will have found out that these modifications in sentencing do not significantly reduce public safety and they will be slow to return to the tough on crime philosophies that have proven so expensive to maintain.

Practical Perspectives

Correctional Administrators Predict the Future

Although the article was published ten years ago, it still has relevance and is very interesting when looking at predictions of the future. Chase Riveland, former head of corrections for the states of Colorado and Washington, polled seven prominent correctional administrators and asked them to look forward to 2025, and predict the changes they see for correctional administration by that time.[21] The following are some of the areas they believed would be major trends and have the greatest impact on what administrators will face by that time.

There were five major themes discussed by these practitioners: prison populations, economics, research into what works, technology, and privatization. The first two are fairly linked in most of the comments, as it was believed that there would be changes in number and makeup of the prison population, but most of this would be driven by cost. Most of the administrators thought the prison population growth would slow, and there would be a reconsideration of our sentencing policies. One expert believed that by 2025, prisons would hold a concentration of high custody, violent, predatory, career criminals, while nonviolent and nondangerous offenders will be supervised in the community. In this sense, prisons will be reserved for those "we are afraid of rather than those we are simply mad at."[22]

As noted, the high cost of prisons and the economics of their increased use will drive much of the change. Competition for public funds from schools, transportation, and other needs will force a relook at how much money we spend on prison, and cost will be the driving factor behind policy reconsideration. Another cost going forward that cannot be reduced and is an anchor to efforts for saving money is the debt service for bonding prisons built over the past decade. One expert simply stated that by 2025, we will not be able to pay the bill for the policies of imprisonment we have implemented today.

Although not as prevalent, there was intrigue with the use of "what works" research or what we now know as evidence based to focus our investments into programs and initiatives that work to reduce crime. Research was also believed to provide answers to what are appropriate sentences for groups of offenders. And research can provide valuable information to improve business processes. Almost everyone touched on the impact of technology over the next twenty-five years. They applauded the early uses of technology to improve corrections, but believed there was much more to come. Technology will not only improve management, quality, and efficiency but will also change how inmates are supervised both in prisons and the community.

There was much discussion of how much the past decade trend of privatization would continue in the future. Although not all supported profit-making companies operating prisons, they all believed it would continue in the future. It will not be an issue of whether the private sector could do a better job, but it is a matter of perceived or real cost savings. But most of the seven experts also believed government could learn from the private sector and become better and more cost-efficient themselves. In a 2010 article regarding the future of privatization, Wright points out that privatization will continue to be a major part of correctional operations, but suggests that instead of quarreling over the merits of private prison performance, we should be focused on how the public correctional systems can benefit from the existence of private prisons.[23]

These opinions by the seven correctional administrators are very consistent with the trends over the last decade, which brings further validity to their predictions for the year 2025. They all believed there would be considerable changes, and it is obvious that this means new challenges for the current students of correctional administration who will be in leadership roles by that time. All agreed that the one thing we know is that things will continue to change.

How will Community Supervision Change?

Over the past thirty years, the "tough on crime" mentality has also impacted how we supervise offenders on probation or parole. Until the late 1960s, probation and parole supervision focused on the casework style of supervision or restoring offenders to the community.[24] However, over the past three decades, there has been an increasing reliance on surveillance or closely monitoring offenders to catch them when they fail to meet all required conditions. Rhine, in describing this change in supervision style, suggests that it brings about a new paradigm in the supervision of offenders in the community:

> Despite their importance to public safety, the past 20 years have witnessed a marked devaluation of traditional probation and parole supervision. Acknowledging this trend, many administrators in the field have adopted a set of practices and a discourse that represent a discernible shift toward risk management and surveillance. This shift in the mission and conduct of supervision reflects a new narrative, the plausibility of which has yet to be established.[25]

Between 1987 and 1996, the percentage of federal offenders with at least one special condition (participation in substance abuse, drug testing, and electronic monitoring) increased from 67 percent to 91 percent.[26] During 2001, states involved in probation and parole supervision reported conducting 6,403,990 drug tests and revoked 90,796 offenders as a result of a positive test for drug use.[27] In 2007, 70 percent of probationers and 84 percent of parolees were on active supervision with weekly or monthly face-to-face contact with their supervision officer.[28]

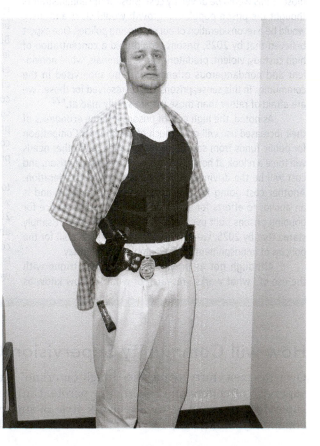

The surveillance style of community supervision even includes "arming" probation and parole officers, the wearing of protective vests, and more of a focus on policing rather than helping.
(Photo by Richard P. Seiter)

As a result of the close surveillance of offenders in the community, the rate of revocations and resulting incarcerations has increased significantly, and most revocations are for only technical violations of supervision rather than commitment of a new felony. According to West and Sabol, 697,975 offenders were admitted to state prisons during 2007.[29] Of this number, 62,510 (9.2 percent) were probation violators, 183,896 (31 percent) were parole violators, and 13,109 (2.2 percent) were violators of some other type of postrelease supervision.[30] Overall, approximately four in ten prison admissions were offenders revoked from community supervision, while in 1980, parole violators constituted only 18 percent of all admissions.[31] In 2006, 50 percent of probationers violated and were sent to prison, and two-thirds of parole violators reimprisoned were for technical violations instead of to serve a new sentence.[32] Some argue that this is good public policy and focuses on public safety. However, it is very expensive and can be shortsighted. Offenders violated for technical reasons are usually returned to prison for a duration of ninety days to one year and when released are seldom better prepared for reentry and have done little to reduce any personal problem such as substance abuse, poor work habits, or family problems.

During these difficult budget times, many states are relooking at whether a surveillance style of supervision is worth the cost in terms of public safety and many other states are changing the style of supervision back to a more proactive treatment-oriented supervision. For example, Maryland moved to an evidence-based supervision model that begins with a risk and need assessment to identify treatment and control needs and makes the supervision officer an instrument for facilitating offender change. This Proactive Community Supervision (PSC) model has resulted in fewer rearrests (30 percent for the PCS and 42 percent for traditional models) among offenders. Maryland believes that supervision styles can be transformed and still achieve public safety goals by focusing on positive offender change.[33]

Another example is of Kansas, which is closing three correctional facilities to save money and targeting a 20 percent reduction in probationers violated and sent to prison. To accomplish this, Kansas implemented behavior modification as a part of probation supervision, which is an intensive version of the casework style of supervision with offenders earning extra privileges and reduced requirements as they make progress on established goals. A Kansas correctional official noted, "It used to be that it was more about waiting for them [probationers] to mess up and send them back to prison. In this time and this economy, you can't afford to keep doing that. There is a better way to do business."[34]

A promising reform of probation that was initiated in the 1990s is gaining a renewed emphasis in an attempt to reduce violations and improve the success of community offenders. Called broken-windows probation, the concept mimics the philosophy of community policing, in which all broken windows in a neighborhood are to be promptly repaired to not allow a belief that there is a lack of community concern that can lead to instability and criminal activity in the neighborhood. Similarly, broken windows probation partners with citizen groups, churches, and other neighborhood organizations to take joint responsibility for supervising offenders. Emphasizing public safety first, broken-windows probation also allocates resources according to risk and need assessments, locates probation officers in the probationers' neighborhoods, and uses graduated sanctions such as house arrest, electronic monitoring, and mandatory substance abuse treatment.[35]

The question posed in this section is "how will community supervision change?" The answer is that we will return to the casework style of supervision and probation and parole officers will take it as their responsibility to make sure offenders succeed in the community, instead of making sure they catch and violate them upon the first failure. Many states (including Colorado, Kentucky, Tennessee, California, Kansas, and Maryland) are focusing their resources on how to keep people out of prison rather than how to put them in. This transformation does not come easy, and there will be political road bumps along the way. Historically, there have been few options to revocation and return to prison that the public sees as effective and contributing to public safety. There has already been and will be instances of serious crime committed by offenders who could have been violated. Yet, states cannot afford to continue the high revocation rates we have experienced and have to make decisions based on the overall effectiveness of the policy and not specific cases so as not to throw out the baby with the bathwater. Unfortunately, correctional administrators often take the brunt of the criticism, yet they cannot give in to the easy decision to retreat to the surveillance style and emphasis on revocations.

What Impact will Technology have on the Future?

Technology continues to be the buzzword of society. Everywhere one looks, there are suggestions for the use of technology to make a job easier or change how things are done. With the information revolution, with personal computers, smart phones, and social networking changing the way people shop, communicate, and work, technology impacts almost everything we do. Automobiles are equipped with high-tech devices to tell people where they are and how to get to where they want to go. There are "smart homes" that can be programmed (or initiated remotely) to do certain tasks and make life easier for owners. Workplaces change almost daily with new equipment and operating systems.

However, corrections has been relatively slow to adopt technological advances, even though there are an amazing variety of innovations that may have application for corrections. While many technological applications are in use throughout corrections, there have been no developments that have recreated the traditional approach to how we supervise and manage offenders. Computers play a much greater role in predicting risk and maintaining information about offenders, and trends of data can help correctional officials be more proactive than reactive. Security systems are much more technologically sophisticated than they were even ten years ago. Telemedicine is being used more extensively to reduce the need to take inmates outside a prison to be seen by a medical specialist. Video cameras are commonly used in prisons to more thoroughly monitor inmate movement and activities. Electronic monitoring of probationers has become an accepted practice in community supervision, and the use of GPS systems are now used to monitor offender movements in real time. Here we address some of the promising initiatives and examine how much these may change corrections in the future.

There are many technology applications that are used in the business world that help corrections to manage more efficiently. Data storage or generation, electronic medical records, office applications to order supplies and pay bills in a paperless fashion, computerized time clocks that automatically create payroll, and identification

The use of GPS systems that can be carried by offenders enables to track their movements and it facilitates the supervision of higher-risk offenders in the community.
(Photo by Richard P. Seiter)

systems to allow and record employee access are all innovations to make the business operations of corrections more efficient just as they do any other government agency or private company.

There are others that improve security in prisons and support community supervision. We can now collect and share criminal or gang intelligence between correctional and law enforcement agencies, better detect and prevent contraband within prisons, use technology to keep staff safer, and aid in supervising offenders in the community. Fabelo suggests that the concept of correctional agencies taking advantage of new technologies to reduce the costs of supervising criminal offenders and minimizing the risk they pose to society is called "**technocorrections.**"[36]

A serious challenge to correctional administrators is the many thousands of prison and jail inmates that are part of criminal networks or gangs in the community. The intelligence that is collected by observing and recording their prison behavior is also useful to law enforcement and homeland security efforts. The Department of Homeland Security spent more than $380 million by the end of 2007 to provide Fusion Centers to state and local governments to collect intelligence information and use it to proactively identify threats to our security.[37] Correctional agencies are beginning to contribute to these Fusion Centers so that their data on criminal or potential terrorist networks can be linked with law enforcement information. Complicated computer systems and programs can sort through large volumes of information and find relevance to a small piece of information at one location and another piece of information at another one.

An interesting development is the use of e-messaging by inmates. A few states are beginning to allow electronic messages to be sent into prisons and may soon allow inmates to respond electronically. This not only reduces the chances of contraband to come into prisons through the mail but also reduces the staff time required to open and search all incoming letters. In 2006, Colorado implemented a system in which inmate families and friends could pay a small fee and thereby e-mail a letter to the prison, which prints it off and delivers it to the concerned inmate just as they would regular mail.[38] Not only does it save staff time, the system is programmed to search for key words that can identify possible criminal or gang activity. Colorado will soon install kiosks in the prisons by which inmates can send e-letters out through a secure system, so that they do not have access to the Internet. Colorado corrections officials point out that this type of system improves security, reduces staff time, does not cost money as the rates charged pay for the system, and increases the contact between inmates and their families.[39]

Technology is also used to detect contraband. Drug are smuggled into a prison through the mail by injecting cocaine into the ink of a gel pen, or placing drops of liquid LSD on the envelope glue. A team from the Sandia National Laboratories developed both a hand-portable and a fixed drug detector that can detect trace amounts of drugs and identify it in less than ten seconds.[40] A serious contraband problem for prisons has been the importation and then use of cell phones by inmates. As cell phones have become cheaper and smaller, they are more easily brought into a prison (staff or visitors smuggle them in or they get them mailed in hidden in other objects) and they are difficult to find and detect. Currently, the Federal Communications Commission (FCC) does not allow cell phone communications to be jammed or blocked, even in a prison, however, they are allowing a few experiments to see if such jamming could occur without "bleeding over" beyond the prison and affecting the general public. Technology is available or being developed to detect cell phone signals to help find and confiscate them, overpower the signal with a stronger one, or intercept the signal and not let it go through.[41] The technology available is expensive and not yet proven, and further advances are required before prisons can be effective at preventing inmate use of cell phones.

Technology can improve staff safety through the use of body armor to protect staff from stabbings better monitoring of inmates.[42] With assistance from the U.S. Department of Defense, a Staff Alarm and Inmate Tracking (SAINT) program helps pinpoint the location and nature of problems such as an assault on an officer within seconds of its occurrence. SAINT is a combination of cameras throughout a facility and a duress alarm worn by an officer. If triggered by the officer or automatically set off if the officer is knocked down, the system sends an alarm and identifies the location in the prison while cameras automatically turn to the assault spot and begin recording.[43]

Community supervision of offenders is also being improved by the use of technology such as GPS tracking and real-time monitoring with alarms if offenders travel outside the geographic areas in which they are allowed. Parole agents in New Mexico track via GPS technology that draws an "invisible fence" or exclusion zone around an area such as a playground that is forbidden for the offender to enter.[44] A **Sex Offender Registry** Information System allows police or correctional officials to identify registered sex offenders who fit descriptions or drive cars similar to those used in a crime.[45] Parole and probation officers use remote kiosks similar to video conferencing to make more frequent checks on offenders in rural or other difficult to get to places.[46]

All of these developments make it seem like technology has significantly impacted and changed corrections. Some say this is true and others believe it has not. There is no doubt that technology has made corrections more efficient, heightened intra- and interagency communications, and made staff safer. But answering the question of what impact technology will have on the future is difficult and must first be put into perspective. Technology will continue to improve efficiency, enhance communications, and make staff safer. However, it is unlikely to reconstruct or seriously modify how corrections staff supervise offenders, hold them accountable for their crimes, or prepare them for success in the community.

The key component of corrections is people who supervise other people, and technology is unlikely to change this paradigm. Perhaps the most complex issue for correctional administrators to consider about technology is whether it can or should replace the people who now carry out correctional functions. Technology can supplement rather than replace staff, but technology is usually not cost effective unless it reduces the number of staff necessary to carry out a function. Corrections has always been a people business. It is people watching people, people communicating with people, and people trying to change people. Some suggest that robots or cameras can replace some staff, but that would also "depersonalize" the correctional environment. Correctional agencies advocate a culture of positive interaction and communications among staff and offenders, knowing that such communications help avoid tension and create an atmosphere conducive to offender rehabilitation. It is unlikely that technology can replace people and maintain this type of environment.

The development of available technology for corrections will continue at a rapid pace. Companies in the technology business see corrections as an expanding market for technology and there will be increased efforts to get correctional administrators to consider and adopt technological advancements. Many offer free installation as a pilot to prove or at least market that their technology is being used in another jurisdiction. However, even though there will be continued use of new technologies in corrections, the answer to the question of what impact technology will have on the future of corrections is "not much."

Will there be a Rebirth of Rehabilitation?

As described in Chapter 13 and in other places throughout this book, the ebbs and flows of support for rehabilitation have been described. Fortunately, over the past few years and for a variety of reasons, there has been a renewed interest in rehabilitation. Through much of the past two decades, a punitive attitude about crime, sentencing, and offenders seems prevalent. Public perceptions were that criminals were treated too softly, and by toughening sentences and making sanctions more punitive, the deterrent effect of criminal sanctions could be increased. In a 1996 review of public attitudes regarding crime control approaches, it was discovered that citizens favored three approaches: (1) harsher sentences for offenders, (2) increased use of the death penalty, and (3) increased gun control. Retribution was ranked as the most important purpose of sentencing adult criminals by 53 percent of respondents, although rehabilitation was ranked as most important by 21 percent of respondents.[47]

This followed a dwindling support for rehabilitation since the mid-1970s review by Martinson and colleagues that found that other than a few isolated correlations between a treatment program and a reduction in recidivism, there were no consistent findings that any single treatment program significantly reduced recidivism.[48] Their "nothing works" conclusion resulted in an abandonment of the medical model that began the momentum to move away from indeterminate sentencing to determinant sentencing with an emphasis on deterrence and incapacitation.

However, many researchers reviewed the work of Martinson and found several limitations in the work.[49] Moreover, there have been improvements in research methodology that have increased researchers' abilities to quantitatively synthesize and assess the impact of research findings. An example is the use of meta-analysis that statistically measures the average effect an intervention has on recidivism across all studies and identifies linkages of treatment and successful outcomes. There were other later studies that did find positive outcomes from treatment.[50] In 1990, Andrews and colleagues found that when categorizing research by the quality of the research design, 40 percent of these studies found that treatment had a "positive effect."[51] A 1993 analysis of correctional treatment identified a 25 percent reduction of recidivism by psychological, educational, and behavioral correctional treatment programs.[52] Another 1995 meta-analyses found that the average impact from the treatment intervention would result in a 10 percent reduction in recidivism.[53] These findings challenged the Martinson conclusion that "nothing works."

Attitudes and acceptance of treatment programs for offenders also began to change. A 1997 survey of citizen attitudes in Ohio indicated strong support not only for correctional treatment programs but also for rehabilitation as the primary purpose for a sentence of imprisonment.[54] Since that time, public opinion polls have continued to find support for treating offenders to improve their chance of success. But the real impetus for a change in attitude about rehabilitation came from the current budget crisis among state governments. As noted in the section above on the modifications of sentencing, elected officials are searching for ways to reduce recidivism and therefore reduce the numbers of offenders in prison. They see putting more money into evidence-based treatment as an investment that will save much more money than it costs. They recognize that we cannot continue to "recycle" offenders through correctional programs only to have them continue to fail when returned to the community or once leaving parole or probation supervision.

The state of Washington is an excellent example of this. Washington faced forecasts that they would need to construct several new prisons in the coming decades. To avoid this, in 2005 the Washington legislature directed the Washington State Institute for Public Policy to find "evidence-based" options that could reduce recidivism and avoid the need for prison construction. The Institute reviewed 571 program evaluations and estimated the benefits and costs of them, and the legislature supported funding programs found to be effective to avoid new prison construction. They estimated savings from avoiding prison construction to be approximately $2 billion.[55] Other states have initiated similar reviews and are expanding programs in hopes of reducing costs.

Therefore, there is a renewed interest in and a rebirth in the rehabilitative philosophy. Unlike when rehabilitation was in its heyday due to belief in the medical model, this is a practical orientation and reason for support. First, there is enough research to determine what types of treatment programs are evidence based. Second, the public supports treatment programming for offenders to improve their chances of becoming productive and law-abiding citizens. And it is believed that funding treatment programs for offenders will save money. These three factors will drive this rebirth in rehabilitation.

SUMMARY

This concludes our discussion of the future of correctional administration and the overall examination of the challenges facing correctional administrators. Throughout this textbook, while there has been a review of history, the primary emphasis has been on looking forward. It is important to understand the past and know how the correctional theories evolved and are integrated into correctional practices. Correctional administrators must understand *why* they do things as well as *how* they are done. By learning from the past and integrating knowledge and experience with predictions of future challenges, correctional administrators will be prepared to proactively set agendas in the future rather than have agendas set by outside forces.

This chapter reviewed many topics. First, you examined the status of correctional administration today. There have been tremendous changes and improvements in correctional administration over the past four decades. Those who have worked in corrections during some of this period are well aware of the changes and should be commended for the increase in sophistication and professionalism that has occurred. Just like any other professional discipline, corrections has experienced a multitude of technological developments, improvements in management and leadership, and progress in staff recruitment and professionalism. However, few disciplines or categories of public or private agencies have advanced as much as corrections. There have been improvements in facilities (new prisons), services (medical, housing, and food service), professionalism, risk analysis and decision making, human resource management (staff training, quality, and diversity), and the ability to plan and prepare for future challenges.

In this chapter you then looked forward as to where we are going. The strongest evidence is that corrections is on a trend in which further reductions in the use of imprisonment are likely. Tight budget combined with successful diversion of offenders to the community has laid the groundwork for a reduced reliance on long sentences as the only way to keep the pubic safe. We can no longer continue to increase the dollars directed to prison operations and take money away from other public needs such as education, health care, growing the economy, and building strong communities. Although the pendulum may not have fully swung away from imprisonment toward community correctional approaches, many believe there will be a change away from the surveillance model of supervision and a return to the casework approach to help offenders be successful and avoid crime.

It is wonderful to see a renewed interest in rehabilitation. Unfortunately, correctional administrators went along with the rejection of rehabilitation as a predominant correctional goal thirty years ago. This was understandable as they felt frustrated that they were unable to force offenders to change, particularly with a lack of research indicating a link between rehabilitation and reduced recidivism and the public's desire to be tough on criminals. Now, however, tight budgets and evidence of success have drawn people back on the rehabilitative bandwagon. This development is very important. A successful correctional environment is one that *balances* the importance of punishment and rehabilitation in correctional practices. With the trend toward punishment as a correctional goal throughout the 1990s, there appeared to be a danger of losing rehabilitation forever as an important part of our correctional practice.

This concludes the study of correctional administration. The goal of this textbook has been to give you an overall understanding of how theory and practice are integrated. The first part of the text provides the foundation for our study by describing the key components of correctional administration, including leadership, management, vision, and strategic planning. In Part II, we move into the important elements that correctional administrators manage, and begin with the most important resource available to them, their staff. Included is how staff are organized, supervised, and empowered.

In Part III, we move to managing the environment in which correctional administrators work or find themselves. We began with budgets and the challenging fiscal environment of the current recession and its impact on corrections. We move to the way they use actuarial predictors of risk to enhance public safety. The final chapter of Part III explains the way modern correctional administrators must affect the external environment of politics, the media, and the public. In Part IV we deal with the specific issues they face in managing prisons, including security, treatment programs, and services.

Finally, in Part V we consider the issues that confront correctional administrators today and how these will play out in the future. It is often said that the best way to predict the future is to look back at the past. This means that issues often recycle. What we try to do here is look at issues today, match them with trends in the environment, and combine them to predict the future. In this last chapter, we ask several questions and then try to use the facts and evolving trends to answer them.

Correctional administration is a profession facing significant challenges, conflicting goals, and increasing visibility in the public and political arena. This text was written because of my career enjoyment of working in corrections for more than twenty-five years. There is fulfillment that results from meeting difficult challenges, yet there is disappointment that results from failure, whether that failure is real or perceived by others. However, there is never a dull day in the life of a correctional administrator. Hopefully, reading this book and studying correctional administration will help prepare you to accept the challenges that will confront correctional administrators for the next several years.

KEY TERMS

Technical violations	Broken-window probation	Sex offender registry
Evidence-based supervision	GPS Systems	Meta-analysis
Behavior modification	Technocorrections	

YOU'RE THE CORRECTIONAL ADMINISTRATOR

1. You are the chief of planning for a state correctional agency that includes both community and institutional corrections. You have been asked by the director of the agency to create an issue paper that speculates into the future and generates a new paradigm for the management of the agency. You are to identify one assumption (for instance, there will be a shift to restorative justice or the agency's primary mission will be the rehabilitation of offenders) that will impact the way the agency is managed in twenty years. Discuss this topic in a small group, and then identify the one major assumption that will drive the agency in the future. Then, describe how the agency should reorganize or change staffing or management to meet this new mission.

2. You are the court administrator for a medium-size county. The judges are very interested in creating a restorative justice model of sentencing. They really do not know much about it nor do they have any idea how to implement it. They ask you to create an organizational model for implementing restorative justice. Who do you involve in a discussion of how a restorative justice model should be implemented, and what role would the individuals or groups play in the discussion? Describe how you would set up a restorative justice model to present to the judges. Include the steps and processes that would be included and the individuals that would be involved. Specifically discuss the role of victims and your recommendations as to whether the victim would ever sit down personally with the offender to discuss ways to repair damages caused by a crime.

WEB LINK EXERCISES

Go to Restorative justice online Web site http://www.restorativejustice.org/whatisslide.

This is a large Web site containing an abundance of good information about the concept of restoration. Click on Introduction to Restorative Justice and after viewing the slides of this presentation, continue viewing the other four slide presentations to see the entire slide show. Note: To advance the slides, click on the slides at the bottom of the viewing window. Do you see this correctional concept growing in the future or is this a passing fad?

Go to American Correctional Association (ACA) www.corrections.com/aca/.

This is the Web site for the ACA. Find the section on accreditation. Identify what the ACA describes as the benefits of accreditation. Which two of the benefits suggested do you think would be the most beneficial to correctional administrators, and why?

GROUP EXERCISES

Each group will address one of the following topics and make a presentation on how it will likely affect the future of corrections: technology, sentencing, restorative justice, supermax prisons, and decreasing incarceration rate.

ENDNOTES

1. John G. Perry and John F. Gorczyk, "Restructuring Corrections: Using Market Research in Vermont," *Corrections Management Quarterly*, 1 no. 3 (1997): 27.

2. These numbers were received by the author from Mark Flowers, Executive Director of the ACA Commission on Accreditation, via email on March 26, 2009.

3. Camille Graham Camp and George M. Camp, *2002 Corrections Yearbook* (Middletown, CT: Criminal Justice Institute, 2003), p. 154.

4. Ibid., p. 155.

5. Ibid., p. 219.

6. Bureau of Justice Statistics, "Prisoners in 2000," *Bureau of Justice Statistics Bulletin* (Washington, DC: U.S. Department of Justice, 2001).

7. William J. Sabol, Heather C. West, and Matthew Cooper, *Prisoners in 2008—Statistical Tables* (Washington, DC: U.S. Department of Justice, December 2009).

8. William J. Sabol, Heather Couture, and Paige M. Harrison, "Prisoners in 2006," *Bureau of Justice Statistics Bulletin* (Washington, DC: U.S. Department of Justice, 2007).

9. Sabol et al., *Prisoners in 2008.*

10. 2010 figures were compiled by the Pew Center for the States in partnership with the Association of State Correctional Administrators. Data reported in Pew Center for the States, *Prison Count 2010: State Population Declines for the First Time in 38 Years* (Washington, DC: Pew Charitable Trusts, March 2010). The 2008 figures come from William J. Sabol, Heather C. West, and Matthew Cooper, "Prisoners in 2008," *Bureau of Justice Statistics* (Washington, DC: U.S. Department of Justice, December 2009).

11. National Governors' Association, 2009. *The State Fiscal Situation: The Lost Decade*, http://www.nga.org/Files/pdf/0911FISCALLOSTDECADE.PDF.

12. J. Warren, *One in 100: Behind Bars in America 2008* (Washington, DC: Pew Center for the States, 2008).

13. Christopher A. Innes, "The Simple Solution for Reducing Correctional Costs," *Corrections Today* 72 no. 1 (February 2010): 32.

14. James Austin, *Reducing America's Correctional Population: A Strategic Plan* (Washington, DC: National Institute of Corrections, 2009).

15. Carol J. Williams, "Justice Kennedy Laments the State of Prisons in California, U.S.," *Los Angeles Times*, February 4, 2010, http://articles.latimes.com/2010/feb/04/local/la-me-kennedy4-2010feb04 (accessed March 27, 2010).

16. National Conference of State Legislatures, Significant State Sentencing and Corrections Legislation in 2009, posted February 9, 2010 on-line website, http://www.ncsl.org/?TabId=19122 (accessed February 23, 2010).

17. Pew Center for the States, *Prison Count 2010: State Population Declines for the First Time in 38* Years, Revised April 2010, p. 3, available at http://www.pewcenteronthestates.org/uploadedFiles/Prison_Count_2010.pdf?n=880 (accessed April 25, 2010).

18. The following studies report that level of reduction of crime based on increased use of incarceration: W. Spelman, "What Recent Studies Do (and Don't) Tell Us about Imprisonment and Crime," *Crime and Justice: A Review of Research*, edited by Michael Tonry (Chicago: University of Chicago Press, 2000), pp. 419–494; S. Aos, *The Criminal Justice*

System in Washington State: Incarceration Rates, Taxpayer Costs, Crime Rates, and Prison Economics (Olympia, WA: Washington State Institute of Public Policy, 2003); W. Spelman, "Jobs or Jail? The Crime Drop in Texas," *Journal of Policy Analysis and Management* 24 no. 1 (2005): 133–165.

19. For a good review of crime control policies, see James Houston and William W. Parsons, *Criminal Justice and the Policy Process* (Chicago, IL: Nelson-Hall, 1997).

20. For a discussion of the value of imprisonment on crime control, see Charles Oliver, "Costs of Crime and Punishment: More Prisons Save Money, But Only up to a Point," *Investors Business Daily* May 20, 1996.

21. Chase Riveland, "Prison Management Trends, 1975–2025," *Crime and Justice* 26 (1999): 163–203.

22. Ibid., p. 193.

23. Kevin A. Wright, "Strange Bedfellows? Reaffirming Rehabilitation and Prison Privatization," *Journal of Offender Rehabilitation* 49 (2010): 74–90.

24. David I. Rothman, *Conscience and Convenience: The Asylum and Its Alternatives in Progressive America* (Boston, MA: Little, Brown, 1980).

25. Edward E. Rhine, "Probation and Parole Supervision: In Need of a New Narrative," *Corrections Management Quarterly* 1 no. 2 (1999): 72.

26. William Adams and Jeffrey Roth, *Federal Offenders under Community Supervision, 1989–1996* (Washington, DC: U.S. Department of Justice, Bureau of Justice Statistics, 1998).

27. Camp and Camp, *2002 Corrections Yearbook*, p. 201.

28. Lauren E. Glaze and Thomas P. Bonczar, *Probation and Parole in the United States 2007* (Washington, DC: U.S. Department of Justice), p. 4.

29. Heather C. West and William J. Sabol, *Prisoners in 2007* (Washington, DC: U.S. Department of Jutice, 2008), p. 3.

30. Camp and Camp, *2002 Corrections Yearbook*, pp. 59–61.

31. Joan Petersilia, "When Prisoners Return to the Community: Political, Economic, and Social Consequences," *Federal Probation* 65 no. 1 (June 2001): 3–8.

32. Glaze and Bonczar, pp. 2 and 7.

33. Faye X. Taxman, "No Illusions: Offender and Organizational Change in Maryland's Proactive Community Supervision Efforts," *Criminology and Public Policy* 7 no. 2 (May 2008): 275–302.

34. Kevin Johnson, "To Save Money on Prisons, States Take a Softer Stance," *USA Today*, March 18, 2009, p. 1.

35. Reinventing Probation Council, " 'Broken Windows' Probation: The Next Step in Fighting Crime," *Civil Report* 7 (1999): 2.

36. Tony Fabelo, "Technocorrections: The Promises, the Uncertain Threats," *Sentencing & Corrections: Issues for the 21st Century*, Papers from the Executive Sessions on Sentencing and Corrections, no. 5 (Washington, DC: U.S. Department of Justice, May 2000).

37. Thomas J. Herzog, *If the World Is Flat, How Come Corrections Is Still Round? Integrating Correctional Authorities into the Fusion Center Rubric*, an unpublished Whitepaper brief of the Corrections Technology Association, September 2007.

38. National Law Enforcement and Corrections Technology Center, "E-Messaging Saves Time, Improves Security," *Tech Beat* (Summer 2008), http://www.justnet.org/TechBeat%20Files/E-Messaging.pdf (accessed August 17, 2009).

39. Ann Coppola, "In the Year 2028," *The Corrections Connection*, posted March 10, 2008 on-line website, www.justnet.org/Pages/RecordView.aspx?itemid=1581 (accessed August 2008).

40. William Falcon, "Special Technologies for Law Enforcement and Corrections," *NIJ Journal* 252 (July 2005): 22–27.

41. National Law Enforcement and Corrections Technology Center, "No More 'Cell' Phones," *Tech Beat* (Winter 2005), http://www.justnet.org/TechBeat%20Files/NoMoreCellPhones .pdf (accessed August 17, 2009).

42. NIJ Staff, "Making Corrections Safer with Technology," *Corrections Today* 70 no. 1 (February 2008): 62–63.

43. Office of Justice Programs, "Duress Systems in Correctional Facilities," *In Short: Toward Criminal Justice Solutions* (Washington, DC: U.S. Department of Justice, June 2006), http://www.ncjrs.gov/pdffiles1/nij/214921.pdf (accessed August 17, 2009).

44. National Law Enforcement and Corrections Center, "On Parole in New Mexico," *Tech Beat* (Spring 2005), http://www.justnet.org/TechBeat%20Files/ParoleNM.pdf (accessed August 17, 2009).

45. Maureen Boyle, "Tracking Sex Offenders Made Easy with New State Computer System," *Enterprise News.com* (March 1, 2008), www.enterprisenews.com/news/x2052203702? view=print (accessed August 17, 2009).

46. Ann Coppola, "Tracking the Event Horizon," *The Corrections Connection* (June 17, 2008), www.justnet.org/Pages/RecordView.aspx?itemid=1633 (accessed August 17, 2009).

47. Timothy J. Flanagan and Dennis R. Longmire, editors, *Americans View Crime and Justice: A National Public Opinion Survey* (Thousand Oaks, CA: Sage Publications, 1996).

48. Douglas Lipton, Robert Martinson, and Judith Wilks, *The Effectiveness of Correctional Treatment and What Works: A Survey of Treatment Evaluation Studies* (New York: Praeger, 1975).

49. Francis T. Cullen and Paul Gendreau, "Assessing Correctional Rehabilitation: Policy, Practice, and Prospects," in *Policies, Processes, and Decisions of the Criminal Justice System*, edited by Julie Horney (Washington, DC: U.S. Department of Justice, National Institute of Justice, 2000), pp. 109–175.

50. Ted Palmer, "Martinson Revisited," *Journal of Research in Crime and Delinquency* 12 (July 1975): 133–152.

51. D. A. Andrews, I. Zinger, R. D. Hoge, J. Bonta, P. Gendreau, and F.T. Cullen, "Does Correctional Treatment Work?," *Criminology* 28 no. 3 (August 1990): 374.

52. Mark W. Lipsey and David B. Wilson, "The Efficacy of Psychological, Educational, and Behavioral Treatment," *American Psychologist* 48 no. 12 (1993): 1181–1209.

53. Friedrich Losel, "The Efficacy of Correctional Treatment: A Review and Synthesis of Meta-Evaluations," in *What Works: Reducing Reoffending*, edited by James McGuire (West Sussex, UK: Wiley, 1995).

54. Brandon K. Applegate, Francis T. Cullen, and Bonnie S. Fisher, "Public Support for Correctional Treatment," *Prison Journal* 77 no. 3 (1997): 237–258.

55. Steve Aos, Marna Miller, and Elizabeth Drake, *Evidence-Based Public Policy Options to Reduce Future Prison Construction, Criminal Justice Costs, and Crime Rates* (Olympia: Washington State Institute for Public Policy, 2006).

Index